THE CAMBRIDGE HISTORY OF

LIBRARIES IN BRITAIN AND IRELAND

*

VOLUME I

To 1640

This volume is the first detailed survey of libraries in Britain and Ireland up to the Civil War. It traces the transition from collections of books without a fixed local habitation to the library, chiefly of printed books, much as we know it today. It examines changing patterns in the formation of book collections in the earlier medieval period, and traces the combined impact of the activities of the mendicant orders and the scholarship of the universities in the thirteenth and fourteenth centuries, and the adoption of the library room and the growth of private book collections in the fourteenth and fifteenth. The volume then focuses upon the dispersal of the monastic libraries in the mid-sixteenth century, the creation of new types of library, and, finally, the steps whereby the collections amassed by antiquaries came to form the bases of the national and institutional libraries of Britain and Ireland.

ELISABETH LEEDHAM-GREEN is a Fellow of Darwin College, Cambridge, and was from 1972 to 1999 Deputy Keeper of Cambridge University Archives. She is a Fellow of the Society of Antiquaries and Vice-President of the Bibliographical Society of London. She is the author of *Books in Cambridge Libraries: Book-lists from the Vice-Chancellor's Court Probate Inventories in the Tudor and Stuart Periods* (1986), and of *A Concise History of the University of Cambridge* (1996), and is co-editor of the series *Private Libraries in Renaissance England* (1992–).

TERESA WEBBER is a Fellow of Trinity College, Cambridge, and University Senior Lecturer in Palaeography and Codicology. She is a Fellow of the Society of Antiquaries and of the Royal Historical Society. She is the author of *Scribes and Scholars at Salisbury Cathedral c.1075–c.1125* (1992), is co-editor of *The Libraries of the Augustinian Canons*, volume VI of the British Academy's Corpus of British Medieval Library Catalogues (1998), and is a General Editor of *Cambridge Studies in Palaeography and Codicology*.

THE CAMBRIDGE HISTORY OF

LIBRARIES IN BRITAIN AND IRELAND

General Editor

Peter Hoare

Libraries pervade the culture of all literate societies. Their history illuminates that culture and many of its facets – the spread of literacy, the growth of scholarship, changes in educational practices – as well as reflecting changing social and political philosophies and practices. As a result, they have often developed in ways which could not have been foreseen by their founders.

The fundamental principle, of collecting for immediate and future use and enjoyment, has usually been combined with a social aim, the sharing of books and information among a wider group, which has become one of the characteristics of libraries today. This is one reason why libraries cannot simply be seen as a discrete phenomenon: throughout their history they must be considered part of the society they serve. This context includes the whole reading environment, the vital connection of libraries with social or cultural development, and the political framework which has become increasingly important in the past hundred years; economic and commercial aspects have also become more significant, as they have for the history of the book. The profession of librarianship has matured, especially in the last century, and has in turn affected the development of libraries: indeed it is the interaction of librarians and users that has provided much of the dynamic for that development. Changing methodologies of scholarship and the vicissitudes of private reading, too, affect the way libraries have developed.

Libraries vary enormously in form, in size and in purpose, and their nature has inevitably changed over the fifteen centuries encompassed in these volumes. In consequence the three volumes have different emphases and reflect different approaches to the historical record, but they share a common theme. This has inspired the project since its first inception on the initiative of Professor Robin Alston (whose library history database has been invaluable to many contributors), and under the aegis of the then Library History Group of the Library Association and its former Honorary Secretary Graham Jefcoate. Notwithstanding these differences in approach, the history of libraries is a continuum, and the divisions between the three volumes of what is essentially a single work are less precise than the volume titles may indicate. Developments for some years around the mid-seventeenth century may be treated in both Volume I and Volume II, though often in different contexts; and a similar overlap for the mid-nineteenth century exists between Volume II and Volume III. Readers concerned with these periods should be sure to consult both volumes.

The Cambridge History of Libraries in Britain and Ireland does not set out to be an exhaustive history of individual libraries, it is, rather, a general history charting the various trends and patterns of development, which studies different types of libraries and individual libraries as part of that broader view. In this way it aims to illuminate not only libraries and their users but also the wider history of the British Isles. Only in understanding their purpose and their context can the role of libraries be properly comprehended.

THE CAMBRIDGE HISTORY OF LIBRARIES IN BRITAIN AND IRELAND

★

VOLUME I

To 1640

★

Edited by

ELISABETH LEEDHAM-GREEN

and

TERESA WEBBER

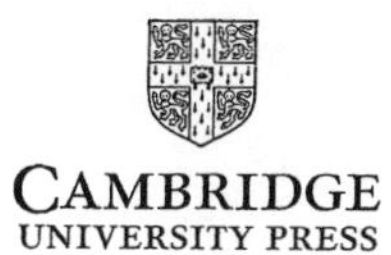

CAMBRIDGE
UNIVERSITY PRESS

CAMBRIDGE UNIVERSITY PRESS
Cambridge, New York, Melbourne, Madrid, Cape Town, Singapore, São Paulo

Cambridge University Press
The Edinburgh Building, Cambridge CB2 2RU, UK

Published in the United States of America by Cambridge University Press, New York

www.cambridge.org
Information on this title: www.cambridge.org/9780521858083

First published 2006

Printed in the United Kingdom at the University Press, Cambridge

A catalogue record for this publication is available from the British Library

ISBN-13 978-0-521-78194-7 hardback
ISBN-10 0-521-78194-9 hardback

Only available as a three-volume set

ISBN-13 978-0-521-85808-3 three-volume set
ISBN-10 0-521-85808-9 three-volume set

Contents

Illustrations

Contributors

J. H. BAKER, St Catharine's College, Cambridge
WILLIAM BARKER, University of King's College, Halifax, Nova Scotia
C. B. L. BARR, formerly (Librarian) of York Minster
DAVID N. BELL, Department of Religious Studies, Memorial University of Newfoundland, St John's, Newfoundland
JAMES P. CARLEY, Department of English, York University, Toronto
CHRISTINE FERDINAND, Magdalen College, Oxford
RICHARD GAMESON, Department of History, Durham University
DAVID GANZ, Department of Classics, King's College, London
TIMOTHY GRAHAM, Institute for Medieval Studies, University of New Mexico, Albuquerque
ARNOLD HUNT, The British Library
KRISTIAN JENSEN, The British Library
PETER MURRAY JONES, King's College, Cambridge
ELISABETH LEEDHAM-GREEN, Darwin College, Cambridge
ROGER LOVATT, Peterhouse, Cambridge
PETER J. LUCAS, Wolfson College, Cambridge
DAVID MCKITTERICK, Trinity College, Cambridge
PÁDRAIG P. Ó NÉILL, Department of English, University of North Carolina at Chapel Hill
NICHOLAS ORME, Department of History, University of Exeter
RICHARD OVENDEN, Bodleian Library, Oxford
JULIAN ROBERTS, formerly of the Bodleian Library, Oxford
CLARE SARGENT, Radley College, Oxfordshire
DAVID SELWYN, formerly of Lampeter University
PAMELA SELWYN, formerly of Lampeter University
RICHARD SHARPE, Faculty of Modern History, Oxford
MARGARET SPUFFORD, Department of History, Roehampton Institute, London
JENNY STRATFORD, Institute of Historical Research, London
TERESA WEBBER, Trinity College, Cambridge

Acknowledgements

A volume of this kind can only be achieved through the efforts, patience and forbearance, as well as the knowledge and expertise, of a great many people. We are especially grateful to all of our contributors who remained throughout graciously tolerant of their editors' cajoling and the unavoidable delays before the volume went to press. The support and patience of our General Editor, Peter Hoare, and of our editors at Cambridge University Press, Caroline Bundy, her successor Linda Bree, and Maartje Scheltens, have also been greatly appreciated, as have the support and advice we have received throughout from David McKitterick. Thanks are also due to Alison Powell and her colleagues at the press for all their help as the volume went through the production process.

Three day-conferences played an important role while the volume was taking shape, and we are grateful to Darwin College and Trinity College, Cambridge, and to the London School of Advanced Studies' Centre for English Studies for hosting them. Warm thanks are also due to Richard H. Rouse, who, at our request, presented valuable advice and comments upon the plans for the volume at the conference in Trinity.

The Cambridge University Library and the Wren Library in Trinity have been heavily used, especially during the latter stages of editing the volume. We are very grateful to the librarians and staff of these two libraries in particular, but also to the librarians and staff of the many libraries whose resources have been used by the contributors over the last decade. We also thank Cadw and English Heritage for permission to reproduce figures from their guides.

A number of individuals kindly responded to requests for assistance and comments, among them Michael Gullick, who read and commented upon two chapters as well as being an unfailing source of advice and bibliographical references; Emily Thornbury, who translated the passages in Old English, and James Willoughby and David Selwyn, who both provided heroic assistance to the editors in time of need. Final thanks must go to Geoffrey and Rachel Webber for their support and forbearance, especially during those months when family life sometimes had to take second place to the history of libraries.

Elisabeth Leedham-Green
Teresa Webber

Abbreviations

ANTS	Anglo-Norman Text Society
ASE	*Anglo-Saxon England*
Bale, *Index*	J. Bale, *Index Britanniae scriptorum*, ed. R. L. Poole and M. Bateson (Oxford, 1902); reissued with a new introduction by C. Brett and J. Carley (Woodbridge and Rochester, NY, 1990)
BAV	Biblioteca Apostolica Vaticana
BC	*Book Collector*
BCI	E. S. Leedham-Green, *Books in Cambridge inventories: book-lists from Vice-Chancellor's Court Probate inventories in the Tudor and Stuart periods*, 2 vols. (Cambridge, 1987)
BJRL	*Bulletin of the John Rylands (University) Library*
BL	British Library, London
BLJ	*British Library Journal*
BLR	*Bodleian Library Record*
BMC	*Catalogue of books printed in the XVth century now in the British Museum* (London, 1908–)
BN	Bibliothèque nationale de France, Paris
Bodleian	Bodleian Library, Oxford
Books, collectors and libraries	N. R. Ker, *Books, collectors and libraries: studies in the medieval heritage*, ed. A. G. Watson (London and Ronceverte, 1985)
BPPB	J. Griffiths and D. A. Pearsall (eds.), *Book production and publishing in Britain, 1375–1475* (Cambridge, 1989)
BQR	*Bodleian Quarterly Review*
BRECP	J. Greatrex, *Biographical register of the English cathedral priories of the province of Canterbury, c. 1066–1540* (Oxford, 1998)
BRUC	A. B. Emden, *A biographical register of the University of Cambridge to 1500* (Cambridge, 1963)
BRUO	A. B. Emden, *A biographical register of the University of Oxford to AD 1500*, 3 vols. (Oxford, 1957–9)
BRUO 1501–1540	A. B. Emden, *A biographical register of the University of Oxford, AD 1501 to 1540* (Oxford, 1974)

Carley and Tite, *Books and collectors*	J. P. Carley and C. G. C. Tite (eds.), *Books and collectors, 1200–1700: essays presented to Andrew Watson* (London, 1997)
CBMLC	Corpus of British Medieval Library Catalogues (London), I. K. W. Humphreys (ed.), *The Friars' libraries* (1990); II. R. A. B. Mynors, R. H. Rouse and M. A. Rouse (eds.), *Registrum Anglie de libris doctorum et auctorum ueterum* (1991); III. D. N. Bell (ed.), *The libraries of the Cistercians, Gilbertines and Premonstratensians* (1992); IV. R. Sharpe *et al.* (eds.), *English Benedictine libraries: the shorter catalogues* (1996); V. W. P. Stoneman (ed.), *Dover Priory* (1999); VI. T. Webber and A. G. Watson (eds.), *The libraries of the Augustinian canons* (1998); VII. J. P. Carley (ed.), *The libraries of King Henry VIII* (2000); VIII. K. Friis-Jensen and J. M. W. Willoughby (eds.), *Peterborough Abbey* (2001); IX. V. Gillespie (ed.), *Syon Abbey*, with A. I. Doyle (ed.), *The libraries of the Carthusians* (2001); X. P. D. Clarke (ed.) (with introduction by R. Lovatt), *The university and college libraries of Cambridge* (2002); XI. Henry of Kirkestede, *Catalogus de libris autenticis et apocrifis*, ed. R. H. Rouse and M. A. Rouse (2004)
CCCC	Corpus Christi College, Cambridge
CCCM	*Corpus Christianorum, Continuatio Medievalis*
CCSL	*Corpus Christianorum, Series Latina*
CHBB I–IV	*The Cambridge history of the book in Britain* (Cambridge), I. R. Gameson (ed.), *The Anglo-Saxon period, c. 600–1100* (forthcoming); II. N. Morgan and R. M. Thomson (eds.), *The manuscript book, c. 1100–1400* (forthcoming); III. L. Hellinga and J. B. Trapp (eds.), *1400–1557* (1999); IV. J. Barnard and D. F. McKenzie (eds.), *1557–1695* (2002)
CIBN	BN, *Catalogue des incunables* (Paris, 1981–)
Clark, *Care of books*	J. W. Clark, *The care of books* (Cambridge, 1901)
CLC	M. S. G. McLeod *et al.*, *The cathedral libraries catalogue, books printed before 1701 in the libraries of the Anglican cathedrals of England and Wales*, I *(Books printed in the British Isles and British America and English books printed elsewhere)*, ed. and completed by K. I. James and D. J. Shaw (London, 1984); D. J. Shaw *et al.*, II *(Books printed on the continent of Europe)* (London, 1998)
CLibR	*Calendar of the Liberate Rolls preserved in the Public Record Office* (London, 1916–)
CMA	[E. Barnard], *Catalogi manuscriptorum Angliae et Hiberniae* (Oxford, 1697)
Coll.	College
CSEL	*Corpus Scriptorum Ecclesiasticorum Latinorum*
CUL	Cambridge University Library

DNB	*Dictionary of national biography*; see also *ODNB*
Durkan and Ross	J. Durkan and A. Ross, *Early Scottish libraries* (Glasgow, 1961)
EETS (ES/OS/SS)	Early English Text Society (Extra Series/Original Series/Supplementary Series)
EHR	*The English Historical Review*
ELM	J. H. Baker, *English legal manuscripts*, 2 vols. (Zug, 1975–8)
ELM/CUL	J. H. Baker with J. S. Ringrose, *Catalogue of English legal manuscripts in Cambridge University Library* (Woodbridge, 1996)
ELM/USA	J. H. Baker, *English legal manuscripts in the United States of America*, Part I, *Medieval and Renaissance* (London, 1985)
EMS	*English Manuscript Studies 1100–1700*
Goff	F. R. Goff, *Incunabula in American libraries: a third census*, repr. with compiler's annotations (Millwood, NY, 1973)
Hbf	*Histoires des bibliothèques françaises* (Paris), I. A. Vernet (ed.), *Les bibliothèques médiévales, du VIe siècle à 1530* (1989); II. C. Jolly (ed.), *Les bibliothèques sous l'Ancien Régime, 1530–1789* (1988)
HBS	Henry Bradshaw Society
HLQ	*Huntington Library Quarterly*
Huntington	Henry E. Huntington Library, San Marino, CA
HUO	*The history of the University of Oxford* (Oxford), I. J. I. Catto (ed.), *The early Oxford schools* (1984); II. J. I. Catto and T. A. R. Evans (eds.), *Late medieval Oxford* (1992); III. J. K. McConica (ed.), *The collegiate university* (1986)
Irwin, *English library*	R. Irwin, *The English library: sources and history* (London, 1966)
Irwin, *Heritage*	R. Irwin, *The heritage of the English library* (London, 1964)
ISTC	*Incunabula short-title catalogue* (database in progress)
James, *ALCD*	M. R. James, *The ancient libraries of Canterbury and Dover* (Cambridge, 1903)
Jayne	S. Jayne, *Library catalogues of the English Renaissance* (Berkeley and Los Angeles, 1956; reissued with new preface and notes, Godalming, 1983)
JEH	*Journal of Ecclesiastical History*
JLH	*Journal of Library History*
JRUL	John Rylands University Library, Manchester
JWCI	*Journal of the Warburg and Courtauld Institutes*
Ker, *Cat. AS*	N. R. Ker, *Catalogue of manuscripts containing Anglo-Saxon* (Oxford, 1957; reissued with supplement, 1990)
Ker, *English MSS*	N. R. Ker, *English manuscripts in the century after the Norman Conquest* (Oxford, 1960)
Lambeth	Lambeth Palace Library, London
Lapidge, 'Booklists'	M. Lapidge, 'Surviving booklists from Anglo-Saxon England', in M. Lapidge and H. Gneuss (eds.), *Learning and literature in Anglo-Saxon England: studies presented to Peter Clemoes on the occasion of his sixty-fifth birthday* (Cambridge, 1985), 33–89

Leland, *Collectanea*	J. Leland, *De rebus Britannicis collectanea*, ed. T. Hearne, 2nd edn, 6 vols. (Oxford, 1774)
Library	*The Library. Transactions of the Bibliographical Society*
LP	J. S. Brewer and others (eds.), *Letters and papers, foreign and domestic, of the reign of Henry VIII*, 21 vols. in 33 and addenda (London, 1862–1932)
Macray	W. D. Macray, *Annals of the Bodleian Library*, 2nd edn (Oxford, 1890)
MÆ	*Medium Ævum*
MGH	Monumenta Germaniae Historica
MLGB	N. R. Ker, *Medieval libraries of Great Britain*, rev. edn (London, 1964); *Supplement*, ed. A. G. Watson (London, 1987)
MLR	*Modern Language Review*
MMBL	N. R. Ker, *Medieval manuscripts in British libraries*, 5 vols. (Oxford, 1969–2002)
MSS at Oxford	A. C. de la Mare and B. C. Barker-Benfield (eds.), *Manuscripts at Oxford: an exhibition in memory of Richard William Hunt* (Oxford, 1980)
Mynors and Thomson	R. A. B. Mynors and R. M. Thomson, *Catalogue of the manuscripts of Hereford Cathedral Library* (Woodbridge, 1993)
NLS	National Library of Scotland, Edinburgh
NLW	National Library of Wales, Aberystwyth
Oates, *CUL*	J. C. T. Oates, *Cambridge University Library, a history*: vol. 1, *from the beginnings to the Copyright Act of Queen Anne* (Cambridge, 1986)
OBS	Oxford Bibliographical Society
ODNB	*The Oxford dictionary of national biography* (Oxford, 2004)
OHS	Oxford Historical Society
Parkes and Watson, *Medieval scribes*	M. B. Parkes and A. G. Watson (eds.), *Medieval scribes, manuscripts and libraries: essays presented to N. R. Ker* (London, 1978)
PBSA	The Papers of the Bibliographical Society of America
PCC	*Prerogative Court of Canterbury*
PL	*Patrologia cursus completus, series latina*
PLRE	R. J. Fehrenbach and E. S. Leedham-Green (eds.), *Private libraries in Renaissance England: a collection and catalogue of Tudor and early Stuart book-lists* (Binghampton, NY, and Marlborough, 1992–5; Tempe, Arizona, 1998–)
PML	Pierpont Morgan Library, New York
Proctor, *Index*	R. Proctor, *An index to the early printed books in the British Museum from the invention of printing to the year MD, with notes on those in the Bodleian Library*, 2 vols. and 4 supplements (London, 1898–1902)
PSAS	*Proceedings of the Society of Antiquaries of Scotland*

RB	*Revue Bénédictine*
Robinson, *Dated MSS in Cambridge libraries*	P. R. Robinson, *Catalogue of dated and datable manuscripts c. 737–1600 in Cambridge libraries*, 2 vols. (Woodbridge, 1988)
RS	Rolls Series
SC	F. Madan *et al.*, *Summary catalogue of western manuscripts in the Bodleian Library at Oxford*, 7 vols. (Oxford, 1895–1953; repr. 1980)
Sharpe, *Latin writers*	*A handlist of the Latin writers of Great Britain and Ireland before 1540* (Turnhout, 1997); *Additions and corrections* (Turnhout, 2001)
STC	*A short-title catalogue of books printed in England, Scotland and Ireland, and of English books printed abroad, 1475–1640, first compiled by A. W. Pollard and G. R. Redgrave. Second edition, revised and enlarged, begun by W. A. Jackson and F. S. Ferguson, completed by Katharine F. Pantzer, with a chronological index by Philip R. Rider*, 3 vols. (London, 1976–91)
Streeter	B. H. Streeter, *The chained library: a survey of four centuries in the evolution of the English library* (New York, 1931)
Survey	*A survey of illuminated manuscripts in the British Isles*, ed. J. J. G. Alexander (London), I. J. J. G. Alexander (ed.), *Insular manuscripts 6th to the 9th centuries* (1978); II. E. Temple (ed.), *Anglo-Saxon manuscripts, 900–1066* (1976); III. M. Kaufmann (ed.), *Romanesque manuscripts, 1066–1190* (1975); IV. N. J. Morgan (ed.), *Early Gothic manuscripts*, 2 vols. (1982–8); V. L. F. Sandler (ed.), *Gothic manuscripts, 1285–1385*, 2 vols. (1986); VI. K. Scott (ed.), *Later Gothic manuscripts, c. 1390–1490*, 2 vols. (1996)
Tanner	T. Tanner, *Bibliotheca Britannica-Hibernica* (London 1748)
TCBS	*Transactions of the Cambridge Bibliographical Society*
TCD	Trinity College, Dublin
Thomson, *Cat. Lincoln*	R. M. Thomson, *Catalogue of the manuscripts of Lincoln Cathedral Chapter Library* (Woodbridge, 1989)
Thomson, *Cat. Worcester*	R. M. Thomson, *A descriptive catalogue of the mediaeval manuscripts in Worcester Cathedral Library* (Cambridge, 2001)
Thorndike / Kibre	L. Thorndike, and P. K. Kibre, *A catalogue of incipits of mediaeval scientific writings in Latin*, 2nd edn (Cambridge, MA, 1963)
TNA	The National Archives
TRHS	*Transactions of the Royal Historical Society*
V&A	Victoria and Albert Museum, London
VCH	*The Victoria History of the Counties of England*
Watson, *Dated MSS in the BL*	A. G. Watson, *Catalogue of dated and datable manuscripts c. 700–1600 in the Department of Manuscripts, the British Library*, 2 vols. (London, 1979)

Watson, *Dated MSS in Oxford libraries*	A. G. Watson, *Catalogue of dated and datable manuscripts c. 435–1600 in Oxford libraries*, 2 vols. (London, 1984)
Willis and Clark	R. Willis, *The architectural history of the University of Cambridge*, ed. J. W. Clark, 4 vols. (Cambridge, 1886)
Wing	D. G. Wing, *Short-title catalogue of books printed in England, Scotland, Ireland, Wales, and British America, and of English books printed in other countries, 1641–1700*, 3 vols. (New York, 1945–51; 2nd edn, revised and enlarged, New York, 1972–98)
Wormald and Wright, *English library*	F. Wormald and C. E. Wright, *The English library before 1700: studies in its history* (London, 1958)

Introduction

ELISABETH LEEDHAM-GREEN AND TERESA WEBBER

The history of libraries in the medieval and early modern periods is a history of shifting collections of books of varied size and function, which differ in significant ways from modern expectations of a library.

The most obvious difference is physical. From the early middle ages until the sixteenth century, the books owned by religious and academic communities as well as those of individuals did not comprise a single physically discrete collection within a designated room, but were housed in chests and cupboards in various locations. The earliest specially designated book-rooms, datable to the twelfth century, were places of storage; library rooms in which books were arranged for consultation *in situ* were introduced in England only from the fourteenth century, and in many instances contained only a part of an institution's holdings.

The modern conception of a library as an organised and comprehensive repository of written knowledge became fully articulated only during the seventeenth century. Indeed, for much of the period covered by this volume, the concept of a library remained ill-defined. Collections of books were assembled in the first instance to serve particular needs. In the early middle ages, these were almost exclusively ecclesiastical: the requirements of the monastic life, the performance of the liturgy, and the delivery of pastoral care. From the thirteenth century, new kinds of need emerged: those of scholars and of mendicant preachers and teachers, and, and by the fifteenth century, of members of the emergent professions, such as doctors and lawyers.

Learned monks and clergy of the earlier middle ages knew the word *bibliotheca* from the references to the great public libraries of the ancient world in late antique and early Christian texts. Occasionally they used this word in their own writings, especially to refer to the more impressive collections of books formed in their own time, despite the obvious differences in physical arrangement and function from the *bibliothecae* of antiquity. Until the end of the twelfth century, however, the majority of references are simply to 'books' rather than to a library. Thereafter, the word *libraria* is found with increasing frequency, first as merely a synonym for *armarium* (which, by this date, had the more general meaning of a collection of books rather than a specific book-chest or cupboard), but, from the late fourteenth century, to refer to a designated room. Nevertheless, until well into the sixteenth century, other collections of books, overlapping in their contents with those in the library room and even extending beyond an institution's walls, might also be considered to form part of the 'library'. Classification marks in late medieval inventories from two cells of Norwich Cathedral Priory (St Leonard's in Norwich and St Nicholas' in Yarmouth) fit within the series used to mark the books of the mother house, 'showing that the library was regarded as a single collection, though some of the books were continuously housed at one of the cells'.[1]

Medieval collections of books are characterised by a surprising degree of fluidity. Little-used volumes might be removed from the principal collections and stored elsewhere or disposed of; books might be sent to dependent cells, or, as happened increasingly from the fourteenth century, to the universities for the use of student monks and canons, where they became vulnerable to more permanent alienation.[2] The dispersal of books from religious houses was thus a phenomenon long before the dissolution of the monasteries in the mid-sixteenth century. The absence of well-defined concepts of ownership regarding books during the earlier middle ages, and, in particular, the apparent lack of any clearly articulated distinction between personal and communal ownership, also contributed to the instability of book collections. During the thirteenth century, however, the particular requirements of the friars as itinerant preachers and teachers prompted the definition of the concept of personal possession but institutional ownership, whereby books were kept and used by individual friars, but reverted to the order at the friar's death.[3] This distinction proved useful to the older orders as well. On the death of Cardinal Simon Langham (1376), a former monk and abbot of Westminster, the prior of Westminster lost no time in travelling to Avignon to recover the Cardinal's effects, including his books.[4]

It may be helpful, when tracing the history of libraries, to distinguish between the shifting 'book collections' of the early and central middle ages, and the emergent 'libraries' of the later middle ages and early modern periods which display some of the characteristic features of the modern library: a designated space, a catalogue, and a greater emphasis upon the collection as a

1 R. Sharpe in CBMLC IV. 289. 2 See below, chapters 5–6.
3 See below, 127–8. 4 CBMLC IV. 613–14.

repository of written knowledge. Nevertheless, to apply a restricted use of the term 'library' too rigidly risks overlooking earlier and different, albeit less well-defined, conceptions of a library. An early medieval religious community, for whom all the books (including those for the liturgy) served a single end, may have thought of their books collectively as a single entity – a library, despite their physically disparate organisation, and the rarity of the use of the words *bibliotheca* or *libraria*. A distinction between the books intended for study and those used for the liturgy or archival purposes, with the consequent narrowing of the meaning of *libraria* to refer to the former, is apparent in religious institutions only by the fourteenth century.

In the early modern period private collections were, obviously, more readily assembled,[5] largely because printed books were more cheaply acquired than many manuscripts, and outlets for them, that is, booksellers, started to proliferate,[6] as did contacts with the continental mainland, the source of the vast majority of scholarly, *belle-lettriste* and, indeed, until the Reformation, liturgical books. The books from the dissolved religious houses were, in the first instance, nearly all absorbed into private libraries.[7] At the same time, institutional libraries surviving the Reformation, whether the few ecclesiastical ones, or those of the universities and colleges, whose further survival was for some years uncertain, clearly lost heart. Not only was there little or no institutional attempt to acquire books, but existing stocks were neglected to the extent that many such libraries fell largely or entirely into disuse.[8]

Nor should we wonder: the dispersal of the ancient collections, coinciding as it did with the increasing availability of printed books, turned the scholarly world upside-down. In the medieval period, and among early modern collectors of manuscripts for whom the notion of *stemmata* was but poorly grasped, it was evident that the older a manuscript was, the closer it must be to the original source. The harbingers of the New Learning, whose works were mostly first known in Britain and Ireland in printed form, were bent on producing more accurate texts in an unfamiliar medium. How could a book printed on paper compare in value with a manuscript, usually on parchment? We know, now, that paper was used for serious texts, but the perception of the time was that vellum was for eternity, it was the medium for muniments, for

5 See below, 292, 297, 351–6, 566.

6 Notwithstanding the essential warnings of the compilers about the distortions of the data arising from alternative spellings and cross-references, the point is well illustrated by the online database of the British Book Trade Index (http://www.bbti.bham.ac.uk), which allows searches in increasing date order.

7 See below, chapter 10.

8 See below, 347–8, 569.

texts for perpetuity. As Johannes Trithemius said in the 1490s: 'For handwriting placed on parchment will be able to endure a thousand years. But how long, forsooth, will printing last, which is dependent on paper? For if in its paper volume it lasts for two hundred years that is a long time.'[9]

Eager scholars had no such reservations: they wanted both the new editions of ancient texts and the latest advances, not only in theology, law and medicine, but also in the subjects of the university curriculum: rhetoric, dialectic, metaphysics, natural philosophy; and the latest advances presented themselves mostly in quarto and in octavo, and even in smaller formats: little books, not the usual occupants of chained libraries and standing desks. Consequently, in the second and third quarters of the sixteenth century, private libraries outstripped those of institutions. Few institutional libraries could compare with those of John Dee in 1583[10] or Andrew Perne in 1589,[11] or even, to go back a generation, with such relatively obscure owners as John Bateman, Master of Arts and a founding fellow of Gonville and Caius College, Cambridge, who died in 1559 possessed of some 500 books.[12] By way of comparison, Cambridge University Library in 1583, after the receipt of substantial donations solicited by Andrew Perne from Matthew Parker, Sir Nathaniel Bacon, Robert Horne (bishop of Winchester), James Pilkington (bishop of Durham) and others, held 464 volumes.[13] For the reasons above, therefore, we have not treated at length with the impact of printing as such. Its impact was gradual rather than dramatic.

Similarly, we have had little to say about the significance of the British presses for reading habits. Relatively few of their products found their way into libraries even late in our period, and they continued to be vastly outnumbered by imported texts throughout it. The attempts of H. S. Bennett[14] and Louis B. Wright[15] to base their analyses of the reading of Englishmen on the productions of the English presses now appear whimsical.[16]

9 J. Trithemius, *De laude scriptorum*, ch. 7, cited by D. McKitterick, *Print, manuscript and the search for order, 1450–1830* (Cambridge, 2003), 20 (and related works cited in his n. 76).

10 J. Roberts and A. G. Watson (eds.), *John Dee's library catalogue* (London, 1990). The editors (p. 22) calculate that in 1583, when the library was at its zenith, it comprised some 3,000 printed books and 500 manuscripts (as against the 1,000 claimed by Dee himself).

11 *BCI*, I. 419–79. At his death Perne's library comprised some 2,900 volumes, mostly printed.

12 *BCI*, I. 234–44. His library is discussed in E. Leedham-Green and D. McKitterick, 'Ownership: private and public libraries', in *CHBB* IV, at 323–4.

13 For an edition and discussion of the 1583 Cambridge University Library catalogue see E. Leedham-Green and D. McKitterick in Carley and Tite, *Books and collectors*, 153–235.

14 *English books and readers, 1475–1640*, 3 vols. (Cambridge, 1952–70).

15 *Middle-class culture in Elizabethan England* (Chapel Hill, NC, 1935).

16 The dominance of Latin is stressed in D. McKitterick, 'Book catalogues: their varieties and uses', in P. Davison (ed.), *The book encompassed: studies in twentieth-century bibliography* (Cambridge, 1992), 161–75, at 162.

Many of the most significant private collections in the early sixteenth century belonged to those who had exerted themselves, at first or second hand, to rescue the holdings of religious houses; but in the second half of the century we see the amassing of very large collections of printed books (Dee, Perne)[17] alongside the collections of men like Sir Robert Cotton, which were concentrated largely on manuscripts. Indeed, with the exception of Cotton, most major collectors of manuscripts from the mid-sixteenth century were also the owners of substantial collections of printed books. Antiquarian and contemporary interests lived side by side just as did works in manuscript and print.[18] When the institutional libraries revived it was, in many cases, the result of their acquisition of large private collections, as in the case of Andrew Perne's bequest to Peterhouse in 1589, or William Sancroft's to Emmanuel,[19] or to a single benefactor, like Sir Thomas Bodley at Oxford, whose library was soon much enhanced by the vast donations of William Laud and John Selden.[20]

The extent of loss and dispersal – the consequence to a great extent but not exclusively of the dissolution of the monasteries – means that the history of medieval and early modern libraries must necessarily begin with the task of reconstruction. In only a tiny handful of cases does a substantial proportion of any medieval library, whether religious or academic, still remain together, either in the same institution or elsewhere, having been transferred *en bloc*. The partial remains of the vast majority are scattered between different national collections, university or college libraries. A substantial number of these books contain no evidence of their former owners. The same is true of all but a few of the major sixteenth- and early seventeenth-century private collections of manuscripts and printed books.

Efforts to identify and describe the scattered remains began just over a century ago, on both a large scale (such as the manuscript catalogues and editions of medieval booklists and catalogues produced by M. R. James), and, at a more local level (T. W. Williams, for example, compiled evidence for medieval libraries in Somerset).[21] These endeavours were complemented by J. W. Clark's and B. H. Streeter's impressive surveys of the physical environment within which books were stored and used.[22] Whereas there has been no

17 See J. Roberts, below, chapter 11.

18 D. McKitterick, *Print, manuscript and the search for order*.

19 H. Carron, 'William Sancroft (1617–93): a seventeenth-century collector and his library', *Library*, 7th ser., 1 (2000), 290–307.

20 See I. G. Philip and P. Morgan, 'Libraries, books and printing', in *HUO* IV. 659–85.

21 *Somerset medieval libraries* (Bristol, 1897).

22 J. W. Clark, *The care of books* (Cambridge, 1901); B. H. Streeter, *The chained library: a survey of four centuries in the evolution of the English library* (New York, 1931).

systematic attempt to revise and supplement the work of Clark and Streeter, the compilation and description of the manuscript and documentary evidence were given a fresh impetus and new scholarly standards with the collaboration of a group of remarkable scholars from the 1930s onwards: the historian Christopher Cheney, the classicist Sir Roger Mynors and the English scholar and palaeographer N. R. Ker. In 1941 the first edition of *Medieval libraries of Great Britain* (*MLGB*) was published, under the editorship of Ker, which brought together lists of the surviving manuscripts of medieval institutional libraries that bore evidence of ownership, and provided information about extant pre-Reformation booklists from those institutions. Its second edition (1964) and *Supplement* (1987) nearly doubled the number of entries, by incorporating those manuscripts that have remained *in situ* in cathedrals and colleges. A complementary project was also envisaged – editions of medieval booklists and library catalogues, including new editions of the lists printed by eighteenth-century antiquaries, such as Hearne, and by James and others from the 1890s. This, however, began to be realised (as the Corpus of British Medieval Library Catalogues) only from 1990, and is now nearing completion. At the time of writing, we still await the publication of editions of some of the most significant lists: from Durham, Christ Church and St Augustine's, Canterbury, as well as from Oxford. These will contribute substantially to our understanding of the book collections of the later middle ages, and of the religious life and learning of those who used them.

In the early modern period the last fifty years have also seen much work achieved on both institutional and private libraries. In this field the father of us all must be Sears Jayne with his *Library catalogues of the English Renaissance*, first appearing in 1956.[23] He lists catalogues of both institutional and private, printed and manuscript catalogues, and the contents of these libraries have started to be investigated.

Among institutional libraries the 1605 catalogue of the Bodleian has been reproduced in facsimile,[24] and the holdings of other repositories have also been made known, ranging from the *Cathedral libraries catalogue* (*CLC*) to the holdings of Shropshire parochial libraries.[25] We hope that the outstanding examples will be found in the bibliography.

23 S. Jayne, *Library catalogues of the English Renaissance* (Berkeley, CA, 1956; reissued with a new preface and notes, Godalming, 1983).

24 *The first printed catalogue of the Bodleian Library, 1605* (Oxford, 1986).

25 Shropshire County Library, *Catalogue of books from parochial libraries in Shropshire* (London, 1971).

Interest in the holdings of early modern institutional libraries has a relatively long history. A catalogue of the Harsnett Library in Colchester, bequeathed to the borough by Samuel Harsnett, archbishop of York at his death in 1631, was published as long ago as 1888, complete with notes on provenance,[26] and we have also seen more or less detailed studies of Cambridge University Library, the Bodleian, and Trinity College, Dublin.

The recording of private libraries has a slightly more recent history, and this concentrated originally on the reconstruction (usually) of the substantial holdings of major collectors, or of persons otherwise well known to fame.[27]

A more recent development has been the investigation of the 'libraries', not so much of the 'common sort', as of the university-educated and otherwise 'middling sort'. Susan Cavanaugh's 'Study of books privately owned in England, 1300–1450'[28] and Leedham-Green's *Books in Cambridge inventories* catalogue the appraised book-holdings of the educated classes, the latter members of the university (including a few 'privileged' persons, like Agnes, husband of Peter and mother of John, Cheke) appearing in inventories proved in the Vice-Chancellor's Court there between 1535/6 and 1760 (the vast majority before 1609). *Private libraries in Renaissance England* (*PLRE*) has devoted most of its volumes to doing the same for the equivalent Oxford court records, currently covering the years 1514 to 1584.[29] The aim of these exercises is to delineate the *mentalité* of the educated classes. This they can do only roughly – statistically the data are to be used only with caution, with due allowance

26 G. Goodwin (ed.), *A catalogue of the Harsnett Library at Colchester* (London, 1888). It is a matter for rejoicing that this library has now been transferred to the local university, where it is undergoing detailed study under the eagle eye of James Raven.

27 E.g. (in order of publication) S. Jayne and F. R. Johnson (eds.), *The Lumley Library: the catalogue of 1609* (London, 1956); A. G. Watson (ed.), *The library of Sir Simonds D'Ewes* [d. 1650] (London, 1966); T. A. Birrell (ed.), *The library of John Morris* (1658) (London, [1976]); D. J. McKitterick, *The library of Sir Thomas Knyvett of Ashwellthorpe, c. 1539–1618* (Cambridge, 1978); J. Roberts and A. G. Watson (eds.), *John Dee's library catalogue* [based on the 1583 catalogue] (London, 1990); D. G. Selwyn (ed.), *The library of Thomas Cranmer* [dispersed 1553] (Oxford, 1996); N. K. Kiessling (ed.), *The library of Robert Burton* [d. 1640] (Oxford, 1998).

28 University of Pennsylvania, PhD dissertation (1980).

29 The first volume is of a different character, comprising *PLRE* 1, the library of bishop Richard Cox (d. 1581) (from an inventory); *PLRE* 2, that of Sir Edward Stanhope (d. 1608), as recorded in his donation to Trinity College, Cambridge; *PLRE* 3, that of Sir Roger Townshend, *c.* 1625, probably recording books moving from one property to another; and *PLRE* 4, that of Sir Edward Dering (d. 1644), derived from an incomplete catalogue (*c.* 1634–45), his 'Booke of Expences', 1617 and 1619–28, and his pocket-book (BL, MS Add. 47787).

made for the recurrence of a single volume in more than one inventory, the idiosyncrasies of the appraisers, mismatches with booksellers' inventories and other incalculable factors. That said, there is beginning to emerge, not so much a picture of that mythical entity the typical library, as a tool whereby an atypical one may be identified.

The present volume is the first full-scale survey of the history of libraries in the islands of Britain and Ireland. Indeed, until 1958 the only surveys of the history of English libraries in the medieval and early modern periods were those in general histories of libraries, and most importantly, for the medieval period, the contribution of Karl Christ to the *Handbuch der Bibliothekswissenschaft*.[30] These, however, were impressively supplemented by a collection of studies, originally given as lectures, published in 1958 as *The English library before 1700*, which thereafter remained the standard introduction to the subject.[31] The extent to which the present volume is able to build upon it is due in no small part to the work of Ker, his colleagues and their early modern counterparts, to the newly available volumes of the CBMLC, *BCI* and *PLRE*, and also to A. B. Emden's monumental *Biographical Registers* of Oxford and Cambridge (*BRUO* and *BRUC*), in which he included references to books associable with individuals who had studied at these universities.

Like its French counterpart, the *Histoire des bibliothèques françaises* (*Hbf*) this volume also reflects the interest in the social, cultural and economic contexts that have shaped the way in which texts have been represented in writing, as well as their circulation and reception, which is commonly referred to as 'The History of the Book'. Close attention to the physical characteristics of books and to their use reveals a richer and more complex picture of how books were conceived and used, collectively as well as singly. A history of libraries that spans the period from the sixth to the mid-seventeenth century can only briefly examine the wider context of book production and reading within which developments in book collections and libraries took place. In the course of our period, for example, the reading classes expanded well beyond the clerisy and the professions: the best-known example is Shakespeare, a grammar-school boy, whose breadth of reading has prompted several to insist that he must have attended a university, notwithstanding the fact that the reading pabulum of university men, so far as we can trace it, consisted of

30 F. Milkau (ed.), *Handbuch der Bibliothekswissenschaft*, 2nd edn, ed. G. Leyh, 4 vols. in 5 (Wiesbaden, 1952–65), III. ch. 5; an English version is K. Christ, *The handbook of medieval library history*, rev. A. Kern, tr. and ed. T. M. Otto (Metuchen, NJ, 1984).

31 In the same year, R. Irwin's *The origins of the English library* also appeared (London, 1958), which was subsequently revised as *The English library: sources and history* (London, 1964).

material quite alien to the Italian novellas and other sources which have been identified as his sources.[32] His reading is metropolitan, not academic.

Other gaps must also be acknowledged: the casualties of unavoidable constraints of space, time and the current state of published research. Most serious is the absence of a late medieval counterpart to Pádraig Ó Néill's contribution on the book collections of Celtic Britain and Ireland, and of the fate of manuscript collections in Wales and Ireland in the sixteenth and seventeenth centuries. This volume of the *Cambridge history of libraries* should therefore be regarded as complementary to the corresponding volumes of the *Cambridge history of the book in Britain* and the projected histories of the book in Scotland and in Ireland, and to the volume of studies on Welsh books and libraries, *A nation and its books*.[33]

Information about the book collections of the 'middling sort' outside the universities remains sparse. Something can be deduced from booksellers' records, for example those of John Foster of York in 1616,[34] and, for other localities, from such sources as Peter Clark's 'The ownership of books in England, 1540–1640: the example of some Kentish townsfolk',[35] and Claire Cross's *York clergy wills 1520–1600*.[36] It has to be remembered, however, that books bequeathed were not always books previously owned – a man might leave a bible to each of his four children, almost certainly not the books themselves, but rather the money to buy them – any more than books in private libraries were necessarily books read by the owner, still less the only books they might have read. Shared access to books among the clergy is discussed by Arnold Hunt,[37] and we have inklings of similar practices among the heterodox, like the Familists.[38] It is likely that there were other groups drawn together by common beliefs or occupations who also held books in common.

The private libraries of women are also notably lacking: apart from the manuscript libraries of princely ladies, evidence for women's libraries in the sixteenth century is scarce. We await a full account of the library of Mildred

32 S. Gillespie, *Shakespeare's books: a dictionary of Shakespeare sources* (London and New Brunswick, 2001).

33 P. H. Jones and E. Rees (eds.), *A nation and its books: a history of the book in Wales* (Aberystwyth, 1998).

34 J. Barnard and M. Bell, *The early seventeenth-century York book trade and John Foster's inventory of 1616* (Leeds, 1994).

35 In L. Stone (ed.), *Schooling and society* (Baltimore, 1976), 95–111.

36 (York, 1989). 37 See below, 403 ff., esp. 409.

38 See C. W. Marsh on William Safford's books in his *The Family of Love in English society, 1550–1630* (Cambridge, 1994), esp. 215, and 92 for communal reading.

Cecil, Lady Burghley,[39] and the few non-noble ladies' libraries that are known to us, like those of Frances Wolfreston (1607–77)[40] and Elizabeth Puckering (1607–76/7),[41] fall towards or beyond the end of our period.

In this volume, we have also tried to trace the evolution of the perception of libraries, and the emergence of the role of librarians culminating in the appearance of the first manuals.[42] Volume II will take these themes further.

39 A useful summary is given by C. Bowden, 'The library of Mildred Cooke Cecil, Lady Burghley', *Library*, 7th ser., 6 (2005) 3–29; a fuller account by Pamela Selwyn is in preparation.

40 P. Morgan, 'Frances Wolfreston and "hor bouks": a seventeenth-century woman book-collector', *Library*, 6th ser., 11 (1989), 197–219; she was collecting from 1631.

41 D. McKitterick, 'Women and their books in seventeenth-century England: the case of Elizabeth Puckering', *Library*, 7th ser., 1 (2000), 359–80. This article contains a very valuable survey of work to date on women's readership and book-ownership.

42 See especially chapters 8, 24 and 25, below.

THE PHYSICAL SETTING

1a

The medieval library (to *c.* 1450)

RICHARD GAMESON

Most 'medieval libraries' were not a single physical entity: rather they comprised a number of collections, often physically discrete, whose contents might shift from one to another, or be reconfigured, in response to changing needs and local conditions. The first library rooms – chambers in which books were not only stored but also consulted – usually held only a portion of the total collection, other parts being stored elsewhere. Throughout our period, where the collections were kept, how they were stored and the principles underlying their organisation were directly connected to their size, function and use. Nevertheless, other, less practical factors, ranging from inertia to the wishes of benefactors, could also come into play. In all but a few of the major religious communities, book collections were usually small, numbering hundreds rather than thousands; and in many institutions a proportion of the books would always be in the hands of individual members, reducing the number for which storage space was required. Most collections grew comparatively slowly (albeit in fits and starts), encouraging a series of *ad hoc* measures and expedients rather than radical restructuring. Thus, once a particular store had been settled upon, it was likely to have a long life. More dramatic change, when it came, was a response as much to new concepts of use as to the practicalities of storage.

Specific details about the practical arrangements for keeping books are frustratingly elusive. The physical evidence is particularly exiguous. Hardly any medieval book-stores (whether chest, cupboard or chamber) or library rooms survive intact. Still less remains of their furnishings.[1] The gaps in the material evidence are only partially remedied by written sources.[2] Few of

1 The material evidence has yet to be fully collated and assessed. The fullest treatments remain the pioneering studies: J. W. Clark, *The care of books* (Cambridge, 1901); B. H. Streeter, *The chained library: a survey in the evolution of the English library* (London, 1931).

2 The most important body of which is being newly (re-)edited for the Corpus of British Medieval Library Catalogues (CBMLC).

the extant medieval booklists and catalogues were intended to act as finding lists, and not many before the fourteenth century provide information about the location of the books. Moreover, such documents are rarely a comprehensive account of all the collections possessed by a community, and by their nature (a record of one particular moment in time) give an artificially static view of those they do list. In addition, the precise meaning of the terms used to describe the places where books were kept is often unclear.

The term most commonly found from the twelfth century onwards is *armarium*, which can refer to a single cupboard, either free-standing (a press) or a wall-recess (aumbrey), but was also used to refer more generally to a collection of books (housed in one or more presses), and even perhaps to a book-room.[3] The word is used in one or other of these latter senses in an inventory of the books of the Cistercian abbey of Meaux, compiled in 1396, part of which comprises a list of books *in communi almario claustri* ('in the common *almarium* of the cloister'), further sub-divided into different *thecae* (cases or cupboards), one above the door, one opposite the door and others evidently against the other walls.[4] Although nothing survives above ground on the site of the abbey, the description is sufficiently detailed to indicate a narrow room within one of the cloister ranges, such as is found at several English Cistercian houses. In other records, however, the mention of a *communis armarium claustri* might refer to a collection accommodated, not in a room, but in recesses built into the cloister wall or in free-standing presses backed against it.

The term *libraria* (or *librarium*) also lacked a single, precise usage. In the fifteenth century, *libraria* was the most commonly used term for a library room, but during the thirteenth and fourteenth centuries it was used in a more general way to refer to a collection of books. A booklist of 1202 from Rochester Cathedral Priory, for example, records the main collection of the works of the Fathers under the heading *Librarium Beati Andree* (the titular saint of the house); this is followed by other collections each also called *librarium*: the *comune librarium*, an *aliud librarium in archa cantoris*, and a *Librarium Magistri Hamonis*.[5] Here, the *archa cantoris* is probably a specific storage space, although of what kind cannot be determined, for while the word itself might lead one to expect a chest, the large number of volumes in the cache in question implies some other form of repository.

3 R. W. Hunt, 'The library of the abbey of St Albans', in Parkes and Watson, *Medieval scribes*, 259; A. J. Piper, 'The libraries of the monks of Durham', in *ibid.*, 217–18.

4 CBMLC III. Z14, nos. 50–363.

5 CBMLC IV. B79.

Book-stores and their location

Reliable evidence for the nature of book storage before the twelfth century is scanty in the extreme. Little relevant physical evidence survives, and only one of the handful of extant booklists records the location of the titles in question. A list from Bury St Edmunds in the time of Abbot Leofstan (1046–65) shows that ten volumes (nine service books and a copy of the *Vita S. Edmundi*) were then kept in the abbey church, eleven liturgical books were in the hands of seven named individuals, while a further thirty books (of unspecified content) were in the keeping of Leofstan himself – for which a single chest or cupboard would have sufficed.[6] Such grander collections as existed prior to the eleventh century are poorly documented, if at all, with the notable exception of that accumulated by Benedict Biscop (d. 689) and Ceolfrith (d. 716) for the twin monasteries of Monkwearmouth and Jarrow.[7] Some impression of the extraordinary number of books they gathered can be gained from the sources used by Bede, but how they were stored and organised is unknown – apart from two of the massive pandects (complete, one-volume bibles) commissioned by Ceolfrith, which he 'had placed in the churches of his two monasteries so that it should be easy for all who wished to read any chapter of either Testament to find what they wanted'.[8] The depiction of an open book-cupboard that appears in the portrait of the Prophet Ezra in a third pandect commissioned by Ceolfrith (the Codex Amiatinus)[9] cannot safely be used as evidence for how books were stored at Monkwearmouth-Jarrow, because the image derives from a continental exemplar (perhaps from Cassiodorus' Vivarium); one can do no more than speculate that the emulation of Mediterranean objects cultivated at Monkwearmouth-Jarrow by Biscop and Ceolfrith might have extended to the imitation of such an item. Be that as it may, and with due regard for artistic purpose and conventions, the image does shed valuable light on the nature of such furniture. Though clearly a substantial cupboard, equipped with five shelves, it does not hold many books; the volumes lie flat on their sides. Both points remain true in later (albeit non-English) depictions of book-cupboards.

From the twelfth century, references to the location of books – especially to *armaria* – begin to multiply. At Ely in 1143, for instance, Bishop Nigel found 'a large number of books in an *armarium*';[10] this may have been a

6 Lapidge, 'Booklists', 33–89, no. VII.   7 See below, 92, 100.

8 C. Plummer (ed.), *Vita Ceolfridi auctore anonymo*, c. 20: *Venerabilis Bedae opera historica*, 2 vols. (Oxford, 1896), I. 395.

9 Florence, Biblioteca Medicea-Laurenziana, Amiatino 1, fol. 'V'r; K. Weitzmann, *Late antique and early Christian book illumination* (New York, 1977), pl. 48.

10 E. O. Blake (ed.), *Liber Eliensis*, Camden Third Series (London, 1962), 294.

free-standing chest or cupboard, or perhaps the twelfth-century wall-recess (of which a fragment is still visible in the north range of the cloister) which was replaced in the thirteenth century by a larger and more elaborate *armarium*.[11] One point that the fuller documentation makes abundantly clear is that books were stored in a variety of locations. Volumes used in the performance of the liturgy or for public reading, for example, were kept in or close to the places where they were used. The list of books that Henry of Blois 'had written for Glastonbury' (where he was abbot from 1126 to 1171) states that a couple of lectionaries were in the chapter house, one breviary was in the infirmary and another in the guesthouse.[12] The catalogue of 1396 from Meaux records eight volumes at the high altar of the church, over seventy in the choir (including thirty-eight small processionals), and seven service-books in the infirmary chapel, 'not counting the other psalters, breviaries and collectanea for the private use of the abbot, the office-holders and the monks'.[13] The late fifteenth-century catalogue from the Augustinian abbey of Leicester offers further precision, listing each volume that lay on the high altar, at ten other altars, at each of the canons' stalls, in the choir, and on the pulpitum, as well as the *cantica organica*, the service-books in the infirmary and those at the abbey's cell at Ingwarby.[14] Texts used for 'public' reading in the refectory sometimes formed a separate small collection, whose contents might change over the course of the year in accordance with the cycle of lections. A rare inventory of such books from Reading Abbey, dating from the late fourteenth century, states that they were kept ready to hand in the dormitory;[15] and volumes marked as belonging to the refectory survive from Bury St Edmunds, Peterborough and elsewhere.[16] At Fountains Abbey there is a small recess in the walling at the entrance to the stairway that leads up to the pulpit within the west wall of the refectory, which may have been the cupboard for the books that were read there.[17] The church itself was sometimes the location for other specialised collections. The Meaux catalogue lists two small caches of manuscripts *in ecclesia*: a collection of texts fundamental to the conduct of Cistercian monasticism,

11 CBMLC IV. 128; *VCH Cambridgeshire* IV. 79; II. 205–6.

12 CBMLC IV. B37.

13 CBMLC III. Z14, nos. 1–21.

14 CBMLC VI. A20, nos. 1699–862. For a similarly detailed list, see the 1506 inventory from Exeter Cathedral: G. Oliver, *Lives of the bishops of Exeter and a history of the cathedral* (Exeter, 1861), 320–76.

15 CBMLC IV. B74; A. Coates, *English medieval books: the Reading Abbey collections from foundation to dispersal* (Oxford, 1999), 66–7, 84–6.

16 E.g. Cambridge, St John's Coll., MS B.13 ('de refectorio monachorum sancti edmundi'); and CCCC, MS 160 ('liber refectorii burg.').

17 For three surviving books from Bury St Edmunds labelled *de refectorio* by Henry de Kirkestede in the mid-thirteenth century, see CBMLC XI. xlix.

which was kept *in communi almario in ecclesia*, and another small group, mainly comprising key texts for biblical study and a four-volume passional, kept 'in aliis almariis officii cantoris in ecclesia'.[18] At St Albans Abbey, the magnificent set of glossed books of the Bible commissioned by Abbot Simon (1167–83) was displayed in a painted cupboard near the tomb of Roger the Hermit (an arched recess in the south wall of the abbey church leading to the cloister), where they commemorated that abbot's love of Scripture.[19] Some books, especially those in precious bindings, were kept in the treasury with other valuables: such was the case at Ely, whose mid-twelfth-century inventory of their treasury includes some eighteen gospel books with lavish bindings.[20] The main collections for personal spiritual reading and study, however, were usually located within the cloister, and are discussed below.

An unusually complete picture of the shifting character of the multiple collections of books created by a religious community to serve its various needs is provided by the surviving records and books of Durham Cathedral Priory.[21] In addition to the various caches sent to its numerous monastic dependencies, over ten collections are documented within the priory itself, in or around the cloister. By the mid-fourteenth century, the principal collection of 'working' books was located in the cloister, while a second major group (comprising volumes that had become outdated and were little used) was kept in the Spendement, a store-room adjoining it; by 1418 a library room had been added above the parlour in the eastern range of the cloister, which was provisioned with books taken from both the cloister and Spendement collections. Volumes continued to be transferred between these three collections, to meet changing needs, over the course of the fifteenth century. Other, smaller caches were similarly fluid. Books to be read at the evening collation formed a separate group in the mid-twelfth century; by the mid-fourteenth century a collection of books to be read aloud in the refectory was kept in a cupboard round the corner from the refectory door, beside the entrance to the infirmary at the south end of the west side of the cloister. Texts for the novices (known from a list of 1395) were kept in the cloister; the collection of archives, once held in the Spendement, were by the Dissolution located in a 'Register' close to the prior's lodging; Prior Wessington (1416–46) held various volumes in a chapel in his lodgings, while the feretrar who looked after the shrine of St Cuthbert had his 'own' cache of books by the late fourteenth century

18 CBMLC III. Z14, nos. 22–49. Such cases must be judged individually, since the word *ecclesia* might sometimes be used to refer to the monastery as a whole.

19 Hunt, 'Library of St Albans', 258.

20 Blake (ed.), *Liber Eliensis*, 290–1.

21 Piper, 'Libraries of the monks of Durham', 213–49, esp. fig. 17.

if not before. Finally, there were the service-books variously located in the cathedral, with additional collections of such texts held by the sacrist and in the infirmary.

The cloister collections

As the focus of their non-liturgical activity (including reading), the cloister was where monastic communities kept their main collections of books for personal study until at least the fifteenth century. The first proper cloister known to have been built in England is that of Edward the Confessor's Westminster Abbey, whereafter it became a standard feature of English monasteries; the earliest reference to lockable *armaria* there appears in the 'Monastic Constitutions' of Lanfranc, archbishop of Canterbury 1070–89.[22] Recesses of different dimensions, suitable for housing books, are found in twelfth-century fabric in approximately the same location (the north end of the east wall of the cloister, beside the south door of the church) at various religious houses in Britain, including the Cluniac priories of Castle Acre and Monk Bretton, the Augustinian abbey of Lilleshall, the Premonstratensian abbey of Dryburgh, and the Cistercian abbeys of Fountains, Kirkstall and Rievaulx. The example at Dryburgh, which is set about 3ft above floor level, is 6ft 8in. wide and 2ft 8in. deep and rises to an internal height of 5ft 4in. at the apex of its gently arched top. Grooves and gouges in the stonework show that the cavity originally had a first shelf 21in. above its base level, with a second shelf 22in. above the first (fig. 1). The stone is also 'rebated' to receive doors.

Physical and documentary evidence confirms the longevity of the use of the cloister as the place for the main reading collection. Four recesses are found in the east range of the cloister of the Augustinian priory of St Andrews, Fife, fabric which probably dates from the early thirteenth century.[23] When the east walk of the cloister at Norwich Cathedral Priory was rebuilt in the early fourteenth century, three elaborately decorated niches were included by the door to the church. In the same position at Worcester are substantial twin recesses, which had been renewed when the cloister was rebuilt in 1372; the floor of these recesses projects forward about a foot, forming a bench-table 16in. above the ground.[24] The custumal of the Augustinian canons of Barnwell (1295×6) is

22 D. Knowles (ed.), *The Monastic Constitutions of Lanfranc*, rev. C. N. L. Brooke, chs. 83–4 (Oxford, 2002), 114.

23 S. Cruden, *Scottish medieval churches* (Edinburgh, 1986), 96–7.

24 Thomson, *Cat. Worcester*, xxxxii, pl. 1.

Figure 1 Dryburgh Abbey, north-east corner of the cloister, showing the doorway into the abbey church and the aumbrey in the wall beside it. (Photo, Gameson)

unequivocal that the cloister (along with the church) is the place for books.[25] The fourteenth-century custumal of St Augustine's Abbey, Canterbury, makes the same assumption.[26] The use of free-standing cupboards and chests as supplements to, or instead of, wall-recesses is apparent from the account of the 1327 incursion into the abbey of Bury St Edmunds, which records that when the townsfolk 'entered the cloister, they broke the chests (*cistulas, id est caroles*) and the cupboards (*armoriola*) and carried off the books along with everything else that was found in them'.[27] Books were subsequently replaced in the cloister, since at least nine surviving Bury volumes contain the location note 'de armario claustri' in the hand of Henry de Kirkestede, librarian at Bury in the mid-fourteenth century.[28] The description in the *Rites of Durham* shows that free-standing *almaria* 'all full of bookes' remained in the north range of

25 J. W. Clark (ed.), *The observances in use at the Augustinian Priory of S. Giles and S. Andrew at Barnwell, Cambridgeshire* (Cambridge, 1897), 64.

26 E. M. Thompson (ed.), *Customary of the Benedictine monasteries of Saint Augustine, Canterbury and Saint Peter, Westminster*, 2 vols., HBS 23, 28 (1902–4), I. 421.

27 T. Arnold (ed.), *Depredatio abbatie Sancti Edmundi*, in *Memorials of St Edmund's Abbey*, 3 vols., RS (London, 1890–6), II. 330; see also III. 38; CBMLC XI. xlii–xliii, xlvii–l.

28 CBMLC XI. xlvii.

Figure 2 Durham Cathedral, north-west corner of cloister. Free-standing *almaria* were in the north range, backing against the south wall of the cathedral; the door to the Spendement is in the west range, close to the corner. (Photo, Gameson)

the cloister there (backed against the south wall of the cathedral nave) up to the Dissolution (fig. 2).[29]

An invaluable description of how the cloister aumbries were fitted out for books is found in the late thirteenth-century Barnwell custumal.

> The press [*armarium*] in which the books are kept ought to be lined inside with wood so that the damp of the walls may not moisten or stain the books. This press should be divided vertically as well as horizontally by sundry shelves on which the books may be ranged so as to be separated from one another, for fear they be packed so close as to injure each other or delay those who want them.[30]

These regulations, combined with the evidence of surviving aumbries and medieval bindings, permit rough calculations of the numbers of books that

29 J. T. Fowler (ed.), *Rites of Durham*, ch. 41, Surtees Soc. 107 (Durham, 1903), 83.

30 Clark (ed.), *Observances at Barnwell*, xlii–xlvi, 64–5. As Clark noted, the wording is closely similar to that in the twelfth-century *Liber ordinis* of the influential Augustinian abbey of Saint-Victor in Paris: *Liber ordinis S. Victoris Parisiensis*, ed. L. Joqué and L. Milis, *CCCM* 61 (Turnhout, 1984), 78–9; see below, 224.

could be accommodated. The presence of titles on the spines of some twelfth- and thirteenth-century bindings concords with other evidence to indicate that books were generally laid flat, with the spine outwards.[31] The Barnwell account gives the impression, even if it does not state so explicitly, that books not only were placed foot to head along each shelf (hence the need for vertical partitions) but were also laid on top of each other; the number of titles listed in a given section of a 'press' in certain library catalogues supports this interpretation. If one allows for the space taken up by the wooden panels and partitions, the Dryburgh recess (fig. 1) might have accommodated some fifty average-sized books – and more, if they were double-stacked. The more substantial twin recesses in the eastern range of the cloister at Worcester, which are 6ft 8in. in height, just over 11ft wide, and 2ft 5in. deep, and might have held five shelves, provide room for some 200–250 volumes each – over 400 in all.[32]

Book-rooms

Some twelfth-century English Cistercian houses, echoing arrangements in certain of their French counterparts, created a book-room in the cloistral complex between the chapter house and the entry to the church (normally at the north end of the eastern range of the cloister); the chamber in question was usually either combined with, or adapted from part of, the sacristy or vestry.[33] At Rievaulx, the room comes off the north-east corner of the cloister, next to the aumbrey, exactly filling the space between the south wall of the south transept and the north wall of the chapter house (fig. 3).[34] Its contents (some 225 volumes) are recorded in a late twelfth-century booklist.[35] At Buildwas, whose

31 G. Pollard, 'The construction of English twelfth-century bindings', *Library*, 5th ser., 17 (1962), 1–22, at 17–18, pls. 1–2; M. Gullick, 'The bindings', in Mynors and Thomson, xxvii, pl. 21. The implications for the form of storage of books with overcovers (the remains of which are found, for example, on many Hereford bindings of different dates), straps and metal furniture, such as clasps and bosses (the latter found on some twelfth-century Cistercian bindings), has yet to be fully considered.

32 Thomson, *Cat. Worcester*, xxxii.

33 For a detailed account of the various structural arrangements made within this area at Bordesley Abbey during the later middle ages, by comparison with those at other Cistercian houses, see S. Hirst and S. M. Wright (eds.), *Bordesley Abbey II: second report on excavations at Bordesley Abbey, Redditch, Hereford-Worcester*, British Archaeological Reports, British Ser., 111 (Oxford, 1983), 116–22. See also M. Aubert, *Architecture cistercienne en France*, 2nd edn, 2 vols. (Paris, 1947), I. 39–51. On the Continent, a designated book-room associated with the cloister can be traced back at least as far as the early ninth century, as at Saint-Wandrille: *Gesta sanctorum patrum Fontanellensis coenobii*, XIII. 5.55: P. Pradié (ed.), *Chronique des abbés de Fontenelle (Saint-Wandrille)* (Paris, 1999), 170.

34 The rear two-thirds of this oblong space was apparently divided off to form a vestry.

35 CBMLC III. Z19.

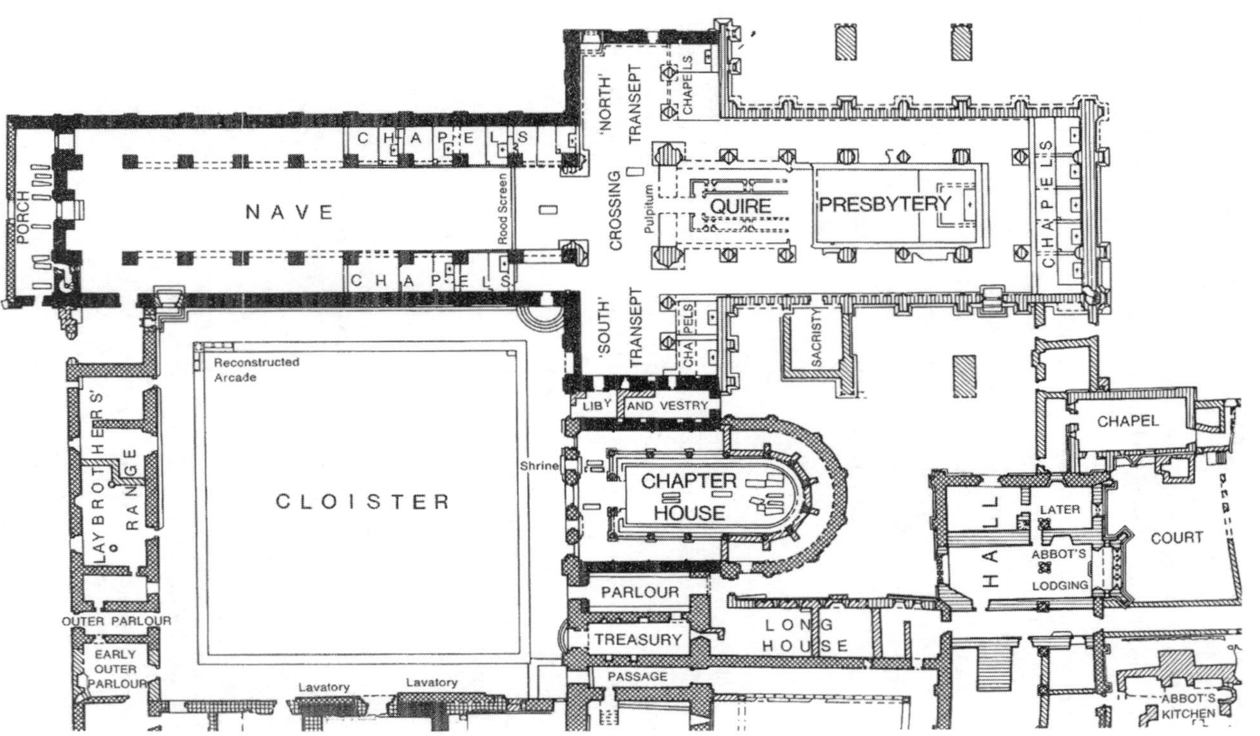

Figure 3 Rievaulx Abbey, plan (detail). The book-store is the small chamber between the south transept and the chapter house. (After Peers 1967)

cloister was to the north of its church, the arrangement was a mirror image of this. Similar provision was made a generation later at Kirkstall, Roche and Strata Florida (fig. 4), and continued (with modest variations reflecting local circumstances) into the thirteenth century, for instance at Tintern, as also at the Premonstratensian house of Dryburgh. Only at the Cistercian abbey of Cleeve does evidence survive of a purpose-built barrel-vaulted library the full depth of the east cloister range, between the sacristy and the chapter house. A variation on the theme was effected at Fountains during the twelfth century, and at Furness in the thirteenth, where a pair of walk-in cupboards was incorporated into the west end of the chapter house (flanking its vestibule) (fig. 5). The earliest known non-Cistercian house in Britain to introduce a store-room for its books was Christ Church, Canterbury, where, some time between 1160 and 1220, the slype (a passage from the east walk of the cloister running beside the north wall of the north transept) was blocked off and roofed to form a chamber for books.[36] The minimal natural lighting afforded in all these rooms confirms that they were used for storage, not for consultation *in situ*.

The principles governing the organisation of the books upon the shelves of the cloister cupboards and book-rooms before the late twelfth century are undocumented. The late twelfth- or early thirteenth-century list from Rievaulx is the earliest known English example in which the books are recorded under a sequence of classes (from A to Q), no doubt reflecting their physical arrangement in the book-room.[37] Catalogues of this kind survive in some number only from the second half of the fourteenth century. That of the Augustinian house of Lanthony-by-Gloucester, compiled in the 1350s and subsequently augmented and amended, provides a clear illustration of the organisation of a medium-sized reading collection.[38] The volumes were divided between five *armaria* with differing numbers of shelves (five, four, four, six and one respectively).[39] The fifth *armarium*, for which only one shelf was itemised, may have been of a different form, or might have been only partly filled at the time the

36 N. Ramsay, 'The cathedral archives and library', in P. Collinson, N. Ramsay and M. Sparks (eds.), *A history of Canterbury Cathedral* (Oxford, 1995), 350.

37 CBMLC III. Z19; R. Sharpe, 'Accession, classification, location: shelfmarks in medieval libraries', *Scriptorium* 50 (1996), 282–3.

38 CBMLC VI. A16.

39 The last leaf of the catalogue (fol. 11) starts with a section headed by the rubric 'libri de phisica continentur in quinto gradu III Armarii'. The three upright strokes probably signify 'III', though one might just argue that they are a sloppily written 'IV'. Be that as it may, the position of this list (out of sequence), allied to the fact that the hand which wrote this leaf is modestly different from that responsible for the main body of the text, implies that it represents an early addition or afterthought.

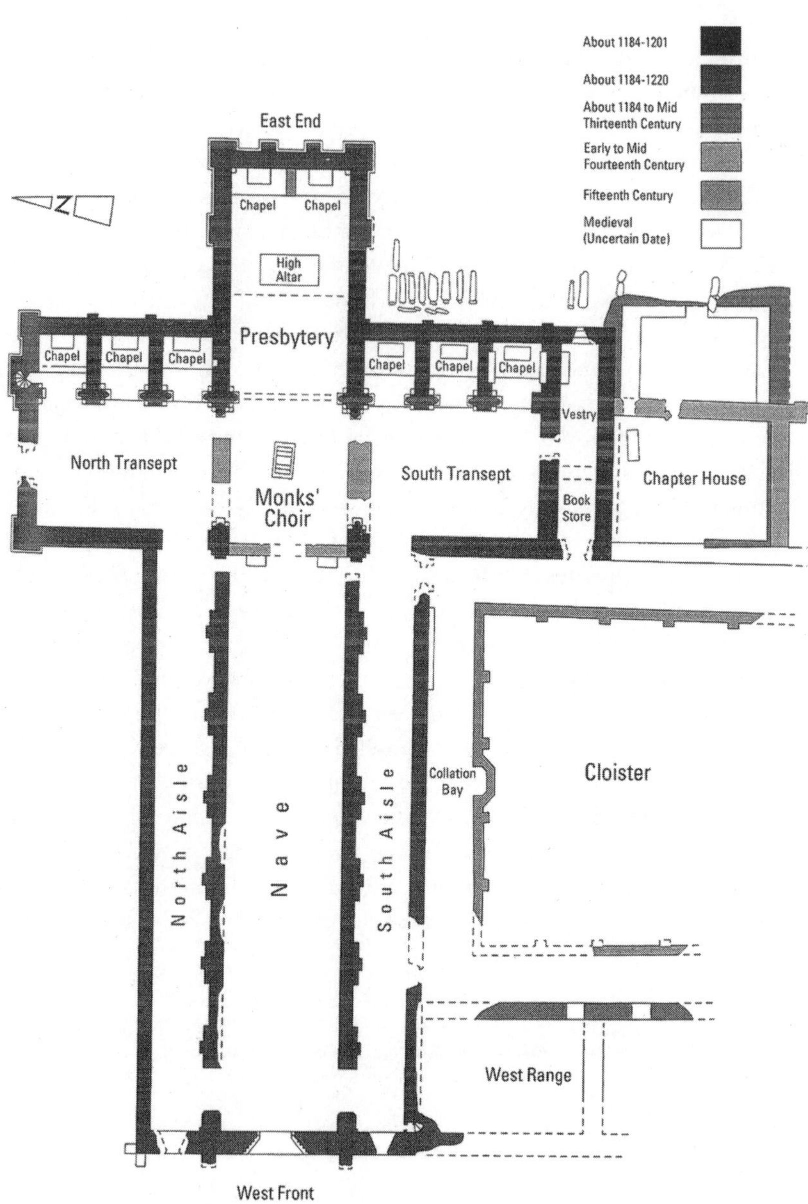

Figure 4 Strata Florida, plan (detail), including book-store between south transept and chapter house. (After Robinson and Platt 1992)

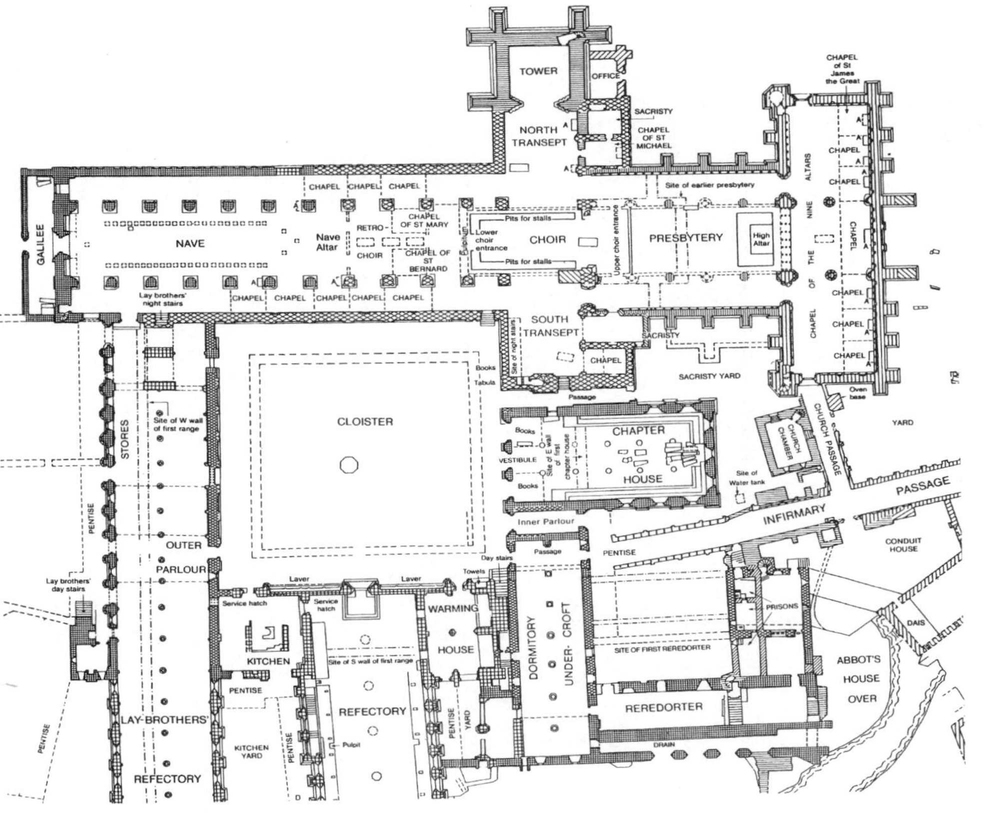

Figure 5 Fountains Abbey, plan (detail), including book storage space flanking the entrance to the chapter house. (After Gilyard-Beer 1986)

catalogue was compiled. Manuscripts of the work of a single author or on a related subject were generally kept on the same shelf. The catalogue describes almost half of the books as either 'large' 'medium-size' or 'small', revealing that whereas books of all sizes appear on the bottom four shelves of most presses, the fifth and sixth shelves – where they occur (namely presses I, IV and possibly also III) – have small and medium volumes only, some of which, moreover, were not in formal bindings. Accordingly, while most of the lower shelves held between twelve and thirty-eight volumes, the fifth and sixth shelves of presses I and IV had forty-five to fifty. The shelf with the largest number of volumes (seventy-two) was the fourth shelf of the fourth *armarium*, which accommodated schoolbooks and works on the liberal arts, typically small-format books; only one volume here is described as 'large'.

The content of the books was clearly the primary factor determining their arrangement, which followed a well-recognised hierarchy of importance reflected in other catalogues: priority was given to the Bible and its study, followed by the works of the Fathers; then came other religious works and canon law, and lastly the secular arts. The first (and undoubtedly the lowest) shelf of Lanthony's first press held bibles; the second and third shelves were devoted to glossed books of the Bible and biblical commentaries; the fourth shelf had glossed psalters and psalter commentaries, and the fifth included less bulky glossed books and other aids to the study of the Bible. The first shelf of the second press contained the works of Clement of Lanthony, an appropriately prominent place for the house author; the other three shelves primarily contained patristic texts. In the third press, the first two shelves were devoted to Augustine, above which are found letter collections and other material, then, on the fourth shelf, sermons and the works of the Augustinian scholar, Hugh of Saint-Victor. The bottom two shelves of the fourth press held canon law, above which were hagiography and *pastoralia*, then (primarily) texts related to the study of the liberal arts, followed by works on grammar, and finally (on the sixth shelf) writings on the quadrivium and a collection of custumals. The single shelf that was recorded for the fifth press held a grand bible, a large two-volume homiliary, and a large passional, together with Peter the Chanter's *Historia scholastica* and sermons, some key grammatical textbooks, a commentary on the Augustinian rule, and books relating to the Office. This might have comprised a 'rapid reference' collection, duplicates of items kept elsewhere, 'outsize' volumes, or some combination of all these. A collection of medical texts appears to have been added shortly afterwards, either to the fifth shelf of the fourth press, or perhaps on an additional fifth shelf in the third press. The arrangement of the collection, considered as a whole, is sufficiently orderly, and the number of volumes sufficiently small, to permit a particular book to be found easily, especially since the various additions, deletions, notes and marks in the catalogue indicate the presence of attentive librarians.[40]

From the fourteenth century also, location marks recording the press (in some cases the shelf as well) were added to the books by certain librarians.[41] For some religious houses, these press-marks can be combined with the evidence of a catalogue to shed light upon the arrangement of the books, although there can also be a puzzling lack of correlation between the two, as a comparison of the catalogue of the books of Christ Church, Canterbury (drawn up by Prior Henry of Eastry, d. 1331), and the press-marks in the books themselves reveals.[42] The unusually detailed catalogues of Dover Priory (1389) and Titchfield Abbey (compiled in 1400) articulate a well-developed concept of a monastic library in which book-room, furniture and the way the volumes were ordered were co-ordinated and carefully recorded both to facilitate finding particular titles and to draw attention to their importance as a spiritual resource.[43] The compiler of the remarkable Dover catalogue, the precentor John Whytefelde, makes this explicit: his catalogue was to 'supply information to the precentor of the house concerning the number of the books and the complete knowledge of them . . . to stir up studious brethren to eager and frequent reading . . . and to point the way to the speedy finding of individual treatises'.[44] The Titchfield document has the added interest that it provides specific details about the nature and location of the four presses (*columnae*): 'there are in the library (*libraria*) of Titchfield four presses in which to place books, of which two (the first and second) are on the east wall; on the south wall is the third; and on the north wall the fourth; and each of them has eight shelves (*gradus*) marked with a letter and number . . .'[45]

In those communities to whose life the cloister was less central, the books might always have been stored elsewhere. For York Minster, which did not have a cloister, this is self-evidently true. But even at Wells, a secular cathedral that did have one, the main book collection seems to have been housed in the

40 Items were added by several hands into the fifteenth century; various volumes, especially on the first shelf of the fourth press, were noted as missing, and several items (especially on the first, second and fourth shelves of the fourth press) are marked with a cross.

41 Sharpe, 'Accession, classification, location', 286–7.

42 James, *ALCD*, no. II, with xxxviii–xliv; N. Ramsay, 'Archives and library', 355–60.

43 CBMLC v (Dover); CBMLC III. P6 (Titchfield).

44 CBMLC v. 15.

45 CBMLC III. 183.

west aisle of the north transept of the cathedral church itself, while a few items, including legal texts, were kept in the treasury (under the chapter house).[46]

The library room

The stimulus to more fundamental changes in the physical setting for collections of books came from the needs of preachers and scholars during the thirteenth century. Many of the books that were owned communally by the convents of the mendicant orders were actually kept in the possession of individual friars for their personal use in preaching and teaching. Provision for scholars at the universities was largely dependent on personal initiative, gradually supplemented by collections of texts available for loan to members of a given college.[47] Over the course of the thirteenth and fourteenth centuries, however, the concept of a fixed reference collection of essential texts available for communal consultation *in situ* – in addition to the loan collection – began to emerge among the mendicant orders. It was soon adopted by academic institutions, often under mendicant influence, though perhaps also in response to practical necessity.[48] Humbertus de Romanis, master general of the Dominican order (1254–63), had envisaged important works being kept in a convenient place within each convent for communal consultation.[49] In 1284, the Franciscan, Archbishop Peckham, enjoined Merton College, Oxford, to acquire three grammatical reference works, which were to be secured to a solid table in a place to which all the fellows would have easy access.[50] Such an arrangement was extended and formalised in the 1292 statutes of University College, Oxford, which stipulated two book collections – one for reference, the other for 'internal' loan.[51]

The formal introduction of a permanent reference collection brought with it a new kind of physical arrangement. Whereas the books available for annual or more extended loan could be accommodated in the traditional way in chests,

46 W. H. B. Bird (ed.), *Calendar of manuscripts of the Dean and Chapter of Wells*, I (London, 1907), 162; and II, ed. W. P. Baildon (London, 1914), 46, 60, 221.

47 Parkes, 'Provision of books', 409–27, 449–58; see below, chapter 6.

48 See below, 166–8. For possible precedents, see D. Nebbiai-Dalla Guarda, 'La bibliothèque commune des institutions religieuses', *Scriptorium* 50 (1996), 254–68.

49 Humbertus de Romanis, *Opera de vita regulari*, ed. J. J. Berthier (Rome, 1888–9), II. 265; K. W. Humphreys, *The book provisions of the mediaeval friars, 1215–1460* (Amsterdam, 1964), 29.

50 C. T. Martin (ed.), *Registrum epistolarum fratris Johannis Peckham archiepiscopi Cantuariensis*, ep. DLXXXIX, 3 vols., RS (London, 1882–5), III. 813; see also J. R. L. Highfield (ed.), *The early rolls of Merton College, Oxford* (Oxford, 1964), no. 12, 225.

51 H. Anstey (ed.), *Munimenta academica or Documents illustrative of academical life and studies at Oxford*, 2 vols., RS (London, 1868), I. 58–9.

cupboards or other forms of book-store, the works for reference required not just a convenient yet secure place but an arrangement which permitted them to be consulted easily. The solution was a library room in which volumes were not only stored but also read. Consequently the rooms had to be equipped with sufficient windows to permit adequate light for reading, while the books were not shelved in presses but placed on lecterns ready for use. They were often chained to the lecterns to ensure that they were not removed. Nevertheless, the distinction in function and use between the two types of collection was not necessarily reflected in their location, for some library rooms were also used as places to store books in chests and cupboards.

The earliest documented example of such arrangements within a university context is at the Sorbonne, whose books were divided into two parts, the *magna libraria* and the *parva libraria*. Volumes from the latter could circulate among the masters, while the former (initially known as the *libraria communis*) was a chained reference library, established in 1289 'for the communal use of the Fellows'.[52] Its influence in England, however, should not be overstated, for here the practices of the friars may have been a more significant impulse. The 1292 statutes of University College, Oxford, likewise identified the need for a common yet secure place in which to keep the reference collection, and this requirement was addressed in the statutes and building activities of many of the foundations at Oxford and Cambridge thereafter.[53] The tortuous history of the Oxford University Library began in 1320, when Thomas de Cobham gave money for a Convocation House beside the University Church of St Mary, with a library room above; because of his straitened circumstances at his death seven years later and the consequent, lengthy dispute between the university and Oriel College, it was to be another ninety years before it finally opened (figs. 19–20).[54] Merton College, Oxford, had a *libraria*, a room in which books were chained, by 1338.[55] The 1350 statutes of Trinity Hall, Cambridge, envisaged a library room (*libraria*) in which 'the books of the Doctors of civil and canon law' (the focus of higher studies there) would be chained, while the legal textbooks that were stored in the same chamber might be available for

52 R. H. Rouse, 'The early library of the Sorbonne', *Scriptorium* 21 (1967), 42–71; rev. repr. in M. A. Rouse and R. H. Rouse, *Authentic witnesses: approaches to medieval texts and manuscripts* (Notre Dame, IN, 1991), 341–408; R. H. Rouse and M. A. Rouse, 'La bibliothèque du collège de Sorbonne', *Hbf* I. 113–23.

53 Anstey, *Munimenta academica*, I. 59.

54 Parkes, 'Provision of books', 470–72.

55 Merton Coll., MS 317, fol. 1^{r}: 'ex dono magistri Nigelli de Wauere . . . quem dedit ad cathenandum in loco communi et inde non transferatur ad usos priuatos'; F. M. Powicke, *The medieval books of Merton College* (Oxford, 1931), no. 270; P. S. Allen and M. W. Garrod (eds.), *Merton muniments* (Oxford, 1928), 33, line 7.

loan.[56] Those of *c.* 1365 for Canterbury College, Oxford (the university cell of Christ Church Cathedral Priory), specified a chamber (*camera*) for books and vestments, in which no volumes were chained, but consultation *in situ* was obligatory for any 'outsider'.[57] Queen's College, Oxford, had a *libraria* under construction in the 1370s;[58] Exeter College, Oxford, which had converted the founder's chapel into a book chamber in 1375, was building a new library room a mere eight years later;[59] and the King's Hall, Cambridge, had one by the 1390s.[60] Merton had meanwhile invested in a new library (the current 'Old Library' in Mob Quad), which was begun in 1371 and completed in 1379. Consonant with the size of the college's book collection, this was an unusually large room, occupying most of the south and west sides of the quadrangle at first-floor level, with a total floor space of around 2,300 square feet, built at a cost of not less than £600 (fig. 6).[61] The example of the mendicants was still apparently influential, for among the sites that the bursar (and later warden) of Merton (John Bloxham) and the master mason (William Humberville) visited in preparation for the project was London, whither they went 'with the purpose of viewing the library of the preaching friars'.[62]

The architectural design of the new facility at Merton was still retrospective in one important respect – the lighting. The windows, though numerous (seven pairs punctuate the west range, ten pairs the south one), are very small in relation to the size of the chamber, which they signally fail to illuminate adequately. Moreover, the spacing of the windows is such that, while a two-sided lectern would fit between them, there was room for only one bench between each pair of lecterns (fig. 7).[63] This aspect of design was remedied at New College, Oxford – the first college in which a library room formed part of the original plan. The college was founded in 1379 and the library seems to have been open within a decade (though construction work continued into the fifteenth century). A substantial first-floor chamber (70ft by 21ft) in the eastern range of the main quadrangle, the room was lit by nine windows on each long side; these faced east–west, thus maximising the light (fig. 8).

56 Willis and Clark, III. 391.

57 W. A. Pantin, *Canterbury College*, 4 vols., OHS, n.s. 6–8, 30 (1947–85), III. 167.

58 H. W. Garrod and J. R. L. Highfield, 'An indenture between William Rede, bishop of Chichester, and John Bloxham and Henry Stapilton, fellows of Merton College, Oxford, London 22 October 1374', *BLR* 10 / 1 (1978–82), 9–19, at 11.

59 C. W. Boase (ed.), *Register of Exeter College, Oxford*, OHS 27 (1894), xlvii.

60 CBMLC X. 316, 319, UC36.

61 H. W. Garrod in *VCH Oxfordshire*, III. 101.

62 Merton College Muniments, Rec. 4102b; J. Harvey, *English medieval architects: a biographical dictionary down to 1550*, 2nd edn (Gloucester, 1984), 153. See also below, 165.

63 Streeter, 13–14.

Figure 6 Merton College, Oxford, Mob Quad, north and east sides. The 'noua libraria' occupied the first floor of both ranges. (Photo, Gameson)

Figure 7 Merton College, Oxford, 'noua libraria', interior view across the top of the post-medieval presses, showing the relatively small spaces between the original window apertures and the small size of the actual lights therein. (Photo, Gameson)

Figure 8 New College, Oxford, in 1675, looking east. The *libraria* occupies most of the first floor of the east range of the main quadrangle. (After Loggan 1675)

Two-sided lecterns, 5ft 6in. high, were fitted on either side between the windows, at right-angles to them, leaving an 'alley' down the centre.[64]

Library rooms continued to be built (or rebuilt) at Oxford and Cambridge during the fifteenth century. Durham College, Oxford (fig. 9), and King's Hall, Cambridge, built libraries (or in the latter case a *noua libraria*) in the second decade of the century; Clare Hall, Cambridge, in the third; Balliol, Oxford, and Gonville Hall and Peterhouse (a *noua libraria*), Cambridge, in the fourth; Queens' College, Cambridge, All Souls and probably Oriel, Oxford, in the fifth. The size of these rooms ranged from the modest 28ft by 18ft of Durham College (figs. 9–10) to the more typical 47ft 6in. by 19ft 6in. of All Souls and 60ft by 20ft of Peterhouse. Like the earlier library rooms, they were generally at first-floor level, and often, although not invariably, ran from north to south, thus having their long walls (with the main ranges of windows) facing east–west to maximise the light – as at Durham College and All Souls, whose long sides were pierced by four and eight windows respectively. As surviving catalogues

64 G. Jackson-Stops, 'The buildings of the medieval college', in J. Buxton and P. H. Williams (eds.), *New College, Oxford, 1379–1979* (Oxford, 1979), 147–92, esp. 182–3; R. W. Hunt, 'The medieval library', in *ibid.*, 317–45.

Figure 9 Durham (now Trinity) College, Oxford, 'Durham Quad', east range. The *libraria* is the first first-floor chamber to the right of the downpipe (cf. fig. 10). (Photo, Gameson)

show, the desks (some with, others without, a lower shelf) that projected into the room between each window held anything from five to nearly thirty books. These principles found their ultimate expression in Henry VI's designs for his foundations of Eton and King's College, Cambridge, projects of the 1440s.[65] The library at Eton was to be the centrepiece of the eastern side of the quadrangle at first-floor level; that at King's was to be a first-floor chamber on the western side of the court. The former was to measure 52ft by 24ft, the latter a magnificent 110ft by 24ft. In the event, neither was built to plan.

While the stone fabric of a number of the library rooms has survived more or less unaltered, the internal furnishings have, not surprisingly, almost entirely disappeared. Lecterns are well attested in documentary sources, especially accounts, which show, for instance, that carpenters from Ely made the lecterns for the new library at Peterhouse, that the carpenter-joiner Richard Tyllock was responsible for 'le deskes in libraria' at All Souls, and that the library at Lincoln College was equipped with some half- or single desks as well as double ones.[66]

65 Willis and Clark, I. 350–80, esp. 356, 360, 370, 374–5.
66 CBMLC X. 444; *VCH Oxfordshire*, III. 183; R. Weiss, 'The earliest catalogues of the library of Lincoln College', *BQR* 8, no. 94 (1937), 343–59.

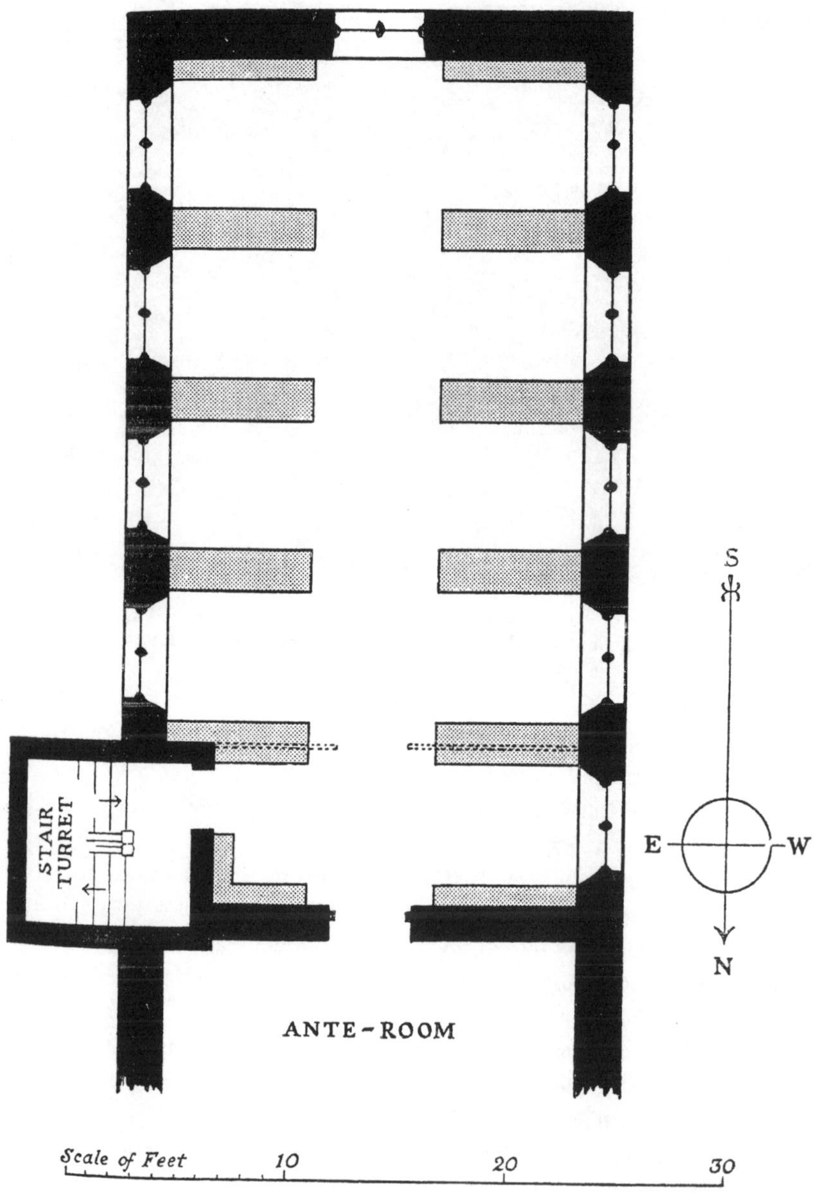

Figure 10 Durham College, Oxford, *libraria*, plan (cf. fig. 9). (After Streeter 1931)

No examples, however, are known to survive from a university context in England. Fortunately, three lecterns survive from the fifteenth-century library room at Lincoln Cathedral. These have a sloping desk on either side, rising to a shelf (where, presumably, chained books that were not being consulted could be temporarily stacked in order to make more space on the desk surface for an opened volume), with a bar running above, to which the chains were attached; a lower shelf was subsequently added to enable more books to be accommodated (fig. 11).[67] Each lectern would seem to have had a bench on both sides, joined to it by cills at floor level.

The books were laid flat on the desks, probably – to judge from the position of fifteenth- and sixteenth-century labels (sometimes covered with horn) that record titles and press-marks – with the lower cover uppermost. An early method of chaining, evident from the marks left by the chain-staples on the boards of the binding or the outermost leaf, involved fixing the chain to a staple near the lower edge of the upper board, usually towards its mid-point.[68] At Oriel and Merton Colleges, Oxford, however, the staple was commonly attached to the lower board; the lower board was also used at Peterhouse and Pembroke College, Cambridge, but the staple was located at the centre of it rather than at the foot.[69]

If chaining might seem an excellent way to preserve a coherent reference collection that was definitively distinguished from the volumes that could circulate among the fellows, this was by no means invariably its function. At New College in 1400, for example, the books to be chained were those left unassigned after the distribution among the fellows: the foundation may have had a fine new *libraria* (fig. 8), but it was being used in effect as a secure book-store.[70] Moreover, donors sometimes specified that their gifts – irrespective of subject-matter – should be chained. Bishop William Rede of Chichester (d. 1385), a former fellow, bursar and sub-warden of Merton and a great patron of Oxford college libraries, is a prime example of the phenomenon. He gave 100 books to Merton and New College, twenty to Exeter, and ten each to Balliol, Oriel and Queen's, expecting them to be 'securely chained' in the

67 Streeter, 16–23; but see also D. N. Griffiths, 'Unfamiliar libraries xv: Lincoln Cathedral', *The Book Collector* 19 (1970), 21–2; Thomson, *Cat. Lincoln*, pl. 1.

68 N. R. Ker, 'The chaining, labelling, and inventory numbers of manuscripts belonging to the old University Library', *BLR* 5 (1954–6), 176–80, repr. in *Books, collectors and libraries*, 321–6.

69 N. R. Ker, 'Chaining from a staple on the back cover', *BLR* 3 (1950–1), 104–7, repr. in *Books, collectors and libraries*, 327–30.

70 Willis and Clark, III. 392; Hunt, 'Medieval library', 318.

Figure 11 Lincoln Cathedral Library, medieval lectern. (Photo, Gameson)

communal libraries: indeed, he left the last four institutions money to do so.[71] The stipulation that volumes be chained owed more to the wish that the benefaction (and hence the spiritual benefit accruing to the donor therefrom) be preserved intact than to the desire to enhance the reference collection *per se*. This was the educational equivalent of a chantry.

Chaining was not the only provision made for the security of the books. In the setting of a university town where many people beyond the walls of a particular community would be interested in and aware of the value of its manuscripts – and those within its walls alive to the possibilities of pawning this valuable resource – measures for security and preservation both of the volumes in the library room (whether chained or not) and of those stored elsewhere were a high priority. The numerous references to locks and keys in college records reflect a preoccupation with security. Archbishop Kilwardby's injunctions for Merton of 1276 required that the books which might be loaned to fellows in return for an adequate security should be kept in a chest with three locks.[72] Similarly, the statutes of Peterhouse of 1344 specified that the books were to be held in 'one or more common chests, each having two locks, one key of which shall for greater security be deposited with the Master, the other with the Senior Dean'.[73] Similar provision was made to ensure the safety of the books in the library room. William of Wykeham's statutes for New College state: 'On the door of the . . . library there are to be two great locks with two different keys which are to be kept continually and carefully in the custody – the one of the Senior Dean, the other of the Senior Bursar, as is proper. A third lock commonly called the "clickett" is to be placed on the aforesaid door – of which lock every fellow of our college may have a single key. The door is to be locked every night with all the three keys aforesaid.'[74] Correspondingly, some of the earliest documented expenses in relation to the *libraria* of the King's Hall, Cambridge (1396/7), were for a lock and thirty-three keys – one each for the warden and thirty-two fellows – at a cost of 5s 8d.[75]

Chaining and library rooms outside the university

References to the chaining of books in cathedrals and religious houses can be found from the fourteenth century. It was undertaken for both practical and

71 Will printed: Powicke, *Medieval books*, 87–91; see also Garrod and Highfield, 'An indenture'. His wishes were sometimes echoed in inscriptions within the volumes themselves, as in New Coll., MS 120.

72 Powicke, *Medieval books*, 1.

73 Willis and Clark, III. 390.

74 Willis and Clark, III. 397.

75 CBMLC X. 316.

spiritual reasons. One may contrast the precentor at Worcester, who, in 1387/8, paid for the lock and chain to fasten his own gradual in the choir (perhaps fed up with other people walking off with it),[76] with Elizabeth Darcy, who stipulated in her will (1412) that her breviary and great psalter be fixed with an iron chain in the chapel of Heynings, Lincolnshire (a priory of Cistercian nuns) and remain there.[77] When in 1369 Bishop Lewis Charlton requested that the glossed Bible, the *Catholicon*, the *Summa summarum* and a couple of other items which he had left to Hereford Cathedral be chained in the church, he was ensuring both their ready availability for reference purposes and their permanence as a memorial to him.[78] The need for such measures to preserve a bequest as intended – or at least to maximise the difficulty of changing it – is shown by cases such as the famous Ormesby Psalter, which was given by the monk Robert of Ormesby to Norwich Cathedral Priory in the late 1320s or 1330s to lie on the desk of the sub-prior in the choir of the cathedral, yet soon came to bear the press-mark 'A.1', indicating that it was subsequently relocated, being shelved as the first of the psalters in the main cloister collection.[79]

Despite the close connections between the major religious houses and the universities – which could extend to the establishment of their own colleges and halls for student monks – monasteries and cathedrals did not generally introduce library rooms into their own complexes until the fifteenth century, or even later. The change in function from the earlier store-rooms is evident from their location and design, for these new chambers were typically at first-floor level and equipped with generous windows. In many places, however, the long-established connection between books and the cloister was maintained. Thus the new library at Durham, constructed between 1414 and 1418 and one of the earliest outside the universities, was located over part of the parlour off the east range of the cloister.[80] During the second and third decades of the fifteenth century, library rooms were built over a length of the cloister at a number of major houses, including the secular cathedrals of Exeter, Hereford, Lincoln and Wells (fig. 12). In 1444–5 the cathedral chapter of Salisbury, apparently aware that they were being left behind, resolved to build 'certain schools suitable for lectures, together with a library for the safe-keeping of books and the convenience of those who wish to study therein, which library up to the

76 Thomson, *Cat. Worcester*, xxxiv.

77 A. Gibbons, *Early Lincoln wills: an abstract of all the wills and administrations recorded in the episcopal registers of the old diocese of Lincoln, 1280–1547* (London, 1888), 117–18.

78 Mynors and Thomson, xx.

79 Bodleian, MS Douce 366, fol. 2^{r}; B. Dodwell, 'The muniments and the library', I. Atherton *et al.* (eds.), *Norwich Cathedral: church, city and diocese, 1096–1996* (London, 1996), 335.

80 Piper, 'Library of the monks of Durham', 223–6, fig. 17.

Figure 12 Wells Cathedral, cloister, *libraria* at the first floor. (Photo, Gameson)

present time they have been without. Such schools and library shall be built as soon as possible over one side of the cloister of the church.'[81] It will be noted that the chapter of Salisbury automatically assumed that the library would be a reading room.

Local circumstances sometimes determined that the library room was located elsewhere. At York Minster, a foundation without a cloister, the library (completed *c.* 1420) was the upper chamber of an annexe that projects west from the south transept of the cathedral (figs. 13–14), while that at Christ Church, Canterbury (completed *c.* 1444), was erected as an extra storey over the prior's chapel (itself above the south side of the infirmary cloister).[82] Abbot Curteys (1429–46) appears to have sited the *libraria* at Bury St Edmunds near to the prior's house, just north of the east end of the abbey church. When the London Guildhall also decided to invest in a library room (1423–5), it was built as a free-standing structure just south of the Guildhall; a chapel was subsequently attached to its northern side.[83]

81 Chapter Act Book 10 'Hutchins', 83. The part designed for lectures was demolished in 1753; for the original appearance, see T. Cocke and P. Kidson, *Salisbury Cathedral: perspectives on the architectural history* (London, 1993), ill. 34.

82 Ramsay, 'Archives and library', 364.

83 C. M. Barron, *The medieval Guildhall of London* (London, 1974), 33–5, fig. 2.

Figure 13 York Minster, looking east towards the south transept. The library occupied the first floor of the two-storey annexe (cf. fig. 14). (Photo, Gameson)

Figure 14 York Minster, the south side of the south transept annexe (cf. fig. 13). (Photo, Gameson)

In general conception these library rooms followed the design of those of academic institutions, being more or less rectangular with a line of generously sized windows piercing both long walls; and, like them, they were presumably equipped with lecterns between the windows, projecting 'inwards' at right angles to the long walls. The chambers varied in size and in the number of books they accommodated. The library room of York Minster measured only 44ft by 24ft, and was lit by four windows in each of its long north and south sides, plus a single larger one in the shorter west wall; in 1421–2 some forty volumes were chained there (figs. 13–14). Durham's library, by contrast, measured 60ft by 16ft 6in., and originally contained 150 volumes, although the number subsequently doubled. The survival at Lincoln of three medieval lecterns as well as three bays of the library that was completed in 1422 provides a unique opportunity to study both a room and its furniture (fig. 11). The chamber was originally of five bays, presumably accommodating eight double-sided lecterns, four on either side. As the lecterns are approximately 7 ft long, there was space for six or seven books per side, or about a dozen per lectern, giving a possible total of around 100 books.[84] This figure accords well with the evidence of the fifteenth-century catalogue of chained books, which enumerates 109 items. A shelf was subsequently added to each of the Lincoln lecterns, below the desk, providing for a modest increase in capacity; volumes kept here were apparently chained to staples fixed in iron plates, the scars indicating that between six and eleven additional titles were thus accommodated. This is also reflected in a second, later set of staple-marks on some Lincoln bindings, near the spine at the top or bottom of the front board, which would suggest that these books were moved from the upper desk to the lower shelf.[85] The eight lecterns at Leicester Abbey must likewise have contained a lower shelf, since the late fifteenth-century library catalogue lists over twenty or thirty volumes for all but the eighth.[86] The same was probably true of the eleven *descae* (lecterns) in the *libraria* of Exeter Cathedral which, an inventory of 1506 reveals, then held a total of 327 volumes.[87] A rare English representation of a reading room, dating from the second quarter of the fifteenth century, shows a couple of desks, each with upper and lower shelves.[88] The substantial library at Christ Church, Canterbury, was furnished with sixteen lecterns, eight on either side of the room. Each had a desk and a shelf (or an upper and lower shelf of some sort) on both sides; since they are described as *sedilia* they probably – like those at Lincoln – included benches as an integral part of their structure.[89] Ingram's list of 1508 records between fourteen and twenty-seven titles per lectern, totalling 293 books in all.

The books were not invariably chained. At Hereford, whose library room was built over the west range of the cloister at an uncertain date in the fifteenth century, the evidence of an unusually large number of medieval bindings reveals that it was only in the early seventeenth century – when the books were stored upright in presses – that chains and chain-staples were affixed.[90] Binding evidence from Worcester indicates that only some of the cathedral priory's books were chained; from their contents they would appear to form a basic theological reference library, but whether this was the main collection in the library room or the theological library that formed part of the Carnery Chapel (rebuilt between 1458 and 1464), near the cathedral's north-west porch, cannot be determined.[91]

84 Thomson, *Cat. Lincoln*, xvii.

85 *Ibid.*, xix. 86 CBMLC VI. 360–80. 87 Oliver, *Bishops of Exeter*, 366–75.

88 BL, MS Cotton Tiberius A. vii, fol. 91^{v} (Lydgate, *Pilgrimage of the life of man*): Hagiography showing books to Pilgrim and Lady Lesson (*Survey*, V/i, 64; ii, no. 89).

89 James, *ALCD*, no. VI. 90 Mynors and Thomson, xxi–xxii.

91 Thomson, *Cat. Worcester*, xxxiv–xxxv.

The construction and equipping of the library rooms of colleges, universities and religious communities alike were extremely costly and could take many years to complete. At King's Hall, Cambridge, the building and furnishing of the *noua libraria* were relatively rapid. Work began in 1416–17; the accounts for 1416–18 suggest energetic building activity, those for 1420–1 imply that the chamber was then being roofed, while those for 1421–2, which all relate to fittings and fixtures (which occupied two carpenters for some fifteen weeks and a bookbinder and his assistant for ten), indicate the final installation of furniture and books.[92] Elsewhere, the process could be far more lengthy. Although the fabric of Durham College's library appears to have been finished in 1418, the room was furnished with 'descae et tabulae et alia necessaria' only in 1431 (at the cost of £6 6s 8d), and one window (most probably, therefore, the single south one) was glazed – or possibly reglazed – in 1436 (for £2 2s 8d).[93] The contract between Peterhouse and the mason John Wassinghale of Hinton, dated 1431, specified that the walls of the new library were to be finished within eighteen months; nevertheless, the fabric was still under construction at the end of the decade, fittings were supplied only in 1447–8, and it was not until 1449–50 that the books were finally installed.[94] The library of Balliol, which was also started in 1431 (after perhaps a quarter-century of fundraising), was plunged back into building work between 1477 and *c.* 1485, when four new bays were added to accommodate the books given and bequeathed by William Gray, bishop of Ely (d. 1478) (figs. 15–16).

The library rooms could be handsomely ornamented. Prior William Sellyng (1472–94) sponsored a handsome ceiling of some kind for the upper chamber at Christ Church; and be-feathered wooden angels still adorn the beams of the surviving portion of Lincoln's medieval library room (fig. 17). The *libraria* of All Souls was well paved with tiles and had magnificent stained glass: each of the sixteen windows contained a pair of figures, the eastern range being dominated by canonised archbishops of Canterbury together with the four Doctors of the Church and the founder, Henry Chichele, the western range boasting a sequence of kings.[95] Just as the windows of the library at All Souls thus articulated the founder's connection with the see of Canterbury, those of

92 CBMLC x. 316–17.
93 H. E. D. Blakiston, 'Some Durham College rolls', in M. Burrows (ed.), *Collectanea* III. OHS 32 (1896), 10, n. 32.
94 CBMLC x. 444.
95 F. E. Hutchinson, *Medieval glass at All Souls College* (London, 1949), 37–61, pls. XIX–XXXI.

Figure 15 Balliol College, Oxford, in 1675, looking north. The library occupied the first floor of the north range of the main quadrangle (cf. fig. 16). (After Loggan 1675)

Figure 16 Balliol College, Oxford, from quad, north side, showing the elevation of the medieval library room. (Photo, Gameson)

Figure 17 Lincoln Cathedral, wooden angel decorating beam in the library room. (Photo, Gameson)

the library at Durham College reflected its northern affiliations, featuring a series of the canonised archbishops of York.[96]

The decoration of such chambers, no less than inscriptions in books, catalogues and on *tabulae*, might commemorate benefactors. The east window of Balliol College library showed Thomas Chace (Master 1412–23) and ten fellows kneeling before their patron saint (Catherine), while each of the side windows contained the coat of arms of a benefactor, including that of Chace, who was also identified as the founder of the building by an inscription.[97] Images of benefactors are documented in the library glazing of the neighbouring Durham College (now Trinity College), and the tracery light in the south window still contains angels bearing aloft the arms of Thomas Hatfield, bishop of Durham, who refounded the college in the 1370s (fig. 18). The arms of Thomas Rotheram were prominently displayed in the many windows of the library within the east front of the Cambridge Schools, which he underwrote in the 1470s. The same practice was followed outside the universities. The shields of arms in the windows in the library of York Minster included those of Thomas Haxley, treasurer at the time the room was built, who gave £26 13s 4d for its roof. The library at Wells Cathedral still preserves original glazing with the arms of its benefactor, Bishop Nicholas Bubwith (d. 1424), while the London Guildhall library was adorned with the arms of Richard Whittington and the initials of William Bury, the 'sponsors' whose executors initiated the project.

After a long delay, the ill-fated common library of the University of Oxford (above the convocation house beside St Mary's) had finally opened in 1412. Its normal hours were 9–11am and 1–4pm (when, even in winter, there would generally be some natural light), but this might exceptionally be prolonged to 'from sunrise to sunset' for VIPs (*notabiles personae*). The room, an uneven-sided rectangle of 45 / 50ft by 19 ft, was then lit by a range of seven evenly spaced windows in both long walls (the north and south) plus one in the east wall, and was equipped with at least sixteen desks, to which the books were chained (figs. 19–20).[98] Their titles were to be displayed (along with the names of benefactors)

96 R. G. Gameson and A. Coates, *The Old Library* (Oxford, 1988), 19.

97 R. A. B. Mynors, *Catalogue of the manuscripts of Balliol College, Oxford* (Oxford, 1963), xvi–xix.

98 University Archives, Registrum C, fols. 113^{v}–115^{r}: Anstey, *Munimenta academica*, I. 261–8. The original fenestration was suppressed when the room was comprehensively reworked in the late fifteenth century, the role of University Library having passed to Duke Humfrey's facility; photographs of its current appearance (e.g. Parkes, 'Provision of books', pl. xvi) are thus misleading.

Figure 18 Durham (now Trinity) College, Oxford, upper light of south window of the *libraria*, with three angels supporting the arms of Thomas Hatfield (azure a chevron or between three lions rampant). (Photo, Gameson)

'on a large and conspicuous placard, written in an elegant hand'. The number of books cannot have been very large (in 1457 the seventeen desks in the common library of the University of Cambridge accommodated 330 books)[99] and measures were deliberately taken to restrict the number of users, but even so the arrangement was not particularly practical: the complaint addressed to Duke Humfrey in about 1445, designed to win sponsorship for a new facility, was that readers got in each other's way.[100]

Thus, by the second half of the fifteenth century, many cathedrals, abbeys and colleges had a purpose-built library room with a permanent reference collection which could be consulted *in situ*. Indeed, the concept of a library room

99 CBMLC x. UC3.

100 University Archives, Registrum F, fols. 71^{v}–72^{r}.

Figure 19 University Church of St Mary, Oxford, eastern elevation in 1896. The university library room was the upper chamber of the annexe – the convocation house – on the north side of the church. (After Jackson 1897)

was sufficiently well established that foundations without one could claim (exaggeratedly) that the lack of such a resource emperiled their books – as did a monk at Fotheringhay College in 1438.[101] With these fixed reference collections and a general store or stores of books available for loan, we might seem to be close both conceptually and physically to modern libraries. Yet in reality we have not moved so very far from where we began. The changes on which this chapter has focused were set against a backdrop of continuity and stasis. Reference collections were fairly small and, once chained, were cumbersome

101 A. H. Thompson (ed.), *Visitations of religious houses in the diocese of Lincoln, 2: records of visitations held by William Alnwick, AD 1436–1449*, 1, Canterbury and York Society 24 (1919), 98.

Figure 20 University Church of St Mary, Oxford, the convocation house, south side, elevation in 1896, showing remains of the original library fenestration. (After Jackson 1897)

(not to mention costly) to reconfigure.[102] In the long-established foundations like the cathedral priories of Christ Church, Canterbury, or Durham, which had accumulated more than 1,000 volumes over the centuries, large numbers of books were preserved, not in the library room, but in other stores, as had been the case previously. At the universities many books were still kept in chests; this was where the unwanted loan books at All Souls, for instance, remained.[103] The practices of most institutions, religious and academic, were marked by a fundamental conservatism. The physical organisation of the books continued to be based on the concept of a comparatively limited and stable body of knowledge, allied to the slow consumption of loaned material. Donations, which were fundamental to the growth of institutional collections, had as much to do with the benefactor's provision for his afterlife as with the needs of cathedrals and universities: symptomatic of this situation is the fact that the university librarian at Oxford was a chaplain who was to combine his oversight of the *libraria* with the duty of praying for the souls of benefactors to

102 See, for example, accounts for chaining and unchaining at King's Hall: CBMLC x. UC40, and below, 163–4, 166–7.

103 E. F. Jacob (ed.), *The register of Henry Chichele, archbishop of Canterbury 1414–1443*, II (Oxford, 1937), 411.

the library and celebrating the customary masses – with the result that on the days of university masses, the library was shut.[104] Equally, benefactors could insist on the chaining of an eccentric selection of books. How would these conservative practices stand up to new pressures in the age of printing?[105]

104 See n. 98.
105 I am very grateful to the librarians and archivists who kindly facilitated my inspection of the surviving library rooms discussed in this chapter.

1b

The early modern library (to *c.* 1640)

CLARE SARGENT

Before we proceed to discuss developments in the physical setting of libraries from the later fifteenth century onwards it is worth clarifying the different names used for different types of book shelving, as the terminology in contemporary records is not consistent. In what follows I use 'lectern' to describe a sloping desk, often double-sided, with a shelf or shelves below it. A 'stall' is, here, a lectern that has shelves superimposed on it at a later date. A 'press' is a shelved cupboard, and a 'bookcase' is the familiar upright shelving of today, often standing in pairs back to back.

The lectern libraries, as we have seen, were seldom capable of accommodating, and were indeed never intended to accommodate, an institution's entire book holdings, and certainly seem often to have been built or first furnished with no idea of expansion. What we know of Leicester Abbey in the late fifteenth century was very likely true of other libraries, and it was certainly so from the early sixteenth century.[1] Neil Ker notes, of the necessity of laying books flat and in piles, that 'almost certainly books were piled thus "subitus", below the desks, during the sixteenth century, in the crowded libraries built originally to house manuscripts and receiving now a flood of printed books'.[2]

The 'public' university libraries founded to provide access to key texts for poor scholars were no longer a sufficient resource as both the nature of books and the manner of studying them evolved. Nevertheless, lectern libraries continued to be set up well into the second half of the sixteenth century, as witness the case of Trinity Hall, Cambridge, discussed below.[3] Why and how did these lectern libraries survive for so long?

1 See above, 16–18, 47–9.
2 N. R. Ker, 'Chaining from a staple on the back cover', *BLR* 3 (1950–1), 104–7; repr. in his *Books, collectors and libraries*, 328. See also his 'The chaining, labelling, and inventory numbers of manuscripts belonging to the old [Oxford] University Library', *BLR* 5 (1954–6), 176–80; repr. in *Books, collectors and libraries*, 321–6.
3 See below, 56.

The answer is, briefly, that for several decades the basic function of such libraries within the university context changed. Those libraries whose primary statutory role was safe storage of the uncirculated books saw increasing redundancy in the stock. Those which were designed to house difficult to obtain texts for seniors saw the collection changing fairly rapidly through purchase in the 1520s and 1530s, but as habits of scholarship now demanded comparison of texts: standing or sitting to consult a book chained to a lectern must have become increasingly unattractive. It became apparent that a corporate collection could not be expected to support the requirements for new texts and of new methods of study, and may have raised the question of whether it should. In addition, studies of the probate wills in Cambridge indicate that, simply among those whose died in residence between 1535 and 1598, 20,000 volumes were circulating among 200 members of the university; as against the 9,305 records (and correspondingly more volumes) circulating among 170 members of Oxford university who died, or fled abroad, between 1507 and 1579.[4]

Illustrations of scholars' studies throughout the sixteenth century show a variety of methods of tackling book storage: chests, desks with cupboards beneath them, book-wheels to enable the scholar to read two (or more) books at one time, and books shelved, upright, flat, fore-edge out, spine out, jumbled on the floor. Those, such as John Dee, who catalogued their collections must have kept them ordered and accessible, and the most space-saving way is upright shelving.

The changes in the curriculum, particularly the increasing diversity of subjects on offer, meant that a limited reference library such as that held in some chained lectern collections was no longer all-sufficient as an educational tool. While the law curriculum hardly changed, and many divinity books continued to be relevant, there were big changes in the undergraduate syllabus, and to some extent in the MA syllabus; but these junior members were scarcely catered for in college libraries at this time, and the books they needed for the new syllabus were usually in small format; they bought them, new or

4 Cambridge data from *BCI*, Oxford data from the cumulative catalogue in *PLRE* v. 309, and from the figures given in the handbook to Research Publications' microfilm of the Oxford inventories, *The social history of property and possessions*. In considering the difference between the figures for the two universities, allowance must be made for the decreasing number of inventories at Oxford from the 1580s and 1590s (16 against 31 from Cambridge), as also for the inclusion of the huge library of Andrew Perne (d. 1589) (2,585 records) at Cambridge. It must always be remembered that an unknown quantity of books may be counted several times as they passed down the generations.

second-hand, and then sold them on.[5] Booksellers abounded. Books, particularly the books of the reformers, were readily available in cheap editions costing pennies, and it is arguable that the booksellers, who ran a brisk second-hand trade, usurped many of what we would now see as the functions of libraries.[6]

Meanwhile, to counter the increasing expense of library rooms and their furniture, lecterns evolved into stalls where, in the memorable image of J. N. L. Myres, 'the top of the mediaeval lectern has, so to speak, burst open like a bud putting forth two and later three superimposed back-to-back shelves on which chained books can stand upright to be read on the desks which, like the calyx of a flower, remain below as vestiges of the split-open lectern tops'.[7]

However, this next stage is not simply an evolutionary leap to solve the problems of the lectern libraries.[8] It is a paradigm shift: the creation of a corporately owned collection aspiring, increasingly, to cover, if not yet the sum of human knowledge, then at least books in the traditional subjects beyond those essential to the syllabus, within a room which promoted study through its architectural form and its furniture, and which for the first time located all the corporate collection in one place, with strict rules governing loans.

The lectern libraries of the fifteenth and sixteenth centuries usually protected the majority of the book stock by chaining from a chain-staple located centrally near the foot or head of either board, although it is possible that some stock lay unchained on shelves below the lecterns, or in chests or cupboards. The stall system introduced from the 1580s had two forms of security: chains now attached to the fore-edge of the books standing upright on the shelves with their spines facing inwards; and grilles, usually ornamental, enclosing entire shelves which usually contained the most valued items. Much smaller books, below octavo in size, were occasionally protected from casual removal by having a form of wooden pelmet attached to the upper edge of the shelf. Apart from early examples such as at Merton College, from 1605 the practice

5 It is notable that the inventories on decease in Cambridge and Oxford show very few texts of the trivium and quadrivium in the libraries of senior members of faculties, except, occasionally, in the libraries of very wealthy men like Thomas Lorkin (d. 1591) (see some of the books kept in his 'nether studie': *BCI*, I. 499–500) or those who were active in teaching, e.g. Philip Johnson (d. 1576): *PLRE* 110 (IV. 212–52).

6 See E. S. Leedham-Green, 'Booksellers and libraries in sixteenth-century Cambridge', in R. Myers, M. Harris and G. Mandelbrote (eds.), *Libraries and the book trade: the formation of collections from the sixteenth to the twentieth century* (New Castle, DE, 2000), 1–14. The hiatus in book acquisitions in the universities in the mid-sixteenth century is discussed further by Kristian Jensen, below, 347.

7 'Oxford libraries in the seventeenth and eighteenth centuries', in Wormald and Wright, *English library*, 238.

8 See also *ibid.*, 252.

in Oxford, introduced from the publicly accessible Bodleian, was to attach the book-chains to an iron rod affixed to the front edge of each shelf, all the bars then fitting into a locking mechanism on the end of the bookcase. This allowed one key to release all the rods. Chaining is an expensive process. It requires the attendance of the smith, and a strong binding on the book itself; and it causes endless headaches for the library keeper: the library statutes of the 1680s at King's College, Cambridge, require fellows when they have finished with a book to put it back again 'without entangling the chains'. The Bodleian's accounts show regular payments to poor scholars to tidy up books, retie the ties and organise the chains. Chains are also heavy; even the relatively well-supported chains of the lectern system caused damage to bindings at Lincoln College, Oxford, in the 1520s.

Although it is generally stated that books came to the colleges by donation, there is increasing evidence that from their foundations the colleges also acquired books by purchase, albeit most often through gifts of money, and also by default as books were left in college rooms or deposited and not redeemed in loan chests. Between the 1520s and 1540s colleges in both universities spent considerable sums on acquiring printed editions of key texts – large scholarly editions, rather than the small, portable texts used by undergraduates.[9] The majority of these purchases are accompanied by a bill for chaining – indeed, frequently the chaining bill is the only indication that books had been acquired and how many.

Unchaining is also significant, indicating either the removal of unwanted books, or occasionally loans. The fate of these unchained books was various: some, as at Merton, joined the loan collection; some were sold; others (as happened with books from Michaelhouse library absorbed into Henry VIII's new foundation at Trinity College, Cambridge) probably ended up inventoried as 'books in the chest'. In all, the colleges maintained the chained libraries in a relatively steady state until the 1540s. Then the books stopped arriving. There are few if any records for library purchases from any Oxford or Cambridge college until the 1570s. This thirty-year gap needs to be examined.

The standard argument has been that this period of religious and political upheaval made fellows reluctant to donate books to corporate collections. The dispersal of the monastic libraries was still ongoing. Presumably purchase was also unwise. However, donations do not stop, only purchases, although the majority of donations to college libraries are seldom of new books. Colleges which received such donations tended to debate their value, chain a few and

9 See below, chapter 13.

either sell the rest or add them to the loan collection. The political and religious upheavals, however, could be said to have diminished by the early 1560s, a decade before purchasing begins again.[10]

The evolution from lectern to stall library is well illustrated at Merton College, Oxford. Throughout the sixteenth century the college retained its medieval manuscript collection intact. This has been attributed to the extreme conservatism of the warden in post in the 1520s. However, throughout the sixteenth century Merton was buying fine examples of printed works, and appears to have absorbed them into the chained lectern library. From 1589 Merton enjoyed the leadership of one of the most cultured and learned men of his century, Henry Savile. A man who knew everybody, travelled to Germany and Italy to buy £100-worth of books at a time for the college, and who nurtured Thomas Bodley as a junior fellow and close friend. From 1575 to 1589 Henry Savile introduced a number of revolutionary initiatives into his college's library: first, he set up a system whereby matriculation fees were paid to the library, thereby endowing it with a regular and predictable income; second, he established a librarian; third, he converted the east end of the lectern library into a stall library; fourth, he called in all the distributed books corporately owned by the college, and, despite much grumbling from the fellowship, he chained them all, regardless of size, in the library.[11]

It is possible that Merton was not the earliest stall library in Oxford; New College had paid for some expensive joinery to house a law collection some years earlier. But Savile certainly organised the removal of half the lecterns at Merton, and replaced them with two-shelf stalls. Merton's library room was still the earlier model of chained lectern library room, with single-light windows and low-level lecterns with a single bench fixed between. These features were retained in the remodelling. The medieval ground-sills, foot-rests and benches remained in place, and flat desks were fitted in front of the bookshelves to allow a seated reader to consult chained volumes in comfort. The stalls were originally fitted with a single central chain bar that allowed the chains, now attached to the fore-edges of the books, to drop through a gap at the back of the desk to attach to the bar.[12] This conversion of the east end into a stall library was a carefully budgeted job, reusing whatever was possible, including buying second-hand medieval tiles to pave the floor. The west end

10 On chaining of books at Coventry, Lewisham and Shrewsbury schools, and unchaining at Eton in 1719, see below, 444, 445–6.

11 G. H. Martin and J. R. L. Highfield, *A history of Merton College, Oxford* (Oxford, 1997), 159–62.

12 G. Barber, *Arks for learning* (Oxford, 1995), 8 and figs. 10 and 11.

of the library retained lecterns until 1624, and presumably the manuscripts remained on their places as they always had done.

Three things always need to be remembered about converted lectern libraries: first, it is impossible to stand up a book which has a staple and chain located centrally in the middle or close to the bottom of one of the boards; second, most medieval binding structures do not well withstand upright shelving; third, the flat desks fitted at Merton and other college libraries such as Corpus Christi, Oxford, and at the newly created Bodleian Library in 1605, are too shallow to support any book larger than a standard folio. The stall libraries, therefore, were expressly designed to house many more volumes in the much more standard dimensions of books printed on paper.

In 1624 the west end of Merton College library was fitted up with more expensive stalls, although ordered to match the earlier work as much as possible; again, parts of the lecterns, particularly the foot-rests, were retained. At this time the manuscripts must have been removed from general access. There is no indication yet where they went, but it is significant that the list of duties of the Merton librarian drawn up by Griffin Higgs, the post-holder in the 1650s, mentions 'the manuscripts he shall bring forth out of their dust and darkness'.[13]

An additional feature of the 1624 Merton conversion needs to be mentioned. As stated earlier, the fourteenth-century windows were single lights and were positioned to give maximum light for copying on the lecterns. The stalls were considerably higher than the lecterns, and shut out the light. Large dormers, facing respectively south and east, were constructed in 1590 and 1624 to solve the lighting problem.

At Merton, Savile placed two bookshelves above a flat desk, with a chain bar located beneath the shelves which was accessed by a gap between the flat desk and the lower shelf. Almost exactly contemporary with Savile's remodelling of Merton was the creation of a new library, in about 1600, at Trinity Hall, Cambridge. Here, the concept of a sloping lectern was retained as the upper section of the stall, with two shelves below it.[14] There is still one central chain bar, attached below the apex of the double-sided lectern. The reader was seated at a fixed double bench between stalls, with the lectern slope at a comfortable height for reading, and the chains, unlike at Merton or the Bodleian, hanging away from the reader, with the chain-staple at the fore-edge.[15]

13 Martin and Highfield, *History of Merton College*, 376–7.

14 Clark, *Care of books*, fig. 65.

15 For illustrations of the various ways of chaining books, see Clark, *Care of books*, esp. 175–7.

It has been conjectured that part of the reason for building a library in the new style at Trinity Hall was the possibility that the college might receive the manuscripts of Archbishop Parker, in lieu of the failure of Corpus Christi College, Cambridge, to look after them satisfactorily. Despite the unlikelihood of such an eventuality, Trinity Hall was instead to receive a large bequest of law books from William Mowse in 1588.

The size of the book collections of individual fellows now needed to be taken into consideration in corporate library planning. Andrew Perne, master of Peterhouse, Cambridge, owned one of the most celebrated collections of books in England, some 3,000 volumes. Perne left his folio and quarto books to Peterhouse, with instructions that they be 'laid and chained' in the library there. In the event Peterhouse obtained some 900 of the 3,000 volumes, but to lay and chain them on lecterns in a building designed for a capacity for 250 volumes was a physical impossibility. Even the new library proposed under Perne's will could not have had the capacity for this. Perne's executors took an executive decision: they created a library for upright shelving, and, despite the provisions of the will, they did not chain the books; none of Perne's extant books shows any evidence of having been chained. It is apparent from his inventory that Perne himself clearly used upright cases, along with all other available flat surfaces, while Whitney's emblem depicting him shows a lectern desk, with books shelved upright below, a standing desk, a double-sided lectern at seating height sufficient for one book on each side, and a shelf of books standing upright, fore-edge out, presumably a depiction of as many possibilities as could be fitted in rather than a recollection of Perne's actual study.[16]

One of Perne's executors was Humfrey Tindall, president of Queens' College, Cambridge, and himself the owner of an extensive library.[17] Tindall was a considerable benefactor to his college, and almost certainly paid for the building of the President's Lodge in the 1580s. Queens' College had a standard college library constructed in 1448, with typical two-light windows and double-sided, two-slope lecterns. In 1613 Tindall masterminded the conversion of the lecterns of Queens' library into double-sided two-shelf bookshelves, without chains. The detailed accounts for this conversion survive.[18]

16 Geffrey Whitney, *A choice of emblemes and other devices* (Leiden, 1586), reproduced in D. McKitterick (ed.), *Andrew Perne: quatercentenary studies* (Cambridge, 1991), 62.

17 For which see *BCI*, I. 569–72; his inventory survives in an incomplete state, so the total extent of his library cannot be ascertained.

18 For what follows, see C. D. Sargent, *The archaeology of a Cambridge library: the records of Queens' College, Cambridge, 1448–1672* (Cambridge, forthcoming).

Here the end faces of each lectern were shaped at some stage to a design very similar to that at Trinity Hall, and it is possible that Queens' accounts of 1613 indicate a second attempt at remodelling, with earlier work, paid for by Tindall, which removed the lower slope and replaced it with two bookshelves, at the same time bringing the overall appearance of the room into contemporary fashion by reshaping the lectern ends. Queens', in parallel with Trinity Hall's gift from William Mowse in 1588, received a large donation of very desirable books from the estate of Sir Thomas Smith in 1585. Remodelling the library to receive them would not have been inconceivable. The work in 1613 was not the final stage in the conversion of the Queens' lecterns: in 1633 Ashley the joiner was paid £30 for 'ledges'. This is almost as much as was paid for more extensive work in 1613, and may indicate either that the upper lectern slope was finally removed, or that a flat desk was added as at Merton. Both the desk at Merton and the lectern and chain-bar at Trinity Hall demonstrate possible solutions to a problem; to read a chained book comfortably there must be somewhere convenient to rest it, even if only to compensate for the weight of the chain. At Queens', however, there is no record of any bill for chaining after 1613, and the latest acquisitions to be chained, both given in 1605, show the traditional centre, lower-back-board chain-staple scar of the Queens' lectern system.

Close analysis of all Queens' accounts from 1448 until 1613 has reconstructed the contents of the chained library at just over 400 volumes in 1613. This is well in excess of the capacity of the lecterns, which had held a library of 200 volumes, the gift of Marmaduke Lumley, at its foundation in 1448. Queens', a leading humanist college, had pursued a steady policy of purchasing throughout the 1520s and 1530s. There is also evidence that Tindall had initiated a fee scheme, similar to that at Merton, from the 1590s. But, despite all this, in 150 years Queens' had acquired 400 volumes, as contrasted with Emmanuel College, Cambridge, which had acquired 500 volumes in the 25 years since its foundation. The upright shelving of the stall system allowed Tindall to build a library with the capacity to accommodate 3,000 books. Corpus Christi College, Oxford, shows the same figures: 400 volumes revelling in the space for 3,000. Tindall cannot have expected to fill the library by rapid purchase on the income available to him, nor did he know another Perne. Queens' donors' book and the entire purchase record are available from 1615 to 1674, when the earliest extant catalogue was drawn up. Comparison of that catalogue with the donors' book and the purchases reveals an anomaly: almost 2,500 titles cannot be accounted for. There can be only one conclusion: Humfrey

Tindall, like Henry Savile in Oxford, called in the distributed collection, and created one corporate library in one location.[19]

At Queens', there is only one mention of *libri distribuendi* between 1448 and 1613: a bill for keys expressly for them in the 1490s, indicating that the book collection was housed in two rooms, and that each of the fellows had his own key and could have access whenever he wished. Generally, therefore, it has been assumed that most distributed libraries faded away and vanished in the early sixteenth century. However, in 1585 Queens' major benefactor of the sixteenth century, Sir Thomas Smith, left to Queens' 'all my Latin and Greek books upon condition that they chain them up in the library or do distribute them amongst the fellows such as will best occupy them'. Among the fellows who received some of Sir Thomas Smith's books was John St George, a noted mathematician. In 1637 St George bequeathed his books to the college, which dutifully recorded them in the donors' book; the majority of his books bear the name and marginalia of Sir Thomas Smith, finally returning to the college twenty-five years after it had abandoned the concept of a loan collection. A further example at Queens' of optimum use of a scholar's books is the will of Walter Bygrave, fellow from 1515 to 1554: 'I wyll allsoe that all the other of my bookes not geven be destributed after the discretyon of myne executours with the advyce and cownsell of Mr Hathwaye but specyally amonges the felows and scholers of the quenes college.'[20]

The library of Emmanuel College, founded in 1584 and possessed of 500 books by 1600, boasted 'nine fayre desks of oake every one having three degrees', interpreted by Frank Stubbings as 'nine bookcases with two shelves and sloping desk-tops', although three shelves seems possible.[21] The books were not chained.

So we come to the concept of the virtual library. A college's books belong to the college wherever they are stored, and the majority of those books were stored in the place where they were of most use, according to their function. The stall libraries indicate a change in this concept of virtual reality. College membership numbers were increasing, and it must have become correspondingly difficult to maintain the idea of a distributed, shared collection. The stall libraries created the space to store the college's entire collection within a single location, and to allow that collection to grow. The next problems to be tackled were access, security and ensuring that the new libraries were used.

19 For an account of distributed collections in colleges, see below, 167–8, 352.

20 *BCI*, I. 144.

21 F. Stubbings, *A brief history of Emmanuel College Library* (Cambridge, 1981).

The accounts of the Cambridge colleges show no evidence of payments for chains after the introduction of the stall system, with the exception of Trinity Hall, previously discussed, and King's. King's has always been anomalous. Henry VI's original plan in 1441 was for a library 110ft in length, over twice the size of any existing college library. Although a much-modified version of the original plan was fitted up in the Old Court, by 1580 its contents had largely disappeared. A new library was set up by Provost Goad in the 1580s in the now redundant side chapels of the great chapel. The new library in the side chapels was located in what was already a major tourist attraction, and chaining the collection was undoubtedly a prudent move in such a public space. In addition, King's was closely associated with Eton, which geographically looked to Oxford, and, under the provostship of Henry Savile, had sent a joiner to examine 'the new library' in Oxford in 1600; this was probably Merton, but could have been any of the new libraries springing up. Certainly Eton chained the books in its fellows' library.

A few books in the libraries of Christ's College and Jesus College, Cambridge, and in the University Library, show evidence of fore-edge chaining.[22] It is possible that it was in use in Cambridge sporadically, or for a short time. A modified version of the Trinity Hall stall system was put up in the new library building at St John's, Cambridge, in 1624, without the chain-bar (see fig. 21).

At Oxford, therefore, the colleges brought the loan collections into the chained library, and chained them. At Cambridge, meanwhile, the colleges unchained the chained collections, and mixed them with the loan collections. But this did not make them loan collections, despite obvious attempts by the fellowship to argue otherwise. A college order from Queens' in about 1635 states rather tetchily: 'that the books are not meant to be removed from the library, is sufficiently evident from the remaining iron chains on the boards, by which they were once attached to their classes'. But locking the books in the library and restricting access is never popular.

A concern for the convenience of readers and the preservation of the books is well manifest in the celebrated letter of 1 February 1598 from Sir Thomas Tresham to Dr John Case relating to the second foundation of the library of St John's College, Oxford. After discussion of the books which he intends to give to the library, Sir Thomas continues:

22 I am indebted to Elizabeth Quarmby Lawrence for the information about Christ's and Jesus, and to Elisabeth Leedham-Green about the University Library.

Figure 21 St John's College Library, Cambridge, bookcase (on left) and stall (on right). (After Clark 1901)

> The binding vp of yor Library bookes is spetially to be respected for the well preseruing of them and reddier vse of them. first wheather in wad or in paste bord I prefer^{r} the past bords, if they be such dooble past bords as we receaue from Paris binding. next wheather clasped or stringed. many make election of stringing then of clasping, in regard of avoyding the anoy of Rushing [*sic*] as in respect of reddylyer repayring them. Then in what leather, and whether all in one colored lether or diuers. Likewise for coloring the Leaues etc. The more diuersitye of coloures and differences, be it in the couerings, false couerings, leaffes or stringes, the better will the same serue for distinguishing between booke and booke, and wth all fitt all other vses so well, as if they had alonely ben of one coloure. Lastly to be resolued whether to haue them wth false couerings or not, such small couerings are of small chardge, will last longe, and redely by any taylor may be renewed. Those will keepe the costely Leather binding from rasing, tearing wearinge and defacing wch cannot be but by that meanes auoyded vnlesse the deskes wheron they are to be placed, were couered over wth cloth. Such couering wth cloth is like or little lesse chardgable, not so longe lasting, and greately subiect to dust and mothes. Therin I rather expounde then advice, leauing it to yor discretions, to geue those directions wch ye shall censure to be therin most conuenient and behouefull.[23]

Neil Ker notes of this passage that 'Tresham's words suggest that he was thinking of a library of lectern-desks', but the same concerns would be relevant in a stall library. It is interesting that Tresham makes no mention here of chaining. Perhaps he just assumed it. Certainly the books *were* chained at St John's.[24]

By bringing together the books, and by implication the readers, into one location, the college changed the role of the library from a repository of undistributed books, a reference collection, or collection of the most desirable and learned books, into a way of providing the greatest number of books for the greatest number of scholars; for the individual colleges, by purchase and by donation, could soon exceed any collection put together by any but the richest or most bibliophile scholars, although many serious scholars might still have in their private collections a greater concentration of specialist texts than was likely to be found in a college library. The library room now became increasingly a replacement for, or an alternative to, the individual studies.

The ideal personal study in gentry households of the later sixteenth and early seventeenth centuries contained books, workspace, family portraits

23 N. R. Ker, 'Oxford college libraries in the sixteenth century', *BLR* 6 (1959), 515, repr. in *Books, collectors and libraries*, 435.

24 I am indebted to Nicolas Barker for confirmation of this.

and cabinets.[25] Now such items began to appear in college libraries: globes; astrolabes; coin collections; portraits of the founder or principal benefactor of the refurbished library, usually behind a curtain; bits of skeleton; 'strange things in glass cases'.[26] The 'portraits' in Duke Humfrey's library at the Bodleian are, perhaps, the best-known British examples of the depiction of worthies. Such things had become essential to the ambience of a scholar, and by extension, to the place of corporate scholarship. It is possible to see this shift in the increasing role played by non-book items placed within the college libraries, which eventually turned them into the equivalent of the college's corporate cabinet of curiosities. A fine example, dating from the early eighteenth century, is Vigani's cabinet, at Queens' College, Cambridge.[27]

However, the first set of curiosities to consider is, in fact, books: the increasingly rare and collectible collections of manuscripts. These had mostly been superseded as tools for learning by the 1600s, although they were beginning to come back into their own with the advent of antiquarian studies. But, for the colleges, they were a problem. Some colleges consigned their manuscripts to the museum, locked away in chests or cupboards, part of the cabinet of curiosities. Others employed the time-honoured librarian's ploy of failing to list them in the public catalogue, so that, just as the distributed collections of the sixteenth century are invisible in the records, so, in the seventeenth century, materials which had previously taken pride of place now disappeared, if not for ever.[28] Either way, they were not visible to the commonality of the fellowship. Those colleges with high-profile manuscript collections, such as

25 For a discussion of the development of gentry library rooms see M. Girouard, *Life in the English country house: a social and architectural history*, 2nd printing, with corrections (New Haven, CT, 1978); for both rooms and furnishings, and fine illustrations, see P. Thornton, *Seventeenth-century interior decoration in England, Holland and France* (New Haven, CT, 1978), 303–15.

26 Andrew Perne (d. 1581), for example, left to Peterhouse, in addition to a choice of his folio and quarto books, 'all my Instrmentes [*sic*] of Astronomye and one kinde of every my mappes and a litell longe box of Woode of Antiquities [coins] of the Emperors in Silver' (*BCI*, I. 421), and to the University Library, his 'greatest black booke of Antiquities of gold & Silver coynes of Emperors and consulls of Rome & other antiquities': McKitterick, *Andrew Perne: quatercentenary studies*, 112. Unfortunately all his collections have been either lost or, in the case of coins, dispersed among the coin collection of the Fitzwilliam Museum. Perne's collection of instruments was truly remarkable, including navigational as well as astronomical devices.

27 For an illustrated account of this cabinet see http://www.quns.cam.ac.uk/Queens/Record/2003/Historical/Vigani.html.

28 For example, a number of manuscripts at Gonville and Caius Library, noted by M. R. James as having been donated before 1569, and which are still in that library, are not listed in the library catalogue of 1569 (E. Leedham-Green, 'A catalogue of Caius College library, 1569', *TCBS* 8 (1981), 29).

the Parker collection at Corpus, Cambridge, built separate library rooms to house them.[29]

The cabinet was just one aspect of the ambience. The other thing essential to encouraging the use of a corporate building is that it should be clean, comfortable and well lit. Lectern libraries, sometimes built as showpieces to demonstrate the wealth and generosity of their principal benefactor, often also had elements of display. Windows were usually glazed, except in the poorest colleges such as Lincoln or Exeter in Oxford, which started with horn and shutters but upgraded to glass as soon as possible. Many of those with glazed windows had fine stained figurative or heraldic glass.[30] Ceilings were either highly decorated beams, as can still be seen in Duke Humfrey in the Bodleian, or at All Souls, where there was a fine plastered barrel vault (since replaced). Floors were admired if they were fine wood, and were frequently tiled.

However, the characteristic of the seventeenth century is the emphasis on cleaning. At Queens', records show that a poor scholar was paid for brooms and dusters from 1615 (i.e. just after the reconstruction). From the 1630s cleaning was done quarterly by the college porter, William Macy. The Bodleian employed an old widow and her daughters to dust the books and sweep the floor regularly from the 1620s.[31] Colleges show a similar pattern of increasing care for the building, which is further exemplified in the amount of small joinery work, constant adjustments to the shelves, and the never-ending stream of repairs to broken glass. The presence of a library keeper may have helped as well. By the 1660s most colleges had established a formal post, well endowed.[32]

If the libraries of the universities and of colleges, and of some cathedrals, are the most fully documented, we are not without occasional glimpses of what was being done elsewhere. In Ipswich, for example, in 1614, when Samuel Ward set about housing the town library, which had previously been kept in an old chest, he first glazed the windows and mended the door between the library room and the Taylors Hall. He then purchased two presses, perhaps better described as a double press, and this was complemented four years later by two more such. By 1705 there were seven double presses. Fortunately, we have drawings of the old presses that were made before the presses were destroyed, and

29 As witness the arrangements for the care of the library after the Parker bequest as detailed in CCCC Archives, Misc.Docs. 139, fols. 1–2 (1576).

30 See, for example, the illustration of the fragments remaining in the time of William Cole, of the stained-glass panels from Thomas Rotherham's extension to Cambridge University Library in the 1470s, in Oates, *CUL*, 46.

31 D. Rogers, *The Bodleian Library and its treasures* (Henley-on-Thames, 1991) 113–14.

32 See below, 570–4.

a drawing of how the library would have appeared in 1614.[33] The books were distributed between the presses on a subject basis and were stored fore-edge out.[34] The library was designed primarily to serve preachers and, no doubt, the resident clergy of Ipswich, and a chained library would clearly not have been appropriate. Presses combined accessibility with a reasonable degree of security.

No building or furnishings are extant in Britain or Ireland which have not received significant alterations over the intervening centuries. In some cases library rooms and furnishings which have been cited as models of their period have been the subject of extensive renovation and archaising in the later nineteenth and earlier twentieth centuries. Other library rooms of significant age spent long periods out of use as libraries and were not returned to that function until relatively recently. One such example is the present Gloucester Cathedral library, now housed in the original late medieval library room of the Benedictine Abbey, suppressed in 1540. In 1646 the mayor and burgesses of Gloucester petitioned Parliament to 'Grant the use of the Chapter House in or belonging to the Colledge of Gloucester as a fitt & Convenient place to be imployed as a Publique Library'. The chapter house was duly fitted up and received much praise for the 'variety of imagery and carved work' of its bookcases. There it remained until 1743, when 'the dampness and inconvenience of the old chapter house' caused the books to be removed to the south side of the choir. In 1764 the books were returned to the chapter house, where they remained until a fire in 1849 led to the building of a new schoolroom, and the rehousing of the library in the old schoolroom, originally the Benedictine's library room. The bookcases of 1646 moved around the building with the books. Thus at Gloucester Cathedral two of the major periods under discussion in this chapter are well represented: a library room of the fourteenth or fifteenth century, and furnishings of the seventeenth. However, the two were not joined until the mid-nineteenth century.[35]

33 J. Blatchly, *The town library of Ipswich* (Woodbridge, 1989), 11–14, figs. 1 and 3.
34 *Ibid.*, 33.
35 D. Welander, *The history, art and architecture of Gloucester Cathedral* (Stroud, 1991), 585–7.

PART ONE

★

THE MEDIEVAL LIBRARY

2

Celtic Britain and Ireland in the early middle ages

PÁDRAIG P. Ó NÉILL

The history of book collections and libraries in the islands of Britain and Ireland begins with Celtic Britain. This area inherited the literary culture of the Roman Empire, while also receiving from the same source in the fourth century the new official religion of Christianity with its book culture centred on the Bible and Christian liturgy. Thus, Celtic Britain had two traditions of literate learning, each with its own type of books: the learning of the late Roman schools with their classical education; and the monastic schools of late antiquity, for whom the highest expression of learning was the study of Scripture. Although no physical evidence for the first type of learning has survived, its existence can be inferred from such British writers as Pelagius and Gildas, both of whom demonstrate in their Latin writings mastery of classical prose style and knowledge of the Roman poets. Both also bear witness to the availability of Christian literature in Celtic Britain, as evidenced by their profound knowledge of the Bible and of Christian writers such as Jerome, Sulpicius Severus and Orosius.[1]

Ireland was never part of the Roman Empire and so did not directly inherit either its classical or Christian learning. Moreover, Ireland's culture was oral during that period, except for the limited use of a specialised script known as *ogam*. In the fifth century, Ireland received Christianity and its concomitant literate culture, most likely from British missionaries such as St Patrick. British influence in the formation of Irish Christian culture is evident in the presence of words in Old Irish borrowed from the British vernacular, many of an ecclesiastical character;[2] the formation of a new alphabet for writing Irish based

1 See M. Lapidge, 'Gildas's education and the Latin culture of sub-Roman Britain', in M. Lapidge and D. Dumville (eds.) *Gildas: new approaches* (Cambridge, 1984), 27–50. On the wide range of works, classical and Christian, available to Gildas, see N. Wright, 'Gildas's reading: a survey', *Sacris erudiri* 32 (1991), 121–62.

2 Damian McManus, 'The so-called *Cothrige* and *Pátraic* strata of Latin loan-words in early Irish', in P. Ní Chatháin and M. Richter (eds.), *Irland und Europa* (Stuttgart, 1984), 179–96.

on the Latin alphabet as it was pronounced by British speakers;[3] and the late antique features of Irish manuscript production and script, presumably based upon British models.[4]

Geographically, the present survey covers Ireland and Britain – in the case of Britain, the whole island for the period from the Roman withdrawal in the early fifth century to the completion of the Anglo-Saxon conquest in the early seventh century; thereafter, only those parts that remained Celtic-speaking, notably, Wales and Cornwall (treated as one cultural region), and Scotland. Scotland had several distinct cultural regions: Gaelic Scotland, centred on the kingdom of Dál Ríata, comprising Argyll and the surrounding islands, with Iona as its ecclesiastical centre – culturally a part of Ireland; British Strathclyde around the valley of the Clyde, with Dumbarton as its capital; and Pictland, covering most of Scotland north of the Clyde and Forth, whose separate language and culture were gradually absorbed by Gaelic neighbours. Not included in this survey is Brittany, which was colonised by Britons in the fifth and sixth centuries and retained strong cultural ties with Celtic-speaking Britain all through the early middle ages. The division between Britain and Ireland is not merely geographical; it signifies major linguistic and cultural differences as well. Ireland (and much of Scotland) belonged to the Goedelic branch of Celtic, in contrast with the British mainland south of the Clyde-Forth line, where Brittonic dialects of Celtic were spoken. And whereas Britain had been under Roman rule for almost four centuries, Ireland remained politically untouched, a difference with potential significance for the development of literacy and collections of books.

Chronologically, the survey covers sub-Roman and early medieval Britain, from the withdrawal of the Romans in the early fifth century to the subjugation of Wales and Scotland to Norman overlordship in the late eleventh and early twelfth centuries. For Ireland, the period begins with the arrival of Christianity in the fifth century and ends with the Norman invasion of the late twelfth century. In both islands political conquest approximately coincided with ecclesiastical reforms that introduced new administrative structures and continental monastic orders. As a result the two regions experienced profound changes in their literary and intellectual traditions that were readily obvious by about 1200 AD.

3 See E. MacNeill, 'Beginnings of Latin culture in Ireland', *Studies: an Irish Quarterly Review* 20 (1931), 39–48 and 449–60.

4 As argued by J. Brown, 'The oldest Irish manuscripts and their late antique background', in Ní Chatháin and Richter, *Irland und Europa*, 311–27; repr. in J. Bately *et al.* (eds.), *A palaeographer's view: the selected writings of Julian Brown* (London, 1993), 221–41.

The search for libraries in Ireland and Celtic Britain during the early middle ages encounters two immediate problems. One is the lack of descriptive terminology from sources of the period. Although the medieval Celtic areas (notably Ireland and Wales) used a variety of words, Latin and vernacular, for books and related paraphernalia, they apparently had no formal terms for a collection of books or for the place where it was kept. No doubt they were familiar with the term *bibliotheca*, denoting a collection and repository of historical documents and ancient texts, from references in the Old Testament,[5] in the works of the Latin Fathers[6] and, in the case of Britain, perhaps from first-hand experience of Roman libraries. They also borrowed into their respective vernaculars a range of Latin words for books: Irish *lebor* ('a book'; Lat. *liber*) and its diminutive, *lebrán*, ('a small book', 'a copy'), *cín* ('a gathering of five parchment leaves', 'a manuscript'; Lat. *quinio*), *pairt* ('a tome'; Lat. *pars*), *scriptuir* ('a book'; Lat. *scriptura*); Welsh *llyfr* ('a manuscript', 'a book'; Lat. *liber*) and its diminutive *llyfryn* ('a small book'). Yet they apparently had no vernacular equivalents for the Latin usage *bibliotheca*, or related words such as *archivum* and *armarium*.

A more serious problem is the lack of direct evidence. No physical remains of libraries in Ireland and Celtic Britain have survived; no catalogues of library holdings or booklists are available, such as one finds for Anglo-Saxon England and medieval Europe. There are scattered references in the literary sources to collections of books, but seldom accompanied by physical details. Given these limitations it will be necessary to rely on indirect sources, notably manuscripts, authors, written works and writing centres, from them drawing inferences about the nature and functions of book collections in Celtic Britain and Ireland.

The obvious place to begin the search for books is in ecclesiastical centres, especially the monasteries. Christianity introduced literacy in Latin, the language of the Bible and liturgy; thereafter, the early medieval Christian church maintained a monopoly on literacy and books. Significantly, when Britain and Ireland adopted (and adapted) the Latin alphabet to write down their Celtic vernaculars, that innovation took place in an ecclesiastical setting. Early Christian Ireland bears witness to the fruits of this literacy in a prolific and distinctive literature composed in both Latin and Irish and transmitted in manuscripts. (Ireland also had a learned class of secular scholars, known

5 For example, Ezra 6. 1 and 2 Maccabees 2. 13.

6 For example, Isidore's definition, 'Bibliotheca est locus ubi reponuntur libri' ('A library is a place where books are stored') in *Etymologiae* xv. v. 5.

as *filid*, but there is no hard evidence that they produced or kept books.)[7] In Celtic Britain the picture is much less clear. Wales is the best-represented area, though the surviving evidence from there is scant by comparison with that of Ireland.[8] Within Scotland the Gaelic-speaking kingdom of Dál Ríata, which formed part of a single Gaelic culture with Ireland, offers considerable evidence of literacy in marked contrast to the neighbouring British kingdom of Strathclyde and the territories of the Picts. Given this imbalance, the present survey will focus mainly on early medieval Ireland (including Dál Ríata) and Wales.

Ireland

The surviving sources of evidence comprise: manuscripts copied in Irish monasteries; works (mainly anonymous) produced in Ireland and composed in both Hiberno-Latin and Irish; and numerous references in early Irish sources (especially the annals) to people whose occupations and activities would imply ready access to collections of books. There is also the archaeological evidence of artefacts connected with the production and conservation of books (mainly metal styli,[9] leather book-satchels, boxes for holding individual manuscripts) and representations of scribes/scholars in manuscripts and on stones. Additionally, the literary sources sometimes refer to the use, acquisition and loss of books.

One is struck by the paucity of surviving manuscripts. Only twelve manuscripts of date older than AD 1000 have survived in Ireland, all of them copies of the Gospels or the Psalms or missals.[10] They probably owe their survival not so much to their religious contents as to their quasi-magical associations with important monastic saints such as Colum Cille; significantly, many were preserved in special boxes (Ir. *cumdach*), indicating that they

7 On the origins and organisation of scholarship in early Ireland, see T. M. Charles-Edwards, 'The context and uses of literacy in early Christian Ireland', in H. Pryce (ed.), *Literacy in medieval Celtic societies* (Cambridge, 1998), 62–82.

8 See now the case for Welsh literature made by P. Sims-Williams, 'The uses of writing in early medieval Wales', in Pryce, *Literacy*, 15–38. On the lack of evidence from Scotland, see K. Hughes, 'Where are the writings of early Scotland?', in her *Celtic Britain in the early middle ages: studies in Scottish and Welsh sources* (Woodbridge, 1980), 38–52; and K. Forsyth, 'Literacy in Pictland', in Pryce, *Literacy*, 39–61.

9 Styli were discovered at the early Irish monastery of Nendrum (Co. Down); see H. C. Lawlor, *The monastery of Saint Mochaoi of Nendrum* (Belfast, 1925), 146.

10 J. F. Kenney, *The sources for the early history of Ireland: ecclesiastical* (New York, 1929); repr. with revisions by L. Bieler (New York, 1966), 9, n. 9, to whose list should be added the two discrete parts of the Stowe Missal (Kenney, no. 555).

were objects of veneration rather than of study. Over fifty other manuscripts (or fragments) that were probably written in Ireland before 1000 have survived on the Continent in libraries of monasteries founded or frequented by the Irish, notably Bobbio, St Gall and Reichenau.[11] For the period AD 1000–1200 ten more manuscripts are preserved in Ireland and some thirty abroad (mostly in Britain). Unfortunately, for the majority of these manuscripts, the place of writing has not been identified. Thus, their value as evidence for book collections in Ireland is limited. Some offer tantalising clues; for example, two copiously glossed eighth-century manuscripts of the Pauline Epistles and of Matthew's Gospel, respectively,[12] have a scribal hand in common. Evidently, at some point they were together in the same Irish writing centre, perhaps in north Leinster.[13]

Of works produced in early medieval Ireland, those in Latin most commonly treat of ecclesiastical concerns, grammar, hagiography, computistics and biblical exegesis. The vernacular (Old Irish) was also being used for religious compositions by the close of the sixth century, as evidenced by the obscure poem *Amra Choluim Cille*, a eulogy on St Colum Cille, the founder of Iona (d. 597). Not surprisingly, the vernacular was also used for secular compositions such as tribal legends, sagas, lore of place-names, genealogies and law tracts. Although this matter was originally the preserve of the secular learned class of the *filid*, its transmission, and perhaps even composition, now belonged firmly in the ecclesiastical domain. Witness the *Cín Dromma Snechta*, a lost manuscript of early eighth-century date and secular contents, which was probably copied from exemplar(s) at the monastery of Bangor, perhaps for the small monastery (Drumsnat, Co. Monaghan) that gave it its name.[14] By the late ninth century the vernacular was the dominant language for both religious and secular literature.

Another type of evidence are the Irish annals (in their various local recensions). A year-by-year record of important local and national events, they often include the obits of prominent ecclesiastical scribes and scholars, usually giving

11 Kenney, *Sources*, 9–10.

12 Würzburg, Universitätsbibliothek, MSS m.p.th.f. 12 and 61.

13 As suggested by their common association with the Irish scholar Sedulius Scottus, who may have hailed from this region. See E. A. Lowe, *Codices Latini antiquiores: a palaeographical guide to Latin manuscripts prior to the 9th century*, 12 vols. (Oxford, 1959), IX, nos. 1403 and 1415.

14 On this manuscript see R. Thurneysen, *Die irische Helden- und Königsage bis zum siebzehnten Jahrhundert* (Haale, 1921), 15–18; and G. Murphy, 'On the dates of two sources used in Thurneysen's Heldensage', *Ériu* 16 (1952), 145–51.

the name of the foundation where they worked. This evidence has been well investigated by Kathleen Hughes,[15] though some caveats are in order. For a survey covering almost four centuries, it is hard to imagine that the nature of the entries on a particular subject remained constant, as if the annals could be analysed as a 'homogenous source'.[16] Her starting date of 730, the generally accepted approximate date for the 'Chronicle of Ireland', the putative common source of all the Irish annals, while commendably cautious, ignores potential evidence for the seventh century, the most productive period in Hiberno-Latin scholarship. Moreover, she makes no mention of Iona, a monastery which probably kept annalistic records from as early as the first half of the seventh century.[17] Finally, not all scribes and centres of book production made it into the annals. Witness, for example, the master scribe Dorbbéne of Iona, whose activity is known only from a colophon at the end of his copy of Adomnán's Life of Columba; or the monastery of Tech Moling (St Mullins, Co. Carlow), whose scribes and scholars never appear in the annals, though other sources indicate that it was a major centre of learning.

However, of the hundreds of monasteries known to have existed in early Ireland,[18] not all should be regarded as significant repositories of books. Some of them were hermitical sites or resting stops on pilgrimage routes; some were active only for a time. Most would have kept the basic books needed for religious observance, copies of the Gospels, the Pauline Epistles, and the Psalms; liturgical books such as missals and hymnals; computistical works, especially an ecclesiastical calendar; penitential handbooks; and perhaps written documents relating to the founder. Monasteries with schools would obviously need larger collections that included instructional books on Latin grammar (notably Donatus and Priscian), natural philosophy (Isidore and Bede), ecclesiastical history (Eusebius in Jerome's Latin translation, and Orosius); and, most importantly, scriptural commentaries, especially those of the Latin Fathers such as Jerome and Augustine. Important monasteries with a vested interest in the larger political scene would in addition have maintained genealogies of the local ruling families and annals of local and national events; they might

15 K. Hughes, 'The distribution of Irish scriptoria and centres of learning from 730 to 1111', in N. K. Chadwick, K. Hughes *et al.* (eds.), *Studies in the early British church* (Cambridge, 1958), 243–72.

16 C. Etchingham, *Church organization in Ireland, AD 650 to 1000* (Maynooth, 1999), 356.

17 J. Bannerman, 'Notes on the Scottish entries in the early Irish annals', in *Studies in the history of Dalriada* (Edinburgh, 1974), 9–26.

18 See A. Gwynn and R. Neville Hadcock, *Medieval religious houses: Ireland* (London, 1970), which lists some 180 monasteries known from the surviving evidence to have been continuously active during the early medieval period, and more than 670 others that were active for some part of the period at least.

also have copied traditional native lore (Ir. *senchas*) in the form of tales and origin legends.

In attempting to identify those monasteries likely to have had significant collections of books, that is, sufficient in number and kind to provide education and promote scholarship, the following four criteria will be employed.

1. Monasteries known to have had specialist scribes.

At the very least, the presence of such scribes implies copying activity and the availability of exemplars: in effect, book production and preservation. In cases where scribes supplied their names in colophons entered at the end of a manuscript or work, their place of writing can often be identified. Notable examples are Dorbbéne of Iona, who copied Adomnán's Life of Columba (*c.* 700), Ferdomnach of Armagh, who copied part of the Book of Armagh (*c.* 807), Máel-Muire of Clonmacnoise, who copied *Lebor na hUidre*, 'the Book of the Dun Cow' (*c.* 1100), and Máel-Brigte hUa Máeluánaig of Armagh, who copied (and glossed) a gospel manuscript in 1138.[19] Such evidence linking scribe and writing centre may also offer insights into the standards of copying and manuscript production that obtained there. But the majority of scribes' names survived in the annals, identified with the formula 'death of X, scribe of [monastery] Y'; for example, the Annals of Ulster (*s.a.* 742), 'Mors Cuidgile, scriba[e] et abbatis Lughmaidh' ['Death of Cuidgile, scribe and abbot of Louth'].[20] Their presence in the annals, which typically note only the most important kinds of people (such as kings, bishops and abbots), and the connotations of learning associated with the term *scriba*, suggests that they were no mere copyists but masters of schools and scholars.[21] Although strictly speaking such obits provide evidence for a writing centre good only for the working lifetime of the specified *scriba*, continuity may reasonably be inferred from later records. For example, the Annals of the Four Masters (*s.a.* 780) record the death of Maelochtraigh mac Conaill, scribe of Cell na Manach (Kilmanagh, Co. Kilkenny),[22] the only mention of a scribe for this foundation. But obits in the same annals of other members of the community at 802, 839 and 843

19 Now BL, MS Harley 1802.

20 S. Mac Airt and G. Mac Niocaill (eds.), *The Annals of Ulster (to AD 1131)*, pt 1 (Dublin, 1983), 196–7 (hereafter abbreviated AU).

21 The exalted status of the Irish *scriba* is probably modelled on examples from the Old Testament. The Irish *scriba* may also have been a scholar of law; see Etchingham, *Church organization*, 174 and n. 1.

22 J. O'Donovan (ed. and tr.), *Annala Rioghachta Eireann: Annals of the Kingdom of Ireland by the Four Masters, from the earliest period to the year 1616*, 7 vols. (Dublin, 1854; repr. New York, 1966), 1. 387 (hereafter abbreviated 'AFM').

indicate institutional, and most likely scribal, continuity. A regular succession of scribes' obits for an institution over a long period points to a stable writing centre. For example, the monastery of Duleek (Co. Meath) had the obits of its scribes recorded in the annals for 872, 907, 920, 929 and 961. That none occurs thereafter may well indicate a decline in Duleek as a centre of learning, probably brought on by the collapse of its local patron, the royal house of Brega.[23] Some of the great monasteries such as Armagh and Clonmacnoise sustained a succession of scribes over several centuries.

2. Monasteries known to have had a master of a school.

The annals record the obits of other types of men of learning with terms such as Latin *sapiens*, Irish *suí*, *senchaidh*, and *fer légind* (literally, 'a man of Latin learning'). The last term had become the most common by the late tenth century with the meaning 'master of a school', usually accompanied by the name of the monastery where he exercised his function. For example, the Annals of Inisfallen (*s.a.* 990) record that the monastery of Ros Ailithir (Ross Carbery, Co. Cork) was attacked by the Danes and its *fer légind*, Airbertach mac Cosse, taken hostage[24] – no doubt his eminent status made him an attractive target. Some of Airbertach's work (in Irish) has survived, including poems on the Psalms and on the geography of the classical world. These two works, presumably intended for his students at Ros Ailithir, show that he drew on a variety of sources, including a treatise on the Psalms in Old Irish (ninth century) and Pomponius Mela's *De situ orbis libri tres*, respectively.[25] The presence of a *fer légind* at a particular monastery – or indeed of a *mac légind* ('student')[26] – implies a centre of learning and a collection of books.

3. Monasteries known to have been the place of writing, or the home, of a manuscript.

Obviously, one manuscript does not make a book collection, but the resources (material and human) required for its production presuppose a scribal tradition and the availability of books as exemplars. Where the manuscript has been skilfully executed, in codicology, layout and script, the case is even stronger. The Book of Armagh, penned in the first decade of the ninth century, bears all the marks of competent scribes working in an organised writing

23 As argued by Hughes, 'Distribution', 256.

24 S. Mac Airt (ed. and tr.), *The Annals of Inisfallen (MS. Rawlinson B. 503)* (Dublin, 1951), 168–9.

25 Kenney, *Sources*, nos. 545–6.

26 For example, at Tealach-Dimain (Tullamaine, Co. Kilkenny), a falling stone from the round tower killed a student (AFM *s.a.* 1121).

centre with access to a good collection of manuscripts.[27] The evidence of a manuscript known to have been simply housed in a monastery is not by itself so compelling, but at the very least it suggests an attempt at book collecting. Using this kind of evidence (as well as that described in no. 4, below), Dom Louis Gougaud attempted to identify the monastic libraries of Ireland from 600 to 1500.[28] In one respect he was too strict, omitting archival documents such as charters, whose very survival implies a repository for preserving such documents; in another too lax, by assuming (with James F. Kenney) that a surviving Life of a monastic founder was necessarily composed at the mother-house. His list includes some thirty monasteries from before 1200 known to have produced or housed manuscripts.

4. Monasteries that can be identified as the location of a known author, even if no copy of his work has survived from that location.

Adomnán's *De locis sanctis*, for example, although preserved only in continental manuscripts, was undoubtedly composed at Iona.[29] Adomnán drew on Jerome's biblical commentaries, the *Chronicon* of Sulpicius Severus, the *Historiae* of the so-called Hegesippus, and Juvencus. In the words of the most recent editor of *De locis*, 'All this indicates a library of relatively wide resources at Iona.'[30] Likewise when Cummian wrote to Ségéne, abbot of Iona, in 632/3, on the Easter question, citing *inter alia* Ambrosiaster, Jerome, Augustine, Gregory, Pelagius and a host of computistical works,[31] he not only demonstrated his own access to a good collection of books (location not yet identified), but also assumed that Ségéne had the same.

Guided by these four criteria, the following historical sketch is proposed. For the initial period after the arrival of Christianity in the fifth century, churches and monasteries would have maintained collections of basic biblical and liturgical books (none has survived). In the second half of the sixth century, evidence of book-learning emerges, concomitant with the founding of monasteries such as Bangor and Clonard as centres of biblical learning. While still at Bangor (before 590) the Irish missionary Columbanus composed a commentary on the Psalms (now lost) and a hymn *Precamur patrem*. The latter gives some

27 See R. Sharpe, 'Palaeographical considerations in the study of the Patrician documents in the Book of Armagh (Dublin, Trinity Coll., MS 52)', *Scriptorium* 36 (1982), 3–28.

28 L. Gougaud, 'The remains of ancient Irish monastic libraries', in J. Ryan (ed.), *Féil-Sgríbhinn Eóin Mhic Néill: essays and studies presented to Professor Eoin MacNeill* (Dublin, 1940), 319–34.

29 Indeed, he mentions in the prologue that he first composed the work on wax tablets before committing it to manuscript.

30 D. Meehan (ed. and tr.), *Adamnan's De locis sanctis* (Dublin, 1958), 14.

31 M. Walsh and D. Ó Cróinín (eds. and trs.), *Cummian's Letter* De controversia Paschali *and the* De ratione conputandi (Toronto, 1988), 226.

idea of the works available to him there: Cassian's *Institutiones*, Caesarius of Arles's sermons, Jerome's letters and possibly Rufinus' translation of Gregory of Nazianzus' *Oratio 3*.[32] When Columbanus later went to the Continent he maintained his scholarly interest in collecting books. In a letter (*c.* 600) to Pope Gregory he asked for a copy of his commentary on Ezekiel and for some comments on the Song of Songs and on the minor prophet, Zechariah, arguing that 'from a small stock [*sc.* of books] less must be lent and from a great one more'.[33] As Columbanus' plea suggests, Ireland during this formative period depended heavily on outside sources for its books. One source was Britain, as suggested by its profound influence on Irish script and codicology.[34] Another source was southern Gaul – to judge by the influence of its scriptural texts and its liturgy on seventh-century Irish works.[35] A third source were late antique books from the Continent, as indicated by the survival of their archaic abbreviations and contractions in later Irish copies.[36]

The seventh century was extraordinarily prolific in literature, especially in the areas of hagiography, computistica and biblical exegesis. Although much of this work is anonymous, some names stand out: Mo Sinu maccu Min of Bangor, and Cummian in the first half of the century, both computists and biblical exegetes; Laidcend mac Baíth Bannaig of Clonfertmulloe (d. 661) who composed an epitome of Gregory the Great's *Moralia in Iob*; the 'Irish Augustine' of Lismore, who composed a highly original work, *De mirabilibus sacrae scripturae* (655);[37] Ailerán of Clonard (?), who wrote at least two commentaries on the Gospels; Banbán of Kildare (+ 686) who commented on the Catholic Epistles; Tírechán of Ardbraccan (Co. Meath), Muirchú of Armagh, and Cogitosus of

32 See C. Stancliffe, 'Venantius Fortunatus, Ireland, Jerome: the evidence of Precamur Patrem', *Peritia* 10 (1996), 81–97.

33 G. S. M. Walker (ed. and tr.), *Sancti Columbani opera* (Dublin, 1957), 10–11.

34 See n. 4 above.

35 Codex Usserianus Primus (Dublin, Trinity Coll., MS 55; early seventh century?) preserves a text of the Old Latin Gospels very close to that used in southern Gaul; likewise, the text of the Gallican psalms preserved on the Springmount wax tablets (Dublin, National Museum, no. S. A. 1914: 2; late sixth century?) has close textual affinities with a psalter from the same region; and a palimpsest sacramentary dated *c.* 650 (Munich, Bayerische Staatsbibliothek, Clm 14429) is heavily Gallican in its liturgy.

36 See W. M. Lindsay, 'The Bobbio scriptorium: its early minuscule abbreviations', *Zentralblatt für Bibliothekswesen* 26 (1909), 302–6; and R. I. Best (ed.), *The commentary on the Psalms with glosses in Old-Irish preserved in the Ambrosian Library (MS. C 301 inf.)* (Dublin and London, 1936), 32–3. For arguments that continental manuscripts had a strong formative influence on Irish script in the second half of the sixth century, see W. O'Sullivan, 'The palaeographical background to the Book of Kells', in F. O'Mahony (ed.), *The Book of Kells* (Aldershot, 1994), 175–82.

37 On the activities of this biblical scholar and his circle, see P. Grosjean, 'Sur quelques exégètes irlandais du VIIe siècle', *Sacris erudiri* 7 (1955), 67–98.

Kildare, hagiographers writing in the second half of the century; and Adomnán of Iona (d. 704), scriptural scholar and hagiographer. Most of these scholars are commemorated in the annals with the title *sapiens*.

The range of sources used by these authors is such that one has to assume ready access to well-stocked collections of books.[38] These evidently contained not only venerable sources (such as Jerome, Sulpicius Severus, Augustine) but also very recent authors. Thus, the works of Gregory the Great were well known in Ireland within a few decades of their composition, as evidenced by Cummian's Letter to Ségéne (632–3)[39] and Laidcend's abridgement of Gregory's *Moralia in Iob*. Even more influential was Isidore of Seville (d. 636). His *De ortu et obitu patrum* was cited by Laidcend, and his *Etymologiae* was known in Ireland *c.* 650.[40] Such ready access to recent works is best explained by a large influx of books from the Continent, almost certainly a result of closer ties with Rome during and after the Easter controversy of the 630s.

The eighth and ninth centuries provide evidence for other kinds of scribal and literary activity: copying, glossing, and commenting on the canonical texts of the monastic schools (notably Latin grammars, the Psalms, Gospels, Pauline Epistles), side by side with composing and redacting vernacular literature (native law, sagas, genealogies, annals). Judging by the obits of scribes in the annals,[41] the main focus of activity during the first half of the eighth century was an area covering the north-east, the east coast and inland from there to the river Shannon. From the late eighth to the early tenth century the distribution of writing centres widens, though concentrated in the centre of Ireland and the east coast in a rectangle bounded on its east side by Carlingford Lough and a little south of Dublin Bay, and on its west side by Roscommon and Roscrea. There were also outlying pockets in the central north and south, and along the north and south coasts of Ireland.

After about 825 the pattern of numerous small centres of scribal activity gives way to a growing tendency towards concentration. This process was accelerated partly by Norse incursions and settlements, and partly by

38 In his encomium on Irish schools of this period, Bede marvels that foreign students received gratis both instruction *and books*: 'quos omnes Scotti . . . libros quoque ad legendum . . . gratuitum praebere curabant', *Historia ecclesiastica* III. xxvii: C. Plummer (ed.), *Venerabilis Baedae Historiam ecclesiasticam gentis Anglorum . . .*, 2 vols. (Oxford, 1896), I. 192.

39 See n. 31 above.

40 A fragment in an Irish hand has survived in St Gall, Stiftsbibliothek, MS 1399.a.1; see M. B. Parkes, 'The contribution of Insular scribes of the seventh and eighth centuries to the "grammar of legibility"', in A. Maierù (ed.), *Grafia e interpunzione del latino nel medioevo* (Rome, 1987), 15–29; repr. in Parkes, *Scribes, scripts and readers*, 1–18.

41 See Hughes, 'Distribution'.

competition from the large monasteries with their formidable financial resources and political connections. The exodus of Irish scholars to the Continent (such as Sedulius Scottus, John Scottus Eriugena, Martinus Hibernesis) also caused a drain of personnel and books (witness the manuscripts left at Würzburg by Sedulius Scottus). More difficult to assess is the effect of the *céli Dé* (literally, 'clients of God') reform movement (late eighth and ninth centuries). Some of its adherents established themselves in the vicinity of the great monasteries, for example at Armagh, and no doubt used their books; others developed writing centres of their own (as at Tallaght), though these seemed to have died out for want of resources. The movement was inward looking and favoured the vernacular, so it is unlikely to have encouraged the acquisition of books from abroad.

Even some of the great monasteries succumbed to these external pressures. Iona and Bangor, which had been thriving centres of learning and book production from the seventh to the ninth century, thereafter declined. Both were casualties of Viking attacks, and Bangor also had to contend with fierce competition from Armagh. Conversely, other early foundations, notably Monasterboice (Co. Louth) and Glendalough (Co. Wicklow),[42] became prominent centres of learning in the tenth and eleventh centuries. During this same period western monasteries (for example, Ardfert, Killaloe, Devenish and Tory) began to appear in the annals as centres of writing and teaching, and this region contributed progressively more names to the total number of writing centres. These western foundations, which survived both ecclesiastical reforms and the Norman invasion,[43] may have played a major role in preserving Irish manuscripts that subsequently became the basis of the great codices of the fourteenth and fifteenth centuries.

Nevertheless, by the twelfth century a relatively small number of ecclesiastical centres had come to dominate, notably Armagh, Clonmacnoise, Glendalough, Kildare and Monasterboice. The character of the manuscripts they produced had also changed: from copies of canonical texts in Latin (mainly biblical and grammatical) to compilations of miscellaneous materials in the vernacular (poems, genealogies, annals, sagas, lives of saints). The new productions, compilatory in character and antiquarian in content,[44] must have

42 On Glendalough, see A. Mac Shamhráin, *Church and polity in pre-Norman Ireland: the case of Glendalough* (Maynooth, 1996).

43 Witness the monastery of Innisfallen (Co. Kerry), which continued to record annals until 1214.

44 Notably, Dublin, Trinity Coll., MS 1441, and Killiney, Franciscan House [now housed at University Coll., Archives, Dublin], MS A. 1 (the *Liber hymnorum*; late eleventh and early

involved an intense search for old books that seem to have been mostly preserved in the Midlands. For example, Áed Húa Crimthaind, *fer légind* at Terryglass (Co. Tipperary), says that he compiled the Book of Leinster from many books.[45]

Yet with no apparent awareness of paradox these same monasteries were also importing books of contemporary scholarship from Europe. Two fragments (early twelfth-century) from Glendalough contain continental school texts;[46] and another manuscript from the second quarter of the twelfth century is glossed with contemporary Platonic scholarship from the so-called School of Chartres. The latter manuscript is composite, incorporating two already existing manuscripts: a copy of Chalcidius' Latin translation of Plato's *Timaeus* made a generation or two earlier (perhaps at Glendalough); and an eighth-century gathering of Irish hymns over which the scribe wrote the text of John Scottus Eriugena's *Periphyseon*. With so many changes in liturgy and the curriculum occurring at this time, such recycling of earlier manuscripts may have been quite common.[47]

The number of Irish ecclesiastical centres that can be shown to have maintained high standards of learning and book production throughout the early medieval period is few: Armagh, Clonmacnoise and Kildare. All three owed their success in large measure to political influence and financial resources. Kildare was already a wealthy and powerful centre of learning by the mid-seventh century, as described by a member of its community, Cogitosus, in his Life of Brigid, the founder. It may have kept its own version of the Chronicle of Ireland;[48] and as late as *c.* 1185 had a beautifully ornamented gospel.[49] Although Clonmacnoise has left no identifiable manuscripts or works from the earliest period, its scribes are among the first to be noted in the annals (*s.a.* 724, 768, 793); one of its scholars, Suibne, even merited an entry in the

twelfth century, respectively); Dublin, Royal Irish Academy, MS 23. E. 25 (1229) (*Lebor na hUidre*; *c.* 1100); Bodleian, MS Rawlinson B. 502, fols. 19–89 (pt II, first half of twelfth century); and Dublin, Trinity Coll., MS 1339 (The Book of Leinster; second half of twelfth century). Compare a similar antiquarian trend in Anglo-Saxon book production during the final quarter of the tenth century.

45 *Aed mac meic Crimthaind ro scrib in leborso 7 ra thinoil a llebraib imdaib*; cited in R. I. Best *et al.*, *The Book of Leinster*, I (Dublin, 1954), xv.

46 L. Bieler and B. Bischoff, 'Fragmente zweier frühmittelalterlicher Schulbücher aus Glendalough', *Celtica* 3 (1956), 211–20.

47 See P. P. Ó Néill, 'An Irishman at Chartres in the twelfth century – the evidence of Oxford, Bodleian Library, MS Auct. F. III. 15', *Ériu* 48 (1997), 1–35.

48 See J. N. Radner (ed. and tr.), *Fragmentary Annals of Ireland* (Dublin, 1978), xiv–xviii.

49 As described by Gerald of Wales, who saw the manuscript and claimed it was written there: J. J. O' Meara (tr.), *Gerald of Wales: the history and topography of Ireland* (London, 1982), 84–5 (pt II, sections 71–2).

Anglo-Saxon Chronicle (*s.a.* 891). Clonmacnoise also kept a version of the Chronicle of Ireland, revised in the tenth century by drawing on its own library of house records, martyrologies, genealogical collections, and materials from Wales (probably via St David's).[50] In the eleventh and twelfth centuries it was a major centre of manuscript production, especially of vernacular texts.[51]

Armagh stands pre-eminent for its almost unbroken tradition of documented scribal and archival activity. As early as the mid-seventh century it was promoting the cult of St Patrick, portraying him as founder of Armagh and Apostle of Ireland. Two Lives of Patrick from the second half of the seventh century and a work known as the *Liber angeli* from same period advanced this agenda. Copies of these works, as well as Patrick's *Confessio*, were kept at Armagh, to be used in the early ninth century by the scribes of the Book of Armagh. Obits of Armagh scribes appear in the first decades of the eighth century and continue in unbroken succession throughout the ninth century. In 899, a century before most other Irish monasteries, the annals record the obit of a *fer légind* at Armagh. Armagh's scriptorium had a recognisable 'house style' of calligraphy and decoration that lasted for centuries.[52] First seen in the Book of Armagh (*c.* 807), and later in the ninth century in the MacDurnan Gospels,[53] it is still evident in the cursive script of a twelfth-century copy of Gregory's *Moralia in Iob*[54] and in the script and decoration of two twelfth-century copies of the Gospels.[55] Such continuity was made possible by Armagh's preservation of its older manuscripts. Some of these apparently belonged to the private collections of former teachers. An early twelfth-century note added to *Lebor na hUidre* acknowledges as a source 'the books of Eochaid Ua Flannacán in Armagh'.[56] Since Eochaid was a scholar at Armagh who flourished in the second half of the tenth century,[57] it seems fair to conclude that he had a private collection of books which he may have left to the school at Armagh.

50 K. Grabowski and D. Dumville, *Chronicles and annals of medieval Ireland and Wales: the Clonmacnoise-group texts* (Woodbridge, 1984), 123 and 225.

51 As evidenced by a version of the Irish World Chronicle (now preserved as Part 1 of Bodleian, MS Rawlinson B.502, fols. 1–12^{v}) and by *Lebor na hUidre*, the compilers of which drew on the books of other monasteries.

52 The term comes from Parkes, *Scribes, Scripts and Readers*, xviii.

53 Now Lambeth, MS 1370.

54 Bodleian, MS Laud Misc. 460.

55 BL, MSS Harley 1023 and 1802. See F. Henry and G. L. Marsh-Micheli, 'A century of Irish illumination (1070–1170)', *Proceedings of the Royal Irish Academy* 62C (1962), 146–52; and F. J. Byrne, *A thousand years of Irish script* (Oxford, 1979), 15–16.

56 R. I. Best and O. Bergin (eds.), '*a llebraib Eochada hui Flandacan i nArd Macha*' (*Lebor na hUidre: Book of the Dun Cow* [Dublin, 1929], 94, lines 2919–20).

57 His death is recorded in AFM (*s.a.* 1003).

Armagh took measures to protect its books. The Annals of the Four Masters (AFM) (*s.a.* 937) report that a special case (*cumdach*) was fashioned for the *Canóin Pátraicc* (the Book of Armagh). The same annals (*s.a.* 1020) note a fire that destroyed much of Armagh – except for the house of the manuscripts (Ir. *teach screaptra*). A less conventional repository at Armagh was the *carcar* (prison); a note in *Lebor na hUidre* states that a famous book of Irish saga materials was missing from there.[58] In the twelfth century Armagh had an official custodian of books; AFM (*s.a.* 1136) records the death of Maelisa Mac Maelcoluim, 'chief keeper of the calendar of Ard-Macha, its chief antiquary and librarian' (Ir. *leabhar-coimhedaigh*; literally, 'keeper of books'),[59] evidently a man who combined the roles of scholar and librarian.

These book collections fulfilled a number of functions. Most obviously, they provided copies of works needed by scholars and students. That role is pointedly illustrated in a famous Middle Irish legend. When the scholar Lon Garad of Cell Gabra (Kilgory, Co. Leix) hid his famous book collection from St Colum Cille, who had a posthumous reputation for secretly copying other scholars' books, the saint cursed the collection so that 'the books remain and no one studies them'.[60] By contrast, the Abbot of Armagh generously lent books to his students; unfortunately, they were lost in the great fire of 1020.[61] Even rare books were made available to students; a note in *Lebor na hUidre* states that a famous book called *in Libur Girr* ('the Short Book') was stolen by a student and taken abroad.[62]

Book collections also served as a repository of exemplars for copying. Abbot Adomnán in his Life of Columba portrayed the community of Iona in the late sixth century as habitually engaged in making copies of their manuscripts. He recorded the scribe Baíthéne's request to Columba: 'I need one of the brethren to help me go through the text of the psalter I have copied and

58 '. . . in Libur Budi testo asin carcar i nArd Macha' ('the Yellow Book that is missing from the prison in Armagh') (*Lebor na hUidre*: Best and Bergin, 94, lines 2921–2). The writer's use of a present-tense verb suggests a recent event.

59 O' Donovan, *Annals*, II. 1052–3. Cf. Late Latin *custos*, 'a librarian'.

60 W. Stokes (ed. and tr.), *Félire Óengusso Céli Dé: the Martyrology of Oengus the Culdee*, HBS 29 (London, 1905; repr: Dublin, 1984), 198–9. For another legend about Lon, see n. 73 below.

61 AFM (*s.a.*), *a liubhair i ttaighibh na mac leighinn*, 'their books in the houses of the students' (O'Donovan, *Annals*, II. 796–7).

62 Best and Bergin, 94, lines 2922–3, and xi, n. 1. Apparently there were several books with this name; see C. Plummer, 'On the colophons and marginalia of Irish scribes', *Proceedings of the British Academy* 12 (1926), 11–44, at 20 and n. 3.

correct any mistakes'[63] – evidently the brother read the exemplar out loud while Baíthéne checked his copy. That a copy was only as good as its exemplar was recognised by another Irish scholar, Calmanus (probably Ir. *Colmán*). In a letter to his student Feradach, he announced that he had recently received *a Romanis* ('from the Romans')[64] improved texts of many Latin works: 'Many exemplars of books written out by the *Romani* have reached us, some of which we have discovered to be more correct [by comparison with] codices of ours that have been corrupted by the negligence of scribes.'[65] He names the *Carmen* and *Opus paschale* of Caelius Sedulius, Isidore's *De officiis ecclesiasticis*, and unnamed *Chronica* (perhaps Isidore's). Two conclusions may be inferred: Colmán was eager to improve the textual quality of his books by collating newly acquired versions with the copies that he already possessed; and he passed on the improved texts to his students so that they could copy them for their collections. Occasionally the name and location of their exemplar(s) are recorded by Irish scribes.[66]

Where were book collections stored? Despite frequent references to the copying, carrying about and reading of books at Iona, Adomnán's Life of Columba never mentions a specific place for keeping them. He uses the Latin word *scrini(ol)um* twice, in contexts that might suggest a coffer for books (the Late Latin usage) rather than a box for holding relics (the normal Hiberno-Latin usage). Speaking of books miraculously retrieved from a river, he claims that the part written by Columba was found to be in excellent condition, 'dry, and not at all injured, as though it had been kept in a coffer'; and 'undamaged, and as clean and dry as if it had remained all that time in a coffer'.[67] A specific building for books is mentioned in the annals (AFM *s.a.* 1020), which record that Armagh's 'house of manuscripts' (Ir. *teach screaptra*) survived a great fire – most likely because the building was made entirely of stone. This type of 'library' building was probably a relatively late and rare development, since

63 R. Sharpe (tr.), *Adomnán of Iona: Life of St Columba* (London, 1995), 129; based on A. O. Anderson and M. O. Anderson (eds. and trs.), *Adomnán's Life of Columba*, rev. edn (Oxford, 1991), bk I, ch. 23 (pp. 50–1).

64 Possibly the inhabitants of Rome, but more likely the seventh-century Irish adherents of Roman practices, especially on the dating of Easter.

65 R. Sharpe (ed.), 'An Irish textual critic and the *Carmen paschale* of Sedulius: Colman's Letter to Feradach', *Journal of Medieval Latin* 2 (1992), 44–54, at 47.

66 Most of these manuscripts are now lost. For some examples, see C. Plummer, 'Colophons', 26–8.

67 'Siccum et nullo modo corruptum, acsi in scriniolo esset reconditum' and 'nitidum et siccum acsi in scrinio tanto permansiset tempore . . .' Anderson and Anderson, *Vita Columbae*, II. 8–9 (pp. 104–7).

stone buildings did not become common in Ireland until the ninth and tenth centuries, perhaps as a reaction to the increased pillaging of monasteries.

For books in common, regular use, the normal method of storage was a leather satchel (Ir. *tiag/tiag libuir*; Hiberno-Latin *scetha*). Although satchels or budgets are attested elsewhere for carrying books, their use as a 'habitual receptacle' for books seems to have been an Irish practice.[68] A seventh-century Hiberno-Latin work, the *Hisperica famina*, describes the student's satchel (*curuana, archimium*) as made of white leather, sewn in the shape of a square, bound by twelve cords and carried around the neck.[69] What the *Hisperica famina* implies, and other sources confirm, is that the book satchel was an essential part of a student's (and scholar's) paraphernalia. For example, Adomnán refers to a young man of the Columban community riding with a satchel of books under his arm, and another student carrying one on his shoulders.[70] Even an eminent master such as Columbanus used a satchel, as reported by his seventh-century continental biographer Jonas, who described him travelling through the woods carrying a book of Holy Scripture on his shoulder, *librum humero ferens*.[71]

The satchel as a method of book storage had several advantages: mobility, since books (including unbound gatherings) could be carried about from place to place without being damaged; convenience, since books could be carried on one's person while other activities were being performed, such as manual labour or travelling; and accessibility, since books could be readily consulted, should the opportunity for reading arise. When not in use, the satchel (and its books) was hung with others on pegs attached to the wall, in effect forming a library. A speaker in the *Hisperica famina* admonishes his fellow students at the end of a day's march: 'Hang your white booksacks on the wall/ set your lovely satchels in a straight line.'[72] A story in the Book of Leinster (*c.* 1160) relates that when the scholar and bibliophile Lon Garad of Cell Gabra died, 'the satchels of Ireland with their gospels and their books of instruction fell from their pegs'.[73] This metonymic reference to the satchel as the repository

68 Three of these Irish satchels have survived; see J. W. Waterer, 'Irish book-satchels or budgets', *Medieval Archaeology* 12 (1968), 70–82.

69 M. W. Herren (ed. and tr.), *The Hisperica famina*: I. *The A-Text: a new critical edition with English translation and philological commentary* (Toronto, 1974), 104–7, lines 513–30.

70 Anderson and Anderson, *Vita Columbae* II. 8 and 9; Sharpe (tr.), *Adomnán*, 160–1.

71 B. Krush (ed.), *Scriptorum rerum Germanicarum in usum scholarum: Ionae Vitae Sanctorum Columbani, Vedastis, Iohannis* (Hanover and Leipzig, 1905), 74, line 17 (section 8).

72 Herren, *Hisperica famina*, 84–5, lines 262–3.

73 A. O'Sullivan (ed.), *The Book of Leinster, formerly Lebar na Núachongbála*, VI (Dublin, 1983), 1690, lines 51886–8, 'IS ed atberar co torchratar tiaga libair hErend 7 a soscelai 7 a llibuir foglamma dia n-aidlenaib in aidchi éitsechta Luin Garad'. The language of the story

of book-learning suggests that it was the normal form of book storage in early Ireland, at least for the most commonly used books such as gospels, psalters and textbooks.[74]

For valuable books various methods of storage were employed. Books could be valuable because of their intrinsic worth (for example, their gold covers, as with the great Gospel of Colum Cille), or their elaborate ornamentation (for example, the gospels at Kildare seen by Gerald of Wales), or their rarity (for example, the *Cín Dromma Snechta*), or some special association with a founding saint (for example, the Book of Durrow, associated with Colum Cille) or some magical powers attributed to them (for example, the psalter called the *Cathach*, which was carried into battle by the O Donnell family). Such books were often kept in specially made boxes or shrines (Ir. *cumdach*) or in elaborately decorated satchels.[75] Another location for books was the round tower, which became a prominent feature of Irish monastic complexes from the tenth century on. Under the year 1097, AFM recorded that 'the round tower of Monasterboice with its books and many treasures were burned'.[76] The so-called Miscellaneous Annals (*s.a.* 1130–1) reported the destruction of the monastery of Druim Both (Drumbo, Co. Down), 'including round tower, oratory and books'.[77] The round tower primarily served to protect against pillage and fire and was relatively inaccessible, so it is likely that any books deposited there were both valuable and outside regular use. In one instance a valuable gospels was kept in the sacristy of the great stone church of Kells, presumably with the sacred vessels.[78]

Wales

As with Ireland, only indirect sources are available. Wales kept annals (*Annales Cambriae*), but unlike their Irish counterparts they offer no evidence about scribal activity or learning or books. The scarcity of manuscripts from Wales is even more severe than that evidenced for Ireland. For the period to 1150, only two manuscripts have survived within Wales (both after 1000) and

is considerably earlier than the twelfth-century date of the manuscript. See also the reference to Lon Garad, 83 above.

74 A late eleventh-century satire on Irish monastic learning, known as 'The vision of Mac Conglinne', relates that after the hero had settled in at the monastic guesthouse of Cork 'he retrieved his book satchel and took out of it his Psalter' (my translation of the Irish text in K. H. Jackson (ed.), *Aislinge Meic Con Glinne* [Dublin, 1990], 5, lines 137–8).

75 See Waterer, 'Irish book-satchels'.

76 O'Donovan, *Annals*, II. 956–7.

77 S. Ó hInnse (ed. and tr.), *Miscellaneous Irish annals (AD 1114–1437)* (Dublin, 1947), 18–19.

78 The measure was not very effective, since the book was stolen (AU *s.a.* 1007).

possibly fifteen more outside Wales (mainly in England).[79] Literary references to book collections are almost unknown.[80] Given these limitations, the attempt to identify book collections and their uses in Wales has to rely on the following indirect evidence: compositions by Welsh authors of the period – in so far as they reveal dependence on or familiarity with written sources current in the early middle ages; manuscripts written in Wales whose contents and scripts imply access to written exemplars; and centres of learning, mainly ecclesiastical, whose activities would necessitate the use of book collections.

The roster of native Welsh writers and their works is quite impressive: Pelagius, whose works (especially his commentary on the Pauline Epistles), although composed in Rome, probably reflect his British education (early fifth century); Gildas's *De excidio Britanniae* (mid-sixth century); the anonymous authors of the *Orationes Moucani* (eighth century?) and the *Historia Brittonum* (early ninth-century); Asser's *Life of King Alfred* (893); the anonymous compilers of the *Annales Cambriae* (tenth century, though perhaps begun in the late eighth century) and the Harleian genealogies (tenth century); and the Welsh-Latin poetry and prose composed by the family of Sulien (second half of the eleventh century). The sources cited by these British / Welsh authors imply ready access to good collections of books. For example, the anonymous author of the *Historia Brittonum* explained in his prologue that because the learned men of Britain had made no record of its history in their books, he collected everything that he found, 'both from the annals of the Romans and from the chronicles of the holy Fathers, that is Jerome, Eusebius, Isidore, Prosper; and from the annals of the Irish and the Saxons'.[81] Asser, the biographer and teacher of King Alfred, showed familiarity with a variety of patristic and historical sources.[82] The family of Sulien at Llanbadarn Fawr produced at least four scholars whose works show that they had studied Virgil, Ovid, Lucan, Juvencus, Boethius, Prudentius, Martianus Capella, Caelius Sedulius and Aldhelm as part of their curriculum of education.[83]

79 There is also mention of four or five lost gospels: Sims-Williams, 'Uses of writing', 21–2.

80 Bodleian, MS Bodley 572, a tenth-century manuscript apparently written in Wales, contains a Latin colloquy (*De raris fabulis*) in which a departing teacher tells his student to guard 'my clothes, gold, silver . . . and our books' (*libros nostros*). The shift from possessive singular to plural (for the books) may indicate that the teacher had charge of (some of) the monastery's collection: W. Stevenson (ed.), *Early scholastic colloquies* (Oxford, 1929), 1–11 (§4).

81 My translation of the Latin text, ed. D. Dumville, '"Nennius" and the *Historia Brittonum*', *Studia Celtica* 10–11 (1975–6), 79.

82 See below, 89.

83 M. Lapidge, 'The Welsh-Latin poetry of Sulien's family', *Studia Celtica* 8–9 (1973–4), 69–70.

The presence of collections of books in Wales is suggested by a long tradition of scribal experimentation and manuscript production. Unlike Ireland, early medieval Wales had inherited an unbroken tradition of literacy (secular and Christian) from its Romano-British past. Although no manuscripts from this period have survived, some of the memorial stones dating from the fifth to the seventh century ('Class I') are carved in a script that owes its origins to the formal letterforms of manuscripts.[84] The surviving manuscripts, despite their small number, bear witness to an extraordinary variety of scripts.[85] Such scribal developments, sustained over a long period, imply the existence of writing centres that were receptive to outside models transmitted in manuscripts. The Book of Llandaff (early twelfth century), a collection of charters whose originals probably range in date from the eighth to the early twelfth century, shows that written records were being maintained in south-west Wales during that period.[86]

The contents of these manuscripts indicate that Wales had copies of well-known Latin works such as one would find in a well-stocked medieval library. They attest to religious works such as the Psalms (*Hebraicum* version) and the Hieronymian martyrology,[87] Augustine's *De trinitate*,[88] Pelagius' Commentary on the Catholic Epistles (a rare work)[89] and Juvencus's versified narrative of the Gospels;[90] to secular works such as Ovid's *Ars amatoria*,[91] Macrobius' commentary on *Somnium Scipionis*,[92] and Martianus Capella's *De nuptiis*;[93] to mathematical and philosophical works, notably Boethius' *De arithmetica*[94] and translation of Porphyry's *Isagoge*;[95] to historical works, such as Bede's *Chronica maiora* and *Chronica minora*;[96] and to computistica, such as the so-called *Liber Commonei*[97] and a computus fragment.[98]

84 Sims-Williams, 'Uses of writing', 18.

85 D. N. Dumville, *A palaeographer's review: the insular system of scripts in the early middle ages*, I, Kansai University Institute of Oriental and Occidental Studies (Kansai, 1999), 123–6.

86 See W. Davies, *The Llandaff Charters* (Aberystwyth, 1979); and the caveats of P. Sims-Williams' review in *JEH* 33 (1982), 124–9.

87 They are found together in the same manuscript; see H. J. Lawlor (ed.), *The Psalter and Martyrology of Ricemarch*, HBS 47–8 (London, 1914).

88 CCCC, MS 199.

89 D. Dumville, 'Late-seventh- or eighth-century evidence for the British transmission of Pelagius', *Cambridge Medieval Celtic Studies* 10 (1985), 39–52.

90 CUL, MS Ff. 4. 42.

91 Part IV of the composite manuscript, Bodleian, MS Auct. F. 4. 32. See the facsimile edition by R. W. Hunt, *Saint Dunstan's Classbook from Glastonbury* (Amsterdam, 1961).

92 BL, MS Cotton Faustina C. i.

93 CCCC, MS 153.

94 CCCC, MS 352 (copied from a Welsh exemplar).

95 Leiden, Universiteitsbibliothek, MS Voss. Q. 2.

96 BL, MS Cotton Faustina C. i.

97 Part III of Bodleian, MS Auct. F. 4. 32.

98 CUL, MS Add. 4543.

The identifiable Welsh authors and the localisable manuscripts can be linked for the most part to ecclesiastical centres. Of these the dominant type was the *clas*, a peculiarly Welsh monastic institution in which the abbacy was hereditary and the members were often married clerks bound by family ties. Such monasteries were probably located near royal centres, the two forming an interdependent relationship, with the first serving the archival and literary needs of the second in return for patronage. According to Bede, the principal ecclesiastical centre of the British in the early seventh century was the monastery of Bangor Iscoed in North Wales, not far from Chester;[99] many learned men from there came to debate with the Roman missionary Augustine (*c.* 600). During the ninth century the court of Gwynedd (north Wales) under Merfyn Vrych (d. 844) and his son Rhodri Mawr (d. 878) emerged as a centre of literary activity which also attracted Irish scholars passing to and from the Continent.[100] St David's monastery on the south-west coast of Wales seems to have had a thriving community in the ninth century. Though none of its manuscripts has survived from that time, its most famous student, Asser, presumably acquired his knowledge of Augustine, Gregory the Great, Virgil, Caelius Sedulius, Aldhelm, Bede and Einhard (Life of Charlemagne) from the books he had studied there.[101] St David's may also have kept a set of annals about this time.[102] Two centuries later it was still flourishing under Bishop Rhygifarch (d. 1099), who composed the first Life of its founder.

Rhygifarch himself hailed from the most important centre of book-learning in eleventh-century Wales, the *clas* of Llanbadarn ('the Church of St Padarn'), located further up the coast, near Aberystwyth. His father, Sulien, had studied in Ireland, whence he brought back a psalter which became the exemplar for the Psalter of Ricemarch (*c.* 1079). Sulien had a school at Llanbadarn, where he educated his four sons. The contents of the three manuscripts produced by this family offer some idea of the range of works available in their book collections. They had access to biblical and liturgical manuscripts, to patristic works, to Neoplatonic philosophy, and to historical works.[103] Their scholarly glosses on these texts reveal another layer of book-knowledge that drew (among others) on the works of Petronius, Isidore of Seville, and Carolingian scholars such as

99 *Historia ecclesiastica* II. 2; Plummer, I. 82.

100 See Kenney, *Sources*, no. 363; and N. K. Chadwick, 'Early culture and learning in North Wales', in Chadwick *et al.*, *Studies in the early British church*, 34–46.

101 S. Keynes and M. Lapidge (eds.), *Alfred the Great* (Harmondsworth, 1983), 53–4.

102 K. Hughes, 'The Welsh Latin chronicles: *Annales Cambriae* and related texts', in her *Celtic Britain in the early middle ages* (Woodbridge, 1980), 67–85.

103 See above, 87.

Helperic and Remigius of Auxerre.[104] In these manuscripts they also entered personal poems that reveal their familiarity with classical Latin poets such as Virgil, Ovid and Lucan. One of the poems, composed by Rhygyfarch in about 1094, laments the imminent destruction by the Normans of this world of book-learning and poignantly marks the end of the tradition: 'neither the law, nor learning . . . not wise teaching . . . none (of these things) retains its station, nor any power'.[105]

Despite the imbalance in their respective bodies of evidence, Ireland and Wales can be seen to have shared similar ideas about the nature and purposes of book collections. Indeed, it is tempting to credit these similarities to the close cultural ties that existed between them all through the period. The British church had introduced the technology of books to the Irish in the fifth and sixth centuries and they in turn had heavily influenced Welsh learning (including scripts) from the eighth century on. For the two areas, a 'library' is best understood as a collection of books serving the needs primarily of ecclesiastical (often monastic) institutions. And in both, the book collection was a product of two complementary activities that took place within the same institution, the writing and the collecting of books. The institutional need for book collections was driven by both secular and religious considerations, reflecting the intimate relations that bound these foundations to the larger society. To fulfil its duties to its lay patrons the institution compiled and copied the genealogies and tribal legends of the ruling family, drew up charters to record land transactions, kept annals to document local history, and composed Lives of saints to confirm its patrimony from the founder. On the religious side, the institution maintained a 'library' to preserve and transmit learning, especially the sacred learning epitomised in the study of the Latin Bible. Although more narrowly focused in purpose than their later medieval counterparts, these ecclesiastical 'libraries' functioned in much the same way: they collected, conserved and circulated books.

104 A. Peden, 'Science and philosophy in Wales at the time of the Norman Conquest: A Macrobius manuscript from Llanbadarn', *Cambridge Medieval Celtic Studies* 2 (1981), 21–45.

105 Ed. and tr. Lapidge, 'The Welsh-Latin poetry', 91.

3

Anglo-Saxon England

DAVID GANZ

Although there were libraries in Roman Britain, there is very little evidence for any continuity between them and the books owned by the Anglo-Saxons. In the Anglo-Saxon era books were assembled at various places for various reasons, but evidence for these collections and their contents is usually lost. The largest collections belonged to religious communities, especially in monasteries or cathedrals, but most evidence for the rules and customs of such communities dates from after the Norman Conquest. We have several detailed twelfth-century booklists, which may include pre-Conquest holdings. But for the five centuries before 1066 neither archaeology, history nor literary investigation can supply many certainties about what libraries may have been. The written evidence from this period does not define the scope or purpose of a library, or distinguish clearly between the various functions of books or collections of books. It therefore seems appropriate in this chapter to use the term 'library' in its most general sense to refer collectively to the books possessed by a community or individual.

Any account of Anglo-Saxon libraries must first consider the Anglo-Saxon terminology in Latin and Old English. *Arca libraria*, the solution to Aldhelm's riddle 89, refers to a chest in which books were kept; few Anglo-Saxon libraries can be shown to have been larger than one or two such chests of books.[1] The Old English equivalent is *bocciste* or *boccest*. *Armaria* ('chest' or 'cupboard') is glossed as *boccysta* in an eleventh-century Old English gloss to Augustine's *Enchiridion* in Cambridge, Trinity Coll., MS O.1.18,[2] and also in a few narrative texts. When Apollonius of Tyre tried to solve a riddle, he opened his 'bocciste'.[3]

1 R. Ehwald (ed.), *Aldhelmi opera*, MGH *auct. antiq.* 15 (Berlin, 1919), 138.

2 A. S. Napier, *Old English glosses*, Anecdota Oxoniensia, Mediaeval and Modern Ser. 11 (Oxford, 1900), 196.

3 'Ac Apollonius þeahhwæðre ær becom to his agenan and into his huse eode and his bocciste untynde and asmeade þone rædels æfter ealra uðwitena and Chaldea wisdome.' ('But Apollonius, however, had previously come to his own [city], and went into his house

A Latin riddle by Hwætberht ('Eusebius'), abbot of Wearmouth-Jarrow from *c.* 716 to 747, has as its subject a book-wallet (*scetha*) in which an individual volume might be kept.[4]

The early ninth-century Corpus Glossary (CCCC, MS 144) glosses *bibliotheca* as *librorum repositio* ('storage-place of books'), and that seems to lie behind *bochord* for the Latin *librorum repositio* in the Latin–Old English glossary, BL, MS Harley 3376 (*Bibliotheca id est librorum repositio. bochord uel fodder*) ['Library: that is, book depository. Book-hoard, or case'].[5] This late tenth- or early eleventh-century glossary also gives *boc gesamnunge* ('book collection') for *Celestis bibliothece*. The Old English word *bibliotheca*, meaning 'library', is found in the Old English translation of Orosius in the account of the library of Alexandria, which had over 400 books: 'þær wæs a swa micel dem geburnen swa on Alexandria wæs þære byrig on hiora bibliotheoco, þær forburnon iiii hund m boca.' ('Just as much destruction was caused there by fire as there had been in the library in the city of Alexandria, where 400,000 books were burnt up.')[6] The same word is used in the Old English Orosius for the library founded by Julius Caesar: 'Æfter an þunor toslog hiora Capitoliam, þæt hus þe hiora godas inne wæron 7 hiora diofolgield, 7 hiora bibliotheoco wearð onbærned from ligette, 7 ealle heora ealdan bec forburnon þærinne' ('Afterwards, a thunderbolt struck their Capitol, the building in which were kept all their gods and the shrines of their devil-worship, and their library was burnt up by lightning, and all their ancient books consumed therein.')[7] But Old English *bibliotheca* more commonly meant the Bible. In Latin, *bibliotheca* could refer to collections of books, when they were thought to be sufficiently impressive to be defined by such a term. This is the word Bede uses to describe Bishop Acca's library of saints' lives at Hexham and the collection built up by Benedict Bishop for his twin foundation of Monkwearmouth-Jarrow.[8] Elsewhere, however, he describes books accumulated by Benedict on his several visits to Rome as large gatherings (*copia*) of books or sacred volumes rather than as a 'library'.[9]

and unfastened his book-chest and interpreted the riddle according to the wisdom of all the philosophers and the Chaldeans.') P. Goolden (ed.), *The Old English Apollonius of Tyre* (Oxford, 1958), 8.

4 F. Glorie (ed.), *Aenigmata Eusebii*, *CCSL* 133 (Turnhout, 1968), no. xxxiii, 243.

5 R. T. Oliphant, *The Harley Latin–Old English glossary*, Janua linguarum, series practica 20 (The Hague, 1966), 29.

6 J. Bately (ed.), *The Old English Orosius*, EETS, SS, 6 (London, 1980), VI. xiv, p. 142.

7 *Ibid.*

8 Bede, *Historia ecclesiastica*, V. xx; *Historia abbatum*, ch. 11: C. Plummer (ed.), *Venerabilis Baedae, Historiam ecclesiasticam gentis Anglorum, Historiam abbatum . . .*, 2 vols. (Oxford, 1896), I. 331, 375.

9 'Innumerabilem librorum omnis genera copiam' (Bede, *Historia abbatum*, ch. 6; Plummer, 369); 'magna quidem copia voluminum sacrorum' (*ibid.*, ch. 9; Plummer, 373).

Evidence for the existence and contents of libraries in Anglo-Saxon England derives from three types of source: the surviving manuscripts, the few extant booklists, and the identified quotations and references in the works of Anglo-Latin and vernacular authors, which make it possible to reconstruct the texts they drew upon; these were presumably sometimes (but not necessarily always) books owned by the author's community. In addition there are occasional references to lost books. Evidence for an Anglo-Saxon volume of Josephus is found in a letter of Herbert de Losinga, bishop of Norwich (1090–1119), asking an abbot Richard to lend him a copy of Josephus: 'You have often made the excuse that the book is falling to bits, but now that it has been corrected and rebound, no pretext is left to you.'[10] A volume 'falling to bits' at this date is likely to have been produced before the Conquest.

The evidence: manuscripts and booklists

The surviving manuscripts have been listed by Helmut Gneuss, and some of them are copied in scripts which can be localised to known centres of book production.[11] This establishes where they were written; when there is later evidence that they belonged to a library at the same place it seems reasonable to assume that they were copied for use there. We have later medieval catalogues and marks of ownership that help to identify books from the libraries at Christ Church, Canterbury, Rochester and Bury St Edmunds, which were all Anglo-Saxon foundations. But some manuscripts changed hands during the Anglo-Saxon period: the Parker Chronicle (CCCC, MS 173) was brought from Winchester to Christ Church, Canterbury, in the early eleventh century,[12] and several major liturgical manuscripts seem to have moved during the late Anglo-Saxon age.[13] When Bishop Leofric established his cathedral community at Exeter, he was able to donate manuscripts which had been copied at Canterbury at least half a century earlier, and which had been studied there.[14]

10 R. Anstruther (ed.), *Epistolae Herberti de Losinga* (London, 1846), *Epistola* 60, p. 107.

11 H. Gneuss, *Handlist of Anglo-Saxon manuscripts: a list of manuscripts and manuscript fragments written or owned in England up to 1100* (Tempe, AZ, 2001). Gneuss is careful to list both the origin and the provenance of the manuscripts.

12 M. B. Parkes, 'The palaeography of the Parker manuscript of the Chronicle, Laws, Sedulius, and historiography at Winchester in the late ninth and the tenth centuries', *ASE* 5 (1976), 171; repr. in his *Scribes, scripts and readers: studies in the communication, presentation and dissemination of medieval texts* (London, 1991), 168.

13 CCCC, MS 146, made at Christ Church, was at Worcester by 1096: Gneuss, *Handlist*, no. 46.

14 Cambridge, Trinity Coll., MS B.11.2; Bodleian, MSS Auct. F.1.15 and Bodley 708: Gneuss, *Handlist*, nos. 174, 533–4, 590.

Other volumes known to have migrated in the late Anglo-Saxon period include BL, MS Royal 4.A.xiv (Jerome) which went from Winchester to Worcester; Bodleian, MSS Hatton 30 (Caesarius on the Apocalypse), taken from Glastonbury to Worcester, and Marshall 19 (Jerome on the interpretation of Hebrew names), taken from Malmesbury to St Augustine's, Canterbury.[15]

Some 640 pre-Conquest manuscripts and fragments survive in English libraries and another 250 are now on the Continent. The majority are gospel books (over seventy-five survive), missals (over thirty), psalters (thirty-four) and other liturgical texts. Gospel books and psalters, finely decorated, were especially suitable for presentation, and hence their place of origin may well have been different from that of their early ownership. Other texts surviving in multiple copies are homilies (fifteen copies of the Latin Homiliary of Paul the Deacon, seventeen of the Old English Catholic Homilies by Ælfric), and school texts often with Latin and Old English glosses (twelve copies of Aldhelm's prose *De virginitate*, five copies of Abbo of St Germain's *Bella Parisiacae urbis* book III, eleven of Prudentius' *Psychomachia*, five tenth-century copies and three eighth-century fragments of Isidore's *Etymologiae*, and fourteen manuscripts of Ælfric's grammar).[16] The major centres from which manuscripts can be shown to have survived are Abingdon; Bury St Edmunds; Christ Church, Canterbury; St Augustine's Abbey, Canterbury; Durham Cathedral; Exeter Cathedral; Winchester Old Minster; Winchester New Minster and Worcester Cathedral.[17] Libraries must also once have existed at Barking; Crowland; Ely; Gloucester; Hereford; Hexham; Lichfield; Muchelney; North Elmham; Ramsey; St Paul's, London; Shaftesbury; Thorney; Wells and Westbury,[18] but only a handful of their manuscripts have been identified.[19] The early ownership of many of the extant books, however, has not been established.

The first reaction to the surviving manuscript evidence for the contents of Anglo-Saxon libraries must be an awareness of the comparative poverty of the holdings. The substantial works of Latin patristic learning, such as the great

15 *Ibid.*, nos. 455, 628, 659. 16 See 'Index I' in Gneuss, *Handlist*, 149–84.

17 D. N. Dumville, 'English libraries before 1066: use and abuse of the manuscript evidence', in M. W. Herren (ed.), *Insular Latin studies* (Toronto, 1981), 153–78; repr. in M. Richards (ed.), *Anglo-Saxon manuscripts: basic readings* (New York, 1994), 169–219.

18 D. Knowles and R. N. Hadcock, *Medieval religious houses: England and Wales* (London, 1971), 463–87, lists Anglo-Saxon religious houses.

19 From Barking: a gospel book (Bodleian, MS Bodley 155); from Ely: a gospel book (CUL, MS Kk.1.24), a pontifical (CCCC, MS 44) and Gregory's *Dialogues* (Lambeth, MS 204); from St Peter's, Gloucester: Bede's *Historia ecclesiastica* (BL, MS Royal 13.C.v); from Lichfield: the Lichfield Gospels (Lichfield Cathedral, MS 1); from Ramsey: perhaps a psalter (BL, MS Harley 2904); from Thorney: Sedulius (NLS, MS Adv. 18.7.7).

biblical commentaries of Augustine and Jerome, together with the theology of Hilary, Augustine or Leo the Great, the major texts of canon law and the works of Carolingian theologians, are conspicuously absent, or virtually absent. As far as we can tell, the range of texts known to Bede was never replicated in the ninth, tenth or eleventh century. In part this is the result of the strength of the vernacular tradition; standard texts like the Psalter and the Rules of Benedict or Chrodegang were studied in the vernacular as well as in Latin.

Surviving booklists, though they are sadly rare, confirm this impression.[20] They are, however, chiefly short inventories, listings of books in wills, or lists of episcopal donations. We do not have any complete Anglo-Saxon library catalogue to compare with the ninth-, tenth- and eleventh-century catalogues from some continental monasteries, and it is therefore difficult to guess from such evidence how large Anglo-Saxon libraries may have been.

Yet any evaluation of these booklists must compare them with the continental material, such as the ninth-century catalogues of Lorsch, St Gall, Murbach or the Reichenau.[21] These lists of some 300 to 500 titles are arranged by authors and subject headings, and reveal a sense of a systematic collection which matches the bibliographies of Cassiodorus (*c.* 485–*c.* 580) or Notker Balbulus (*c.* 840–912). If these titles are set beside the surviving manuscripts from Anglo-Saxon England, several serious gaps are evident. Augustine's *Confessiones*, *De civitate Dei* and *De Genesi ad litteram*, although known to Bede, do not survive in copies written or owned in Anglo-Saxon England. Of the major biblical commentaries there are no copies of Ambrose on Luke, or of Jerome on Jeremiah or on Isaiah, and only two early fragments of Jerome on Matthew.[22] There are no pre-Conquest copies of Bede's commentaries on the Song of Songs or Mark and only one of the commentary on the Apocalypse. Of standard monastic texts there are large collections of the sermons of

20 T. A. M. Bishop, *English Caroline minuscule* (Oxford, 1971), xiii: 'Something like a characteristic English pre-Conquest book-list can be recognized; but it is characterized mainly by its limitations, and represents a fraction of what circulated on the Continent.' The lists have been re-edited and discussed by Lapidge, 'Booklists', 33–89. The lists from Bury, Glastonbury, Worcester and Peterborough are now included in the Corpus of British Medieval Library Catalogues (CBMLC IV. B12, B36, B114; VIII. BP1).

21 P. Lehmann (ed.), *Mittelalterliche Bibliothekskataloge Deutschlands und der Schweiz*, I (Munich, 1918), 55–146 (St Gall); 222–74 (Reichenau); A. Häse, *Mittelalterliche Bücherverzeichnisse aus Kloster Lorsch: Einleitung, Edition und Kommentar*, Beiträge zum Buch und Bibliothekswesen 42 (Wiesbaden, 2002); W. Milde, *Die Bibliothekskatalog des Klosters Murbach aus dem neunten Jahrhundert* (Heidelberg, 1968). See also R. Kottje, 'Klosterbibliotheken und monastische Kultur in der zweiten Hälfte des elften Jahrhunderts', *Zeitschrift fur Kirchengeschichte* 80 (1969), 145–62.

22 Shrewsbury, Shropshire Record Office, 1052/1, and Worcester Cathedral, MS Add. 2: Gneuss, *Handlist*, nos. 755 and 770.5.

Caesarius, but only one manuscript each of Cassian's *Collationes*, his *De institutis monachorum*, and the elementary grammar of Donatus.

Classical texts are even more rare. There are no copies of Horace or Lucan and only one Welsh manuscript of Ovid. The study of Virgil seems to have been neglected, were we to judge from the surviving manuscript evidence alone; a tenth-century Worcester manuscript (Rome, Biblioteca Apostolica Vaticana, MS Reg. lat. 1671) with some Latin glosses, and fragments of a Carolingian manuscript from Canterbury and of an English manuscript from Bury are the only surviving witnesses.[23] Worcester was also the home of a glossed manuscript of Statius' *Thebais*, and late Anglo-Saxon glossed copies of Persius and Juvenal survive from St Augustine's, Canterbury.[24]

Before judging the contents of Anglo-Saxon libraries too harshly, however, it is important to realise quite how small these religious communities were. Evesham had only twelve monks in 1059, Winchester New Minster about forty in 1040, Gloucester eleven in 1072 and Abingdon twenty-eight in 1100.[25] By contrast, the great ninth-century continental monasteries such as Corbie had some 300 monks, and Fulda over 600.

The monastic customs of Fleury (Saint-Benoît-sur-Loire) describe the librarian (*armarius*) as also the head of the school.[26] Regarded by the brothers as equal to an apostle equipped with the knowledge of all truth, he also wrote charters for the abbey. He was responsible for the care of the books and of all of the tools of the scriptorium, parchment, threads for sewing the codices and skins of deer to bind the books. Lastly he was responsible for correcting the books, fixing the office lessons and defending the faith, refuting heretics, and all that concerned purity of doctrine. We have no comparable Anglo-Saxon texts, though it is possible that the influence of Fleury on monastic reformers in tenth-century England may have encouraged the same links between the school and the library. If we use manuscript evidence to try to associate the resources of the library with the school and its masters, we find Anglo-Saxon glosses to Aldhelm's prose and verse *De virginitate*, to Bede's verse Life of Cuthbert, to Boethius' *Consolation of Philosophy*, Prosper's *Epigrammata*,

23 Bodleian, MS Lat.class c.2, fol. 18 and five other fragments from the same copy (see Gneuss, *Handlist*, no. 648), and the palimpsest leaves in London, College of Arms, MS Arundel 30 (*ibid.*, no. 503). But see also M. Lapidge, 'The study of Latin texts in late Anglo-Saxon England (1): the evidence of Latin glosses', in N. Brooks (ed.), *Latin and the vernacular languages in early medieval Britain* (Leicester, 1982), 101.

24 Gneuss, *Handlist*, nos. 766 and 195.

25 D. Knowles, *The monastic order in England*, 2nd edn (Cambridge, 1963), 712–13.

26 K. Hallinger (ed.), '*Consuetudines Floriacenses antiquiores*', in his *Consuetudinum saeculi x/xi/xii monumenta non-Cluniacensia*, Corpus Consuetudinum Monasticarum 7 (Siegburg, 1984), 16–17.

Prudentius and Sedulius. A few vernacular glosses are found in three copies of Isidore's *Synonyma* and two copies of the *Excerptiones de Prisciano*.[27] Most of these manuscripts also contain Latin glosses. There are also Anglo-Saxon glosses in four copies of Felix's Life of Guthlac.[28] So the texts carefully studied were chiefly the monuments of Christian Latin poetry.

But to lament the lack of erudition is to misunderstand the function of the monastic library. The Rule of St Benedict, which formed the basis for the *Regularis concordia*, a monastic customary drawn up by Bishop Æthelwold of Winchester, and given official sanction in about 973, prescribed readings in winter from 5.00am until Matins at 6.00 and from 2.45pm until Vespers in the early evening, and in summer from 5.00 to Prime (at 6.00), after which 'they shall leave the church and meditate on holy reading for the profit of their souls', and from 9.30am until Sext (at 11.30).[29] During Lent, the rule required each monk to read a complete book, as the Latin and Old English versions specify.[30] Continental monastic custumals, such as those of Cluny, explained that this was to be done by assembling the books on a carpet, with a list of titles, and distributing them to the monks, who might later be questioned on what they had read, but lists of the texts distributed do not survive from Anglo-Saxon England.[31]

Prescriptive texts from Anglo-Saxon England suggest that priority was accorded to the provision of service books. The prologue to Ecgberht's Penitential, Ælfric's letter to Bishop Wulfsige, and his Latin and Old English letters to Archbishop Wulfstan all list those books which a priest ought to own.[32] Chrodegang's rule for canons has a similar list.[33] There is evidence that these

27 Ker, *Cat. AS*, nos. 210, 228, 400 (Isidore), 2, 371 (Priscian).

28 *Ibid*., nos. 29, 66, 251, 266.

29 T. Symons (ed.), *Regularis concordia Anglicae nationis monachorum sanctimonialiumque* (London, 1953), 15, 22, 26–7; Knowles, *Monastic order*, Appendix XVIII.

30 'On þam dagum lænctenfæsten, hiderfan ealle ænlepige bec of boccystan þa hi be endebyrdnesse eall abutan rædan. þa bec synd to syllanne on anginne fæsten.' ('During the Lenten season, let everyone individually receive books from the book-chest: these should be read in order all through. These books should be given out at the beginning of the fast.') H. Logeman (ed.), *The Rule of St Benet*, EETS 90 (London, 1888), 83. Note the use of OE *boccysta* for the Latin *bibliotheca*.

31 See below, 223, 243.

32 Ælfric lists a psalter, epistolary, gospel book, missal, gradual (*sangboc*), manual (*handboc*), computus and/or calendar (*gerim*), pastoral (*pastoralem*), penitential and lectionary (*rædingboc*): B. Fehr (ed.), *Die Hirtenbriefe Ælfrics in altenglischer und lateinischer Fassung*, Bibliothek der angelsächsischen Prosa 9 (Hamburg, 1914); repr. with supplement by P. Clemoes (Darmstadt, 1966), 13, 51, 126–7. See also H. Gneuss, 'Liturgical books in Anglo-Saxon England and their Old English terminology', in M. Lapidge and H. Gneuss (eds.), *Learning and literature in Anglo-Saxon England: studies presented to Peter Clemoes* (Cambridge, 1985), 91–141.

33 A. S. Napier (ed.), *The Old English version of the enlarged rule of Chrodegang together with the Latin original*, EETS 150 (London, 1916), 84.

provisions were obeyed. A list of seven service books of the church of Sherburn-in-Elmet in Yorkshire was copied into the York Gospels around 1020. It comprises two gospel books, one *Aspiciens* (antiphonary), one *adtelevavi* (gradual), the epistles, a sacramentary, a psalter and a hymnal.[34]

We get a sense of those books used for celebrating the mass and office from the *Monasteriales indicia*, the sign language used in monasteries, found in BL, MS Cotton Tiberius A. iii, from Christ Church, Canterbury. This gives signs for the books to be used at divine service: a gradual, a sacramentary, an epistolary, a troper; at Matins: a bible, a martyrology, a psalter, a hymnal, and in chapter: a small martyrology and the rule (texts also prescribed by the *Regularis concordia* for reading in chapter).[35] A list from Bury St Edmunds datable to 1044–65 shows service books in use: four gospels, one sacramentary, epistles, psalter, homiliary, collectar, and the *Passio* of St Edmund.[36] It also records books in the hands of certain individuals: Blakere has one lectionary (*winterraedingboc*), Brihtric one sacramentary, and two lectionaries – winter and summer, Siuerth a sacramentary, Leofstan a manual, Æþeric a sacramentary and a collectar, Durstan a psalter, and Oskytel a sacramentary and a gradual.[37] A second Bury list, on a scrap bound into Bodleian, MS Auct. D. 2.14, also lists books in the possession of named individuals.[38] Salomon *preost* has a homiliary, a martyrology, a psalter, a chronicle and a troper; Wulfmer *child* a gradual, an epistolary, a hymnal, a collectar, a homiliary, and another title (now erased). The priest Sigar has a medical book, Æilmer a large psalter, a small troper damaged by fire, and a work by Donatus.

It has been suggested that this second list may be a record of loans. In some cases service books, as well as other kinds of books, might have been regarded as the possessions of individuals. The will of Bishop Ælfwold of Crediton (*c.* 1016) records five titles. Although he left three service books (a sacramentary, a pontifical and an epistolary) to the church at Crediton, copies of Hrabanus and a martyrology were given to one Ordulf.[39] Anglo-Saxon ownership inscriptions of any kind are extremely rare. Nevertheless, the

34 A. J. Robertson (ed.), *Anglo-Saxon charters* (Cambridge, 1939), 248; Lapidge, 'Booklists', 56–7.

35 D. Banham, *Monasteriales indicia: the Anglo-Saxon monastic sign language* (Frithgarth, 1996), 26–8 and 30; Symons, *Regularis concordia*, 17.

36 Lapidge, 'Booklists', 57.

37 *Ibid.*, 57–8.

38 *Ibid.*, 74–5; Robertson, *Anglo-Saxon charters*, 250, 510.

39 Lapidge, 'Booklists', 55–6. See also D. N. Dumville, 'Liturgical books for the Anglo-Saxon episcopate: a reconsideration', in his *Liturgy and the ecclesiastical history of late Anglo-Saxon England* (Woodbridge, 1992), 66–95. Particularly helpful is R. W. Pfaff, 'The Anglo-Saxon bishop and his book', *BJRL* 81 (1999), 3–24.

earliest extant inscription (an early eighth-century entry on the endleaf of a manuscript now at Würzburg) appears to be a record of personal ownership: 'Cuthsuuithae boec thaerae abbatissan'; this Cuthswith has been identified as a seventh-century abbess of Inkberrow in Worcestershire.[40] *Bald's Leechbook*, preserved as a copy in a mid-tenth-century manuscript (BL, MS Royal 12.D.xvii), has a Latin colophon implying that Bald had ordered the book (perhaps the Royal manuscript's exemplar) to be made, and that it belonged to him. He must have owned other books, for he says, 'There is nothing as dear to me as the excellent treasure than the dear books which the grace of Christ adorns.'[41] A cryptic inscription in a book of prayers and other texts datable to between 1023 and 1031 (now BL, MSS Cotton Titus D. xxvi + xxvii) concludes with the statement that it belonged to Ælfwine monk and deacon (*Ælfwinus monachus aeque decanus me possidet*). Since Ælfwine was a member of the reformed Benedictine community of the New Minster, Winchester, this inscription raises questions about ownership practice within monastic communities, and the extent to which books that can be localised to a particular place would have been perceived as forming part of the possessions of the community.

Libraries in Anglo-Saxon England

In attempting to identify libraries in Anglo-Saxon England, we can expand the evidence of booklists and surviving manuscripts by examining the literary evidence and the sources which authors writing in Anglo-Saxon England had used. In some cases such evidence adds substantially to the picture. Bede's *Ecclesiastical history* tells of how Pope Gregory the Great sent very many manuscripts with Mellitus and Justus to Augustine at Canterbury in 601.[42] The gift is associated with church ornaments, vestments and relics, so we are probably dealing with service books. It is just possible that a tiny fragment of one of these manuscripts, a papyrus copy of Gregory's own Gospel Homilies, may have survived as a Cotton manuscript.[43] In the eleventh century, manuscripts traditionally linked to Gregory were kept on the altar at Canterbury Cathedral,

40 Würzburg, Universitätsbibliothek, M.p.th.q. 2, fol. 1. P. Sims-Williams, 'Cuthswith, seventh-century abbess of Inkberrow near Worcester, and the Würzburg manuscript of Jerome on Ecclesiastes', *ASE* 5 (1976), 1–22.

41 BL, MS Royal 12.D.xvii, fol. 109r: R. Gameson, *The scribe speaks? Colophons in early English manuscripts*, H. M. Chadwick Memorial Lectures 12 (Cambridge, 2001), 37.

42 Bede, *Historia ecclesiastica*, 1. xxix; Plummer, 63.

43 R. G. Babcock, 'A papyrus codex of Gregory the Great's *Forty Homilies on the Gospels* (London, Cotton Titus C. xv)', *Scriptorium* 50 (2000), 280–9.

though the only one which we can securely identify, the Vespasian Psalter (BL, MS Cotton Vespasian A. i), was copied in Kent in the eighth century. Theodore and Hadrian, according to Bede, gave instruction in the books of Holy Scripture, the art of metre, astronomy and computus, implying that Canterbury had an important teaching library.[44] Bede's picture has been amplified by the publication of glosses linked to Theodore discovered by Bernhard Bischoff.[45] Bede also praised Aldhelm, who had studied at Canterbury, and lists his writings.[46] But the only explicit mention of a library in the *Ecclesiastical history* is at Hexham: 'Acca has built up a very large and most noble library (*bibliotheca*), assiduously collecting histories of the passions of the martyrs as well as other ecclesiastical books.'[47]

Quotations from patristic and classical authors found in Bede's own writings provide the main source for the exceptional resources available to him at Jarrow during the early eighth century. The list of texts identified by Laistner reveals a collection that is hard to parallel anywhere in the early middle ages.[48] Of classical authors Bede quotes Eutropius, Lucan, Macrobius' *Saturnalia*, Pliny's *Natural History*, Vegetius, and a wide range of grammarians. The Christian texts comprise: Ambrose's *De fide, De Noe, De Spiritu sancto, Hexaemeron, Expositio evangelii secundam Lucam*; Augustine's *Confessiones, Contra Faustum, De civitate Dei, De consensu evangelistarum, De doctrina christiana, De Genesi ad litteram, Enarrationes in Psalmos, Tractatus in Iohannem*; Basil's *Hexaemeron* and Cassiodorus' *Expositio in Psalmos*, Jerome on Daniel and his *Adversus Jovinianum*; Gregory, Dionysius Exiguus, Fulgentius' *Ad Thrasamundum*, Josephus's *Antiquitates iudaicae*, Orosius, Victorinus of Pettau, Primasius, Tyconius, Juvencus, Prudentius, Sedulius, Arator, Prosper and Cyprianus Gallus, Eusebius' *Chronicle* and *Ecclesiastical history*, in the translations of respectively Jerome and Rufinus; Gregory of Tours, and the *Liber Pontificalis*. Sadly, other than the manuscripts or fragments identified as products of a scriptorium at Monkwearmouth-Jarrow, which presumably drew for their exemplars upon books already available there, only one manuscript from Bede's library has been identified, a bilingual (Latin–Greek) copy of Acts.[49]

44 Bede, *Historia ecclesiastica*, IV. ii; Plummer, 204–5.

45 B. Bischoff and M. Lapidge (eds.), *Biblical commentaries from the Canterbury school of Theodore and Hadrian* (Cambridge, 1994).

46 Bede, *Historia ecclesiastica*, V. xviii; Plummer, 320–1.

47 *Ibid.*, V. xx; Plummer, 331.

48 M. L. W. Laistner, 'Bede as a classical and a patristic scholar', *TRHS*, 4th ser., 16 (1933), 69–94.

49 Bodleian, MS Laud Gr. 35; M. B. Parkes, *The scriptorium of Wearmouth-Jarrow*, Jarrow Lecture (Jarrow, 1982); repr. in his *Scribes, scripts and readers: studies in the communication, presentation and dissemination of medieval texts* (London, 1991), 93–120.

Our knowledge of the great library at York depends on the authors mentioned in Alcuin's poem on the bishops, kings and saints of York, describing the holdings around 778, which Alcuin tells us had been assembled by Archbishop Ælberht.[50] This section of Alcuin's poem is a versified booklist, but it cannot be considered a catalogue, since, like a very similar versified list in a poem of Venantius Fortunatus,[51] it supplies only the names of authors, not their works. He lists Jerome, Hilary, Ambrose, Augustine,[52] Athanasius, Orosius,[53] Gregory and Leo, Basil, Fulgentius, Cassiodorus, John Chrysostom (perhaps his *De reparatione lapsi* or his commentaries),[54] Aldhelm, Bede, Victorinus and Boethius.[55] Also listed are the historians Pompeius (in Justinus' *Epitome*),[56] Pliny,[57] Aristotle and Cicero rhetor (presumably the *De inventione*); the poets Sedulius, Juvencus, Avitus, Prudentius, Prosper, Paulinus, Arator, Fortunatus, Lactantius,[58] Virgil, Statius and Lucan; the grammarians Probus, Phocas, Donatus, Priscian, Servius, Eutyches and Cominianus,[59] and many others described as 'teachers outstanding for their learning, art and style'.

The list can be supplemented by other sources: Alcuin knew the works of Gildas and Isidore before he left York,[60] and in 780–1 sent works of Priscian and Phocas to Beornrad of Sens.[61] The letters of Boniface request copies of the works of Bede from York.[62] But no manuscript which can be securely attributed to York has survived.[63]

From elsewhere in eighth-century England, we have only meagre manuscript survival, which provides a very fragmentary indication of the texts present in largely unidentifiable religious centres. The earliest surviving manuscripts from this century include a poetic anthology (CCCC, MS 173 part 2) with Sedulius' *Carmen Paschale*, poems of Damasus and versifications of the Sibylline prophecy, including that transmitted in Augustine's

50 P. Godman (ed.), *Alcuin: the bishops, kings and saints of York* (Oxford, 1982), 122–6; D. A. Bullough, *Alcuin: achievement and reputation* (Leiden, 2004), 260–86.

51 See Godman, *Alcuin*, 124.

52 Bullough, *Alcuin*, 261–6.

53 *Ibid.*, 267; Orosius is also mentioned in Alcuin's letter 245.

54 Fragments of an eighth-century Northumbrian copy of Chrysostom, *De compunctione cordis*, survive as Düsseldorf, Universitätsbibliothek, Fragm. K1: B 215, K2: C 118 and K15: 00. Bullough, *Alcuin*, 260.

55 *Ibid.*, 268–70.

56 *Ibid.*, 259–60.

57 *Ibid.*

58 On Alcuin's knowledge of the Christian poets: *ibid.*, 277–9.

59 On his knowledge of the grammarians: *ibid.*, 282–3.

60 *Ibid.*, 271–4.

61 Alcuin, *Carmen*, iv: D. Dümmler (ed.), MGH *Poetae latini aevi Carolini*, 1 (Berlin, 1881), 220–3.

62 M. Tangl (ed.), *Die Briefe des heiligen Bonifatius und Lullus*, MGH *Epistolae selectae*, 1 (Berlin, 1916), nos. 75, 91, 125, 126.

63 The Moore Bede (CUL, MS Kk.5.16), taken to Charlemagne's court, must be a potential suspect.

City of God. Fragments of Augustine's *De trinitate* survive as a palimpsest in Edinburgh, National Library of Scotland, MS Adv. 18.7.8, and fragments of his *De consensu evangelistarum* in BL, MS Cotton Cleopatra A. iii. Further fragmentary survivals are Junilius' *Instituta regularia divinae legis* (BL, MS Cotton Tiberius A. xv, fols. 175–80), and Jerome on Matthew (Shrewsbury, Shropshire Record Office,1052/1) and on Daniel (Marburg, Hessisches Staatsarchiv, Hr 2, 17). A Paterius fragment (Worcester Cathedral, MS Add. 4) and the Douce Primasius *In Apocalypsin* (Bodleian, MS Douce 140), used by St Boniface,[64] are further cases of the survival of those patristic commentaries, which were subsequently to be supplanted by writings of Bede and his Carolingian successors.

The most substantial evidence for a library in ninth-century Anglo-Saxon England is the group of texts drawn upon by the Old English martyrologist, who compiled materials on the lives of saints commemorated during the year. Nothing is known of when or where he worked.[65] He cites books of the Old and New Testaments (including Maccabees), Bede's *Historia ecclesiastica*, Aldhelm's *De virginitate*, Adomnán's *De locis sanctis*, Gregory's Homilies on the gospels, an 'old' and 'new' sacramentary (*ealdran mæssebocum* and *niwran sacramentorium*). Unnamed sources include a calendar (or calendars), legendary and homiliary; Bede's Life of Cuthbert, his *Historia abbatum*, *De temporum ratione* and *Martyrologium*; ps.-Isidore, *De ordine creaturum* and Isidore's *De ortu et obitu patrum*; the *Liber pontificalis*, the *Vitas patrum*, the *Dialogues* of Gregory, Jerome's Life of Paul the Hermit and Athanasius' Life of Anthony.

Compared with the previous centuries, the forms of evidence from the tenth are more plentiful, but the picture is still far from complete, even as regards the texts available to the leading monastic reformers of the period: Dunstan (archbishop of Canterbury 959–88), Æthelwold (bishop of Winchester 963–84) and Oswald (bishop of Worcester 961–92 and archbishop of York 971–92). Dunstan's first biographer stresses the importance of the books brought to

64 M. B. Parkes, 'The handwriting of St Boniface: a reassessment of the problems', *Beiträge zur Geschichte der deutschen Sprache und Literatur* 98 (1976), 161–79; repr. in his *Scribes, scripts and readers*, 121–42.

65 J. E. Cross, 'On the library of the Old English martyrologist', in Lapidge and Gneuss, *Learning and literature*, 227–49. A ninth-century date for this writer has been suggested on the evidence of the earliest manuscript (BL, Add. MS 23211), which dates from the late ninth century. The dialect of the text is Mercian. But, for a new argument, published after this volume went to press, that the text is a ninth-century translation of an eighth-century Latin compilation, see M. Lapidge, 'Acca of Hexham and the origin of the Old English Martyrology', *Analecta Bollandiana* 123 (2005), 29–78; and his *The Anglo-Saxon library* (Oxford, 2006), 46–8, 233–7. The latter is a comprehensive survey and listing of texts known in Anglo-Saxon England based upon the evidence of surviving manuscripts, booklists and the sources used by Anglo-Saxon authors.

Glastonbury by Irish pilgrims, where Dunstan taught Æthelwold *grammatica ars et metrica* and *volumines divina*, according to the latter's biographer.[66] Recent claims for Æthelwold's learning, which might shed light on books at Winchester, await proof, but we do have a record of a gift he made to Peterborough (963–84) recorded in the Peterborough *Liber niger*.[67] It is a rather limited range of texts: Bede on Mark, a *Liber miraculorum*, Jerome's *Liber interpretationis Hebraicorum nominum*, Julian of Toledo, Augustine's *Contra academicos*, Paulinus of Nola's Life of Felix, the *Synonima* of Isidore, a *Vita Eustachii*, Abbo of St Germain on the siege of Paris, a *Medicinalis*, the *De XII abusivis*, sermons on the Psalms, a *commentum super Canticum Canticorum* which may be by Bede, a *De eucharista*, a commentary on Martianus Capella,[68] the poems of Avitus, *Liber differentiarum*, Cyprianus (presumably his letters), *De litteris Grecorum* (presumably a Greek–Latin glossary), and a *Liber bestiarum*. (Some of the Latin titles resist secure identification.)

An indication of the texts used for teaching within one monastery is provided by an Old English list of the books of a grammarian, Æthelstan, recorded in a mid-tenth-century copy of Isidore's *De natura rerum* from St Augustine's, Canterbury.[69] They comprise the *De natura rerum*, Persius, Sedulius, Donatus' *Ars maior* and *Ars minor*, an unidentified commentary on Donatus, a *De arte metrica* (perhaps that of Bede), *Excerptiones de metrica arte*, an unspecified work of Alcuin (presumably one of his grammatical texts), *Glossa super Catonem* (probably the commentary of Remigius), a *libellus de grammatica arte que sic incipit terra que pars*, a computus which belonged to the priest Alfwold, a text called *Dialogorum*, which may be Gregory's *Dialogi*, but which in this context is more likely to be scholastic colloquies, and an *Apocalypsin*. Æthelstan was presumably a teacher at St Augustine's, and his collection may be compared with the groups of books left to the cathedral at Laon by those who taught there, which include not only schoolbooks but also works of scriptural exegesis and pastoral topics, including patristic texts.[70]

66 W. Stubbs (ed.), *Memorials of Saint Dunstan, archbishop of Canterbury*, RS (London, 1874), 10–11; Wulfstan of Winchester, *Life of St Æthelwold*, ed. M. Lapidge and M. Winterbottom (Oxford, 1991), 14–15.

67 Lapidge, 'Booklists', 116–20; see also M. Lapidge, 'Æthelwold as scholar and teacher', in B. Yorke (ed.), *Bishop Æthelwold: his career and influence* (Woodbridge, 1988), 103–4.

68 Perhaps the commentary of Remigius. Fragments of an early tenth-century copy, perhaps produced in Winchester, survive as Cambridge, Magdalene Coll., Pepys Library, MS 2981 (5): M. B. Parkes, 'Fragments of an early tenth-century Anglo-Saxon manuscript and its significance', *ASE* 12 (1983), 129–49; repr. in his *Scribes, scripts and readers*, 171–85.

69 BL, MS Cotton Domitian i, fol. 55v: Lapidge, 'Booklists', 50–2.

70 J. Contreni, *The cathedral school of Laon from 850 to 930: its manuscripts and masters* (Munich, 1978), 95–164.

As is the case for earlier periods, the sources drawn upon by late Anglo-Saxon authors provide a fuller picture of the texts available to a few, perhaps exceptional, scholars. Byrhtferth of Ramsay (d. *c.* 1020), in his *Enchiridion* (an extensive work on computus), quotes from the Old and New Testaments and from the New Hymnal, from Servius and Priscian, Bede's *De arte metrica* and *De schematibus et tropis*, Isidore's *Etymologiae*, Cato, Sedulius, Arator, Aldhelm, the *De natura rerum* of Isidore and of Bede, Boethius' *De consolatione philosophiae*, Macrobius, Abbo's *De differentia circuli et sphaerae*, Hrabanus' *De computo*, Helperic's *De computo ecclesiastico*, Bede's *De temporum ratione*, Jerome's *Liber interpretationis Hebraicorum nominum* and *In Matthaeum*, Gregory's Homilies on the Gospels and *Moralia in Iob*, Isidore's *Sententiae*, and Haimo of Auxerre's *Homiliae*.[71] This is an impressive list of schoolbooks, including advanced works by authors such as Macrobius and Abbo. Byrhtferth was clearly aware of current continental computistical learning and of rather more Latin verse than one might have expected. Furthermore, these sources do not correspond to all of Byrhtferth's reading; his hagiography used other Latin sources.[72]

The only other evidence of a comparable range of reading in the late tenth and early eleventh centuries is that yielded by the sources used by Ælfric, abbot of Eynsham (d. *c.* 1010). His Catholic Homilies draw heavily on the homiliaries of Paul the Deacon and of Haimo of Auxerre,[73] and his homilies on the lives of saints make use of several of the lives found in the mid-eleventh-century Cotton-Corpus legendary,[74] a great collection of the lives of 165 saints, derived from a collection or collections assembled on the Continent and brought to England perhaps by the late tenth century.[75] Homiliaries and other compilatory texts, such as Smaragdus' *Diadema monachorum*, were an important indirect source for knowledge of patristic and Carolingian writings in late Anglo-Saxon England, but Ælfric may also have known at first hand Ambrose's *Hexaemeron*, Augustine's *De civitate Dei*, *De bono coniugali* and his Homilies on John, Jerome on Matthew, Amalarius' *Liber officialis*, Pelagius on

71 P. S. Baker and M. Lapidge (eds.), *Byrhtferth's Enchiridion*, EETS, SS, 15 (Oxford, 1995), lxxiv–xciv.

72 P. S. Baker, 'The Old English canon of Byrhtferth of Ramsey', *Speculum* 55 (1980), 22–37; M. Lapidge, 'The hermeneutic style in tenth-century Anglo-Latin literature', *ASE* 4 (1975), 67–111.

73 J. Pope, *Homilies of Ælfric: a supplementary collection*, 2 vols., EETS 259–60 (Oxford, 1967–8), I. 50–77; M. Clayton, 'Homiliaries and preaching in Anglo-Saxon England', *Peritia* 4 (1985), 207–42. J. Hill, 'Ælfric and Smaragdus', *ASE* 21 (1992), 203–37; M. Godden, *Ælfric's Catholic Homilies: introduction, commentary and glossary*, EETS, SS, 18 (Oxford, 2000), xxxviii–lxii.

74 CCCC, MS 9 + BL, MS Cotton Nero E. I, pt II.

75 P. Jackson and M. Lapidge, 'The contents of the Cotton-Corpus legendary', in P. Szarmach (ed.), *Holy men and holy women: Old English prose saints' lives and their contexts* (Albany, NJ, 1996), 131–46.

the Pauline Epistles, the *Prognosticon* of Julian of Toledo, the *Historia ecclesiastica* of Eusebius-Rufinus, Cassiodorus' *Historia tripartita*, Smaragdus' *Expositio libri comitis*, Isidore's *De ecclesiasticis officiis*, Bede's Commentary on Acts, Theodulf's *De ordine baptismi*,[76] and a sermon of Martin of Braga. This is a wide range of texts, including significant works of Carolingian theology.

From the end of the Anglo-Saxon period we have more substantial records associated with named individuals who assembled book collections. Sæwold, formerly abbot of Bath, gave thirty-three volumes in or around 1070 to the abbey of Saint-Vaast, Arras, some of which have survived (most of which are now in the Bibliothèque municipale at Arras).[77] Lapidge regards them as the personal library of an English ecclesiastic at the time of the Conquest, although some volumes may have been acquired after he went into exile. They comprise a gospel book bound in silver, a sacramentary, the Heptateuch, twenty of the thirty-three books of Gregory's *Moralia*, the first part of the Homiliary of Haimo, Claudius of Turin on Matthew (Arras, MS 889), the Rule of Benedict bound with Smaragdus' *Diadema monachorum*, Gregory's *Dialogues* (Arras, MS 681), the *Vitas patrum* (apparently the early eighth-century manuscript, Brussels, BR, 9850–2, which shows no evidence of having been in England), Ambrose on Psalm 118 (Arras 899, also a continental manuscript with no detectable English provenance), Ambrose's *De mysteriis* and *De sacramentis* with Palladius' *De moribus Brachmanorum* and Isidore's *De officiis* (Arras, MS 1068), Julianus Pomerius (Arras, MS 435, a continental manuscript), Ambrose's *Hexaemeron* (Arras, MS 346 probably copied at Abingdon), Prosper, Bede on the Catholic Epistles, a *Liber epistolarum Bacarii, Augustini, Eubodii, Macedonii* (they are recipients of letters of Augustine), saints' Lives including the Life of Dunstan (Arras, MS 1029), *De assumptione* (Arras 732), *Liber canonum* (Arras 644), Bede's *Historia ecclesiastica gentis anglorum*, (perhaps the Northumbrian fragment in New York, Pierpont Morgan Library, MS M 826), a *Liber medicinalis*, Cassiodorus' *De orthographia*, a *Liber parabolorum Salamonis* (Arras, MS 1079 with commentaries), Aldhelm, Prudentius, Juvencus and Sedulius, Hrabanus Maurus on Judith and Esther (Arras, 764, a continental manuscript which had passed through England) and Cassiodorus' *Historia tripartita*.

Our best evidence of the library of a community is the list of sixty-six books given to the canons of Exeter Cathedral by Bishop Leofric between 1069 and

76 The text survives in a late tenth-century St Augustine's, Canterbury, manuscript, BL, MS Royal 8.C.iii.

77 Lapidge, 'Booklists', 58–62.

1072. It is preserved in two versions.[78] Several of the books have survived, and have been identified from contemporary inscriptions recording Leofric's donation – evidence of ownership largely unparalleled in manuscripts from elsewhere in England before the twelfth century – and from the presence of the hands of Exeter scribes.[79] The donation lists start with an account of the lands restored and added to St Peter's, Exeter, before proceeding to the books: two great ornamented gospel books (Bodleian, MS Auct. D.2.16, containing a list of Leofric's donations), two sacramentaries (perhaps Bodleian, MS Bodley 579, and Westminster Abbey, MS 36), a collectar containing chapters of Scripture and collects (BL, MS Harley 2961, which once contained a donation inscription), two epistolaries, two *fulle sang bec* (probably books for the Office), an antiphonary for the night office (*niht sang*), an *adtelevavi* (gradual), a troper, two psalters (presumably containing the Gallican version, to judge from the next entry), a psalter *se þriddan swa man singð on rome*, two hymnals, one precious pontifical or benedictional (perhaps BL, Add. MS 28188, copied by Exeter scribes), three other (presumably less precious) pontificals/benedictionals, a gospel book in Old English (CUL, MS Ii.2.11 with the donation inscription), two summer lectionaries and one winter lectionary, and Chrodegang's *Regula canonicorum* (CCCC, MS 191, written at Exeter), a martyrology (CCCC, MS 196, written at Exeter), a canon law collection (*canon on ledan*), a penitential in English (probably CCCC, MS 190, written at Exeter), one full homiliary in Old English (*i full spell boc wintres 7 sumeres*: perhaps CCCC, MS 421, partly written at Exeter, and Lambeth, MS 489), Boethius (presumably the *Consolation of Philosophy*) in Old English, and the Exeter Book of Old English poetry (*i mycel englisc boc be gehwilcum þingum on leoðwisan gewohrt*). All of these books are clearly designed to meet the needs of priests. After this the list relates that when Leofric took charge of the minster he did not find any more books except one capitulary, one very old nocturnal antiphoner, one epistolary and two very old and worn out office-lectionaries.

78 Bodleian, MS Auct. D. 2. 16, fols. 1^r–2^v, and on two leaves of a quire that once formed part of a book containing the West Saxon Gospels (CUL, MS Ii.2.11), which is now Exeter Cathedral, MS 3501, fols. 0–7 (the list is on fols. 1^r–2^v), and is reproduced in facsimile by R. W. Chambers, M. Förster and R. Flower (eds.), *The Exeter Book of Old English poetry* (London, 1933); Lapidge, 'Booklists', 64–9. The Auct. manuscript can now be viewed on the Bodleian Library website: http://image.ox.ac.uk.

79 M. Förster, 'The donations of Leofric to Exeter', in Chambers, *The Exeter Book*, 10–32; R. Frank and A. Cameron, *A plan for the dictionary of Old English* (Toronto, 1973), 193. For scribal identifications, see E. M. Drage, 'Bishop Leofric and the Exeter Cathedral Chapter 1050–1072: a reassessment of the manuscript evidence', unpublished DPhil thesis, Oxford University (1978).

Leofric also obtained a number of Latin books for the canons, which form the latter half of the list: Gregory's *Regula pastoralis* (Bodleian, MS Bodley 708 with the donation inscription), his *Dialogues*, a book of 'the four prophets' (Isaiah, Jeremiah, Ezekiel and Daniel), the original Latin text of Boethius' *Consolation of Philosophy* (Bodleian, MS Auct. F.1.15 with the donation inscription), Porphyry's *Isagoge*, a passional or lectionary, Prosper, Prudentius' *Psychomachia*, *Cathemerinon* and *Peristephanon* (Bodleian, MS Auct. F.3.6, written at Exeter and with the donation inscription) Ezekiel, Song of Solomon, Isaiah, *Etymologies* of Isidore, Passions of the Apostles, Bede on Luke, Bede on the Apocalypse (Lambeth, MS 149), Bede on the Catholic Epistles (Bodleian, MS Bodley 849), Isidore on the Old and New Testaments, Isidore's *De miraculis Christi* (i.e. his *De fide catholica contra Iudaeos*: Bodleian, MS Bodley 394), a *liber oserii*, Maccabees, Persius (Bodleian, MS Auct. F.1.15 with the donation inscription), Sedulius, Arator, a *liber de sanctis patribus*, Smaragdus' *Diadema monachorum* (this item is only found in the copy of the list in Auct. D.2.16), glosses on Statius (presumably a copy of the *Thebaid* with glosses), Amalarius' *Liber officialis* (Cambridge, Trinity Coll., MS B.11.2 with the donation inscription). The list ends, like the donation inscriptions, with a stern anathema: 'and whoever may wish to deprive God and St Peter of these gifts and this grant may he be deprived of the heavenly kingdom and may he be cast down eternally into damnation'.

The lack of booklists comparable in scale to the record of Leofric's donation, combined with an absence of substantial numbers of manuscripts localisable to more than a handful of religious houses, makes it very difficult to identify local differences in the size of collections or emphases in their contents. Nevertheless, the Exeter list confirms the impression derived from shorter and perhaps more partial records, such as the list of eleven books (almost all in the vernacular) probably from Worcester,[80] and from surviving manuscripts. Two significant points emerge. First, service books were essential, with only a small and somewhat limited range of schoolbooks and biblical commentaries. Secondly, the library at Exeter contained a large number of works either in Anglo-Saxon with a full Anglo-Saxon translation, reflecting England's flourishing vernacular culture, by contrast with all other countries in Europe. Practical

80 CCCC, MS 367, fol. 48^{v}: a legendary in Old English, a martyrology, two copies of Werferth's Old English translation of Gregory's *Dialogues* and two copies of Alfred's Old English translation of Gregory's *Pastoral care*, the Old English Rule of St Benedict, two psalters in Old English, the *Visio S. Baronti monachi* and '*Oddan boc*' (presumably a book belonging to one Odda): Lapidge, 'Booklists', 62–4.

pastoral concerns were especially important with vernacular homilies and a vernacular Gospel translation which was used for liturgical reading. The Rule for canons and the *Pastoral care* were also available in Old English, as was a penitential.

Only the *Isagoge* of Porphyry and the glossed Persius and Statius show the sorts of intellectual interests we can find in some eleventh-century continental collections. Nicholas Brooks's study of the books which were copied at, and in many cases for, Christ Church, Canterbury, reveals a similarly limited picture. He notes the presence of multiple copies of certain basic works: Aldhelm's prose *De virginitate*, Prosper's *Epigrammata*, Prudentius' hymns, Sedulius and Juvencus, but the absence of works of theology or exegesis, or of Christian history.[81] The sources drawn upon by Byrhtferth and Ælfric, and the books given by Abbot Sæwold to Saint-Vaast, are suggestive of wider learned interests, but a comparable range of Latin, and especially patristic, literature appears only to have become more widespread among even the larger religious houses and cathedrals in England from the final decades of the eleventh century.

81 N. P. Brooks, *The early history of the Church of Canterbury* (Leicester, 1984), 266–76.

4

Monastic and cathedral book collections in the late eleventh and twelfth centuries

TERESA WEBBER

The late eleventh and twelfth centuries witnessed a significant increase in the scale of book collections owned by monasteries and cathedrals.[1] It was an achievement commemorated by twelfth- and thirteenth-century chroniclers, and is well attested by surviving books and records of book ownership.[2] Such evidence permits a detailed examination of the contents and other aspects of these collections to an extent that is not possible for earlier centuries.[3] In this respect, the period marks a turning point in the history of libraries in England, at least; a dearth of evidence remains for the rest of Britain and Ireland. More difficult to establish is the extent to which growth was accompanied by changes in the use and organisation of these collections, and developments in the concept of a library.

The marked growth in the holdings of religious communities was one aspect of a phenomenon common to western Europe during the later eleventh century and first half of the twelfth: a desire, expressed in various ways, to restore and perfect the form and practice of the religious life. It contributed

1 N. R. Ker, *English MSS*, 4–9; R. M. Thomson, *Books and learning in twelfth-century England: the ending of* 'Alter orbis' (forthcoming); R. M. Thomson, 'The Norman Conquest and English libraries', in P. Ganz (ed.), *The role of the book in medieval culture*, 2 vols. (Turnhout, 1986), II. 27–40; repr. in Thomson, *England and the twelfth-century renaissance* (Aldershot, 1998), no. XVIII; R. Gameson, *The manuscripts of early Norman England (c. 1066–1130)* (Oxford, 1999), 5–20.

2 For surviving books, *MLGB* and *Supplement*; Gameson, *Manuscripts of early Norman England*. For medieval booklists: CBMLC III–IV, VI, VIII. Forthcoming volumes of CBMLC will supersede existing editions of the booklists from Christ Church, Canterbury, and from Durham, and will provide editions of the scantier remains from Scottish religious houses and from the secular cathedrals.

3 C. R. Cheney, 'English Cistercian libraries, the first century', in his *Medieval texts and studies* (Oxford, 1973), 328–45; A. Coates, *English medieval books: the Reading Abbey collections from foundation to dispersal* (Oxford, 1999); R. M. Thomson, 'The library of Bury St Edmunds Abbey in the eleventh and twelfth centuries', *Speculum* 47 (1972), 617–45, repr. in Thomson, *England and the twelfth-century renaissance*, no. I; Thomson, *Manuscripts from St Albans Abbey, 1066–1235*, 2nd edn, 2 vols. (Woodbridge, 1985); T. Webber, *Scribes and scholars at Salisbury Cathedral c. 1075–c. 1125* (Oxford, 1992).

to an unprecedented expansion in the number of religious communities.[4] In England alone the number increased from sixty-one in 1066 to 400 by 1154.[5] New or enlarged churches and other buildings, many in stone, were the most substantial and visible signs of the piety and patronage that lay behind such expansion, but books were also accorded a high priority. The obit composed for the liturgical commemoration of the achievements of Lanfranc, archbishop of Canterbury (d. 1089), for example, celebrates his endeavours to supply the community with 'the precious gift of books, many of which he had corrected himself', as an achievement second only to his enhancement of every part of the fabric of the cathedral priory.[6] Such activities were praised by William of Malmesbury in his accounts of post-Conquest prelates in his *Gesta pontificum*, and are likewise recorded in several other twelfth- and thirteenth-century chronicles.[7] The significance of the books is also reflected in their inclusion in formal records of endowments, privileges and property, such as the *Textus Roffensis*, compiled at Rochester Cathedral Priory some time after 1123, and the late twelfth-century cartulary of Reading Abbey, in which a booklist accompanies a list of the abbey's relics.[8] At the Augustinian abbey of Cirencester, the names of the abbot, precentor and scribes were added to volumes produced by members of the house,[9] an act which may have been associated with some kind of liturgical commemoration of those responsible for providing the community with books such as was practised at the beginning

4 G. Constable, *The reformation of the twelfth century* (Cambridge, 1996), esp. 44–87.

5 D. Knowles and R. N. Hadcock, *Medieval religious houses, England and Wales*, 2nd edn (London, 1971), 494; D. Knowles, *The monastic order in England*, 2nd edn (Cambridge, 1963), 100–252; E. Cownie, *Religious patronage in Anglo-Norman England, 1066–1135* (London, 1998); J. Burton, *The monastic order in Yorkshire, 1069–1215* (Cambridge, 1999), for a detailed regional study.

6 'Pretioso insuper ornamento librorum. ecclesiam istam apprime honestauit. quorum quamplurimos per semetipsum emendauit.' M. Gibson, *Lanfranc of Bec* (Oxford, 1978), 227–9.

7 William of Malmesbury, *De gestis pontificum Anglorum*, ed. N. E. S. A. Hamilton, RS (London, 1870), 184, 195 and 431–2 (on Osmund, bishop of Salisbury, John de Villula, bishop of Wells, and Godfrey, abbot of Malmesbury); Symeon of Durham, *Libellus de exordio atque procurso istius, hoc est Dunhelmensis, ecclesie*, ed. D. Rollason (Oxford, 2000), 244–5 (on William of Saint-Calais, bishop of Durham); *Excerptiones . . . de abbatibus Abbendonie*, in J. Stevenson (ed.), *Chronicon monasterii de Abingdon*, 2 vols., RS (London, 1858), II. 289 (on Faricius, abbot of Abingdon, 1100–17); H. T. Riley (ed.), *Gesta abbatum sancti Albani*, 3 vols., RS (London, 1867–9), I. 57–8, 70, 76, 94, 106, 179, 184, 192 (on the late eleventh- and twelfth-century abbots of St Albans); Thomas of Marlborough, *History of the abbey of Evesham*, ed. J. Sayers and tr. L. Watkiss (Oxford, 2003), 178–9, 182–3, 186–7 (on Abbots Walter, Reginald and Adam).

8 CBMLC IV. B77, B71; Coates, *English medieval books*, 20–1.

9 For example, Oxford, Jesus Coll., MSS 52, 53, 63, 67, 68 and 70; Watson, *Dated MSS in Oxford Libraries*, nos. 798–803.

of Lent by another English Augustinian priory, Barnwell, near Cambridge, and at the Bendictine abbey of Peterborough.[10]

The most striking aspect of these endeavours, not only in Britain but throughout Europe, was the extensive copying or acquisition of the writings of the early Church Fathers, regarded as the authoritative teachers of Christian truth and essential guides to the meaning of Scripture and the conduct of the religious life.[11] The final chapter of the Rule of St Benedict, for example, stressed their importance:

> for him who would hasten to the perfection of the monastic life, there are the teachings of the holy Fathers, by observing which a man is led to the summit of perfection. For what page or what utterance of the divinely inspired books of the Old and the New Testament is not a most unerring rule of human life? Or what book of the Catholic Fathers is not manifestly devoted to teaching us the straight road to our Creator?[12]

The rule, however, named only a limited number of texts, all concerned primarily with the conduct of the monastic life through exhortation or example, such as Cassian's *Collationes* and the *Vitas patrum*. For more detailed guidance on the Fathers and their writings, communities turned to the authoritative lists and recommendations of late antiquity. In England, a group of such works circulated widely as a corpus of bio-bibliographical texts. Some eleven late eleventh- or twelfth-century English copies survive that derive from a ninth-century continental manuscript, now Hereford Cathedral, MS O.iii.2, imported to England perhaps during the second half of the eleventh century.[13] It contains a cumulative list of the Fathers (the *viri illustres*) comprising Jerome's *De viris illustribus* and the continuations by Gennadius and Isidore, together with the pseudo-Gelasian *De libris recipiendis et non recipiendis* (a text that had come to be regarded as a papal document, and was incorporated into canon law as the authoritative statement of which biblical and other writings were to be deemed 'authentic' and those which were not), and Augustine's *Retractationes* (a list of his own writings and a commentary upon them). Additional guidance was provided by the first book of Cassiodorus' *Institutiones*, the first known attempt to provide a thorough programme for the study of the Bible

10 J. W. Clark (ed.), *The observances in use at the Augustinian Priory of S. Giles and S. Andrew at Barnwell, Cambridgeshire* (Cambridge, 1897), 62–3; CBMLC VIII. xlvi. See also below, 224.

11 Gameson, *Manuscripts of early Norman England*, 20; Thomson, *Books and learning*; Webber, *Scribes and scholars*, 31–9.

12 R. Hanslik (ed.), *Regula S. Benedicti*, ch. 73, CSEL 75, 2nd edn (Vienna, 1977), 180, J. McCann (tr.), *The Rule of St Benedict* (London, 1970), 78.

13 R. A. B. Mynors (ed.), *Cassiodori Senatoris Institutiones* (Oxford, 1937), xv–xvi, xxxix–xlix.

and the patristic reading appropriate for it. The manuscript ends with four introductory texts by Isidore on the interpretation of the Bible.

To judge from surviving books and booklists, no community in England fulfilled all of Cassiodorus' recommendations or acquired the full works of any one of the Fathers.[14] It is possible, however, that the incomplete state of the evidence may conceal the full extent of what was achieved; even records that purport to list the books possessed by a community may not be comprehensive. A late twelfth-century list from Burton Abbey headed 'Hos habet libros ecclesia Burtone' ('The church of Burton has these books'), for example, does not include a single text by Jerome, a surprising gap which may indicate that the list is not a full record.[15] At least thirty-five surviving books known to have been owned by Bury St Edmunds Abbey in the twelfth century are not listed in what otherwise appears to be a detailed account of the community's books.[16] Despite the apparent absence of comprehensive programmes of acquisition, there is evidence of sustained activity.[17] Prolonged or spasmodic periods of intense copying over two or more decades took place at Christ Church, Canterbury; Salisbury; and perhaps also St Augustine's, Canterbury, from the 1080s;[18] Durham, from the 1090s;[19] Rochester, from around the turn of the eleventh and twelfth centuries; and numerous other communities during the first half of the twelfth century,[20] continuing into the second half at more recently founded Cistercian and Augustinian houses, such as that of the Augustinian canons at Cirencester.[21] The close textual relationships between copies of the same work made at different places indicate communication and co-operation between communities, as they sought to acquire desired texts.[22]

14 T. Webber, 'The patristic content of English book collections in the eleventh century: towards a continental perspective', in P. R. Robinson and R. Zim (eds.), *Of the making of books: medieval manuscripts, their scribes and readers: essays presented to M. B. Parkes* (Aldershot, 1997), 192.

15 CBMLC IV. B11.

16 CBMLC IV. B13; Thomson, 'Library of Bury St Edmunds', 618.

17 Thomson, *Books and learning*.

18 Ker, *English MSS*, 25–30; M. Gullick, 'The scribal work of Eadmer of Canterbury to 1109', *Archaeologia Cantiana* 118 (1998), 173–89; Webber, *Scribes and scholars*, 8–30.

19 M. Gullick, 'The scribes of the Durham cantor's book (Durham, Dean and Chapter Library MS B.IV.24) and the Durham martyrology scribe', in D. Rollason, M. Harvey and M. Prestwich (eds.), *Anglo-Norman Durham, 1093–1193* (Woodbridge, 1994), 93–109; M. Gullick, 'The hand of Symeon of Durham: further observations on the Durham martyrology scribe', in D. Rollason (ed.), *Symeon of Durham, historian of Durham and the North* (Stamford, 1998), 14–31, 358–62, supplementing and modifying R. A. B. Mynors, *Durham Cathedral manuscripts to the end of the twelfth century* (Oxford, 1939), 32–63.

20 Ker, *English MSS*, 30–2.

21 Thomson, *Books and learning*.

22 *Ibid.*; Ker, *English MSS*, 11–15; M. P. Richards, 'Texts and their traditions in the medieval library of Rochester Cathedral Priory', *Transactions of the American Philosophical Society* 78/3 (1988).

The importance accorded the writings of the Fathers at this time is apparent in several formal records of book-ownership and narrative accounts of book production, in which they are placed second only to the Bible. Their authority as the fundamental guides to the study of Scripture was indicated primarily by the order of the entries in the booklists, sometimes reinforced with headings naming each author. The incomplete list that forms part of the *Textus Roffensis* almost certainly originally began with books of the Bible; it now starts midway through the entries recording volumes of Augustine, followed by groups of entries devoted to books containing the works respectively of Jerome, Ambrose and Gregory, each new section introduced by a heading naming the author: for example, 'Libri beati Ieronomi sunt isti'.[23] Fragments of a contemporary or slightly later document from Rochester are arranged and articulated in a similar manner: 'De libris beati Augustini. habemus eiusdem'.[24] A fragmentary mid-twelfth-century list from Durham Cathedral Priory likewise begins with the Old and New Testament followed by three well-defined sections devoted respectively to Jerome, Ambrose and Augustine, while in another, slightly later list from Durham, entries recording texts by respectively Jerome, Augustine and Ambrose are grouped together, following the opening sections that record biblical volumes and canon law.[25] A late twelfth-century account of the book production initiated by Faricius, abbot of Abingdon (d. 1117), also singles out the Fathers by name, their authoritative status emphasised by the title *doctor*: 'Scriptores uero hos libros scribebant, Augustinum de ciuitate Dei. Omelias sancti Augustini super Iohannem, et multa alia uolumina ipsius doctoris' ('The scribes wrote these books, Augustine, *De civitate Dei*; St Augustine's homilies on John, and many other volumes of this *doctor*'), a formula repeated for Gregory, Ambrose, John Chrysostom and probably (the wording is ambiguous) Jerome.[26]

The initiatives in England were paralleled elsewhere on the Continent, where they likewise accompanied the introduction or restoration of regular discipline and religious renewal, at the heart of which was the study of Scripture. In Normandy, a reform movement first inspired by the Cluniac William of Volpiano (d. 1031) stimulated the copying or acquisition of the writings of the Fathers at William's own monastery of Fécamp and at Mont Saint-Michel during the mid-eleventh century, and at several other Norman monasteries by

23 CBMLC IV. B77.1–51.   24 CBMLC IV. B78.

25 A. J. Piper, 'The libraries of the monks of Durham', in Parkes and Watson, *Medieval scribes*, 213–16.

26 CBMLC IV. B2.1–9.

the end of the century.[27] During the late eleventh and early twelfth centuries, monasteries in south-east Germany influenced by the reforms of William of Hirsau (*c.* 1026–91) also undertook similar programmes of copying and acquisition in which the writings of the Fathers were prominent.[28] For the Carthusians, too, the production and careful correction of books were important aspects of their regular discipline. According to Guibert of Nogent, by contrast with their ideal of complete poverty, they gathered together the richest of libraries ('ditissimam tamen bibliothecam coaggerant'); while the compiler of their rule (the *Constitutiones Carthusiae*), Guigo, fifth prior of the Grande Chartreuse (d. 1137), was assiduous in acquiring and producing corrected texts of various works of the Fathers, including the letters of Jerome, Augustine and Ambrose, as well as Hilary on the Psalms and the writings of Gregory of Nazianzus and John Chrysostom.[29]

It was not just monastic reformers, however, who emphasised the importance of the Fathers. Discussion and dispute about matters of doctrine, such as the Eucharist, about the moral reform of the clergy, and about the relationship between ecclesiastical and secular authority gave urgency to the appeal to written authority – patristic as well as biblical and canonical – by those involved in the active as well as the contemplative life.[30] Certain texts of canon law, such as the *Panormia* of Ivo of Chartres and the Pseudo-Isidorian Decretals and Canons of Councils, first brought to England by Lanfranc, became widely disseminated. In England, during the late eleventh and early twelfth centuries, two non-monastic cathedral communities, Salisbury and Exeter, acquired substantial holdings of the writings of the Fathers and other texts necessary for understanding biblical truth and orthodox doctrine, presumably for practical application in their active ministry as canons, priests, pastors and

27 G. Nortier, *Les bibliothèques médiévales des abbayes bénédictines de Normandie* (Paris, 1971); B. Branch, 'Inventories of the library of Fécamp from the eleventh and twelfth centuries', *Manuscripta* 23 (1979), 159–72; J. J. G. Alexander, *Norman illumination at Mont Saint-Michel, 966–1100* (Oxford, 1970); Webber, 'Patristic content', 198–9.

28 R. Kottje, 'Klosterbibliotheken und monastische Kultur in der zweiten Hälfte des 11. Jahrhunderts', *Zeitschrift für Kirchengeschichte* 4: 18 (1969), 145–62, at 149–52; C. J. Mews, 'Monastic educational culture revisited: the witness of Zwiefalten and the Hirsau reform', in G. Ferzoco and C. Muessig (eds.), *Medieval monastic education* (London, 2000), 183–91.

29 Guibert of Nogent, *Monodiae*, pr. *PL* 156, 854; tr. as *Self and society in medieval France: the memoirs of abbot Guibert of Nogent (1064?–c. 1125)*, ed. J. F. Benton (New York, 1970), 61; P. Lehmann, 'Bücherliebe und Bücherpflege bei den Karthäusern', *Miscellanea Francesco Ehrle: scritti di storia e paleografia*, v, Studi e testi 41 (Rome, 1924), 366–9; repr. in Lehmann, *Erforschung des Mittelalters*, III (Stuttgart, 1960), 122–5.

30 Webber, 'Patristic content', 197, n. 26.

ecclesiastical administrators.[31] The unusually large number of manuscripts of this period that survive from Salisbury indicate that the recommendations of Cassiodorus' *Institutiones* and the other bibliographical texts that circulated with it were followed closely, perhaps as an aspect of the canonical discipline encouraged by the bishop, Osmund (1078–99).[32]

From the mid-twelfth century, religious houses in England, as elsewhere, were taking advantage of new resources for biblical study emanating from the schools of northern France, in particular Paris. Most important were glossed books of the Bible, which, by this time, had come to constitute a comprehensive reference tool, the *Glossa ordinaria*, in which was assembled the inherited wisdom of the Fathers, supplemented by the teaching of Carolingian and subsequent scholars. The relevant extracts (*auctoritates*) were organised according to the order of each book of the Bible, and presented in the form of interlinear and marginal glosses accompanying the biblical text.[33] The Bible in its entirety was not necessarily disseminated as a complete set of glossed books. Instead, volumes of individual books, or groups of them, were copied or acquired piecemeal or in smaller sets, eventually resulting at some houses, such as Durham Cathedral Priory, in a complete set.[34] At Bury St Edmunds, a list of books entered in a glossed copy of Genesis and the Song of Songs (now Cambridge, Pembroke Coll., MS 47) during the third quarter of the century and revised later in the century, contains blocks of entries recording glossed books.[35] Several of these books survive, together with others not recorded in the list; the palaeographical evidence suggests that almost all of them were the product of a sustained programme of copying at Bury during the third quarter of the twelfth century.[36] Some thirty locally produced glossed books also survive at Hereford Cathedral.[37] According to the thirteenth-century St Albans chronicler, Matthew Paris, Abbot Simon (1167–83) employed a team

31 Webber, *Scribes and scholars*, 129–39; R. Gameson, 'The origin of the Exeter Book of Old English poetry', *ASE* 25 (1996), 153–60; Thomson, *Books and learning*.

32 Webber, *Scribes and scholars*, 113, 129–39.

33 M. T. Gibson, 'The twelfth-century glossed bible', *Studia Patristica* 23 (Leuven, 1989), 232–44; repr. in her *'Artes' and bible in the medieval West* (Aldershot, 1993), no. XIV; C. F. R. de Hamel, *Glossed books of the bible and the origins of the Paris booktrade* (Woodbridge, 1984).

34 De Hamel, *Glossed books*, 11–13; Thomson, *Books and learning*.

35 CBMLC IV. B13.120–42, 138–48, 216–32.

36 Thomson, 'Library of Bury St Edmunds', 635–9; T. Webber, 'The provision of books for Bury St Edmunds Abbey in the 11th and 12th centuries', in A. Gransden (ed.), *Bury St Edmunds: medieval art, architecture, archaeology and economy*, British Archaeological Association Conference Transactions 20 (1998), 189–90.

37 R. M. Thomson, 'Robert Amiclas: a twelfth-century Parisian master and his books', *Scriptorium* 49 (1995), 240, n. 16; repr. in his *England and the twelfth-century renaissance*, no. III.

of professional scribes and commissioned 'fine books and volumes of both the Old and New Testaments, glossed and corrected, faultlessly finished, which we have not seen bettered'.[38] Other houses, such as Christ Church, Canterbury, Durham Cathedral Priory and the Cistercian abbey of Buildwas were the beneficiaries of substantial donations of glossed books by individuals who had studied at the schools in Paris.[39] In such instances it is not altogether clear where the initiative to acquire the copies may have lain – with the student donor or with a senior member of the community. Other works that acted as tools to aid the study of the Bible, and that conveniently brought together the inherited wisdom of the past and the more recent teaching of the schools, were also quickly acquired, such as Peter Lombard's *Sentences* (composed *c.* 1155–8), the *Historia scholastica* of Peter Comestor (d. *c.* 1179), and the *Verbum abbreviatum* of Peter the Chanter (d. 1197), as well as the biblical commentaries and other writings of Hugh, abbot of the Augustinian abbey of Saint-Victor in Paris (d. 1142).[40]

The provision of copies of the writings of the Fathers and other texts ancillary to the study of the Bible accounts for the greater part of the copying and acquisition of books by religious communities in England during the late eleventh and twelfth centuries, but it is also evident that the book collections required for every aspect of communal life were enhanced during this period. The provision of books for the Office remained a priority. For example, it is liturgical books that are specified in detail in the account of the books produced for St Albans at the initiative of Abbot Paul (1077–93) as part of his renewal of monastic discipline at St Albans in accordance with the observances outlined in Lanfranc's *Monastic constitutions*.[41] Around the turn of the late eleventh and early twelfth centuries, copies of the expanded homiliary of Paul the Deacon were made by or acquired for several communities to supplement existing resources for the lections of the night office and the public reading at mealtimes and at collation.[42] The provision of a complete copy of the Bible, in two or more large and sometimes lavishly decorated volumes, intended for public reading in the refectory and elsewhere within the community, was another

38 Thomson, *Manuscripts from St Albans Abbey*, I. 51–2, citing Matthew Paris, *Gesta abbatum Sancti Albani*, pr. as part of H. T. Riley (ed.), *Gesta abbatum sancti Albani*, I. 184.

39 De Hamel, *Glossed books*, 12–13; Mynors, *Durham Cathedral manuscripts*, 78–9; J. M. Sheppard, 'Magister Robertus Amiclas: a Buildwas benefactor?', *TCBS* 9 (1988), 281–8; Thomson, 'Robert Amiclas', 238–43; Thomson, *Books and learning*.

40 Thomson, *Manuscripts at St Albans Abbey*, I. 65.

41 *Ibid.*, I. 13, citing Matthew Paris, *Gesta abbatum Sancti Albani*, I. 57–8.

42 Thomson, *Books and learning*.

major undertaking typical of the late eleventh and twelfth centuries,[43] as were usually more modest volumes or booklets containing one or more saints' Lives. New impulses in religious practice and personal devotion were also met, with the acquisition of the spiritual writings of Aelred of Rievaulx, Bernard of Clairvaux and the Victorines, for example.[44] The books for the education of the novices were supplemented to keep pace with developments in the studying of the liberal arts, especially grammar. A detailed list of such texts (many of them in multiple copies) was drawn up at Christ Church, Canterbury, in the late twelfth century. It includes not only texts that had formed part of the young monks' curriculum in the late tenth and early eleventh centuries, such as the satires of Juvenal and Persius, but also those that became popular in England only during the late eleventh and twelfth centuries, such as the works of Horace, six copies of which are listed.[45] In addition to the books that served all these core requirements, texts of a more miscellaneous kind were also copied and acquired in a more *ad hoc* manner to meet various practical needs and more local or individual interests.[46]

Because of the scale of losses from female communities and from religious houses in Scotland, Wales and Ireland, it is difficult to discern in any detail how far their collections were shaped by developments in religious culture during the late eleventh and twelfth centuries. Literary evidence, such as the *Liber confortatorius* written by Goscelin of Saint-Bertin for the recluse, Eve, and the letters of Osbert of Clare to nuns at Barking Abbey, hints that the more highly educated and aristocratic nuns and recluses in England may have been capable of a level of Latin spiritual reading akin to that of their male counterparts.[47] This was demonstrably the case in some Bavarian communities, but

43 Examples survive complete or in part from Durham (Durham Cathedral Library, MS A.II.4, late eleventh century), Rochester (San Marino, CA, Huntington Library, HM 62, vols. I–II, late eleventh century), Lincoln (Lincoln Cathedral, MS 1, and Cambridge, Trinity Coll., MS B.5.2, before 1110); Bury St Edmunds (CCCC, MS 2, before 1138), Dover Priory (CCCC, MSS 3–4, mid-twelfth century) and Winchester (Bodleian, MS Auct. E. inf. 1–2, mid-twelfth century, and Winchester Cathedral, MS 17, second half of the twelfth century).

44 For example: *Speculum caritatis*: CBMLC III. Z19.46 (Rievaulx), CBMLC IV. B11.29 (Burton-on-Trent), B80.15b (Rochester); CBMLC VI. A4.34 (Bridlington); *De spiritali amicitia*: CBMLC III. Z19.40a (Rievaulx), CBMLC VI. A4.35 (Bridlington).

45 James, *ALCD*, 7–12.

46 For example, the small group of books containing medical texts and natural science from Bury St Edmunds, and those (now lost) at Waltham Abbey, or the Latin version of the astronomical tables of al-Khwārizmī, copied at Worcester: see C. Burnett, *The introduction of Arabic learning into England* (London, 1997), 25, 29, 39–40.

47 C. H. Talbot (ed.), 'The Liber confortatorius of Goscelin of Saint Bertin', *Analecta monastica*, Series 3, Studia Anselmiana 37 (1955), 80–1; E. W. Williamson (ed.), *The Letters of*

the absence of similar numbers of books and booklists from England makes comparison impossible.[48] As far as Scotland, Wales and Ireland are concerned, the meagre evidence needs to be assessed within the wider context of the distinctive ecclesiastical and religious structures and learned culture of each of these areas, and the complex history of their interactions with movements of reform on the Continent and with ecclesiastics and religious houses in England, especially, in the case of Wales and Ireland, in the wake of conquest and colonisation.[49] The *Registrum*, an early fourteenth-century 'union catalogue' of primarily patristic texts, compiled by the Oxford Franciscans, records a substantial number of such texts at the Cistercian abbey of Margam, Glamorganshire (242 titles), and reasonable numbers at the Scottish border abbeys of Jedburgh (Augustinian, 82 titles), Kelso (Benedictine, 96 titles) and Melrose (Cistercian, 102 titles), as well as 95 titles at the Augustinian cathedral priory of St Andrews.[50] Only one volume whose contents were recorded has been identified as surviving, a thirteenth-century compendium of Augustine from St Andrews.[51] Nevertheless, given the patterns of acquisition elsewhere, it is likely that many of these texts were acquired during the twelfth century.[52] The remainder of the evidence permits only a study of individual books, not of collections.[53]

Osbert of Clare, prior of Westminster (London, 1929), *epp.* 21–2, 40–1: pp. 89–91, 135–40; A. Barratt, 'Small Latin? The post-Conquest learning of English religious women', in S. Echard and G. R. Wieland (eds.), *Anglo-Latin and its heritage: essays in honour of A. G. Rigg on his 64th birthday* (Turnhout, 2001), 51–65.

48 A. Beach, *Women as scribes: book production and monastic reform in twelfth-century Bavaria* (Cambridge, 2004); D. N. Bell, *What nuns read: books and libraries in medieval English nunneries* (Kalamazoo, MI, 1995).

49 On this wider context, see, for example, F. G. Cowley, *The monastic order in South Wales, 1066–1349* (Cardiff, 1977); H. Pryce, 'Church and society in Wales 1150–1250, an Irish perspective', in R. R. Davies (ed.), *The British Isles, 1100–1500: comparisons, contrasts and connections* (Edinburgh, 1988), 27–47; A. Gwynn, *The Irish church in the eleventh and twelfth centuries*, ed. G. O'Brien (Dublin, 1992); D. Bethell, 'English monks and Irish reform in the eleventh and twelfth centuries', *Historical Studies* [Irish Conference of Historians] 8 (1971 for 1969), 111–35; M. Philpott, 'Some interactions between the English and Irish churches', *Anglo-Norman Studies* 20 (1998 for 1997), 187–204; P. Ó Néill, 'The impact of the Norman invasion on Irish literature', *Anglo-Norman Studies* 20 (1998 for 1997), 171–85.

50 CBMLC II. 289–91, 303–7; J. Higgitt, 'Manuscripts and libraries in the diocese of Glasgow before the Reformation', in R. Fawcett (ed.), *Medieval art and architecture in the diocese of Glasgow*, The British Archaeological Association Conference Transactions 23 (Leeds, 1999), 102–10, esp. 102–4.

51 St Andrews, University Library, MS BR 65. A 9.

52 A twelfth-century copy of Augustine's sermons, not identifiable in the *Registrum*, survives from Kelso, Dublin, Trinity College, MS 226; *MLGB*, 105.

53 D. Huws, 'The medieval manuscript in Wales', in P. H. Jones and E. Rees (eds.), *A nation and its books: a history of the book in Wales* (Aberystwyth, 1998), 25–39; *Five ancient books of Wales*, H. M. Chadwick memorial lecture 6 (Cambridge, 1996); 'A Welsh manuscript of Bede's *De natura rerum*', *Bulletin of the Board of Celtic Studies* 27 (1976–8), 491–504; all

The formation of new or enhanced collections of books was possible only with considerable wealth and the availability of competent scribes. The scale of the need prompted sustained programmes of production within many religious communities during the final decades of the eleventh century and the first half of the twelfth. The copying was carried out either by the monks or canons themselves or by craftsmen remunerated in some fashion for their work. At several houses formal arrangements were instituted to supply the necessary materials and scribes, sometimes by assigning specified revenues to the precentor (although other office-holders might also be assigned revenues to cover some of the expenses involved).[54] The extent of such arrangements depended in part upon the economic resources of the community and its abbot or prior. Forty-three volumes were made for Glastonbury Abbey during a period of about ten years, thanks to the wealth and patronage of Henry of Blois, who held the abbacy in plurality with the bishopric of Winchester.[55] The elaborate arrangements instituted by a succession of abbots at St Albans, for example, and the quality of the books produced there, were aided by the usually low assessment of their military obligation, the *servitia debitum*.[56] By the end of the twelfth century, however, in-house book production was being increasingly supplemented or supplanted by other means of provision, in particular donation and bequest. Growing numbers of students and masters were able to acquire books at the places where they studied, either by copying the texts themselves or by paying others to produce them, subsequently donating or bequeathing these books to religious houses. The new centres of higher learning at Paris and Oxford, both places in which there were concentrations of masters, students and other professionals, provided favourable conditions for the beginnings of commercial, if *ad hoc*, arrangements for the provision of the materials and skills involved in book production.[57]

The greater part of the expansion of communal book collections during this period was intended to meet needs outside the formal liturgy of the Office,

repr. in his *Medieval Welsh manuscripts* (Cardiff, 2000), 1–23, 65–83, 104–22. Histories of the book in Scotland and in Ireland are in hand.

54 M. Gullick, 'Professional scribes in eleventh- and twelfth-century England', *EMS* 7 (1998), 1–24.

55 CBMLC IV. 160–5 (B37.1–34).

56 Gullick, 'Professional scribes', 7, 12–14; Thomson, *Saint Albans*, I. 13, 15, 22, 52–3; B. Golding, 'Wealth and artistic patronage at twelfth-century St Albans', in S. Macready and F. H. Thompson (eds.), *Art and patronage in the English Romanesque* (London, 1986), 107–17.

57 De Hamel, *Glossed books*, 62–3; R. H. Rouse and M. A. Rouse, *Manuscripts and their makers: commercial book producers in medieval Paris, 1200–1500*, 2 vols. (Turnhout, 2000), I. 17–49; M. B. Parkes, 'The provision of books', *HUO* II. 413.

and, in particular, to deepen understanding of divine truth revealed in Scripture with the provision of the authoritative writings of the Church Fathers and other aids. It is not easy, however, to determine with any precision from surviving volumes or from booklists how the books were read, publicly or privately, and, if the latter, as part of the individual devotional reading required of each monk or canon, or for reference purposes with an intellectual or practical application in mind.

In communities that followed the Rule of Benedict, public reading took place in the chapter house, at mealtimes in the refectory, and at the evening collation.[58] Augustinian custumals likewise provide regulations for reading at mealtimes.[59] This public reading comprised largely biblical texts, homilies, saints' Lives and texts on the conduct of the religious life.[60] A rare list of books read at collation comes from Durham, written in a mid-twelfth-century hand, its eleven titles corresponding with the kinds of texts recommended as models for the conduct of the religious life in the final chapter of the rule: for example, the *Vitas patrum*, Cassian's *Collationes*, Gregory's *Dialogi* and *Cura pastoralis*; Isidore's *Sententiae* and Smaragdus' *Diadema monachorum*.[61] Nevertheless, surviving books indicate that a wider range of the writings of the Fathers and subsequent works of exegesis may have been produced for the purposes of public as well as private reading. The size of handwriting and, in some instances, a two-column layout of many copies of such works would have enabled them to be read aloud from a lectern. Furthermore, some books were also supplied with accents to assist correct pronunciation and comprehension by distinguishing stressed from unstressed syllables where confusion might arise.[62] Such accents have been observed in several late eleventh- and twelfth-century Durham manuscripts, including, for example, copies of Augustine's *De civitate Dei* and *Enarrationes in Psalmos* and the *Hexaemeron* of Ambrose.[63]

It is, however, reasonable to assume that the increase in the scope of the patristic holdings was primarily intended to widen the range of the personal,

58 Hanslik, *Regula S. Benedicti*, chs. 38, 42, pp. 106–8, 114–6.

59 For the regulation at Barnwell, for example, see Clark, *Observances*, 64–7.

60 D. Nebbiai-dalla Guarda, 'Les listes médiévales de lectures monastiques', *RB* 96 (1986), 271–326.

61 Durham Cathedral, MS B.IV.24, fol. 1v: Piper, 'Libraries of the monks of Durham', 230; *Catalogi veteres librorum ecclesiae cathedralis Dunelm.*, Surtees Soc. 7 (London, 1838), 9–10.

62 L. E. Boyle, *'Vox Paginae': an oral dimension of texts* (Rome, 1999).

63 *Ibid.*, 32–3; Mynors, *Durham Cathedral manuscripts*, pls. 21–2, 34. See also, Piper, 'Libraries of the monks of Durham', 231, pl. 71, for a fourteenth-century inscription in an early twelfth-century copy of Florus of Lyons on the Pauline Epistles (Durham, Dean and Chapter Library, MS B.II.34, fol. 1r), which states that it was formerly used for reading in the refectory.

devotional reading. Within communities that followed the Rule of Benedict, each monk had a formal requirement to receive one book at the beginning of Lent, which was then returned at the next Lenten distribution. On the Continent, from the ninth century onwards, the regulation in Chapter 48 of the rule was commented upon and elaborated, not least in order to monitor the performance of this requirement.[64] The earliest such evidence from England is Lanfranc's *Monastic constitutions*, but no borrowing lists earlier than the fourteenth century are known to survive.[65] A mid-eleventh-century list, however, survives from Cluny (whose customs, as they are extant from the twelfth century, correspond very closely with those of Lanfranc's, although the exact nature of the relationship is unknown),[66] which records the books distributed to sixty-four monks. A substantial proportion contained works of biblical exegesis and theology, of varying levels of difficulty, and just under half were copies of patristic texts.[67]

A monk's personal reading was first and foremost a spiritual activity, of which the goal was the deeper understanding of biblical truth.[68] The spiritual benefit to the community was also the principal aim of the ostensibly scholarly activity of correcting copies of the biblical and other texts that provided spiritual nourishment for the community – an activity that was regarded as an important aspect of regular discipline. Lanfranc's biography (attributed to Milo Crispin), for example, describes in detail Lanfranc's correction of copies of the Old and New Testaments, the works of the Fathers, and other books used by the community, while Eadmer, in his portrayal of Anselm's praiseworthy acts of personal discipline, describes his nightly vigils, engaged in correcting books and meditating.[69] Corrected or variant readings can be found between the lines and in the margins of numerous late eleventh- and twelfth-century books made for communal use, in many instances carried over from the exemplar, but sometimes added by the scribe or corrector.[70]

64 For example, Hildemar, *Expositio regulae*, ed. R. Mittermüller, *Vita et regula SS. P. Benedicti una cum expositione regulae a Hildemaro tradita* (Regensburg, 1880), 481–6.

65 See below, 223, 243–4.

66 D. Knowles (ed.), *The Monastic Constitutions of Lanfranc*, rev. C. N. L. Brooke (Oxford, 2002), xxxix–xlii, 28–31.

67 A. Wilmart, 'Le convent et la bibliothèque de Cluny vers le milieu du xie siècle', *Revue Mabillon* 11 (1921), 89–124.

68 F. Vandenbroucke, 'La lectio divina du xie au xive siècle', *Studia monastica* 8 (1966), 267–93.

69 Milo Crispin (attrib.), *Vita Lanfranci*: *PL* 150, 55; Eadmer, *Vita Sancti Anselmi archiepiscopi Cantuariensis*, ed. R. W. Southern (London, 1962), 14–15, esp. 15, n. 1. For manuscripts containing copies of texts corrected by Lanfranc (with the colophon 'Lanfrancus hucusque correxi'), see Gibson, *Lanfranc*, 40. See also Constable, *Reformation*, 154–5.

70 For examples from Durham and Salisbury, Gullick, 'Hand of Symeon', 16, 21, 25–9; Webber, *Scribes and scholars*, 12. Most examples of such activity, however, are represented

For some members of the religious communities, the requirement of the annual Lenten distribution may have been difficult to meet, but others evidently had more frequent recourse to their community's books, either to supplement their spiritual reading or for more immediate practical or intellectual purposes. Annotations in books from Christ Church, Canterbury, and from the secular cathedral of Salisbury indicate the close scrutiny of the written authority contained in canon law and the Fathers for practical application in ecclesiastical and pastoral administration.[71] William of Saint-Calais, bishop of Durham, when mounting his defence at his trial, drew upon his knowledge of the contents of a copy of the Pseudo-Isidorian Decretals and Canons of Councils that he gave to the newly restored community at Durham.[72] In his letter *De incestis coniugibus*, Ernulf, bishop of Rochester and former prior of Christ Church, Canterbury, under Lanfranc, appears to have drawn directly from a number of patristic texts as well as from collections of canon law.[73] Book collections were also drawn upon by the authors and compilers of works of edification and instruction, such as chronicles, saints' Lives, sermons and florilegia, all of which proliferated during this period. The best-attested example is William of Malmesbury, although he may have been exceptional in the extent to which he not only used the resources already available at Malmesbury but also sought out new texts.[74]

During the second half of the twelfth century, numerous scholars who had studied at Paris and other schools of higher learning became members of religious communities in England, often attaining high office. They put their professional knowledge and techniques of argument (acquired as part of their academic training in theology, canon and civil law) to practical purposes, especially in defending the rights, privileges and jurisdiction of their communities. Their expertise was especially valuable at a time when appeals to Rome were proliferating in the face of the encroachments of episcopal, royal and

by copies in which corrected or variant readings have been transcribed by the scribe from his exemplar.

71 Z. N. Brooke, *The English church and the papacy from the Conquest to the reign of John* (Cambridge, 1931), ch. 5; Webber, *Scribes and scholars*, 132–9.

72 Cambridge, Peterhouse, MS 74, M. Philpott, 'The *De iniusta uexatione Willelmi episcopi primi* and canon law in Anglo-Norman Durham', in Rollason, Harvey and Prestwich (eds.), *Anglo-Norman Durham*, 131–2.

73 P. Cramer, 'Ernulf of Rochester and early Anglo-Norman canon law', *JEH* 40 (1989), 498–9.

74 William of Malmesbury, *Gesta regum Anglorum*, bk II, prologue; ed. Mynors, Thomson and Winterbottom, I. 151–2; R. M. Thomson, *William of Malmesbury*, 2nd edn (Woodbridge, 2003), esp. ch. 3; N. Wright, 'William of Malmesbury and Latin poetry: further evidence for a Benedictine's reading', *RB* 101 (1991), 122–53; N. Wright, '"Industriae Testimonium": William of Malmesbury and Latin poetry revisited', *RB* 103 (1993), 482–531.

abbatial authority.[75] Even the Cistercians, who engaged more reluctantly in such studies, recognised the utility of the reference books of canon law, albeit imposing restrictions upon access to them.[76]

With hindsight, the late eleventh and twelfth centuries may be perceived as representing an important stage in the emergence of institutional libraries as more permanent, if not necessarily coherent or physically discrete, entities. Not only did the number of the communally owned books increase dramatically, but the collections appear to have gained a greater level of institutional stability. The practice of supplying books with an inscription of communal ownership was beginning to become more common by the end of the twelfth century, especially among the Cistercians and Augustinians.[77] Many of the volumes of the Fathers and later works of exegesis, the glossed books of the Bible, and the textbooks of the higher studies made or acquired during the late eleventh and twelfth centuries subsequently came to form the core of the late medieval cloister collections, or the reference collections shelved upon lecterns in the new library rooms of the fifteenth century. The growing numbers of books sometimes placed strains upon existing arrangements, and may explain why, at Christ Church, Canterbury, for example, the slype was adapted as a room in which to house books during the later twelfth century.[78] At about this same time, identification marks in the form of one or more letters of the alphabet and other symbols were supplied on the right-hand side of the upper margin of the first text page of many Christ Church books, including service-books.[79] Surviving manuscripts containing Jerome's exegetical works, for example, are marked with a sequence of letters from .a. to .p., and volumes of Ambrose, likewise from .R. to .V. Copies of school texts and the liberal arts were marked with pairs of letters and other symbols, which were also recorded against the relevant entries in a late twelfth-century booklist added to a copy of Boethius' *De arithmetica* and *De musica*.[80] These are the earliest marks of identification known from England, and their significance, beyond identifying a particular volume or copy of a text, has not yet been established. Nevertheless, their introduction may have owed something to the growth in the scale of the Christ

75 Thomson, 'Library of Bury St Edmunds', 641.

76 Cheney, 'English Cistercian Libraries', 343.

77 *MLGB*, xvi; see also below, 232–3, 241.

78 See above, 23.

79 *MLGB*, 29; M. Gullick and R. W. Pfaff, 'The Dublin Pontifical (TCD 98 [B.3.6]): St Anselm's?', *Scriptorium* 55 (2001), 288 and n. 8.

80 CUL, MS Ii.3.12, fols. 74–6; reproduced in James, *ALCD*, 3–6. Entries in another late twelfth-century Christ Church list recording liturgical books (mostly graduals) are also marked with such symbols (BL, MS Cotton Aug. ii.32): *MLGB*, 29; Gullick and Pfaff, *ibid.*

Church book collections, and perhaps to the introduction of new arrangements for storing the books.[81]

The greater institutional stability of book collections in the twelfth century may be regarded as a product of the ideals of religious reform, which involved a more rigorous application of the monastic discipline of communal ownership of all kinds of rights and property, including the books. This may be reflected in the far greater numbers of booklists that survive from the twelfth century by comparison with the Anglo-Saxon period, and the formal character of some of them. The lists may have acted as practical checklists, although the movement of books from one location to another would have rendered their utility only temporary. The classified order of lists such as that in the *Textus Roffensis* has led to their being described as catalogues, yet the arrangement may not have reflected the order of the volumes on the shelves, nor may such lists have been intended to facilitate the location of a copy of a particular text, since details about location are not specified, as they would be in some of the more elaborate and detailed catalogues of the late fourteenth and fifteenth centuries. The lists may, therefore, have carried a symbolic meaning, as a record of the community's possession of written authority, worthy of remembrance alongside its material property and rights, and (as in the Reading Abbey cartulary) its relics.[82]

Despite the greater emphasis upon communal ownership of books, and those that aided the study of Scripture most especially, the concept of a 'library', which comprised a certain category or categories of texts but not others, does not yet appear to have been defined. Books continued to be variously grouped, stored, and listed according to use and convenience, and might be moved from one collection or location to another as need arose. There was no clear-cut distinction between books used for public reading and those distributed for prolonged personal reading, still less between the books distributed for personal reading and a permanent reference collection for consultation *in situ*. Neither is there evidence for a well-defined bipartite categorisation of the books as 'liturgical' and 'non-liturgical', the latter constituting the library. Contemporary terminology reinforces the impression of an absence of such distinctions. The term *bibliotheca* is found both as a synonym of *armarium* as a general term for a collection of books and occasionally also in a seemingly more qualitative sense to refer to a collection of books deemed worthy of the

81 N. Ramsay, 'The cathedral archives and library', in P. Collinson, N. Ramsay and M. Sparks (eds.), *A history of Canterbury Cathedral* (Oxford, 1995), 350–1.

82 CBMLC IV. 421.

name.[83] The great majority of descriptions in customaries, historical narratives and booklists, however, refer simply to books in general, rather than using the term *bibliotheca*: for example, 'Hii sunt libri' ('These are the books') or similar wording is the most common formula in those booklists that begin with a heading.[84]

By the end of the twelfth century, however, developments were under way that would bring about more significant changes in the ways in which religious communities perceived, organised and used their books during the later middle ages. The scholars who brought to religious communities books and skills acquired at the schools represent the informal beginnings of what would become formal links between the larger monastic houses and the universities. Such contacts provided channels through which new practices in the organisation and use of books that had developed in response to the needs of preachers and scholars would eventually be transmitted also to the monasteries and cathedrals.

83 'Bibliotheca . . . scilicet armarium': John Beleth (d. after 1182), *Summa de ecclesiasticis officiis*, ed. J. Douteil, *CCCM* 41A (Turnhout, 1976), ch. 60, p. 109; 'Libri conscripti nonnulli, vel potius bibliothecae primitiae libatae' ('Some books were written, or rather the foundations of a library were laid') William of Malmesbury, *De gestis pontificum*, 431; tr. D. Preest, as William of Malmesbury, *The deeds of the bishops of England* (Woodbridge, 2002), 296 (on Godfrey, abbot of Malmesbury, 1081–1105). This latter use of the term is more common in continental narratives: see, for example, Guibert of Nogent on the Carthusians, above, 114.

84 CBMLC IV. B11: 'Hos habet libros . . .' (Burton Abbey, *c.* 1175); B71 'Hii sunt libri . . .' (Reading Abbey, 1192); B75 'Hii libri habentur . . .' (Leominster, cell of Reading, 1192); CBMLC III. Z19: 'Hi sunt libri . . .' (Rievaulx Abbey, s. xii/xiii).

5

The libraries of religious houses in the late middle ages

DAVID N. BELL

A medieval library was not a place so much as a process, a shifting accumulation of changing materials housed in diverse locations, which responded, to a greater or lesser degree, to a variety of trends in the cultural, educational, social, economic, political and intellectual milieux of its time and place. To trace its evolution, therefore, among all orders, from Augustinians to Premonstratensians, both male and (where applicable) female, is a daunting task and in some cases (for lack of information) simply impossible. Yet a careful examination of the surviving evidence enables us to draw a number of informed conclusions, and the broad lines of development, like the song the Sirens sang, are not beyond all conjecture.[1]

The period with which we are concerned was one of dramatic change in the complex life of the islands of Britain, and it was not a period of unalloyed peace and prosperity. The period spanning the fourteenth and early fifteenth centuries, for example, was one of major climatic change, when Britain was ravaged repeatedly by famine and disease. Book collections do not develop in a vacuum, and we cannot blame a Cistercian abbot whose monks are dying from plague or whose sheep are dying from liver-rot for neglecting his library. But towards the end of the fifteenth century, there was a remarkable recovery in prosperity and a significant increase in disposable income, and since, in a number of areas, child labour now became dispensable, schooling improved and literacy grew. It is no coincidence that this was a period of intellectual and cultural reawakening, when we see 'an increase in the demand for, availability and ownership of books of all kinds'.[2]

Much of this intellectual reawakening was due to the ever-increasing importance of the universities,[3] and university education had an all-pervasive impact

1 T. Browne, *Hydriotaphia: Urne-Buriall* (London, 1658), ch. v.
2 D. Pearsall, 'Introduction', in *BPPB*, 7.
3 K. Jensen, 'Text-books in the universities: the evidence from the books', in *CHBB* III. 354–79.

on the content, form, production and distribution of medieval books.[4] By the fifteenth century, religious of all orders regularly attended university, though interest in university education naturally varied from order to order. In the case of the friars, preaching and the defence of doctrine were their *raison d'être*, and, since those who had ideas contrary to the official teaching of the church were often intelligent and well educated, their adversaries also had to be intelligent and well educated. Since heresy commonly arises at the cutting edge of theology, friars of whatever colour needed up-to-date libraries and training to deal with it. By the end of the thirteenth century, university teaching in theology and philosophy was dominated by Dominicans and Franciscans, while about 40 per cent of all incunabula titles were written by friars.[5]

Furthermore, the friars themselves, especially at Oxford and certain major European universities, made their own contributions to university education, not least in the areas of the commentary and practical aids to study and preaching.[6] Members of these orders were often away from their home bases for extended periods, and, since they needed a certain minimum of relevant texts about their person, they made extensive use of what, in the later middle ages, was the growing practice of personal use but communal ownership. To this idea, one of the most important developments in book ownership in the period under consideration, we shall return in due course.

The monastic orders, on the other hand, were generally receptive rather than creative in the realm of university studies. This is not to suggest, however, that they were intellectually stagnant. Some monks were studying subjects 'on the very fringes of the arts curriculum'[7] – J. G. Clark cites mathematics and astronomy;[8] we could also add French and certain of the occult pseudo-sciences[9] – but it seems, in general, that the monk scholars preferred the works of authors who belonged to an earlier tradition: writers like Bede, Hrabanus

4 See C. H. Talbot, 'The universities and the medieval library', in Wormald and Wright, *English library*, 66–84 (useful, but now dated); E. Leedham-Green, 'University libraries and book-sellers', in *CHBB* III. 316–53; and M. B. Parkes, 'Provision of books', *HUO* II. 407–83.

5 R. Hirsch, *Printing, selling and reading* (Wiesbaden, 1967), 129, citing (critically) E. Schulz, *Aufgaben und Ziele der Inkunabelforschung* (Munich, 1924) and J. M. Lenhart, *Pre-Reformation printed books* (New York, 1935).

6 See R. H. Rouse and M. A. Rouse, '*Statim invenire*: schools, preachers, and new attitudes to the page', in R. L. Benson and G. Constable (eds.), *Renaissance and renewal in the twelfth century* (Cambridge, MA, 1982), 201–25, repr. in their *Authentic witnesses: approaches to medieval texts and manuscripts* (Notre Dame, 1991), 191–219; *eidem*, 'The development of research tools in the thirteenth century', in their *Authentic witnesses*, 221–55.

7 J. G. Clark, 'University monks in late medieval England', in G. Ferzoco and C. Muessig (eds.), *Medieval monastic education* (London, 2000), 62.

8 Clark, 'University monks', 62.

9 See n. 20 below.

Maurus, the Victorines and Stephen Langton.[10] It is clear, too, that the book collections of their colleges and home cloisters were not always adequate for their needs, and the monk scholars both compiled and used a variety of summaries, epitomes, anthologies and reference works.[11] Sometimes the Oxford notebooks of earlier monk scholars found their way back to the abbey, where they could be profitably used by later generations.[12] A small number of monk scholars produced original treatises on rhetoric and dictamen,[13] but, in general, they seem to have preferred to study older works, and to use newer academic approaches – disputations, quodlibets, and so on – to elucidate the essential principles of traditional monastic life.[14]

Monks who had studied at university naturally had an impact on the libraries of their mother-houses. Not only did the collections have to cater – not always successfully – to their needs, but their own books regularly reverted back to the abbey (or, in the case of friars, to the province) on their deaths.[15] The Benedictine abbey of Ramsey provides a number of examples. The mid-fourteenth-century catalogue informs us that Nicholas of Baston left works by Aristotle, commentaries on Aristotle by Thomas Aquinas and Robert Kilwardby, corrections to Aquinas by William de Mara, a commentary on Peter Lombard's *Sentences*, a biblical concordance, and half a dozen volumes of law, both civil and canon.[16] A similar collection came from Hugh of Aylington.[17] The books left at Arbroath in 1473 by its former abbot, Richard Guthrie, tell much the same story.[18] But we must note that, despite the late date of the list from Arbroath, all the works it contains were written before 1300. Then as now, university education did not always keep pace with the times.

Well-educated monks normally expected to occupy important positions in the monastic hierarchy,[19] and a university-trained abbot or prior with a love of books could have a profound influence on the intellectual atmosphere of his abbey. William Slade, abbot of the Cistercian abbey of Buckfast at the beginning of the fifteenth century, is an excellent example. He himself wrote

10 Clark, 'University monks', 63. 11 *Ibid.*

12 A. Bellenger, 'A medieval novice's formation: reflection on a fifteenth-century manuscript at Downside Abbey', in Ferzoco and Muessig, *Medieval monastic education*, 37; J. Greatrex, 'From cathedral cloister to Gloucester college', in H. Wansbrough and A. Marett-Crosby (eds.), *Benedictines in Oxford* (London, 1997), 59; and Parkes, 'Provision of books', 450–1.

13 Clark, 'University monks', 65–6. 14 *Ibid.*, 64.

15 K. W. Humphreys, *The book provisions of the mediaeval friars, 1215–1400* (Amsterdam, 1964), 18–89 *passim*; Parkes, 'Provision of books', 432–4, 452–5.

16 CBMLC IV. 362–3 (B68.103–116). 17 CBMLC IV. 363–4 (B68.117–125).

18 D. N. Bell, 'Monastic libraries, 1400–1557': in *CHBB* III. 233; Parkes, 'Provision of books', 448–9.

19 W. Sheehan, 'The religious orders 1220–1370', in *HUO* I. 217–18; C. H. Talbot, 'The English Cistercians and the universities', *Studia monastica* 4 (1962), 203.

quaestiones on Aristotle and Lombard; the Buckfast library contained a number of rare and interesting scholastic texts; and Richard Dove, a monk of the abbey, has left us his Oxford notebook containing texts on mathematics, astronomy, astrology, mensuration, physiognomy, chiromancy, magic, and French.[20]

At an earlier date, learned or bibliophilic abbots at houses like Bury St Edmunds, Cirencester, Evesham, Malmesbury, Meaux or St Albans could and did transform the collections,[21] but the tradition continued until the very eve of the Dissolution. There are good examples among the abbots of Bury St Edmunds and St Albans in the fourteenth century,[22] and Prior More of Worcester is an obvious example from the sixteenth.[23] But even at Cistercian Hailes in 1538, abbot Stephen Sagar (or Whalley) bought a bible printed in 1532 and sixteenth-century printed editions of Bede, Denys the Carthusian and Peter Lombard. They were intended for the collection in the chapter house.[24]

University education also reflected and created new approaches to study. The traditional, ruminative approach to biblical study had been replaced (not without protest) by the logical precision of the scholastic method, but in none of the orders was the sanctity of Scripture denied or the study of Scripture neglected. It was studied in a new way, to be sure, but although there were some – perhaps many – who, like Lot's wife (wrote Alexander Nequam in the early 1200s), seem to have been changed into men who preferred *amor saecularium litterarum* to the *deliciae paginae celestis*, who would rather hear about Martianus Capella's *Marriage of Philology and Mercury* than about Christ and his church,[25] they do not appear to have been the majority. In 1336 Pope Benedict XII had issued the bull *Summa magistri*, which demanded, among other things, that each Benedictine monastery must provide within its walls instruction in the 'primitive sciences', grammar, logic and philosophy.[26] The requirement was later extended to the Cistercians and regular canons, and although the response varied dramatically from house to house, the principle behind it was widely accepted. Grammar now became of first importance in the formation of novices,[27] and, from about the end of the twelfth century,

20 CBMLC III. 10–12 (Z3); D. N. Bell, 'A Cistercian at Oxford, Richard Dove of Buckfast and London, B. L., Sloane 513', *Studia monastica* 31 (1989), 69–87.

21 See above, chapter 4. 22 CBMLC IV. 46, 541–2, 552. 23 See n. 121 below.

24 D. N. Bell, 'Printed books in English Cistercian monasteries', *Cîteaux, comm. cist.* 53 (2002), 152–5.

25 Alexander Nequam, *Comm. in Cant. Cant.*, BL, MS Royal 4.D.xi, fols. 169va and 51vb.

26 Clark, 'University monks', 57.

27 Bellenger, 'A medieval novice's formation'; J. Greatrex, 'The scope of learning within the cloisters of the English cathedral priories in the later middle ages', in Ferzoco and Muessig, *Medieval monastic education*, 44–7, and Clark, 'University monks', 61.

grammar, which was not always distinguishable from rhetoric and dialectic, was as much concerned with etymology as with syntax and accidence. In 1395 the *armarium* of the Durham novices contained basic works by Priscian, Papias, William Brito and others,[28] and a similar situation – including contemporary works by Oxonian grammar masters – could be witnessed at a number of other abbeys.[29] Even at conservative Cistercian Pipewell, two monks were studying a copy of William Horman's *Vulgaria* printed in London in 1519.[30] In other words, as Dom Aidan Bellenger has pointed out, 'grammar and dictionaries had their place on the path to perfection',[31] and, for later medieval monks and friars, *meditatio* and *lectio* were intimately associated with the lexical and grammatical analysis of appropriate texts, especially the Scriptures. We may see the same progression in the way in which the old biblical glosses, the staple spiritual food of an earlier age, gave way to the commentaries of the Dominican Hugh of Saint-Cher (d. 1263), later supplemented by the popular *postilla* of the Franciscan Nicholas de Lyra (d. 1340).

Furthermore, since the standard form of university teaching was the commentary, and since commentaries were being produced in ever greater number and at ever greater length, there developed a need for concordances, indexes and *tabulae* (a word of wide meaning) to guide one through the mass of material.[32] Such aids to study were also essential in preaching, which, from the second half of the thirteenth century, came to occupy a position of major importance, not only among friars and Bridgettines,[33] but also among members of the monastic orders.[34] The vast numbers of sermons that one finds in virtually all later monastic library catalogues (at Syon, they were the single largest genre in the realm of printed books)[35] are not there by chance; and as the newer commentaries superseded the older ones, the now out-of-date books might be dismembered and used for the repair of more up-to-date volumes.[36] Thus, when the community at Durham sent a collection of glossed books of the Bible to their confrères at Durham College at Oxford in the early 1400s, the gift was less generous than it appears. The mother-house had kept

28 Greatrex, 'The scope of learning', 44–5.

29 Clark, 'University monks', 61.

30 Bell, 'Printed books', 157–8; see also 151–2 (no. 14, from Hailes).

31 Bellenger, 'A medieval novice's formation', 39.

32 See n. 6 above.

33 For Bridgettine interest in preaching, see V. Gillespie, 'Syon and the New Learning', in J. G. Clark (ed.), *The religious orders in pre-Reformation England* (Woodbridge, 2002), 80–1, and CBMLC IX. xxxii–xxxiii.

34 J. Greatrex, 'The English cathedral priories and the pursuit of learning in the later middle ages', 45 (1994), 396–411.

35 Gillespie, 'Syon and the New Learning', 93, and CBMLC IX. lxiii.

36 See, e.g., C. E. Wright, 'The dispersal of the libraries in the sixteenth century', in Wormald and Wright, *English library*, 148–9.

them in the Spendement, a sort of genizah for superseded volumes, and was probably happy to be rid of them.[37]

The first biblical concordance had been compiled by the Dominicans of Saint-Jacques in Paris in the 1230s, and the first *distinctiones* (which appeared in increasing numbers in the course of the thirteenth century) likewise reflect the demands of preaching and what K. W. Humphreys has called 'an almost aggressive appetite' for easy access to information.[38] But the principle was clearly a sound one, and it was not long before it was applied to subjects other than theology, especially law. In 1396 the Cistercians of Meaux possessed a substantial collection of biblical *distinctiones*;[39] a similar collection could be found in the library of the Leicester Augustinians;[40] there were *distinctiones causarum* at (possibly) Bermondsey;[41] and the nuns of Barking – or, more probably, their steward – owned a 'booke of the distinctions of the lawe' at the Dissolution.[42]

We might also add that university books needed to be 'immediately useful, practical, convenient for carrying around, relatively inexpensive and without frills and flourishes',[43] and to cater to this demand we see changes in the size and style of handwriting, the use of *peciae* as exemplars, and the burgeoning of the book trade in Britain.[44] Furthermore, the fact that books had to be relatively inexpensive was much helped by what R. J. Lyall has called 'the paper revolution'.[45] Paper was cheaper than parchment, and the difference in price became ever greater as the technology of paper-making developed. In 1400 one could buy twenty-five sheets of linen paper for about the price of a single skin; by the 1450s the cost had halved; and by the end of the century it had halved again.[46] This obviously had an impact on the price of books, and, when that was taken with the professionalisation of book production during the same period, the cost of books decreased dramatically. They were never cheap and they were always something of a luxury (it is not uncommon to find them pawned or used as pledges for loans),[47] but, as M. B. Parkes has said, 'the production of cheaper books meant that they could become a luxury

37 A. J. Piper, 'The libraries of the monks of Durham', in Parkes and Watson, *Medieval scribes*, 220, 246.

38 K. W. Humphreys, 'The effects of thirteenth-century cultural changes on libraries', *Libraries and culture* 24 (1989), 17.

39 CBMLC III. 324.

40 CBMLC VI. 549.

41 CBMLC IV. 26 (B.10.40).

42 CBMLC IV. 15 (B7.10).

43 Talbot, 'The universities', 66; C. de Hamel, *A history of illuminated manuscripts*, 2nd edn (London, 1994), 108–41.

44 Parkes, 'Provision of books', 428–31, 462–70; Bell, 'Monastic libraries', 235, n. 36.

45 R. J. Lyall, 'Materials, the paper revolution', in *BPPB*, 11–29.

46 Lyall, 'Materials', 11.

47 See, e.g., Parkes, 'Provision of books', 409–14, 451–2; D. N. Bell, *What nuns read: books and libraries in medieval English nunneries* (Kalamazoo, MI, 1995), 20; CBMLC III. 32–4 (St Mary of Graces).

for poorer people'.[48] Students, by definition, are poor. The decrease in price coupled with an increase in prosperity towards the end of the fifteenth century meant that more people could buy more books, and that would clearly have a significant effect both on personal or communal ownership and, as we shall see, on bequests and donations. You cannot give what you do not have.

There can be no doubt, then, that university education had the most profound effect on the nature and content of later medieval book collections, yet it was not the only formative influence on their development. Another major factor, not wholly separate from the growth of the universities, was the impact of three reforming church councils, and a considerable number of reforming statutes on the part of the religious orders. Of the councils, Lateran IV (1215), Vienne (1311–12) and Constance (1414–18) all recognised that the church of the time was in need of correction and improvement; all recognised a need for sound instruction on the part of preachers and teachers; all acknowledged the need for an informed laity; and all shared a maniacal, though arguably justified, fear of heresy. Sometimes the councils selected specific individuals or groups for condemnation: the Beguines at Vienne, for example, or John Wyclif at Constance.[49] Indeed, the virulent condemnation of Wyclif and all his works probably resulted in the theological cleansing of the library at Syon. The index to the early sixteenth-century catalogue mentions several of Wyclif's works; many of them are missing in the list of actual holdings.[50]

The demand for a better-educated clergy had already been made at the Third Lateran Council in 1179,[51] but the results had been disappointing. It was therefore reiterated in 1215, and a century later, at Vienne, the council emphasised the need for good preaching and sound explanation of the word of God. To assist in this, the council called for the establishment of university chairs in Hebrew, Aramaic and Arabic (the religious houses were to contribute to the salaries of the lecturers),[52] but the libraries of the religious houses show little interest in Hebrew / Aramaic studies. Prior Gregory of Ramsey was clearly interested in Hebrew and Greek (he had bought his Hebrew books in 1290 when their Jewish owners had sold them at auction),[53] and a century

48 M. B. Parkes, 'The literacy of the laity', in his *Scribes, scripts and readers: studies in the communication, presentation and dissemination of medieval texts* (London, 1991), 287. On the cost of books, see W. L. Schramm, 'The cost of books in Chaucer's time', *Modern Language Notes* 48 (1933), 139–45; H. E. Bell, 'The price of books in medieval England', *Library*, 4th ser., 17 (1936–7), 312–32; D. N. Bell, 'The library of Cîteaux in the fifteenth century, *primus inter pares* or *unus inter multos?*', *Cîteaux: comm. cist.* 50 (1999), 125–6.

49 N. P. Tanner (ed.), *Decrees of the Ecumenical Councils*, I: *Nicaea I to Lateran V* (London and Washington, 1990), 374 (Beguines), 411–16 (Wyclif).

50 Gillespie, 'Syon and the New Learning', 86, and CBMLC IX. lvi.

51 Tanner, *Decrees*, 220. 52 *Ibid.*, 379–80. 53 CBMLC IV. 330, 336–7.

or so later a monk of the abbey, Lawrence Holbeck, used them to compile a Hebrew dictionary.[54] But books like these, together with Hebrew grammars at Exeter and Syon, a copy of David Qimchi at Norwich and the printed Hebrew concordance at Syon, are no more than intriguing curiosities and do not here warrant extended discussion.[55] As for Arabic, if we discount the abundant translations from Arabic authors,[56] it had no impact on the contents of any monastic library in the later middle ages.

The question of languages leads us naturally to the question of literacy, especially vernacular literacy. Apart from scattered texts in Greek and Hebrew (and a small but important group of works in Welsh, Irish and Scots), the books of the religious orders were written in Latin, French or English. Latin, obviously, accounts for the vast majority of treatises, but in the later middle ages the decline of French and the rise of English are matters which, for a moment, must claim our attention.

Between the middle of the fourteenth century and the early sixteenth there was a dramatic increase in literacy in England, and it was an increase as dramatic among women as among men.[57] It was, however, primarily vernacular literacy, and it is significant that although about three-quarters of all incunables were written in Latin, almost 60 per cent of titles printed in England (excluding broadsides) were written in English.[58]

This growth in English literacy coincided with a decrease in the use of French, though the nuns of Lacock were still speaking French of a sort – it was 'moche like the frenche that the common Lawe is writen in'[59] – in the early sixteenth century. By this time, however, French had been moribund in England for 150 years, and the statement by M. D. Legge that French survived longest in the ports[60] is incorrect. It survived longest in the nunneries. But the French language and French literature had always played a greater role in women's houses than in men's.[61]

French had been superseded by English by the middle of the fifteenth century. The process had actually begun about two centuries earlier, but it took time for the trickle to become a flood.[62] It is no coincidence, therefore, that

54 CBMLC IV. 330, 417.

55 *MLGB*, 85 (Bodleian, MS Bodley Oriental 135), 138 (Cambridge, St John's Coll., MS 218), 186 (Oxford, Merton Coll. 76.b.11 and 77.a.20).

56 See, e.g., F. J. Carmody, *Arabic astronomical and astrological sciences in Latin translation: a critical bibliography* (Berkeley, 1956).

57 Bell, 'Monastic libraries', 232, n. 19. 58 *Ibid.*, n. 20. 59 Bell, *What nuns read*, 147.

60 M. D. Legge, 'Anglo-Norman as a spoken language', in R. A. Brown (ed.), *Proceedings of the Battle conference on Anglo-Norman studies*, II, 1979 (Woodbridge, 1980), 116.

61 Bell, *What nuns read*, 67–71. 62 *Ibid.*, 57–8.

whereas some eighteen volumes, or about 8 per cent, of the books recorded at Titchfield in 1400 are in French (excluding a number of legal texts), the brothers' library at Syon could boast no more than four volumes out of a total of more than 1,400.[63]

In the course of the fourteenth and fifteenth centuries English came into its own as a versatile language as well adapted for theology and spirituality as for romance and poetry. The development and dissemination of devotional literature in English have been considered elsewhere,[64] and it is hardly surprising to see its effects on the holdings of monastic libraries. It is true that it took time to offer any real challenge to Latin, but a glance at surviving manuscripts from religious houses reveals a wide variety of treatises in English. There are gospels both apocryphal and canonical (some in Wycliffite translations), psalters, lives of saints, translations of the major patristic and medieval works of exegesis and doctrine, chronicles, medical tracts, poems, hymns, monastic rules, a great deal of devotional material, masterpieces of fourteenth-century English spirituality (Rolle and Hilton are well represented), and such classics as Robert Mannyng's *Handlyng synne*, John Lydgate's *Brut*, Nicholas Love's *Mirror of the blessed life of Christ*, the *Prick of conscience*, the *Book of the craft of dying*, the *Chastising of God's children*, the *Cleansing of Man's soul*, the *Ancrene riwle*, *Cursor mundi*, and the *Cloud of unknowing*.[65]

Almost all the manuscripts date from the fifteenth century (I exclude here the early English texts at Christ Church, Canterbury, and Worcester, and at smaller houses such as Tavistock and Thorney),[66] and – as with French – the English texts they include were more important for nuns than for monks and friars. Of the non-liturgical books which have survived from English nunneries, almost a quarter are in Latin and about a tenth are in French, but no fewer than two-thirds are in English.[67] With this we may contrast the brothers' library at Syon. Of the 1,421 titles listed in the catalogue, only twenty-six are in English.[68] From a theological point of view, however, this, for the nuns, may have been no disadvantage. Their ignorance of Latin (which has certainly been exaggerated)[69] forced them to cultivate the fertile soil of religious literature in English, and, as a consequence, their theological and devotional life may have been richer and more up to date than that of their more Latinate confrères.[70]

63 Bell, 'Monastic libraries', 232.

64 H. S. Bennett, 'The production and dissemination of vernacular manuscripts in the fifteenth century', *Library*, 5th ser., 1 (1946–7), 167–78; V. Gillespie, 'Vernacular books of religion', in *BPPB*, 317–44; M. C. Erler, 'Devotional literature', in *CHBB* III. 495–525.

65 See, e.g., Bell, *What nuns read*, 37–8, 71–2, 74–5, 223–30.

66 See *MLGB*, 29–39, 188–9, 210–15.

67 Bell, *What nuns read*, 36.

68 *Ibid.*, 75.

69 *Ibid.*, 57–79.

70 *Ibid.*, 75–7.

In general, however, the fifteenth century was not a productive period for men's houses. There were exceptions, especially at Syon and some larger Benedictine abbeys – St Albans and Bury St Edmunds are two excellent examples;[71] Westminster somewhat less[72] – and towards the end of the century some other houses (Cistercian Kirkstall, for instance)[73] enjoyed a resurgence of scholarly activity, especially, but by no means exclusively, in hagiography and history.[74] But, as Joan Greatrex has pointed out, the impressive historical output from St Albans and Bury has no parallel among the cathedral priories,[75] and theology and philosophy were the prerogative of the universities. We may see a reflection of this diminished productivity in the limited numbers of fifteenth- and sixteenth-century manuscripts acquired by the monasteries and convents, for if we examine the dates of the 5,000 or so surviving manuscripts from men's houses, we find that only about 13 per cent were copied in the fifteenth or early sixteenth century.[76] We may contrast this with the 50 per cent which survive from the nunneries.[77] Only the Carthusians seem to have been different, though our knowledge of their libraries is sadly incomplete.[78] Nevertheless, I think it significant that, of about 150 manuscripts and books traced to ten Carthusian houses (Axholme, Beauvale, Coventry, Hinton, Kingston-upon-Hull, London Charterhouse, Mount Grace, Perth, Sheen and Witham), about 60 per cent of the manuscripts date from the fifteenth and early sixteenth centuries, and if we include with these the printed books the proportion increases to no less than 90 per cent.[79] We know the names of a number of fifteenth-century Carthusian scribes,[80] and there were certainly others, whose identities are now unknown.

The Carthusians may also have evinced a greater interest in works in English than most of their confrères. Of all the surviving volumes (including printed books) which have been traced to Carthusian houses, about a tenth are in

71 J. G. Clark, 'Thomas Walsingham reconsidered: books and learning at late-medieval St Albans', *Speculum* 77 (2002), 832–60, and the works cited in his n. 24.

72 See B. Harvey, 'A novice's life at Westminster Abbey in the century before the Dissolution', in Clark, *The religious orders*, 66.

73 J. E. Krochalis, 'History and legend at Kirkstall in the fifteenth century', in P. R. Robinson and R. Zim (eds.), *Of the making of books: medieval manuscripts, their scribes and readers: essays presented to M. B. Parkes* (Aldershot, 1997), 230–56.

74 A. I. Doyle, 'Book production by the monastic orders in England (*c.* 1375–1530)', in L. L. Brownrigg (ed.), *Medieval book production: assessing the evidence* (Los Altos Hills, CA, 1990), 1–19, and his 'Publication by members of the religious orders', in *BPPB*, 109–23.

75 Greatrex, 'The scope of learning', 50.

76 Bell, 'Monastic libraries', 243.

77 Bell, *What nuns read*, 76.

78 CBMLC IX. 609–10.

79 The figures in Bell, 'Monastic libraries', 244, require revision.

80 See, e.g., A. I. Doyle, above, n. 74; his 'Stephen Dodesham of Witham and Sheen', in Robinson and Zim, *Of the making of books*, 94–115, and CBMLC IX. 614.

English, and of twenty-four books borrowed from the London Charterhouse by John Spalding on his return to Kingston-upon-Hull in the late fifteenth or early sixteenth century, almost half are in English.[81] But, as we have said, we are working here from very limited data, and it is dangerous to draw too broad a conclusion.

The mention of printed books leads us ineluctably to a discussion of the impact of printing with movable type. This was introduced into Europe in the mid-1450s, but it took some decades for it to have a major impact. As L. J. McCrank has said, 'the impact of printing on medieval library development was pervasive, although, rather than revolutionary, change was evolutionary'.[82] There were two reasons for this: first, the innate conservatism of the monastic orders (manuscripts were still highly prized),[83] and second, the question of cost. Until about the 1470s, printed books could be extremely expensive, and when we compare their cost with that of contemporary manuscripts (which had been diminishing in price since about 1400), the difference was by no means as great as many would think.[84] By 1512–17, however, the Fifth Lateran Council could state that one of the great benefits of printing was that now, 'at small expense, one may possess a great number of books'.[85] And many people did.

With the exception of Syon,[86] the response of the religious orders to the printing revolution was, in general, enthusiastic but slow. Printing presses were installed at the Benedictine abbeys of Abingdon and Tavistock in 1525 and 1528 respectively, and, just possibly, at the Carthusian priory of Mount Grace;[87] but it is probable, as I have suggested elsewhere, that an analysis of surviving volumes presents a seriously inaccurate picture of the impact of printing on religious establishments, and that many houses were more interested in acquiring printed books than might be suggested by the meagre number of survivors.[88] To that suggestion I still subscribe. But I also suggested that printed volumes 'did not find their way into the libraries in any quantity until the early sixteenth century',[89] and that suggestion needs some revision.

81 CBMLC IX. 614–20 (C2). Only two or three of these seem to have been printed.

82 L. J. McCrank, 'Libraries', in J. R. Strayer (ed.), *Dictionary of the middle ages* (New York, 1986), VII. 563.

83 Bell, 'Library of Cîteaux', 125.

84 *Ibid.*, 125–6

85 Tanner, *Decrees*, 632; M. L. Ford, 'Private ownership of printed books', in *CHBB* III. 205–28.

86 Gillespie, 'Syon and the New Learning', 87–8, and CBMLC IX. li–liii.

87 W. K. Sessions, *A printer's dozen: the first British printing centres to 1557 after Westminster and London*, 2nd edn (York, 1983), 69–74 (Tavistock), 75–7 (Abingdon), 108–10 (Mount Grace).

88 Bell, 'Monastic libraries', 247–50, 253.

89 *Ibid.*, 249.

Three hundred and forty-eight dated printed books are recorded in N. R. Ker's *Medieval libraries of Great Britain* and its *Supplement*,[90] and of this number only two pre-date 1470. Both are copies of Cicero, one from Cistercian Woburn, printed at Mainz in 1466, and one from Benedictine Westminster, printed at Rome in 1469.[91] But, lest it be thought that the English Cistercians exhibited a precocious interest in purchasing incunables, the book in question was bought by Robert Hobbes, abbot of Woburn, in 1523. The other books are distributed by date thus:

1470–9	4.3 per cent	1510–19	17.6 per cent
1480–9	19.4 per cent	1520–9	10.1 per cent
1490–9	27.8 per cent	1530–9	5.5 per cent
1500–9	15.3 per cent		

The high percentages between 1480 and 1500 may suggest that the acquisition of printed books by religious houses began somewhat earlier than I had previously suggested, though the evidence of the catalogues – especially from Syon and Monk Bretton[92] – also implies that numbers increased substantially in the early fifteenth century. We must also note that books were being bought right up to the time of the Dissolution (1536–40). Abingdon bought a volume of Primasius printed at Lyon in 1537, Evesham bought an English bible printed at Antwerp in the same year,[93] and, as we have seen, the abbot of Hailes was still buying books for the chapter-house library in 1538.[94]

The great majority of the books came from the Continent.[95] The largest number came from Paris; after Paris we have books from Basel, Venice, Lyon, Strasbourg, Cologne and Nuremberg before we arrive at London, Westminster and Oxford. Still fewer – between one and five – came from Abingdon, Alcalá, Antwerp, Augsburg, Bologna, Brescia, Deventer, Fano, Florence, Gouda, Hagenau, Leipzig, Leyden, Mainz, Milan, Naples, Padua, Reggio, Rome, Rouen, Speier, Treviso, Tübingen, Urach and Zwolle. Books printed in England account for a fraction over 10 per cent.

90 I have not included printed books from Scotland, which presents a special case: see M. L. Ford, 'Importation of printed books into England and Scotland', in *CHBB* III. 179–201.

91 BL, IB.118 (Woburn) and IA.17230 (Westminster).

92 Bell, 'Monastic libraries', 247–9 and CBMLC IX. li–lvi.

93 Cambridge, Pembroke Coll., 4.18.8 (Abingdon); Evesham, Almonery Museum (Evesham).

94 See n. 24 above.

95 Ford, 'Importation'.

Printed books inevitably displaced manuscripts. There was, as we have seen, some initial hesitation, some personal copying of printed texts (no doubt to save money),[96] and a few arch-conservatives who remained faithful to the old handwritten tradition;[97] but, in general, a printed edition tended to be regarded as more accurate and more authoritative than its manuscript equivalent, printed editions of an author's collected works were more convenient to use, and – especially in the realm of law[98] – the superior indexing and cross-referencing in the printed volumes led to the disuse and, in many cases, destruction of older manuscript compilations.

Let us now turn from these general considerations and glance at the collections of some specific houses. In a study complementary to this I have taken the reader on a guided tour of the libraries of the Cistercians of Meaux in 1396 and the Premonstratensians of Titchfield in 1400,[99] and there is no need to retrace our steps in this present essay. Let us instead look at the small library of an obscure house in Lincolnshire and see what it has to tell us of the nature of monastic libraries in the period which is here our concern.

The Benedictine priory of St James at Deeping was a cell of Thorney. It was never a large or important house and little is known of its history, but the fourteenth-century register, now BL MS Harley 3658, contains an inventory of its twenty-six books.[100] They present us with a microcosm of a conservative monastic library and deserve more than a passing glance.

The list begins, as was usual for the time, with a bible, and then we find the ubiquitous *Moralia* of Gregory the Great. Gregory's homilies on the Gospels appear later. There are three historical works, Peter Comestor for biblical history, Geoffrey of Monmouth's *Historia regum Britanniae* for British history, and the third book of the much rarer *Liber Eliensis* for local Fenland history. There is a copy of the Rule of St Benedict, a computus, and two books of canon law, the Constitutions of Benedict XII and the *Constitutiones Clementinae*. Overlapping with canon law is the less common *Sacramentale* of William de Montlauzun, given to Deeping by John Swarby, sometime rector of

96 E.g. BL, MS Sloane 779, a 1484 copy of Caxton's *Game and playe of the chesse* and *Cordyal*, see M. C. Erler, *Women, reading, and piety in late medieval England* (Cambridge, 2002), 140–1.

97 See n. 83 above.

98 See Gillespie, 'Syon and the New Learning', 84–5, and CBMLC IX. lv.

99 Bell, 'Monastic libraries', 237–41. On the Titchfield library and Premonstratensian collections in general, see now J. A. Gribbin, *The Premonstratensian order in late medieval England* (Woodbridge, 2001), ch. 5.

100 CBMLC IV. 606–8 (B102).

St Guthlac's in Deeping, and a *tractatus de confessione* by Robert Grosseteste. There is also a *liber de vitiis et virtutibus*, common grammatical / lexicographical works by Hugutio of Pisa and William Brito (both the gift of John Tiryngham, of whom nothing is known) and a small collection of service books.

If we take the contents of this collection, increase the numbers, augment the major patristic and medieval works of exegesis and doctrine, add a few more grammatical texts for the novices (and others too, especially in abbeys offering elementary schooling) and add some classical texts, we have a blueprint for the basic collection of almost any average house of contemplative monks or regular canons at the period in question. Medical and scientific works always present a special case.[101] Deeping also represents those numerous smaller houses whose numbers did not require them to send monks to university, though even here there were exceptions. The poor and tiny priory of Tynemouth, for example, continued to receive novices, send students to Oxford and expand its library into the early sixteenth century – but only under the wing of its mother-house, St Albans.[102]

Let us also note four other points about the Deeping list. First, as with a multitude of other houses, we have a collection of standard or common texts interspersed with rarer items. Second, we may see in the *tractatus de confessione* and *liber de vitiis et virtutibus* a reflection of that 'wave of enthusiasm for confession and penance set in motion by the Fourth Lateran' in 1215.[103] Third, although only three books are known to have been donated to the house, three books out of twenty-two is not insignificant. And fourth, although the list was compiled in the fourteenth century, only two fourteenth-century writers are represented: Benedict XII, who died in 1342, and William de Montlauzun, who died a year later. The Constitutions of the former may have entered the collection as a planned acquisition; the *Sacramentale* came perhaps by chance, as a donation. Apart from the early Fathers, the other writers named are all of the twelfth or thirteenth century. In other words, the collection tended to look to the past, but this is not to say that it was old-fashioned. There was a universal reverence for the standard authorities, and the monks of Deeping might have found their small book collection quite satisfactory for the purposes of spiritual development – especially if none of them was attending university.

101 P. M. Jones, 'Medicine and science', in *CHBB* III. 433–48.
102 J. G. Clark, 'The religious orders in pre-Reformation England', in Clark, *Religious orders*, 10; *MLGB*, 191.
103 M. D. Legge, *Anglo-Norman in the cloisters: the influence of the orders upon Anglo-Norman literature* (Edinburgh, 1950), 69.

Indeed, during the subsequent century there was a significant resurgence of enthusiasm for twelfth-century spiritual writings.[104]

Similarly, if we visit the libraries of the Benedictines of Dover or Canterbury (Christ Church and St Augustine's), or the Augustinians of Leicester, or the Carmelites of Hulne, or the Cistercians of Meaux, or the Premonstratensians of Titchfield, we find ourselves in familiar surroundings. The numbers, obviously, are larger – twenty-six books at Deeping; more than 1,800 at St Augustine's – and the variety of authors is correspondingly greater, but the principles of organisation remain much the same. We are bound to come across a greater number of rare and curious volumes, and it is likewise inevitable that a bibliophile such as William Charyte of Leicester – a man with a deep interest in astronomy – would leave his mark on his library;[105] but the Wycliffite works present at Leicester, or Gerald of Wales's *De instructione principis*, or a work on arboriculture by Nicholas Bollard, and so on, are simply the exceptions that prove the rule.[106] All these libraries, whatever the date of their catalogue, give a certain sense of age – 'tradition' might be a better word; few of the authors they contain are any later than the first half of the fourteenth century.[107] The catalogues themselves, however, are quite a different matter, and are sometimes of greater interest than the collections (see below, chapter 8).

Even a fifteenth-century foundation like Syon remained anchored to its patristic and medieval past. It is true that the order of books listed in the catalogue is new: we begin with grammar and classics, then move on to medicine and astrology and proceed to philosophy, and it not until *distinctio* E that we find the bibles and concordances which, elsewhere, invariably head the list. But the large proportion of printed works (just under a third of the brothers' library) and the obvious impact of the writers of the Renaissance,[108] must not blind us to the abundance and importance of the traditional patristic and medieval authors. *Distinctio* D of the catalogue is devoted to the *Sentences* and the standard commentators. In *distinctio* E there are copies of the Bible, biblical commentaries and concordances, the *Moralia* of Gregory the Great and a large collection of the common *postilla* of Hugh of Saint-Cher and Nicholas

104 G. Constable, 'Twelfth-century spirituality and the later middle ages', in *Medieval and Renaissance Studies* 5 (1971), 27–60, and his 'The popularity of twelfth-century spiritual writers in the late middle ages', in A. Molho and J. A. Tedeschi (eds.), *Renaissance studies in honor of Hans Baron* (Firenze, 1971), 5–28; both repr. in his *Religious life and thought (11th–12th centuries)* (London, 1979), nos. XV and XVI.

105 CBMLC VI. 107–8. For his astronomical instruments, see pp. 324–5.

106 CBMLC VI. 231 (A20.611–2), 237 (A20.645), 269 (A20.858), 270–1 (A20.862f).

107 See also Bell, 'Monastic libraries', 242–3.

108 *Ibid.*, 246, and CBMLC IX. lvi–lxiv.

de Lyra. Just the same sort of material continues through *distinctiones* F, G, H and I. The brothers of Syon might have responded more eagerly than many to the printing revolution and the New Learning (though whether they actually read the new writings of Renaissance scholarship is a moot point),[109] but their library was established on a solid foundation of traditional authorities and there was (if we may quote Pearl Kibre) 'no sharp line of cleavage' between their interests and those of earlier centuries.[110]

With the library of the Austin friars of York we are plunged into the world of university learning.[111] The catalogue, compiled in 1372 and later, begins, as usual, with bibles and biblical commentaries, and then moves on to concordances and the usual authorities. But when we move to the section headed *Historie gencium* we find Caesar's *Gallic Wars*, the *Trojan War* of Dictys Cretensis, and, cheek by jowl with Joachim of Fiore, the *De excidio Troiae historia* of Dares Frigius. There is a large selection of *summae* on the *Sentences*, and a profusion of the *distinctiones*, *sententiae*, *quaestiones*, *quodlibeta*, *repertoria* and *tabulae* so typical of the period. There is an abundance of Aristotle, a whole library of Latin classics, a variety of Arabic writers, and even a few works on magic and divination. It was a formidable collection and well reflects the friars' needs and interests, but it was also an unusual one and owed much to an extraordinary donation by John Ergome, a religious of the York convent in 1372 who went on to become regent at the *studium generale Curie* in Naples.[112] Ergome gave more than 200 books (many containing a substantial number of separate treatises) to the convent, but, as K. W. Humphreys has observed, his 'gift was both outstanding and unusual among private libraries in England in the fourteenth century. With the books already in the convent's own collection it made York potentially one of the great centres for scholarship late in the century.'[113] It also shows what impact a large donation might have.

Books might be acquired by a religious house in three main ways: by copying, purchase or donation. Copying was of fundamental importance in the eleventh and twelfth centuries, but after about 1200 it played a diminishing role; although there was more copying in later centuries than is sometimes supposed (especially by Carthusians and Bridgettines), the quantity of material produced was much less than was either bought or given.[114]

109 Gillespie, 'Syon and the New Learning', esp. 79–80, and CBMLC IX. lvi–lxiv.
110 P. Kibre, 'The intellectual interests reflected in libraries of the fourteenth and fifteenth centuries', *Journal of the History of Ideas* 7 (1946), 297.
111 CBMLC I. 11–154. 112 CBMLC I. xxix–xxx. 113 CBMLC I. xxviii.
114 See n. 74 above, and Bell, 'Monastic libraries', 235–6.

Purchase, in the later middle ages, was common. The friars regularly bought books;[115] Cistercians from Biddlesden, Boxley, Byland, Croxden, Abbey Dore, Furness, Hailes, Holme Cultram, Kirkstall, Meaux, Medmenham, Pipewell, and London, St Mary Graces, were certainly buying them;[116] and much the same can be said for the other orders, though there is a paucity of evidence for the Premonstratensians and Carthusians.[117] Sometimes, as at Syon, the purchases were of second-hand books;[118] sometimes, as at Westminster, the purchases were in-house. That is to say, an older monk with no further need for a particular volume sold his copy to a younger novice of the same abbey.[119] Yet more interesting are the cases of monks purchasing their own personal copies of books which were already to be found in the main collection of the convent.[120] Merely borrowing a copy was clearly deemed inadequate for their needs, though on their deaths, as was the custom, these personal copies reverted to the common collection of their house. There is every reason to believe that purchases increased with the advent of printing, especially in the first half of the sixteenth century, when the variety of titles increased dramatically, prices fell and – as we have seen – printed editions came to be preferred over the older manuscripts. Prior More of Worcester, a prime example, was buying collected editions of Ambrose, Augustine, Basil, Bernard of Clairvaux, Bruno the Carthusian, Cyprian, Fulgentius, Gregory the Great, Hilary, Hugh of Saint-Victor, Jerome, Ludolf the Carthusian, Philo and Seneca, all recently printed in Europe.[121] But volumes such as these were still expensive and certainly beyond the purchasing power of smaller and poorer houses, especially women's houses. On the other hand, of the abbeys visited by John Leland and the anonymous compiler of the Lincolnshire lists,[122] many contained 'numerous printed books of little interest';[123] what these were we do not know.

Donations, therefore (and among donations I include bequests and reversions), were of major importance, and they played an ever increasing role from the thirteenth century on. In the sixteenth century, almost 86 per cent of the holdings of the brothers' library at Syon was the result of donations.[124] There were two reasons for this, one pragmatic, one theological. From a pragmatic

115 Humphreys, *Book provisions*, 19–82. 116 See *MLGB*, 226–321, and *Supplement*, 76–113.
117 Gribbin, *The Premonstratensian order*, 164–5; Doyle, 'Book production', 13.
118 CBMLC IX. xl–xli. On the second-hand book trade in Oxford, see Parkes, 'Provision of books', 418–24.
119 Harvey, 'A novice's life', 67. 120 *Ibid*., 72. 121 CBMLC IV. 662–74 (B117).
122 CBMLC III. xxvii–xxx.
123 See, e.g., CBMLC III. 154–6 (G2, G4–5). There are numerous other examples.
124 C. F. R. de Hamel, *Syon abbey: the library of the Bridgettine nuns and their peregrinations after the Reformation* (London, 1991), 80.

point of view, the larger numbers of books donated reflected the larger numbers of books owned by members of an increasingly literate society. From a theological point of view, the increasing importance of the doctrine of purgatory – and, more importantly, the question of how to escape it – led to an ever greater value being attached to acts of charity, however they were defined. It was possible, therefore, to benefit from one's books while one was alive, and to benefit from them even more when one was dead. We need not be surprised, therefore, to find that Prior Eastry's catalogue of Christ Church, Canterbury, the fourteenth-century catalogue of Ramsey, and probably the lost 1315 catalogue of Norwich,[125] were all arranged by donor.

Donations, however, were as unreliable as they were unregulated. Sometimes, as with the books of John Ergome at York or Cardinal Langham at Westminster,[126] they could transform an entire library. Sometimes they could transform a particular section of it, such as the books on canon law left to the Augustinians of Lanthony by John Lecche in 1355–60.[127] On the other hand, a generous donation might be of little use. The French romances given to the Cistercian abbey of Bordesley in 1306 by the Earl of Warwick were hardly appropriate reading for Cistercian monks, and it is possible that the books were sold and the money put to better use.[128] Donation and reversion also tended to produce large numbers of duplicate copies of common works. If a monastery was also operating as a school, this might be useful; if not, shelves might simply be encumbered with a superabundance of popular piety.

Donations, however, certainly played a fundamental role in enlarging the size of later medieval libraries, and it was a role as fundamental for women as for men. Marilyn Oliva, for example, examined some 3,000 wills from the diocese of Norwich in order to determine the extent of patronage of nunneries by the local parish gentry and yeoman farmers. Her conclusions were that the testators undoubtedly preferred friars to any other group, but that nuns ranked second. The reason, she suggests, is 'the simplicity and poverty of their lives, the services their convents provided, and the absence of the kinds of scandals that plagued their male counterparts'.[129] None of the recorded donations of books, however, is very numerous. The largest of which I am aware is the bequest of twelve books in Latin given to the Cistercian nunnery of Swine

125 CBMLC IV. 330–415 (B67–8); N. R. Ker, 'Medieval manuscripts from Norwich Cathedral Priory', *TCBS* 1 (1949–53), 6.

126 See nn. 112–13 above, and CBMLC IV. 613–25 (B105).

127 CBMLC IV. 94–102 (A17).

128 CBMLC III. 4–10 (Z2). See also, below, 208.

129 M. Oliva, 'Patterns of patronage to female monasteries in the late middle ages', in Clark, *Religious orders*, 157.

by Peter, vicar of Swine, in the late fourteenth or early fifteenth century.[130] Whether the great houses of Shaftesbury, Amesbury, Barking and Dartford ever received larger donations is unknown. If, however, we consider the total number of surviving volumes which certainly or very probably come from nunneries, we find that about twenty-eight of them (about 15 per cent) contain inscriptions indicating that they were received as gifts.[131] Fifteen per cent is by no means negligible, and, for a small and poor nunnery, even a single psalter might have been a useful addition.

Larger libraries naturally demanded more elaborate administration. The eighty books at Cistercian Flaxley at the beginning of the thirteenth century would not have been difficult to administer,[132] but the larger the collection, the greater the need for effective cataloguing and the greater the need for careful control of what books were where. Developments in library cataloguing in the later middle ages are dealt with elsewhere in this volume (chapter 8), but the matter of keeping track of books is of importance here with regard to the ways in which the books were used.

The libraries of the religious orders in the later middle ages could never, of course, be regarded as public lending libraries. Lending books was always a serious matter, theologically as well as economically,[133] and what was lent to whom, and how willingly, varied from house to house. The Dominicans, according to Richard de Bury, were particularly generous in lending their holdings;[134] the Franciscans of Oxford were not.[135] Nevertheless, the development, in the later middle ages, of a greater degree of individualism and privacy was reflected, in religious houses, in the desire for private rooms and workspaces, and, to whatever extent it could be reconciled with communal ownership, the personal possession of books. In the case of the eremitic Carthusians, private chambers and personal possession had always been part of their way of life; but in the case of those orders which emphasised any form of communal living – especially the orders based on the Rule of St Benedict – the idea of a room of one's own was theologically and canonically inappropriate. The trend, however, was inexorable. Private workspaces – carrells – are

130 CBMLC III. 144–6 (Z25). Other donations are listed in Part II of Bell, *What nuns read*.

131 Bell, *What nuns read*, 39. The numbers have been adjusted to take account of the additional books listed in Appendix I of Erler, *Women, reading, and piety*, 139–46.

132 CBMLC III. 15–26 (Z7).

133 L. Smith, 'Lending books: the growth of a medieval question from Langton to Bonaventure', in L. Smith and B. Ward (eds.), *Intellectual life in the middle ages: essays presented to Margaret Gibson* (London, 1992), 265–79. See also below, chapter 9.

134 M. Maclagan (ed.), *Philobiblon Richardi de Bury: the text and translation of E. C. Thomas* (Oxford, 1960), ch. 8; see also Humphreys, *Book provisions*, 34.

135 J. Catto, 'Franciscan learning in England, 1450–1540', in Clark, *Religious orders*, 100.

known at numerous houses from the second half of the thirteenth century;[136] at Christ Church, Canterbury, Prior William Sellyng (1472–94) used them to house (among other things) the Greek books he had introduced into the monastic collection.[137]

Private chambers in religious houses appeared ubiquitously in the course of the fourteenth century, though there are numerous examples from an earlier date. In general, the principle began with enclosed spaces for senior obedientiaries (office-holders), and gradually spread to the rank and file of the other religious. Private chambers were not generally approved (in the first half of the fourteenth century the pope himself, Benedict XII, demanded their removal),[138] but there was no chance of reversing the tide. Nevertheless, the Cistercian General Chapter gave up the struggle only in the seventeenth century.[139] The architectural details of these private rooms are not here our concern – they generally began with the partitioning of dormitories and then, as monastic populations decreased, involved the adaptation and refurbishing of now vacant buildings (especially infirmaries) – what is significant, however, is their relationship to the use of books. If religious were going to study in their own rooms or carrells, it is reasonable to assume that they would want their books with them, and the established practice of returning them to a central depository at the end of every day was grossly inconvenient.

In the later middle ages, therefore, borrowing books became ever more popular, and borrowing was not confined to religious.[140] Books might also be loaned *extra claustrum*, though only to those considered worthy and reliable. Even then, the loan might be secured by a formal indenture with a severe penalty if the books were not returned on time.[141] Sometimes, as at Eynsham in the 1360s, this was not the case, and the abbot was accused of lending books to outsiders without due care.[142] But the general practice of monasteries 'opening out to society' in the later middle ages led to important devotional networks of religious and lay readers which, as M. C. Erler has shown, were as important for women as for men.[143]

A number of library catalogues indicate items on loan,[144] and borrowers' lists are not uncommon. The most important of these, for our present

136 Clark, *Care of books*, 83–92. His list is by no means complete.
137 Bellenger, 'A medieval novice's formation', 38.
138 L. Lekai, *The Cistercians: ideals and reality* (Kent, OH, 1977), 373–4.
139 *Ibid.*, 374.
140 See below, chapter 9.
141 See, e.g., CBMLC IV. 534–7 (B83).
142 CBMLC IV. 153.
143 Erler, *Women, reading, and piety*. See also B. Thompson, 'Monasteries, society and reform in late medieval England', in Clark, *Religious orders*, 183.
144 E.g., CBMLC I. 160 (Hulne Carmelites).

purposes, are the lists from Augustinian Anglesey, dating from 1314, Benedictine Thorney, dating from 1324–30, and St Albans, dating from between 1420 and 1437.[145] At Anglesey, nine canons had thirty-one books in their personal keeping. At Thorney, the names of thirty monks and more than fifty titles are listed, and most of the books were borrowed more than once. This has led to the suggestion 'either that the collection was a small one or that only certain volumes were available for loan'.[146] We might also note that the books borrowed tended to be standard patristic or twelfth-century works: texts by Ambrose, Augustine, Jerome, Cassian, Ephraem Latinus, Isidore, Bernard of Clairvaux, Hugh of Saint-Victor, Peter Comestor, and the like, though one monk was studying the Aristotelian *Logica nova* and another was reading the *Roman de sept sages de Rome* in French.

Even more interesting is the St Albans list, in which we find the titles of books borrowed by seven monks of the abbey. The numbers range from two to twenty-five. At the time, the total number of monks at St Albans was about fifty, and if many or most of them had books on loan, safely secured in their own cells, the main book collection must have been sadly depleted.[147] In other words, there can be no doubt that the development of the private chamber and private workspace had a profound impact on the housing of books in the later middle ages, and it is quite possible that, in some houses, there was little left in the main collections but outmoded volumes of little interest.

Sometimes, of course, books were borrowed and not returned, and this may have been a particular problem among those religious who attended university. When Alan Kirkton, a Benedictine monk of Spalding, went up to Oxford in the early 1430s, he took with him twelve books from the priory library; in 1438, three years after he had left Oxford, they had still not been returned.[148] But this should not surprise us, students and book theft have been bedfellows for centuries.

Nevertheless, despite the scattering of books among individual religious and its inevitable effect upon the main collection, in the first half of the fifteenth century (which saw remarkable cultural and intellectual advances) there was a spate of activity among librarians.[149] But although their main interest seems to have been recataloguing older volumes rather than purchasing

145 CBMLC VI. 3–5 (A1) (Anglesey); CBMLC IV. 597–604 (B100) (Thorney); 554–63 (B87) (St Albans).

146 CBMLC IV. 599; see also Humphreys, 'Thirteenth-century cultural changes', 8, and R. Sharpe, below, 223 and n. 17.

147 CBMLC IV. 555.

148 CBMLC IV. 592–3 (B95), and Bell, 'Monastic libraries', 234.

149 See also below, 240.

new works by contemporary authors,[150] in many houses (depending, naturally, upon resources) we see the building of new *librariae* in response to changing circumstances and changing times.

In the later middle ages, we might add, *libraria*, as the designation for a dedicated book-room, seems to become ever more popular.[151] The old classical term *bibliotheca* can still be found, but the increasing use of the Middle English *librarie* and its variants may have played a role in this matter. *Libraria* as a bookshop can be found in classical Latin, but only became common as a term for a book-room in a monastery from the late fourteenth century, although it had been used earlier to refer more generally to a collection of books.[152] Between 1381 and 1500, the term is used to refer to a book-room by the Carmelites of Aylesford, the London Greyfriars, the Benedictines of Bury, Rochester, St Albans and Westminster (and also Gloucester College, Oxford), the Premonstratensians of Titchfield, the Augustinians of Leicester and the Bridgettines of Syon.[153] The term usually refers to the main book-room of the house, though at Leicester, as may have been common elsewhere, the *libraria* was only one of a number of places in which books were kept. Others were the *scriptoria*, refectory and other unnamed locations.[154] Even after the building of the new *libraria* at St Albans in the first half of the fifteenth century, the abbot still had his own collection, as did the sacrist and the archdeacon.[155]

At an earlier date, the usual place for books was an *armarium* or *armariolum* in the north cloister, but it did not take long before the increasing size of collections necessitated additional space. The main collection of the Cistercians, for example, spread from the *armarium* to part of the sacristy, then, in some cases (Furness and Hailes are good examples), from the sacristy to part of the chapter room, and thence (in Europe at least)[156] to the construction of new libraries. The separate book-room at Cleeve, tucked in between the sacristy and the chapter room and dating from the mid-thirteenth century, appears to be unique among the English Cistercians.[157]

150 As I have observed in 'Monastic libraries', 242, fifteenth-century library catalogues are not catalogues of fifteenth-century books.

151 *Librarium* is a rare alternative: see, e.g., CBMLC IV. 169.

152 See above, 14. The account by Folcuin (d. 990) of the deeds of the monk Gunbert, in his cartulary of Saint-Bertin, contains an unusually early use of the term, *PL* 136, 1222C.

153 CBMLC I. 157, 216; CBMLC III. 183; CBMLC IV. 48, 464, 564, 611; CBMLC VI. 104, 360; CBMLC IX. xlii, xlv. These are no more than examples. On the library rooms of the monastic colleges at Oxford, see above, 32–4.

154 CBMLC VI. 105–6. Such a scattering of books was by no means uncommon: see above, 16–18.

155 CBMLC IV. 543.

156 Bell, 'Library of Cîteaux', 123–4.

157 Other early examples may be found in Germany and Scandinavia.

But from the later fourteenth and early fifteenth centuries the situation changed dramatically. A new *libraria* was built at Worcester in about 1376–7 (although its precise function is not known). Library rooms were built in the other great monasteries and cathedrals, both Benedictine and secular: Bury St Edmunds, Canterbury, Durham, Exeter, Gloucester, Hereford, Lichfield, Lincoln, London (St Paul's), St Albans, Salisbury, Wells, Winchester and York.[158] It is at this period that we see the transformation of a book-room from being a simple storage space (or, more accurately, one of many storage spaces) to a library as a place for reading and study, something which had been anticipated by the friars.[159] At St Albans, for example, the new library had reading desks to which were chained selected volumes,[160] and at Syon the brothers and sisters each had their own library (*library* or *lybrary* in Middle English), where silence was to be kept 'in tyme of study' for the brothers and 'whyls any suster is there alone in recordyng of her redynge' for the sisters.[161]

The principle behind these new, large study spaces may have conflicted with the idea of personal possession. The provision of a central location for books and desks on which to study them may have moved some to question why any religious should have his or her own collection. This might well have been in the mind of Abbot William Curteys of Bury St Edmunds (1429–46) when he ordered all books in the personal keeping of his monks to be returned to the conventual library.[162] Likewise, at some time between 1396 and 1401, Abbot John Moote of St Albans ordered the return of the abbey's books from its cell at Hertford.[163] In this case, the new library had not yet been built, but the abbot seems to have been gathering all the books together in preparation for it.

Much, naturally, depended on circumstances. Small, impoverished houses (especially women's houses) could never have afforded new libraries, and, since they were unlikely to benefit from lavish donations, they presumably made do with what they had. Changes in monastic institutions (such as the decline of lay-brotherhood among the Cistercians) and changes in monastic population (as a consequence of the Black Death, for example) left many monasteries with empty spaces and unused rooms, but how the inhabitants accommodated to the new circumstances varied depending on time and place. Even in houses

158 See, e.g., D. Knowles, *The religious orders in England*, 3 vols. (Cambridge, 1955), II. 352–3.
159 Humphreys, 'Thirteenth-century cultural changes', 15–16, and his *Book provisions*.
160 See CBMLC IV. 543. On chaining, Streeter remains the classic study, but much has been added to our knowledge since 1931.
161 J. Hogg (ed.), *The rewyll of seynt Sauioure* (Salzburg, 1980), III. 45 (brothers); IV. 72 (sisters).
162 CBMLC IV. 47. 163 CBMLC IV. 552.

with substantial accumulations, much would have depended on the personal initiative of the librarian. In monasteries with large collections and interested librarians – Thomas Swalwell at Durham,[164] for example, or John Whitfield at Dover[165] – we may see major developments in librarianship, cataloguing, archival work, bibliography and monastic studies. But we are wholly ignorant of what happened at a host of houses, from Benedictine Abbotsbury, whose library is commemorated only by Leland and three surviving manuscripts,[166] to Yarmouth Carmelites, of whose library we know nothing whatever, though the convent was enlarged in 1378 and John Tylney, prior of the house from about 1430 to 1455, was a distinguished professor of divinity at Cambridge and a respected author in his own right.[167]

On the other hand, with the exception of a few houses like Durham or Worcester, the number of surviving books tells us nothing about the size of a collection and little about its overall contents. Indeed, it is difficult to overemphasise the danger of drawing too firm conclusions from too little evidence. Take, for example, the case of the Augustinian priory of St Peter at Thurgarton.[168] Until recently, the only memorials of the library were two manuscripts and an early printed book,[169] but the identification of a fifteenth-century booklist in BL, MS Sloane 3548, has revolutionised our knowledge of the collection. The list reveals an extraordinarily interesting range of books, though quite how we are to interpret them is a moot point. There are standard theological works, biblical *distinctiones*, and some common chronicles and volumes of canon law. But among the *vitae sanctorum* we find not only the Lives of Wulfric of Haslebury and Godric of Finchale, but also, and much more unusually, Lives of Elizabeth of Spalbeek, Christina the Astonishing and Mary of Oignies. A number of the devotional works listed are likewise uncommon, texts by Mechthild of Hackeborn, Catherine of Siena, and Birgitta of Sweden, and treatises by Richard Rolle, Walter Hilton, Henry Suso and Jan van Ruusbroec. There are a number of medical works, including texts by John of Parma, John Arderne and John of Gaddesen. Astronomical works include Chaucer's *Treatise on the astrolabe* in English and other works on the astrolabe in Latin. There is also a *liber de sortibus et alkymia fratris Carmelite*.

It is not certain that this intriguing list comes from Thurgarton, though it seems very probable, and, if we did not know its provenance, we might have guessed that it represented the collection of a Carthusian house. It

164 A. J. Piper, 'Dr Thomas Swalwell, monk of Durham, archivist and bibliophile (d. 1539)', in Carley and Tite, *Books and collectors*, 71–100.
165 CBMLC V. 166 CBMLC IV. 3–4 (B1). 167 *VCH*, *Norfolk*, II (1906), 437.
168 CBMLC VI. 414–26 (A36). 169 *MLGB*, 190, *Supplement*, 65.

certainly reflects a significant interest in later medieval devotional reading, and a careful examination of the late fifteenth-century catalogue of Leicester Abbey reinforces this conclusion. But, as Teresa Webber has pointed out, 'it would be dangerous to generalize about the spiritual vigour of English Augustinian houses during this period from this evidence alone'.[170] That is true. But, however we are to interpret it, the Thurgarton list is a salutary reminder of the danger of extrapolating from too little information, and some of the conclusions we have drawn in this chapter will undoubtedly need to be amended in the wake of further research. Yet if there is one thing which stands out among the revelations of recent scholarship, it is the re-evaluation of the nature and practice of the religious life at the end of the middle ages. The old myth of lax and decadent religious who 'turned lazie, then, getting wealth, waxed wanton, and at last endowed with superfluity, became notoriously wicked'[171] has now been laid to rest – or should have been laid to rest – and the research of the last several years has clearly revealed what J. G. Clark has called an 'ambitious re-invention of monastic studies',[172] which transformed the social and intellectual climate of religious houses in the later middle ages.

This revitalisation of religious life is reflected in the history of later medieval libraries. The nature and use of books, their means of acquisition, their housing and cataloguing, their lending and borrowing, and so on, all alike reflect the changing intellectual climate; and although the prurient will not find it difficult to find examples of true decadence, they are, in general, the exceptions that prove the rule. Monastic reformers over the centuries, writes Christopher Harper-Bill, 'had argued that the primitive observance of the various orders was a norm from which there should be no deviation, but in reality, in an age when recruitment was so wide, and perhaps so indiscriminate in terms of commitment to spiritual excellence, it was hardly surprising that the life of the cloister should be influenced by its wider environment'.[173] Book collections, too, do not develop in a vacuum. The location, contents, housing and operation of the collections of all religious houses in the sixteenth century were obviously

170 T. Webber, 'Latin devotional texts and the books of the Augustinian canons of Thurgarton Priory and Leicester Abbey in the late middle ages', in Carley and Tite, *Books and collectors*, 35.

171 T. Fuller, *The church-history of Britain; from the birth of Jesus Christ, until the year MDCXLVIII* (London, 1655), 265.

172 Clark, 'The religious orders', 12.

173 C. Harper-Bill, *The pre-Reformation church in England, 1400–1530*, rev. edn (London, 1996), 39.

different from their location and so on in the years immediately following their foundation, but to say that the new situation was better or worse than the old is a modern value judgement of little relevance. Times had changed, and religious life had changed with them. What might have happened had the Dissolution not occurred, and the new flame of religious fervour not been quenched, is a matter for visionaries, not for scholars.

6

College and university book collections and libraries

ROGER LOVATT

At some point during the middle years of the fifteenth century a monk of the Yorkshire Cistercian house of Meaux sold two theological texts, one a work by Aquinas. Appropriately enough, given the character of the two books, the purchaser would seem to have been a Cambridge academic, William Wylflete, sometime fellow and later master of Clare College. Subsequently Wylflete came to doubt whether the monk possessed the authority to dispose of the volumes and he returned them to the community of Meaux. Shorn of its apparently happy outcome, the story is characteristic and could be repeated many times over. Prior to 1500, former monastic books were to be found in considerable numbers throughout the collegiate libraries of both Oxford and Cambridge.[1] But the transaction was also emblematic. It is a commonplace in the history of later medieval Europe that the previous intellectual leadership of the monasteries had tended to pass into the hands of the universities, and indeed that in some respects monastic intellectual life had become dependent on that of the universities. The change is symbolised in the foundation of monastic houses of study at the universities and in the way in which, under papal direction, the most talented monks of the day came to spend their most formative years at university. Many signs of this transition are apparent in the history of libraries. The major formative age of the monastic libraries had now in a sense largely passed. Of course, the change was not immediate or total. Monastic libraries continued to grow, often substantially. A number of monasteries, particularly the larger ones, continued to be involved in the production of books, sometimes from their own resources but perhaps more frequently on a commercial basis.[2] The activities of Henry de Kirkestede at

1 Bodleian, MS Digby 77, fol. 147^{v}. For the general phenomenon, and many Oxford examples, see N. R. Ker, 'Oxford college libraries before 1500', in his *Books, collectors and libraries*, 314–16.

2 J. G. Clark, 'The religious orders in pre-Reformation England', in Clark (ed.), *The religious orders in pre-Reformation England* (Woodbridge, 2002), 3–33, esp. 23.

Bury St Edmunds in the 1360s and 1370s and of John Whitfield at Dover Priory in the 1380s remind us that dedicated bibliographical activity persisted and flourished in some monastic houses.[3] In a few cases, such as the Bridgettine community at Syon or the new charterhouses, totally new monastic libraries often of a rather different character were being established.[4] Yet such well-informed men as Richard de Bury, bishop of Durham, writing in the 1340s, and a century or so later Thomas Gascoigne, sometime chancellor of Oxford, were equally clear that an earlier impetus to monastic book production had by their day markedly diminished.[5] Hence the role of creating, stocking and managing libraries had to a degree passed in later medieval England into the hands of the universities. This change is apparent in the way in which the monasteries came to use their monk students and their university houses of study as channels through which to acquire the new academic texts which were now being produced and circulated within the universities.[6]

In the history of libraries, change is rarely decisive or rapid. In this case the friars, particularly in their houses of study, played a crucially formative and innovatory role in both library provision and organisation. The corporate production in the early years of the fourteenth century of the *Registrum Anglie*, appropriately by the Franciscans of Oxford, in itself provides the most striking evidence of their creative and organisational bibliographical expertise.[7] The new university libraries owed a great deal to mendicant example. Nevertheless, in creating their new libraries the universities also deployed methods of acquiring books and of regulating them which were both different from those of the monks and a development of those of the friars. They were methods which naturally reflected the distinct demands of a predominantly academic environment.

A library was central to the purpose of an academic institution in a way that it was not for a monastery. Of course, books were fundamental to monastic life; the tag 'claustrum sine armario castrum sine armamentario' ('a cloister without a book collection is a castle without an armoury') embodied a deep truth derived from the words of St Benedict himself. Yet monastic attitudes to books, characterised by the annual distribution envisaged in many customaries, were not at heart those of academics. For monks, books were an aid to

3 CBMLC IV. 44–5; CBMLC V. 6–13. 4 CBMLC IX.

5 M. Maclagan (ed.), *Philobiblon Ricardi de Bury* (Oxford, 1960), 52–7; T. Gascoigne, *Loci e libro veritatum*, ed. J. E. T. Rogers (Oxford, 1881), 73.

6 M. B. Parkes, 'Provision of books', *HUO* II. 407–83, esp. 448–55.

7 CBMLC II; Parkes, 'Provision of books', 431–45; K. W. Humphreys, *The book provisions of the mediaeval friars, 1215–1400* (Amsterdam, 1964).

devotion; for scholars, they were of the essence. Within the university environment books multiplied rapidly. University study was distinctively based on the close reading of texts and their comparison with other texts. The most characteristic form of academic writing was the commentary on another text. This mentality is exemplified by the way in which many founders saw it as part of the very act of foundation to provide their colleges with a collection of books. Physical and intellectual endowment went hand in hand. Even more was this appropriate because, for most within the universities, unlike those within a monastery or friary, access to books for long depended on their own individual initiative. Institutional provision did not exist. Colleges were for a favoured few and substantial university libraries did not appear until the fifteenth century. Hence as early as the 1280s Bishop Hugh of Balsham, the founder of the first Cambridge college, bequeathed to it *libros . . . plures theologice et quasdam aliarum scientiarum*; that is, well before his new college possessed its own hall and some 350 years before the building of its own chapel.[8] Almost 200 years later the process culminated, as it were, when Bishop Waynflete prefaced a visit to his new foundation of Magdalen by sending the college some 800 volumes.[9] Naturally, the details varied. Bishop Bateman's gifts to Trinity Hall included books which were close to him. One, he records, he had studied since he was a youth; some he described as fine volumes; others were his own textbooks. Indeed, so loth was he to part with some, particularly the works of theology, that he kept them by his side until his death, while carefully distinguishing those books which were eventually destined for his college.[10] On the other hand Henry VI seems to have simply diverted to his new foundation of King's College books which had previously belonged to Humfrey, duke of Gloucester, and were probably intended for Oxford, and which had by chance fallen into the king's hands following the duke's arrest and death.[11] Nevertheless the phenomenon was ubiquitous, as true for William of Wykeham and New College or Archbishop Chichele and All Souls at Oxford as it was for Edward II and King's Hall or Robert Wodelarke and St Catharine's at Cambridge:[12] so much so that even its aristocratic foundress gave to Clare College books as academic in flavour as a volume of Gregory IX's *Decretales* and Bradwardine's *De causa Dei contra Pelagium*, and a century and a half later

8 Bodleian, MS Laud misc. 647, fol. 175r.

9 V. Davis, *William Waynflete: bishop and educationalist* (Woodbridge, 1993), 91–5.

10 CBMLC x. 634–47.

11 *Ibid.*, 283–4.

12 CBMLC x. 317–18, 593–602; A. F. Leach, 'Wykeham's books at New College', *Collectanea*, 3rd ser., OHS 32 (1896), 213–44; N. R. Ker, *Records of All Souls College Library, 1437–1600*, OBS, n.s. 16 (1971), 3–17, 122.

the Lady Margaret was to follow suit at Christ's.[13] What is more, in a process remarkably similar to that in which sub-tenants also customarily made benefactions to their lord's monastic foundation, so the more lowly associates of a college founder tended to follow his example in this respect. The sentiment is most clearly articulated by William Byconyll, a lawyer within the Canterbury administration and one of Chichele's executors, who bequeathed books to All Souls specifically in recompense for the benefits which the archbishop had conferred on him.[14] Henry Penwortham, one of Chichele's most faithful servants, his registrar and treasurer, also made the same point by leaving books to the archbishop himself for transmission to his college. Similar sentiments doubtless motivated the gifts of books by other members of Chichele's circle, such as John Lyndfeld and John Lovelich, who were also both leading lawyers in the Canterbury administration, or Richard Andrewe, not only sometime official of the court of Canterbury and another of Chichele's executors but also the first warden of All Souls.[15] Exactly the same pattern is visible at New College, where two of William of Wykeham's relations gave books to his college, as did both his former official and his former chancellor in the Winchester diocese and even one who had served as his clerk in the office of the Privy Seal.[16] Here, as elsewhere, a powerful founder brought to his college not only his own resources but those of his retinue.

The universities of Oxford and Cambridge, of course, had no founders in a collegiate sense and their libraries were hence unable to benefit from this form of initial benefaction. Similarly, they lacked the funds to be able to compensate from their own resources. Indeed, it is symptomatic that the libraries of the oldest colleges long antedated those of the two universities. Oxford appears to have possessed perhaps a handful of volumes by about 1300, but a series of subsequent attempts during the fourteenth century to establish a library proper either came to nothing or foundered on collegiate imperialism. What is more, these efforts were at times made by external episcopal patrons rather than by the scholars themselves.[17] As a result the university library was not fully established until 1412. The story at Cambridge is similar. A few books given to the university during the course of the fourteenth century did not

13 CBMLC x. 110–17, 674–5.

14 Ker, *Records of All Souls College Library*, 106, 160; *BRUO* I. 330.

15 Ker, *Records of All Souls College Library*, 108, 122; *BRUO* I. 34–5; II. 1167, 1190; III. 1459–60.

16 *BRUO* I. 635–6 (John Elmer); II. 1042–3 (Robert Keton); III. 1925 (William de Tyrington), 2110–12 (John Wykeham, Nicholas de Wykeham); Leach, 'Wykeham's books at New College', 237–41.

17 Parkes, 'Provision of books', 470–2; A. C. de la Mare and S. Gillam (eds.), *Duke Humfrey's library and the divinity school, 1488–1988* (Oxford, 1988), 14–15.

start to take shape as a recognisable library until the 1420s. In contrast, both Exeter and Merton had built themselves new libraries by 1385. New College owned at least 300 books when its founder died in 1404 and at about the same time the library of Merton amounted to some 500 volumes.[18] At Cambridge the catalogue of the university library, which records the development of its collection between about 1424 and *c.* 1440, lists some 122 volumes. This may be a slight underestimate, but a few years earlier the library of Peterhouse contained more than twice as many books.[19]

Yet, despite this contrast in the way in which they were initially established, the subsequent history of the growth of both university and college libraries follows an almost identical pattern. In a word, both relied almost entirely on gifts of books, virtually exclusively from their former members. Hence it embodies a universal truth that the first catalogue of the Cambridge university library should be headed 'Registrum librorum per varios benefactores . . . collatorum'.[20] No university or college statute obliged its members to donate their books. The closest we come to a formal statement of obligation occurs in Archbishop Kilwardby's visitation injunctions to the fellows of Merton in 1276, an obligation which may well be derived from his own experience of the mendicant concept of corporate ownership but individual possession. The archbishop laid down that any books brought to the college by a fellow, or acquired during his residence, should remain there. If a fellow died, a sufficient number of his books might be sold to settle his debts but the residue should remain the property of the college. If a fellow entered the religious life, his books should revert to the college. Finally if a fellow left the college and took a living, then he might retain the use of his books for his lifetime but only on the understanding that they would be bequeathed to the college or a 'just compensation' paid in lieu.[21] The archbishop's words, although never repeated elsewhere in official, legislative terms, represent a leitmotiv in the history of university libraries during the period. Their moral force weighed on all sorts and conditions of members of the universities and manifested itself in a multitude of different ways. Indeed, this reliance on the generosity, or sense of obligation, of their former members to sustain their expansion is one of the most striking features of these libraries, distinguishing them in turn from their monastic and mendicant counterparts.

18 Leach, 'Wykeham's books at New College', 213–44; *Books, collectors and libraries*, 304, 312.
19 CBMLC x. 7–31, 443–548.
20 *Ibid.*, 9; see also CBMLC x. 110–18 (Christ's), 133–40 (Clare), 416–42 (Pembroke).
21 H. W. Garrod (ed.), *Merton College: injunctions of Archbishop Kilwardby, 1276* (Oxford, 1929), 14.

Its importance can be expressed in simple numerical terms. In the relatively short time between its establishment in the 1420s and the end of the period, the university library at Cambridge is known to have received gifts of books from some sixty individuals.[22] The university could call on a wide field of potential benefactors. Yet even a moderately sized college such as Peterhouse could also attract book donations from about the same number of donors; and at Pembroke and Gonville Hall the count of known donors is only slightly less at about fifty.[23] The picture at Oxford is identical. The first known donation of books was made to Balliol by 1276, little more than a decade after the college was founded.[24] Both of the first two wardens of Merton gave books to their college, and when a list of 250 of the college's theological books was compiled in the middle of the fourteenth century it revealed that they were derived from no fewer than forty-nine separate donors.[25] Merton was exceptionally well endowed, but even a more modest college such as Oriel shows a similar pattern with well over forty identifiable donors.[26] The same picture holds good for later colleges. Books were given regardless, apparently, of the scale of the founder's original provision of a library. Indeed, there are some signs that, the more wealthy and distinguished a college, the more it attracted benefactors; to him that hath, indeed. Hence, despite William of Wykeham's generous initial provision of books, by the end of the fifteenth century New College had acquired at least 300 more books from over fifty benefactors, and the number of donors was only slightly smaller in the case of All Souls, a college whose origins were even more exalted.[27] Yet a much more modest college like Lincoln could also be given books by more than thirty individuals during the seventy-odd years after its foundation.[28]

The phenomenon was ubiquitous and fundamental, and essentially unchanging until the end of the fifteenth century. Nevertheless, it is possible to distinguish some shifts of emphasis. The overwhelming majority of donations tended to consist initially of a handful of volumes, often only one or two books, and they were made to a single beneficiary. This continued to

22 CBMLC x. 5. 23 *Ibid.*, 445, 372, 256.

24 R. A. B. Mynors, *Catalogue of the manuscripts of Balliol College, Oxford* (Oxford, 1963), xii.

25 F. M. Powicke, *The medieval books of Merton College* (Oxford, 1931), 3, 95.

26 The Oriel figures are derived from C. L. Shadwell, 'The catalogue of the library of Oriel College in the 14th century', *Collectanea*, 1, OHS 5 (1885), 59–70; and G. C. Richards and H. E. Salter (eds.), *The Dean's Register of Oriel, 1446–1661*, OHS 84 (1926), 386–97.

27 R. W. Hunt, 'The medieval library', in J. Buxton and P. Williams (eds.), *New College, Oxford, 1379–1979* (Oxford, 1979), 317–45, esp. 323–4. The figures for All Souls are derived from Ker, *Records of All Souls College Library*, esp. 105–11, 122–5.

28 Figures for Lincoln are largely derived from R. Weiss, 'The earliest catalogues of the library of Lincoln College', *BLR* 8 (1937), 343–59.

be the case, but towards the end of the fourteenth century two new forms of gift began to appear. A few much larger benefactions were made and gifts were at times distributed among several institutions. The process began in the 1370s and 1380s when Bishop Rede of Chichester gave more than 130 books to Merton, another 100 to New College and smaller collections to Balliol, Exeter, Oriel and Queen's.[29] Donations on a similar scale were mirrored elsewhere. The most spectacular example was undoubtedly the gift of well over 280 volumes made by Humfrey, duke of Gloucester, to Oxford in the 1430s and 1440s, but scarcely less impressive was Bishop Gray's donation of more than 180 books to Balliol.[30] And at Cambridge Archbishop Rotherham's gift to the university library must have amounted to about 200 volumes.[31] These were great men with massive resources, but men of lesser means also gave what must have represented almost their complete libraries. Thomas Markaunt, who remained a mere fellow of Corpus Christi until his death, left seventy-five books to his college.[32] Walter Crome, whose ecclesiastical career rose no higher than a London rectory, gave almost 100 volumes to Cambridge, as well as a handful to Gonville Hall, and another theologian of similar status, John Warkworth, master of Peterhouse, endowed his college with more than fifty volumes.[33] Lesser men also emulated Bishop Rede's example in starting to distribute quite small collections of books among several beneficiaries. Hence in Oxford Thomas Gascoigne gave small numbers of books to All Souls, Balliol, Lincoln, Oriel and New College, and in Cambridge this was matched by John Hurt's equally modest benefactions to the University Library, Clare, Godshouse and King's.[34] Yet, whatever minor changes in their pattern may have occurred, the essential role of donations remained constant.

Why were so many made? Evidence for them normally appears in wills (although the ultimate destination of such bequests was not always straightforward), in donors' lists or inscribed on the books themselves, and usually it is merely the fact of donation that is recorded. But sometimes conditions were attached. The institutional library might be merely a reversionary beneficiary, with the use of a book passing initially to another for his lifetime.[35] Donors frequently specified that their gift must be placed in the chained library or, more

29 Powicke, *Medieval books of Merton College*, 87–92; *BRUO* III. 1556–60.

30 The best account of Duke Humfrey's gifts, and the sources for it, is in *Duke Humfrey's library and the divinity school*, 18–49. For Bishop Gray, see Mynors, *Manuscripts of Balliol College*, xxiv–xlv; *BRUO* II. 809–14.

31 *BRUC*, 489–91; CBMLC X. 74, 728–9; Oates, *CUL*, 37–50.

32 CBMLC X. 184–207.

33 *Ibid.*, 33, 683–4, 534–48, 743–4; *BRUC*, 168, 618–19.

34 *BRUO* II. 745–8; CBMLC X. 703–4.

35 E.g. CBMLC X. 430 (no. 113), 470 (nos. 107, 109).

rarely, that it should be available for borrowing.[36] One donor even stipulated that his gift might be lent only to one of his relations.[37] Walter Crome reserved the right to sell any of the books that he had bequeathed to Cambridge if he needed financial support during his last illness.[38] The donor of a medical text to New College laid down that any fellow studying medicine should be allowed to take the book outside the college when summoned to visit the sick, and a benefactor of Magdalen left books to two fellows of the college on condition that they occupied his present room.[39] More normal were two related stipulations. The first was designed to ensure the safe keeping of the gift and took both practical and spiritual form. The donor's books were often, although not invariably, to be chained and an anathema was pronounced against those who alienated them. Such provisions were widespread and had the incidental but important consequence that, with the accumulation of donations over time, the chained books tended to increase in numbers in relation to those that could be borrowed. But this provision represented much more than the donors' natural desire to safeguard their benefactions. It was closely related to the second stipulation, namely that in return for gifts of books the college or university – and even the individual reader – should pray for the repose of the souls of the donors. In this context books lost meant prayers lost, and the chaining of one's benefaction was not merely a matter of library administration but a contribution to one's eternal salvation. At times these concerns were articulated in unusually precise terms. In his will of 1458 Robert Rooke bequeathed sixteen books to be chained in Balliol library but on condition that his name was inscribed on the college's *Rotulus Benefactorum*, which was read out every Friday in chapel after Antiphon.[40] Some were less self-regarding. When the rector of Stoke Bruerne left a book to the University of Oxford he requested prayers not only for himself but also for his parents and even for his parishioners.[41] An inscription of gift which, although lengthy, can stand for hundreds of others in its essential sentiments is attached to one of the massive series of volumes of the works of Hugh of Saint-Cher bestowed on Exeter

36 E.g. Balliol College, MS 197, fol. 4^{v}; CBMLC x. 726–7. Compare CBMLC x. 658–9 (Ayscogh), 744 (Warmyster).

37 Bodleian, MS Auct. F.5.28 (erased inscription); *MLGB*, 292 (Oriel College: Cobuldik).

38 CBMLC x. 33, 683–4.

39 Hunt, 'The medieval library', 333; W. D. Macray (ed.), *Register of the members of St Mary Magdalen College* 8 vols. (London, 1894–1915), I. 107–8.

40 *BRUO* III. 1589; A. B. Emden, *The last pre-Reformation 'Rotulus benefactorum' and list of obits of Balliol College* (Oxford, 1967), 3.

41 Oxford, St John's College, MS 172, fol. 322^{v}; *Duke Humfrey's library and the divinity school*, 55 (illus.), 56, 58; *BRUO* I. 29 (Alward).

College during the 1450s and 1460s by Roger Keys, precentor of Exeter Cathedral. The books were given to the rector and fellows to be chained in their library for the use of the fellows and their successors '*in eodem studere volencium*'; in return the college undertook for all time to celebrate the donor's obit with sung exequies and a requiem mass. The books were not to be removed from the library without the express consent of the rector and all the fellows, absent as well as present. Those who did so were anathematised not only by the authority of Almighty God and of the blessed apostles, Peter and Paul, but finally by the bishop of Exeter himself.[42]

This combination of practical charity – support for poor scholars – and spiritual insurance brings us to the core of the motivation of donors. The combination is exemplified by the way in which at both Oxford and Cambridge the university librarians were also its chaplains, entrusted with the joint, indeed inseparable, task of caring for its books and praying for the repose of the souls of its benefactors.[43] And it was this same combination which, because it embodied some of the deepest spiritual aspirations of the day, proved so attractive to benefactors and explains in turn why colleges were so successful in attracting gifts of every sort that they came to dominate the life of the two universities.[44] Of course, more immediate considerations played their part. The vast majority of donors were former members of the institutions that they enriched and many felt genuine gratitude and affection towards them. In some respects the universities acted as social solvents in the period, a means by which men of relatively humble origin might rise to the highest positions in church and state. No wonder that Cardinal Morton left a substantial sum to enable poor boys to attend both Oxford and Cambridge. On a lesser scale many clearly shared his sentiments. No doubt practical concerns also weighed on some. A measure of social emulation can explain why gifts of books from great men so often stimulated lesser gifts from others. And the enforced celibacy of so many members of the two universities meant that there were no familial rivals for their generosity. Yet entirely characteristic, if exuberantly expressed, were the words which John Somerset inscribed in his gift of a copy of Avicenna's *Canon* to his former college of Pembroke: 'Blessed therefore be that noble Hall,

42 Exeter College, MSS 51–68, esp. MS 53, fol. 1^v: A. G. Watson, *A descriptive catalogue of the medieval manuscripts of Exeter College, Oxford* (Oxford, 2000), 85–108.

43 H. P. Stokes, *The chaplains and the chapel of the University of Cambridge*, Cambridge Antiquarian Society, Octavo ser. 41 (1906), esp. 1–30; S. Gibson (ed.), *Statuta antiqua Universitatis Oxoniensis* (Oxford, 1931), 165–6, 216–21.

44 On this topic, central to the theme of this chapter, see R. Lovatt, 'The triumph of the colleges in late medieval Oxford and Cambridge', *History of Universities* 14 (1998, for 1995–6), 95–142.

in which I was educated as a pupil, and its most devout Foundress, the Lady Mary of St Pol; may she live with Christ in eternity; thanks be to God.'[45]

Needless to say, gifts were not always as spontaneous as they might seem. Donations might be directly solicited. Richard Caudray, warden of King's Hall, petitioned Henry VI as its patron for a grant of books, citing the college's poverty, the inadequacy of its library and the resulting damage to the scholars' academic progress. His plea was rewarded, although only with a collection of books captured some years earlier at the siege of Meaux by Henry V.[46] Sometimes the approach was more subtle. The sustained and flattering courtship of Humfrey, duke of Gloucester, by Oxford was clearly as much intended to inspire future gifts of books as it was to express gratitude for past donations.[47] But, as the eventual fate of Humfrey's library proved, death threw all such expectations into disarray. Hence many of the most exigent letters were addressed not to donors but to their executors and associates, claiming that gifts had been promised but that death had supervened. As early as about 1320 Oxford was writing in these terms in an attempt to obtain the books of its deceased former chancellor.[48] And in 1437 the university was seeking the assistance of its most powerful friends in what seems to have been an unsuccessful effort to secure some books supposedly promised to it seventeen years previously by Henry V.[49] Similar letters occur frequently in the university's abundant correspondence during the rest of the century, and in 1470 Oxford and Cambridge seem to have been rivals in pursuit of their claims to books belonging to the recently executed earl of Worcester.[50] Colleges followed suit. In 1484 the fellows of Merton wrote to the brother and executor of a former fellow claiming that he had frequently promised them his copy of Bredon's *Trifolium* and asking that it should be given to the college.[51] Similarly, inducements were available which offered benefactors more worldly recognition than the promise of prayers. Just as Oxford decreed in 1412 that its new library should contain a grand, conspicuous board on which the names of its benefactors were to be finely inscribed lest their memory should be forgotten, so the large windows of the new libraries of the fifteenth century, at Balliol, New

45 Cambridge, Pembroke Coll., MS 137, fol. 389ᵛ. 46 CBMLC X. 351–60.

47 H. Anstey (ed.), *Epistolae academicae Oxon.*, 2 vols., OHS 35–6 (1898), I, esp. 114–15, 177–84, 197–9, 202–5, 232–7, 244–6.

48 H. E. Salter, W. A. Pantin, H. G. Richardson (eds.), *Formularies which bear on the history of Oxford, c. 1204–1420*, 2 vols., OHS, n.s. 4–5 (1942), I. 56–7.

49 Anstey, *Epistolae academicae*, I. 150–1.

50 *Ibid.*, I. 251–62; II. 389–90; S. M. Leathes (ed.), *Grace book A*, Cambridge Antiquarian Society (Cambridge, 1897), 84; Oates, *CUL*, 30.

51 H. E. Salter (ed.), *Registrum annalium Collegii Mertonensis, 1483–1521*, OHS 76 (1923 for 1921), 47–8, 131.

College and University College as at Gonville Hall and Cambridge University Library, contained some form of visual representation of their donors. In this way readers would be graphically reminded of their benefactors, whose posthumous fame was in turn assured.[52]

From request and inducement to direct purchase is a short step, and indeed a step that could be elided. In 1447 the fellows of King's and Eton addressed a remarkable petition to their founder, Henry VI. Pleading the inadequacy of their libraries, they asked the king to grant their agent, a royal chaplain with the assistance of a well-known London bookseller, rights of pre-emption over all books for sale in his kingdom.[53] King's was wealthy enough to envisage expenditure on this scale. Most university libraries were not. Nevertheless, it would be wrong to allow emphasis on the importance of donations entirely to eclipse the existence of purchases. In this respect the library economy could be paradoxical. Richer colleges, such as All Souls, with wealthy founders and benefactors could rely on their generosity and had little need to buy books. Poorer institutions like the two universities themselves might have greater need of books but lacked the resources for anything but the occasional purchase. Nevertheless, where relatively full accounts have survived it is possible to see that colleges in particular did buy books, albeit usually on a limited scale. Merton began to purchase books as early as the 1280s, and in the 1330s its fellows clearly felt that it was natural to ask that some canon law texts should be acquired by the library.[54] Similarly, the 1316 statutes for Exeter instruct the fellows that any increase in the college's resources should be applied, among other things, to the purchase of books. The detailed accounts of Exeter show that books were already being bought by the college in the 1320s and sporadic purchases continued subsequently. In 1446 the college even went to the lengths of exploiting its links with the West Country and commissioning a book from a scribe in the distant Devon house of Plympton.[55] The similarly comprehensive records of King's Hall reveal an almost identical picture. On

52 Gibson, *Statuta antiqua*, 220; Mynors, *Manuscripts of Balliol College*, xvii–xix, xliv. G. Jackson-Stops, 'Gains and losses: the college buildings, 1404–1750', in Buxton and Williams, *New College*, 193–264, see 194; *VCH, Oxfordshire*, III. 72; C. Brooke, *A history of Gonville and Caius College* (Woodbridge, 1985), 25–8; Oates, *CUL*, 44.

53 A. N. L. Munby, 'Notes on King's College Library in the fifteenth century', *TCBS*, I (1949–53), 280–6, esp. 281–2.

54 J. R. L. Highfield (ed.), *The early rolls of Merton College, Oxford* (Oxford, 1964), 213, 225–6; P. S. Allen and H. W. Garrod (eds.), *Merton muniments*, OHS 86 (1926), 35.

55 F. C. Hingeston-Randolph (ed.), *The register of Walter de Stapeldon, bishop of Exeter, 1307–1326* (London and Exeter, 1892), 307; C. W. Boase (ed.), *Register of rectors and fellows . . . of Exeter College* (Oxford, 1879), 172, 174; C. W. Boase (ed.), *Registrum Collegii Exoniensis*, OHS 27 (1894), xxxv–xxxvii.

quite a number of occasions the accounts show the college purchasing or commissioning books. Books were bought from fellows, or from their estate. Works of Augustine and Lyra were commissioned. At another point a copy of Lyndwood's *Provinciale* was purchased, explicitly with the consent of the fellows.[56] When Peterhouse bought half a dozen books in about 1430 the compiler of the catalogue noted that they were *ad usum et proficium sociorum*, and, as was to be expected, such purchases were often more specifically purposive than gifts might be.[57] When the master of Corpus bought a bible in 1380 at the unlikely venue of the Northampton parliament it was expressly for reading in hall.[58] Similarly, in 1481 Magdalen bought a book particularly for the use of the college lecturer.[59] So it is not surprising to find an Oxford college acquiring five volumes of the works of Hugh of Vienne at St Frideswide's fair, but undoubtedly a more accurate impression of the role of purchases in the creation of university libraries is provided by the mid-fourteenth-century list of Merton's theological books. Merton was a wealthy college, well able to buy books.[60] Yet out of the 250 books mentioned, only eleven had been bought.

This is not to say that money was not spent. Quite the opposite was the case. Paradoxically, a library economy based on benefactions entailed substantial expenditure. In the first place, donors frequently died some distance away from the intended recipients of their books, leaving the institutions to bear the cost of carriage. When John Neuton, its former master and later canon and treasurer of York Minster, gave a substantial number of his books to Peterhouse, the college had to shoulder the expense of transporting them from York to Cambridge.[61] In 1365 King's Hall paid for a bequest of books to be brought to Cambridge from London.[62] All Souls had to pay for transporting books from London, Devon and York and many other places as well as offering wine and a meal to one donor.[63] Exeter College suffered from its regional connections. Many of its benefactors came from the West Country, and the cost of transporting their gifts was correspondingly high. In 1381 the college hospitably gave breakfast to one who brought books given by the archdeacon of Cornwall.[64] And wherever detailed college accounts have survived, the picture is the same. There are frequent references to expenditure on the transport of donated books. But such books also, as it were, had to be 'accessioned'. This in turn, given the physical arrangements of the libraries concerned, might well be costly. All too often donors requested that their books should be chained,

56 CBMLC x. 319, 360–8, 687, 723, 726. 57 *Ibid.*, 474. 58 *Ibid.*, 184.
59 Macray, *Register*, 7. 60 *Ibid.*, 32; Powicke, *Medieval books of Merton College*, 3.
61 Peterhouse Archives, Computus Roll, 1411–12. 62 CBMLC x. 361.
63 Ker, *Records of All Souls College Library*, 113–16. 64 Boase, *Registrum*, lvi, n.

as a way of safeguarding the memory of their generosity. Yet the cost of this chaining fell on the beneficiary. Furthermore, chaining regularly also entailed rebinding, because chains had to be attached to stout wooden boards, whereas flimsier bindings seem to have been adequate for private use. Hence a generous gift of books frequently brought in its train expenditure on repairs, binding and chains. Entirely characteristic are the events at Exeter in 1410, when it was left a number of books by a former fellow, Robert Rygge. The college had to pay for bringing the books to Oxford, the cost of chaining and the wages of Robert Bokbynder for binding and repairs.[65] Later, Magdalen defrayed the cost of bringing a book from the founder's palace at Bishop's Waltham, and then employed a binder for at least six days, undoubtedly in consequence of Wayneflete's massive recent gift to the library.[66] Similarly generous donations to the Cambridge University Library in the 1470s entailed similar expense. When some fourteen volumes arrived in 1470–1, chains and clasps had to be bought and attached to the books. The books had to be rebound and the normal thin horn label had to be attached to them in order to display the donor's name. Finally, a new stall had to be constructed to accommodate them.[67] The financial burden falling on the university in connection with the much larger donation made by its chancellor, Thomas Rotherham, was even greater, involving not only the normal carriage of books, repairs, binding, labelling and chaining, but even the compilation of a catalogue of the existing library. This was sent to Rotherham to act, it would seem, as a form of 'desiderata list in reverse'.[68] Indeed, at Merton a number of individual fellows themselves paid for the repair and rebinding of books given to the college by others.[69]

Yet this expenditure was merely preparatory. It was a response to the arrival of individual gifts of books. Cumulatively such gifts came to pose a much more expensive problem, that of their accommodation. Hence the very success of the economy of benefactions involved the even more expensive undertaking of constructing library buildings. The process is clear and, because it was a response to the same problem, remarkably consistent across both universities. The initial small collections of books were simply stored in chests, and later a particular room might be set aside for them. As the number of books grew, such an arrangement posed obvious problems in terms of access, security and readers' convenience. The solution was the construction of new, purpose-built library rooms. Hence during the century after about 1370, the two universities and apparently all of their colleges constructed their own libraries. The older

65 *Ibid.*, 11. 66 Macray, *Register*, 6. 10. 67 Leathes, *Grace book A*, 84.
68 *Ibid.*, 122–4. 69 Powicke, *Medieval books of Merton College*, 118, 128, 135 and *passim*.

colleges had to fit these libraries into the pattern of their existing buildings by conversion or extension. But, from the establishment of New College in 1379, a library formed an integral part of the planning of any new college's buildings. Where accounts survive, as at King's Hall or Exeter and elsewhere, it is possible to follow almost day by day the progress of the work.[70] Sometimes it was protracted. The University of Oxford lacked resources and relied on benefactors to finance an ambitious building, with the result that its library took some forty years to complete.[71] The construction of many college libraries occupied ten to twenty years. But the pressure of increasing numbers of books was so great that a number of libraries were extended not long after they had been completed. At Balliol a library first built shortly after 1430 was enlarged by four bays some fifty years later in order to provide for the massive gift of books from Bishop Gray, and at New College a separate library, leading off the main library, was built in 1480–1 to house a large donation of law books.[72] At Cambridge the university constructed three new libraries during the middle years of the fifteenth century, again partly, at least, to provide for the substantial quantity of books given by Archbishop Rotherham.[73]

Not only were these libraries a response to a common problem, but they were also constructed to a common pattern. Indeed, there are at times signs of direct emulation. When the new library of Merton was being planned, the bursar and the master mason together visited the library of the Dominican house in London, an obvious model as one of the best-equipped collections of theological books outside Oxford and a striking example of mendicant stimulus to collegiate development.[74] Then a century later Bishop Wayneflete explicitly instructed that the windows in his new library at Magdalen should be as good as or better than those at All Souls.[75] Although by no means unique to the universities, this common pattern of design was complex and subtle, based to some extent on classical precepts and carefully attuned to the needs of both books and readers. In general these new libraries were situated away from the main entrance of the college and the noise of the street, and were

70 Willis and Clark, III. 387–471; CBMLC X. 316–17; Boase, *Registrum*, 344–8; Peterhouse Archives, Computus Rolls, 1438–50.

71 S. Gillam, *The divinity school and Duke Humfrey's library at Oxford* (Oxford, 1988), 3–29.

72 Mynors, *Manuscripts of Balliol College*, xliv; Hunt, 'The medieval library', 330.

73 CBMLC X. 1–3; Oates, *CUL*, 3–43.

74 G. H. Martin and J. R. L. Highfield, *A history of Merton College, Oxford* (Oxford, 1997), 88–9.

75 C. Ferdinand, 'Magdalen College and the book trade: the provision of books in Oxford, 1450–1550', in A. Hunt, G. Mandelbrote and A. Shell (eds.), *The book trade and its customers, 1450–1900: historical essays for Robin Myers* (Winchester, 1997), 175–87, see 176. For what follows, Willis and Clark, III. 387–471; Streeter, *passim*.

placed on the first floor in order to protect against damp. Where possible they seem to have been built on a north–south axis, with windows facing east and west in order to give the best light to the early and late reader. This pursuit of light, so essential to readers deprived of both adequate spectacles and artificial illumination, also explains the universal presence of large two-light windows placed regularly and uniformly along both sides of the room. Indeed, at both New College and All Souls the external string-course was dropped to enable the depth of the library windows to be increased compared with the other windows in the quadrangle. The same large size and configuration also made the windows suitable frames for a developing library iconography, where donors or their arms and appropriate emblematic figures were portrayed in stained glass. These new libraries were uniformly rectangular in shape with a central walkway running down the middle of the room. Between the windows, desks shaped in the fashion of reading lecterns were placed endways against the walls and projected out into the room. At New College the deeply canted window recesses enabled window seats to be provided; elsewhere benches for readers were situated against the windows and between each pair of desks. The books themselves were placed on the desks and chained to them. As the collections grew, further books were laid flat on shelves situated underneath the sloping top of the lectern-desks, until towards the end of the sixteenth or beginning of the seventeenth century the demands for extra space provoked by the increasing influx of printed books rendered these arrangements impractical and the medieval desks were replaced by upright shelving on bookcases.

The appearance of dedicated, planned library rooms was an indication not only of substantial expenditure but also of the application of greater care and thought to the management of collections of books. But in this respect they were symptomatic of increasingly detailed and complicated administrative structures which characterise all university libraries during the later middle ages and which are a similar response to the success of the economy of benefactions. By no means all of these were unique to university libraries. The example and stimulus of the friars, with their major houses of study within the universities themselves, were potent forces. Yet, even where the scholars were following mendicant precedents, they tended to adapt them in detail in order to suit their particular requirements. Most fundamental of all was the division of the book collections in the colleges, but less in the university libraries, into two categories: the reference section and the borrowing section, or in contemporary language the chained library and the *electio* library. In its origin this process of division entailed a global assessment of the whole collection of books and the application to it of a principle articulated in its most moralistic form towards the end of the thirteenth century at the library of the Sorbonne. It might be convenient for individuals that books should be available for borrowing, but the good of the community is greater than the good of the individual.[76] More specifically, this meant that the best copy of each work, or the only copy, was extracted from the collection and placed in the chained library, while the rest were made available for borrowing. In practice and over time, matters were rarely so straightforward. The composite manuscript, containing several diverse items, only one of which might be unique to the collection, defied easy categorisation. Donors, anxious that their benefactions should not be lost and with them the prayers for their souls, often specified that their books should be chained, with the result that the chained library tended to grow in an unsystematic fashion. And college statutes, mindful of the need to reassure donors, insisted that their wishes in this regard must be respected. Books might be moved from one category to another, often for no very obvious reason. Some colleges practised their own refinements of the system. At Trinity Hall, a college for lawyers, poor scholars might borrow the texts of canon and civil law but the volumes of their commentators were to remain chained.[77] In consequence the proportions in the two categories varied sharply between colleges. At King's Hall in about 1400 some four-fifths of the books appear to have been borrowable, whereas at Peterhouse a little later the proportion fell to only about a third.[78]

All colleges appear to have allowed their members to borrow books. Notably, the university libraries did not, save in rare and exceptional circumstances and then only by special permission. Sometimes a college's statutes or a particular donor laid down a formal procedure for lending. At Pembroke the college statutes envisaged a particularly detailed and apparently unusual procedure.[79] Yet such rules tended to be there to be forgotten or evaded. In a few cases, notably at Merton, Corpus Christi, Gonville Hall and King's Hall, the ephemeral and informal records of some series of loans have happily survived.[80] Elsewhere the odd book bears a note to the effect that it had been borrowed by a particular fellow. Some features of the system were universal.

76 P. Glorieux, *Aux origines de la Sorbonne*, I: *Robert de Sorbon* (Paris, 1960), 214–15.

77 *Documents relating to the university and colleges of Cambridge*, 3 vols. (London, 1852), II. 432.

78 CBMLC X. 333–5, 445–8.

79 J. Ringrose, 'The medieval statutes of Pembroke College', in P. Zutshi (ed.), *Medieval Cambridge: essays on the pre-Reformation university* (Woodbridge, 1993), 116.

80 Powicke, *Medieval books of Merton College*, 60–82, 247–52; N. R. Ker, 'The books of philosophy distributed at Merton College in 1372 and 1375', in P. Heyworth (ed.), *Medieval studies for J. A. W. Bennett* (Oxford, 1981), 347–94; CBMLC X. 184–211, 256–73, 323–33, 345–51; C. R. Cheney, 'A register of MSS borrowed from a college library, 1440–1517', *TCBS* 9 (1987), 103–29.

First, borrowing books from a college library was an occasion, not a way of life. It took place at a specific time and place. Secondly, it was a collective matter, usually involving the whole college and articulating its corporate identity. Finally, it was far from spontaneous, but was normally controlled, or supervised, by a senior college officer. But within these norms practice differed to a surprising degree.[81] The *electio*, or formal borrowing of books, usually took place every year in the Michaelmas Term, although the timing varied slightly from college to college. The procedure was normally overseen by a college official such as the dean or bursar, but at Corpus three *custodes* were specifically elected for the purpose.[82] Every fellow was obliged, under the threat of various sanctions, to attend and to return the books that he had previously borrowed. The choice of books then took place usually, it would seem, in order of seniority, so that the most senior chose a book, followed by the next senior and so forth, until all those present had selected one book, at which point the sequence of choice was renewed. Books not selected were then often kept in chests, or chained, until the next *electio*. Choice was by no means always unfettered. At Merton, which had an exceptionally large stock of books and where they seem to have been held irregularly, there were separate *electiones* for the artists and the theologians, so that the one group of fellows could not borrow books required by the other. Furthermore, the sub-warden seems to have managed the artists' *electio* in such a way that every fellow was provided with a complete set of the basic texts.[83] Some other colleges were similarly *dirigiste*, instructing the artists not to borrow the theology books or giving preference to the lawyers with regard to their primary texts, but elsewhere the choice seems to have been unrestricted.[84] Where detailed records exist it is possible to see that individual fellows often essentially preserved their *sortes*, or choices, from year to year, occasionally returning the odd volume and borrowing another one. But, as might be expected, the pattern of borrowing was often as random as the needs or interests of individual fellows. The one fairly consistent thread, equally predictably, is that these *electio* books have tended not to survive in comparison with their chained counterparts. As ever, access and security proved incompatible.

The division of libraries in this way was a reaction to their expansion and also to the accompanying need to control and manage an increasing stock of books. So equally was the catalogue. In some cases the production of a

81 For an account of a characteristic *electio*, see *Documents relating to . . . Cambridge*, II. 44–5.

82 CBMLC X. 187–90.

83 Ker, 'Books of philosophy', 350.

84 *Documents relating to . . . Cambridge*, II. 432 (Trinity Hall); *Statutes of the colleges of Oxford*, 3 vols. (Oxford, 1853), I. New College, 98; Lincoln College, 21.

catalogue might be associated with the completion of a new library building. At other times it was itself a direct response to a substantial gift of books, or even initially no more than a list of the gift itself. Indeed, the flow of donations to the university library at Cambridge was so great that a catalogue initially compiled across the period around 1424–40 had to be completely replaced in 1473.[85] Merton had produced a catalogue of its arts books by about 1330 and a comprehensive list of the books owned by Oriel seems to have been drawn up by about 1350.[86] Subsequently, library catalogues became essentially universal and in later colleges the compilation of a library catalogue was often a statutory requirement.[87] Of course, library catalogues are not uncommon at this time and in many respects university catalogues follow a common form. Some are mere inventories, of little use to a reader seeking to locate a specific book; others approximate to finding lists. Most record only the main item in a particular volume, although others are more detailed. Books are precisely identified by the conventional *dicta probatoria*, the unique opening words of the second folio sometimes accompanied by the opening words of the penultimate, or even other, folios, and are normally, but not invariably, arranged in the traditional subject order, beginning with theology and ending with arts.[88] But in other respects these catalogues show some distinctive, if not unique, features characteristic of their origins. College libraries were divided between chained and *electio* sections and their catalogues normally reproduce this fact, either by dividing their entries in some way into the two categories or by listing only the books in one category. Fellows who failed to return *electio* books were liable to be fined their value. The catalogues are therefore rather more likely to record the monetary value of these books, although these values were at times artificially inflated in order to deter the careless.[89] Above all, university catalogues exhibit the crucial importance of donors. Some are no more than lists of benefactors with the titles of their books added, as it were, as an afterthought. Many go to unusual lengths to record the names of the donors of their books.[90] Others show – an often justified – faith in the continuance

85 CBMLC x. 7–62.

86 Powicke, *Medieval books of Merton College*, 2–3, 47–51; Shadwell, 'Catalogue of the library of Oriel College', 59–70. For a revision of Shadwell's dating, W. J. Courtenay, 'The fourteenth-century booklist of Oriel College Library', *Viator* 19 (1988), 283–90.

87 *Statutes of the colleges of Oxford*, I: All Souls, 55; Queens' College Archives, Book 79 (Statutes), fol. 12r.

88 For more than usually detailed *dicta probatoria*, see CBMLC x. 168–84, 449–548.

89 *Ibid.*, 187–210, 329–30, 607–11. For the principle of valuing all books before distribution, *Documents relating to . . . Cambridge*, II. 44; for deliberate 'overvaluation': H. Anstey (ed.), *Munimenta academica*, 2 vols., RS (London, 1868), I. 58.

90 CBMLC x. 9–31, 134–40, 376–97.

of benefactions by leaving substantial spaces in their lists in order to record future gifts.[91] And occasionally the compilers of these catalogues reveal that personal interest in their books which might be thought to characterise the academic.[92]

A dedicated library building, the organisation of the stock of books into a chained and a borrowing section, and the preparation of a catalogue, represent the three fundamental elements in the emergence of mature university libraries. Other developments are merely symptomatic. Embodying them is the emergence of the office of librarian, combined in the case of the two universities with that of chaplain. At Oxford the duties of the librarian-chaplain were first laid down in about 1320 by Bishop Cobham as part of his plan for a university library, but the scheme proved abortive and the office did not finally take shape until 1412.[93] Cambridge certainly had a librarian-chaplain by 1463, and probably since at least about 1420, assisted by a servant who was to sleep in the building.[94] Colleges took the same path. At Merton the sub-warden was effectively acting as librarian by about 1350, and at Pembroke the first version of the statutes of about that date speaks of a *custos librorum* and lays down uniquely detailed arrangements by which he should control lending. These statutes may soon have lapsed, but librarians, under various guises, appear in a number of other colleges during the next century.[95]

Librarians exist to administer libraries and their emergence is paralleled with accounts of their duties and hence of library rules. Almost all university libraries insisted on annual, or even termly, book checks, followed by reports to the relevant authorities, and most college statutes forbade removal of their books from the college except for repair and occasionally for use in lectures. There was much concern with chains, locks and keys, and in the same vein a number of colleges came to insist, not always successfully, that their books should be marked with an *ex libris* inscription.[96] Naturally, the behaviour of readers was also controlled. Bishop Cobham had insisted that no one should enter his library with damp clothes, pen and ink or a knife, but allowed a wax tablet and stylus to take notes. The detailed Oxford statute of 1412 not only

91 For good illustrations of this phenomenon, CBMLC x. pls. 4 and 5.

92 Particularly CBMLC x. 168–84; but also 634–47.

93 C. L. Shadwell and H. E. Salter, *Oriel College records*, OHS 85 (1926), 24–7; Gibson, *Statuta antiqua*, 216–21.

94 Oates, *CUL*, 31–4; Stokes, *Chaplains . . . of the University of Cambridge*, 1–19.

95 H. W. Garrod, 'The library regulations of a medieval college', *Library* 8 (1927–8), 312–35, esp. 322; Ker, 'Books of philosophy', 350; Ringrose, 'Medieval statutes of Pembroke College', 116; CBMLC x. 319–20.

96 *Documents relating to . . . Cambridge*, II. 435; *Statutes of the colleges of Oxford*, I. All Souls, 55; II. Magdalen, 62.

laid down the librarian's terms of employment and the exact opening hours of the library but insisted that all readers must swear to treat the books properly, making no erasures or blots in the text. And similar rules might insist that books should be closed after use or windows and doors secured at the end of the day.[97] In the light of such precautions it is sobering to contemplate the depredations inflicted on their libraries by so many fellows and the astonishing rate of losses sustained by even so well ordered a college as Merton.[98]

The rules also often stipulated who might use these libraries and in so doing raise the most fundamental question of what was their role within and also beyond their own institutions. In its most concrete terms this is a question of access. Paradoxically, the two university libraries, while their buildings expanded and their holdings grew, actually restricted access. Indeed, the two processes were related. The Oxford statute of 1412, which limited admission to masters, bachelors in academic dress and religious *possessionati* of a certain seniority, specifically associated the need for these restrictions with the increasing throng of readers.[99] And the somewhat similar Cambridge statute of the 1470s seems to have sprung from the same considerations.[100] Yet, paradoxically again, both statutes were soon moderated in various ways. Exemptions were granted, often on payment of a contribution to the library, and at Cambridge in 1499–1500 all monk students were given free access.[101] In any case it is doubtful in general whether the excluded undergraduates would actually have profited from being able to use the chained books. The position in the colleges is not always straightforward. At Merton the bachelor fellows were not originally allowed to use the chained library. This was a subject of complaint and in 1484 the restriction was finally lifted.[102] But Merton possessed an exceptionally large collection of books and was able to provide its fellows with ample reading by means of its *electiones*. Elsewhere, as one would expect, fellows normally had access to all of their colleges' books, whether chained or not. What is also important is the extent to which these libraries were open to outsiders. Access to the library of University College seems to have been dependent on the consent of only one fellow, but other early college statutes

97 Shadwell and Salter, *Oriel College records*, 25; Gibson, *Statuta antiqua*, 216–22.

98 Powicke, *Medieval books of Merton College*, 16, 247–8; Salter, *Registrum annalium*, 360, 441–2.

99 Gibson, *Statuta antiqua*, 218.

100 *Documents relating to . . . Cambridge*, I. 403; Leathes, *Grace book A*, 90.

101 M. Bateson (ed.), *Grace book B, parts I and II* (Cambridge, 1903–5), I. 133, 161; II. 118. Compare W. A. Pantin and W. T. Mitchell (eds.), *The register of congregation, 1448–1463*, OHS, n.s. 22 (1972), 33, 81, 83, 91, 94.

102 Allen and Garrod, *Merton muniments*, 34; Salter, *Registrum annalium*, 102–3.

are silent on the matter or seem to exclude visitors, and the fact that in 1451 even the registrar of Oxford had to obtain a special grace permitting him to use a non-graduate to copy texts in the university library suggests that entry restrictions were being maintained.[103] Yet many later college statutes, such as those of King's and St Catharine's at Cambridge or All Souls and Magdalen at Oxford, explicitly allow for visitors or even copyists and merely insist that they should be adequately supervised.[104] The scholarly activities of Dr Thomas Gascoigne point in the same direction. His habit of annotating his reading and the survival of his commonplace book both indicate that he had ready access to any college library in Oxford that interested him as well as to the university library at Cambridge.[105] It might be thought that Gascoigne was scarcely characteristic, being a distinguished theologian, sometime chancellor of the university of Oxford and, although not a fellow of a college, a benefactor of many of the libraries that he used. Yet his experiences were shared by many others. The distinguished Italian humanist Poggio Bracciolini, on his visit to England in the 1420s, certainly assumed that he would have easy admission to libraries in Oxford, even though in the event he probably did not take advantage of the opportunity.[106] Similarly the antiquarian William Worcester, although an Oxford man, gained entry to at least four college libraries in Cambridge, and Erasmus, a little later, was able to study a volume of Seneca in the library of King's College.[107]

Access is only partly a matter of visits; it can equally well be achieved by lending. Here again the evidence is contradictory or too fragmentary to sustain even an incomplete account. The very early statute of 1292 for University College appears to envisage that any scholars who were engaged in certain academic exercises might freely borrow the college's books, while others could do so only with the universal consent of the fellows and on deposit of a more valuable pledge.[108] Such provisions are not found elsewhere and may reflect a stage when books were in short supply and when the university itself, which actually established the college, wished to make its library more widely accessible. Later college statutes are at best ambiguous. Some preclude external

103 Anstey, *Munimenta academica*, I. 59; Pantin and Mitchell, *Register of congregation*, 83.

104 *Documents relating to . . . Cambridge*, II. 601–2; H. Philpott (ed.), *Documents relating to St Catharine's College in the University of Cambridge* (Cambridge, 1861), 25–6; *Statutes of the colleges of Oxford*, I. All Souls, 56; II. Magdalen, 62–3.

105 Dr Robert Ball (pers. comm.), who is preparing a detailed study of Gascoigne's bibliographical activities.

106 Poggio Bracciolini, *Lettere*, ed. H. Harth (Florence, 1984), I. 20, 35, 44.

107 BL, MS Cotton Julius F. vii, fols. 59v, 64r, 121–2, 201r; D. F. S. Thompson (tr.) and H. C. Porter (ed.), *Erasmus and Cambridge* (Toronto, 1963), 207–8, 211.

108 Anstey, *Munimenta academica*, 58–9.

lending altogether; others allow books to be taken out of the college subject to formal consent, but are not clear whether the concession applies only to fellows or to other scholars. What is certain is that in 1439 Oxford set aside a number of arts books given by Humfrey, duke of Gloucester, and allowed them to be borrowed not only by the masters lecturing in these subjects but also by the principals of halls for the use of their students if no relevant lectures were being given.[109] Elsewhere there are merely spasmodic references to particular loans. A fourteenth-century donor to Oriel College gave a book on condition that it might be lent only to one of his relations, but in the next century, the college was lending a book to a fellow of another college merely against a deposit.[110] At Merton, where the records are as full as was its library, it is possible to see that lending was not unusual by the end of the fifteenth century, but that it normally required formal consent and a pledge of some sort and was not without its hazards.[111] Similar conventions probably obtained at many other colleges, particularly where the borrower was a man of standing.

Such questions of access are merely the superficial, or microcosmic, aspects of the fundamental question of how these libraries served the interests of their institutions. An initial answer to such a question must lie partly in the nature of their contents. In this respect it is not merely banal to stress that they were academic libraries, libraries for scholars, and that their books reflect that fact above all. Of course, there are many exceptions to such generalisations, but it follows that the overwhelming majority of their books were in the academic language of Latin, few were in the vernacular and even fewer in Greek or Hebrew. Similarly, their contents were academic in nature. Literary and historical writings were relatively sparse; devotional works were much more likely to figure in private libraries, and liturgical texts tended to be confined to chapels. Conversely, the focus was on the subjects of the syllabus. Here the major higher faculties predominated: theology, canon law and civil law, with medicine coming a poor fourth. Some libraries were relatively well stocked with books for the arts course, the *trivium* and *quadrivium*, but as most colleges were predominantly focused on higher studies their libraries tended to reflect this fact. Nowhere was the symmetry between syllabus and library more vividly revealed than in the matter of the common law. The subject was not taught in the universities and its literature did not intrude upon its libraries.

This same symmetry informs the economy of benefactions. It might be thought that libraries which were stocked by gifts could have no accessions

109 Gibson, *Statuta antiqua*, 259–62.
110 Bodleian, MS Auct. F.5.28, erased inscription; *BRUO* I. 643 (Epworth).
111 Salter, *Registrum annalium*, 62, 69, 128, 140; and, for the obvious hazards, 431, 436, 442.

policy. At best this is no more than a half-truth. In the numerous cases where a founder also endowed his college with books, the benefaction naturally, indeed inevitably, reflected his intentions for his college. Hence Bishop Bateman provided his new college of Trinity Hall with a splendid assemblage of law books (mainly canon law), and conversely Robert Wodelarke launched the library of St Catharine's with a collection which was predominantly theological in character and, by design, contained no law books whatever.[112] In both instances the library mirrored the proposed character of the college, as did the more diverse collection of books given by William of Wykeham to New College.[113] Similar considerations apply to the very numerous later gifts made to university and college libraries. These were far from random. The vast majority were made by present or former members of the institutions concerned. Their academic careers would have taken shape within these institutions and they were ideally placed to know which particular gifts of books might be appropriate or which would meet particular needs. A striking example is that of King's Hall. The college's concentration on legal, and especially civil law, studies was to make it predominant in this area in medieval Cambridge. Its library had not received any substantial initial endowment of books but was created by a long series of piecemeal gifts from individual benefactors. Yet, as a result of this harmony between donor and recipient, it was to become one of the best specialist legal libraries in the university.[114] An accessions policy was thus achieved, albeit indirectly. And a similar broad congruence between the academic interests of scholars and the contents of their college library, achieved by the same means but across a broader range of subjects, is noticeable in Cambridge at Gonville Hall, Peterhouse and Queens', as it is in Oxford at All Souls, Merton and New College and in the early libraries of Balliol and Lincoln.

Of course, these symmetries were not always complete or permanent. The economy of benefactions could at times be whimsical and libraries might change as they expanded. Given the statutory character of the particular colleges, the libraries of Corpus Christi in the 1370s and of Clare in the 1440s might seem to contain, as it were, too many law books.[115] Sometimes a donor might not be content merely to reinforce the existing character of a library but sought to use his benefaction to effect some change. Roger Marchall's careful allocation of his medical books to selected Cambridge colleges seems

112 CBMLC x. 593–602, 636–47.

113 Leach, 'Wykeham's books at New College', 223–44; Hunt, 'The medieval library', 321–2.

114 CBMLC x. 315–68, esp. 333–5; for a comprehensive survey of donors to Cambridge libraries: 655–742.

115 *Ibid.*, 120–33, 168–84.

to have been specifically intended to strengthen their holdings in this area. Indeed, Marchall himself provided helpful lists of contents to his manuscripts, which revealingly tended to omit all but those items, particularly medical, which interested him.[116] And Andrew Holes specifically instructed his executors to distribute his law books to those Oxford colleges which lacked them.[117] But others were more ambitious. The massive donation of Humfrey, duke of Gloucester, to Oxford, although more diverse than is sometimes assumed, was clearly an aspect of his plans to modernise the arts syllabus and to stimulate humanist studies within the university. While the arts course was, at least in theory, modified and Humfrey's books certainly attracted attention, it is difficult to see that any fundamental change was effected.[118] The same picture holds good elsewhere. Robert Flemyng donated a substantial collection of humanist texts to Lincoln College, and William Gray gave a number of similar books, among others, to Balliol.[119] Yet the fellows of both colleges appear to have remained remarkably resistant to the enticements which such works offered. Books alone could not achieve such a cultural transformation. Gifts which were too alien to the nature of their recipients tended to fall on stony ground.

University libraries did change their character over time, but such change was gradual, partial and, above all, organic. As the number of donations accumulated, it was inevitable that their holdings should become more heterogeneous. Merton's original concentration on arts and theology was supplemented by books on law and medicine. The gift to the college of a volume of Marco Polo, exceptionally rare in the Oxford of the day, exemplified this change.[120] A few more texts of the Latin classics appeared in Cambridge University library during the half-century between its first and second catalogues.[121] All Souls acquired some medical works and even a book in French.[122] Not surprisingly, works of current theological controversy arrived, writings associated with the Wycliffite controversy or attacks on Bishop Pecock.[123] This growing diversity was enhanced by the appearance of substantial benefactors

116 L. E. Voigts, 'A doctor and his books: the manuscripts of Roger Marchall', in R. Beadle and A. J. Piper (eds.), *New science out of old books: studies in manuscripts and early printed books in honour of A. I. Doyle* (Aldershot, 1995), 249–314, esp. 263–4, 265–7.

117 *BRUO* II. 949–50.

118 Anstey, *Epistolae academicae*, I. 64–5; J. M. Fletcher, 'Developments in the Faculty of Arts, 1370–1520', *HUO* II. 315–45, esp. 323–5.

119 Weiss, 'Earliest catalogues', 343–59; Mynors, *Manuscripts of Balliol College*, xxiv–xlv.

120 Powicke, *Medieval books of Merton College*, 127–8.

121 CBMLC X. 32.

122 Ker, *Records of All Souls*, 20–1, 123; All Souls College, MS 182 (Ker, no. 594).

123 For works concerned with the Wycliffite controversy at Queens' College, see CBMLC X. 570–1, also 59 (no. 288).

who were also bibliophiles, like William Bateman, William Rede, William Gray and, archetypically, Humfrey, duke of Gloucester. Not only did such men give large numbers of manuscripts but their interest in fine volumes and in rarer texts also served to increase the range of books available. Similarly, whereas most of the books available in the early libraries of both universities would seem to have been written in England by English scribes, it is noticeable that many fifteenth-century donations consist of books either written abroad or written by foreign scribes working in England.[124] In this area, as elsewhere, expansion also amplified variety. Yet in one respect, in Cambridge at least, expansion also consolidated. Here, perhaps slightly unexpectedly, the representation of theology in many of its libraries steadily increased as their holdings grew across the fifteenth century. This is noticeable in the long established colleges of Clare, Corpus Christi and Peterhouse, to a lesser degree in the university library and even at the law college of King's Hall. At Peterhouse, for example, whereas the numbers of arts and theology books were roughly equal in 1418, the theology books had become substantially more numerous by 1500.[125] And the trend was reinforced by the appearance of the new libraries of Queens' and St Catharine's, which were overwhelmingly theological, and even anti-Lollard, in emphasis.[126] It is hard not to associate such a development with the broader transformation of Cambridge in this period into a bastion of orthodoxy, as opposed to the nest of heresy at Oxford, and with the associated foundation of new Cambridge colleges explicitly to produce a clergy better educated to defend the church against its enemies.

In this respect, as in many others, the reliance on benefactions from their own members meant that university libraries tended to reflect their own institutions. They did not, could not, change them because they were by and large a product of them. The sum of a large number of relatively small gifts tended to embody, as it were, a lowest common denominator. Hence most of these libraries amply mirrored the diluted, second-hand Scotism which was the intellectual commonplace of the day. The novel and unexpected, however distinguished, were much less likely to be represented. Hence the striking absence of the work of the 'Mertonians', even from their own college's library, and the similar disregard for the writings of the later Oxford logicians, despite

124 Ker, 'Oxford college libraries', 307, 313–17. For Cambridge, see, for example, CCCC, MS 68; Gonville and Caius Coll., MS 114/183; Peterhouse, MSS 87, 188.

125 CBMLC x. lxxxv–lxxxvi, 8, 32 (on the assumption that UC2 is incomplete in its omission of civil law texts), 447.

126 *Ibid.*, 562, 592. For the important general context of this change: A. B. Cobban, 'Robert Wodelarke and St Catharine's', in E. E. Rich (ed.), *St Catharine's College, Cambridge, 1473–1973* (Cambridge, [1973]), 1–32.

their fame on the Continent. But this merely exemplified a wider neglect of these achievements. In the same way, dependence on donations, usually in the form of legacies, tended to impart a *retardataire* character to these libraries. This is particularly noticeable in the relatively late appearance of printed books. As has been well said, the old men who bequeathed their books had not bought printed texts, while the younger men who did had not yet died. But did this matter? The chained manuscript book was a robust, resilient object, good for centuries of use. When books two or three hundred years old, including an Augustine and a Josephus, were given to Merton in 1493 they were welcomed as *perpulcra satis et manu et materia*.[127] Equally, the universities were slow to change their syllabuses, with the result that the books of a former age did not rapidly lose their relevance. So these libraries were in tune with their environment and not simply in the most obvious sense. Poor colleges raised money, often for building schemes, by collectively pawning their books.[128] Books could be used as a deposit against the purchase of a building. A spell in the library, writing comments on Aristotle's *Generationes*, might even be a suitable punishment for an errant fellow.[129] When founders gave books and William of Wykeham and his successors incorporated libraries into their initial building plans, they were articulating this view of libraries as integral to their communities and representative of both their faults and their virtues. No more and no less.

127 Powicke, *Medieval books of Merton College*, 219.

128 Mynors, *Manuscripts of Balliol College*, xvi–xvii; Boase, *Registrum Collegii Exoniensis*, xlviii–xlix, 34–5; A. F. Butcher, 'The economy of Exeter College, 1400–1500', *Oxoniensia* 44 (1979), 38–54, esp. 41–5; Brooke, *History of Gonville and Caius College*, 22–3; CBMLC x. 291–2.

129 Macray, *Register of the members of Magdalen College*, I. 72.

7

Bishops and kings: private book collections in medieval England

JENNY STRATFORD AND TERESA WEBBER

Any attempt to trace the history of the book collections of individual men and women in England during the middle ages meets with difficult, indeed often insuperable, problems of evidence and interpretation.[1] The evidence for true book collections belonging to individuals, embryo libraries, as opposed to small clutches of books, is at best partial and scattered. Much of it remains uncollated and unedited, while the physical evidence for storage and use has usually disappeared. Where individual owners are concerned, the catalogues, press-marks and other written evidence that shed light on how both religious and academic communities perceived, organised and used their books as collections are almost completely lacking. Between the second half of the twelfth century and the fifteenth century, more and more men and women can be shown to have owned books, but how many, of what kind, and how far, if at all, their owners thought of them as a collection, can be only imperfectly pieced together from the instances where the evidence is more complete, and by comparison with the more extensive surviving records of both lay and ecclesiastical book-owners in continental Europe.

These difficulties might seem enough to rule out the book collections of individual medieval people from this volume. Yet personal book collections are fundamental to the early history and development of libraries. Until the fourteenth century, if not later, some learned men owned as many and as wide-ranging books as some academic and religious institutions, and their gifts of books had a direct impact on the creation, growth and development of the communal libraries. Moreover, especially where religious houses are concerned, the distinction between personal books and communal collections is often ill-defined. Within the universities and other places of learning, communal collections were only one element in book provision; individual

1 K. Harris, 'Patrons, buyers and owners: the evidence for ownership and the role of book owners in book production and the book trade', in *BPPB*, 163–99, esp. 163–7.

initiative played at least an equal if not a greater part. Donations had always been an important way for institutions to increase their stock of books; from the thirteenth century onwards, donations became the primary route, books being either given *en bloc* or dispersed among different beneficiaries. Some of the major donors were themselves influential in shaping the character of the emerging institutional libraries. It is for these reasons that this chapter, with all its limitations, must be included.

Paradoxically, most of the documentary evidence for private ownership of books was compiled at the time the books changed hands. Private owners are most often named as testators. In Susan H. Cavanaugh's pioneering compilation for the study of private book-ownership in England, 1300–1450, wills make up the overwhelming majority of the records.[2] Next in number come the donation lists drawn up by the institutions who received the gifts (perhaps the most accessible form of documentary evidence for personal collections before the fourteenth century), and finally, among other miscellaneous sources, are a few precious inventories, some taken after forfeiture of an attainted traitor's goods to the Crown. Almost all these records were made at, close to or after death, so that the surviving documents are limited in two ways. Not only are they a fraction of those originally made, but they also paint an incomplete picture of the books owned by an individual. Because the vast majority of these records were made at the end of the owner's life, they cannot reveal changes in the pattern of book-ownership during his or her earlier years. Furthermore, wills present a misleadingly low impression of the number of books owned by a testator at death.[3] Other forms of evidence reveal that substantial numbers of books escape mention. This is especially true of lay wills, but true also of many wills of the learned elite: for example, of William Waynfleet, bishop of Winchester.[4] Relatively few wills record more than a handful of books. Their contents are not fully specified, if at all. Many of the books named are liturgical or devotional, tied to provisions for prayers for the testator's soul; but service-books do not belong to the history of later medieval libraries.

2 S. H. Cavanaugh, 'A study of books privately owned in England 1300–1450', 2 vols., unpublished PhD thesis, University of Pennsylvania (1980).

3 Cavanaugh, 'Books privately owned', I. 9–20, with references to the pioneering work of H. R. Plomer, 'Books mentioned in wills', *Library* 7 (1904), 99–121, and M. Deanesly, 'Vernacular books in England in the fourteenth and fifteenth centuries', *MLR* 15 (1920), 349–58, and her *The Lollard Bible* (Cambridge, 1920), 220–2, 391–8; Harris, 'Patrons, buyers and owners', 163–5; J. T. Rosenthal, 'Clerical book bequests: a *vade mecum*, but whence and whither', in C. Barron and J. Stratford (eds.), *The Church and learning in later medieval society: essays in honour of R. B. Dobson* (Donington, 2002), 327–43.

4 V. Davis, *William Waynfleet: bishop and educationalist* (Woodbridge, 1993), 91.

Published editions of wills and other testamentary records sometimes introduce a further deceptive element of selection.[5]

Donation records compiled by communities are a source of more substantial lists of books, but their evidence can also be incomplete and difficult to interpret. Only exceptionally do they include donations by the same individual to other recipients, whether private persons or institutions. Moreover, both wills and donation lists may mention only large and handsome books, humbler volumes and booklets being disposed of in other ways or not considered worthy of recording. The wording of headings often blurs the distinction between a gift of books formerly owned by an individual as well as used by him, and books obtained on behalf of the community. Phrases such as *fecit transcribere* ('caused to be written') suggest communal provision, but terms such as *acquisivit* ('acquired') are more difficult to interpret.[6] A list of forty-one books with the heading 'Hii sunt libri Roberti de Aldesword' ('These are the books of Robert of Aldsworth'), supplied during the thirteenth century on the front endleaf of a one-volume bible owned by Gloucester Abbey at least by 1284 (CCCC, MS 485), might be assumed to represent Robert's personal collection. But a second inscription in the same book reveals a more complicated picture:

> Hunc librum fecit scribi Robertus de Aldeswyrth:
> Sum de communi; nolo fieri specialis.
> Tradar sic uni quod cunctis sim generalis.
>
> (Robert of Aldsworth had this book written.
> I am for the community; I do not want to be kept private.
> Let me thus be handed over to one, that I may be common for all.)

All the books in the list may, like the bible, have been acquired by Robert on behalf of the community at Gloucester, although, perhaps for a time, they were reserved for his own personal use.[7] Books were sometimes acquired solely for the purpose of donation, and hence had never formed part of a book collection in use by the donor. King Æthelstan (d. 939), for example, seems to have acquired books partly as gifts to religious communities in return for their prayers and favour.[8] Similar caveats may apply to some of the donations

5 J. B. Friedman, *Northern English books, owners and makers in the late Middle Ages* (Syracuse, NY, 1995), 4–5, on the bequests of Thomas Langley, bishop of Durham.

6 Cf. CBMLC IV. B37, 'De libris quos Henricus fecit transcribere Glastonie', and B53.

7 CBMLC IV. B47.

8 S. Keynes, 'King Athelstan's books', in M. Lapidge and H. Gneuss (eds.), *Learning and literature in Anglo-Saxon England: studies presented to Peter Clemoes on the occasion of his sixty-fifth birthday* (Cambridge, 1985), 143–201.

made to colleges and universities in the fifteenth century.[9] Wills sometimes made provision for the return of communally owned books on loan but this may not always be explicitly stated.[10]

The most substantial lists of books in personal ownership are in inventories, where the context is often of key importance; printed extracts may distort the evidence. For late medieval France, it has been estimated that some 160 such collections are known from surviving inventories. A comparatively detailed picture can therefore be drawn of the book collections of lay and ecclesiastical magnates.[11] Partly because of differences in administrative procedures, relatively few inventories listing large English book collections are known.[12] It would be dangerous to generalise from the few survivors. Nevertheless, the contrast between the far richer information given in these inventories, especially about secular books and cheaper books, as compared with wills, benefaction lists and other forms of evidence, underlines how incomplete our knowledge usually is.[13]

Surviving books may provide evidence of individual ownership, but present their own difficulties.[14] Privately owned books have survived far less well than books owned by communities, and are more difficult to identify. Many are likely to have been in a small format; some were no doubt merely booklets, stitched together in a limp parchment wrapper, or never bound at all. They were fragile and might disintegrate through use, and were rarely mentioned in a bequest, especially if the subject-matter was secular. Privately owned books stood the greatest chance of survival if they passed to an institution, so that the distortions of the documentary evidence are compounded by the surviving books.[15] Unless there is unambiguous heraldic evidence or an *ex libris* inscription, the books of private owners are also much harder to recognise. They lack the clues in many books once belonging to communities: anathemas, press-marks and other library marks, or the apparatus of titles and contents sometimes supplied by assiduous monastic custodians. In privately owned

9 See above, 158–62. 10 See below, 189, on the will of Richard de Gravesend.

11 L. Delisle, *Le cabinet des manuscrits de la Bibliothèque (impériale) nationale*, 4 vols. (Paris, 1868–81; repr. Amsterdam, 1969); P. Stirnemann, 'Les bibliothèques princières et privées aux xiie et xiiie siècles', in *Hbf* I. 173–91; F. Robin, 'Le luxe des collections aux xive et xve siècles', in *ibid.*, 193–213; G. Hasenohr, 'L'essor des bibliothèques privées aux xive et xve siècles', in *ibid.*, 215–63.

12 Harris, 'Patrons, buyers and owners', 165, and n. 15.

13 Contrast, for example, the ninety-odd volumes recorded in the inventory of Richard de Gravesend with the mere two mentioned in his will: below, 189.

14 Harris, 'Patrons, buyers and owners', 165–7.

15 E. Leedham-Green, 'University libraries and booksellers', in *CHBB* III. 339–43; Jensen, 'Text-books in the universities: the evidence from the books', in *CHBB* III. 354.

books *ex libris* inscriptions are less often to be found. Unambiguous statements of ownership are rare; more common are inscriptions of temporary possession added to the books assigned to the use of monks and friars, and various forms of *ex dono* inscription.[16] Coats of arms or other heraldic devices integral to the original decorative schemes of some later medieval manuscripts may provide evidence of the first owner, but books decorated with the patron's arms were also made for presentation to a chantry or a community.[17] Added heraldry must be considered carefully; as must names, added, for example, in the margins. They are not necessarily evidence of ownership.[18]

The history of private book collections in England during the middle ages is much less well understood than that of religious and academic communities. A satisfactory overview remains a distant aspiration. Whereas the few extant Anglo-Saxon booklists have been comprehensively edited, the Corpus of British Medieval Library Catalogues is, at the date of writing this chapter, limited to the records of institutional collections,[19] although these include some lists of books donated by individuals. There is no database of surviving manuscript books containing evidence of private ownership, such as Margaret Ford's study of printed books in private possession.[20] Yet scattered scraps of evidence of personal book-ownership gradually come to light from many classes of document as well as from extant manuscripts, especially for the later middle ages. There are good resources for specific categories of book-owners. Lists of books belonging to the learned can be compiled from A. B. Emden's magisterial biographical registers of the universities of Oxford and Cambridge. Men and women associated with extant manuscripts acquired by academic, monastic and cathedral communities and parish churches are identified in the appendixes to Ker's *Medieval libraries of Great Britain* and its supplement.[21] Book-ownership by women religious has been surveyed by David N. Bell, Anne Clark Bartlett and Mary Erler.[22] The body of published

16 *MLGB*, xvii–xviii. 225–325; *Supplement*, 75–114.

17 Harris, 'Patrons, buyers and owners', 167–70.

18 See, for example, K. Harris, 'The origins and make-up of Cambridge University Library MS Ff.1.6', *TCBS* 8 (1983), 299–333; J. Tschann and M. B. Parkes, *Facsimile of Oxford, Bodleian Library, MS Digby 86*, EETS, SS 16 (Oxford, 1996), lvi–lx.

19 The one exception is the libraries of Henry VIII: CBMLC VII.

20 M. L. Ford, 'Private ownership of printed books', in *CHBB* III. 205–28. A database of privately owned manuscripts from urban contexts from the period 1300–1476 is currently being compiled as part of the Urban Manuscripts Project, under the direction of Professor Felicity Riddy at York.

21 *MLGB*, 225–325; *Supplement*, 75–114.

22 D. N. Bell, *What nuns read: books and libraries in medieval English nunneries* (Kalamazoo, MI, 1995); A. C. Bartlett, *Male authors, female readers: representation and subjectivity in Middle*

material from wills grows all the time.[23] Cavanaugh's invaluable compilation surveying private ownership in England between 1300 and 1450 was almost entirely based on records in print at the time of writing. As she makes clear, it is inevitably incomplete, and she was able to re-edit only a few of the lists she included.[24]

Because of these difficulties, it is hardly surprising that the main focus of recent scholarship has been on studies of individual owners, on single books or texts, or on groups of books and their readers (for example, the gentry or women), not on whether or how these books were perceived, acquired and used as collections.[25] Given the partial and disparate nature of the evidence, and the current state of published research, it would be premature and misleading to attempt to present here a general survey. Instead, this chapter will focus primarily upon two kinds of owner: bishops (who are by far the best represented in the surviving evidence), and lay members of the royal family (whose ownership of books has received more attention to date than any other group within the laity).[26]

Episcopal book collections

All bishops needed books to fulfil their office as diocesans and pastors. Until the later eleventh century, most books associated with bishops are those that deal directly with the episcopal office, such as the copies of the English translation of Gregory the Great's handbook, the *Cura pastoralis*, supplied by King Alfred to each of his bishops as part of his programme for the revival of learning. Some twenty-odd pontificals (the principal liturgical volume containing the services

English devotional literature (Ithaca, NY, 1995), 149–71; M. C. Erler, *Women, reading and piety in late medieval England* (Cambridge, 2002); see also J. H. M. Taylor and L. Smith (eds.) *Women and the book: assessing the visual evidence* (London and Toronto, 1997).

23 In addition to the works cited by Harris, 'Patrons, buyers and owners', 184, n. 4, see Friedman, *Northern English books*, and Rosenthal, 'Clerical book bequests'.

24 See also R. H. Bartle, 'A study of private book collections in England between *c.* 1200 and the early years of the sixteenth century, with special reference to books belonging to ecclesiastical dignitaries', unpublished BLitt thesis, Oxford University (1956).

25 See, for example, the contributions on the books of women, scholars, members of the professions, and the gentry in *CHBB* III, chs. 18–25. See also Parkes, 'The literacy of the laity', in D. Daiches and A. K. Thorlby (eds.), *Literature and western civilization: the medieval world* (London, 1973), 555–76; repr. in his *Scribes, scripts and readers: studies in the communication, presentation and dissemination of medieval texts* (London, 1991), 275–97; Harris, 'Patrons, buyers, and owners'.

26 For the book collections of members of the professions, see below, chapters 13–20, and *CHBB* III, chs. 18–21.

performed by a bishop) are precious survivals from the late Anglo-Saxon period.[27] It is not always clear, however, whether liturgical and sometimes other books were regarded as the personal property of the bishop or were deemed to belong to the office. Richard Swinefield's bequest of books, including a pontifical, a gradual and a troper, to his successor bishops of Hereford in 1317, might either reflect normal practice or indicate that he could dispose of such books as he wished.[28]

Bishops had the means to accumulate books to serve their scholarly interests as well as their practical duties as pastors and administrators within their diocese and as royal advisers and administrators. The only such collection known from before the mid-eleventh century was compiled by Ælberht, archbishop of York (766/7–779/80). It is celebrated in Alcuin's poem on the saints of York, and included works both by the early Church Fathers and by classical authors, such as Cicero, Virgil, Statius and Lucan.[29] Identifying a bishop's own books before the later twelfth century is complicated because the division between his own books and those of his cathedral community was not always clearly defined. Archbishop Ælberht's books did not pass to the cathedral *familia* at York, but were bequeathed to Alcuin. After becoming abbot of Tours, Alcuin made arrangements for them to be brought to him from York. The monastic and clerical reform movements of the tenth and eleventh centuries seem to have prompted bishops to identify their needs and resources, including books, more closely with those of their cathedral community. The list of books donated by Bishop Leofric (1050–72) to his cathedral at Exeter, and the donation inscriptions in a number of the surviving volumes, might give the appearance of a personal book collection, but many of these books were produced as a collaborative endeavour by scribes who may themselves have been members of the community.[30] The collection was almost certainly intended for the use of the community from the start. A similar picture of collaborative effort is presented by William of Malmesbury's description of Bishop Osmund (1078–99) at Salisbury, an impression confirmed by the

27 Gneuss, 'Liturgical books in Anglo-Saxon England and their Old English terminology', in Lapidge and Gneuss, *Learning and literature*, 131–3; D. N. Dumville, *Liturgy and the ecclesiastical history of late Anglo-Saxon England* (Woodbridge, 1992), 66–95; R. W. Pfaff, 'The Anglo-Saxon bishop and his book', *BJRL* 81 (1999), 3–24.

28 Mynors and Thomson, xx; Roger Martival, bishop of Salisbury (d. 1330), made the same provision for the descent of his pontifical (Bodleian, MS Rawlinson C. 400): *MLGB*, ix.

29 Lapidge, 'Booklists', no. I. 45–9.

30 Lapidge, 'Booklists', no. X. 64–9; E. M. Drage, 'Bishop Leofric and the Exeter Cathedral Chapter (1050–1072): a reassessment of the manuscript evidence', unpublished DPhil thesis, Oxford University (1978).

evidence in the extant books of close collaboration between a large number of scribes, who were also perhaps canons.[31]

From the middle of the twelfth century, throughout England and northern France, the distinction between a book collection owned and used by the bishop and that of the cathedral becomes clearer. Small collections of about a dozen books, comprising, for the most part, the new textbooks and reference works of the twelfth-century schools, performed a practical function for bishops, whose administrative activities were becoming increasingly complex. A few, however, went beyond such practical needs and reflect a desire for visual display and the learning of the cultivated man of letters.[32] By far the largest such collection known belonged to Philippe d'Harcourt (d. 1164), bishop of Bayeux and a former dean of Lincoln. It comprised at least 140 books, which he bequeathed to the Norman monastery of Bec.[33] Thomas Becket left at least seventy books to Christ Church, Canterbury. Among them were large and lavishly decorated glossed books of the Bible as well as classical texts.[34] Such collections did not have a purely private aspect but were part of the currency of spiritual friendship and shared interests between a learned elite of scholars, ecclesiastics and religious both within the episcopal household and further afield, being consulted by visitors and learned members of the *familia*, or being drawn upon as exemplars for rarer texts. The contents of Becket's collection may well reflect something of the learned interests of members of his *familia*, such as Herbert of Bosham, a pupil of Peter Lombard, and John of Salisbury (d. 1180), who himself, as bishop of Chartres, left a substantial collection of some thirty books to his own cathedral.[35]

The number of personal collections, both small and large, of bishops and other clergy, grew during the thirteenth century in response to new scholarly and pastoral needs. From the thirteenth century onward it became increasingly common for members of the episcopate in particular to have studied at university, and often to have taken one or more of the degrees of the higher faculties, especially theology and canon and civil law. Expertise in these subjects was

31 William of Malmesbury, *De gestis pontificum Anglorum*, ed. N. E. S. A. Hamilton, RS (London, 1870), 183; T. Webber, *Scribes and scholars at Salisbury Cathedral c. 1075–c. 1125* (Oxford, 1992), 8–30.

32 Stirnemann, 'Les bibliothèques princières', 174.

33 M. A. Rouse and R. H. Rouse, '"*Potens in opere et sermone*": Philip, bishop of Bayeux, and his books', in their *Authentic witnesses: approaches to medieval texts and manuscripts* (Notre Dame, IN, 1991), 33–59.

34 C. F. R. de Hamel, *Glossed books of the Bible and the origins of the Paris booktrade* (Woodbridge, 1984), 38–54.

35 *Ibid.*; C. J. Webb, 'Note on books bequeathed by John of Salisbury to the cathedral library of Chartres', *Mediaeval and Renaissance Studies* 1 (1941–3), 128–9.

deemed particularly appropriate for bishops to aid them in the enhanced perception of their pastoral duties following the Fourth Lateran Council of 1215. They were charged with improving the competence of their diocesan clergy, with combating the perceived threat of heresy, as well as dealing effectively with the increasing complexity and litigious nature of their administrative duties within the diocese and in the wider world. Candidates for the higher degrees in canon and civil law and in theology were required to own copies of the prescribed texts.[36] The lack of institutional resources for scholars at the major *studia* at this time placed the onus upon individual initiative in acquiring copies of the set texts they needed as well as ancillary texts. New kinds of reference work and compendia proliferated, designed for individual use. Reference tools such as concordances and *tabulae*, as well as preaching aids, created especially to meet the scholarly and preaching requirements of the itinerant friars, soon proved useful to other religious and members of the secular clergy.[37] The physical character and appearance of the books also underwent changes to suit the demands of regular personal consultation and increased portability. Books of smaller format became more common. They were able to accommodate considerable amounts of text, by being written on thinner parchment and in smaller script with a far heavier incidence of abbreviations. Their contents were also articulated visually in more complex ways to facilitate use for reference purposes.[38]

Some of these features are represented in the book collection made by Robert Grosseteste, bishop of Lincoln from 1235 to his death in 1253. He had previously been the first lector of the Franciscan convent at Oxford (established in 1229/30), and chancellor of Oxford, although the details of his own earlier academic training are unknown. In his time there was no library in Oxford to provide the extensive materials he needed for his theological and scientific writings and for his later Greek translations. All the evidence suggests he himself owned a large number of learned books – probably many more than the forty volumes which would have constituted a considerable collection in his day. Exceptionally, they included Greek as well as Latin texts and also a Hebrew psalter. The extraordinary scope of Grosseteste's reading can be

36 M. B. Parkes, 'Provision of books', in *HUO* II. 407.

37 D. L. d'Avray, 'Portable *vademecum* books containing Franciscan and Dominican texts', in *MSS at Oxford*, 61–4.

38 R. H. Rouse and M. A. Rouse, '*Statim invenire*: schools, preachers, and new attitudes to the page', in R. L. Benson and G. Constable (eds.), *Renaissance and renewal in the twelfth century* (Cambridge, MA, 1982), 201–25; repr. in their *Authentic witnesses: approaches to medieval texts and manuscripts* (Notre Dame, IN, 1991), 191–219; 'The development of research tools in the thirteenth century', in their *Authentic witnesses*, 221–55.

gauged from the theological subject index he compiled together with his friend, the Franciscan, Adam Marsh. For it they devised an elaborate system of some 400 symbols. The key survives incomplete in a bible in Lyon, but lacks the works on cosmology Grosseteste would have used. While Grosseteste is unlikely to have owned all the works tabulated, he certainly owned some of them.[39] The range extends from the Latin and Greek Fathers through medieval authors including Bede, Hrabanus Maurus, Anselm of Canterbury, Bernard of Clairvaux and Hugh of Saint-Victor, to classical and late antique, Greek and Arabic authors. Its contents are untypical of thirteenth-century personal collections. There is an overwhelming emphasis upon the full texts of the Fathers and other authoritative writers, rather than upon the organised selections compiled from them and discussed by the twelfth- and thirteenth-century masters, such as Peter Lombard and Stephen Langton, which formed the theological core of most thirteenth-century scholars' book collections. The books themselves, however, share the physical and visual features developed to facilitate individual use and reference.[40]

Eleven books once in his possession have been identified, and were demonstrably used by him. A single volume contains both Augustine's *De civitate Dei* and Gregory the Great's *Moralia in Iob*, texts which had each run to two or more volumes in the copies made for communal use in the late eleventh and twelfth centuries.[41] The leaves of parchment are noticeably thinner than those of twelfth-century monastic books, and the script is much smaller and more compressed, with an abundant use of abbreviations and more drastically simplified forms of words. This book was probably made for Grosseteste; its wide margins contain his annotations and indexing symbols for rapid identification of passages on individual theological topics. Three Greek manuscripts Grosseteste once owned are a tenth-century copy of the *Testamenta XII Patriarcharum* he used for his translation, a twelfth-century gospels, and the writings of the Pseudo-Dionysius copied from a manuscript at Saint-Denis.[42] According to Nicholas Trevet, Grosseteste left his books to the Oxford Franciscans out of affection for Adam Marsh; it is reasonable to assume that, in so doing, he intended the collection to be preserved as a scholarly resource for the study of theology. References to a further nine books of Grosseteste's once owned

39 P. W. Rosemann (ed.), 'Tabula magistri Roberti Lincolniensis episcopi . . .', in J. McEvoy (ed.), *Opera Roberti Grosseteste Lincolniensis*, I, *CCCM* 130 (Turnhout, 1995), 235–43.

40 R. W. Southern, *Robert Grosseteste: the growth of an English mind in medieval Europe*, 2nd edn (Oxford, 1992), 186–90.

41 Bodleian, MS Bodley 198.

42 CUL, MS Ff.1.24, Cambridge, Gonville and Caius Coll., MS 403/412, and Bodleian, MS Canon. Gr. 97.

by the convent are known, several from the citations of his fifteenth-century admirer, the Oxford theologian Thomas Gascoigne, who used the collection.[43]

By the late thirteenth and early fourteenth centuries, it had become more common for English bishops to possess substantial book collections of between at least forty and ninety books, while increasingly other scholars who had proceeded to the higher degrees accumulated smaller collections. Their books contained mainly theology and canon and civil law, but, as a few examples will demonstrate, they were far less uniform than they appear at first sight.[44]

Prior Eastry's catalogue of the books of the cathedral priory of Christ Church, Canterbury, records forty-five volumes once owned by Archbishop Robert Winchelsea (1293–1313). Archbishop Winchelsea had studied arts in Paris and was rector of the university in 1267. He was strongly influenced by Thomas Aquinas and may have attended his lectures at the convent of Saint-Jacques in 1269 to 1272. By 1288 he was a doctor of theology at Oxford and until 1289 chancellor of the university. He also lectured in theology at the important London cathedral school at St Paul's.[45] Not surprisingly, given Winchelsea's eminence as a theologian active in contemporary debate, his books included many volumes of Aquinas. Seven of his books are known to survive.[46] The notarial instrument attached to Winchelsea's will specifies that *tota libraria sua*, all his books kept in his cathedral church at Canterbury, were to remain there. It is impossible to know whether he had others elsewhere.[47]

A rather different collection of more than ninety books belonged to Walter Stapeldon, bishop of Exeter (1307–26), treasurer of England and loyal servant of Edward II. After his murder in London, they were listed as part of an inventory of his goods, and valued for his executors at over £200. While Winchelsea's collection was dominated by works of theology, Stapeldon's, by contrast, was especially strong in canon and civil law, reflecting his training in both subjects at Oxford and at least to some extent his official duties on behalf of the Crown. There is a little information about where he obtained his books. His *Novum digestum* had been bought in Oxford, others had previously belonged to clerics

43 R. W. Hunt, 'The library of Grosseteste', in D. A. Callus (ed.), *Robert Grosseteste: scholar and bishop* (Oxford, 1955), 121–45 and pl. 1; R. Weiss, 'The private collector and the revival of Greek learning', in Wormald and Wright, *English library*, 125–6.

44 K. Edwards, 'Bishops and learning in the reign of Edward II', *Church Quarterly Review* 138: 275 (1944), 57–86, esp. 69–71, 85.

45 W. J. Courtenay, *Schools and scholars in fourteenth-century England* (Princeton, NJ, 1987), 91–106; his *Quaestiones disputatae apud London* survive in Oxford, Magdalen Coll., MS 217.

46 Cambridge, Trinity Coll., MSS B.16.6–9 and 11; Bodleian, MSS Bodley 214 and 379; Oxford, University Coll., MS 68.

47 James, *ALCD*, 135–7; *BRUO* III. 2057–9.

in his diocese. Some were apparently duplicates. Perhaps he made his books available for others to use, or perhaps the executors had brought together sets of books from different residences. None, however, is known to survive. Two carrying chests for the books were separately valued.[48]

The book collections of the bishops of London in the early fourteenth century are comparatively well attested. Richard de Gravesend, bishop from 1280 to 1303, left a large collection of ninety-eight volumes mainly of theology and canon law.[49] Its full extent is known from a probate inventory, drawn up and valued for his executors. His will, by contrast, mentions only a book on loan and two of his own finest books: a set of decretals and a multi-volume bible. Gravesend's books were stored in his Wardrobe after his death and were valued at the very large sum of nearly £117. The two named in the will went to two of his executors, both future bishops of London: a thirteen-volume bible valued at £10 to his nephew Stephen de Gravesend, who later became a benefactor of the libraries of his cathedral and of Merton College, Oxford, and a set of decretals worth £6 13s 4d to Richard de Newport, then archdeacon of Colchester.[50] Almost all Bishop Richard's other books were sold. The most valuable was a two-volume *Summa Hostiensis* (the *Summa* on the decretals by the bishop of Ostia) at £13 6s 8d, while a copy of Aristotle's *Libri naturales*, worth only 3s, was given to a poor scholar, who was to pray for the bishop's soul. He also provided in his will for the return to Lincoln Cathedral of the gospel book with the glosses of Aquinas.[51]

It is only very rarely possible to glimpse the books a man was using at a particular time, or where and how they were kept. Ralph Baldock, dean of St Paul's from 1294, was bishop of London from 1304 to his death in 1313 and briefly chancellor of England in 1307. A month before he died, an inventory was taken at his manor at Stepney, Middlesex. It lists twenty-eight books in his study there – an unusual and precious reference to the whereabouts of a man's books. Apart from a small bible 'bene correcta', the others the bishop had at hand were canon law, sermon collections, his own chronicle, and several books of a practical nature: a medical compilation, and registers concerning the administration of his diocese. Books of reference and administrative records

48 F. C. Hingeston-Randolph (ed.), *The register of Walter de Stapeldon, bishop of Exeter, 1307–1326* (London and Exeter, 1892), 563–5; *BRUO* III. 1764–5.

49 Cavanaugh, 'Books privately owned', I. 382–5; *BRUO* II. 804–5.

50 *BRUO* II. 805–6, 1357–8.

51 W. H. Hale and H. T. Ellacombe, *Account of the executors of Richard, bishop of London 1303*, Camden Soc., n.s. 10 (London, 1874), 50–3; 113–16; *BRUO* II. 804–5; F. M. Powicke, *The medieval books of Merton College* (Oxford, 1931), 51.

were often kept together.[52] Some were bound in red covers, others in white or black. This was only a fraction of his book collection. A memorandum records 126 volumes bequeathed to St Paul's, greatly enriching its library and 'more than adequately covering Oxford and Parisian texts in arts and theology of the thirteenth century'.[53] Moreover, Baldock's executors had to substitute seven books for those they could not find, presumably from a yet larger stock. His bequest included complete bibles, scholastic commentaries, canon and civil law, sermons and works of pastoral theology, medicine, astronomy and an illustrated apocalypse. The list ends with two works reflecting St Paul's role as a centre of historical writing, Baldock's own chronicle, which was seen by Leland, but lost by the seventeenth century, and the chronicle of Henry of Huntingdon.[54] Among Baldock's books was also an unusual liturgical psalter of around 1300 (St Paul's Cathedral, MS 1), with added obits for the Baldock family and 'liturgical doodles', perhaps autograph, suggesting he worked on his cathedral's liturgy.[55]

Collections with similar contents but on a smaller scale were accumulated by other clergy, regulars as well as seculars, who had studied in the higher faculties. By the end of the thirteenth century even monks who were not office-holders were permitted a personal income. It became increasingly common for them to acquire books, especially while studying at university, provided that their books passed to the community at their death.[56] John of Taunton, abbot of Glastonbury (1274–91), left to his community what his contemporaries regarded as a 'librarium . . . optimum, pulcherimum, et copiosum', some twenty-four volumes of theological textbooks and reference works.[57] William de Bernham, abbot of Bury St Edmunds (1335–61), left books to the abbey valued at 100 marks. His successor, John of Brinkley (1361–79), who studied law at Oxford, gave books worth £150.[58] Seculars were under no such obligation, and might choose to make provision for more than one beneficiary. The will of Henry de la Wylie (d. 1329), chancellor of Salisbury and fellow of Merton

52 Stirnemann, 'Les bibliothèques princières'.
53 Courtenay, *Schools and scholars*, 101.
54 *BRUO* III. 2147–9; N. R. Ker, 'Books at St Paul's Cathedral before 1313', in *Books, collectors and libraries*, 235–6, for the chronicle no. 124a; A. Gransden, *Historical writing in England, c. 550 to c. 1307* (London, 1974), 523; J. Taylor, *English historical literature in the fourteenth century* (Oxford, 1987), 26; D. E. Greenway, 'Historical writing at St Paul's', and N. Ramsay, 'The library and archives to 1897', both in D. Keene, A. Burns and A. Saint (eds.), *St Paul's: the cathedral church of London 604–2004* (London, 2004), 153 and n. 14, 414.
55 R. W. Pfaff, 'Bishop Baldock's book, St Paul's Cathedral, and the use of Sarum', in his *Liturgical calendars, saints and services in medieval England* (Aldershot, 1998), no. XI. 1–20; Ker, 'Books at St Pauls', 235, 4a.
56 Parkes, 'Provision of books', 452–5; see also above, 152.
57 CBMLC IV. B40.
58 CBMLC IV. B15.

College, is unusually detailed about the destination of his book collection of at least thirty-seven books.[59] Fifteen largely exegetical and theological volumes were bequeathed to his cathedral. Eight of these survive, and in addition a ninth not mentioned in the will.[60] Six volumes of patristic and later theology went to Merton, and four of natural philosophy to Balliol, while pastoralia and liturgical books were reserved for canons of Salisbury. To his brother Robert de la Wylie Henry left a small bible, as well as four volumes of theological set texts. These were to pass to Merton on Robert's death.

Many of the eighty-five bishops during the reign of Edward III (1327–77) were university men, and it is not unreasonable to assume that they possessed more or less substantial collections of the kind already described.[61] A few, however, compiled collections on an even larger scale, and to fulfil more ambitious aims, perhaps influenced by continental precedent. Three names stand out: the bibliophile Richard de Bury, bishop of Durham, the learned John Grandisson, bishop of Exeter, and the Benedictine monk, Cardinal Simon Langham, bishop of Ely and subsequently archbishop of Canterbury. All three men had long lives in which to accumulate their books. Bury died in 1345, some three years before the first outbreak of the Black Death. Grandisson was by his own reckoning seventy-eight when he died in 1369; Langham who was already a monk at Westminster by 1340, died in Avignon only in 1376. All three had been at the papal curia at Avignon, and must have known the outstanding papal library there, which by 1369 numbered some 2,059 volumes.

By his own joyous account in the *Philobiblon*, Richard de Bury (1287–1345) was a man who loved books for their own sake and owned an enormous number of them. His description of Paris as the 'Paradisum mundi' centred on the opportunities for the book-lover in its libraries and bookshops. Adam Murimuth claimed that he had amassed enough to fill more than five carts, a staggering collection for the mid-fourteenth century. Bury came from a knightly family, and became tutor to the future Edward III. He amassed the riches to make his immense book collection through his career in royal service, crowned as keeper of the privy seal and briefly as chancellor, and then as bishop of the rich see of Durham from 1333. Until 1340, when Bury retired from royal service and moved to Durham, his household was in London at Durham Inn,

59 Cavanaugh, 'Books privately owned', I. 238–42.

60 Salisbury Cathedral, MSS 2, 18(?), 19–20, 54, 62 (+ BL, MS Sloane 1056A), 72, 82 and 93. The endleaf of Bodleian, MS Bodley 516, that bears an inscription of his bequest, did not originally form part of the manuscript: *MLGB Supplement*, 109.

61 J. R. L. Highfield, 'The English hierarchy in the reign of Edward III', *TRHS*, 5th ser., 6 (1956), 124–32.

but he went to Avignon several times on diplomatic missions; on one visit he met Petrarch. He had studied at Oxford between about 1302 and 1312 but he did not incept;[62] some contemporaries judged him only moderately learned, but his curiosity seems to have been boundless, and he may have had at least a smattering of Hebrew and Greek. Among his *familia* at various times were the philosopher Walter Burley, the future archbishop Thomas Bradwardine, and many other scholars who enjoyed his patronage. These able clients lived with Bury, accompanied him on his frequent travels and no doubt helped him to obtain his books.[63]

Bury has left a vivid account in the *Philobiblon* of the ways he obtained his books in England and abroad, revealing how rich men could add to a stock of new and second-hand books.[64] He wrote openly of accepting books in return for favours. These he regarded as the normal perquisites of office. Such were the five service-books and nine 'libri diversi', titles unspecified, granted to him in 1328 from the store in the royal Wardrobe during his tenure as its keeper and treasurer.[65] He borrowed books from individuals and from religious houses, no doubt for copying or collating by the friars he states that he employed for these purposes, and as exemplars for the scribes, illuminators and binders he kept busy in one of his manors. Three books Bury had on loan at one time probably came from Bermondsey Abbey; on another occasion Anthony Bek, dean of Lincoln and bishop of Norwich, asked for the return of his own copy of a rare work, as well as two books from Lincoln Cathedral.[66]

Many books came from St Albans. According to Thomas Walsingham in the *Gesta abbatum*, Abbot Richard of Wallingford (1328–36?) gave Bury, then keeper of the privy seal, four books from St Albans library, a Terence, a Virgil, a Quintilian and Jerome's *Contra Rufinum*, hoping for preferment at court.[67] He sold him thirty-two more from the library for £50. Bury wrote his name in these books, but gave some back after he became bishop of Durham. After Bury's death in 1345, Abbot Michael of Mentmore (1336–49) bought back some more, and also purchased other books from Bury's executors which had not previously been at St Albans. An inscription in a very handsome copy

62 *BRUO* I. 323–6.

63 Courtenay, *Schools and scholars*, 133–7.

64 For an example on a smaller scale of the diverse means of acquiring books by a scholar at Oxford in the early fifteenth century, see Parkes, 'Provision of books', 423–4, on Richard Calne.

65 BL, Add. MS 60584, fols. 17^{v}, 18^{v}; J. Stratford, 'The early royal collections and the Royal Library to 1461', *CHBB* III. 259–60 and n. 15.

66 Powicke, *Merton books*, 227–8, no. 1189; CBMLC IV. B10. 109–13, pp. 22–3, 32; C. R. Cheney, 'Richard de Bury, borrower of books', *Speculum* 48 (1973), 325–8.

67 H. T. Riley (ed.), *Gesta abbatum sancti Albani*, 3 vols., RS (London, 1867–9), II. 200; CBMLC IV, 541–2.

of works of John of Salisbury made for Abbot Simon probably before 1173 (BL, MS Royal 13.D.iv) records that the abbot bought it back in 1346. A twelfth-century Pliny (Oxford, New College, MS 274) and a theological miscellany, datable to before 1107 (Bodleian, MS Laud Misc. 363), both with Bury's *ex libris*, seem not to have been recovered. The abbot also bought from the executors the *Tabula originalium sacre scripture*, which had been written for Bury in London (BL, MS Royal 8.G.i). It was kept in the abbot's study.[68] Three more St Albans manuscripts seem to have belonged to Bury. He wrote his name in a twelfth-century Terence (Bodleian, MS Auct. F. 2.13). The others are an early thirteenth-century copy of Odo of Morimond, and an anthology of Aristotelian texts of about the same date.[69]

Bury wanted to found a college in Oxford, where he had taken his MA and BD, and to bequeath it his books, intending them also to be available on loan to other scholars. Perhaps for shortage of cash, Bury's executors sold his books and the college was never founded. The catalogue compiled on his orders is lost.[70] He was no doubt influenced by the precedent of the great Sorbonne library, as well as the friars' libraries. Bury's intentions were in response to the lack of communal provision of books in Oxford. His perception of this need was shared by other fourteenth-century bishops. A little earlier, Thomas de Cobham, bishop of Worcester, had intended to bequeath his books to Oxford for the use of poor scholars. In 1320 Cobham had provided a congregation house for the university on the north side of St Mary's church. His books were supposed to be chained in the upper room and were meant to act as a permanent reference collection. After a prolonged dispute caused by a shortage of funds at Cobham's death in 1327, the books were finally installed as he had wished in 1413.[71]

Another great man who bequeathed books for the use of poor scholars at Oxford from his own impressive collection was John Grandisson, bishop of Exeter (1327–69). His will, drawn up in 1368, a year before his death, brings his love of learning vividly to life, revealing his attitude towards his books and the use that should be made of them. Munificence was a virtue expected of the

68 N. R. Ker, 'Richard de Bury's books from the library of St Albans', *BLR* 3 (1950–1), 177–9; R. M. Thomson, *Manuscripts from St Albans Abbey, 1066–1235*, 2nd edn, 2 vols. (Woodbridge, 1985), I, nos. 34, 48, 60; CBMLC IV. 541.

69 Thomson, *ibid.*, nos. 41, 42, 56; J. G. Clark, *A monastic renaissance at St Albans: Thomas Walsingham and his circle c. 1350–1440* (Oxford, 2004).

70 M. Maclagan (ed.), *Philobiblon Richardi de Bury: the text and translation of E. C. Thomas* (Oxford, 1960), ch. 19, 168–9; N. Denholm-Young, 'Richard de Bury (1287–1345) and the *Liber epistolaris*', *TRHS*, 4th ser., 20 (1937), 135–68; repr. in *Collected papers of Denholm-Young* (Cardiff, 1969), 1–4, 24–41; Weiss, 'The private collector', 113–15; *BRUO* I. 323–6.

71 Parkes, 'Provision of books', 470–1.

great, and Grandisson was munificent with his books as well as with his other possessions.[72] His finest academic books of theology were carefully divided to enhance the resources of the major churches and the scholars of his diocese. Nicholas de Lyra, and Nicholas Trevet on the psalms (the latter Bodleian, MS Bodley 738), were destined for the cathedral, together with the best *originalia* (the works of the Fathers) not in its *libraria* – here again meaning the book collection rather than a room – to remain there 'in archivis'. His theological books of modest value were to be divided between poor scholars in theology and Stapledon Hall, afterwards Exeter College. For the Dominicans of Exeter he intended all the works of Thomas Aquinas. Any residue was to go to the collegiate churches of Ottery, Crediton and Bosham. Reserved for his successors as bishop were the ordinal he had compiled and other books kept in his chamber and chapel. Among them were the Meditations and Prayers of Anselm and Augustine in a large volume, his best bible and two books of homilies. Two of his gospel books were magnificently bound in silver-gilt: the gospel of St John 'in ancient script' was left to the cathedral and a gospel lectionary was intended for his successors as bishop. The lectionary had raised images of the crucifixion, Mary and John on the upper cover, with the coronation of the Virgin in niello on the lower, iconography reminiscent of his ivory triptych in the British Museum.[73]

Other bequests, perhaps of more personal books, reflect Grandisson's aristocratic connections. Grandisson was a member of a great baronial family from Savoy who had settled in England in royal service. He had lifelong connections at court and at the papal curia. His studies probably began with civil law at Oxford in 1306. In Paris he studied theology between 1313 and 1317 under the Cistercian Jacques Fournier, the future Benedict XII, then theology at Oxford from 1326 to 1327. Grandisson was consecrated at Avignon in 1327 by John XXII, to whom he owed his advancement. Throughout his career, he retained strong links with the papacy. After his elder brother died in 1358, he became very rich. Like the *familia* of Richard de Bury, his *familia* included scholars, men such as Richard Fitzralph, archbishop of Armagh (1347–60), and Thomas Buckingham, who died in 1349 as chancellor of Exeter, no doubt from

72 *BRUO* II. 801. See also *MMBL* I. 275; II. 711, 809–10, 819, 820, 844, 845; III. 659; F. Rose-Troup, 'Bishop Grandisson: student and art lover', *Transactions of the Devonshire Archaeological Association* 60 (1928), 249–55; M. W. Steele, 'A study of the books owned or used by John Grandisson bishop of Exeter (1327–1369)', unpublished DPhil thesis, Oxford University (1994).

73 *BRUO* II. 800–1; Hingeston-Randolph, *Reg. Grandisson*, III. 1549–58; *Survey*, IV/ii. no. 165; N. Stratford, 'Bishop Grandisson and the visual arts', in M. Swanton (ed.), *Exeter Cathedral, a celebration* (Exeter, 1991), 145–55.

the Black Death. He left a copy of Bernard's sermons to Pope Urban V and gave the copy of Anselm's *Epistolae* he had collated to Archbishop Islip of Canterbury in 1364 (BL, MS Cotton Claudius A. xi), later confirming the gift to future archbishops. A copy of the *Similitudines Anselmi* (BL, MS Cotton Cleo. C. xi) passed to Abbey Dore, Hereford, where his mother was buried, and a great concordance was given to Lewis Charlton, bishop of Hereford. His late thirteenth-century illuminated psalter, prefaced with an added shield of his arms, was left to Isabella, eldest daughter of Edward III (BL, Add. MS 21926).

A comparatively large number of Grandisson's books, mainly of theology, have survived. Many have autograph annotations in the bishop's distinctive large hand, evidence of the use he made of them. Some notes relate to provenance and to donations. In a second-hand copy of Augustine, *Opuscula*, formerly belonging to Robertsbridge and with an anathema (Bodleian, MS Bodley 132), Grandisson wrote that he did not know where that was, but that he had come by the book honestly. He composed a Life of Thomas Becket and a legendary (Exeter Cathedral, MSS 3504 and 3505), the latter written and decorated for him, probably in London, where he lived from time to time at Exeter Inn. Besides the two volumes of his legendary, an Isidore and a selection of decretals are still at Exeter. Eleven further volumes bequeathed to his cathedral, mainly works of theology and a Hebrew grammar, are now divided between the Bodleian Library, Lambeth Palace and Trinity College, Cambridge. Also at Trinity is the copy of William of Malmesbury's *De gestis pontificum* that Grandisson had borrowed and returned to Malmesbury Abbey (Trinity, MS R.5.36). A volume with the commentaries of Nicholas Trevet and Thomas Waleys on Augustine's *De civitate Dei* was designated for poor scholars and was at Merton College, Oxford, by 1382 (Merton, MS E.1.6).[74] The notes in the magnificent thirteenth-century Amesbury Psalter (All Souls, MS 6), suggest it may have belonged to him.[75]

The large book collection of Simon Langham, who died as cardinal bishop in Avignon in 1376, must have been shaped by his residence close to the papal curia and its great library.[76] He had been abbot of Westminster after the Black Death from 1349 to 1362, before becoming bishop of Ely, then archbishop of Canterbury, 1366–8, serving briefly as treasurer and chancellor of England. Among his possessions sent back from Avignon to Westminster Abbey after his death were

74 *MLGB*, 128; *Survey*, IV/i. no. 60; Powicke, *Merton books*, 137, no. 362.

75 *Survey*, IV/ii. no. 101; A. G. Watson, *A descriptive catalogue of the medieval manuscripts of All Souls College Oxford* (Oxford, 1997), 13–15.

76 *BRUO* II. 1095–7; J. A. Robinson and M. R. James, *The manuscripts of Westminster Abbey* (Cambridge, 1909), 4–7.

eighty well-chosen volumes, mainly works of theology and canon law. They filled seven chests and were valued during transport by merchants via Bruges at some 1,100 francs. A collection estimated to be of equal if not greater size (perhaps at least 228 books) was donated to Norwich Cathedral by Adam Easton, Langham's secretary at Avignon from 1368 to 1376. Easton, a fellow Benedictine, was a future cardinal, who remained at the papal curia until his death in 1397.[77] If this estimate is correct and since the number of Richard de Bury's books cannot be determined, only one other fourteenth-century personal collection exceeded Easton's in size. The friar John Ergome (d. 1385) possessed around 300 volumes; they were bequeathed to the Austin friars of York.[78]

By the second half of the fourteenth century certain bishops stand out as donors of major book collections to the Oxford colleges and for the part they played in shaping the development of those collections. The important contributions to the formation of the libraries of respectively Merton, New College, Lincoln, All Souls, Balliol and Madgalen by William Rede, bishop of Chichester, William of Wykeham, Richard and Robert Flemyng, Archbishop Chichele, Bishop Gray and Bishop Waynflete, are discussed above (chapter 6). Their bequests were supplemented by smaller donations from less eminent men. By the later fourteeth century, cheaper books, both new and second-hand, became available, enabling lesser clergy and monks to possess collections on a scale which had been possible only for prelates in the later twelfth century. Master Thomas de Lexham, canon of Hereford and rector of Feltwell (d. 1382), for example, left a total of fifty-one books.[79] The majority (thirty-three) he bequeathed to Clare Hall.[80] The remainder reflected his connections in Norfolk and the West Midlands: seven went to Castle Acre, four to Hereford, and the remainder in ones and twos to religious houses and churches in King's Lynn, to his own church at Feltwell and to Worcester Cathedral.

The book collections of clergy and scholars were first and foremost accumulated as practical tools that served religious and scholarly needs. By the later medieval period, members of the emergent professions had also come to need specific books as 'tools of the trade', although, for some, a single book or a mere handful of volumes might suffice.[81] For other members of the laity many different requirements – and perhaps accidents – influenced what books they owned. In the earlier middle ages, little can be known of lay book-ownership.

77 *BRUO* I. 620–1; N. R. Ker, 'Medieval manuscripts from Norwich cathedral priory', *TCBS* I (1949–53), 10, 17, 18; repr. in his *Books, collectors and libraries*, 253–4, 260–1, 271–2; CBMLC IV. 290–1.

78 See above, 141.

79 Cavanaugh, 'Books privately owned', I. 512–18.

80 CBMLC X. UC143.

81 See below, chapters 13–20.

But from the twelfth and thirteenth centuries, the evidence slowly begins to accumulate.

Royal books and book collections

Our knowledge of royal book collections in England between the twelfth and the fourteenth centuries is fragmentary. Although there are well-known examples of learned kings, very little can be discovered about their books before the thirteenth century. But it is almost certain that by the twelfth century, if not earlier, apart from the service-books used in the royal chapels and the itinerant *capella*, books for devotion, instruction and entertainment were kept within the royal household. The grandchildren and great-grandchildren of William I belonged to an Anglo-French elite in which learning as well as literary and scholarly patronage was increasingly considered a fitting attribute. Between the years 1066 and 1204 the rulers of England also held extensive territories in the French kingdom: the duchy of Normandy, the county of Anjou and the great duchy of Aquitaine, which was the inheritance of Eleanor, wife the Angevin king Henry II. Some of these kings, among them Henry I and Henry II, had a reputation for learning, for to be *litteratus* in the twelfth century meant to be literate in Latin, but very little is known about their books. Queens, such as Adeliza of Louvain, second wife of Henry I, are known to have read works presented to them by clerical authors.[82] There has been much debate, however, about the extent to which Henry II and his wife Eleanor commissioned works in Latin or the vernacular. They have been closely associated with the so-called earliest *romans d'antiquité* as with the historical *romans de Brut* and *de Rou* (i.e. Rollo, the first 'Norman ancestor' of the Anglo-Norman and Angevin kings). If accepted, this controversial hypothesis could imply the existence of a book collection.[83]

The books and literary works that have been associated with the princely couple Count Henry the Liberal of Champagne (1127–81) and his wife Marie may provide a point of comparison.[84] An early fourteenth-century inventory lists forty-nine non-liturgical books kept in the uppermost treasury of the collegiate church of Saint-Etienne at Troyes, a church lavishly endowed by Henry,

82 M. D. Legge, *Anglo-Norman literature and its background* (Oxford, 1963), 22–3, 364.

83 K. M. Broadhurst, 'Henry II of England and Eleanor of Aquitaine: patrons of literature in French?', *Viator* 27 (1996), 53–84; P. Damian-Grint, '*En nul leu nel truis escrit*: research and invention in Benoît de Sainte-Maure's *Chronique des ducs de Normandie*', *Anglo-Norman Studies* 21 (1999 for 1998), 11–30; *The new historians of the twelfth-century Renaissance: inventing vernacular authority* (Woodbridge, 1999).

84 J. F. Benton, 'The court of Champagne as a literary center', *Speculum* 36 (1961), 551–91.

and his burial place. By matching this list with the identifiable surviving volumes, the majority of them dating from the second half of the twelfth century, it has recently been proposed that these patristic, classical and medieval works in Latin constituted the library of Henry himself, rather than, say, a library constituted by or for the canons he so liberally endowed. They have been linked to a common centre on the grounds of their decoration and ornament.[85] One of these books, a Valerius Maximus, contains the colophon of the scribe Willelmus anglicus, stating that he wrote at Provins on the orders of Count Henry in 1172.[86] Literary references in vernacular works suggest that Marie also had a book collection. Although no direct connections can be made, it is surely relevant that Marie was the daughter of Queen Eleanor by her first husband, Louis VII of France, and that she was one of the earliest patrons of the great vernacular poet Chrétien of Troyes. Marie de Champagne has also been associated with the enigmatic Andreas Capellanus and is a central figure in his notorious treatise on love, *De amore*.[87]

Count Henry's court was especially renowned, but its literary and learned connections were not unique.[88] Small collections of books, perhaps produced by scribes from neighbouring religious houses or by secular artisans, probably existed, to judge by the literary references to the patronage of the Anglo-French aristocracy. The surviving Insular French literature reveals these magnates to be precocious in their taste for devotional and romance literature in French.[89] These works sometimes refer to books in individual ownership, although only one direct reference to lay ownership of more than a single volume is known.[90] Hue de Rotelande, in his *Protheselaus* (written between 1180 and 1190 for Gilbert FitzBaderon, lord of Monmouth), claimed that Gilbert's castle was well stocked with books in both Latin and French.[91] The lack of direct evidence of books may be explicable by the exceptionally poor survival of books that did not pass into institutional ownership and also by the possibility that copies

85 Stirnemann, 'Une bibliothèque princière', 36–42.

86 BN, ms lat. 9688: 'Titulus scriptoris. feliciter emendavi descriptum Pruuini. iussi illustris comitis Henrici. Willelmus Anglicus. anno incarnati verbi MCLXVII. Indictione XV'. See P. D. Stirnemann, 'Quelsques bibliothèques princières et la production hors scriptorium au XIIe siècle', *Bulletin archéologique du CTHS*, n.s., 17–18 (1984), 7–38.

87 Andreas Capellanus, *On love*, ed. and tr. P. G. Walsh (London, 1982); Benton, 'Court of Champagne', 578–82, 587–9; Broadhurst, 'Henry II', 78–80.

88 On the book collection of Baldwin, count of Guînes, see Stirnemann, 'Les bibliothèques princières', 177.

89 I. Short, 'Patrons and polyglots: French literature in twelfth-century England', *Anglo-Norman Studies* 14 (1992 for 1991), 229–49, esp. 237–49.

90 *Ibid.*; Parkes, 'Literacy', 276–8.

91 A. J. Holden (ed.), *'Protheselaus' by Hue de Rotelande*, 2 vols., ANTS 47–8 (London, 1991), II. 174. vv. 12696–12710: 'Dount sis chastels est mult manauntz / E de latyn e de romaunz.'

of twelfth-century vernacular texts were in booklet form and not copied as, or bound into, more substantial volumes.[92]

During the 200 years from the accession of King John to the deposition of Richard II (1199–1399), all too little is known about royal books, let alone a royal library. Much of the evidence, such as it is, comes from written sources. By the thirteenth century, royal records were more systematically compiled and they have survived in increasing numbers over the succeeding centuries. Scattered references can be found to the titles of royal books or to their movement in and out of store, but these are notoriously difficult to interpret. Books in store in the Wardrobe or the Treasury were not and may never have been for the personal use of the king or his household. Other archival references are to scribes, illuminators and binders in royal employment – within the households of Eleanor of Castile, wife of Edward I; Isabella, wife of Edward II; and Philippa of Hainault, wife of Edward III, for example. The cost of the materials with which they were provided is known, but not what was being written, decorated and bound.[93] There are only a few extant royal books; most of those that have survived have done so because they are exceptional illuminated manuscripts.[94] Some works in verse and prose have dedications to one or another king or queen, but most of these are known from copies, not the presentation manuscript. Yet the cumulative impression is that English kings and queens were by no means indifferent to books, even though incontrovertible evidence of a more or less coherent and stable royal book collection, as opposed to shifting assemblages of books, is lacking before the fifteenth century.

King John (1199–1216), the son of the cultivated and learned Henry II, may have possessed a book collection. An enigmatic entry in the Pipe Roll for 1203 records the cost of 'chests and carts to take the king's books overseas', perhaps a book collection of some size. Were these service-books, books for leisure, devotion or instruction, books for the king's administrative business, or all of these? Were they intended for the use of the king himself?[95] In 1205 John had a 'romance' (an Anglo-Norman text) of the history of England sent to him at Windsor, perhaps the lost version of the *Brut* by Gaimar. Like other

92 For a different perspective, see R. M. Thomson, *Books and learning in twelfth-century England: the ending of* 'Alter orbis' (forthcoming).

93 Cavanaugh, 'Royal books', 304–16; M. A. Michael, 'English illuminators *c.* 1190–1450: a survey from documentary sources', *EMS* 4 (1993), 70–1 and Appendix 2.

94 J. J. G. Alexander, 'Painting and manuscript illumination for royal patrons in the later middle ages', in V. J. Scattergood and J. W. Sherborne (eds.), *English court culture in the later middle ages* (London, 1983), 141–62.

95 *Pipe Roll 5 John*, Pipe Roll Society Publications, n.s. 16 (1938), 139; W. L. Warren, *King John*, 2nd edn (London, 1964), 300; for what follows, see M. T. Clanchy, *From memory to written record: England, 1066–1307*, 2nd edn (Oxford, 1993), 161–2.

educated laymen, he enjoyed history in the vernacular.[96] English kings from Henry II onwards were also literate in the sense of having been taught at least some Latin. In 1208 Reading Abbey returned John's own copy of Pliny in Latin ('librum nostrum'). And a few days earlier, just before Easter, he had obtained from the abbey fourteen Latin books, among them a complete Old Testament, the *Sentences* of Peter Lombard, Hugh of St Victor on the sacraments, and patristic texts of Augustine, Origen and others. These books probably belonged to Reading. They could have been intended for John himself or for members of his religious household. It has been suggested that they may have been required to bolster arguments in the king's dispute with Stephen Langton over clerical privileges.[97]

It may be an accident that so little is known of the books of Henry III (1216–72), or of his wife, Eleanor of Provence. Records of payments survive for service-books for the royal chapels at Hereford, Nottingham, Winchester and Windsor, but 'a great book of romances' in a binding with silver clasps is also mentioned in 1237.[98] This could be the 'great book in French' containing 'the deeds of Antioch and of the kings' delivered to Eleanor thirteen years later, in 1250. It was then in store with the Knights Templar, probably as part of a royal Wardrobe.[99] Matthew Paris wrote of several meetings with the king in his chronicle, and of Henry's request to him to report the ceremonies at Westminster on the feast of Edward the Confessor, 13 October 1247. Henry is well documented as a patron of building works and of monumental painting, but Matthew Paris also recorded the king's keen interest in ensuring that there was a written record of events in which he himself took part.[100] Eleanor of Provence was the dedicatee of vernacular works: Matthew Paris's verse translation of *Estoire de Seint Aedward le Rei* and John of Howden's mystical poem *Rossignos*. Eleanor bequeathed a book she had owned in old age to her son Edward I, and in 1298 it was delivered by a minstrel to her grandson Edward II. This is a rare documented reference of a royal book passing through three successive generations.[101]

According to Rustichello of Pisa, Henry's son Edward I (1272–1307) 'took' a volume of Arthurian romances on crusade to the Holy Land in 1271. Kings

96 T. D. Hardy (ed.), *Rotuli litterarum clausarum*, 2 vols. (London, 1833–44), I. 29.

97 *Ibid.*, 108; Legge, *Anglo-Norman literature*, 108; *MLGB*, 154–5.

98 Clanchy, *From memory to written record*, 161–2, citing *CLibR 1240–5*, 29, 296; *CLibR 1251–60*, 11; *CLibR* 1226–40, 419; *Cal. Close Rolls* 1247–51, 162; *CLibR 1226–40*, 288.

99 Clanchy, *ibid.*, 161.

100 Clanchy, *ibid.*, 101; R. Vaughan, *Matthew Paris*, 2nd edn (Cambridge, 1979), 3–4, 13.

101 Legge, *Anglo-Norman literature*, 233–4; 269; H. Johnstone, *Edward of Carnarvon* (Manchester, 1946), 108.

and great nobles undoubtedly took books in their baggage on campaign, but this is probably a literary fiction. Rustichello asserted in the prologue to his *Roman de Tristan* and *Roman de Palmede* that Edward's book was his source, but told a different story at the end of his work.[102] Appropriately enough for a future soldier king, an Anglo-Norman translation of Vegetius, datable to around 1265–72, is among the few extant books associated with Edward. Another is the Douce Apocalypse. The fragmentary French apocalypse which precedes the Latin texts is introduced by an initial with the arms of Edward and his queen, Eleanor of Castile.[103] The Alphonso Psalter was originally ordered for Edward's eldest son, who died in 1284.[104] The small groups of books documented in the Wardrobe in 1295–6 and still there in 1299–1300, and those stolen from the treasury in the chapter house at Westminster in 1303, however, were not in current use. They were packed up in coffers with other valuables. A gospel book in a leather case, for example, 'on which the magnates were accustomed to swear their oaths of loyalty to the crown', was stored with a *mappa mundi* on a cloth, a mixed bag of gold coins from old wardrobe stock, broken pieces of an ancient royal sceptre and gold rings of religious which had returned to the Crown.[105]

A few of the books needed for Edward II's education as Prince of Wales are recorded; once again, those stored in the Treasury of the Exchequer in 1313 and 1323 are unlikely to have been in use by the king or his court.[106] An exceptional document, on the other hand, has survived from the end of Edward's reign and from the reign of his son, Edward III. The account of John Flete, keeper between 1324 and 1341 of the Privy Wardrobe in the Tower, lists some 340 books and unbound quires stored there at different times with other valuables. Some of the titles in Latin and French are recorded, as well as a good deal about the bindings and a few scraps about illumination, but almost nothing about

102 E. Löseth (ed.), *Le roman en prose de Tristan, le roman de Palmède et la compilation de Rusticien de Pise* (Paris, 1891), 423–4; S. H. Cavanaugh, 'Royal books: King John to Richard II', *Library*, 6th ser., 10 (1988), 307; M. Prestwich, *Edward I* (London, 1988), 118, 123; F. Cigni, *Il romanzo arturiano di Rustichello da Pisa* (Pisa, 1994), nos. 1, 236, with facsimiles of BN, ms fr. 1463.

103 *Survey*, IV/ii, nos. 150, 153.

104 *Survey*, V, no. 1.

105 BL, Add. MS 7965, fols. 145, 145–145^{v}, 146^{v}, Wardrobe account for 1296 to 1297 with *remanencia* for the previous year; *Liber quotidianus contrarotulatoris garderobae 28 Edward I, AD 1299–1300* (London, 1787), 347–9, 351; Clanchy, *From memory to written record*, 256 for the gospel book.

106 Johnstone, *Edward of Carnarvon*, 18; *Cal. Close Rolls* 1313–18, 10; F. Palgrave (ed.), *The antient kalendars and inventories of the Treasury of her Majesty's Exchequer . . .* , 3 vols. (London, 1836), I. 104–6, esp. nos. 95–101; p. 116; A. Breeze, 'A manuscript of Welsh poetry in Edward II's library', *The National Library of Wales Journal*, 30/2 (1997), 129–31; P. R. Robinson, *Catalogue of dated and datable manuscripts c. 888–1600 in London libraries*, 2 vols. (London, 2003), no. 129 and pl. 46.

the contents. Soon after Flete took office in 1324, a French psalter and fourteen 'romances', meaning either books in the vernacular or romances in the modern sense, were issued to the clerk of Edward II's Chamber. A few more secular and liturgical books were sent to other household and Chamber clerks. This suggests that some of the books could have been read in the king's household, although not necessarily by Edward himself. It has been proposed that these books constituted a royal 'library'. This hypothesis can be accepted only with important reservations.[107]

The books came from different sources, and not all had a royal provenance. Sixty-six 'libri diversi' and other quires sealed in a canvas sack and stored in a chest, and quantities of other secular and liturgical books, stored in other chests, all received at the Tower at one and the same time, may have been sent from the king's Chamber or the Great Wardrobe. The seal of Thomas Ouseflete was fixed to the sack; Ouseflete was clerk and controller of the king's Chamber from 1319 to 1323 and keeper of the Great Wardrobe from 1323 to 1326. Another group, books of canon and civil law, came from the bishop of Winchester in 1326, probably John Stratford. Yet more books were among the valuables confiscated from great magnates and bishops implicated in the political troubles of Edward II's reign. After Edward III's accession in 1327, many of these were returned to their original owners or their heirs with their other valuables. Most of the books had been dispersed when Flete left office in 1341.

The books from this stock obtained by Richard de Bury have already been mentioned. Books also went to other favoured royal clerks. Soon after her return to power, in March 1327, Queen Isabella, mother of Edward III, received from Flete seven books in French from the stock in the Tower, all bound in red, white or green leather. Among them were the romances of *Renard* and *Meraugys and Sado*, a copy of Vegetius in French, and an illuminated book with clasps containing *historie . . . de heremitis et pluribus aliis titulis*. Two other romances, *Perceval* and *Guy of Warwick* were delivered on her orders at the same time to Thomas Ouseflete, still styled clerk of the Wardrobe.[108] We cannot know for certain if these books were for Isabella's own use, for her son's, or for some quite other purpose. But there is no question that Isabella, the daughter of Philip IV of France, ordered, owned and read books. Payments from her household in 1357 suggest as much. They are for parchment, some of

107 BL, Add. MS 60584; J. Vale, *Edward III and chivalry: chivalric society and its context, 1270–1350* (Woodbridge, 1982), 49–50, App. 9, 10; Stratford, 'The early royal collections', 257–60.

108 BL, Add. MS 60584, fol. 27^{v}.

the finest quality, for azure, to a scribe and to an illuminator.[109] She owned at her death Arthurian and other romances, and other vernacular books such as Brunetto Latini's *Trésor* in a volume with a *Brut*. Isabella had a comprehensive collection of service-books for her chapel, some of the use of Paris, as well as missals of Franciscan use, and two quires with an office of Corpus Christi. In her chamber were her more personal devotional works: a two-volume bible in French, an *apocalipsis in gallicis videlicet de vitiis patrum*, three books with matins of the Virgin (one unfinished), a book of 'imagery', and a psalter, perhaps identifiable as Munich, Bayerische Staatsbibliothek, Cod. gall. 16, in French and Latin. Most of her books were divided at her death between her daughter Joan, queen of Scotland, and Edward III.[110]

Edward III had a conventional princely education, including instruction in Latin, supervised by his tutors John Paynel and Richard de Bury. Shortly before he came to the throne in 1327 as a boy of fourteen, two Latin manuscripts, designed and illuminated as a pair, were begun for him by Walter de Milemete, fellow of King's Hall, Cambridge: the pseudo-Aristotelian *Secreta secretorum* (BL, Add. MS 47680) and Walter's own compilation, *De nobilitatibus sapientiis et prudentiis regum* (Oxford, Christ Church, MS 92). They belong to the 'mirror of princes' genre and were adapted to reflect Edward's new status as king. In neither was the lavish decoration completed.[111] Another compilation in French is associated by the heraldry with Edward and Philippa of Hainault around the time of their betrothal in 1326. This manuscript has been dismembered at various times during its history and now contains only the *Livre du trésor* of Brunetto Latini, the *Secrets des secrets*, and Raoul le Petit, the *Dit de Fauvain* (BN, ms fr. 571). A table of contents at the beginning of the manuscript lists other lost texts, among them a *Livre de Julius Cesar* and the statutes of England, perhaps the copy now in Harvard Law Library (MS 12).[112] The only items recorded as

109 BL, MS Cotton Galba E. xiv, *necessaria*; E. A. Bond, 'Notices of the last days of Isabella, Queen of Edward II, drawn from an account of the expenses of her household', *Archaeologia* 35 (1854), 465.

110 'Romances': TNA: PRO, E101/393/4, fol. 8; partly printed by E. Rickert, 'Richard II's books', *Library*, 4th ser., 13 (1933), 145; chapel books: PRO, E 101/333/29 and E101/393/4, fols. 6^{v}, 8, 9, partly printed by Palgrave, *Kalendars*, III. 239, nos. 88–90, pp. 244, 245; Cavanaugh, 'Royal books', 309–11; *Survey*, v, no. 27.

111 M. R. James, *The treatise of Walter de Milemete* (London, 1913); *Survey*, v, nos. 84 and 85; *Age of Chivalry*, no. 682; M. A. Michael, 'The iconography of kingship in the Walter of Milemete treatise', *JWCI* 57 (1994), 35–47; F. Lachaud, 'Un "miroir au prince" méconnu: le *De nobilitatibus, sapienciis et prudenciis regum* de Walter Milmete (vers 1326–1327)', in J. Paviot and J. Verger (eds.), *Guerre, pouvoir et noblesse au Moyen Age: mélanges en l'honneur de Philippe Contamine* (Paris, 2000).

112 M. A. Michael, 'A manuscript wedding gift from Philippa of Hainault to Edward III', *Burlington Magazine* 127 (1985), 230–2; *Survey*, v, no. 96; F. Avril and P. D. Stirnemann, *Manuscrits enluminés d'origine insulaire, viie–xxe siècle* (Paris, 1987), no. 187.

being delivered for Edward's own use (*opus*) from the stock of books in the Privy Wardrobe, as opposed to those sent to officers of his household, seem to have been four rolls 'of mappa mundi and other portraitures', which were issued in 1338.[113]

Edward spent money on books, but the scrappy documentary evidence mainly concerns service-books, such as an expensive missal and antiphoner bought in 1362 for St Stephen's Chapel and an ordinal given to St George's Chapel, Windsor, for example. Archbishop John Stratford may have left a valuable troper to Edward in 1348.[114] Books seized by the sheriffs of London in 1365 from Henry de Tatton were retained because 'they related to the solemnity of the feasts, and were of great value', but included a Juvenal and three 'romances'.[115] The psalter, Oxford, Bodleian, MS Douce 131, dating from around 1340, may have belonged to him, whereas the tiny psalter in Dr Williams' library – beyond question a personal book – was probably made for Philippa.[116] Some copies of Mandeville in French have a Latin dedication to Edward. He bought a volume of 'romance' in 1335 from Isabella of Lancaster, a nun at Amesbury, where Eleanor of Provence had lived at the end of her life. It was kept in the Chamber, may have been a family heirloom, and presumably had a valuable binding, since it cost the enormous sum of 100 marks (£66 13s 4d). Some of the other romances recorded in Edward's possession at his death may well have been inherited from his mother.[117] But it is improbable that we have a true picture. It was, after all, Edward who decreed that the finances of the Chamber, that is his personal expenditure, should be protected from scrutiny by exemption from accounting at the Exchequer.

'In no case is our ignorance of the details of English royal book-collecting more frustrating than in Richard II's,' wrote Professor R. F. Green in 1976. He demonstrated that the fourteen books listed in a memoranda roll of 1384/5 had been inherited from Edward III and therefore could not safely be used, as they

113 BL, Add. MS 60584, receipt, fol. 6^{v}, '[Et de] iiij rotulis de mappa mundi et aliis purtreituris'; fols. 7^{v}, 12^{v} (also receipt) and delivery, fols. 22^{v} (twice), 34^{v}, described as 'De rotulis de mappa mundi iiij'.

114 F. Devon (ed.), *Issue rolls of the Exchequer* (London, 1837), 177; M. F. Bond, *The inventories of St George's Chapel, Windsor Castle, 1384–1667* (Windsor, 1947), 32, no. 18 (1384–5), 103, no. 19 (1409–10); *BRUO* III. 1796–8.

115 Devon, *Issues*, 187.

116 O. Pächt and J. J. G. Alexander, *Illuminated manuscripts in the Bodleian Library, Oxford*, 3 vols. (Oxford, 1966–73), III. no. 590; Alexander, 'Royal patrons', 142; London, Dr Williams' Library, MS Anc. 6; *Survey*, v, no. 106; no. 74, 102 × 70 mm.

117 E.g. BL, Royal MS 20.A.i. 15th century; Devon, *Issues*, 144; fourteen books listed in Rickert, 'Richard II's books', 144–7; cf. R. F. Green, 'King Richard II's books revisited', *Library*, 5th ser., 31 (1976), 235–9.

previously had been, to judge Richard's library or his literary tastes.[118] We know that three of these books, a two-volume bible, perhaps a *Bible historiale*, a *Roman de la Rose* and a *Romance de Percivall et Gawayn*, had been sent to the Chamber of the twelve-year old Richard in 1379. It is improbable, as Green concluded, that 'a king who could number Chaucer, Usk, Granson, Clanvowe, and Montague amongst his servants', and to whom Gower dedicated the first version of the *Confessio amantis*, had no interest in books and literature.[119] The few extant books associated with Richard are in Latin and French, not in English. Two copies are known of the *Libellus geomancie* written for Richard in 1391. This type of prognostic text is recorded in many European princely collections of the fourteenth and fifteenth centuries. Other short texts associated with kingship are with it in Oxford, Bodleian, MS Bodley 581; it is the only text in BL, MS Royal 12.C.v, but neither is certainly the presentation manuscript. Roger Dymock's Latin tract against Lollard heresy, *Liber contra duodecim errores*, on the other hand, with the king's portrait, arms and badges, is the presentation copy.[120] In 1395, at the time of the negotiations for peace with France, Charles VI, the French king, sent Richard the *Epistre au roi Richard*, composed by Philippe de Mézières, and written and illuminated in Paris. This is a rare example of a codex which beyond question belonged to an English king before Edward IV, was recorded in the first known list of English royal books, those seen by a French visitor to Richmond Palace in 1535, and is still today among the Old Royal Collection in the British Library (BL, MS Royal 20.B.vi).[121] Around the same time, Charles VI sent Richard the exquisite two-volume Belleville Breviary, afterwards given by Henry IV to the duke of Berry (BN, mss lat. 10483–4). Richard may well have had the reputation in France of being a bibliophile. Some details of Froissart's account of his second visit to England in

118 Green, 'King Richard II's books revisited'.

119 *Ibid.* See also Cavanaugh, 'Books privately owned', II. 725–33; V. J. Scattergood, 'Literary culture at the court of Richard II', in Scattergood and Sherborne, *English court culture*, 32–3; for Bodleian, MS Eng. hist. C. 775, see also K. Harris, 'Patrons, buyers and owners', 194 and n. 89; and C. Meale, 'Patrons, buyers and owners: book production and social status', in *BPPB*, 202 and 222, n. 5; C. M. Meale, 'The Morgan Library copy of *Generides*', in *Romance in medieval England*, ed. M. Mills, J. Fellows and C. M. Meale (Cambridge, 1991), 91.

120 BL, MS Royal 12.C.v, and Bodleian, MS Bodley 581, see Pächt and Alexander, *Illuminated manuscripts*, III. no. 673; *Survey*, v, no. 152; Cambridge, Trinity Hall, MS 17, see N. Saul, *Richard II, king of England* (New Haven, CT, 1997), 303 and pl. 10.

121 BL, MS Royal 20.B.vi. See Philippe de Mézières, *Epistre au roi Richart*, ed. G. W. Coopland (Liverpool, 1975); J. Stratford, 'Gold and diplomacy: England and France in the reign of Richard II', in J. Mitchell (ed.), *England and the Continent in the Middle Ages: studies in memory of Andrew Martindale* (Stamford, 2000), 224–5; Stratford, 'The early royal collections', 260; CBMLC VII. H1.79.

1395 have been shown to be unreliable, but his narrative of Richard's favourable reception of his book of poems at Eltham, seated on a bed of state, admiring the rich binding and reading aloud from several pages, rings true. Even if it was not, it was credible to Froissart's audience.[122] And in 1415 Pierre de Vérone (Pietro Sacchi da Verona), who was a bookseller in Paris and at one time 'librarian' of the duke of Berry, defended himself against a trumped-up charge of spying for the English. He agreed that he had gone to England some fifteen years earlier to see King Richard, but said it was to try to sell him a bible.[123]

Our limited knowledge of Richard's books contrasts with the much fuller records of the books of his uncle, Thomas of Woodstock, duke of Gloucester, youngest son of Edward III.[124] This is because Thomas of Woodstock's goods were forfeited to the Crown after his attainder for treason and murder in 1397, and were accordingly inventoried by escheators during confiscation, not necessarily because he possessed a larger book collection than Edward III or Richard II. Thomas of Woodstock is, however, one of the few medieval English noblemen to have put his name to a book, a short businesslike treatise on the order of battle in the Court of Chivalry dedicated to Richard II. The inventory, taken at his principal seat, Pleshy Castle, in Essex, survives in more than one version. More than forty service-books were seized, some new ('Libri pro capella'). After forfeiture the liturgical books were auctioned off in the Exchequer, many at higher values than the escheator's. At least eighty-three other books as well as a few pamphlets and rolls were at Pleshy, the great majority in French, some in Latin, a few in English. Among them were romances in our modern sense, works of piety, and a bible in English; the escheator listed all the non-liturgical books indiscriminately as 'Livres de divers rymances et estories'. These too may have been auctioned, but the document at Stafford listing these transactions is now incomplete. Another thirteen liturgical and

122 BN, mss lat. 10483–4; F. Baron (ed.), *Les fastes du Gothique: le siècle de Charles V* (Paris, 1981), no. 240; J. W. Sherborne, 'Charles VI and Richard II', in J. J. N. Palmer (ed.), *Froissart: historian* (Woodbridge, 1981), 50–63; Jean Froissart, *Oeuvres*, ed. K. de Lettenhove, 26 vols. (Brussels, 1867–77), XV. 167.

123 J. Guiffrey, *Inventaires de Jean duc de Berry (1401–1416)*, 2 vols. (Paris, 1896), I. 285–6 and no. 1093; R. H. Rouse and M. A. Rouse, *Manuscripts and their makers: commercial book producers in medieval Paris, 1200–1500*, 2 vols. (Turnhout, 2000), II. 115–16.

124 J. Stratford, '"La Somme le Roi" (Reims, Bibliothèque municipale, ms 570): the manuscripts of Thomas of Woodstock, duke of Gloucester, and the scribe, John Upton', in M.-C. Hubert, E. Poulle and M. H. Smith (eds.), *Le statut du scripteur au moyen âge: actes du XIIe colloque scientifique de paléographie latine* (Paris, 2000), 267–82, esp. 268–71; cf. J. E. Krochalis, 'The books and reading of Henry V and his circle', *The Chaucer Review* 23 (1988), 50–2.

secular books in Latin and French were confiscated at the duke's house in London. They are listed in an inventory taken by Richard Whittington, then mayor.[125]

The copy of Higden's *Polychronicon* that Thomas of Woodstock had adapted for the chantry college he established at Pleshy (Bodleian, MS Bodley 316) is extant, as are some of his own books. Three are of a comfortable size for an individual to read. The compact *Roman de la rose* (BL, MS Royal 19.B.xiii) bought from the executors of the courtier Sir Richard Stury, and the copy of Brunetto Latini's *Livre du trésor* (Bodleian, MS Douce 319) given to Thomas by William Montagu, second earl of Salisbury, belong to this category. So, too, does a *Somme le Roi* (Rheims, Bibl. mun., MS 570) which was written for Thomas, probably within his household, before being decorated in London. The Wycliffite bible in English (BL, MSS Egerton 617–618), also written for the duke, is, on the contrary, a large book designed to be read on a lectern. Both these specially written books are embellished with the duke's arms.[126] Thomas of Woodstock's widow Eleanor, duchess of Gloucester, retained or recovered some books before her death in 1399. She was co-heiress of the book-loving earls of Bohun with her sister Mary, wife of Henry, earl of Derby (the future Henry IV), and her inheritance may have helped to stock the library at Pleshy. In her will dated 9 August, that is before Richard II's deposition, she bequeathed five books, among them a swan romance, associated with her Bohun ancestors, and three other books, all in French, to her son, Humphrey, as well as a psalter with swans enamelled on the clasps, which had belonged to her father. To each of her three daughters she left books: a *Golden legend* in French to Anne; a two-volume French bible, perhaps a *Bible historiale* and a set of decretals in French to Isabelle, a minoress at the London house at Aldgate; and to Joan, queen of Scotland, the illuminated psalter hours she had used for her own devotions. The latter survives (Edinburgh, National Library of Scotland, Adv. MS 18.6.5).[127]

125 Pleshy inventory: Viscount Dillon and W. H. St John Hope, 'Inventory of the goods and chattels belonging to Thomas, duke of Gloucester . . .', *Archaeological Journal* 54 (1897), 275–308; partly printed by Cavanaugh, 'Books privately owned', II. 844–51; another incomplete version of the Pleshy inventory is Stafford, Staffordshire Record Office, D641/1/3/2. London inventory: TNA: PRO, C 257/8, no. 6A; *Calendar of inquisitions miscellaneous, 1392–1399*, 223–5, no. 372.

126 BL, Egerton MSS 617–18, is the original second volume, now divided. The first is lost. A. I. Doyle, 'English books in and out of court from Edward III to Henry VII', in Scattergood and Sherborne, *English court culture*, 168; Stratford, 'La Somme le Roi', 269, 279–80.

127 *Survey*, v, no. 142; Lambeth, Reg. Arundel, I. fols. 163–4, partly printed in Nichols, *Royal wills* (1780), 177–86; Stratford, 'La Somme le Roi'.

Everything known about lay book-owners among the higher aristocracy during the thirteenth and fourteenth centuries suggests that Thomas of Woodstock's books of edification, devotion and leisure (as opposed to his service-books) were typical in being mostly in French. This was still the main language of the nobility, although by the first half of the fourteenth century trilingual compendia using Latin, French and English for different purposes are also to be found.[128] This linguistic bias is well illustrated earlier in the fourteenth century by a list of the books of Guy Beauchamp, earl of Warwick, who was buried at Bordesley Abbey in Worcestershire in 1315. In May 1306 he transferred to Bordesley some twenty-seven volumes containing about fifty separate French titles. They embraced biblical and devotional works, courtly romances and epics, didactic and historical literature, all categories of books to be found in literate lay households. The act of donation, which survives in a seventeenth-century copy, specified an inalienable gift in perpetuity, but the earl was careful to allow for borrowing rights of two or three books at a time for himself or for his family 'pur solas aveyr'. This seems to imply that the books, characterised by Legge as 'old-fashioned', were in fact still read and enjoyed. Indeed, the donation may not have been all that it seems.[129] Monastic houses were used for safe keeping by the magnate families closely associated with them.

Some of Guy of Warwick's books were probably modest volumes, as were some of Thomas of Woodstock's. The escheator priced the most valuable of the duke's books at £10. The least expensive were estimated at only 6d. This was still the equivalent of a day's wages for a master mason, but, as has been observed, 'increasing demand, better-organized production, cheaper hand-writing and the introduction of paper, led in the long run to cheaper books . . . Books were always a luxury in the Middle Ages, but . . . cheaper books meant that they could become a luxury for poorer people.'[130] By the late fourteenth century more and more lay men and women wanted to read for devotion, recreation and profit. This inevitably stimulated the supply and ownership of books, both new and second-hand.[131] Books (excluding

128 R. J. Dean and M. B. M. Boulton, *Anglo-Norman literature: a guide to texts and manuscripts*, ANTS Occasional publications series 3 (London, 1999); Parkes, 'Literacy', 276–8; Short, 'Patrons and polyglots', 229–49; T. Turville-Petre, 'Three languages: traditions in the south-west Midlands', in his *England the nation: language, literature, and national identity, 1290–1340* (Oxford, 1996), 181–221.

129 M. Blaess, 'L'abbaye de Bordesley et les livres de Guy de Beauchamp', *Romania* 78 (1957), 511–18; CBMLC III. 4–10, correcting the date.

130 Parkes, 'Literacy', 286–7.

131 See, for example, W. Scase, 'Reginald Pecock, John Carpenter and John Colop's "Common Profit" books', *MÆ* 61 (1992), 261–74.

service-books) in French and Latin still had a place in the collections of kings and magnates, but the books of people of lesser social status were by and large in English by the second half of the fifteenth century.[132] These collections, however, lie beyond the scope of this chapter.

Royal book collections and a royal library from Henry IV to Edward IV

The apparent contrast between what is known of the books of English kings, queens and princes, and the libraries of other European rulers, especially the Valois during the reigns of Charles V of France (1364–80) and his son, Charles VI (1380–1422), is probably an accident, a matter of different administrative procedures and of documentary survival and loss. In England by the second half of the fourteenth century, the Chamber, the department which after 1318 had come to deal increasingly with the personal expenditure of the Crown, was accountable only to the king and was exempted from accounting at the Exchequer. Lists of the king's books in current use cannot therefore be found among the central records of the Crown. There is no equivalent in England until the Tudor period of the remarkable inventories of books and other valuables produced in the *Chambres de comptes* of the Valois. The earliest known inventory of the books of an English king is the brief list of 143 manuscripts and printed books seen by an anonymous French visitor to Richmond Palace in 1535.[133]

From the accession of Henry IV (1399–1413), and during the reigns of his son and grandson, more is known about royal books and – significantly – of special provisions for housing them. In 1401–2, soon after Henry usurped the throne, he furnished a new study ('novum studium') attached to his chamber at Eltham, one of his favourite palaces. It had a fireplace and a wooden ceiling and was lit by seven stained-glass windows. Two desks were sent down from London for the study, one with two 'stagez' to keep books in.[134] There are many points of similarity with the 'estude' of Charles V at Vincennes, his favourite palace to the east of Paris. Henry had a keeper of his books, 'custos librorum', one Ralph Bradfield, gentleman, the first known English royal 'librarian'. Bradfield seems to have been a yeoman of the Chamber by

132 J. T. Rosenthal, 'Aristocratic cultural patronage and book bequests, 1350–1500', *BJRL* 64 (1982), 522–48; Meale, 'Patrons, buyers and owners', 207–9, 218–19; Parkes, 'Literacy', 287–96; P. J. Lucas, 'The growth and development of English literary patronage in the later middle ages and early Renaissance', *Library*, 6th ser., 4 (1982), 240–4.

133 Stratford, 'The early royal collections', 255–7.

134 *Ibid.*, 260–1.

1405–6, that is, a man of modest status. He is named in a suit brought in 1419 against the London stationer Thomas Marleburgh, concerning nine books of Henry's that had been missing since 1413, the year of his death. They included a volume by Gower and a *Polychronicon* as well as a 'smale cronykles', presumably in English, what must have been a Wycliffite bible and another bible in Latin, two psalters, Gregory's *Moralia in Iob* and a *Catholicon* (a Latin grammar and dictionary).[135] The impression of Henry's Latin learning conveyed by these books is reinforced by the education he gave his children and by a newly identified large volume made for him before he became king, now bound with quires made for him as king before 1406 (Cambridge, Trinity College, MS B.2.16). This compendium contains moral and devotional Augustinian and other texts and is introduced by a Latin version of Louis IX's moral testament to his son Philip III.[136]

There can be little doubt that Henry V possessed a considerable number of learned books even before he obtained well over 100 volumes through his victory at the Market of Meaux in 1422.[137] The principal evidence comes from Henry's will of June 1421 and its codicils of 1422. Not all of the books seem to have been for his own use or intended for a 'royal library'. He bequeathed some to his new monastic foundations, the double house of Brigettines at Syon and the Carthusian monastery at Sheen, as well leaving specific books to Christ Church, Canterbury, and to other individuals. Syon was to have all his books for preaching, and Sheen any for meditation which were not bequeathed elsewhere. It must be a reflection of the number of books Henry possessed that he specified in a codicil that neither house was to have any duplicates. Henry intended to leave his legal and scholastic books to the 'common library' of the University of Oxford, but they had not arrived by 1437. Nevertheless, in a significant phrase, Henry decreed that his unborn child was to have the whole residue of his books not left to others, 'pro libraria sua'. The context makes it clear that he was thinking of books within the royal household and Chamber. In addition, the child was also to have the service-books from the household chapel. The celebrated 'Old Hall' manuscript (BL, Add. MS 57950) may have

135 *Ibid.*, 261–2; H. R. T. Summerson, 'An English Bible and other books belonging to Henry IV', *BJRL* 79 (1997), 109–15.

136 Henry's arms are in the lower border of fol. 4; arms of the livery of Lancaster are in the lower border of fol. 107. For a preliminary account of the manuscript, see P. Binski and S. Panayotova (eds.), *The Cambridge Illuminations: ten centuries of book production in the medieval West* (London and Turnhout, 2005), 258–9, no. 118.

137 P. Strong and F. Strong, 'The last will and codicils of Henry V', *EHR* 96 (1981), 79–102; G. Harris, 'Henry V's books', in K. B. McFarlane (ed.), *Lancastrian kings and Lollard knights* (Oxford, 1972), 233–8; Stratford, 'The early royal collections', 262–3.

been among them. Some books for the chapel probably had as personal a resonance for Henry and his son as the service-books Charles V of France kept in his great Chamber at Vincennes, or as the superbly illuminated Bedford Hours (BL, Add. MS 18850), given to Henry VI at Christmas 1431 by Anne of Burgundy, duchess of Bedford, his aunt, with the consent of her husband, his uncle.[138]

All four of Henry IV's sons were, as Gower put it, 'wel boked' and it is not surprising that they too owned books. The second son, Thomas, duke of Clarence, who was killed in a rash engagement at Baugé in 1421, seems to have loved books as well as music. He owned an exquisite copy of Machaut's works, and the 'Old Hall' manuscript may originally have been made for him before it passed to Henry V; the book of hours made after his death for his wife Margaret was in the finest style available in London.[139] Henry's two younger sons were both bibliophiles on the scale of their contemporaries at French and Italian courts. John, duke of Bedford (1389–1435), who became regent of France after Henry's death in 1422 for his infant nephew, Henry VI, bought the great Louvre Library of Charles V and Charles VI of France, then containing some 843 volumes, a very large collection indeed in the early fifteenth century. Until 1429, when the English left Paris, Bedford left these books at the Louvre in the library Charles V had constructed on three floors in the Tour de la Fauconnerie, the north-east angle tower. He then moved them to a refurbished room in the castle at Rouen, the new centre of the English administration. This 'grete library that came owte of France' did not, however, then become the basis for an English royal library, but, after Bedford's death, was dispersed in London by his executors. Bedford's standing as a bibliophile also emerges from the twelve surviving Latin and French illuminated manuscripts made or adapted for him in London and in Paris or with dedications to him.[140] At least two outstanding manuscripts from the Louvre Library, a French translation of Livy and the *Songe du Vergier*, both written and illuminated for Charles V,

138 J. Backhouse, 'A re-appraisal of the Bedford Hours', *BLJ* 7 (1981), 47–69; *The Bedford Hours* (London, 1990).

139 Machaut, BN, ms fr. 9221: see E. Taburet-Delahaye (ed.), *Paris 1400: les arts sous Charles VI* (Paris, 2004), no. 15, pp. 55–6; 'Old Hall': see R. Marks and P. Williamson (eds.), *Gothic art for England* (London, 2003), no. 14, p. 157; Clarence Hours (private collection, Cologne), Sotheby's sale cat. 12 Dec. 1967, lot 46; 19 June 1989, lot 3018: see Scott, *Survey*, VI/ii. no. 56; J. M. Plotzek *et al.* (eds.), *Ars vivendi, ars moriendi: die Kunst zu sterben* [exhibition catalogue, Diocesan Museum, Cologne] (Munich, 2002), no. 16.

140 J. Stratford, 'The manuscripts of John, duke of Bedford: library and chapel', in D. Williams (ed.), *England in the fifteenth century: proceedings of the 1986 Harlaxton Symposium* (Woodbridge, 1987), 329–50; *The Bedford inventories: the wordly goods of John, duke of Bedford, regent of France (1389–1435)* (London, 1993), C 95 and pp. 95–6.

were acquired by Bedford's younger brother Humfrey, duke of Gloucester (1390–1447).[141]

Some of Duke Humfrey's books, those from the Louvre library among them, reflect a traditional enough aristocratic taste for slightly old-fashioned if beautiful books. Others reflect his interest in the new, humanistic learning and the classics, inspired or reinforced by his role as 'protector' of Oxford University. Duke Humfrey's humanist manuscripts were acquired or specially written for him through the Italian humanist Piercandido Decembrio, who sent four manuscripts from Milan in around 1439 to 1441, all written on the same batch of parchment, and the duke's secretaries, the Ferrarese, Tito Livio Frulovisi, who was in his household from 1436 to 1438, and Antonio Beccaria of Verona, who remained with him longer, from about 1439 to 1446. By December 1430 at the latest, the duke was actively involved in helping Oxford. Between May 1435 and February 1444, he gave well over 280 books to the university, some perhaps always intended for that purpose. Not all are recorded by title, but 274 volumes (most of them lost) are listed in the surviving copies of indentures the duke sent with his munificent donations. He no doubt wished to bequeath the residue of his Latin books to Oxford, but after his arrest and sudden death, Henry VI diverted them to King's Hall, Cambridge, by 1452.[142] The late A. C. de la Mare aptly wrote: 'To judge from the surviving books and from the titles listed in the University's indentures with Duke Humfrey, some of the books came from his personal library – they were gifts to him from friends or admirers, or translations specially made for him, or have annotations by him or his secretary – but others were probably commissioned or bought to give to Oxford.'[143]

During Henry VI's childhood the minority council seems to have carried out his father's wishes. He no doubt inherited most if not all the books his father intended for his 'library', but during his unsettled reign he gave many books away as well as so much else. Some 140 learned books in Latin remained in the Treasury until 1440, well after Henry had assumed personal rule. The

141 Paris, Bibl. de Ste-Geneviève, ms 777: see F. Avril and J. Lafaurie, *La librairie de Charles V* (Paris, 1981), no. 189 and col. pl. 189; BL, MS Royal 19.C.iv: see Baron, *Les fastes du Gothique*, no. 282; Taburet-Delahaye, *Paris 1400*, no. 11.

142 A. C. de la Mare and R. W. Hunt (eds.), *Duke Humfrey and English humanism in the fifteenth century* (Oxford, 1970); A. Sammut, *Unfredo duca di Gloucester e gli umanisti italiani* (Padua, 1980); A. C. de la Mare and S. Gillam (eds.), *Duke Humfrey's library and the divinity school, 1488–1988* (Oxford, 1988); S. Saygin, *Humfrey, duke of Gloucester (1390–1447), and the Italian humanists* (Leiden, 2002); D. Rundle, 'Two unnoticed manuscripts from the collection of Humfrey, Duke of Gloucester', *BLR* 16 (1998), 211–24; 299–313.

143 De la Mare and Gillam, *Duke Humfrey's library*, 20.

majority – 110 – came from Meaux and probably had been written in France. Seventy-seven of the Meaux books, for example, were given in perpetuity to King's Hall, Cambridge.[144] Another large group of twenty-seven books, some of English origin, went to All Souls College, Oxford.[145] After these dispersals, small groups of Latin books, some of them duplicates, remained in the Receipt of the Exchequer, rather than in the king's own possession. Some of these were given to bishops and clerks within the royal circle. Others were lent out, returned, then lent again, thus constituting a small lending library in our modern sense, a library belonging to the Crown, but in all likelihood administered with only nominal royal consent.

As expressed in the elegant and learned introduction to Warner and Gilson's catalogue of the Royal Collection in the British Library: 'The Old Royal Collection is of respectable, though not of extreme antiquity. Its real founder was Edward IV.'[146] In spite of the piecemeal evidence for earlier royal book collections which has been briefly surveyed in this chapter, Edward IV (1461–83), and Henry VII (1485–1509) are with good reason often considered to be the true founders of the Old Royal Library as we know it today. Some of their books were recorded in the earliest known list of any part of the English royal library, the French works seen at Richmond Palace by an anonymous visitor in 1535. Many of this group are among the books George II presented to the nation in 1757 and are still in the British Library today. Some forty-five massive illuminated manuscripts, produced or adapted for Edward IV in the commercial workshops of the Burgundian Netherlands, can be recognised today in the Old Royal Collection. Edward may have owned other books; we have no list of his collection. All the known manuscripts are secular works in French in ambitious large-scale copies. Edward imported most of them towards the end of his reign, between 1478 and 1480. In 1479, a foreign merchant, Philip Maisertuell, received £80 in part payment of the very large sum of £240 for books 'to be provided to the kinges use in the partees beyond the see'.[147] In 1480 the Josephus and other books of the king were given splendid bindings by a London stationer, Piers Bauduyn, and a London silkwoman, Alice Claver. In the same year some were transported to Eltham Palace. Edward, like Henry IV,

144 Stratford, 'The early royal collections', 262–6.

145 R. Weiss, 'Henry VI and the library of All Souls College', *EHR* 57 (1942), 102–5; N. R. Ker (ed.), *Records of All Souls College Library, 1437–1600*, OBS, n.s., 16 (London, 1971), 1–2.

146 Gilson, in G. F. Warner and J. P. Gilson (eds.), *Catalogue of western manuscripts in the Old Royal and King's Collections*, 4 vols. (London, 1921), I. xi.

147 TNA: PRO, E404/76/4/135.

refurbished a study at Eltham and some of his books may well have been kept in it.

Edward's manuscripts are mainly prose and are weighted towards histories and works of moral and practical instruction. In this they resemble other northern European princely and noble collections of the same period. Ancient history is represented by a two-volume Josephus (London, Soane Museum, MS 1), a Xenophon (BL, MS Royal 16.G.ix), the *Romuléon* (BL, MS Royal 19.E.v), the *Faits des Romains* (MS Royal 17.F.ii) and Valerius Maximus (MSS Royal 18.E.iii–iv); modern history includes William of Tyre's *History of the Crusades* (MS Royal 15. E.i), the chronicles of Froissart (MSS Royal 18.E.i–ii) and one book of Wavrin's *Croniques d'Angleterre* (MS Royal 15.E.iv). Theology, encyclopaedias and literature are among the other works. Among 'practical' texts is a popular French translation of the *De rustica* (MS Royal 14.E.vi) by Petrus de Crescentiis.

Edward's 'Flemish' acquisitions were no doubt influenced by his exile in the Burgundian Netherlands between 1470 and 1471, by his contacts in exile in Bruges with the bibliophile Louis of Gruuthuse, and by the marriage in 1468 of his sister Margaret of York (herself a patron of books) to Charles the Bold, the last Valois duke of Burgundy (1467–77). The arms and badges in the broad borders around the miniatures associate some of these large manuscripts with Edward alone. In others, such as *La grande histoire Cesar* (BL, MS Royal 17.F.ii), the heraldry belongs to both Edward and his sons, the 'princes in the Tower'.[148] Given the size and weight of these imposing books, they must have been read aloud from a lectern. Edward probably intended them for entertainment at court as well as for his sons' education. In some other very similar volumes in the Old Royal Collection, the spaces left for heraldry are left blank. The arms in yet others belong to members of Edward's Court, such as Sir John Donne (BL, MSS Royal 15.D.iv, 16.F.v and 20.B.ii) and Lord Hastings (MS Royal 18.E.i).

Henry VII added manuscripts, but more especially printed books, to the Old Royal Collection. Among manuscripts with his arms and badges and those of Elizabeth of York is a very large copy of the poems of Charles d'Orléans and other works (BL, MS Royal 16.F.ii). Recently it has been suggested that this book

148 J. Backhouse, 'Founders of the royal library: Edward IV and Henry VII as collectors of illuminated manuscripts', in D. Williams (ed.), *England in the fifteenth century: proceedings of the Harlaxton Symposium for 1986* (Woodbridge, 1987), 23–41; 'The royal library from Edward IV to Henry VII', *CHBB* III. 267–73; S. McKendrick, '*La grande histoire Cesar* and the manuscripts of Edward IV', *EMS* 2 (1990), 110; 'The Romuléon and the manuscripts of Edward IV', in N. Rogers (ed.), *England in the fifteenth century: proceedings of the 1992 Harlaxton Symposium* (Stamford, 1994), 149–69; see also McKendrick, in T. Kren and S. McKendrick (eds.), *Illuminating the Renaissance* (Los Angeles and London, 2003), 295–303.

may in fact have been begun for Edward IV rather than for Henry VII. Another tentative hypothesis is that it could reflect the commission of a wealthy London citizen. This arises from the depiction of London landmarks in the celebrated paining of Charles d'Orléans in the Tower, which gives prominence to London Bridge and to the Old Custom House.[149] Henry acquired forty-two editions published by Vérard, some on paper, others expensive copies on vellum. Eight were specially adapted for him with the addition of arms and badges or with his title substituted in dedications intended originally for the French king.[150] This move towards printed books and away from manuscripts is paralleled in other libraries of these decades and may offer clues to Henry's taste in personal reading. It is significant that Henry appointed a royal librarian in 1492. He was Quentin Poulet, a native of Lille, who served until at least 1506. Poulet himself wrote for Henry the *Imaginacion de vraie noblesse* he signed and dated at Sheen in 1496. Poulet was not, however, as is often said, the first man to hold this post under an English king. According to the *Liber niger*, one of Edward IV's yeomen of the Crown would have been appointed 'to kepe the kinges bookes'. Apart from Ralph Bradfield, the yeoman in office under Henry IV, and John Burnham, also a yeoman of the Chamber, who is cited as keeper of the late King Henry's books in 1425, we do not know the names of Poulet's predecessors.[151]

The bits and scraps of evidence that have been pieced together suggest that royal book collections in England, large and small, probably existed throughout the medieval period and that they came into being, albeit in a transitory fashion, considerably earlier than either the surviving manuscripts or the documents can reveal. In common with many other private book collections, the royal books seem to have taken on a permanent character as a library only in the late fifteenth century. This seemingly fluid existence of the book collections of both lay and ecclesiastical private owners contrasts with those of religious and academic communities. Regulars were obliged to donate their books to their houses, as were some scholars to their colleges. There was no such obligation on the laity. On the other hand, some books, especially devotional books, but also secular works, were sometimes passed down from generation to generation within the same family. Examples are not frequent within our

149 J. Backhouse, 'Illuminated manuscripts associated with Henry VII and members of his immediate family', in B. Thompson (ed.), *The reign of Henry VII: proceedings of the 1993 Harlaxton Symposium* (Stamford, 1995), 175–8; McKendrick, in Kren and McKendrick, *Illuminating the Renaissance*, no. 119.

150 M. B. Winn, *Anthoine Vérard: Parisian publisher, 1485–1512* (Geneva, 1997), esp. 138–53.

151 For Burnham, see N. H. Nicolas (ed.), *Proceedings and ordinances of the Privy Council of England*, 6 vols. (London, 1834–37), III. 168.

period, but include the book of romances once owned by Eleanor of Castile and both liturgical and secular manuscripts of members of the Bohun family. Other secular books belonging to the laity, some of a practical nature, as well as administrative records and estate documents, were no doubt preserved over time within the same family.

For the reasons outlined in the introductory section of this chapter, references to books being given away or bequeathed are common: given to win favour; given and bequeathed to reinforce 'networks', that is, family and social relationships, and in the hope of prayers for the donor's soul.[152] It must be remembered that, by the fourteenth century, if not earlier, at least in royal and magnate households, liturgical books for the chapel were regarded as distinct and kept separately. They were presumably charged to a chaplain or other representative of the religious establishment, witness the inventory of Thomas of Woodstock. But it is by no means certain how far the other non-liturgical books would have been regarded as a 'library' in our modern sense, or whether they would have been separately housed, even though groups of texts might be put together in a single volume, forming a kind of 'library' of useful texts for the family or household.[153] Bequests in wills hint that, close to a testator's hour of death, he or she might see his or her devotional books as spiritual objects whose significance was profoundly personal, not as part of a coherent book collection.

The Richmond list of 1535 and the Westminster inventory of 1542 provide the earliest evidence from England of permanently designated library spaces for the royal books, whereas in France the Louvre Library is known to have functioned with its librarian Giles Malet from 1367. The book-desks Henry IV ordered in London for his study at Eltham Palace were designed to hold books. They no doubt resembled the book-desk depicted in Charles V's copy of John of Salisbury's *Policraticus* in French translation (Paris, BN, ms fr. 24287, fol. 1). Edward IV refurbished a study at Eltham. His transfer of books there is suggestive, but no lists exist to establish where his books were stored. The introduction of the library room within academic and religious communities by the fourteenth century, followed naturally from the needs of scholars for sizeable permanent reference collections to use *in situ*. Books for a wide

152 For the various reasons which determined to whom books were bequeathed, see, for example, M. C. Erler, 'Devotional literature', *CHBB* III. 495–525, especially 521–5.

153 J. Boffey and J. T. Thompson, 'Anthologies and miscellanies: production and choice of texts', *BPPB*, 279–315. Volumes of this kind can be shown to have stayed within a single family for a number of generations: Parkes, 'Literacy', 292–5.

variety of purposes, for devotion, instruction and entertainment, were no doubt available within royal, noble and gentry households. With the possible exception of the royal books and of the books of some great magnates, they cannot have been on a comparable scale or have been put to the kind of use to need a special room. Pending further discoveries, private book collections in England, including books within the royal household, are perhaps best described as just that, book collections, not libraries.

8

The medieval librarian

RICHARD SHARPE

If we may use the word 'librarian' to refer to the person responsible for the care and administration of a collection of books owned by a medieval institution, we must bear in mind that the role was very different in different libraries. Variation through time is one part of this: while some books from the eighth and ninth centuries might be preserved in the same library for centuries, neither the library nor its use remained constant. Wide variation in book provision is another. Institutions of different kinds kept libraries of different kinds and managed them in different ways. At one level the differences between institutions are obvious. Religious houses such as those of the Benedictines or Augustinians had substantial libraries in many cases, and these might remain substantial over long periods, in some cases changing in their organisation, in others remaining largely unaffected by change over long periods. But similar rules need not imply similar book provision; other houses of the same religious orders might have very minor libraries. Their management would clearly differ, yet one can find evidence of the most advanced librarianship in a quite modest library such as that of Dover Priory, a small Benedictine house dependent on Canterbury Cathedral Priory. Religious orders with a different culture from that of the Benedictines, such as the Cistercians, nonetheless maintained libraries of a similar kind though generally on a smaller scale. With a few prominent exceptions, nunneries were mostly small; their book provision does not run in parallel to that in monasteries for men, however, since the literacy of religious women seems to have declined in the early Norman period, at exactly the period when men's abbeys were investing in their libraries. Secular institutions, ranging from well-endowed cathedrals to small and underfunded colleges, had much lower levels of book provision; their canons were able to own their own books for study or business. From the thirteenth century the libraries of the friars vary across both scales: large friaries in centres of study would have major book collections, comparable in scale if not in content with those of well-equipped monastic houses; small friaries might have no more books than a poor secular college. University colleges sometimes chose to imitate the customs of religious orders, particularly the friars, but more often their libraries were managed very differently as a circulating stock of core texts on long-term loan to fellows of the college.

What is common to all medieval libraries, however, is that their need of management was very small. The role of the librarian generally resembled that of prefect or monitor in a school library more than that of librarian. The most important duty was to be present where the books were kept at times when readers were allowed access, so that books could be both handed out and returned to their places. At most times the stock was unchanging. Accessions were occasional and for the most part accidental, by bequest or gift, and most libraries at most periods had no policy of collection development. There is no evidence that librarians in ordinary circumstances had sufficient resources at their disposal to acquire books. Security against loss or theft was a more pressing issue, leading to regulations as to who might hold the keys to the book-cupboards or book-room. Other matters of active library administration were always optional. If they take up a disproportionate space in the discussion below, it should nonetheless be remembered that libraries were for the most part not actively managed at all or, when they were, it was only for a brief period. It is not surprising, therefore, that the person of the librarian is an elusive figure.

The only continuous need was the maintenance of an adequate supply of books to meet the demands of the liturgy in religious institutions. Many priories, nunneries, colleges and hospitals owned few books, if any, beyond those required for the liturgy. Books used in services were susceptible to wear and tear, and the earliest evidence of a managerial role is that the precentor, the person responsible for the liturgy in monastic houses, had a duty to ensure that there were enough service-books and that they were kept in good repair. No work has been done to answer questions such as how many service-books were needed for the liturgy in, say, a Benedictine abbey with a certain number of monks or an Augustinian priory with a certain number of canons. Some abbeys had considerable numbers. At Ely Abbey there were seventy-two monks in 1093, when an inventory shows that seventy-nine books out of 287 were for liturgical use; there were twenty-two psalters, nineteen missals, twelve graduals, nine antiphonaries, eight lectionaries, seven breviaries and two benedictionals.[1] At Ramsey Abbey around 1330 an inventory records, 'the number of psalters, all told except St Oswald's Psalter, one hundred at least',

1 E. O. Blake (ed.), *Liber Eliensis*, II. 139, Camden 3rd ser. 92 (1962), 223–4.

besides some seventy breviaries, thirty-three tropers, thirty-two graduals (ten of them bound with psalters already counted) and twenty-nine processionals, as well as other types of liturgical book in smaller numbers.[2] This may reflect a higher effective provision of liturgical books or merely an accumulation of books over time, some of them old and useless but not actually broken up. Bishop John Grandisson's statutes (1339) for his college of priests at Ottery St Mary provide a remarkable witness to the use of books during services and to the hazards of the correcting of words or music by the inexpert.[3] It is not known how long a missal or breviary might be in continuous use, how often new ones had to be added to the stock, old ones repaired to keep them in use, or worn-out ones disposed of. Changes in liturgical custom would also, from time to time, have required the acquisition of new books and left others obsolete.

There is evidence that the only regular provision of income to the precentor was concerned to meet needs of this kind, and there is no religious house where the precentor had regular funds sufficient to build up a library of books for study. The earliest evidence comes from Ely, where the abbey became a cathedral priory in 1109. At the beginning of 1134 the new bishop, Nigel, commissioned a survey of the priory, which reported many books in the *armarium*.[4] Soon after that, several offices were instituted as obediences in the priory, and it may well have been in this connection that Nigel gave to the prior and monks the revenues of several parish churches, which were to be dedicated to the precentor and his successors as endowment 'ad faciendos et emendandos libros ecclesie nostre' ('to make and repair the books of our church'). This expression denotes service-books rather than library books. A later confirmation by the bishop, datable between 1158 and 1168, assigned the same income 'scriptorio ecclesie Elyensis ad libros eiusdem ecclesie faciendos et emendandos' ('to the writing-office of the church of Ely to make and repair the books of the same church').[5] At Evesham Abbey in 1214 revenues were allocated to the prior 'to buy parchment and to support copyists so that

2 CBMLC IV. 414–15.

3 The statutes were printed by J. N. Dalton, *The collegiate church of Ottery St Mary* (Cambridge, 1917), 33–259; see especially §§ 8, 68 (how the men were to stand around the books to see words and music), § 30 (position and number of service-books in the choir), §§ 28–9 (copying and correction of service books), § 33 (careful handling of books).

4 Blake, *Liber Eliensis*, III. 50 (p. 294). After copying out a detailed inventory of plate and vestments, the compiler chose not to copy the list of books: 'in the *armarium* such a number of books as would bore the reader if he were held up by its recitation'.

5 N. E. Karn (ed.), *English episcopal acta 31, Ely 1109–1197* (Oxford, 2005), 53–4, 68–70 (nos. 32, 44). The latter is one of very few references to a monastic *scriptorium* in medieval England. On the institution of obediences, see Karn's discussion, pp. xcviii–xcix.

books may be written', while the precentor had to provide parchment for documents but ink for all purposes within the house and 'colours for illumination and everything needed for binding books'.[6] The production of ink was apparently a noxious process likely to leave an unpleasant smell around the whole monastery. This fact led custumals sometimes to regulate the process under the precentor's supervision.[7]

In the early middle ages, the offices of librarian and precentor may have been distinct. From the early ninth century, libraries expanded in scale in some continental houses, and here for a time we find the *armarius* ('keeper of the bookcase') mentioned alongside the *cantor* ('precentor') in monastic custumals. The elaboration of the liturgy, however, during the eighth, ninth and tenth centuries required the support of books, so that the precentor had to have book-related skills as well as musical skills and also the resources to provide for the writing or copying or repairing of service-books. By the eleventh century *armarius* and *cantor* are usually the same person.[8] Custumals, however, which seek both to describe and to regulate the practices of religious houses, provide much detail on his liturgical role and rather little on the care of library books. Nonetheless, in the Benedictine and Augustinian traditions, responsibility for the library was subsumed in the office of precentor from the eleventh century until the dissolution of the monasteries in England.

As well as having responsibility for the arrangement of the liturgy and, as occasion demanded, composing words and music for special masses and offices, the precentor also seems to have had a particular role in maintaining the hagiographical pretensions of a Benedictine house by writing lives of saints; and monastic custumals show that the precentor also wrote the notices of deaths that were circulated to neighbouring communities. We know of several literary precentors from that particularly fruitful time for manuscript production at the end of the eleventh century and in the early twelfth, when many Anglo-Norman monasteries devoted considerable resources to build up their library collections.[9] Among this company might be mentioned Osbern of Canterbury (d. 1094), a man of Norman origin who was precentor of Christ

6 Abbot Ranulf's customs (1214), quoted in CBMLC IV. 132; also in Thomas of Marlborough, *History of the abbey of Evesham*, §§ 409, 411, ed. J. E. Sayers and tr. L. Watkiss (Oxford, 2003), 392, 394.

7 Custumals of St Augustine's Abbey, Canterbury (*c.* 1330), and Westminster Abbey (*c.* 1266): E. M. Thompson (ed.), *Customary of the Benedictine Monasteries of Saint Augustine, Canterbury and St Peter, Westminster*, 2 vols., HBS 23, 28 (1902–4), I. 82; II. 97.

8 M. E. Fassler, 'The office of the cantor in early western monastic rules and customaries: a preliminary investigation', *Early Music History* 5 (1985), 29–51.

9 Case studies based on Canterbury by Ker, *English MSS*, and on Salisbury by T. Webber, *Scribes and scholars at Salisbury Cathedral,* c. *1075*–c. *1125* (Oxford, 1992).

Church and author of saints' lives as well as of liturgical music;[10] Eadmer (d. 1124), an Englishman, who followed him as precentor of Christ Church and wrote devotional works, hagiography, history and (best-known) the biography of Archbishop Anselm;[11] their older contemporary Goscelin of Canterbury (d. after 1114), a Fleming, who after many years in England as a travelling hagiographer settled at St Augustine's Abbey at Canterbury, where he wrote the Lives of St Augustine and the early archbishops as well as composing for the liturgy;[12] Nicholas of Worcester (d. 1124), an Englishman originally named Æthelred, friend of Eadmer, who trained in Canterbury before becoming precentor of Worcester Cathedral;[13] and last and greatest in this company, William, monk and precentor of Malmesbury (d. 1143), historian, hagiographer and one of the most voracious readers of his time.[14] William surely took good care of the library at Malmesbury, though to judge from the surviving books they were not marked even with an *ex libris*.

There was no tradition of making the role of librarian an office or 'obedience' within the monastic tradition. The duty always fell on the precentor, though in some larger institutions his office was sub-divided, and some responsibility for the library was shared with his deputy, the succentor. So, for example, at Abingdon in the late twelfth century the library was in the keeping of the *cantor*, but in his absence the *succentor* should take care of the keys, if he were reliable; otherwise the precentor should leave them with a superior officer, the prior or the sub-prior. On the other hand, the succentor ordinarily held the keys of the cupboards in which the *libri annuales* and the *libri cantus* were kept.[15] The latter were service-books in the church, while the 'annual books' are those allocated to individual monks for their daily reading from Lent to Lent. The underlying assumption appears to be that from day to day the need for books could be met by the presence of the succentor in the cloister; the precentor was too busy elsewhere to act as library prefect, but only he had the authority to distribute books.

10 J. C. Rubenstein, 'The life and writings of Osbern of Canterbury', in R. G. Eales and R. Sharpe (eds.), *Canterbury and the Norman Conquest* (London, 1995), 27–40; *BRECP*, 248.

11 R. W. Southern, *Saint Anselm and his biographer* (Cambridge, 1963), 229–40, 274–354, 367–74; Sharpe, *Latin Writers*, 104–5; *BRECP*, 142–3.

12 Sharpe, *Latin Writers*, 151–4; M. Lapidge and R. C. Love, 'The Latin hagiography of England and Wales', in G. Philippart (ed.), *Hagiographies*, vol. 3 (Turnhout, 2001), 225–33.

13 Sharpe, *Latin Writers*, 400; *BRECP*, 154, 858.

14 R. M. Thomson, *William of Malmesbury*, 2nd edn (Woodbridge, 2003).

15 The Abingdon custumal: J. Stevenson (ed.), *Chronicon monasterii de Abingdon*, 2 vols., RS (1858), II. 373–4. The same distinctions are made in the thirteenth-century Eynsham custumal: A. Gransden (ed.), *The customary of the Benedictine abbey of Eynsham in Oxfordshire*, Corpus consuetudinum monasticarum 2 (Siegburg, 1963), 166.

The Rule provides that each monk should study a book, and the distribution of books for study takes place on the first Monday of Lent each year.[16] This is the context in which custumals will most often mention the role of librarian. It was generally the custom that the precentor presided over this distribution, and he had to keep a list of which book each brother had had last year, and which he took this year. From Thorney Abbey there survive unique examples of such records, much washed out and overwritten, on the back of an old mortuary roll that was then, eventually, reused in the binding of another book.[17] Still legible are the notes for four years, 1324, 1327, 1329 and 1330. The arrangement of each list in two columns, for the abbot's side and the prior's side, perfectly illustrates the detailed description of the process in the custumal of nearby Peterborough Abbey.[18] The similarity is not accidental. Cluniac customs of the early eleventh century were widely influential in shaping the practice of other Benedictine houses in northern Europe – the custom of gathering the books remaining in the cupboards on two carpets in the chapter house, and each brother rising in alternating turns, from the abbot's side and the prior's side, to show the book he has read before adding it to one or other pile – but one must take care not to make too much of what one custumal has to say about this without knowing the sources on which it is based. At Evesham in the fourteenth century the precentor was supported by young members of the community; his role appears to be one of keeping a continuous record of books issued to monks for their own study and of checking that his assistants had not left any books out when the period in the cloister came to an end:

> It is the duty of the precentor to commend the keeping of the book-cupboards to the young men (*iuuenibus*) and to keep them in good repair. Whenever the monks shall sit in the cloister, he must go round the cloister after the bell has been rung to put away any books that may have been forgotten through someone's lack of attention. He shall have the care of all the monastery's books and he shall have them in his keeping, provided that he shall have sufficient learning and inclination to study to be a fit person to have care of the books. No one shall take a book unless it is entered in his roll, nor shall anyone exchange books without an appropriate and sufficient memorandum, which must be entered in his roll.[19]

16 R. Hanslik (ed.), *Regula S. Benedicti*, ch. 48. 14–16, *CSEL* 75, 2nd edn (Vienna, 1977), 117.
17 R. Sharpe, 'Monastic reading at Thorney abbey (1323–1347)', *Traditio* 60 (2005), 243–78.
18 J. M. W. Willoughby in CBMLC VIII. xliii–xlvi.
19 Printed from BL, MS Cotton Vitellius E. xvii by J. Stevens, *The history of the ancient abbeys* (London, 1722–3) and quoted, CBMLC IV. 132. It is also quoted in translation by Clark, *Care of books*, 69.

Augustinian custumals often make more detailed specifications than do Benedictine custumals for the physical care of books. In England, since J. W. Clark edited the late thirteenth-century customs of Barnwell Priory, the requirement for wooden linings to the book-cupboards has been quoted from the Barnwell customs – without reference to the fact that the passage derives from the twelfth-century *Liber ordinis* of Saint-Victor in Paris, a very detailed and influential Augustinian custumal.[20] The same passage, and its wider context, are also quoted by modern historians of libraries from the work of Humbertus de Romanis, the French Dominican.[21] It is quite clear that, in his guidance on the keeping of books, the Dominican had also turned to the customs of Saint-Victor as a model. Something of the reality can be found in Benedictine records too. For example, the still visible stone *armarium* in the north range of the cloister at Ely was repaired in 1396–7, when the precentor paid for 'thirty boards of wainscot'.[22]

Frustratingly, apart from the duty to keep the books safe, and the procedures relating to the Lenten election of books, there is almost nothing to be got from custumals that sheds light on what we may be interested in as contributing to the management of libraries as collections of books. For this we must turn to the limited evidence that can be derived from those books that have survived, a matter we shall return to below.

I note here, however, one interesting point of contact. Some custumals require the precentor or librarian to write into books the name of the donor, usually a monk of the house, together with a prayer for his soul. For example, the fourteenth-century custumal from St Augustine's Abbey, Canterbury, gives a firm ruling that before a book can be accessioned into the library the precentor is to write into it the name of the brother whose book it was.[23] Donor

20 The Barnwell custumal: J. W. Clark (ed.), *The observances in use at the Augustinian Priory of S. Giles and S. Andrew at Barnwell, Cambridgeshire* (Cambridge, 1897), xlii–xlvi, 64–5; compare his *Care of books*, 70–1. The source will be found in L. Jocqué and L. Milis (eds.), *Liber ordinis S. Victoris*, c. 19, 'De officio armarii', *CCCM* 61 (1984), 78–86. See also L. Jocqué, 'Les structures de la population claustrale dans l'ordre de Saint-Victor au XIIe siècle: un essai d'analyse du *Liber ordinis*', in J. Longère (ed.), *L'Abbaye Parisienne de Saint-Victor au moyen âge* (Paris and Turnhout, 1991), 74–9.

21 R. D. Taylor-Vaisey, 'Regulations for the operation of a medieval library', *Library*, 5th ser., 33 (1978), 47–50; K. W. Humphreys, *The book provisions of the mediaeval Friars, 1215–1400* (Amsterdam, 1964), 32. Humbert's Latin can be found in his *Opera de vita regulari*, ed. J. J. Berthier (Rome, 1888–9), II. 263–6, and was also printed by Humphreys, *Book provision*, 135–6.

22 M. Gullick, *Extracts from the precentors' accounts of Ely Cathedral Priory concerning books and bookmaking* (Hitchin, 1985), 13.

23 Thompson, *Customary*, 362: 'libri quos habet de librario, et alii libri de acquisicione sua, omnia ista liberentur precentori; et ipse scribere faciet nomen fratris in quolibet libro de sua acquisicione, antequam portentur in librarium'.

inscriptions of this type are quite common in Benedictine books, and from around 1170 until around 1340 accession by donor was the most common route by which monastic libraries enlarged their stock. This is sometimes reflected in catalogues arranged in accession order by donor, such as the large early fourteenth-century catalogues from Ramsey Abbey and from Christ Church, Canterbury. At Ramsey the surviving portions of the two witnesses to the catalogue – one in roll format, the other part of a booklet – use the names of donors as headings, beneath which are grouped the books that came to the library from each source.[24] Most of the donors were monks of the house whose books had passed into the collective stock. The few surviving books from Ramsey show that the donor's name was also entered in the book, and a short list of books on loan identifies particular copies of a work by the donor's name, for example, 'Regula sancti Benedicti Iohannis abbatis', 'Decretales Iohannis abbatis'.[25] It is clear that in this way a particular copy of a certain text could be recognised and retrieved. For the cathedral priory of Christ Church, Canterbury, the fullest catalogue is a document of about 1326 copied into the register of Prior Henry of Eastry. Although the first part of the catalogue is arranged alphabetically by the author or title of the first work in a manuscript, the later and larger part is arranged under donor headings. Several different hands are at work in this later stage of the catalogue, recording gifts that were received after the time that the main hand had finished its stint and on leaves left blank for that purpose, from which it is clear that, if only for a short while, the catalogue was kept up to date as the library grew.[26]

A catalogue arranged in this manner had a natural advantage when it came to absorbing new accessions. Whether the books themselves were kept together in the batches of their accession is impossible to say, though clearly the donor's name was the important identifier. This approach could not provide any subject classification, and so for the retrieval of a particular text it must have been a clumsy system. However, a library of even 500 books is a library that one could know well, and although it is an aspect of the librarian's work that is now quite lost from view, we should not overlook the potential for a librarian to know

24 CBMLC IV. B67–8.

25 *Ibid.*, B69. 5, 7; the books also appear in the catalogue roll among about forty books listed under the heading 'Libri dompni Iohannis abbatis', B68. 79, 47. John of Sawtry was abbot of Ramsey from 1285 to 1316. This manner of marking the Ramsey books led the sixteenth-century bibliographer John Bale to confuse ownership with authorship in his discussion of Gregory of Huntingdon; R. Sharpe, *Titulus: identifying medieval Latin texts* (Turnhout, 2003), 124–5.

26 Eastry's catalogue is found in BL, MS Cotton Galba E. iv, fols. 128^r–147^v; James, *ALCD*, 13–142; a new edition by J. M. W. Willoughby is in hand for CBMLC.

his books quite intimately, to recognise them from their external appearance, and to understand in which chest or cupboard and in which book he could find a particular text. Indeed, it is this very familiarity with the contents of the *armaria*, which we might imagine would grow naturally out of his duty of care, that made the precentor-librarian the indispensable figure, holding the keys to the library figuratively as well as physically.

In cases such as those from Ramsey and Canterbury, where the evidence is an *ex dono* inscription in a book or a catalogue arranged by donor, the hand of an active librarian can be inferred, an officer who received books on behalf of a community and accessioned them to the library. In this we approach something of the routine activity of the medieval librarian. Besides donor inscriptions, there are two other categories of evidence that attest the role played by an official whom we may call the librarian in the custody of medieval monastic libraries. On the one hand, there are library records. The most important form of document in this category is the inventory or catalogue, such as those from Canterbury and Ramsey already referred to. A catalogue can provide a snapshot of the contents of a particular library at a particular moment, and the most complete catalogues can be very detailed. Their detail and their organisation are also important evidence for how well the librarian could describe his books and how they were arranged and stored. Occasional records, such as those already mentioned that have survived by chance from Thorney, can also provide a valuable witness. On the other hand, there is the variety of evidence that can be drawn from the actual books that have survived from medieval monastic libraries; often they can show how they were handled by their medieval custodians, from which further aspects can often be inferred of the way in which the library was cared for.

First, the evidence of inventories and catalogues must be considered, of which different species can be identified.[27] The form of the booklist and the detail included in it always reflects to some extent the reasons for making the record and the bibliographical knowledge of the person making it, although complexities in the presentation were circumstantial and practice developed over time. One of the earliest species of list – although the format had currency throughout the middle ages – was the simple inventory of a collection of books arranged usually by subject and author, such as might have been held by the precentor and used by him at the time of the annual audit of the library. (There was no requirement in the customs that the precentor should keep a list of

27 R. Sharpe, 'Medieval library catalogues and indexes', in N. J. Morgan and R. M. Thomson (eds.), *CHBB*, II (forthcoming).

the books in the library, but the custom of doing so was widespread.) Since the precentor also had the charge of the Lenten distribution, he had another reason for knowing not only what texts his monks had but which physical book. Many booklists from the twelfth century onwards therefore make an attempt to list subsidiary contents of a volume, and sometimes make reference to simple, even outward, aspects of a book's condition (not necessarily the most significant aspect for someone interested in the texts contained). A list from Glastonbury Abbey, for example, written in 1247/8 and showing numerous revisions as well as later audit marks (crosses and dots) next to the entries, consistently notes the status of each book, be it good or bad, new or old: 'Libri dialogorum Gregorii duo, unus bonus alius inutilis.'[28] A refinement of this type of list makes a more serious attempt to record every text in each book, but these catalogues, particularly those from the twelfth and thirteenth centuries, still offer no way of working from the physical book to its entry in the catalogue or indeed vice versa. A practical improvement in this direction was provided by the adoption of *dicta probatoria*, two or three words, sometimes just one, taken from the beginning of a particular page, usually the recto of the second folio. Between manuscript books, written by hand and therefore unlikely to fit the same number of words to each leaf, this was a diagnostic that was intrinsic to the book and allowed a control that the same book was returned as had originally been loaned.[29] The practice, ubiquitous in the later middle ages, is first found in two documents from the later thirteenth century from the Sorbonne;[30] a later ordinance of 1321 stated that the reason for noting the second folio was to identify books on loan precisely and to ensure that the borrower did not substitute a copy of the same work but of lower value.[31] The earliest English booklist to incorporate the second folio is a list of philosophy books from Merton College in Oxford, datable between 1318 and 1334.[32] The ease with which individual books could be identified by use of the second folio caused the principle to be taken up very widely, and allowed university colleges for the first time to manage a library, with a sometimes considerable circulating stock as well as or instead of chained textbooks, without the mediation of a librarian.

28 CBMLC IV. B39. 80.

29 For orientation, see D. Williman and K. Corsano, 'Tracing provenances by *dictio probatoria*', *Scriptorium* 53 (1999), 124–45.

30 An inventory and a register of borrowed books which cite the second folio are dated to *c.* 1275 and *c.* 1283 respectively by R. H. Rouse, 'The early library of the Sorbonne', *Scriptorium* 21 (1967), 51–4, 57.

31 This ordinance of 1321 is ed. L. Delisle, *Le cabinet des manuscrits de la Bibliothèque nationale* 2 (Paris, 1874), 188, n. 2, and cited by Rouse, 'The early library', 229.

32 F. M. Powicke, *The medieval books of Merton College* (Oxford, 1931), 47–51.

This species of list, however, remains akin to an inventory of property. It is only when a booklist also cites letter-marks that correspond to marks in a book that we can speak of location registers, and it is with catalogues such as these that we come most fully into contact with the administration of a medieval library.

Documents for which the word 'catalogue' is appropriate are rare in the middle ages, but the few examples that exist show a precocious sophistication which in England would not be met with again until the seventeenth century. The largest and most sophisticated library catalogue from medieval England is that from St Augustine's Abbey outside the walls of Canterbury.[33] This catalogue, listing over 1,800 books, was compiled around 1375 to 1380; it was augmented over the years, though the additions did not conform to the original, very systematic, organisation by author and work, with cross-references to other copies elsewhere in the library. That original worked-over copy was recopied in the later fifteenth century and anomalies in the grouping of texts reveal where entries had been added in the archetype. Adaptation to include shelf-marks was imperfectly superimposed on it. The librarian who organised this remarkable catalogue is not known by name, though one librarian of St Augustine's is known. Clement Canterbury has left his hand in quite a number of books from the library, sometimes initialling his notes in the front of books.[34] There is no documentation to confirm that he was officially the librarian, but his markings are so extensive that, if he was not, then he was (in Bruce Barker-Benfield's words) 'a library malefactor of diabolical persistence'. Clement Canterbury may have been the late fifteenth-century librarian for whom the interpolated catalogue was recopied.

In 1389, only a few years after the librarian of St Augustine's had made his theoretical advance, John Whitfield, monk of Dover Priory, compiled an extraordinary tripartite catalogue of the rather modest library of his priory.[35] The first part of the catalogue is a shelf-list by case, shelf and book, recording for each volume the author or title of the first text, the number of folios in the volume and the number of texts. Also provided for each are *dicta probatoria*, not always from the second folio. The second part of the catalogue records the same books in the same order, but this time lists all the contents of each

33 Dublin, Trinity Coll., MS 360; the catalogue was edited by James, *ALCD*, 174–406; a new edition by B. C. Barker-Benfield, who has been able to date the catalogue a century earlier than James suspected, is in hand for CBMLC.

34 B. C. Barker-Benfield, 'Clement Canterbury, Librarian of St Augustine's Abbey, Canterbury', in *MSS at Oxford*, 83, 88–92.

35 CBMLC v.

volume, with the folio number for where each text began and an incipit. The third part is an alphabetical index by author and title, with a location register giving case number, shelf number, volume number, folio number, and on which side of the folio, recto or verso (a or b), the text began. In settling on his tripartite arrangement, Whitfield showed a nice sensitivity to the different requirements of the readers in his community. The first part was designed for the precentor or an officer taking stock of the library: he was supplied with an inventory by which each individual book could be identified. The second part was intended for the brothers of the priory, who were encouraged to browse. The third part was designed to be a help to scholarly monks who might be looking for particular texts. The catalogue is even linked to the markings in the books. Each book has its shelf-mark on the outside and again with a table of contents inside the front of the book. The first part of the catalogue noted which folio was used for the *dicta probatoria* and, in each book, the shelf-mark was entered in the lower margin of that folio; in this way the assistant handling the books during a check would quickly be able to find the right leaf while the librarian followed in the catalogue. All this effort, together with an explanation of the use of the catalogue, was bestowed on an undistinguished collection of about 400 books, from which some twenty-four survive, a meagre 6 per cent. At least we can be sure that we could recognise any other survivors from this collection.

William Charyte, Augustinian canon of Leicester Abbey, at the end of the fifteenth century compiled a less distinguished catalogue of a much larger though still unexciting library.[36] Both these librarians had the 'listing gene': they were men innately disposed to making lists. Both compiled rentals of their houses' property and other kinds of lists. An extreme case of this was the unnamed Premonstratensian canon of Titchfield who compiled a catalogue of the library, explanatory but not detailed, as well as cartularies, rentals, and even an estate survey that measures land down to fractions of an inch. He included five such compilations in his library catalogue, which is dated to the year 1400, and four of them still exist.[37] Alas, he does not tell us his name.

The librarian who shows most interest in what his books contained is Henry de Kirkestede, monk and later prior of Bury St Edmunds, in the mid-fourteenth century. He compiled a catalogue which does not survive. He assigned

36 CBMLC vi. A20. The catalogue is organised in several parts, including a subject classification and a locations list, imperfectly cross-referenced.

37 Besides the catalogue itself, CBMLC iii. P6, now BL, MS Add. 70507, one should note P6. 202–6. All except P6. 205 (papal letters and Premonstratensian documents) have survived.

class-marks to the books, according to the initial letter of the author's name or of its subject – A for Ambrose, Augustine, Anselm; B for Bible – with numbers. These marks were entered in the books together with a note of the contents and sometimes a short biographical note about the author. His notes occasionally refer to other books by their class-mark, for example 'in registro librorum in J. 35', indicating that there was a written catalogue.[38] Even though it is lost, Henry's numbers allow us to estimate the size of the library in his time, by adding up the largest number of each letter-class in surviving books: A. 229, B. 385, C. 78, and so on to Y. 28; the total comes to at least 2,100 separate entries in his register. He also compiled a bio-bibliographical catalogue of some 674 authors, assimilating it to the shape of the Franciscan union catalogue *Registrum Angliae*, with incipits and explicits, and copying the numeral code by which the compilers of the *Registrum* indicated where copies of the work in question might be found, sometimes adding references to copies elsewhere (more to footnote his sources than to guide his monks to visit other libraries). With large collections of the letters or sermons of Augustine and Jerome, he went so far as to itemise and alphabetise headings for individual texts.[39]

The evidence that Henry has left for the extent of his reading and his interest in what he read is exceptional for the middle ages. To answer the question of how much monastic librarians would ordinarily know about the texts in the books in their care, our evidence is less straightforward. Contents lists entered at the front of books reveal a tidy-minded interest in knowing what the books contain, and often cataloguers drew on this information to provide a synoptic view of the contents of the whole library.[40] Confusion was easily achieved in the process, since medieval books use varying ascriptions and inconsistent titles for texts, and librarians, lacking the *incipitaria* and handbooks that are available to modern bibliographers, did not possess the means or often show the persistence that would enable them to identify the text before them accurately. John Whitfield at Dover spelled out in his preface the problems he faced, and he used the incipit as his clue to the informed reader. But not all cataloguers knew their books. Other booklists refer to the incipit as a way of patching over ignorance as to what a text is: for example, 'Alius liber

38 R. Sharpe, 'Reconstructing the medieval library of Bury St Edmunds Abbey: the lost catalogue of Henry of Kirkstead', in A. Gransden (ed.), *Bury St Edmunds: medieval art, architecture, archaeology, and economy*, British Archaeological Association Conference Transactions 20 (1998), 204–18. For Henry's practice as librarian, see also CBMLC XI. xlii–lxiv.

39 Henry's *Catalogus de libris autenticis et apocrifis* is edited by R. H. Rouse and M. A. Rouse, CBMLC XI; their edition of *Registrum Anglie* is CBMLC II.

40 Sharpe, 'Medieval library catalogues'; CBMLC VIII. 53, 57, 63.

qui sic incipit, *Herbarum quasdam*'.[41] The wandering practice of a cataloguer at Peterborough Abbey can be observed quite closely in his late fourteenth-century *Matricularium*, a puzzling, partial document.[42] For his description of a book from the library that has survived, a small miscellany now CCCC, MS 459, he had no contents list to guide him, but his entries in the *Matricularium* match the scribal titles and rubrics in the manuscript, or are otherwise abbreviations of them. On folio 30^{v} a text begins without rubric but is announced in the margin as 'Diffinicio confessionis', which the cataloguer took over as the title for his entry. This tract is, however, Robert Grosseteste's *De confessione* (*serm.* 15), which appears in the *Matricularium* several times, usually with its incipit 'Quoniam cogitacio' quoted alongside. It would seem that the cataloguer, even when possessed of the means to make an accurate identification of the text in front of him, did not always *apply* that knowledge and could be led astray by scribal titles in the manuscript.

Surviving catalogues such as this one nonetheless provide a picture of a library of a certain kind in a certain period, and allow a library to be reconstructed without the evidence of extant books, and some catalogues attest unusually good libraries. They all show different librarians at work at different times, each alive, to a different extent, to the issues of book classification, access and storage. The other means of approaching what were the practical professional concerns of the librarian take the form of interventions in the surviving books themselves, and we turn now to these. The entering of donor inscriptions into books is only one such intervention. Others include the numbering of folios, the writing of *ex libris* inscriptions, contents lists and shelf-marks. There is even, occasionally, evidence that the librarian read books. John Whitfield at Dover tells us, in his catalogue, that he had personally added *tabulae* in some thirty volumes. At the house of Augustinian friars at Gorleston on the Norfolk coast, the prior John Brome (d. 1449), who had already much enriched a notable library and had apparently been dispensed from the cure of souls in 1424 so as to be able to devote his time to the books, drew up indexes to every book in the collection.[43]

41 CBMLC iv. B10. 32. In this case, the incipit is enough to identify the text as 'Macer Floridus', *De uiribus herbarum*, sometimes attributed to Odo of Meung, an unknown figure; Sharpe, *Titulus*, 49.

42 J. M. W. Willoughby in CBMLC viii. 53.

43 John Bale, *Scriptorum illustrium maioris Brytanniae catalogus*, 2 vols. (Basel, 1557–7; facs. repr. Farnborough, 1971), i, 591: 'Directoriaque seu tabulas, ut uocant, aliorum scriptis per totam fere bibliothecam illam, docte et laboriose addidit'; F. Roth, *The English Austin friars, 1249–1538: History*, Cassiciacum 6 (New York, 1966), 518–19; *BRUC*, 95.

When observed simply as phenomena, the forms of custodial markings such as *ex libris* inscriptions, shelf-marks and even tables of contents conform to a spectrum from familiar, common types to rare or unique types. When understood as the work of a librarian, it becomes apparent that some librarians were learning their techniques from their colleagues in other institutions while others were devising their own solutions to problems shared with their colleagues.

There are, for example, numerous examples of marks that combine a letter and a number, but the signification of such marks, when properly understood, varies widely in spite of their similar appearance.[44] They may, for example, designate cupboards and the books inside, a probable interpretation at many institutions. Indeed, Franciscan houses appear generally to have used marks in this form, and extant examples show only a few letters in use, A to F. At Norwich, however, letter-classes, which in the first place may have designated cupboards, were added to over a long period, so that they came also to reflect accessions and the evolution of the collection.[45] Some letter-classes comprised large numbers of volumes – class X, the books acquired from Cardinal Adam Easton, amounted to at least 228 volumes. At Bury, as we have seen, Henry de Kirkestede's marks, similar in appearance, designate author- and subject-classes. There are also cases where the logic of letter and number is inverted. So, at St Mary's Abbey, York, the number designates the desk, and the preceding letter identifies a particular book at that desk.[46]

As with shelf-marks, so with *ex libris* inscriptions. These are often formulaic, and the same or similar formulas were used in different institutions at great distances apart. A strongly centralised order such as the Cistercians appears to have exercised clear direction: they used very much the same formula everywhere, 'Liber sancte Marie Rieuallis', 'Liber sancte Marie de Fontibus', 'Liber sancti Marie de Dulci corde'. Some Benedictine abbeys, on the other hand, vary the wording in every generation. In some houses the wording of an *ex libris* might be distinctive and inventive and could incorporate an anathema against the book's removal.[47] So many letter-marks and inscriptions seem to

44 For the many and various systems of marking books to reflect different requirements of organisation, see R. Sharpe, 'Accession, classification, location: shelfmarks in medieval libraries', *Scriptorium* 50 (1996), 279–87.

45 N. R. Ker, 'Medieval manuscripts from Norwich cathedral priory', *TCBS* I (1949–53), 1–28, repr. in his *Books, collectors and libraries*, 243–72.

46 CBMLC IV. 678–84.

47 M. Drogin, *Anathema! Medieval scribes and the history of book curses* (Totowa, NJ, 1983). There is a real need for more study of the wording of *ex libris* inscriptions, and much

be *sui generis* that one cannot help but receive the impression that while, to some degree, favourable experience could be transferred from one place to another, in many cases it was not transferred or only superficially.

In most books that bear notes of this kind, it is rare to find more than one mark of the same type; that is not in itself significant. If a book already had an *ex libris*, there would usually be no reason to add a second one. Similarly, it is rare to find two shelf-marks, though there are many reasons to think that different librarians had different ideas about the scheme of marking they would choose. At Durham the reorganisation of shelving arrangements in the fourteenth century and again in the early fifteenth, when the dedicated library room was built next to the chapter house, led to a reorganisation of letter-classes, and some books show the accumulated marks of two separate systems on the same page.[48] From Ely Cathedral Priory the evidence is more fragmentary and the picture more confused: around forty books have been assigned to Ely by Ker and Watson, a quarter of them with a query. Among the remainder, eleven have the early fifteenth-century *ex libris*, distinctively entered at both back and front of the book, while a good many others were liturgical books or books of domestic history, both categories that need not have been treated as library books at all. Nine books have what M. R. James termed 'the Ely mark', a cross symbol distinctively written on the first leaf, of which six also have the *ex libris* and three do not; this Ely mark appears in books datable to the ninth, twelfth and fourteenth centuries, but not in any later books, and it probably dates from the fourteenth century, earlier than the *ex libris*.[49] Some of the Ely books have added titles from the fourteenth century, and some have a press-mark, though no more than four press-marks have been identified from Ely, and they do not obviously reflect a single system

more attention to whether the same hand or a diversity of hands over time has entered them in books from a single foundation. In her *Bibliothèques cisterciennes dans la France médiévale: répertoire des Abbayes d'hommes* (Paris, 1991), and her *Bibliothèques de l'Ordre de Prémontré dans la France d'Ancien Régime* (Paris, 2000), A. Bondéelle-Souchier goes much further than N. R. Ker in *MLGB* in recording the significant variety of *ex libris* from the same institution. We must take notice, too, of those places from where a list of recognised survivors may be drawn up on other evidence but which wholly lack *ex libris*. Places where the most basic librarian's input was never found necessary provide a meaningful negative testimony.

48 A. J. Piper, 'The libraries of the monks of Durham', in Parkes and Watson, *Medieval scribes*, 218–28, and pls. 67–8.

49 Nine copies listed by Ker, *MLGB*, 77; James notes five examples of the mark in CCCC, MSS 44 (s. xi) [pontifical made at Canterbury; 15th-cent. Ely *ex libris*], 393 (s. xii) [Ely *ex libris*], 416 (s. xii) [no *ex libris*, early 16th-cent. numerical mark]; Cambridge, Pembroke Coll., MS 308 (s. ix) [Ely *ex libris* and 'the mark † which I have learnt to be characteristic of Ely books']; Cambridge, Trinity Coll., MS O. 2. 1 (cat. 1105) (s. xii^{2}) [no *ex libris*].

of marks.[50] Here, then, we appear to have several layers of activity, none of it apparently applied to the whole collection – though we must remember that Ker's perception of provenance may well have jumbled together books that formed part of distinct collections at Ely. More typically, marks are rare or absent. And where the librarians' *ex libris* dates from about 1500 in a twelfth-century book, we must be aware that for more than 300 years the book was unmarked.

Ex libris inscriptions are the most widespread evidence of librarians' activity, and in some sense the most basic, marking the ownership of a book as property. Summaries of the contents of a book, added, usually, to its flyleaf or sometimes written on a label attached to the cover, would be the second most prevalent intervention, while the inclusion of shelf-marks is far less frequent. What is perhaps surprising in these circumstances is how rarely there is unambiguous evidence for continuity of a traditional practice within a particular institution. In more than a few houses from which we have *ex libris* inscriptions, it is apparent that during the whole attested period of the middle ages there was only one campaign to enter marks of ownership in the books. At Reading Abbey, for example, founded by King Henry I as his burial church, a librarian in the mid-thirteenth century wrote a distinctive *ex libris* in all the books then in the library.[51] They had not been marked before, and they were not marked again, nor (it seems) were subsequent accessions at Reading marked at all. A consequence of that is that if books survive from a date later than this librarian's campaign, they cannot be recognised as Reading books. For other houses – including notable monasteries that might be expected to have owned decent libraries, such as Abingdon, Bath, Evesham, Peterborough, Tewkesbury – the situation is harder yet, for these houses seem never to have marked their books at all.[52] The same principle of a single campaign can be observed in other forms of marking. At Bury St Edmunds, for example, Henry de Kirkestede's class-marks were never superseded, even when a new library was built in the 1420s

50 Bodleian, MS Bodley 762 (s. xii) [no *ex libris*] and Oxford, Balliol Coll., MS 49 (s. xiii/xiv) [Ely *ex libris*] have large numerical press-marks, '6. 32' and '8. 17'. The simple numerical mark '108' in CCCC, MS 416 (s. xii) [no *ex libris*] was dated to the early sixteenth century by M. R. James and may reflect a different system. Bodleian, MS Bodley 582 (s. xii) [Ely *ex libris*] has the press-mark 'M. 23' (formerly taken for a Bury class-mark), which might reflect another system or a single system in which some locations were lettered and others numbered. For discussion, see N. Ramsay, 'The library and archives 1109–1541', in P. Meadows and N. Ramsay (eds.), *A history of Ely Cathedral* (Woodbridge, 2003), 157–68.

51 A. E. Coates, *English medieval books: the Reading Abbey collections from foundation to dispersal* (Oxford, 1999), 53 and pl. 9.

52 Ker, *English MSS*, 5.

with a very different regime for storage and access to the books, which had been moved out of the numerous cupboards and chests in the cloister into a dedicated library room.[53] It is quite clear that many institutions seem to have managed their books with little or no evidence of marking of any kind by their custodians. These 'silent' books may deny us a view of the medieval librarian at work, but we cannot assume that they once had marks on flyleaves or bindings that have disappeared. The inference instead must be that active interest in the library in medieval institutions was fitful, haphazard and in no sense a necessity.

There is sometimes also obvious physical evidence of the librarian's work: he would have books bound or rebound, and bindings are sometimes distinctive of a particular library. Likewise, external marks that show whether a book was once chained may show something specific about their pattern or position that is no less distinctive of the practice of a particular institution. At Lincoln Cathedral, which has kept much of its medieval library, the books show two distinctive types of chain-staple marks relating to the disposition of books in the new library that had been constructed over the cloister in the early fifteenth century. The older type is trapezoidal and always found near the middle of the foot of the front board, showing that the book was chained to one of the sloping desks. The available space on the desks was quickly taken, and at a later date an extra shelf was added below each desk to which newly acquired books were chained. The marks left by this arrangement are smaller, rectangular and found at either the top or foot of the front board, towards the spine.[54] External labels for ease of identification were added in a few places, and these are likely to reveal a single campaign of modifying the books, which, combined with other evidence, would show that one librarian had seriously changed the recognisability of the books in his custody. At Syon Abbey, near London, during just such a period of curatorial activity in the late fifteenth century associated with the *custos librarie* Thomas Betson, the books, often newly rebound, were given descriptive labels indicating their contents; these were placed on the lower boards and covered with horn shields that were nailed in place. Each volume received a shelf-mark which corresponded to a full descriptive entry in a remarkable classified and indexed catalogue drawn up by Betson.[55] Also characteristic of the care that was taken at Syon to make books accessible to readers are the fore-edge tabs that mark each new text

53 CBMLC IV. 47–8. 54 Thomson, *Cat. Lincoln*, xix.

55 M. C. Erler, 'Syon Abbey's care for books: its sacristan's account rolls 1506/7–1535/6', *Scriptorium* 39 (1985), 293–307. Betson's catalogue is ed. V. A. Gillespie, CBMLC IX; for his work as librarian, see pp. xlvi–li.

in composite volumes (and this is a feature also of Betson's own catalogue, sub-divided alphabetically by press).[56] Such aspects of physical appearance not only show how a librarian looked after the books in his keeping but can also help to disclose provenance; it would be possible to reclaim Syon books for Syon even were we to lack the control of Betson's descriptive catalogue.

Sometimes medieval bindings are not as old as the manuscripts they contain, the natural situation where a book has seen heavy use and has needed repair, or indeed where a formerly unbound book has for whatever reason come to acquire covers. The situation would also pertain where there has been a deliberate policy of rebinding a collection, either *en bloc* and at one time, where the intention might have been to make the books outwardly uniform, or as a process that continued *ad hoc* over a period of time, as was the case at Worcester Cathedral Priory, where there appear to have been near continual campaigns of repair and rebinding of the books from the mid-fifteenth century until the Dissolution.[57] While these campaigns were carried out under the supervision of different librarians, the books at Worcester also show evidence of one single unifying campaign, dating from around 1530, when labels listing the contents of each book were pasted to the back cover.[58]

In these cases of practical curatorship it is easy enough to detect the hand of the medieval librarian; but there are other areas of responsibility which we might naturally regard as belonging to his part where his role is less easily discerned, and one of these is the formulation of an accessions policy. We might ask whether it was due to the librarian to initiate a period of acquisition, or whether he merely carried out the instructions of abbot or prior in this respect. Certainly in Anglo-Norman England, where many monasteries were caught up in a trend of collection development, the enlargement of their libraries was decided upon as a deliberate policy, and the production of books was a corporate enterprise with monies directed towards the support of the work. At later periods, in individual houses where it is possible to discern a period of substantial investment in new books, or indeed in rehousing or rebinding books, the costs involved would likewise have demanded a resolution by the convent as a whole. Where monastic histories refer to such developments, they are usually associated with the abbot under whose leadership they took place. The Evesham chronicle attributes the acquisition of books to successive abbots in the eleventh and twelfth centuries: from as early as Abbot Ælfweard

56 CBMLC IX. xli and pl. 3.

57 M. Gullick, 'The bindings', in R. M. Thomson, *Cat. Worcester*, xxxviii–xlvii.

58 Illustrated by Thomson, *Cat. Worcester*, pl. 20a–b. Ker, *MLGB*, 206–15, indicates with an obelus which books – some 150 – still show a label, or traces of one.

(d. 1044), who bought books in London – surely the earliest reference to the London book trade – and sent them to Evesham, down to Abbot Adam, who acquired the Old and New Testaments glossed.[59] Histories from Abingdon and St Albans similarly credit abbots with increasing the library.[60] At Peterborough Abbey the record of books given by abbots extends from 1193 to 1396.[61] The abbots of Bury in the period when Henry de Kirkestede was active, William de Bernham (1335–61) and John Brinkley (1361–79), are said to have spent at least 100 marks and £150 respectively on books for the abbey.[62] If the initiative tended to come from the librarian, however, at times when that role was filled with unusual energy, we shall never know. But there would always be more detailed questions requiring choices to be made. Who made decisions about what books to buy, what works to have copied, during periods of major internal growth in the early twelfth century or in the mid- and later fourteenth century? For other periods there are nice questions regarding what proportion of books was produced to bespoke requests rather than acquired because the books were available, and what proportion exists as the private miscellanies of the readers who copied texts for their own use. Where a book was written to order, who instructed the copyist regarding what should be copied, according to what layout, and in combination with what other texts? An unusual and personal note written by a monk and dating to around 1248–9 survives in a book from Reading Abbey; W. de Wycombe, the author of the note, lists certain books that he had copied for the precentor and for the sub-prior: these are liturgical books, including music. Others in the list must have been intended for the library collection, such as a copy of Isidore's *Synonyma*, but direction for these is unattributed. He also compiled books of excerpts from Gregory, and these probably represent a personal selection drawn from his own reading.[63]

It is commonly assumed that medieval libraries showed the steady accumulation of the centuries and that there was no deliberate deaccessioning from their shelves, but this is a perilous assumption and almost certainly incorrect. The many leaves of broken books, recovered from the fifteenth-century bindings of books from Lambach and now at Yale, provide a dramatic illustration

59 Thomas of Marlborough, *De constitutione Eueshamensis coenobii et benefactoribus et malefactoribus et abbatibus eiusdem ecclesie*, chs. 146, 182, printed as part of his *History of the abbey of Evesham*, 152, 186; CBMLC IV. 131–2.

60 CBMLC IV. 4–5, 539–42.

61 CBMLC VIII. BP3 (Abbot Benedict, 1177–93)–BP19 (Abbot Nicholas Elmstow, 1391–6).

62 Sums recorded in a list of benefactors in whose memory the abbey bells were rung; extracts in CBMLC IV. B15, 90–4.

63 CBMLC IV. B76. The note is written in Bodleian, MS Bodley 125 (s. xii), a copy of the *Collationes* of Odo of Cluny.

of how scores of superannuated books were turned into mere binding-leaves during a period of renewed investment in the library.[64] In the early sixteenth century at Syon, more than 200 books were carefully removed from the catalogue and the space was used to enter newer acquisitions. From the index, which was not brought up to date, and with some use of ultraviolet light, it has proved possible to recover what these deaccessioned books contained.[65] But we can only guess at the administration of this restocking. The second-hand trade in books in the middle ages would also be intensely interesting, if only it were possible to recover more information about it. There are, for example, three twelfth-century books surviving with inscriptions showing that these books were acquired by Thomas Netter and presented to the Carmelites in London in the early fifteenth century.[66] One of these and one other owned by the London Carmel demonstrably came from the Cistercian abbey of Buildwas, far away in Shropshire, and it appears certain that Netter, head of the Carmelites in England, was buying books that had been deaccessioned by older monastic libraries.[67] These were not obsolete books. The texts, the style of script and the language were by no means useless to those with an interest in monastic reading, but perhaps recruits to a rural Cistercian house in the early fifteenth century had no use for them; better perhaps to sell them into the London trade and allow the friars to enjoy them. It is surely not necessary to speculate that these were stolen books that fell into the hands of a dealer.

The issue of security, however, then as now, was an important concern of librarians. In the management of the book collections of university colleges, security was central. Instead of the situation that pertained in the monasteries, where the monks were themselves cloistered, and the librarian, who knew the books better than his confrères, had the exclusive keeping of the collection, in colleges, where fellows might carry books out of college with them, it was usual to have three keys to the book-chests and three fellows keeping the keys, who had to be present together to open them. Obviously it was feared that one fellow with unsupervised access on his own might make mischief with the books of the college. Similar provisions were made for other secular institutions outside the universities. These institutions, unlike the university

64 R. G. Babcock, *Reconstructing a medieval library: fragments from Lambach* (New Haven, CT, 1993).

65 CBMLC IX. SS2.

66 Bodleian, MS Bodley 730, Cambridge, St John's Coll., MS 221, and Oxford, Trinity Coll., MS 58.

67 Bodleian, MS Bodley 730 (John Cassian), and NLS, MS 6121 (mainly Augustine); J. M. Sheppard, *The Buildwas books: book production, acquisition and use at an English Cistercian monastery, 1165–c. 1400*, OBS, 3rd ser., 2 (1997), 85, 62.

colleges, were isolated from general learned society and so their provisions are often more explicit on the role of the figure who can be recognised as the librarian. For example, the library that was established in 1464 in the guild church of All Saints, Bristol, by Bishop John Carpenter of Worcester was governed by the joint custodianship of the prior of the guild clergy, the mayor, and the rural dean of Bristol, but daily responsibility for the books was firmly vested in the prior. The library was to stand open every weekday, 'for two hours before noon and two after noon', for the use of any of the local clergy who wished to study there, at which times the prior was to remain on hand both to supervise the room and to be ready to explain obscure points of Scripture. Each of the three officers was to hold a copy of the inventory of books and perform an annual audit every autumn, between Michaelmas and All Saints Day; the prior was bound to replace any book which was found to be lacking.[68] Hospital foundations rarely owned the numbers of books that would bring urgency to questions of practical librarianship, although the books in such collections were often quite widely accessible; when they might be borrowed, then security again was the pressing issue. The priest who served the almshouses built around 1400 in Saffron Walden was provided with a small house whose oratory contained a small collection of chained books. Any priest in the surrounding district was entitled to consult these books, and was permitted, on receipt of a suitable pledge, to carry a book away for up to three months.[69] In such a case as this the librarian's role was that of custodian only, and similar examples are numerous.

Monastic librarians were not paranoid, and there is little evidence that security was a major concern to them, though there are many complaints in visitations about the prodigal loan of books. Definite cases of theft can be observed. In the thirteenth century the sacrist of Reading sent out a circular describing an augmented pocket bible, stolen from the cloister in July 1253, in the hope that it might be retrieved.[70] Ely Cathedral Priory around 1330 suffered the theft of some expensive books which were later found in Paris and identified as belonging to the monks of Ely; the official of the bishop of Paris took charge of the books, and he must have contacted the monks, though he was not swift to accede to their *procurateur*'s request to get the

68 N. I. Orme, 'The Guild of Kalendars, Bristol', *Transactions of the Bristol and Gloucestershire Archaeological Society* 96 (1978), 32–52; repr. and abbreviated in his *Education and society in medieval and Renaissance England* (London, 1989), 209–19.

69 The statutes of the almshouse were edited by F. W. Steer in *Transactions of the Essex Archaeological Society*, new ser. 25 (1955–60), 166–202; also J. M. W. Willoughby and N. L. Ramsay (eds.), *The libraries of secular colleges and hospitals*, forthcoming for CBMLC.

70 CBMLC IV. B73; Coates, *English medieval books*, 63–5, 83.

books back.[71] In the universities the danger was much greater. We can see that in the fifteenth century the main loss of books from the library of Canterbury Cathedral was through monks who went to university: books were transferred from Canterbury itself to its dependency, Canterbury College, at Oxford, for the use of student monks, but many were borrowed and never returned, being pawned, sold or otherwise alienated.[72]

There is no evidence that any librarian at Canterbury Cathedral ever asserted himself to reclaim these books scattered into the university market, or tried to keep a stricter control over them. In contrast, Abbot William Curteys of Bury St Edmunds (1429–46) did make an effort to assert control over the disposition of the abbey's books in two ordinances of the 1420s, which were copied into his register. Certain of the brethren had shown themselves remiss in their keeping of the community's books, 'lent to them for the purpose of study through the precentor or through another brother associated with him in his official responsibility'; some monks had given books as pledges for loans, some had loaned or even sold books outside the monastery. A number of these books had been recovered, 'some by request, others by purchase, some only with great effort and at excessive cost, even to the considerable indignation of those into whose hands they had come'. To safeguard the library in the future, brethren who were found to have alienated books or erased *ex libris* inscriptions were to be confined to the abbey, to eat all meals in the refectory (rather than enjoy the richer diet of the misericord), and to have certain other privileges removed, such as being bled. And because such crimes 'were able to take place a long time before they came to the notice of the said precentor or his deputy', sentence of major excommunication was passed on transgressors until in the judgement of the abbot or prior the crime had been sufficiently redeemed. A second ordinance demanded that at the end of fifteen days all library books in the possession of the monks were to be brought together in one place before the abbot.[73]

It was during William's abbacy that the monastery built a dedicated library room, fitted with desks to which books were chained.[74] In making this change Bury was conforming to the fashion of the period; since perhaps as early as the 1370s the book provisions of the religious orders had begun to imitate those of

71 BL, MS Add. 41612, fol. 74r; R. Sharpe, 'Books stolen from Ely Cathedral Priory and found in Paris *c.* 1330', *Library*, 7th ser., 6 (2005), 76–9.

72 C. F. R. de Hamel, 'The dispersal of the library of Christ Church, Canterbury, from the fourteenth to the sixteenth century', in Carley and Tite, *Books and collectors*, 263–79.

73 BL MS Add. 7096, fols. 182v, 192v; M. R. James (ed.), *On the abbey of St Edmund at Bury*, Cambridge Antiquarian Society, Octavo Publications 28 (Cambridge, 1895), 109–11.

74 CBMLC IV. 47–8.

the universities, with which they had interacted since early in the fourteenth century. Worcester Cathedral's *domus librarii*, completed in 1377, may be the earliest datable example.[75] Such libraries were built at many abbeys during the first half of the fifteenth century.[76] It was a development which encouraged new and freer arrangements for readers' access to the books. A category of documentary evidence that reflects the need to adapt management to the new situation is that of what we might call library rules, a rarer and more specialised form of document, presumably entirely prescriptive in intention. Secular bodies, particularly the university colleges of Oxford and Cambridge, had more reason to frame such rules than religious ones, but they clearly borrowed from monastic traditions and from the library arrangements of the friars. This aspect of library organisation is treated more fully elsewhere in the present volume.[77]

The fitful signs of management, even in books that were held by the same library over some hundreds of years, show how sporadic active librarianship was at this time. Precentors and their assistants for the most part managed their libraries for the here and now. Few of them held office for long periods, and no doubt, guided by their own lights, most were satisfied simply to have kept the books secure and in good repair during the period of their stewardship. The evidence for the habits of active librarianship – the marking of books with shelf-marks, *ex libris* inscriptions and contents lists – is widespread. The way in which it is brought together in Ker's *Medieval libraries of Great Britain* makes it appear more the norm than was in reality the case. It is evidence that demands careful interpretation to take due account of the occasional interest that led some librarians sometimes to place marks in their books. There is a wider lesson, too, that we should be very chary of thinking of a medieval library as a collection of books founded along with its host institution and developing by stages thereafter in a linear manner. The chances of personal intervention help to explain why the evidence of library catalogues and of marks in books is so individual. This evidence is crucial to our capacity to reconstruct medieval libraries, and the consequence of personal chances may be as important as the accidents of preservation in influencing the conclusions we draw from it. Medieval libraries varied enormously in their character, their purpose and their management, and they varied over time. Medieval librarians were the unintentional witnesses to much of this, but the diversity and inconsistency of their activities must warn against easy generalisation.

75 Thomson, *Cat. Worcester*, xxxiii–xxxiv.

76 See above, 38–42.

77 See above, 170–2.

9

Borrowing and reference: access to libraries in the late middle ages

PETER J. LUCAS

In coenobitic monasteries books provided intellectual and spiritual fodder. Provision for internal borrowing had existed from the beginning. St Augustine of Hippo's *Ordo monasterii* (*c.* 397) laid down in article 3 that reading should be pursued from noon until three, when the books should be returned.[1] The Augustinian rule stated that 'books will be available every day at the appointed hour, and not at any other time'.[2] St Benedict of Nursia laid down in his rule (*c.* 535–45) that reading was to occupy certain periods of time daily on a set pattern.[3] At the beginning of Lent, reading was given particular emphasis: monks were to receive books and they were to read them right through.[4] The Benedictine rule, widely influential from the sixth century, came to dominate western monasticism from the ninth century onwards, while the Augustinian rule became more and more important from the late eleventh century as it was adopted by many communities of canons and by the Dominican and Augustinian friars.

For advice on the writing of this chapter I am grateful to Professsors T. P. Dolan, K. O'B. O'Keefe, R. H. Rouse and R. Sharpe, Drs A. J. Fletcher and P. Zutshi, and the editors, and to Dr Webber in particular for commenting in detail on a draft of this chapter. I am solely responsible for the views expressed and for any errors.

1 'A sexta usque ad nonam uacent lectioni, et ad nonam reddant codices': G. Lawless, *Augustine of Hippo and his monastic rule* (Oxford, 1987), 74.

2 'Codices certa hora singulis diebus petantur; extra horam qui petierit, non accipiat' (ch. v. 10): Lawless, *Augustine,* 96; L. Verheijen (ed.), *La règle de Saint Augustin* (Paris, 1967), 433.

3 Ch. xlviii. 4, 10, 13, 14, 22–3: R. Hanslik (ed.), *Regula S. Benedicti*, *CSEL* 75, 2nd edn (Vienna, 1977), 126–30.

4 'In quibus diebus quadragesimae accipiant omnes singulos codices de bibliotheca, quos per ordinem ex integro legant' (ch. xlviii. 15–16): Hanslik, *Regula*, 129. The phrase 'de bibliotheca' is ambiguous, and could have meant 'from the Bible': see A. de Vogüé and J. Neufville, *La règle de Saint Benoît*, ii, Sources Chrétiennes xxxv (Paris, 1972), 602–3, n. 15; also D. Knowles (ed.), *Decreta Lanfranci monachis Cantuariensibus transmissa*, Corpus Consuetudinum Monasticarum 3 (Siegburg, 1967), 19, note to lines 12–13.

Gradually these basic provisions were embellished. Since we do not know what elaborations may have been introduced to English monasteries by the tenth-century monastic reformers, our earliest detailed evidence comes from the *Constitutiones* drawn up around 1077 by Lanfranc, archbishop of Canterbury, for the monks of Christ Church, arrangements that probably derive from the customs of Cluny.[5] Each monk was to read one book a year. On the first Monday of Lent:

> before the brethren go in to chapter, the librarian should have all the books save those that were given out for reading the previous year collected on a carpet in the chapter-house; last year's books should be carried in by those who have had them . . . The librarian shall read out a list of the books which the brethren had the previous year. When each hears his name read out he shall return the book which was given to him to read, and anyone who is conscious that he has not read in full the book he received shall confess his fault, prostrate, and ask for pardon. Then the aforesaid librarian shall give to each of the brethren another book to read, and when the books have been distributed in order he shall at the same chapter write a list of the books and those who have received them.[6]

The books on the carpet were a selection and corresponded to the number of the community. There is a list from Cluny, dating from the mid-eleventh century, of sixty-four books and their recipients, where they range from Augustine's *De Trinitate* for Gualo to a psalter *(psalterium suum)* for the less learned Stephen.[7] From Thorney (Cambridgeshire) in 1324–30 there is a list of fifty-one or more volumes distributed among thirty-eight monks; one Iohannes (the sixth of that name) retains a copy of the Pentateuch over the seven years.[8] There is also a list from Christ Church, Canterbury, itself, dating from 1338,

5 See D. Knowles (ed.), *The monastic constitutions of Lanfranc*, rev. C. N. L. Brooke (Oxford, 2002), xxviii–xlii.

6 'Priusquam fratres intrent capitulum, custos librorum debet habere congregatos libros in capitulo super tapetum extensum, praeter eos, qui praeterito anno ad legendum dati sunt; illos enim intrantes capitulum ferre debent, quisque suum in manu sua . . . librorum custos legat breue, qualiter praeterito anno fratres habuerunt libros. Cum uero audierit unusquisque nomen suum pronunciari, reddat librum, qui ad legendum sibi alio anno fuerat commendatus. Et qui cognouerit se non perlegisse librum quem recepit, prostratus culpam dicat, et indulgentiam petat. Iterum praedictus librorum custos unicuique fratri alium librum tribuat ad legendum. Distributis per ordinem libris, praefatus librorum custos in eodem capitulo inbreuiet nomina librorum et eos recipientium': Brooke and Knowles, *Monastic constitutions of Lanfranc*, 29–31.

7 P. Dinter (ed.), *Liber tramitis aevi Odilonis abbatis*, Corpus Consuetudinum Monasticarum 10 (Siegburg, 1980), 261–4.

8 CBMLC IV. 598–604 (B100); R. Sharpe, 'Monastic reading at Thorney Abbey (1323–1347)', *Traditio* 60 (2005).

and referring to about twenty-four monks, which shows books ranging from Aquinas to a psalter of the Virgin Mary.[9] A fragmentary list survives from St Albans from between 1420 and 1437, in which the monks have between two and twenty-five books each, ranging from works of the Church Fathers to antiphoners.[10] Lanfranc's *Constitutiones* were copied and adopted as a model in other English Benedictine monasteries, appearing, for example, in the ordinale and customary of the nunnery at Barking Abbey as late as 1404.[11] Arrangements modelled on Lanfranc's were also put into practice by the Gilbertines (*c*. 1140).[12]

Among the Augustinian canons a particularly clear set of regulations survives from Barnwell Priory (Cambridgeshire), which were modelled on those in use at Saint-Victor in Paris;[13] in their present form they date from 1295–6.[14] Again, the librarian (*armarius*) was the precentor, whose duty it was to keep the service-books correctly pointed, dusted and in good repair. He was also responsible for a lending collection, which he was to know thoroughly by the titles. As with Lanfranc's provisions, the librarian was to show the books at the beginning of Lent, and distribute the books which the brethren saw fit to use, keeping a record of who had which book and taking a pledge if appropriate.[15] Passing the books on to another was forbidden, and there is considerable

9 For the full list see J. B. Sheppard (ed.), *Literae Cantuarienses: The letter books of the monastery of Christ Church, Canterbury*, RS 85, 3 vols. (London, 1887–9), II. 146–52. For discussion (by N. Ramsay) see P. Collinson, N. Ramsay and M. Sparks, *A history of Canterbury Cathedral* (Oxford, 1995), 361–2.

10 R. W. Hunt, 'The library of St Albans', in Parkes and Watson, *Medieval scribes*, 254–7, 273–6; CBMLC IV. 554–63 (B87).

11 J. B. L. Tolhurst, *The ordinale and customary of the Benedictine nuns of Barking Abbey*, HBS 65–6 (London, 1927–8), I. 67–8. See also Brooke and Knowles, *Monastic constitutions*, xliii–xlix, liv; Wormald and Wright, *English library*, 21.

12 W. Dugdale, *Monasticon Anglicanum*, ed. J. Caley, H. Ellis and B. Bandinel, 6 vols. (London, 1846), VI. xxix–xcvii, at xxx. See also K. Christ, 'Mittelalterliche bibliotheksordnungen für frauenklöster', *Zentralblatt für Bibliothekswesen* 59 (1942), 6, and his *The handbook of medieval library history*, rev. A. Kern, trs. and ed. T. M. Otto (Metuchen, NJ, and London, 1984), 24; B. Golding, *Gilbert of Sempringham and the Gilbertine Order c. 1130–c. 1300* (Oxford, 1995), 180–1.

13 L. Delisle, *Le cabinet des manuscrits de la Bibliothèque Nationale*, 4 vols. (Paris, 1868–81), II. 224–7.

14 J. W. Clark, *The observances in use at the Augustinian Priory of S. Giles and S. Andrew at Barnwell, Cambridgeshire* (Cambridge, 1897). For the date, see p. xi, and for the indebtedness to the provisions at Saint-Victor, see pp. xlii–xlvi. The same provisions applied in Grönendaal near Brussels, as noted by Clark, *Care of books*, 60, n. 3. See also above, 224.

15 'Fratribus eciam debet libros quos sibi uiderint oportunos tradere, et nomina librorum et recipiencium in rotulo suo annotare; de quibus, cum fuerint requisiti, debent respondere': Clark, *Observances*, 62. In 1339 Benedict XII laid down that the distribution of books

emphasis on the taking of pledges of value equal to the book.[16] Presumably this provision implies that books could be lent outside the house.[17] Certainly some five books from the Augustinian Priory at Lanthony (Gloucestershire) were borrowed by a vicar of Cherington (a manor held by the priory in East Gloucestershire).[18]

As early as 1212 efforts were made to promote the lending of books beyond the confines of the monastery. Robert de Courçon, an Englishman at the university of Paris, who became a cardinal the same year, records that a Council in Paris decreed:

> We forbid those who belong to a religious Order to formulate any vow against lending their books to those who are in need of them; seeing that to lend is enumerated among the principal works of mercy.[19]
>
> After careful consideration, let some books be kept in the House for the use of brethren; others, according to the decision of the abbot, be lent to those who are in need of them, the rights of the House being safe-guarded.
>
> From the present date no book is to be retained under pain of incurring a curse [for its alienation], and we declare all such curses to be of no effect.[20]

How much notice was taken of this decree it is difficult to say; the fact that it was felt necessary to promulgate it presumably indicates some dissatisfaction with the parsimony of monastic houses in lending books beyond their walls. Smith has argued that the approach of the Parisian Council stems from

could be at any suitable time: *Bullarum diplomatum et privilegiorum sanctorum Romanorum pontificum Tauriensis editio*, 24 vols. (Turin, 1857–72), IV. 439.

16 'Nec ipse armarius debet libros accommodare nisi accipiat equiualens memoriale, et tunc debet nomen recipientis, et libri traditi, et memorialis accepti, in rotulo suo annotare': Clark, *Observances*, 62.

17 Cf. CBMLC VI. 6.

18 CBMLC VI. 35.

19 Luke 6.35: 'lend, expecting nothing in return': see L. Smith, 'Lending books: the growth of a medieval question from Langton to Bonaventure', in L. Smith and B. Ward (eds.), *Intellectual life in the middle ages: essays presented to Margaret Gibson* (London, 1992), 265.

20 J. D. Mansi, *Sacrorum conciliorum nova et amplissima collectio* (Venice, 1778), XXII: Concilium Parisiense AD 1212, pt ii, ch. 23, col. 832: 'Interdicimus inter alia viris religiosis, ne emittant juramentum de non commodando libros suos indigentibus, cum commodare inter praecipua misericordiae opera computetur. Sed adhibita consideratione diligenti, alii in domo ad opus fratrum retineantur; alii secundum providentiam abbatis, cum indemnitate domus, indigentibus commodentur. Et a modo nullus liber sub anathemate teneatur: & omnia praedicta anathemata absolvimus.' The injunction is repeated from pt i, ch. 7, col. 821, where it applies to secular clergy. The translation is by Clark, *Care of books*, 64–5, who cited the passage from L. Delisle, 'Documents sur les livres et les bibliothèques au moyen âge', *Bibliothèque de l'Ecole des chartes* 3/1 (1899), 225. The decree was repeated in 1214 at a Council at Rouen also presided over by Cardinal Robert de Courçon: G. Bessin, *Concilia Rotomagensis Provinciae* (Rouen, 1717), Concilium Magistri Roberti de Corcon legati, apud Rotomagum celebratum, pt ii, ch. 26, sig. $P3^v$–4^r (pp. 118–19).

the views of Peter the Chanter (d. 1197), whose teaching in Paris focused on practical questions of ethics; she adduces evidence of similar thinking from Thomas of Cobham (*c.* 1220) and Stephen Langton, archbishop of Canterbury (1207–28), both of whom, like Robert de Courçon, were taught by Peter the Chanter. Langton expressed the view forcibly in his commentary on Deuteronomy 5.17, the sixth commandment: 'You shall not kill', 'not to lend books is a type of homicide'.[21] In this light it is appropriate to note evidence from Christ Church, Canterbury, of a book containing a *Brut* chronicle and St John Chrysostom's *De laude apostoli* being lent to Master Laurence de St Nicholas (d. *c.* 1237), rector of Terrington, after whose death it apparently went to Anglesey Priory.[22] The approach evidently persisted and spread among the Benedictines. Roger of Huntingfield, rector of Balsham, near Cambridge, had eleven books on loan for life from Ely Cathedral when he died in 1329, and they were fetched personally by the precentor/librarian.[23] From 1338 there is a list from Christ Church, Canterbury, of fifty-four books lent (and some not returned), of which sixteen went to seculars, and two had gone to Edward II (who had died in 1327).[24] However, the thinking reflected by Peter the Chanter's pupils and subsequent practice evidently faded as the mendicant orders of friars came to dominate the teaching of theology. From 1363–6 there is record of a complaint against Geoffrey Lambourn, abbot of Eynsham, by the visitor, Thomas de la Mare, abbot of St Albans, that, *inter alia*, he had carelessly lent the abbey's books to outsiders.[25] Although Lambourn answered the charges more or less convincingly, the fact that they were brought at all indicates a climate different from that pertaining a generation earlier. Nevertheless, there are exceptions. In 1369 Thomas Southam, who was in the service of Simon Langham, archbishop of Canterbury (1366–8), borrowed books on canon law from Westminster Abbey.[26] An indenture from 1390 whereby Rochester Cathedral lent books and vestments to John Mory, rector of Southfleet, may be a special case, as is suggested by the degree of legal formality in the arrangement.[27] Later, curses continued to be added to books in Benedictine houses. For example, a fifteenth-century hand has added to a manuscript that belonged to

21 Smith, 'Lending books', 268, n. 16: 'Ergo genere homicidii est quaternos non accommodare.'

22 J. Burtt, 'Notes upon ancient libraries', *Notes and Queries* I (1849–50), 21–3.

23 CBMLC IV. 129–30 (B27).

24 For discussion (by N. Ramsay) see Collinson, Ramsay and Sparks (eds.), *Canterbury Cathedral*, 361.

25 CBMLC IV. 153–5 (B33).

26 CBMLC IV. 611–13 (B104). On Southam see *BRUO* III. 1733.

27 CBMLC IV. 534–7 (B83).

the Benedictine abbey of Saint-Jacques (Liège) after 1419 the following three hexameters:

Ad claustrum	sancti Jacobi	spectat liber iste
Si quis eum	ferat hinc alibi	te vindice Christe
Grande malum	pariare sibi	succrescere iuste.[28]

(This book belongs to the cloister of St Jacques. If anyone bears it from here to somewhere else, with you Christ as avenger, (may he suffer Him) justly to beget a big calamity for himself to make retribution.)

By this time the regulations at Saint-Jacques had been influenced by those of the Dominicans, as promulgated by their fifth master general, Humbertus de Romanis (1254–63),[29] who drew on those of the Augustinian canons of Saint-Victor in Paris.[30] No doubt, curses were added in the fifteenth century in England too.[31]

In friaries there were generally up to four collections of books – one in the choir or sacristy, one in the refectory, a chained reference collection, sometimes called the *libraria conventus*, and the books in the communal library, essentially a working collection, from which friars might borrow items, sometimes called the *libraria studencium*;[32] it is the last that is our concern here. From about 1246 the Dominicans usually had a librarian, whose responsibility it was to carry out an inspection once or twice a year. The communal library was to be available at a stated time each day, and the librarian was to keep an account of the books lent.[33] Members of the order could borrow books *ad vitam* (when they would be returned to the order anyway, because all the books held by a friar reverted to his order on his decease);[34] examples of such loans from the London friary to John Beauchamp and from the Chester friary

28 Maynooth, Co. Kildare, Russell Library MS RB16, fol. 232^{v}/b/35ff. The manuscript (Engelbert of Admont, *Commentarius in Psalmum* CXVIII, formerly attributed to Alexander of Hales) passed to St Jacques after the death of Johann von Wallenrode (bishop of Liège) in 1419. For assistance in deciphering and in the (provisional) elucidation of the verses I am grateful to Mrs A. M. Lucas, Dr D. Money and Professor H. Sauer.

29 P. Volk, *Der liber ordinarius des Lütticher St Jakobs-Klosters*, Beiträge zur Geschichte des alten Mönchtums und des Bendiktinerordens 10 (Münster, 1923), lxxi, 44–5.

30 For the use of curses at Saint-Victor see Delisle, *Cabinet des manuscrits*, II. 227.

31 On book curses generally see M. Drogin, *Anathema! Medieval scribes and the history of book curses* (Totowa and Montclair, NJ, 1983), 46–111.

32 CBMLC I. xix. The Latin names are Franciscan: see Parkes, 'Provision of books', in *HUO* II. 436.

33 K. W. Humphreys, *The book provisions of the mediaeval friars, 1215–1400* (Amsterdam, 1964), 31–2.

34 Some books were inscribed as belonging (presumably by reversion) to the order, e.g. BAV, MS Ottoboni lat. 210 (Alexander of Hales, *Summa*), 'Iste liber est conuentus fratrum predicatorum': see Parkes, 'Provision of books', 434 and n. 133.

to Adam of Knutsford are respectively BL, MS Royal 5.C.vii (Augustine) and Shrewsbury School, MS xxiv (Peter Comestor).[35] A book could go outside the order to a layman provided that a pledge or 'memoriale' was given; such a pledge could be another book.[36] Among the Augustinian friars, all *studia generalia* (i.e. houses with advanced educational facilities where ordinands were prepared for university) were to have a librarian. He was to supervise borrowing, which could also be outside the order if permission was obtained and a pledge given,[37] but from 1482 loans of books were not favoured, as the general chapter at Perugia decided to excommunicate any librarian who loaned a book without a receipt signed by the borrower and a pledge of twice its value.[38] The Cistercians and Carthusians also provided for the loan of books to extraneous persons under certain conditions.[39]

Although St Francis himself (d. 1226) was not a great enthusiast for promoting the study of books as a priestly pastime,[40] in 1230 the bull *Quo elongati* of Gregory IX provided for Franciscan friars to have the use (but not the ownership) of property,[41] so that the order could assemble collections of books to support study, which it did avidly. Consequently, Franciscan friaries usually had a library, the contents of which were *in potestate ordinis*, and books left over after those required for essential study had been distributed could be borrowed under the supervision of a custodian.[42] Every friar could borrow from the friary library with the consent of the provincial minister. If a book was assigned *ad vitam*, the consent of the custodian was required as well; a thirteenth-century example of such a loan from the Cambridge friary to Simon of Hunton is BAV, MS Ottoboni lat. 442 (Caesarius of Arles).[43] Books had to be

35 BL, MS Royal 5.C.vii, fol. 1^{v}: 'Iste liber est de conuentu fratrum predicatorum London assignatus fratri Iohanni Beauchamp'; and Shrewsbury School, MS xxiv, fol. 1^{r}: 'Iste liber est de communitate fratrum ordinis predicatorum cestr' concessus fratri Ade de Knotesford' ad terminum vite', see Parkes, 'Provision of books', 432 and n. 124.

36 Humphreys, *Book provisions*, 33–4. On Dominican practice see also W. A. Hinnebusch, *The early English Friars Preachers* (Rome, 1951), 180–6.

37 Humphreys, *Book provisions*, 74.

38 F. Roth, *The English Austin friars, 1249–1538*, 2 vols. (New York, 1961–6), I. 377.

39 Clark, *Libraries*, 16.

40 Neither the earlier rule nor the later rule of St Francis makes any provision for study as part of the daily routine: see, e.g., R. J. Armstrong and I. C. Brady, *Francis and Clare: the complete works* (New York, 1982), 107–45.

41 J. H. Sbaralea *et al.* (eds.), *Bullarium Franciscanum Romanorum Pontificum*, 4 vols. (Rome, 1759–68), I. 68–70.

42 On the regulation of access to books among the Franciscans, see B. Roest, *A history of Franciscan education (c. 1210–1517)* (Leiden, 2000), 215–22.

43 Ottoboni lat. 442, fol. 1: 'Iste liber est de domo cantebrigie concessus fratri Simone de Hunton' ad vitam suam', see Parkes, 'Provision of books', 432 and n. 124. For Hunton see *BRUC*, Appendix, 678.

shown once a year, when an inventory was made. In Florence, books were to be returned each fortnight or month at the ringing of a bell.[44] Similarly, with the Carmelites, the study of books was subject to strict regulation. During the fourteenth century, books could be borrowed *in casu necessitatis*, so presumably most books were kept for reference. Friars who did borrow books were encouraged to pass them on (with the prior's knowledge).[45]

It was characteristic of all the orders of friars that no secular person could borrow a book as of right, and nowhere was the reluctance to lend greater than among the Franciscans. As St Bonaventure (minister general OFM 1257–74) or his close associate argued, reluctance to lend books is justified because much lent to others becomes lost:

> He who is quickest to ask is slowest to return; and having been asked repeatedly gives it back with much murmuring and ingratitude in return for kindness shown. Often the book has been written in or torn; or it will be lent to someone else without your permission, who lends it again, and this fourth person does not know who you are or how to return it to you. Or this person may move too far away to return it. It cannot be entrusted to a messenger or he fears it will be destroyed on the journey. Or else the person who is supposed to return it wants to read it himself or lends it to another, and *he* ends up by denying he ever had it. Sometimes the book is bound in a volume with other works and the thing is pulled apart to get at the section the borrower wants. Or if you agree to lend the book to one person, others will be angry that you did not lend it to them too, so you are compelled to wait a long time until they all see it; or finally, having passed through many hands, it comes back dirty or destroyed altogether.[46]

44 For Franciscan practice see Humphreys, *Book provisions*, 55–63.

45 Humphreys, *Book provisions*, 78–80.

46 Cited in translation by Smith, 'Lending books', 274–5, from [Bonaventure,] *Determinationes Quaestionum*, pt 2, qu. 21 (Cur Fratres scripta sua tam difficulter aliis communicent), in *S. Bonaventurae opera omnia* (Quaracchi, 1898), VIII. 372: 'Item, sunt in petendo multi valde importuni, sed in reddendo tardi, quod saepius pulsati, vix tandem cum murmure concessa reddunt et pro beneficio ingratitudinis verba impendunt. Item, saepe per scriptores polluuntur quaterni et libri et lacerantur vel aliter male tractantur sic concessi. Item, unus concedit ulterius alii, irrequisito eo qui ei scriptum concessit, et ille forsitan iterum alii, donec tandem ille nescit, a quo reposcere debeat, et sic elongatur ab eo, quod nullus directe ei inde respondet . . . Aliquando etiam ille vel iste de loco mutatur, et tam longe unus ab altero disiungitur, quod non potest concessum per nuntios repetere, vel timet in via destrui . . . Ille autem, quibus talia restituenda committuntur, quandoque volunt sibi rescribere, priusquam illi restituant, vel commodant aliis, vel alicubi restituant, vel commodant aliis, vel alicubi relinquunt, donec oblivioni tradunt, et postea negant, sibi fuisse commissa . . . Aliquando scriptum aliquod est ligatum in volumine cum aliis operibus, et si illud Frater alicui concederet, oporteret, eum totum librum dissolvere, cum gravi damno expensarum et laborum in ligando factorum. Saepe etiam cum uni rescribendum conceditur, alii, nisi et sibi concedatur, indignantur, et per hoc aut diu cogitur ille scripto suo carere, aut per plures manus transiens sordidatur et perditur.'

This possessiveness regarding books caused frustration. In his *Philobiblon* (1344–5), Richard de Bury (bishop of Durham 1333–45), a renowned 'borrower' of books,[47] records that books were heaped up unused in friaries: 'Whenever it happened that we turned aside to the cities and places where the mendicants . . . had their convents, we did not disdain to visit their libraries . . . there we found heaped up amid the utmost poverty the utmost riches of wisdom.'[48] Bury also found that the Dominicans were 'above all the religious most freely communicative of their stores without jealousy',[49] a statement of praise ('Praedicatores . . . extollimus merito speciali') that probably implies some criticism of others.[50] This criticism was taken up by Richard FitzRalph (archbishop of Armagh 1346–60),[51] who had previously benefited from Bury's patronage, and who became involved in a bitter dispute with the Franciscans of Dundalk and Drogheda during 1352–6.[52] In a sermon preached at St Paul's Cross in London on 12 March 1357, FitzRalph complained that the friars 'have more books, and finer books, than any prelate or doctor'.[53] Later that year, on 8 November, in a sermon preached before the pope and curia at Avignon he elaborated his complaint. The mendicant friars have become so numerous

> that . . . one can scarcely find any useful book for sale; for they have all been bought up by the friars, so that every convent has a large and noble library, and every friar with standing in the *studia* . . . has a noble library. Thus, I sent

47 C. R. Cheney, 'Richard de Bury, borrower of books', *Speculum* 48 (1973), 325–8; CBMLC IV. 32 (B10).

48 M. Maclagan (ed.), *Philobiblon Richardi de Bury: the text and translation of E. C. Thomas* (Oxford, 1960), 90–1: 'Cum vero nos ad civitates et loca contingeret declinare, ubi . . . pauperes conventus habebant, eorum armaria . . . visitatare non pinguit . . . ibi in altissima paupertate altissimas divitias sapientiae thesaurizatas invenimus.'

49 *Philobiblon*, 92–3: 'eos [Praedicatores] prae cunctis religiosis suorum sine invidia gratissime communicativos invenimus'. Later (1473) Thomas Bloxham gave Merton a book (Peter of Poitiers on the *Sentences*, now MS 132) that previously belonged to the Oxford Dominicans, as noted by Ker, 'Oxford college libraries before 1500', in his *Books, collectors and libraries*, 316 and n. 74; whether Bloxham borrowed it or not is moot. For Bloxham, see *BRUO* I. 204–5.

50 For some comparative remarks about the position of the Dominicans *vis-à-vis* the Franciscans, see Smith, 'Lending books', 276–7.

51 K. Walsh, *A fourteenth-century scholar and primate: Richard FitzRalph in Oxford, Avignon and Armagh* (Oxford, 1981); A. Gwynn, 'Archbishop FitzRalph and the Friars', *Studies: An Irish Quarterly Review* 26 (1937), 50–67.

52 On the inception and growth of criticism of the friars see L. Hammerich, *The beginnings of the strife between Richard FitzRalph and the mendicants* (Copenhagen, 1938), and C. Erikson, 'The fourteenth-century Franciscans and their critics', *Franciscan Studies* 35 (1975), 107–35, 36 (1976), 108–47. See also P. R. Szittya, *The antifraternal tradition in medieval literature* (Princeton, NJ, 1986).

53 Gwynn, 'FitzRalph and the Friars', 59. For the manuscript sources of this material see Gwynn, 'The sermon-diary of Richard FitzRalph, archbishop of Armagh', *Proceedings of the Royal Irish Academy*, 44C (1937), 1–57, esp. 45–7.

> three or four of my rectors to the schools, and I was told that they were unable to find there any usable Bible or other books of theology suitable for them and so they returned home.[54]

FitzRalph's complaint was that books were not available to purchase because the friars had bought them all up.

His complaint was elaborated by the Lollards, who after about 1382 circulated a set of sixty-five Latin *quaestiones* aimed at the friars, one of which concerned books and libraries. Although the original *quaestiones* have not survived, an (expanded) Middle English version survives in *Jack Upland*: 'Frere, what charite is it to gadere vp þe bokis of Goddis lawe, many mo þanne nediþ ȝou, & putte hem in tresorie, & do prisone hem fro seculer preestis & curatis, wher bi þei ben lettid of kunnynge of Goddis lawe to preche þe gospel freli?'[55] The theme is taken up again in other Wycliffite writings.[56] For example, article 17 in *How religious men should keep certain articles* says: 'þat þei drawen not noble bokis of holy writt & holy doctouris & oþere nedeful sciencis . . . in-to here owene cloistris . . . & suffre hem be closed þere & waxe rotyn, & neiþer ȝeue hem ne lene hem ne selle hem to curates & clerkis, þat myȝtten . . . teche it [holy writ] frely for loue of mennus soulis.'[57]

Hoarding of books was condemned. The anonymous *Of clerks possessioners* criticises all religious in orders: 'þes possessioners ben þeues . . . for þei han manie bokes, and hyden hem from seculer clerkis & suffren þes noble bokes

54 M. A. Rouse and R. H. Rouse, 'The Franciscans and books: Lollard accusations and the Franciscan response', in their *Authentic witnesses: Approaches to medieval texts and manuscripts* (Notre Dame, 1991), 413. The Latin text printed in R. FitzRalph, *Defensio curatorum* (Lyon, J. Trechsel, 1496 = Proctor, *Index* no. 8611), sig. 2A5^{v}, reads, 'quod non reperitur . . . aliquis vtilis multum liber venalis, sed omnes emuntur a fratribus: ita vt in singulis conuentibus sit una grandis ac nobilis libraria, vt singuli fratres habentes statum in studijs . . . nobilem librariam. Vnde etiam de meis subiectis rectoribus tres aut quattuor misi ad studium. & dictum est mihi quod nec bibliam eis utilem, nec libros alios theologie venales eis congruos ibi poterant reperire ad suam patriam sunt reuersi.'

55 P. L. Heyworth (ed.), *Jack Upland, Friar Daw's reply and Upland's rejoinder* (London, 1968), 70, lines 373–6: 'Friar, what charity is it to gather up the books of God's law in much larger numbers than you need, and put them in your treasury, and hold them secure from secular priests and curates, so that they are prevented from acquiring knowledge of God's law with which they could freely preach the gospel?'. For a Latin version used by William Woodford, see J. I. Catto, 'William Woodford, O.F.M.', unpublished DPhil thesis, Oxford University (1969), 31–6.

56 For a full treatment of this topic, see Rouse and Rouse, 'Franciscans and books'.

57 F. D. Matthew (ed.), *The English works of Wyclif hitherto unprinted*, EETS, OS, 74 (London, 1880), 221, lines 25–32: 'that they should not withdraw noble books of holy writ and by holy doctors and on other necessary areas of knowledge into their own cloisters, and allow them to be kept there and rot and neither give them nor lend them nor sell them to curates and scholars in holy orders who might freely teach holy writ for the love of mens' souls'. The exact date of this anonymous work is not known.

wexe roten in here libraries, and neiþer wolen sillen hem ne lenen hem to oþere clerkis þat wolden profiten by studiynge in hem & techen cristene peple þe weie to heuene.'[58] But the mendicant friars receive the fiercest criticism: 'in þis defaute ben religious mendynauntis as principal þeuys & forgoeris of anticrist . . . lord siþ þes bokis ben more nedeful to mannys good lif þan gold or siluer . . . hou moche more ben þes religious out of charite, þat helpen not seculer clerkis & curatis of þes bokis neiþer be ȝifte ne lenyng ne sillyng for no money.'[59]

The Franciscans were sufficiently shaken by the accusations, which were really part of a smear campaign aimed at portraying the friars as robbers, to produce a rejoinder. In 1395/6 William Woodford from Greyfriars at Oxford wrote a *Defensorium fratrum mendicantium contra Armachanum*, in which he answered FitzRalph and the Wycliffite charges categorically if not entirely convincingly.[60] Woodford made three points regarding the hoarding of books: (1) all religious houses hold on to their own books; (2) books must be secured against mutilation and theft; and (3) books must be kept for study by the friary's own inmates. Of course, the first point is what gave rise to the criticisms in the first place, although the Franciscan philosophy of possession without ownership was a particular irritant. As for the second point, the distinction between books in the chained reference library and those in the lending library had effectively broken down, and many books were chained just to keep them secure.[61] While the third point is fair enough, a balance between keeping books available for brother friars and allowing others to make use of them was not an unreasonable demand, but pledges had always been required, and it was precisely the indigent who could not afford them. In fact there is evidence that Oxford Greyfriars did allow others to use their books.[62] 'Chancellor Harclay had used Grosseteste's books by 1317; Richard de Bury or his agents knew the

58 Matthew, *Wyclif*, 128/16–23: 'These possessioners [persons belonging to a religious order] are thieves . . . because they have many books . . . and hide them away from secular clerks and allow these noble books to rot in their libraries, and they will neither sell them nor lend them to other scholars in holy orders who would profit from studying them, and would teach christian people the way to heaven'.

59 Matthew, *Wyclif*, 128/23–129/2, where the reading 'leuyng' has been considered erroneous for 'lenyng': 'In this fault, the mendicant orders are the principal thieves and heralds of Anti-Christ . . . Lord! Since these books are more necessary to man's godly life than gold or silver . . . how much more are these religious in orders out of charity, who do not help secular scholars in holy orders and curates to obtain these books, either by gift or by lending or by selling for any amount of money.'

60 Rouse and Rouse, 'Franciscans and books', 415–18. On Woodford, see *BRUO* III. 2081–2.

61 Humphreys, *Book provisions*, 87. However, in some friaries even the 'select' books were lent: Parkes, 'Provision of books', 439–40, regarding Greyfriars at Oxford.

62 One borrowed book was never returned, Cambridge, Gonville and Caius Coll., MS 403/412, inscribed on fol. 1^{r} 'Iste liber est de communitate fratrum minorum Oxonie'

library in the first half of the century; Henry de Kirkestede, a Benedictine of Bury St Edmunds, recorded titles from this library in his *Catalogus* in the 1370s; and Wyclif himself seems to have had extended access to it.'[63] And another user was Thomas Gascoigne (1403–58), who worked on Grosseteste's books and others in 1433–4.[64] But none of these were paupers. The implicit Wycliffite belief in books as a public service commodity,[65] a belief foreshadowed only superficially by the thinking of Peter the Chanter, because at that time potential borrowers would all have been beneficed clergy, was not shared by the institutions who held them, any more than modern Oxford and Cambridge colleges would allow campers to pitch tent on their courts and quadrangles.

Because of the difficulty in obtaining books, three developments took place: (1) students in the universities had to try and borrow books from elsewhere; (2) religious foundations provided for their own book collections in the universities; and (3) secular foundations were forced to set up their own libraries.

(1) Although borrowing from elsewhere was difficult, some members of Oxford University succeeded. In 1300 Henry de Shorne borrowed a copy of Justinian's *Codex* from Christ Church, Canterbury.[66] In 1334 Thomas Duraunt, a fellow of Merton, borrowed a copy of Nicolas de Gorran's *Super psalterium* from Rochester Cathedral.[67] But, as is to be expected from what has been said above, after about 1350 the evidence for borrowing directly from Benedictine houses runs out. Before 1385 we find Nicholas de Stenington borrowing a copy of Bede's *Historia ecclesiastica* from the Augustinian priory of St Frideswide, Oxford, in return for the pledge of another book, Nicholas Trevet on Leviticus.[68] Other loans seem to have been personal ones. Henry Abingdon, warden of Merton, lent another fellow, John Hanham, twelve books from his personal collection in the 1430s.[69] Around 1440 Thomas Burton, a former fellow of New

(cited by Parkes, 'Provision of books', 439 and n. 159), was lent to Master Richard Brynkley (*BRUC*, 103), but he was himself a Franciscan, a member of the Cambridge friary.

63 Rouse and Rouse, 'Franciscans and books', 420.

64 R. M. Ball, 'The opponents of Bishop Pecok', *JEH* 48 (1997), 245; at least one book which Gascoigne had (borrowed?) from Greyfriars, Oxford, was left by him to Lincoln College, where it is now MS lat 31 (Ker, 'Oxford college libraries before 1500', in his *Books, collectors and libraries*, 315 and n. 73). On Gascoigne, see below, 261–2.

65 M. E. Aston, 'Lollardy and sedition 1381–1431', *Past and Present* 17 (1960), 1–44.

66 James, *ALCD*, 148; *BRUO* III. 1696–7; Parkes, 'Provision of books', 412.

67 BL, MS Royal 2.C.v, fol. 1, *BRUO* I. 611–12; Parkes, 'Provision of books', 412.

68 Now Merton College, MS 188, with inscription on the verso of fol. i: Parkes, 'Provision of books', 412; *BRUO* III. 1771; F. M. Powicke, *The medieval books of Merton* (Oxford, 1931), 135.

69 Powicke, *Medieval books of Merton*, 76; *BRUO* I. 7–8; II. 866; Parkes, 'Provision of books', 412.

College, lent his copy of Justinian's *Institutiones* to a current fellow, Thomas Clyffe.[70] In 1448, on completing his studies at Oxford, Isaac Ledbury, a Benedictine from Worcester, lent the cathedral copy of John Duns Scotus on the Lombard's *Sentences* to Thomas Jolyffe, who subsequently had it returned to Worcester.[71] In 1458 Thomas Gascoigne who lodged in Oriel recorded in his will that he also had lent a copy of Scotus on the *Sentences* to Thomas Wyche, a fellow.[72] In 1485 John Smyth, a fellow of Balliol, borrowed a copy of Robert Holcot's *Super Sapientiam* from Merton.[73]

(2) The Dominican regulations put in place by Humbertus de Romanis in the third quarter of the thirteenth century encouraged the exchange of books between houses.[74] This practice could be utilised when a friar went to study at university. For example, when John Swan OP went to study at Oxford he was granted the use of a copy of the *Sentences* from Blackfriars in London.[75] The bull *Summi magistri* of Benedict XII, issued in 1336, obliged all monasteries to send suitable monks to university,[76] and to support these students they were to make appropriate books available. In Oxford the Benedictines established three colleges, Canterbury College (1361), Durham College (refounded 1381), and Gloucester College (1291), and the Cistercians Rewley Abbey (1282) and the college of St Bernard. In his *Philobiblon* Richard de Bury set out his ideas for lending books from his putative Durham College in chapter xix. Only duplicates were to be lent, in return for a pledge that exceeded the value of the book borrowed. Books with no duplicate could be consulted in house. No book was to be allowed outside the college walls for copying, no book was to be passed on without the consent of three (out of five) superintendents, and no book was to leave Oxford. There was to be an annual audit and inspection once a year in the first week of July.[77] Archbishop Courtenay's

70 Now New College, MS 174, with inscription on fol. 2v: quoted by Parkes, 'Provision of books', 412; *BRUO* I. 321, 448.

71 Now Worcester Cathedral, MS F.39, with inscription on the endleaf: quoted by Parkes, 'Provision of books', 412; *BRUO* II. 1120, 1020–1; on Ledbury see also *BRECP*, 832–3.

72 H. E. Salter (ed.), *Registrum cancellarii Oxoniensi 1434–1469*, OHS 93–4 (1932), I. 406; *BRUO* III. 2102; Parkes, 'Provision of books', 412–13.

73 *BRUO* III. 1717; Parkes, 'Provision of books', 412–13.

74 As noted by Christ, *Handbook*, 22, from Humbertus, *De vita regulari*. The practice later spread to other orders, e.g. the Augustinian canons, witness the fifteenth-century record of two books from St Peter's Priory at Thurgarton (Notts) at St James's, Northampton (CBMLC VI. 415, 435).

75 BL, MS Royal 9.B.x, with inscription on fol. 260v: quoted by Parkes, 'Provision of books', 435 and n. 137.

76 *Bullarium Romanum*, IV. 362; D. Wilkins, *Concilia Magnae Britanniae et Hiberniae* (London, 1737), II. 597; W. A. Pantin, *Canterbury College, Oxford*, OHS, n.s. 6–8, 30 (1950–85), IV. 155.

77 Maclagan, *Philobiblon*, 168–73.

statutes for Canterbury College (1384) provided for the succentor of Christ Church to send to the warden of the college the books set aside for a new student (with a note of them), so that he could then pass them on to the student monk, and carry out an inspection once a year.[78] This system was a kind of long-arm extension of the Lenten *electio librorum* described in Lanfranc's *Constitutiones*. For example, there is a fifteenth-century note in a Bury copy of Anselm that it was assigned to John Wykham while he was a student at Oxford.[79] Alan Kirkton, a monk from Spalding Priory, took twelve books with him to study in Oxford and had still not returned them, three years after completing his course, in 1438.[80] Thomas Wybarn, a monk from Rochester, probably lodged in Canterbury College to study in Oxford around 1467–8, and had at least three Rochester books with him, which he inscribed in verse.[81] Wybarn pledged one of them to another student, William Goldwin, in exchange for Scotus on the *Sentences*, thus widening the scope of the books sent from the parent house.[82] There is a list of thirty books from Worcester Cathedral presumably deposited at Gloucester College between 1436 and 1444.[83] The practice of one monk student borrowing books from another was encouraged by the federal structure of the colleges, especially, in the first place, Gloucester. William de Brok, from Gloucester, the first Benedictine to incept at Oxford (1298), borrowed a copy of a commentary on Aristotle's *Ethics* from Worcester.[84] Richard de Bromwich, from Worcester Cathedral, who studied in Oxford around 1302–12, left two books in the safe keeping of Geoffrey de Kylminton, fellow of Merton, for the use of Alexander de Sprouston, a monk of Norwich, who studied in Oxford 1309–10, or any other resident monk from Norwich (where a fire had decimated the library in 1272).[85] Two books from

78 Pantin, *Canterbury College*, III. 172–83.

79 Now CCCC, MS 135, with inscription on fol. 167^{v}: quoted by James, *Corpus*, I. 309; Parkes, 'Provision of books', 450; *BRUO* III. 2113.

80 CBMLC IV. 593 (B95).

81 BL, MSS Royal 2.C.i, 5.B.iv, and 6.D.ii: as noted by Parkes, 'Provision of books', 450, citing *BRUO* III. 1098–9; see also *BRECP*, 649–50. Other possible examples are given by Parkes, 'Provision of books', 449–51, on which this paragraph draws.

82 Royal 2.C.i (Comestor), with inscription on fol. 2^{r}: Parkes, 'Provision of books', 452. Goldwin may be the fellow of All Souls who had medical interests: *BRUO* II. 787.

83 CBMLC IV. 659–62 (B116).

84 As noted in Worcester Cathedral, MS F.4, fol. 234^{r}: *BRUO* I. 272; Parkes, 'Provision of books', 447.

85 Worcester Cathedral, MS F.101 (Aquinas, *Summa*) has 'Memorandum quod M[agiste]r Galfridus de Kellinton' habet in custodia sua istum librum et librum Magistri H. de Gand[avo] in quo continentur vii quodlibeta eiusdem [Henry of Ghent, *Quodlibeta*, now Worcester Cathedral, F.79], quos ac[cepit de manibus] fratris Ric. de b[romwyca . . .] et tradantur domino Alexandro monacho vel alicui socio de Nortwych Oxon' commoranti': quoted by A. G. Little and F. Pelster, *Oxford theology and theologians c. AD 1282–1302*, OHS

Malmesbury Abbey were borrowed by Roger de Swyneshed, a monk of Glastonbury (who was at Oxford in about 1360), and his abbot returned them in 1365.[86]

(3) The libraries of the secular foundations replicated the organisation and regulations of those in the houses belonging to the orders. They built up their collections by stipulating that every fellow should leave his books to his college. The division into two parts, a reference collection (*libri concatenati*), and a lending collection (*libri distribuendi*), is a universal feature among colleges and other secular foundations in Oxford and Cambridge up to the fifteenth century. At Oxford the statutes of University College (1292) required the best copy of each work (or the sole copy if there was only one) to be chained in the community library (*libri communitatis*), while the rest could be lent out to fellows.[87] Whereas student friars could borrow books from their order, and student monks could borrow books from the collection sent by their order to the university from the parent house, secular students could borrow from their college only when there was a surplus. In Oxford, beginning with Oriel in 1329, the colleges held annual meetings for the return and redistribution of books, which were borrowed in exchange for a pledge (*cautio*, usually another book). The arrangements in Oriel called for the annual meeting on All Souls Day (2 November), when each fellow (in order of seniority) could choose (*eligere*) one book; then, if there were more books available than fellows, each fellow could choose again.[88] Similar arrangements came into being in Merton (1339),[89] Queen's (1372), Exeter (1382) and New College (1400).[90] Those in Merton, where

96 (1934), 241; Parkes, 'Provision of books', 447, n. 193. For Bromwich, see *BRUO* I. 277–8, and *BRECP*, 782–3; for Sprouston, see *BRUO* III. 1747, and *BRECP*, 557; for Kylminton, see *BRUO* II. 1068. On Norwich, see Ker, *Books, collectors and libraries*, 248.

86 Noted in *BRUO* III. 1837, following J. A. Weisheipl, 'Roger Swyneshed, OSB, logician, natural philosopher, and theologian', in R. W. Southern (introd.), *Oxford studies presented to Daniel Callus*, OHS, n.s. 16 (1964), 241–2, who cites BL, MS Arundel 2, fol. 80^{v}, and, *ex informatione* N. R. Ker, identifies the first book as Cambridge, Trinity Coll., MS O.5.20 (Eriugena, *De divisione naturae*); Parkes, 'Provision of books', 447 and n. 194, where the second book is identified as Bodleian, MS Auct. F.3.14, a collection of computistical texts.

87 R. W. Hunt, 'The manuscript collection of University College, Oxford, origins and growth', *BLR* 3 (1950), 14. This practice paralleled that of the Sorbonne, which was reorganised with the chaining of books in the *magna libraria* in 1289–92: see R. H. Rouse, 'The early library of the Sorbonne', *Scriptorium* 21 (1967), 61. When books were chained, their removal could be effected only by agreement of the whole community.

88 *Statutes of the colleges of Oxford*, 3 vols. (Oxford and London, 1853), I. 14–15 (Oriel).

89 Powicke, *Medieval books of Merton*, 12–16.

90 For references, see Parkes, 'Provision of books', 457, and for New College, R. W. Hunt, 'The medieval library', in J. Buxton and P. Williams (eds.), *New College, Oxford, 1379–1979* (Oxford, 1979), 317–45.

the stock of books built up faster as a result of the injunctions issued in 1276 by Robert Kilwardby OP, who as archbishop of Canterbury was the college visitor,[91] were more generous than Oriel's, though still more restricted than those of the religious orders. Books were divided into two categories, *electio librorum in philosophia* and *electio librorum in theologia* (following the two categories of fellows established by the founder's statutes in 1274, 'philosophers', who studied for the arts degreee, and 'theologians', who studied for the higher degree in theology), and were distributed at variable intervals.[92] The *electiones* took place in the hall (philosophical), and the warden's lodge (theological), under the supervision of the sub-warden, who assigned the books (rather than the fellows choosing them), sometimes as many as forty per fellow, each fellow becoming in effect a sub-librarian, responsible for keeping his books until the next *electio*. The method of assignment seems to have been based on perceived faculty needs, what any student would require for the course, rather than on a particular fellow's individual needs. Because so many books were assigned, the need for fresh *electiones* was diminished, and they occurred at relatively infrequent intervals, with gaps of up to nine years between them. The system did not work well, and was apparently discontinued in 1519. In Cambridge the books of Gonville Hall, Pembroke, Peterhouse, St Catharine's and Trinity Hall could apparently be borrowed by members by arrangement,[93] but Trinity Hall and Gonville Hall never lent to outsiders,[94] and Pembroke did so only when there was a majority of the fellows in favour.[95] Trinity Hall and Gonville Hall also stipulated that no book in quires (i.e., unbound, or bound in a membrane or paper wrapper) was to be lent to anyone, even a fellow, for the purpose of making a copy.[96] At the end of a year, or when a course finished if sooner, books were to be returned. Pembroke had an annual audit on the Feast of the Translation of St Thomas (7 July).[97] Trinity Hall and Gonville Hall had audits twice a year, at the same times as the general audit of accounts (in Michaelmas and Easter terms).

91 H. W. Garrod (ed.), *Injunctions of Archbishop Kilwardby, 1276* (Oxford, 1929). N. R. Ker, 'Oxford college libraries before 1500', in his *Books, collectors and libraries*, 304, calculates that in 1372 Merton owned about 500 books, five times more than Oriel.

92 H. W. Garrod, 'The library regulations of a medieval college', *Library* 4/8 (1927), 312–35, 320–31.

93 Willis and Clark, III. 389–92; Clark, *Care of books*, 134–7; Humphreys, *Book provisions*, 88.

94 Willis and Clark, III. 391; D. R. Leader, *A history of the University of Cambridge*, I: *The University to 1546* (Cambridge, 1988), 74.

95 J. Ringrose, 'The medieval statutes of Pembroke College', in P. Zutshi (ed.), *Medieval Cambridge: essays on the pre-Reformation University* (Woodbridge, 1993), 116. The statutes date from the third quarter of the fourteenth century.

96 Willis and Clark, III. 391.

97 Ringrose, 'Pembroke', 116. Cf. Clark, *Care of books*, 139.

None of these arrangements really satisfied the needs of poor scholars. It was their needs that sowed the seeds of a university library. In 1320 Thomas de Cobham (*c.* 1255–1327), bishop of Worcester, who had studied in Oxford from about 1291 to 1300, funded the erection of a two-storey extension on the north side of St Mary's Church in Oxford to provide a congregation room and a *solarium* above it where books were to be chained for the use of poor scholars.[98] Nearly 100 years later the project came into being, when the library was to be open six days a week for two hours in the morning and three in the afternoon. Once the library was in existence, gifts began to come in, most notably those of Humfrey, duke of Gloucester (1435, 1439, 1441, 1444), and the consequences were far-reaching. However, this library did not allow borrowing, a practice that has died hard. In Cambridge there was a *communis libraria* in the fifteenth century and a building to put the books in by 1438, borrowing being recorded from 1487.[99]

Although Trinity Hall and Gonville Hall in Cambridge put a particular ban on borrowing books to make a copy, among the friars copying by their own brethren was allowed, even by the Franciscans, albeit without borrowing. Foreign student friars at Oxford made copies of works they found in the libraries there. In 1393 in Greyfriars, Oxford, Jacopo (Giacomo) Fey OFM from Florence copied Stephen Patrington's *Compilacio diversorum argumentorum a diversis doctoribus*.[100] In 1412, also presumably at Greyfriars, Oxford, Johann Sintram OFM from Würzburg copied a sermon collection and the *Fasciculus morum*.[101] In 1402, presumably at Blackfriars, Oxford, Tomaso di Venezia OP made an unsystematic copy of passages from Robert Holcot's commentary on the *Sentences*.[102] There is also evidence suggesting that one religious order borrowed from another to make a copy. John of Beverley OSB, a Durham monk at Durham College, Oxford, deposited the Durham copy of Hugutio of Pisa with the Oxford Franciscans as a pledge for their Joachim of Fiore *Super Apocalypsim*; the Hugutio is now back in Durham

98 On Cobham, see *BRUO* I. 450–1.

99 Oates, *CUL*, 1–4, 52.

100 Florence, Biblioteca Medicea Laurenziana, MS Plut. xvii sin.cod. 10 has the inscription 'scripta per me fratrem I. Fey de Florentia Ordinis Minorum in Conuentu Oxonie anno Domini MCCCXCIII die sequenti festum 40 Martyrum': Parkes, 'Provision of books', 442, n. 171; *BRUO* II. 682.

101 Leeds University Library, Brotherton MS 102 + Princeton University Library, MS Garrett 90 contains the sermons, with an inscription on Brotherton 102, fol. 1r, 'Librum istum scripsit Iohannes Sinttram de herbipoli', *MMBL* III. 65 (with references); Parkes, 'Provision of books', 442, n. 172. The *Fasciculus morum* is PML, MS 298. For Sintram see *BRUO* III. 1703.

102 Padua, Biblioteca Universitaria, MS 1925, *BRUO* III. 1945; Parkes, 'Provision of books', 442.

(Cathedral Library, MS C.i.20) and it is likely that the Joachim was borrowed to make a copy of it.[103] But evidence of this kind of activity in England is rare. The practice may have been used more extensively on the Continent.[104] The *pecia* system was put into practice by the Dominicans in Paris in the second half of the thirteenth century.[105] Although there were earlier precedents in England,[106] by the second half of the fourteenth century the system was in decline even in Paris, was not favoured by Bury,[107] and was evidently not popular in Cambridge.

Evidence from library users about the facilities they used is not common either. Literary writers were capable of exaggeration. For the compilation of his *Brut* in the first half of the twelfth-century

Laȝamon gon liðen wide ȝond þas leode,
And biwon þa æðela boc þa he to bisne nom.[108]

(Laȝamon travelled far and wide throughout this land, and obtained the excellent books which he took as a model.)

He refers to just three books, one by Bede, perhaps the *Historia ecclesiastica* in its Old English translation, another in Latin by St Albin and Augustine, which has puzzled commentators, and the third by Wace, presumably the *Roman de Brut*, which was Laȝamon's main source. Perhaps the apparent distance Laȝamon says he had to travel reflects the difficulty in finding a copy of Wace in particular which he could borrow. William of Malmesbury travelled widely in England in search of books to provide him with the historical sources he required.[109]

Detailed study of an author's sources is certainly one way of acquiring more information relevant to the theme of the present chapter. For example, Richard de Mores (Morins), prior of Dunstable (Austin canons), borrowed a manuscript of Ralph de Diceto's *Abbreviationes chronicorum* from the library of St Albans

103 As argued by Parkes, *ibid.*, 468, with quotation of the pledge note on 447, n. 196. For Beverley see *BRUO* i. 183. On pledges see G. Pollard, 'Medieval loan chests at Cambridge', *Bulletin of the Institute of Historical Research* 17 (1940), 113–29, and his 'The loan chests', in W. A. Pantin and W. T. Mitchell, *The register of congregation, 1448–63*, OHS, n.s. 22 (1972), Appendix iii, 418–20.

104 Parkes, 'Provision of books', 468–70.

105 R. H. Rouse and M. A. Rouse, 'The book trade at the University of Paris ca. 1250–ca. 1350', in L. J. Bataillon, B. C. Guyot and R. H. Rouse, *La production du livre universitaire au Moyen Age: exemplar et pecia* (Paris, 1988), 41–113.

106 C. H. Talbot, in Wormald and Wright, *English library*, 68.

107 See above, 254.

108 W. R. J. Barron and S. C. Weinberg (ed. and tr.), *Laȝamon Brut or Hystoria Brutonum* (London, 1995), 2, lines 14–15.

109 R. Thomson, *William of Malmesbury* (Woodbridge, 1987), 72–4.

Abbey in 1209/10, from which he made excerpts in his *Annales prioratus de Dunstaplia.*[110] For his *Abbreuiacion of Cronicles* John Capgrave OSA (1393–1464) used a version of Thomas Walsingham's St Albans Chronicles that has not survived.

> From 1295 . . . to 1376 Capgrave followed a version of Walsingham's *Chronica Maiora* . . . antecedent to and slightly fuller than that preserved in the best surviving manuscript. From 1376 to 1417 he followed a version of Walsingham's *Short History* . . . antecedent to and slightly fuller than that preserved in the best surviving manuscripts, and containing some details not preserved even in the *Chronica Maiora* . . . Very possibly Capgrave had just one manuscript of Walsingham's chronicles containing the *Chronica Maiora* to 1376 and the *Short History* from 1376 onwards.[111]

Presumably Capgrave, who, apart from studies in Cambridge, spent most of his life in the Augustinian friary at (King's) Lynn,[112] borrowed such a manuscript.[113] English authors seeking sources on the Continent apparently met with co-operation on a scale not recorded in England. In a country such as Italy, the rulers of city-states vied with each other in magnificence, including the scale of their libraries and patronage of literature.[114] In 1378 Geoffrey Chaucer went on a diplomatic mission to Bernabò Visconti, lord of Milan and *scourge of Lumbardye,*[115] and presumably paid his respects to Bernabò's brother, Galeazzo II, lord of Pavia, where the tombs of Augustine and Boethius were to be found in the church of San Pietro in Ciel d'Oro. There he visited the Visconti library, where his hosts were noted for their generosity in allowing manuscripts to be copied, and provided scribes for that purpose, and he almost certainly had a copy made of Boccaccio's *Teseida* from that in MS 881 (now lost) in the 1426

110 The borrowed Diceto manuscript was BL, MS Royal 13.E.vi. See C. R. Cheney, 'Notes on the making of the Dunstable annals, AD 33 to 1242', in T. A. Sandquist and M. R. Powicke (eds.) *Essays in medieval history presented to Bertie Wilkinson* (Toronto, 1969), 79–98.

111 P. J. Lucas (ed.), *John Capgrave's Abbreuiacion of Cronicles*, EETS, OS, 285 (Oxford, 1983), lxxxvi–lxxxvii.

112 On Capgrave, see P. J. Lucas, *From author to audience: John Capgrave and medieval publication* (Dublin, 1997).

113 Alternatively, Capgrave may have made an extended period of study in a library that possessed such a manuscript, but this explanation seems less probable than that the book went to Lynn.

114 On magnificence in relation to literary patronage, see Lucas, *From author to audience*, 256–8.

115 M. M. Crow and C. C. Olson, *Chaucer life-records* (Oxford, 1966), 53–61. The quotation is from Chaucer's *Monk's tale*, line 2399, in L. D. Benson *et al.* (ed.), *The Riverside Chaucer* (Oxford, 1988), 247.

inventory of manuscripts at Pavia,[116] with omissions corresponding to matter omitted in Chaucer's *Knight's Tale* (which is based on the *Teseida*).[117] In this light the frustration of Pietro del Monte, an Italian resident in England, in his attempts to borrow a Seneca manuscript from Nicholas Bildeston, dean of Salisbury (1435–41),[118] can be appreciated. In Italy itself, no less a religious institution than the Vatican allowed manuscripts to be borrowed by approved readers, although the records begin only in 1475 and the users were mostly beneficed clergy, including bishops.[119]

The best-documented example of a user of manuscripts in England is that of Thomas Gascoigne (1403–58), a scholarly rediscoverer of old theology who was briefly chancellor of Oxford University. He left notes in the margins of manuscripts that he consulted, which show that he read in a number of libraries. In Oxford he used the libraries of Durham College, where he read St Bernard's *De amando Deo*, Balliol, Exeter, Lincoln and Oriel Colleges, and Duke Humfrey's university library, where he read Hugh of Saint-Victor's *De potestate clavium*.[120] He also consulted a number of works held by the Oxford Austin friars.[121] His favourite Oxford library was that of Greyfriars at Oxford, where he revered the works of Grosseteste. There he also read Jerome, Augustine and Alexander of Hales.[122] Just outside Oxford Gascoigne visited the library of the Augustinian canons at Osney, where he found Bede's *In parabolas Salamonis* and a Hugh of Saint-Cher, another favourite author.[123] He also visited the Benedictine monasteries at Abingdon, Evesham and Peterborough, where he consulted (respectively) what are now Lambeth, MS 42 (John of Worcester),

116 E. Pellegrin, *La bibliothèque des Visconti et des Sforza ducs de Milan, au XVe siècle* (Paris, 1955), 269. The incipit and explicit identify the work as Boccaccio's *Teseida* without the prologue and epilogue.

117 R. A. Pratt, 'Chaucer and the Visconti libraries', *English Literary History* 6 (1939), 191–9; W. E. Coleman, 'Chaucer, the *Teseida*, and the Visconti library at Pavia, A hypothesis', *MÆ* 51 (1982), 92–101; R. Delasanta, 'Chaucer, Pavia, and the Ciel d'Oro', *MÆ* 54 (1985), 117–21.

118 D. Rundle, 'Two unnoticed manuscripts from the collection of Humfrey, duke of Gloucester: Part II', *BLR* 16 (1997–9), 304. For Bildeston, see *BRUO* I. 187–8.

119 M. Bertòla, *I duè primi registri de prestito della Biblioteca Apostolica Vaticana, codici vaticani latini 3964, 3966* (Vatican City, 1942).

120 On Gascoigne see W. A. Pronger, 'Thomas Gascoigne', *EHR* 53 (1938), 606–26, 54 (1939), 20–37, and *BRUO* II. 745–8, from whom the following particulars are taken. As for the manuscripts: Durham College, noted in Oxford, Lincoln College, MS 117, fol. 260^{r} (Pronger, 620, n. 7); Balliol: Bodleian, MS Bodley 252, formerly at Balliol, and Balliol, MSS 4, 129, 156, 212; Duke Humfrey's library: noted in Oxford, Lincoln College, MS 117, fol. 586^{v} (Pronger, 619, n. 6).

121 Listed by Pronger, 'Gascoigne', 621. See also Ball, 'Opponents of Pecok', 257.

122 Listed by Pronger, 'Gascoigne', 621–2.

123 Pronger, 'Gascoigne', 620. Gascoigne annotated Cambridge, Gonville and Caius Coll., MS 481/477 (Hugh of Saint-Cher), which was formerly at Osney Abbey.

Bodleian, MS Rawlinson A. 287 (Haimo of Auxerre), and Lambeth, MS 202 (Isidore). There are also annotations of his in a Worcester manuscript (now BL, MS Royal 4.B.xiii (Bede)) and a manuscript formerly at Christ Church, Canterbury (now Bodleian, MS Bodley 160 (Bede)), so presumably he visited those libraries too.[124] In London he visited the library of the Carmelites, and in Middlesex the library at Syon Abbey,[125] where the order was dedicated to Gascoigne's favourite saint, St Bridget of Sweden. In Gascoigne we see the precursor of the itinerant textual scholar. Although he wrote in manuscripts that he read (anathema to modern conservationists), he loved them and took pains to keep them carefully and bestow them on good homes. His approach was very different from that of a century later, when Archbishop Parker split manuscripts and transferred leaves from one manuscript to another, discarding others in the process.[126] Parker, too, was an avid reader of manuscripts, and loved them enough to take pains to 'borrow' them and preserve them, but he had his own political agenda, and the awe and the reverence had gone.

124 For Canterbury, see Ker, *Books, collectors and libraries,* 320, note to p. 319. It is possible that a manuscript such as that from Worcester might have been deposited in Oxford under the arrangements indicated above, 255.

125 Cf. Ball, 'Opponents of Pecok', 259.

126 R. I. Page, *Matthew Parker and his books* (Kalamazoo, MI, 1993); see also below, 328–32.

PART TWO

★

REFORMATION, DISSOLUTION, NEW LEARNING

10

The dispersal of the monastic libraries and the salvaging of the spoils

JAMES P. CARLEY

Relatively little concrete evidence remains concerning the contents of the English monastic libraries in the years leading up to the major dissolutions of the second half of the 1530s, and the only complete catalogue compiled after 1500 still extant is that of the brothers' library in the Bridgettine house of Syon (*c*. 1500–*c*. 1524).[1] The booklists which do survive, primarily those compiled by John Leland, were selective in nature and throw more light on the interests of the compiler than on the material contained in the monasteries themselves.[2] In his *De uiris illustribus*, or *Commentarii de scriptoribus*

C. E. Wright, 'The dispersal of the libraries in the sixteenth century', in Wormald and Wright, *English library*, remains the seminal work on this topic, but see also my 'Monastic collections and their dispersal', in *CHBB* IV. 339–47. The most recent account is found in N. Ramsay, '"The manuscripts flew about like butterflies": the break-up of English libraries in the sixteenth century', in J. Raven (ed.), *Lost libraries: the destruction of great book collections since antiquity* (London, 2004), 125–44. Dr A. I. Doyle, Dr J. Clark, Professor A. G. Watson and Mr J. Willoughby read the present essay in manuscript form and provided many helpful suggestions.

1 Ed. V. Gillespie, in CBMLC IX. 4–566; see also D. N. Bell, 'Monastic libraries: 1400–1557', in *CHBB* III. 230–1. It should be noted, however, that a catalogue for St Augustine's, Canterbury, was copied shortly before 1500 and it had later additions. The situation for secular cathedrals (which were not monastic and do not therefore fall into the scope of this chapter) – and the former cathedral priories, which continued on as cathedrals of new foundation – is, of course, different from that of the monasteries, and many were relatively unaffected: the library at Exeter, for example, remained basically intact right up to the seventeenth century. Archbishop Tobie Matthew, formerly dean (1583–95) and then bishop (1595–1606) of Durham, abstracted a number of monastic books, some of which went to the public library he founded at Bristol in 1614: see A. I. Doyle, 'The printed books of the last monks of Durham', *Library*, 6th ser., 10 (1988), 217–18. At Wells, Samuel Ward (d. 1643) – Master of Sidney Sussex College, Cambridge, and a prebendary at Wells – obtained at least one medieval manuscript which had remained *in situ* until the early seventeenth century: see J. P. Carley and V. Law, 'Grammar and arithmetic in two thirteenth-century English monastic collections', *The Journal of Medieval Latin* 1 (1991), 140–67.

2 In 1533 Leland received a commission to travel throughout the kingdom searching out rare and valuable books. The precise nature of his commission has been much debated, but he was certainly armed with some sort of letter (*diploma*) from the king, and his mission was similar to that of Jean de Gagny, who in 1537 recalled having told Francis I that 'there

Britannicis as it was called by its eighteenth-century editor, Leland included several brief sketches of monastic libraries, and these suggest widely differing conditions from house to house and order to order. For the most part, the Benedictines were singled out for praise, and Leland was lyrical in his evocation of the well-stocked library at Glastonbury, which he visited in the summer of 1533:

> A few years ago I was in Glastonbury, Somerset, where the oldest and the most famous abbey of our whole island is found. Wearied by the long labours of research I was refreshing my spirits by the kindness of Richard Whiting, abbot of the place, until a certain enthusiasm for reading and learning should inflame me afresh. This enthusiasm came sooner than I had expected, and so I betook myself at once to the library (which is not open to all comers) in order to turn over the relics of venerable antiquity, of which the number there is not easily matched anywhere else in Britain. Indeed, I had hardly crossed the threshold when the mere sight of the ancient books left me awestruck, stupefied in fact, and because of this I stood hesitating a little while. Then, having saluted the *genius loci*, I spent some days searching through all the bookcases with the greatest curiosity. (*Scriptores*, 41)[3]

At Bath he was impressed by the ancient books which had survived up to his time (*Scriptores*, 160), and he mentioned that the famous library at St Albans was likewise stocked with ancient books (*Scriptores*, 166). The cathedral

were forests of material in your kingdom which their custodians did not allow access to. You promised to help and gave me a letter (*diploma publicum*) which empowered me to examine the libraries of your kingdom . . . I began to sweep the libraries (*librarias verrere*) of the monasteries which I came near while travelling in your company and found near a hundred volumes of no less worth (*non inferioris notae*) than the Primasius. You conceived the plan not only of building up a library but of publishing *in commune philologiae bonum* the most important, and I chose Primasius.' See R. W. Hunt, 'The need for a guide to the editors of patristic texts in the 16th century', *Studia Patristica* 17.1 (1982), 368; P. Petitmengin and J. P. Carley, 'Malmesbury – Sélestat – Malines: les tribulations d'un manuscrit de Tertullien au milieu du XVIe siècle', *Annuaire des amis de la Bibliothèque humaniste de Sélestat* (2003), 63–74; J. P. Carley and P. Petitmengin, 'Pre-Conquest manuscripts from Malmesbury Abbey and John Leland's letter to Beatus Rhenanus concerning a lost copy of Tertullian's works', *ASE* 33 (2004), 195–223.

3 This and subsequent translations are taken from a forthcoming edition and translation of the *De uiris illustribus* (henceforth *Scriptores*) to be published by Oxford Medieval Texts. On the library at Glastonbury, see also Leland's comments in the chapter on Tatwine (*Scriptores*, 131). During this same journey he visited the nearby cathedral library at Wells, observing that it 'had been magnificently furnished with no small number of books by the bishops and canons of that city in former times' (*Scriptores*, 387). Leland was a patriot, it should be pointed out, and to some extent his enthusiastic descriptions of monastic libraries (especially during the early years of his journeys) may reflect his pride in Henry's England.

priory at Norwich, he stated, was 'crammed with good books' (*Scriptores*, 247),[4] and he saluted Ramsey as a 'storehouse of ancient authors' (*Scriptores*, 264).[5] St Augustine's, Canterbury, was described as 'a rich storehouse of ancient manuscripts' in spite of a terrible fire in 1168 and later depredations by ignorant monks (*Scriptores*, 299–301). The library at Abingdon had been neglected, but nevertheless Leland found a particular gem, a copy of Joseph of Exeter's lost *Antiocheis*, while rooting through 'the dust and moths' (*Scriptores*, 238).

Among the Cistercian houses, Jervaulx was singled out for praise, the library being 'well filled with books' (*Scriptores*, 74).[6] Warden's library was 'crammed with ancient manuscripts'; among other works he found a finely illuminated manuscript of Nicholas Stanford's now lost *Moralitates super Genesim* (*Scriptores*, 343, 234). In London the best library was that of the Carmelites: 'although the number of books has now markedly declined, there is still no library in London to compare with that of the Carmelites for the number or the antiquity of its manuscripts' (*Scriptores*, 441).[7]

Not all collections were as well maintained, and Leland's search for writings by Roger Bacon was frustrating. Although Bacon's writings

> were once disseminated in many copies and kept religiously in libraries all over Britain; now – I am ashamed to say – some of them have been removed from their bookcases and stolen as a result of the negligence of their guardians; others have become mutilated, with quires torn out here and there; in fact, they appear so seldom that it would be easier to collect the Sybilline leaves than the names of the books which he wrote. (*Scriptores*, 258)

4 According to Leland's own account, a friend preceded him and made a preliminary examination of the libraries in Norwich, thus allowing him to work more quickly once he got there (*Scriptores*, 301). In his epitome of the *Scriptores* (now Cambridge, Trinity Coll., MS R. 7. 15) John Bale identified himself as this friend (fol. 61^{v}).

5 He particularly admired the Hebrew books in this 'noble' library and pointed out that the Oxford Hebraist, Robert Wakefield (d. 1537), had seized a Hebrew dictionary compiled by Lawrence Holbeach, a monk of Ramsey in the time of Henry IV: see *Scriptores*, 452. On Wakefield as a book-collector see Carley, 'Religious controversy and marginalia: Pierfrancesco di Piero Bardi, Thomas Wakefield and their books', *TCBS* 12.3 (2002), 206–45.

6 As in several other passages, Leland here referred to the persuasive power of his *diploma* from the king: 'Once he had read the king's letter [the abbot] showed me every kindness and took me immediately into his library.'

7 After its suppression, the Tudor humanist, propagandist and diplomat Richard Morison (?1514–1556) acquired the library as well as other portions of the house.

Bacon was a Franciscan and Leland's strongest disapproval was directed at the library of the Oxford Franciscans. When he asked to see the library,

> several asses gawped at me, braying that hardly any mortal man was allowed to approach such a holy precinct and sanctuary to see the mysteries, except the Warden – for so they call their head – and the bachelors of his sacred College. But I pressed them and, armed with the king's letter, more or less forced them to open up their shrines. Then at last one of the senior donkeys, with much humming and hawing, reluctantly unlocked the doors. Good God! What did I find there? Nothing but dust, cobwebs, bookworms, moths, in short filth and destitution. I did find some books, but I should not willingly have paid threepence for them. So, searching for diamonds I found nothing but cinders. (*Scriptores*, 286; see also *Collectanea* IV.60)

He assumed that the missing books had 'been illicitly taken away by the Franciscans themselves, travelling or rather straying like vagabonds from place to place as their rule demands', and he ironically concluded, 'Go ahead, bishops, leave your treasured books to the care of friars of this sort.' Not surprisingly, then, the mendicant orders as a whole fared badly in Leland's account, and he referred to 'the dust of the Dominican library in Oxford' (*Scriptores*, 330). Cursing the thief, he also observed that a manuscript containing Adelard of Bath's *Problemata* and other works which he had seen in the library of the London Dominicans had subsequently been stolen (*Scriptores*, 201–2).

Leland was, in modern terms, a bio-bibliographer and he judged libraries by the antiquity of the collections and the rarity of the contents. The religious themselves had quite different criteria, as might be expected, and most of the monastic libraries contained working collections which had evolved over the generations, outmoded books being recycled or disposed of in other ways.[8] It is clear, too, that by the sixteenth century, printed books were replacing the older and bulkier handwritten codices.[9] At St Albans, things progressed even further and in the 1530s John Herford established his press within the precincts of the abbey. By 1539, when the house was dissolved, he and the last abbot, Richard

8 See Leland's own disparaging comments concerning conditions at St Augustine's: 'The age which followed [the fire of 1168] inflicted a far greater injury on the books, for the unlearned monks plucked pieces out of the Greek manuscripts, which they did not understand, and those Latin ones which were made unattractive by old age, for odd jobs around the bookshelves, to say nothing worse' (*Scriptores*, 300–1).

9 As J. G. Clark has observed, monks seem to have been some of the first purchasers of printed books in England: see 'Print and pre-Reformation religion: the Benedictines and the press *c.* 1470–*c.* 1550', in J. Crick and A. Walsham (eds.), *The uses of script and print, 1300–1700* (Cambridge, 2004), 76–7.

Boreman, had collaborated on six different books.[10] In particular, the post-Dissolution collections of individual monks, perhaps sometimes representing significant portions of the libraries of their former houses, indicate some degree of replacement of manuscripts by printed books.[11]

Early dispersals and the formation of the royal library

Even before the 1530s, Thomas Wolsey had suppressed religious houses (and he was not the first to do so), ordering the closure of a number of institutions between 1524 and 1529. Small establishments were particularly vulnerable under Wolsey's programme.[12] From around 1527, Wolsey's policies became increasingly dominated by the question of the validity of Henry's marriage to Catherine of Aragon, and he, like his royal master, turned to historical precedent on the matter of papal jurisdiction.[13] It seems almost certain, moreover, that it was he who gathered a group of at least thirty-one medieval manuscripts, all but two now contained in the modern Royal Collection, which carry a TC monogram (i.e. Thomas Cardinalis).[14] These manuscripts, for the most part

10 See J. G. Clark, 'Reformation and reaction at St Albans Abbey, 1530–58', *EHR* 115 (2000), 297–328. There was also a close association between the printer Wynkyn de Worde and the Bridgettine house of Syon: see most recently V. Gillespie, 'Dial M for mystic: mystical texts in the library of Syon Abbey and the spirituality of the Syon brethren', in M. Glasscoe (ed.), *The medieval mystical tradition: England, Ireland and Wales* (Cambridge, 1999), 241–68.

11 During the sixteenth century, monks – especially those who had been to university – built up their own collections primarily of printed books, which they would have no doubt viewed as personal property, quite separate from the communal libraries, which would still have been dominated by older manuscripts. The books acquired by Prior William More of Worcester Cathedral Priory between 1519 and 1534 (printed in CBMLC IV. B117) give a good sense of the sort of material being purchased during the last days of the monasteries.

12 See D. Knowles, *Bare ruined choirs: the dissolution of the English monasteries* (Cambridge, 1976), 58–62; also R. W. Hoyle, 'The origins of the dissolution of the monasteries', *The Historical Journal* 38/2 (1995), 275–305, who has observed that 'there was in the later 1520s a reform programme within the church which owed nothing to Lutheranism or foreign example' (283). Hoyle has also edited a 1529 petition from the Commons which advocated 'disendowment of the church . . . to achieve the restoration of true priestly values' and also 'called upon the king to resume part of the temporal property of the church to provide his nobility with the wherewithal to resist the Turk' (285).

13 For a more detailed discussion of the growth of the royal library under Henry VIII see J. P. Carley, in CBMLC VII. xxx–xliii.

14 The exceptions are Bodleian, MSS Bodley 245 and Bodley 458. Both of these form part of a cache of books extracted from the royal library by Sir Thomas Copley in the second half of the sixteenth century. They were given to Sir Thomas Bodley in 1604 by Charles

dealing with historical and theological topics, all appear to have come from religious houses. After their acquisition, they were undoubtedly stored at Wolsey's chief residence, Hampton Court, and must have been sequestered for Henry with other goods when the great cardinal fell in 1530.

Wolsey was just one of the agents employed in Henry's antipapal manoeuvres, and, around 1530, libraries in three of the royal palaces, Westminster, Hampton Court and Greenwich, were refitted as storehouses for monastic books.[15] BL, MS Royal Appendix 69, which consists of an undated list of almost 100 manuscripts found in Lincolnshire houses, was compiled at roughly the same time. After its compilation the list was given to some person in authority who placed a cross beside approximately forty items, which were then transferred to the Royal Collection, where most of them can still be found.[16] As in the case of the Wolsey cache, there is a copy of Ralph of Flaix's commentary on Leviticus, a text especially relevant to Henry's concerns between 1527 and 1533 in its strict forbidding of marriage to one's brother's widow. The copy of William of Malmesbury's *Gesta pontificum Anglorum* from Thornton-on-Humber (now BL, MS Harley 2) has marginal notes, some possibly by Henry himself, on councils, on the authority of bishops and popes, and on the question of marriage to one's brother's widow. The acquisition of these Lincolnshire books, then, mirrors precisely the emerging scheme of Henry's future archbishop of Canterbury, Thomas Cranmer, for searching out old documents for opinions on consanguinity and the pope's authority.[17]

Royal Appendix 69 is the only list of this type to survive, but it cannot have been unique, as the privy purse expenses make clear. On 27 November 1530 a list of books was sent to Hampton Court from Reading Abbey. Even if the document itself no longer survives, it can be assumed that it was examined

Howard, earl of Nottingham, who had acquired them from his father: see J. P. Carley, 'Sir Thomas Bodley's library and its acquisitions: an edition of the Nottingham benefaction of 1604', in Carley and Tite, *Books and collectors*, 357–86.

15 Leland affirmed this in his unpublished *Antiphilarchia*, presented to the king after 1541 (CUL, MS Ee.5.14, 335–6). Although there is no inventory as such for Greenwich and Hampton Court, a list of 910 titles of books contained in the Upper Library at Westminster in 1542 still survives. The list is arranged in alphabetical order and each book had a characteristic inventory number entered in it. Soon after Henry's death in 1547, books were brought from other palaces and integrated into the Westminster collection. The books coming to Westminster were in turn alphabetised and given inventory numbers; these ranged from 911 to 1450: see CBMLC VII. H2.

16 Several were subsequently abstracted; one of these (Bodleian, MS Bodley 419) came to Nottingham.

17 On Cranmer's own acquisition of monastic books see D. G. Selwyn, 'Thomas Cranmer and the dispersal of medieval libraries: the provenance of some of his medieval manuscripts and printed books', in Carley and Tite, *Books and collectors*, 281–94.

and marked up precisely in the manner of the Lincolnshire document, since an abbey servant was paid 40s on 29 November – that is, just two days later – for delivering books to Hampton Court.[18] Five books with Westminster inventory numbers come from Reading and there are ten other books in the Old Royal Library which derive from this house.[19] Two other Reading manuscripts, both glossed gospel books, were rebound in velvet for Henry; they were subsequently deaccessioned and are now found in Queen's College, Oxford (MSS 317 and 323). It is not certain that all these books arrived in one batch, but if they did, a total of seventeen manuscripts, most of which deal with canon law and biblical commentary, were brought to Hampton Court from Reading in 1530. On 27 January 1531 a servant of the abbot of Ramsey was paid 20s for bringing books to Westminster, and on 26 January 1532 one of his servants received 40s for transporting books to the king.[20] There are ten identified Ramsey books in the modern Royal Collection, primarily theology and law, and all have Westminster inventory numbers.[21] Of the five known survivors from Sempringham, four have royal inventory numbers and were almost certainly part of the group for which a servant of the prior was paid 30s on 12 February 1531 to bring to Westminster.[22] On 27 February 1531 the abbot of Gloucester was paid 10s for transporting books to Westminster.[23] Four Gloucester books with royal inventory numbers are found in the royal library and there is one other, now Royal 5.A.xi, which also arrived during these years.[24] On 4 June 1531 the prior of Spalding's servant received 40s for transporting books to the king and there are four Spalding books with Westminster numbers.[25] Slightly earlier, on 18 March 1531, the servant of the abbot of Evesham was paid 40s for delivering books to the 'king's grace'.[26] Of the surviving Evesham books, only three got to Westminster.[27] There are, however, two other Evesham survivors which went to Henry and were later removed from the royal library – one formed part of the earl of Nottingham's bequest in 1604, now Bodleian, Auct. D. 1. 15, and one, as in the case of Reading books, is found at Queen's College, Oxford, now MS 302. What is characteristic of the Evesham books is that they can be identified as Evesham books, not from a medieval *ex libris*, but

18 N. H. Nicolas (ed.), *The privy purse expenses of King Henry the Eighth* (London, 1827), 89.

19 *MLGB*, 156; CBMLC VII. xxxvi–xxxvii.

20 Nicolas, *Privy purse expenses*, 106, 190.

21 *MLGB*, 154; CBMLC VII. xxxvii.

22 Nicolas, *Privy purse expenses*, 109; *MLGB*, 177; CBMLC VII. xxxvii.

23 Nicolas, *Privy purse expenses*, 112.

24 *MLGB*, 92; CBMLC VII. xxxvii. One of the books, now Royal 11.D.viii, has marginal annotations in a sixteenth-century hand on fols. 3^r, 81^r, 87^r, 136^r, etc., concerning matters of consanguinity, authority of the church hierarchy, and related issues.

25 Nicolas, *Privy purse expenses*, 137; *MLGB*, 182; CBMLC VII. xxxvii.

26 Nicolas, *Privy purse expenses*, 116.

27 *MLGB*, 81; CBMLC VII. xxxvii.

from a sixteenth-century one taking the form 'Liber monasterii Eveshamie'. Ten manuscripts from Worcester also bear a similar sixteenth-century *ex libris*: 'Liber monasterii Wygornie'. Of these, seven carry Westminster inventory numbers; the eighth has been damaged in the place where the number would have been placed. The ninth, Bodley 862, is part of the Nottingham bequest; and the tenth, CCCC, MS 217, has a characteristic label under horn and velvet binding associated with Henrician books. An eleventh book with this *ex libris* is still at Worcester, which suggests that the provenance mark was applied *in situ* rather than when books got up to London. Finally, although no payment survives to the abbot of Pershore, five of his books were transported to Westminster and one to another royal library; this latter, now Bodley 209, came to Oxford from Nottingham.[28]

The early phase of monastic acquisitions was conducted over a very brief period and was a direct result of Henry's attempt to rid himself of Catherine of Aragon. This issue lost its relevance by early 1533, when Henry took matters into his own hands and married Anne Boleyn without having obtained the requisite annulment. To do so, however, he was forced to challenge the pope's authority directly and this led inevitably to the assertion of imperial status for England. The wording of the Preamble of the Act in Restraint of Appeals of April 1533 is pertinent: 'Where by divers sundry old authentic histories and chronicles it is manifestly declared and expressed that this realm of England is an empire, and so hath been accepted in the world, governed by one Supreme Head and King having the dignity and royal estate of the imperial Crown of the same . . .'[29] The seed of the revolution planted in the late 1520s had, in other words, fallen on fertile soil, and the 1533 Act led quite naturally to the Act of Supremacy in 1534, where, once again, 'divers sundry old authentic histories' were used as supporting documents.

John Leland's role

According to Leland's own account, the lost commission which enabled him 'to peruse and dylygentlye to searche all the lybraryes of monasteryes and collegies of thys your noble realme'[30] was granted in 1533, that is, in the same

28 *MLGB*, 150; CBMLC vii. xxxix.

29 See G. R. Elton (ed.), *The Tudor constitution: documents and commentary*, 2nd edn (Cambridge, 1982), 353.

30 *The laboryouse journey & serche of Johan Leylande, for Englandes antiquitees geuen of hym as a New Yeares gyfte to Kynge Henry the VIII. in the XXXVII. yeare of his reygne, with declaracyons enlarged by Johan Bale* (London, 1549; repr. Amsterdam and Norwood, N J, 1975), sig. B.viii^r.

year that Parliament denied the pope his traditional appellation and called him instead 'Bishop of Rome'.[31] The official repudiation of the pope's authority led to further examination of the monastic libraries, and there are at least two letters to Leland's patron, Thomas Cromwell, which pertain specifically to this endeavour.[32] On 3 October 1535, John Draper, prior of the Augustinian house at Christchurch, Hampshire, wrote to Cromwell, stating: 'I send you Beda *de Ecclesiastica Historia*, and another chronicle, whose author I do not know, wherein is also another treatise *de Gestis Pontificum Anglorum*. The other book which you desire, *de Gestis Anglorum*, cannot yet be found; but as soon as I may have him, if he be within our house, I will send him without delay' (*LP* 9. 529). Leland had visited Christchurch in 1533, taking extracts from a copy of William of Malmesbury's now lost *Vita S. Patricii*, and it is possible that it was he who alerted Cromwell to the existence of these other books.[33] On 25 September 1535, William Holleway, the prior of Bath, wrote to Cromwell stating, 'I have send your maistershipp hereyn an old boke *Opera Anselmi* which one William Tildysleye after scrutinye made here in my librarye willed me to send unto youe by the kynge ys grace and commawndment' (*LP* IX. 426). Tyldesley was, in fact, the royal librarian, but both Leland and the monastic visitor Richard Layton had been at Bath before him and had examined the library.[34]

Citing a now lost document among the 'Papers of State', Anthony Wood observed that Leland wrote to Cromwell on 16 July 1536, only a matter of months after the passage of the bill for the suppression of all religious houses with an annual income of less than £200, requesting assistance to preserve books which were fast being dispersed: 'whereas now the Germanes perceiving

31 On 5 June 1534 Sir George Lawson wrote to Cromwell describing how in Leland's company he defaced a *tabula* at York Minster because it contained a reference to the pope's authority in England: see *LP* VII. App. 23.

32 Thomas Cromwell was appointed vicegerent on 21 January 1535 for the purpose of undertaking a general ecclesiastical visitation, which in turn resulted in the *Valor ecclesiasticus*. Cromwell had been acquiring monastic books even earlier, and in 1533, for example, Robert Catton, abbot of St Albans, seems to have given him a copy of the monastery's foundation charter. The other monks were not pleased: see J. G. Clark, 'Reformation and reaction at St Albans Abbey, 1530–58', *EHR* 115 (2000), 308–9.

33 See Leland, *Collectanea*, III. 273–5. Immediately before the extracts from the *Vita S. Patricii* come others from the *Gesta regum Anglorum* (234ff.), and the *Gesta pontificum Anglorum* (243ff.). This conjunction of texts may suggest that Leland saw all three works while he was at Christchurch. BL, MS Arundel 222, which is heavily annotated by Leland, contains an unattributed copy of Bede's *Vita S. Cuthberti* followed by the *Gesta pontificum* and the *Miracula beati Andreae* (actually by Gregory of Tours). According to Bale (*Index*, 42, 136) Leland owned copies, probably multiple, of all three of these texts and no doubt his references (at least in part) are to Arundel 222.

34 Leland had a low opinion of Layton, whom he called a pettifogger and whom he blamed for the fire which partially destroyed the library at Christ Church, Canterbury, in 1535: see *Scriptores*, 483.

our desidiousness and negligence, do send dayly young scholars hither, that spoileth them, and cutteth them out of libraries, returning home and putting them abroad as monuments of their own country'.[35] In fact, there is little evidence that Leland (or anybody else) made concerted efforts to rescue books on a major scale during the second half of the decade.[36] Certainly no pattern of monastic retrieval can be perceived from the Henrician collection as it exists,[37] and, as N. R. Ker long since pointed out, it tends to be a disappointment from an antiquarian point of view.[38] The situation must have been, to some degree, the one so gloomily described by Bale: 'But thys is hyghly to be lamented, of all them that hath a naturall loue to their contrey, eyther yet to lerned Antiquyte . . . That in turnynge ouer of the superstycyouse monasteryes, so lytle respecte was had to theyr lybraryes for the sauegarde of those noble and precyouse monumentes.'[39]

Leland continued to search out books even after the monasteries had fallen, as his transcription of a letter by an unknown individual dated 9 November – the year not stated – from Barnwell makes clear:

> And whereas Master Leylande at this praesente tyme cummith to Byri to see what bookes be lefte yn the library there, or translatid thens ynto any other corner of the late monastery, I shaul desier yow apon juste consideration right

35 See P. Bliss (ed.), *Athenae Oxonienses*, 4 vols. (London, 1813–20), I. 198. No doubt Leland was thinking in particular of Simon Grynaeus, who visited England in 1531, and borrowed ancient manuscripts.

36 Considerable research has been undertaken on individual antiquaries. Among the monastic visitors, for example, Sir John Prise (1502/3–55) collected books from Bury St Edmunds, Cirencester, Evesham, Gloucester, Hereford, Pershore and Winchcombe: see N. R. Ker, 'Sir John Prise', in *Books, collectors and libraries*, 471–96. Ker suggested that Prise may have gathered books for the royal library as well as for himself (476, n. 5). Leland's friend Robert Talbot (*c*. 1505–58), who had an interest in Old English, annotated manuscripts (or perhaps removed them) from Norwich Cathedral, where he was a prebendary: see Ker, 'Medieval manuscripts from Norwich Cathedral Priory', 246. Nicholas Brigham (d. 1558), the single most quoted source in Bale's *Index*, retrieved vernacular materials as well as Latin texts. For other examples see T. Graham and A. G. Watson (eds.), *The recovery of the past in early Elizabethan England* (Cambridge, 1998), and chapter 23 below.

37 The one exception is Rochester from which more than 100 books in the Westminster collection derive, no doubt coming to the throne with the other sequestered goods of John Fisher, bishop of Rochester (d. 22 June 1535): see Carley, in CBMLC VII. xl–xli.

38 See *MLGB*, xii: 'Some great national store-house of ancient manuscripts may have been dreamt of by Leland, but the reality was a rather small collection of selected books, not truly of the first interest and drawn from a restricted area.' On books which may have got to the Royal Collection during Henry's reign and then later have escaped, see below.

39 *The laboryouse journey*, sig. A.vii[v]. In the unpaginated preface to his *De antiquitate Britannicae ecclesiae*, published in 1572, Archbishop Matthew Parker observed that the agents sent out by Henry VIII to select ancient manuscripts from the monastic houses acted *leuiter et perfunctorie* and that many choice items had afterwards to be rescued from the shops of apothecaries and cooks.

> redily to forder his cause, and to permitte hym to have the use of such as may forder hym yn setting forth such matiers as he writith for the kinges majeste.[40]

The Benedictine house at Bury St Edmunds was dissolved on 4 November 1539 and the buildings were despoiled three days later, the plate and best ornaments being taken into the custody of the king.[41] One of the commissioners was Sir John Prise, who appropriated at least three manuscripts.[42] Leland himself had visited Bury on another occasion earlier in the decade, when he had listed twenty-two books from the library, none of which was abstracted for the royal library.[43] By the end of the decade, however, times had changed and Leland was no longer simply perusing books at Bury and elsewhere; he was now returning to the libraries to 'have the use of them', that is to gather them up and rescue them from destruction – or, as he would put it himself several years later: 'Fyrst I haue conserued many good authors, the whych otherwyse had ben lyke to haue peryshed, to no small incommodyte of good letters' (*The laboryouse journey*, sig. C.ii^{r}).

Leland had three potential destinations for these salvaged books. First, so he stated, 'parte remayne in the most magnificent libraryes of your royall palaces' (*The laboryouse journey*, sig. C.ii^{r}). As we have seen, remarkably few books still in the Old Royal Collection were brought there by Leland and his claim might at first seem to be another example of the vainglory of which his enemies accused him. In mid-century, however, massive reorganisation of the Royal Collection took place and at this time there was significant weeding out.[44] This state of flux continued right up to the Civil War, and some of

40 Quoted in L. Toulmin Smith (ed.), *The itinerary of John Leland in or about the years 1535–1543*, 5 vols. (London, 1906–10), II. 148. There are a number of cases of books being transported to 'corners' of dissolved monasteries and being rescued considerably later. One R. Ferrar recovered two Anglo-Saxon manuscripts from Tavistock Abbey for Francis Russell, second earl of Bedford, in 1566, and monastic books could still be found in the buildings at St Augustine's, Canterbury, into the seventeenth century: see A. G. Watson, 'John Twyne of Canterbury (d. 1581) as a collector of medieval manuscripts: a preliminary investigation', *Library*, 6th ser., 8 (1986), 135–6; repr. in his *Medieval manuscripts in post-medieval England* (Aldershot, 2004), IV.

41 See R. Sharpe, in CBMLC IV. 48. It is quite possible, as John Chandler suggests, that the Barnwell letter should be dated to 1539, that is, immediately after the dissolution: see his *John Leland's itinerary: travels in Tudor England* (Stroud, 1998), xxxi.

42 On Prise, see above, n. 36.

43 His list is printed in CBMLC IV. B16; see also M. R. James, *On the abbey of St Edmund at Bury*, Cambridge Antiquarian Society 28 (1895), 10–11. James believed that Leland's list was compiled subsequent to the Barnwell letter, but at least one item was gone by November 1539; Prise had already acquired no. 18, *Leges Langobardorum* (now Bodleian, MS Laud; Misc. 742).

44 This process was overseen by Edward VI's librarian, Bartholomew Traheron, a Protestant of advanced views. Traheron got rid of duplicates, no doubt, but it is also possible that

Leland's most significant acquisitions were thus vulnerable to depredation, which must account in part for the disparity between his assertions and the 'reality' of the modern Royal Collection. In the *Scriptores,* for example, Leland referred to a copy of *De synodis pontificiis* which he saw at Bath and which he removed to the royal library after inscribing verses linking it to Æthelstan on a flyleaf. The manuscript survives, although without the verses, as BL, MS Cotton Claudius B. v.[45] Presumably it was displaced from the royal library during a series of exchanges between Sir Robert Cotton and the royal librarian Patrick Young early in the seventeenth century, although it does not appear in any of the surviving lists.[46] BL, MS Royal 1.A.xviii, which is a tenth-century gospel book given by Æthelstan to St Augustine's, Canterbury, was brought by Leland to Henry and it had the verses quoted in the *Scriptores* inscribed in it. It must have left soon afterwards, however, and it later found its way into the Lumley library.[47] Bodleian, MS Bodley 354 is a twelfth-century copy of part of the Cotton-Corpus legendary which went from Henry VIII's collection to Nottingham and ultimately to Sir Thomas Bodley. It must have come to Henry via Leland, however, since he has written a set of verses on its flyleaf. I imagine it was Leland, too, who acquired the ninth-century copy of Bede on Luke, now Bodley 218, which formed part of the Nottingham bequest.[48]

The second location to which Leland transported monastic books was his own library – 'Part also remayne in my custodie' (*The laboryouse journey*, sig. C.ii^{r}) – and his collection was a major one. In his *Index* Bale listed more than 200 titles *ex bibliotheca Ioannis Lelandi*, and this accounts for the British component

he oversaw the destruction of other manuscripts in the manner recommended by the Edwardian Act against Superstitious Books and Images of 1550 and the order in council of 1551 for 'the purging' of superstitious books. A variety of individuals benefited from the Edwardian deaccessions, including Sir Thomas Pope, who acquired more than fifty books, printed and manuscript, from Hampton Court and Greenwich, with which he stocked his new library at Trinity College, Oxford: see Carley, in CBMLC vii. lxxiv–lxxvi.

45 See S. Keynes, 'King Athelstan's books', in M. Lapidge and H. Gneuss (eds.), *Learning and literature in Anglo-Saxon England* (Cambridge, 1985), 159–65.

46 On the exchanges see C. G. C. Tite, *The manuscript library of Sir Robert Cotton* (London, 1994), 13. The lists are printed in Tite's *The early records of Sir Robert Cotton's library* (London, 2003); for Claudius B. v, see p. 123.

47 See Keynes, 'King Athelstan's books', 165–70. At least three books from Westminster – Royal 14.C.vii, Royal 13.D.v and Royal 12.C.xiii – came to John, first baron Lumley, through his father-in-law, Henry FitzAlan, twelfth earl of Arundel. Concerning the first of these, Matthew Paris's *Historia Anglorum*, Bale complained in a letter written to Matthew Parker of 30 July 1560 that 'thys chronycle remayneth in the custodye of my lorde of Arundell, beynge a fayre boke, and written in an olde Latyne lettre. It belongeth to the quenes maiestyes lybrary, lent by Bartylmew Trihearon, suche tyme as he had the kepynge of that lybrarye in kynge Edwardes tyme': see Graham and Watson, *The recovery of the past*, 29–30.

48 See Carley, 'Sir Thomas Bodley's library and its acquisitions', 371, 372.

only. Some of Bale's titles can be matched with surviving manuscripts. One of Leland's copies of Bede's Lives of St Cuthbert, now Cotton Vitellius A. xix, was possibly written at St Augustine's Canterbury (*Index*, 42).[49] He owned a copy of Giraldus Cambrensis, *De instructione principis*, now Cotton Julius B. xiii, fols. 48–173 (*Index*, 425);[50] as well as a composite manuscript, now Cotton Faustina B. ix, containing the Melrose chronicle and a chronicle misattributed to William Rishanger (*Index*, 402, 471).[51] The unique surviving copy of the *Cronica regum Mannie et insularum*, now Cotton, Julius A.vii, fols. 3–54, from Rushen Abbey, was found in his library (*Index*, 484). Apart from historians, he was interested in poets and possessed BL, Cotton Titus A. xx, which is made up of sixty-nine separate Latin poems;[52] also a copy of Walter of Wimborne's *Marie carmina*, possibly now Bodleian, MS Laud Misc. 368 (*Index*, 111).[53] He got hold of a manuscript from Crowland, now Douai, MS Bibliothèque municipale 852, containing Robert of Shrewsbury's *Vita S. Wenefredae*, Felix of Crowland's *Vita S. Guthlaci*, Goscelin's *Vita S. Iuonis* and other works.[54] His copy of Roger of Crowland's *Compilatio de vita S. Thomae* is now Paris, BN, MS lat. 5372 (*Index*, 401).[55] Although Leland asserted St Augustine's, Canterbury, to be a major source for his books (*Scriptores*, 301), there is no real discernible pattern among surviving books from his library. Most of his books were gathered entirely for practical purposes, as part of his scheme to reclaim the British past and to bring key texts into print; there is little evidence that he collected books for their illustrations or on other aesthetic grounds, although he did own BL Royal 2.D.xxxv, a thirteenth-century copy of the Gospel of St Matthew in St Jerome's version with an illuminated initial, which is one of the few books containing his *ex libris*: 'Liber Ioannis Leylandi Londinensis'.

It is not possible to detect a precise relationship between the lists of monastic books drawn up by Leland and the books he owned. Almost inevitably the

49 On his marginalia in this manuscript see Ker, *Cat. AS*, no. 217.

50 On his marginalia see Wright, 'The Elizabethan Society of Antiquaries and the formation of the Cottonian library', in Wormald and Wright, *English Library*, 212, n. 56. For other components of the manuscript, also owned by Leland, see J. Harrison, 'The English reception of Hugh of Saint-Victor's *Chronicle*', *eBLJ* (2002), 7–8.

51 See Carley, '"Cum excuterem puluerem et blattas": John Bale, John Leland and the *Chronicon Tinemutensis coenobii*', in H. Barr and A. M. Hutchison (eds.), *Text and controversy from Wyclif to Bale* (Turnhout, 2005), 163–87.

52 *Index*, 108–10 (under Walter Map), etc.; on this compilation see A. G. Rigg, 'Medieval Latin poetic anthologies, 1: Titus A.xx and Rawlinson B.214', *Mediaeval Studies* 39 (1977), 292–4; for a description of its contents see Rigg, *A history of Anglo-Latin literature, 1066–1422* (Cambridge, 1992), 308.

53 See A. G. Rigg (ed.), *The poems of Walter of Wimborne* (Toronto, 1978), 7.

54 For a description see Carley, 'John Leland . . . Lincolnshire', 351–2.

55 See Graham and Watson, *The recovery of the past*, J2.67.

former were compiled before the suppressions, often before there was any hint that there would be a wholesale disbanding of monastic life in England, and Leland seemed on good terms with many of the religious authorities, referring to Richard Whiting, abbot of Glastonbury, as *homine sane candidissimo ac amico singulari meo*.[56] It would seem unlikely, therefore, that he removed books on a large scale during his original travels, although he did acquire some books for himself – as well as those items which found their way into the Royal Collection – during this early phase, stating, for example, that Whiting presented him with a now lost copy of Stephen of Ripon's *Vita Wilfridi episcopi* (*Scriptores*, 107). His copy of Henry of Huntingdon's *Historia Anglorum*, now BL, MS Arundel 48, was lent to him by the canons of Southwick and he kept it.

Books belonging to Leland as well as autograph copies of his own works went to other scholars, some before his death in 1552.[57] According to his own account, John Dee purchased six manuscripts at a London sale of Leland's books in 1556.[58] Dee's list indicates that Leland's interests were much wider, more scientific in the most general sense, than the selected references in Bale's *Index* might suggest.[59] The date of the sale, 18 May 1556, is unexpectedly late, since Leland had died in 1552, and it is possible that there is a relationship between it and Cheke's arrest on the Continent on 15 May 1556.[60] Cheke himself

56 He would later delete this phrase: see Bodleian, MS Top. gen. c. 4, p. 34.

57 Around 1548 John Foxe referred to 'the history of Leland "De Catalogo virorum illustrium"; which book, being borrowed of Master Cheke, I myself did see in the hands of the aforesaid John Bale, what time we were both together, dwelling in the house of the noble lady the Duchess of Richmond': S. R. Cattley (ed.), *The acts and monuments of John Foxe*, 8 vols (London, 1837–41), III. 705. Sir John Cheke apparently was given charge of Leland's collections after his insanity: see Oliver Harris, '"Motheaten, mouldye, and rotten": the early custodial history and dissemination of John Leland's manuscript remains', *Bodleian Library Record* 18/5 (2005), 462–5.

58 Five are listed under the heading 'Ex bibliotheca Laelandi emi pro 30 solidis hos sequentes libros 1556 18 Maii Londini': [1] Mineralium Alberti libri quinque. Robertus de Kilwardby de ortu scientiarum. Tractatus de Tempore. Tractatus de Relationibus (now BL, MS Harley 57; s. xiii); [2] Urso de commixtionibus elementorum. Aphorismi Ursonis cum aliis (now Cambridge, Trinity Coll., MS O.2.50; London Dominicans, s. xiv/xv); [3] Summa Anglicana Joannis Eschuyden (?now London, Royal Coll. of Physicians MS 390; s. xiv ex); [4] Haly haben ragel de Judiciis (?now Oxford, Corpus Christi Coll., MS 151; AD 1380); [5] Messahalah de astrolabio. Planisphaerium Ptolomaei. Euclidis de speculis. Jordanus de ponderibus. Practica geometriae cum aliis variis in medicina (now TCD, MS D.2.29 (403); s. xv). A sixth is Bodleian, MS Digby 76, fols. 1–109, containing works by Roger Bacon and others. M. R. James believed that Dee also acquired Oxford, Corpus Christi Coll., MS 236 from Leland but there does not seem to be any evidence to substantiate this: see J. Roberts and A. G. Watson (eds.), *John Dee's library catalogue* (London, 1990), CM38–42, DM113, M85.

59 BL, MS Sloane 3744, an alchemical collection, has the name 'Leyland' on fols. 117^{r} and 124^{r}, but it is an old-fashioned hand and does not resemble Leland's italic script.

60 See Roberts and Watson, *Dee's catalogue*, 6.

appropriated books from Leland's collections, and Bale affirmed that Leland's copy of Sicardus of Cremona's now lost Lives of the popes came into Cheke's possession.[61] Cheke may also have got copies of Henry of Huntingdon, William of Malmesbury's *Gesta regum*, *Gesta pontificum* and *Historia nouella*, John Bever's *Brutus abbreuiatus*, and Nicholas Trevet's *Historia ab orbe condita* from Leland's library, since Bale cites it as a source for these titles and they later turn up in Cheke's ownership.[62] Presumably, too, it was Leland's copy of Walter of Coventry's *Memoriale*, now CCCC, MS 175, which passed to Lady Cheke and thence to Matthew Parker.[63] Apart from CCCC 175, Parker subsequently obtained the Annals of St Neots, now Cambridge, Trinity Coll., MS R. 7. 28, which Leland had earlier appropriated from St Neots.[64]

The Oxford scholar Thomas Keye (d. 1572) is given as the source for nearly thirty titles in Bale's *Index*. In a number of cases, Keye and Leland are listed as the sole possessors of manuscripts of works by relatively obscure writers, the circulation of which would have been extremely limited. Given that Keye greatly admired Leland and owned manuscript copies of the latter's own writings, and given that Bale's *Index* was composed over a number of years, it seems likely that, in cases where both individuals are listed, Bale is actually citing a single manuscript which passed from Leland to Keye. For example, Godwin of Sarum's *Meditationes* survives uniquely in Bodleian, MS Digby 96, which is probably the copy seen by Leland at Abingdon.[65] Bale recorded a copy in Leland's library, almost certainly the Abingdon manuscript, and also one in Keye's library (*Index*, 96). The description of Keye's manuscript is fuller – it lists *De tribus habitaculis* – and this corresponds precisely to Digby 96. Bale attributed a poem on the martrydom of Thomas Becket to William of Cherbourg based on a manuscript found in Leland's and Keye's libraries, and this is almost certainly Digby 65, the only manuscript in which this attribution occurs.[66] A further example might be the copy of the *Epistola Cuthberti de*

61 Graham and Watson, *The recovery of the past*, Bn32; see also J2.6.

62 *Ibid.*, Bn110; also J2.36–7, 84.

63 *Ibid.*, J2.69. Leland probably owned a copy of Walter of Guisborough's *Chronica*, possibly the one he saw at Wells Cathedral, and took extracts from it (*Collectanea*, III. 314–5); this may be the manuscript which passed to Lady Cheke: see Graham and Watson, *The recovery of the past*, J2.86. Likewise it was no doubt his copy of Asser which was later owned by Lady Cheke (J2.26). Parker's copy, which may be the same, is probably the badly burnt Cotton Otho A. xii.

64 See D. Dumville and M. Lapidge (eds.), *The annals of St Neots with Vita prima Sancti Neoti*, *The Anglo-Saxon Chronicle: a collaborative edition*, 17 (Cambridge, 1985), xiv, xxi.

65 See CBMLC IV, B4. 2.

66 Bale also gives Keye's library as the source for a number of other works contained in this poetical anthology.

obitu Bedae that Bale saw in Keye's library; somewhat earlier, Leland had come across a copy of this text in Henry's library and took excerpts from it (*Index*, 57; *Collectanea*, IV. 77–80). The manuscript to which Leland refers can be identified as BL MS Arundel 74; possibly he obtained it from the royal library and then Keye later got hold of it. There are other examples of books which went from Leland to Keye, such as the letter commanding Aelred of Rievaulx to write his *Speculum caritatis*, falsely attributed to Gervase of Louth (*Index*, 86), but the actual manuscripts have not been identified.

According to Leland, some books went to a third location: 'Farther more part of the exemplaries, curyously sought by me, and fortunately found in sondry places of this youre dominion, hath bene emprynted in Germany, and now be in the presses chefely of Frobenius.'[67] In his commentary to the *New Year's Gift* Bale expressed himself uncertain about the identity of these manuscripts,[68] but at least one can be shown to have existed. Among the books Leland saw at Malmesbury in 1533 was a copy of writings by Tertullian.[69] In his entry for Aldhelm in the *Scriptores*, he was more detailed in his description of this manuscript, pointing out that it contained 'de Spectaculis, de Ieiunio' (*Scriptores*, 100). On 13 June 1539, he wrote a letter to the continental humanist scholar Beatus Rhenanus concerning the latter's edition of Tertullian published by Hieronymus Froben earlier in the year.[70] According to the letter, he had handed over an ancient manuscript of Tertullian, which he had found at Malmesbury, to Damião de Gois to convey to Rhenanus.[71] Sigismund Ghelen, who was an associate of Froben, brought out a revised edition of Tertullian's works in 1550, and in the preface he singled out the Malmesbury manuscript discovered by Leland, describing the incapacitated antiquary as *feliciori dignus ualetudine* ('deserving of better health'). Nor does the story end here, since the manuscript passed to Thomas More's former protégé and Leland's friend, John

67 *The laboryouse journey*, sig. C.iiii^r. In his chapter on Joseph of Exeter, Leland complained that Joseph's *Bellum Troianum* had been (badly) printed by the Germans, who attributed it to Cornelius Nepos (*Scriptores*, 239). His reference is to the Basel edition of 1541. See also above, n. 35.

68 'Of the bokes which shoulde be in the handes of Hieronymus Frobenius, can I nothyng heare. Yet haue I made thydre most instaunt sute and labour by diuerse honeste men, at the least to haue had but theyr tytles; but I neuer coulde obtayne them. Whiche maketh me to thinke, that eyther they haue peryshed by the waye, or els that they are throwne a syde in some corner, and so forgotten' (*The laboryouse journey*, sig. C.iiii^v).

69 CBMLC IV. B54. 23; Carley and Petitmengin, 'Pre-Conquest manuscripts from Malmesbury Abbey'.

70 For an edition of this letter and a discussion of the circumstances surrounding its composition see Petitmengin and Carley, 'Malmesbury – Sélestat – Malines'.

71 This was apparently done at the request of Richard Morison, on whom see above, n. 7.

Clement, during the latter's first exile in Edward VI's reign and was consulted by Jacques de Pamèle in the preparation of his 1583/4 edition.[72]

Like Leland, Bale had connections with continental printers. When he fled from Ireland to the Continent on the accession of Mary in 1553, he left many of his books behind him.[73] By 1556 he had joined a number of exiles in Basel, and he may have brought with him a copy (acquired from the royal library) of the manuscript making up the so-called *Collectanea* falsely attributed to Bede.[74] If this is the case, Johann Herwagen the Younger must have made use of this manuscript in his 1563 *omnium gatherum* edition of Bede's works. Bale may also have been the source for a copy of Byrhtferth's commentaries on Bede's computistical writings used in this same edition.[75]

Other contemporary salvaging

In the mid-1530s, as many as 200 medieval manuscripts, almost all from the houses of the Austin, Dominican and Franciscan friars in Cambridge, were packed up and transported abroad, coming into the possession of Cardinal Marcello Cervini (1510–55); they now form part of the series of Codices Ottoboniani.[76] Eugene J. Crook has suggested two possible explanations for the removal of these books: either they were sent for safe keeping to Cervini, protector of the Servite and Austin friars, shortly before the houses fell, or they were sold off by Dr John Hardyman, the last prior of the Cambridge Austins, who seems actively to have sympathised with the reform movement. In light of the demoralised state of the houses and the fact that, well before

72 Much earlier, Clement provided Simon Grynaeus with the manuscript which formed the basis of his edition of Proclus' *De motu* (1531), and during his second exile, begun soon after Elizabeth's accession, he sent Pamèle readings from his own manuscript for the latter's edition of Cyprian (1568).

73 See W. O'Sullivan, 'The Irish "remnaunt" of John Bale's manuscripts', in R. Beadle and A. J. Piper (eds.), *New science out of old books: studies in manuscripts and early printed books in honour of A. I. Doyle* (Aldershot, 1995), 374–87, and the references cited therein.

74 See P. Jackson, 'Herwagen's lost manuscript of the *Collectanea*', in M. Bayless and M. Lapidge (eds.), *Collectanea Pseudo-Bedae* (Dublin, 1998), 114–20.

75 See M. Gorman, 'The glosses on Bede's *De temporum ratione* attributed to Byrhtferth of Ramsey', *ASE* 25 (1996), 232.

76 See N. R. Ker, 'Cardinal Cervini's manuscripts from the Cambridge friars', in *Books, collectors and libraries*, 437–58; E. J. Crook, 'Manuscripts surviving from the Austin friars at Cambridge', *Manuscripta* 27 (1983), 82–90; J. P. Carley, 'John Leland and the contents of English pre-Dissolution libraries: the Cambridge friars', *TCBS* 9 (1986), 90–100; CBMLC I. A2, D2, F2. The manuscripts date from the twelfth to the fifteenth centuries and most are standard biblical commentaries, commentaries on the *Sentences*, church historians, works by Augustine, Gregory the Great, Bernard and Thomas Aquinas, and similar works.

the offical dissolutions in 1538, the priors of all three houses had already begun dismantling the buildings and selling off land and building materials, the latter explanation would perhaps appear more likely.[77]

Christ Church, Canterbury, had one of the largest book collections in England at the end of the middle ages, and Christopher de Hamel has published a detailed analysis of the post-Dissolution fate of part of the library.[78] Soon after the cathedral priory was suppressed in 1540, private collectors – including John Twyne, Thomas Cranmer, William Darrell, John Bale, Nicholas Wotton, William Lambarde and William Bowyer – obtained manuscripts, but none of these came from the upper library, a list of whose books had been drawn up by William Ingram in 1508. After he became archbishop of Canterbury in 1583, John Whitgift acquired some fifty-two manuscripts from Christ Church. Whitgift had been the master of Trinity College, Cambridge, and he bequeathed these to Trinity College when he died in 1604.[79] Another twenty-four were given to Trinity by his successor as master, Thomas Nevile, who was appointed dean of Canterbury in 1597.[80] Both these groups, unlike the others, were drawn

77 See, however, J. Catto, 'Franciscan learning in England, 1450–1540', in J. G. Clark (ed.), *The religious orders in pre-Reformation England* (Woodbridge, 2002), who sees a possible link between the situation at Cambridge and that at Oxford. Concerning Leland's description of the Franciscan library at Oxford, above, 268, he points out: 'True, the remaining bookworms, if we can take them seriously, do rather imply that there had been books about not long before, which may have been disposed of like the plate and the lead on the convent roof, out of necessity or the desire to thwart the King's commissioners; the latter possibility may be the reason why so many books of the various Cambridge friaries, only two of them apparently seen by Leland, ended up in the Ottobuoni collection in the Vatican' (97).

78 'The dispersal of the library of Christ Church, Canterbury, from the fourteenth to the sixteenth century', in Carley and Tite, *Books and collectors*, 263–79. De Hamel has also observed how a number of books from Canterbury College, brought by monks from Christ Church itself, appear to have been used as waste by Oxford binders: see 267–9. This ties in with Bale's lamentations in *The laboryouse journey* concerning the ultimate fate of many monastic books: 'some they [the purchasers of the monastic sites] sent ouer see to the bokebynders, not in small nombre, but at tymes whole shyppes full' (sig. Bi^{r}).

79 At the time of his death Whitgift owned at least 200 medieval manuscripts: see P. Gaskell, *Trinity College Library: the first 150 years* (Cambridge, 1980), 80. Around fifty of these, some of which were from Canterbury, went to Richard Bancroft (1544–1610), his successor as archbishop of Canterbury, who in turn left his collection for the foundation of Lambeth Palace Library. There does not seem to be any real logic to the way Whitgift divided up his manuscripts between Trinity and Bancroft, and in at least one case two parts of a former Christ Church book (Cambridge, Trinity Coll., MS B. 3. 14 and Lambeth, MS 62) went to different destinations: see Carley, '"A great gatherer together of books": Archbishop Bancroft's library at Lambeth (1610) and its sources', *Lambeth Palace Library Annual Review* (2001), 58–60.

80 See de Hamel, 'The dispersal', 273–4, who has observed that Nevile 'completed the job' begun by Whitgift. However, as William O'Sullivan has pointed out ('Archbishop Whitgift's library catalogue', *Times Literary Supplement*, 1956, 468), Nevile did present Trinity manuscripts formerly belonging to Whitgift.

from the upper library, and the reason for this, so de Hamel postulates, is that it had probably been boarded up ever since the fire of 1535 and was rendered accessible again only in 1569, when funds were set aside for the restoration of the former prior's buildings.

The situation of the Cambridge friars and the one at Christ Church were, as far as we can tell, unusual and do not provide parallels for other groups of books which stayed intact after the Dissolution.[81] More common is what Leland described at Sherborne, where the prior 'lying yn the toun can bring me to the old librarie yn Shirburne'.[82] Basing his argument on this sort of clue, N. R. Ker has speculated:

> The removal of books by individual inmates at the moment of the Dissolution caused, no doubt, a wider dispersal of the libraries of some houses than of others . . . And I guess that individual monks and nuns played a part in preserving books from Fountains, Glastonbury, Hailes, Southwark, Syon, and the charterhouses, without being able, however, to produce more in the way of evidence than names in the extant books, the general character of the books, and their present wide dispersal. This sort of evidence needs collecting and weighing. I do not feel justified in drawing conclusions from it at present.[83]

81 As pointed out above, n. 1, there was generally speaking much greater continuity at the former cathedral priories (where many of the monks became canons in the new cathedral chapters). A. I. Doyle has analysed Durham books and has concluded that 'the evidence is also strong that a large number of previous monks' books not bearing the survivors' names remained in the precincts of the Cathedral in individual or communal custody into the reign of Elizabeth, besides the communal monastic collections of manuscripts and those printed books explicitly assigned to the new cupboard or registry. For although there were alienations of important manuscripts in this period, the number of losses may not have reached its peak till later in the century, and it is obvious that a chained library at least of printed books was intended to continue' ('The printed books of the last monks of Durham', 214–16).

82 *Leland's itinerary*, I. 153. One of the books seen by Leland at Sherborne during an earlier visit was a copy of Wulfstan Cantor's *Narratio metrica de Sancto Swithuno* (CBMLC IV. B94.9). This survives as Bodleian, MS Auct. F. 2. 14 and has marginal annotations in Leland's hand.

83 Ker, 'The migration of manuscripts from the English medieval libraries', in *Books, collectors and libraries*, 469. As Doyle has pointed out, moreover, there had been some blurring of the distinction between personal and institutional books even before the Dissolution: 'It is clear from many other books from the [Durham] Cathedral Priory, and from other monastic communities, that before their abolition monks were allowed to have books for their individual use, and to buy and give them, though to members of their own community only; after its dissolution and their secularisation they felt free to keep anything they had, including items marked more specifically as from the institutional collections, and even from the chained library, which must have been broken up'. See 'The library of Sir Thomas Tempest: its origins and dispersal', in G. A. M. Janssens and F. G. A. M. Aarts (eds.), *Studies in seventeenth-century English literature, history and bibliography* (Amsterdam, 1984), 85.

Recent research, at least for Yorkshire, where much work has been done, supports Ker's supposition.[84] In his will of 23 May 1542, Richard Barwicke, formerly of the Benedictine abbey at St Mary's, York, bequeathed to Sir John Pott, another former monk of St Mary's, a copy of John of Genoa's *Catholicon* and Angelus de Clavasio's *Summa angelica de casibus conscientiae*; to Robert Brawshay he left a copy of the *Chronicles of England*, and to his parish church at Escrick, Ludolf of Saxony's *Meditationes uitae Iesu Christi*, Peter Comestor's *Historia scholastica*, and a *Legenda sanctorum*. After the suppression of the Cluniac (later Benedictine) house at Monk Bretton on 21 November 1538, the last prior, William Browne (d. 1557), established himself at Worsborough in a kind of community in exile along with Thomas Frobisher, sub-prior (d. March 1557), and two former monks, Thomas Wilkinson (d. before 1564?) and Richard Hinchcliff (d. 1574).[85] They managed to acquire some 148 books from their monastery, and when Browne died he passed them on to two of these monks and five other former colleagues, although he requested that, if the monastery were reconstituted, the books and other goods be '*restored* to the sayd monastre of Monke Bretton and bretheren there without any delay' (emphasis mine).[86] On 21 July 1558 an inventory was made, presumably by Hinchcliff, listing the books – almost all of which appear to be printed books.[87] It is possible that the collection next went to the last surviving monk, Robert Scoley, alias Kirkby,

84 See C. Cross and N. Vickers (eds.), *Monks, friars and nuns in sixteenth-century Yorkshire* (Leeds, 1995); Cross, 'Community solidarity among Yorkshire religious after the Dissolution', in J. Loades (ed.), *Monastic studies: the continuity of tradition* (Bangor, 1990), 245–54; also her 'Monastic learning and libraries in sixteenth-century Yorkshire', in J. Kirk (ed.), *Humanism and reform: the church in Europe, England, and Scotland, 1400–1643*, Studies in church history, Subsidia 8 (Oxford, 1991), 255–69, where she has argued that 'sufficient records have survived to suggest that a significant number of erstwhile monks and friars were . . . redistributing medieval books around Yorkshire in the generation after the Henrician Reformation' (255). See also P. Cunich, 'The ex-religious in post-Dissolution society: symptoms of post-traumatic stress disorder?', in Clark, *The religious orders*, 235–7. Cunich, who describes the attempt to maintain informal communities as 'avoidance', lists a number of ex-religious who stayed together and mentions several who, in their wills, 'made provision for the return of personal possessions [including books] to their former communities should they ever be re-founded' (236). According to a visitation book of 1567, 'ther is in a howse within a vawte of the said Churche [of Ripon] yet remaininge reserved . . . xlix bookes, some Antiphoners, and suche bookes as ar condemned by publique auctoritie': see J. T. Fowler (ed.), *Memorials of the Church of SS. Peter & Wilfrid, Ripon*, 4 vols., Surtees Soc. 74, 78, 81, 115 (Durham, 1882–1908), III. 344.

85 See Cross and Vickers, *Monks, friars and nuns*, 22, 78; also Cross, 'A medieval Yorkshire library', *Northern History* 25 (1989), 282.

86 Quoted in Cross, 'A medieval Yorkshire library', 283. Browne died during Queen Mary's reign, when the possibility of a refoundation may well have seemed a viable possibility.

87 CBMLC IV. B55. In a private communication James Clark has informed me that in 1558 there were a number of bequests at St Albans to support a refoundation and he suggests that the prospects for further restorations on the Westminster model may have seemed likely that summer.

who, in his will of 10 January 1579, left his books to his godson Robert Helm, on condition that the latter become a priest.

The Yorkshire Cistercians provide a number of examples. After Kirkstall surrendered on 22 November 1539, Edward Heptonstall acquired books. When he made his will on 3 August 1558 he gave to the parish church at Leeds a copy of Johannes Herolt's *Sermones discipuli de tempore*; to his nephew he bequeathed the books in a chest at the foot of his bed and all the other books in his custody which had once belonged to the abbey. If, however, the house were to be revived, the books should be *restored* to it.[88] Richard Hall, alias Gilling, formerly of Rievaulx, possessed a number of books, several of which he left in his will of 1 March 1566 to individuals who may have been former monks of St Mary's, York and Byland.[89] The commissioners allowed the former abbot of Roche Abbey, Henry Cundall (d. 1555), to retain his books after the surrender of the house on 23 June 1538.[90] Cundall kept in touch with his former colleagues and as late as 1554 referred to himself as 'the abbot of Roche'.

The Cistercian house at Byland was dissolved on 30 November 1538. The prior, Robert Barker, may have been the individual presented to the vicarage of Driffield on 15 December 1541.[91] If so, then it is likely that the remarkable collection of books left by a second Robert Barker, who was vicar of Driffield from 1558 until his death in 1581/2, came from Byland through the agency of the first Barker. The second Barker appointed John Nettleton (d. 1597) and his son Edward as trustees of approximately 150 medieval books until such time as his natural kin were of an age to understand them.[92] John Nettleton, who also owned medieval manuscripts from Fountains, Rievaulx and York Minster, later obtained many of Barker's Byland books and a number ultimately went to Henry Savile of Banke (d. 1617).[93]

88 Cross and Vickers, *Monks, friars and nuns*, 146; also Cross, 'A medieval Yorkshire library', 283. Once again, the date this will was drawn up seems significant.

89 Cross and Vickers, *Monks, friars and nuns*, 176–7.

90 *Ibid.*, 188–9.

91 See Cross, 'A medieval Yorkshire library'; M. A. Hicks, 'John Nettleton, Henry Savile of Banke, and the post-medieval vicissitudes of Byland Abbey library', *Northern History* 26 (1990), 212–17; Cross and Vickers, *Monks, friars and nuns*, 101.

92 Cross, 'A medieval Yorkshire library', 285–90.

93 On Savile of Banke see A. G. Watson, *The manuscripts of Henry Savile of Banke* (London, 1969). By Hickes's reckoning, all of the Byland books in the Savile collection, of which there are fourteen, derived from Barker. In his opinion, Nettleton gave the books to the elder Henry Savile of Banke (d. 1607), a known recusant, to be returned if the monastery were ever refounded. There are other examples of recusants becoming custodians of monastic books. For example, Doyle has argued that books which were acquired by the Tempest family came from two relations who were former monks, of whom one went abroad during Elizabeth's reign: 'it would hardly be surprising if this line of Tempest

Like the Cistercians, Yorkshire Augustinian canons retained books. After the Dissolution a monk of Guisborough, John Clarkson, became curate in the local parish church.[94] According to his will, drawn up in 1556, he possessed a number of books, most of which were to be distributed at the discretion of former colleagues in the priory. Robert Collynson, former prior at Haltemprice, which surrendered on 12 August 1536, drew up a will on 28 March 1552 in which he described himself as priest at Cottingham.[95] He left the parish church a Latin bible, the works of Origen, Gregory's *Moralia in Iob*, Ludolf of Saxony's *Meditationes uitae Iesu Christi*, Peter Lombard's *Sententiarum libri* IV, Peter Comestor's *Historia scholastica*, *Parati sermones de tempore et de sanctis*, William Durandus the Elder's *Rationale diuinorum officiorum* and other works. William Barker, the former sub-prior of the Augustinian priory at Newburgh, got a dispensation to hold a living in 1539; in his will drawn up on 31 August 1548, he left his brother all his books, except his copy of Raymond of Pennafort's *Summa de casibus poenitentiae*, which went to Sir Richard Hall, perhaps a former Rievaulx monk, and one other book, Guido de Monte Rochen's *Manipulus curatorum*, to a chaplain.[96]

Five of the six known surviving books from the Hull Charterhouse are printed books and belonged to the former prior Ralph Malevory (d. 1551), who described himself as a priest of Seaton in the will in which he left some of his books to the former Hull Carthusians William Browne and William Remington.[97] William Bee, who had been a brother at the Mount Grace Charterhouse and who kept in touch with his former colleagues after its dissolution on 18 December 1539, left Leonard Hall, also one of the brothers, all his books at Wakefield and Newcastle when he drew up his will on 27 March 1551.[98] Hall joined the re-established charterhouse of Sheen in 1556 and then went abroad after Elizabeth's accession. Edmund Skelton, of the Grandimontine priory at Grosmont, became a curate at Egton after the fall of his house on 31 August 1539. In his will he left his books – a set of postills, works by Cassiodorus, a copy of John of Genoa's *Catholicon* and a bible in Latin – to remain at Egton church for ever. He also bequeathed certain other unspecified books to a former colleague, Robert Holland.[99] Finally, the former

should have also remained attached to the ancient faith and have kept the books which embodied the monastic tradition of theological learning, still of potential utility to clergy with a scholastic training, as well as representing family alliances': 'The library of Sir Thomas Tempest', 87.

94 Cross and Vickers, *Monks, friars and nuns*, 273–4.

95 *Ibid.*, 287.

96 *Ibid.*, 316–17.

97 *Ibid.*, 219–20. On Malevory's surviving books, *MLGB*, 106; *Supplement*, 40.

98 Cross and Vickers, *Monks, friars and nuns*, 227, 229–30.

99 *Ibid.*, 238.

warden of the York Franciscan friary, William Vavasour, drew up a will on 13 November 1544, in which he set aside twenty-six books for various York priests, reserving the remainder of his library for his former colleague Ralph Clayton.[100]

The evidence from these Yorkshire wills is remarkably uniform: the religious normally took away printed books, generally in Latin, but they did remove manuscripts too.[101] The deaccessions consisted primarily of bibles and commentaries on the Bible, although there was a smattering of historical works. Some books may have been acquired when individuals were pursuing their studies at university and some were useful in pastoral work. When collected in large numbers, the books appear to have been held in the hope of the re-establishment of the dissolved houses – a possibility which must have seemed particularly realistic during Mary's reign – but the small collections ultimately passed to parish churches, local priests and grammar schools as well as to family and friends. Little trace remains of these books; apart from the manuscripts from Byland, few can be identified with modern survivors.

Even if wills have not yet been consistently scrutinised in other parts of the country, similar patterns do emerge.[102] At Pershore the last abbot, John Stonywell (d. 1551), wrote to Cromwell on 23 February 1539, requesting permission to keep his books.[103] These were probably printed books and none has been identified.[104] At the time of his death in 1557 Philip Hawford, the last abbot of Evesham, owned some seventy-five books, most acquired while he was a monk.[105] The great majority of the surviving manuscripts from the priory of Augustinian canons at Lanthony are now found in Lambeth Palace and formed part of Archbishop Richard Bancroft's bequest.[106] When Lanthony surrendered on 10 March 1538 – 'with as much quietness as might be desired' according to William Petre – the former prior Richard Hart, alias

100 *Ibid.*, 455. John Dee subsequently owned books which Vasavour had transcribed: see Roberts and Watson (eds.), *John Dee's library catalogue*, M162–3, M169.

101 It should be observed, however, that a certain percentage of the printed books bequeathed by the ex-religious could have been ones they got after their secularisation.

102 Scholars have gathered more provenance information about former monastic manuscripts than about the printed books and the evidence may therefore be slightly skewed.

103 See J. Youings, *The dissolution of the monasteries* (London, 1971), 174–5.

104 Lambeth, MS 761, a thirteenth-century copy of Aelred of Rievaulx's *Vita S. Edwardi regis et confessoris*, was owned in 1538 by Richard Beerley, another Pershore monk.

105 See E. A. Barnard, 'Philip Hawford, pseudo abbot of Evesham and dean of Worcester: his will and inventory', *Transactions of the Worcestershire Archaeological Society*, NS 5 (1928), 52–69. Hawford, the former cellerer, obtained the abbacy in 1538 through Cromwell's intervention: see Knowles, *Bare ruined choirs*, 224–5.

106 For what follows see T. Webber and A. G. Watson, in CBMLC VI. 35.

Hempstead, was given the right of residence at Brockworth, near Gloucester, a former monastic holding. He took some or all of the priory's books with him, and when he died he bequeathed 'all his bookes of latyn' to Thomas Morgan, about whom nothing is known. One of his executors was Thomas Theyer, from the collection of whose grandson, John Theyer of Cooper's Hill, Brockworth, Lanthony books found their way into the royal library. How the Morgan books were acquired by Bancroft, however, 'is a mystery which seems unlikely ever to be solved'.

Seventeen manuscripts from the Cistercian abbey of Buildwas in Shropshire, now at Trinity College, Cambridge, are listed in *Medieval libraries of Great Britain*, and another eight are rejected. Six of Ker's rejects have subsequently been attributed to Buildwas, and three other Trinity books unknown to Ker have been shown to have come from Buildwas.[107] Virtually all the Trinity cache derives from Whitgift.[108] At Lambeth Palace there are five further former Buildwas books which were given by Bancroft, who, in turn, acquired them from Whitgift. Whitgift, in other words, obtained a group of more than thirty books belonging to Buildwas, and it is likely that he did so while he was bishop of Worcester (1577–83) and vice-president of the Council of the Welsh Marches (?1577–80).[109] Given that Buildwas was suppressed in 1536, there must have been a forty-year hiatus between the dissolution and Whitgift's acquisition of the collection. The books would have remained intact as a group, either because they were acquired by an individual collector around the period of the dissolution, or because they were taken away by a departing monk.[110]

A former monk of Bury, Aylot Holt, provided John Bale with the only known copy of the *Catalogus scriptorum ecclesiae* of Henry de Kirkestede ('Boston of Bury'), and he removed other books as well, of which Bale listed four.[111] Holt was a member of a local family, and his will, dated 8 July 1570, survives in the

107 J. M. Sheppard, *The Buildwas books* (Oxford, 1997), xlix; also *MLGB Supplement*, 5.

108 The one anomaly is B. I. 29, presented by Nevile, but no doubt Nevile acquired it from Whitgift rather than independently.

109 Gaskell, *Trinity College Library*, 80–1.

110 Ker noted the similarities of content between this group and the so-called Reading group, collected by Sir Francis Englefield, the Bury group, collected by William Smart, and the Cirencester group, collected by Sir John Prise. He concluded therefore that in each case they were 'the chosen acquisition of an individual collector' ('The migration of manuscripts', 467).

111 See *Index*, xxv. Bale later obtained another of his manuscripts, now CCCC, MS 135. He appears in the list of pensions as Ailot Halstede, alias Holte, receiving £6 13s 8d (*LP* XIV / 2, no. 462). See also R. H. Rouse and M. A Rouse (eds.), *Henry of Kirkestede's Catalogus de libris autenticis et apocrifis*, CBMLC XI. clxxxi–clxxxii.

Suffolk Record Office (W1/10/219).[112] Describing himself as Eliot Holt, clerke, he left his goods to various members of his family, including 'R. Holt precher', who was the recipient of all his books, except for his Testament. It was no doubt from this latter that Jeremiah Holt, also of Suffolk, acquired some of the medieval manuscripts which, as rector of Stonham Aspall, he gave to St John's College, Cambridge, in 1634.[113] According to an inscription in a thirteenth-century bible, now Lambeth, MS 90, it was given after the Dissolution by another Bury monk, John Yxworth, to Roger Duckett, 'then scolar of the gramer scole there'. William Smart (d. 1599), portreeve of Ipswich, obtained as many as 150, if not more, manuscripts from Bury, and he donated these to Pembroke College, Cambridge, in 1599.[114] He himself could not have acquired the books directly from the monastery – he was not born until about 1529 – and they may have come from his father (as Blatchly postulated in his study of the Ipswich Library), although no books are mentioned in the father's will. James, on the other hand, suggested that he 'must have bought these books *en bloc*, it would seem, either at Bury or in its neighbourhood'.[115] From whom he (or his father) may have bought them, whether former religious or local antiquary, cannot be ascertained.

Reading Abbey fell on 19 September 1539, and in 1550 custody of the former monastic site and its lands passed to Edward Seymour, duke of Somerset.[116] In Mary's reign, Sir Francis Englefield, who was appointed high steward and keeper of the abbey, acquired a number of manuscripts, presumably stored until then in the portion of the buildings being used as a royal palace. He was related through marriage to Clement Burdett, to whom he must have handed over the manuscripts at some point before he went into exile in 1559.[117]

112 I thank Dr John Craig for this reference.

113 Of the ten manuscripts donated by Jeremiah Holt seven certainly come from Bury, and James suspected two others did as well. He was less sure about the tenth, although he opined that it had been owned by an East Anglian monastery.

114 See J. Blatchly, *The town library of Ipswich* (Woodbridge, 1989). At least three Bury manuscripts now in the Ipswich Library also derive from Smart and it is possible, as Blatchly suggests (7), that some of the Ipswich printed books came from Bury. See also Rouse and Rouse in CBMLC XI. clxxx–clxxxi. On Bury manuscripts which have strayed from Pembroke see A. Gransden, 'Some manuscripts in Cambridge from Bury St Edmunds Abbey: exhibition catalogue', in A. Gransden (ed.), *Bury St Edmunds: medieval art, architecture, archaeology and economy*, British Archaeological Association Conference Transactions 20 (Leeds, 1998), 229.

115 *On the Abbey of St Edmund*, 22.

116 See A. Coates, *English medieval books: the Reading Abbey collections from foundation to dispersal* (Oxford, 1999), 122–42.

117 Coates has suggested that the books were given to Burdett in anticipation of the refoundation of the monastery (*ibid.*, 136).

Many of these later passed to Clement's nephew William Burdett, and, of the thirty-four manuscripts William presented to the Bodleian in 1608, some twenty-eight probably derive from Reading.[118]

No catalogue survives from the house of Augustinian canons at Merton, Surrey, which was dissolved on 16 April 1538, but there were at least two waves of removals, and these are representative of the ways in which books were dispersed in general. Around 1530, some eight books were taken from the monastery to Henry VIII's library and they now carry Westminster inventory numbers. John Ramsey, the last prior, owned at least seven books, of which five were printed books possibly purchased by Ramsey for his own use. Two, however, were medieval manuscripts which he must have carried off in 1538. One of his printed books, now Oxford, St John's College, .1.32, came into the hands of his colleague, Thomas Paynell (d. *c.* 1564), and is one of almost 150 books bequeathed by Paynell to St John's College, in 1563/4.[119] Most of the books were bought by Paynell himself, but at least four, all printed, had been previously owned by the priory.

Of the seventeen identified manuscripts from the Cistercian house at Warden (surrendered 4 December 1537), thirteen are now at Trinity College, Cambridge.[120] In one of these books (Cambridge, Trinity Coll., MS B. 4. 15) there is a list of thirty-two titles in a sixteenth-century hand, compiled by one R. Manley. Manley's hand, which shows no sign of italic influence, would appear to date to the first half of the sixteenth century. Many of the books in his list cannot be traced, but thirteen can be identified as Warden books, and all but one of these (Bodleian, MS Laud Misc. 447) are at Trinity. One item appears in a list of nineteen titles compiled by Leland shortly before the dissolution – the corresponding manuscript is Cambridge, Trinity Coll., MS B. 4. 32 – and we can assume, therefore, that the manuscripts were still in the library in the mid-1530s.[121] The organisation of Manley's list suggests that it may have been taken from an earlier catalogue of the library. It is quite possible, then, that Manley drew up a list, possibly at the very moment of the dissolution, and managed to acquire some, if not all, of the items he listed. The books did not get to Trinity until considerably later; they figure in a group of twenty-four manuscripts and eleven printed books which may have been acquired in the

118 On the ways in which other 'Englefield' books were dispersed see Coates, *English medieval books*, 136–42.

119 See W. H. Stevenson and H. E. Salter, *The early history of St John's College, Oxford*, OHS, n.s. 1 (1939), 133–6. In 1540 Paynell was presented to the rectory of Cottingham and he became rector of All Hallows, Honey Lane, in London, in 1545 in succession to another former canon of Merton. He was also a chaplain to the king.

120 *MLGB*, 193–4.

121 Leland's list has been edited by D. N. Bell, in CBMLC III. Z26.

1630s as a payment for debt.[122] It is not possible to establish Manley's identity,[123] but his list shows an interest in theology and biblical interpretation with a strong emphasis on the Fathers. Indeed, this list provides a fascinating contrast with the bio-bibliographical bias in Leland's list of books at Warden. With one exception, every title noted by Leland was chosen because it was written by an English author – Gilbert of Hoyland, Odo of Canterbury, Nicholas Stanford, *ps*. Robert Grosseteste, Thomas Waleys, Alcuin, Richard Pluto, and Godfrey of Winchester. The single overlap, MS B. 4. 32 (Alcuin's *Interrogationes et responsiones in Genesim* and other works), emphasises the difference: it appealed to Leland because the author was British; for Manley it was important as a piece of biblical exegesis. In the two lists we also get a hint of what sorts of manuscripts would survive: Leland and his friends were collecting antiquarian material of patriotic and historical, sometimes legal, value; Manley and his like were preserving theology. Taken together, these lists bear out Ker's observation that 'the kinds of books which had on the whole the best chance of surviving were historical, patristic, and biblical, and mainly of the twelfth and thirteenth centuries'.[124]

122 See Gaskell, *Trinity College Library*, 83–4.

123 He does not appear to have been a monk at the time of the Dissolution and his name does not appear in any of the published parish registers of Old Warden. (I thank Julian Harrison for his assistance in this matter.)

124 Ker, 'The migration of manuscripts', 464.

11

Extending the frontiers: scholar collectors

JULIAN ROBERTS

The collectors whose achievements are described in this chapter possess some or all of a number of qualities which enable them to be seen as the creators for the first time in England of libraries as opposed to collections of books. The notion of extending has been deliberately introduced into the title, and it is size, generated particularly by the development of printing, which is the most obvious quality which these collections have in common. The collectors will be perceived not only to have crossed the physical dimension of owning 1,000, 2,000 or 3,000 volumes, but an intellectual dimension in which the possible interests or research needs of a single individual have been exceeded; posterity and a future scholarly community have been envisaged.

The phrase 'for the first time' must immediately be qualified. A library embodies an agreement, tacit or explicit, to hold books in common for mutual and future benefit. This is not a novel idea in the sixteenth century; community, direction and anticipation appeared in the creation and enlargement of monastic libraries, certainly after the Norman Conquest. After the dissolution of the monasteries, however, these concepts had to be reinvented, often in a secular context. Renaissance England, in common with other European countries, did indeed reinvent them, with one vital difference: the availability, from the mid-fifteenth century, of books which could be multiplied indefinitely through the art of printing.

At the beginning of the period, there is something tentative and experimental about a library; at the end of it, founding a library is a normal and natural aspect of the scholarly behaviour of our collectors. Nevertheless, the Civil Wars seem to have brought new uncertainties into their plans for the future. Richard Holdsworth, who died in 1649, seems to have had a clearer vision than John Selden, who accumulated books on a comparable scale, but who died five years after him.

This chapter will begin by considering the common factors in the collecting of those who may be said to have extended the frontiers. It will then consider in greater detail the creation, use and fate of individual libraries.

The most immediate distinction of these libraries is their size. It would clearly be wrong to put a lower limit on the number of books in a collection destined to become a library. Nevertheless, it will be seen that most of them can be shown to have contained 1,000 or more books. Sir Robert Cotton, otherwise exemplifying every quality to be sought in the pioneering creator of a library, did in fact own fewer than 1,000 manuscripts; but he also owned an indeterminate and less well-documented number of printed books.

More important than a shelf-count is the simple fact that by the middle of the sixteenth century it was possible for one man to accumulate more books than one man needed in the course of his own intellectual inquiry. The history of libraries is full of those who brought together specialised collections of books clearly of value in their profession; doctors – such as the Cambridge physicians John Hatcher and Thomas Lorkin[1] – and lawyers had large collections relevant to their professional practice. Leedham-Green notes that Lorkin had a gentleman's collection, moving beyond his medical preoccupations. But if there is much evidence of intellectual inquiry, not only by our subjects but by those whom they envisaged as taking advantage of their provision for research, there is very little evidence of bibliophily. The size of English collections may approach that of the more numerous contemporary French collections, but our collectors, while they might personalise their books, with a very few exceptions, took no great pleasure in beautiful books in beautiful bindings.

The extent to which the frontiers of learning were being pushed back is perhaps most evident at the end of our period, when, for example, Archbishop William Laud employed his political power to make the merchants of the Levant Company bring back Arabic books, which were destined for his university; he did not himself understand the language. John Selden seems to have had an interest in printing in exotic languages, which were beyond even his linguistic competence.

Perhaps beyond the scope of this chapter is the consideration of the historical perspective of collectors. Systematic possession of manuscripts certainly indicates a knowledge that the written text antedated the printed, and might thus claim a greater authority. Yet one must wait, in England at least, for the appearance of Humfry Wanley for the establishment of a more sophisticated

1 *BCI*, I. 367–82, 492–508.

and scholarly understanding of the relative age and authority of handwritten texts. Britain and Ireland were also home to at least three languages with an exceptionally long written history. Acquaintance with the history of the book was perhaps equally uncertain. In 1583, John Dee – or his cataloguer, Andreas Fremonsheim – designated incunabula as '*vetust*'. Somewhat later, two major collectors, Holdsworth and Selden, both owned significant numbers of fifteenth-century books, and, since English books were then more accessible than foreign books, we probably owe to them the preservation of a significant part of the nation's literary and bibliographical heritage.

In the mid-sixteenth century the status of books in English was low in contrast with that of books in the 'learned languages'. John Rastell, an owner and a printer of English books, makes the point:

> For though many make bokys yet unneth ye shall
> In our englyshe tonge fynde any warkys
> Of connynge that is regardyd by clerkys.[2]

This may also have been true for collectors of books in other European vernaculars, such as Jacques-Auguste de Thou,[3] though attempts were made to approximate them to the learned languages, for example by Joachim du Bellay in his *Defence et illustration de la langue françoise* (1561). The defenders of the English language followed, and the Welsh language was also celebrated with Renaissance rhetoric by John Davies of Mallwyd.

It is characteristic of the period 1550–1640 that the proportion of English books in libraries gradually rises from the negligible to the dominant, and with this growth goes the readiness to record the presence of books in English in collections. John Dee in 1583 was unusual in according the same degree of cataloguing detail to his weightiest volumes in the learned languages as to his most ephemeral publications in English.

The ordered accumulation of large numbers of learned books called for established lines of supply of books printed abroad. The 'Latin trade', particularly important in the growth of learned libraries, has already been described in the relevant volumes of *The Cambridge history of the book in Britain*. In brief, there existed a group of specialised booksellers, usually working through the port of Antwerp and, after that port was closed, through lesser Flemish, Dutch and German ports, drawing their stock largely from the biannual Frankfurt fairs, and after 1564 making use of the printed fair catalogues and the

2 R. Axton (ed.), *Three Rastell plays* (Cambridge, 1979), 33.

3 A. Coron, '"Ut prosint aliis"; Jacques-Auguste de Thou et sa bibliothèque', in *Hbf* II. 101–25.

London reprints of them. Collectors who are known to have possessed or used these catalogues include John Dee, Archbishop Tobie Matthew, Archbishop James Ussher and John Selden. The set in the Bodleian derives partly from Robert Burton, and partly from those used within the library. Most of those engaged in the import of printed books were at first aliens (though William Caxton was a substantial importer), the Birckmanns of Cologne, Ascanius de Renialme, his stepson James Rimius and his apprentice Adrian Marius. The participation of aliens was, in theory, limited to wholesaling under the Act concerning the printers and binders of books of 1534. At the turn of the seventeenth century, native English booksellers, such as John Norton, John Bill (who worked for Sir Thomas Bodley) and Henry Fetherstone, came to dominate the trade.

Essential, however, to the planned growth of the kind of libraries we are considering was the ability to buy older, second-hand books. At first this branch of the trade seems not to have been highly regarded, but a considerable trade became concentrated in parts of London, such as Duck Lane and Little Britain, and in the university cities. Provenances common to Holdsworth and Selden suggest that both frequented the same London bookshops. Robert Beaumont of Little Britain was named in Holdsworth's will as 'trusty', and as a cataloguer of his books. Holdsworth also named Robert Littlebury, a servant of Laurence Sadler of Duck Lane.[4]

Libraries have already been characterised as the result of an agreement to hold books in common, in perpetuity. The extent to which these early libraries grew, and developed into places of research, is described elsewhere in this volume. There is thus nothing new in the emergence of libraries as opposed to collections of books, before 1540 – particularly since books as vehicles of learning were largely concentrated in the hands of religious, who were, in theory, inhibited from owning personal property. The dissolution of the monasteries, and the dispersal of their libraries, represented an erasure of the national memory, but did not entail a complete discontinuity with the past, because the Anglican cathedrals retained, in some important instances, their pre-Reformation collections (though they were often, to their loss, visited by the 'new' collectors whose activities will be described later). Some, indeed, enlarged their libraries; Bishop Edmund Geste (d. 1577) bequeathed his library to Salisbury Cathedral. There were also those curious survivors from a semi-monastic past, the colleges of Oxford and Cambridge, and it is noticeable how often, in the succeeding centuries, the libraries of these corporations became

4 Oates, *CUL*, 309.

the beneficiaries of gifts and bequests, not only from alumni and other secular donors but also from a still largely celibate clergy.[5]

The collectors of books and creators of libraries whose work is described in this chapter were all collectors of manuscripts, many of which derived from monastic libraries, though not directly. The question must be asked, 'Why did this not happen earlier?' Why, between the dissolutions of 1536–41 and the *Supplication* of John Dee in 1556, was no one – with the exceptions of John Leland and the King's Commissioner, Sir John Prise – eagerly taking significant numbers of books off the unguarded monastic shelves into his own library? Or, as John Bale wrote in 1549, 'If there had bene in euery shyre of Englande, but one solempne lybrary, to the preseruacyon of these noble workes and preferrement of good lernynges in oure posteryte, it had been yet sumwhat.'[6] The date of Bale's preface to Leland's *The laboryouse journey* (1549) narrows the dates between which Bale could have rescued monastic books from the ignoble uses which he vividly describes. Was there, however briefly, an intellectual fashion, perhaps linked to Protestant humanism, when these books were despised, unless they could be used to prove a doctrinal point?

For the royal library (whose fortunes are described elsewhere), whatever its purpose, was not the 'solempne lybrary' for which Bale called. It was an issue-driven library – or libraries – and the dominating issues under Henry VIII were the King's Great Matter, his divorce and, subsequently, the royal supremacy. Much of it remained for George II to give to the nation, but there are enough strays from it to suggest that it also served as a quarry for opportunistic courtiers and officials from Sir Thomas Pope through Archbishop Bancroft to John Selden.[7] While Henry VIII and his successors did not lack advice, there is no statement from the library's proprietors or custodians of what they thought its functions were, and any direction or purpose they imparted must be sought in its accessions and inferred from its catalogues. Historians of the royal library are on much firmer ground with the coming of the more bookish James I and VI and his elder son.

5 A number of such bequests, including those of Parker, Perne and Whitgift, are listed in J. C. T. Oates, 'The libraries of Cambridge, 1570–1700', in Wormald and Wright, *English library*, 213–15, 217–18. Oxford collegiate bequests include those of Archbishop Edmund Grindal to Queen's College and the purchase of Bishop John Jewel's library by Magdalen College in 1572.

6 Quoted in Wormald and Wright, *English libraries*, 153, from Bale's 1549 edition of Leland's *The laboryouse Journey & serche of Johan Leylande for Englandes Antiquitees*.

7 Bancroft's depredations, which were deplored shortly after his death by the royal librarian Patrick Young, are described by James Carley, '"A great gatherer together of books"', *Lambeth Palace Library Annual Review* (2001), 51–5.

If the royal library in the intervening period proves to be little more than a receptacle – albeit, as Professor Birrell has shown, a very interesting receptacle[8] – for the books which preoccupied or interested royalty, that period is also richer in statements of purpose in the creation of libraries. In reprinting John Dee's *Supplication* of 1556 to Queen Mary, Andrew Watson and I attempted to show that while the *Supplication* was addressed to those who were, within two years, to lose political power by death or deposition, Dee himself was able to achieve something of what he had urged upon the queen.[9] By 1556 there was perhaps common ground between Catholics – in Dee's case, a temporary and accommodating Catholic – and reformers, about the shame and loss brought by the dispersal of the monastic libraries. Dee combines a lament for destruction comparable in sentiment, if not in eloquence, with that of Bale, with a search for dispersed monuments and their restitution (if possible) for their placing and copying within a furnished royal library and for the copying of similar monuments in libraries overseas, notably those in Italy. Dee's provisions also include the importation of printed books 'which likewise shall be gotten in wonderfull abundance'. It was this wonderful abundance that was to mark the growth of libraries in the century after Dee's *Supplication*. The tentative and uncertain development of the royal library is in strong contrast to the assured statements of Thomas Bodley and the archbishops Bancroft and Abbot, and to the actions of Archbishop Laud in support of Bodley's foundation. The founding of Sion College Library suggests that by 1623 (the date of Thomas White's will, under which the college was set up) the augmentation of a college with a library was a normal development.[10]

A recurrent theme of statements of the purpose of libraries is that of the recovery of knowledge that once existed and has been lost or deliberately concealed. The Renaissance and the Reformation both presuppose such a loss; a mark of the Renaissance is the quest for texts of the Greek and Latin classics and for a perfect rendering – and even pronunciation – of the languages; while the Reformation and Counter-Reformation seek the 'original' text and interpretation of the Scriptures, and the interpretation of them, by writers as near as possible to the time of Christ. Bodley's first librarian, Thomas James, was perhaps the most extreme exponent of the belief that these texts had been deliberately corrupted by his Catholic opponents. English libraries had been unsuccessfully and half-heartedly searched for classical survivals in the fifteenth century, and John Dee was unusual (and almost certainly wrong) in believing

8 T. A. Birrell, *English monarchs and their books: from Henry VIII to Charles II* (London, 1987).
9 J. Roberts and A. G. Watson (eds.), *John Dee's library catalogue* (London, 1990).
10 E. H. Pearce, *Sion College and library* (Cambridge, 1913), 17.

that Cicero's much-sought *De republica* had survived at Canterbury.[11] Serious English quest for classical manuscripts was largely a thing of the future, but William Laud actively sought for Greek Orthodox, Hebrew and Arabic books through expanding English trade links, and Selden seems to have been aware of a frontier beyond even the Christian and Islamic East. Although the libraries of the period – notably Dee's, Lumley's and Perne's – were rich in material in the natural sciences, there is little intimation that it might be possible to know things which Aristotle had not known.

The possession of manuscripts was, then, a factor common to all the scholar collectors of this period. This is hardly surprising, since most of the collectors were of an antiquarian cast of mind, sharing a sense of regret at the spoiling of the monastic libraries, and having similar views on the importance of Greek and Latin culture, and the witness of antiquity to the Christian faith. Most of the manuscripts were at first from English sources, though the subjects might vary from the historical and theological collections of Parker, Cotton and Perne; Dee's had a 'scientific' bent, with an interest in Roger Bacon, and it is also possible to detect a 'British' (that is, Welsh) strain in it.[12] He was baffled by his 'arabick book' or 'Book of Soyga'.[13] If it was indeed an Arabic book, it would not have perplexed the next generation of scholars. A realisation of the importance of early manuscripts in English was also common to these scholar collectors; it would perhaps have been better for the preservation of literature in English if women, less overawed by the dominance of classical culture, had held more economic and educational power. The English and Italian books of Elizabeth Grey, countess of Kent, formed a distinct part of the library of John Selden as it was inventoried in 1654.

While Dee foresaw the arrival of printed books on a large scale, and himself kept and catalogued books of all sizes and subject-matter (with the curious exception of the religious and devotional books which he must have possessed), he and his fellow collectors do not seem to have regarded large books as more appropriate to libraries than small ones. Andrew Perne is the exception, discriminating in his will against books in octavo and decimosexto as not proper to a library.[14] Perne was also unusual among scholar collectors in the embellishment, modest though it was, which he applied to his books. Although

11 Dee's *Supplication*, in Roberts and Watson, *John Dee's library catalogue*, 194.

12 R. J. Roberts, 'John Dee and the matter of Britain', *Transactions of the Honourable Society of Cymmrodorion* (1991), 129–43.

13 Roberts and Watson, *John Dee's library catalogue*, DM166 and *Additions and corrections*, 4.

14 E. S. Leedham-Green, 'Perne's wills', in D. McKitterick (ed.), *Andrew Perne: quatercentenary studies* (Cambridge, 1991), 105.

his library was shown to the French ambassador in 1571 as the 'worthiest in all England',[15] the ambassador might well have thought its appearance more monochrome than the collections he had known at home. Only the royal library, intermittently, and relatively small-scale collectors, such as Thomas Wotton or Robert Dudley, earl of Leicester, could have made any display for their friends to enjoy.[16] The use of the tag *et amicorum*, with its connotation of display and humanistic community, is relatively uncommon in England.[17]

The presence of artefacts other than manuscripts and books has been discussed in several articles in the *Histoire des bibliothèques françaises*. The impact of the Renaissance on France was certainly sharper than upon England, and was intensified by French incursions into Italy in the late fifteenth century. Jean Grolier's library is, bibliographically, only the most obvious example of this impact.[18] English collectors had had, up to this period, fewer opportunities to acquire the monuments of the classical past. There were, simply, fewer relics of the Roman empire in Britain than in France, and the thoroughness of the Anglo-Saxon cultural impact upon lowland Britain obliterated most of what remained, so that Sir Thomas Browne could write in *Hydriotaphia* in 1658 that the funeral urns of Norfolk had survived 'the drums and tramplings of three conquests'. Andrew Perne's library – its owner never ventured abroad – contained a 'longe box of Antiquities' and coins.[19] Cotton, in William Camden's company, travelled in 1600 to the Roman military zone around Hadrian's Wall, bringing many inscriptions back, not to his library in Westminster, but to his manor at Conington. But as David McKitterick points out, 'in forming collections of coins and inscriptions, to accompany his manuscripts and printed books, he was assembling a library in which each of these various forms was expected to complement the others'.[20] Selden, likewise, owned Greek inscriptions and sculpture, which he bequeathed to Oxford University.[21] Many, if not all, of these he owed to the quest for antiquities in Asia Minor, in which English diplomats, such as Sir Thomas Roe, and merchants were involved in the first

15 Oates, *CUL*, 92.
16 H. M. Nixon and M. M. Foot, *The history of decorated bookbinding in England* (Oxford, 1992), 33–6.
17 G. D. Hobson, 'Et amicorum', *Library*, 5th ser., 4 (1949), 87–99. Some further English examples are given by David Pearson, *Provenance research in book history: a handbook* (London, 1998), 25.
18 H. M. Nixon, *Bookbindings from the library of Jean Grolier* (London, 1965), xi–xii.
19 Leedham-Green, 'Perne's wills', 112.
20 D. McKitterick, 'From Camden to Cambridge: Sir Robert Cotton's Roman inscriptions, and their subsquent treatment', in C. J. Wright (ed.), *Sir Robert Cotton as collector* (London, 1997), 105.
21 J. Selden, *Opera omnia*, ed. D Wilkins (London, 1726), I. liii.

half of the seventeenth century. It is often difficult to distinguish, within the various national and academic collections, which coins derive from collectors such as Perne and Cotton. Archbishop Laud certainly regarded coins as proper objects of collection in a library, since among his gifts to the Bodleian were five cabinets of coins in 1636.[22] Some at least of the coins collected at this time were of local origin; Sir Thomas Browne's *Hydriotaphia* demonstrates that finds of coins were common, and treasure-hunting is a recurrent theme in John Dee's *Diaries*.

The statements of intent with which scholar collectors inaugurated their libraries, or with which they sought to secure their future, have already been mentioned. John Bale's backward-looking call for 'in euery shyre of Englande but one solempne lybrary' is perhaps the earliest, and contrasts with the confident tone of Dee's *Supplication* of 1556. The latter has the ring of a plausible and well-connected young man, drawing a line under the tragic events of the previous twenty years, writing, probably, from the household of the bishop of London, Edmund Bonner, and ready to enlist not only his support, but that of the queen and the cardinal archbishop of Canterbury. The *Supplication* embraced either the restitution of 'monuments' to their previous possessors, or their copying, and the placing of original or copy in the queen's library. There was to be a wider role for Dee himself in that his travel to the great libraries of Europe would be financed, and that from these travels further copies would flow into the royal library, and that these copies would be accompanied by the importation of abundant printed books.

We attempted to show, in our edition of his library catalogue, that although Dee's ambitions for the royal library were frustrated by the death of the queen and cardinal, and by the deposition of Bonner, he nevertheless attempted, in the formation of his own library, to carry out something of what he had urged upon the queen.[23] The facsimile of the catalogue showed that in 1583 Dee owned nearly 300 manuscripts. We believed that this part of the catalogue was incomplete, and that a further 169 could be associated with him; this figure, though again incomplete, is lower than the thousand that Dee claimed to own. Many of these were of monastic or collegiate origin, and those from the latter source were often acquired by what would now be called scrounging. By comparison with other contemporary collectors, Dee collected little theology

22 Macray, 84.

23 We did not know, when we discussed Dee's intentions in our edition of the library catalogue, that Dee had in fact visited Rome in July 1563, a fact revealed in his annotations to Ramusio's *Navigationi* (no. 273, copy in TCD). He would at least have run less risk as a relapsed heretic in 1563.

(or more accurately, if he did, it does not appear in the catalogue), in either manuscript or printed form. He favoured natural philosophy, including Roger Bacon and the Merton school, and alchemy. Research, largely subsequent to the publication of the library catalogue, revealed the depth of his interest in Welsh ('British') history, and in the great fabrication of Geoffrey of Monmouth.[24] The printed books numbered, in 1583, nearly 2,300, a large number of which he took with him on his travels of 1583–9. These returned with him, apparently intact; but we were unable to identify any survivors from the books he might have been expected to acquire on his travels. His library suffered during his absence from the depredations of John Davis and Nicholas Saunder; ironically, many of those stolen by Saunder have survived in the library of the Royal College of Physicians.

Dee's methods of acquisition of manuscripts, somewhat crudely characterised above, may well have been employed in accordance with his *Supplication* to Queen Mary of 1556. The purchase of printed books is more clearly illustrative of the sources open to an English collector who travelled abroad, and his useful early practice of dating and placing his purchases documents his movements from his Cambridge student days, through the Netherlands and France in 1548–51, back to London, and his travels in the Netherlands and Italy in 1562–4. His booksellers in London included the major importing house of the Birckmanns of Cologne.

The absence of theology among his books has already been noted. His principal interests have been the subjects of two excellent studies.[25] The catalogue of 1583 suggests that his *externa bibliotheca* was divided first between bound and unbound books, and then by size; but some sub-headings, such as 'Historici libri ad navigationem pertinentes',[26] 'Paracelsici libri', 'Hebraici, chaldaici & syriaci libri, &c.', in the catalogue, must indicate a particular interest.

Although he owned, at least before the 1583 raid on his library, scientific and navigational instruments, at no time does he mention coins or other antiquities. He left, apparently, no will; his library became, upon or even before his death in 1609, in some way, and perhaps in return for financial support,

24 Roberts, 'John Dee and the matter of Britain', 129–43; R. G. Gruffydd and R. J. Roberts, 'John Dee's additions to William Salesbury's Dictionary', *Transactions of the Honourable Society of Cymmrodorion*, n.s. 7 (2001), 19–43.

25 N. H. Clulee, *John Dee's natural philosophy: between science and religion* (London and New York, 1988); W. H. Sherman, *John Dee: the politics of reading and writing in the English Renaissance* (Amherst, MA, 1995).

26 It is curious that two relevant books, recently discovered, and very heavily annotated, were not placed in this section. These are Ramusio (above, n. 23), and no. 1101, F. Colombo (copy in BL).

the property of his heir John Pontois, and the only indication of his intentions was a statement that some of his 'monuments' were destined for the Tower.[27] The lack of a will seems, upon Pontois's death in 1624, to have given rise to litigation (between whom, we do not know). This was evidently settled, to permit first the acquisition of some books by Pontois's own heirs, John Woodall and Patrick Saunders, and secondly an open sale by London booksellers, at which Sir Robert Cotton, Brian Twyne, Archbishop James Ussher, Richard Holdsworth, John Selden and other collectors were eager participants.

The text of Dee's *Supplication* was in Cotton's library (MS Vitellius C. vii, fols. 310–11) and it may have coloured the petition which Cotton himself drew up in the later years of Queen Elizabeth, at approximately the same stage in his life. This is discussed below.

There seems, however, to be no connection between the proposals in the *Supplication* of 1556, and the measures associated with the circle of Archbishop Matthew Parker in the next reign. Dee's position in Bonner's household can hardly have endeared him to the reformers. The holdings of manuscripts which Dee's collecting, scrupulous or otherwise, had left him, were evidently unknown to John Bale when, in 1560, he replied to a letter, now lost, 'concernynge bokes of Antiquite, not printed'.[28] Less than a year after his consecration, Parker had received through the queen a request from the Magdeburg Centuriators regarding historical materials in England relating to church history and church councils. The extent of Bale's knowledge and his efforts as a collector of manuscripts 'in tyme of the lamentable spoyle of the lybraryes of Englande' were evidently already known to Parker. Bale's long letter to him of 30 July 1560[29] lists both his own – which he had lost in Ireland – and those that he knew to be in the hands of other collectors; the theme of books held by private persons, who might conceal them for reasons of religious or political disaffection, is a recurrent motif in the documents by Dee, by Bale, and later by Cotton.

The scope and success, albeit limited, achieved by the initiatives of Parker and his circle by the time of his death in 1575 are amply described elsewhere.[30] The weight and significance of these initiatives lay in their coming from the archbishop himself, at the centre of government. They were backed by a letter from the Privy Council of 7 July 1568, which proclaimed the queen's interest

27 Roberts and Watson, *Dee's catalogue*, 197.

28 T. Graham and A. G. Watson, *The recovery of the past in early Elizabethan England: documents by John Bale and John Joscelyn from the circle of Matthew Parker* (Cambridge, 1998).

29 CUL, MS Add. 7489: Graham and Watson, *The recovery of the past*, 17–30.

30 See below, chapter 12.

and the archbishop's special care for them. Their direction is clear from the lists of sources for Anglo-Saxon and medieval English history drawn up by John Joscelyn, Parker's chaplain and secretary by 1567,[31] and by the texts published under Parker's direction.[32]

What is significant for the history of libraries is that, from these initiatives, two libraries in Cambridge became the recipients of the manuscripts and books that formed an essential part of these activities. Despite the Privy Council's concern, there was to be no national repository for nearly 200 years. The security that lay in the colleges of the universities and their efficacy as repositories during the later sixteenth century have already been noted. It was to the college, Corpus Christi, of which he had been master, that Parker looked for the preservation of his library. But not wholly; Parker's support had also been enlisted by Andrew Perne, master of Peterhouse, for the restoration of Cambridge University Library, and Parker's gift in 1574 of twenty-five manuscripts and seventy-five printed books was, as much as his greater benefaction to his college, a sign that the libraries of a university were, in default of a national collection, to be the proper and permanent custodians of the national memory. Perne's own collecting, and the consideration that he gave to its ultimate bestowal, were confirmations of this sign. The printed books given by Parker and others in 1574 were, as Oates points out, the first that the University Library had received since 1529.[33]

Andrew Perne is, in many ways, paradigmatic of the scholar collector and library-creator of the sixteenth century.[34] Possessed of ample financial means, he accumulated a very large number of books, many in subjects unconnected with his apparent immediate needs and interests; indeed, he published little, being responsible only for the translation of Ecclesiastes and the Song of Solomon in the Bishops' Bible of 1568. He had a care for the manuscript legacy, probably preserving on his own shelves such manuscripts as remained from the gifts and bequest by Walter Crome to the University Library in the previous century. Yet by far the larger part of his library was printed, deriving both from the local trade and from his contacts with the principal importers of foreign learned books, among them the Birckmanns of Cologne.[35] His concern that Lord Lumley's gifts towards Oxford University's library should not be overgenerous was in an enduring Cambridge tradition.[36] Posterity now sees in Perne's concern for continuity and stability in his university something more

31 Graham and Watson, *The recovery of the past*, 55–109. 32 See below, 335–6.
33 Oates, *CUL*, 97. 34 This account is greatly indebted to McKitterick, *Andrew Perne*.
35 D. McKitterick, 'Andrew Perne and his books', in McKitterick, *Andrew Perne*, 44.
36 Oates, *CUL*, 148.

estimable than some of his contemporaries saw. These qualities were indeed essential for the development of libraries.

David McKitterick notes the wide extent of Perne's collections in theology, and in particular his study of Melanchthon's Greek and Latin Bible of 1545, yet Perne's published output is very limited in subject, by contrast with his ownership of many contemporary scientific, medical and topographical works. Though he owned scientific instruments, and seems to have dabbled in medicine, he never travelled abroad, and it is difficult to avoid the conclusion that Perne was creating a general library of that learning which seemed important to him, and that he was seeking some form of permanence for it. His will is clearly the result of a long process of decision;[37] a new library was to be built for Peterhouse, and it was to contain 'one of the best and largest sort of all my books of divinitie Lawe, Physicke or of any other Sciences that I haue at Cambridge in folio & in quarto of every sort of Authors'. The duplicates, and smaller books, 'not so meete for a library', were left to his nephew, while 'all the old doctors and Histories that I haue in written Hande' were left to the University Library. Perne was thus making a distinction between a working scholarly library of large books, proper to his college, and the University Library as a repository of manuscripts.

The growth, development, use and ultimate disposal of the library of Sir Robert Cotton are together a topic of such major importance in the history of English libraries in this period that separate treatment is warranted. Yet any statement of intent in the creation of a scholarly library may be considered here. Dee's intentions at the age of twenty-nine can be ascertained from his *Supplication* (though his final intentions, if any, are deeply obscure), whereas Perne's can be divined only from his actions and from his will. Cotton was perhaps about the same age as Dee when he drew up his petition to Queen Elizabeth 'for the erecting of her library and an academy'.[38] Colin Tite suggests that Cotton had begun to acquire manuscripts in 1588,[39] and that the foundation of the first Society of Antiquaries took place in 1586, when Cotton was at Cambridge. The petitioner seems to envisage the elevation of the society into an academy, with a governor or president, two annually elected guardians of the library, and a number of fellows. The library would include not only books concerning history and antiquity from the existing royal library and books now in the hands of private gentlemen, but 'other excellent monuments whereof there is no record now extant'. The academy would have (in contrast with

37 Leedham-Green, 'Perne's wills', 79–119.

38 BL, MS Cotton Faustina E. v, fols. 89–90.

39 C. G. C. Tite, *The manuscript library of Sir Robert Cotton* (London, 1994), 5.

the contemporary Society of Antiquaries) a corporate existence and premises; Cotton suggests that space might be found in the Savoy, or in the late dissolved monastery of St John of Jerusalem. In its corporate status, it would not be hurtful to either of the universities, because it would be concerned for the preservation of history and antiquity, and would not meddle with the arts, philosophy or other university matters.

Although the queen, like her sister before her, was not to be persuaded, Cotton's petition, with its emphasis on the manuscript book, on history and antiquities, and on the service that might be done to the Crown, does bear a notable resemblance to what Cotton himself achieved. Unlike Dee and Perne, he paid little attention to the printed book. He certainly did own them, one iron press and nine presses of them,[40] but their nature and whereabouts are largely unknown.[41]

Cotton's reluctance for his proposed academy to usurp the functions of the universities is in ironical contrast with what Perne had attempted to do, with limited success, for Cambridge, and with what Thomas Bodley was at that very time forcefully setting up for Oxford. Another bequest which perhaps illustrates the relative value placed upon manuscripts and printed books (quite unlike Perne's tripartite distinction) was that of Archbishop John Whitgift in 1604.[42] More than one third of the 150 manuscripts left by Whitgift to Trinity College, Cambridge, came from the library of his own cathedral at Canterbury. Philip Gaskell comments, 'In removing Canterbury manuscripts to Cambridge, Whitgift followed the example of Archbishop Parker. No doubt the two archbishops – and Dean Nevile after them – believed that Canterbury's monastic books would be safer in academic libraries in Cambridge.' Whitgift's bequest also included a number of manuscripts from Buildwas Abbey.[43] Whitgift's printed books remained at Lambeth, somehow to be incorporated in the library founded there by his successor, Richard Bancroft.

Perne's ambivalent support for university and college was not emulated by Thomas Bodley. Bodley had been a scholar at Magdalen and a fellow of Merton. Although he was in sufficient awe of the warden of Merton, Sir Henry Savile, to press his librarian Thomas James to waive the prohibition on lending from the library in favour of Savile,[44] it was to the vice-chancellor that his offer

40 C. G. C. Tite, 'A catalogue of Sir Robert Cotton's printed books?', in Wright, *Sir Robert Cotton as collector*, 183–93.

41 The matter is currently under further investigation by Colin Tite.

42 P. Gaskell, *Trinity College Library: the first 150 years* (Cambridge, 1980).

43 J. M. Sheppard, *The Buildwas books* (Oxford, 1997).

44 G. W. Wheeler (ed.), *Letters of Sir Thomas Bodley to Thomas James* (Oxford, 1926), 43, 174, 196.

of refounding the library was made, and it was the university as a whole which was the unequivocal target of his energies and his generosity. The history of the refoundation of Oxford University's library is properly a part of that of academic libraries. But the impact of Bodley's intentions was upon a national scale, and these at least must be considered here. In contrast to the intentions of other creators of libraries, Bodley's purposes are well known, both from his brief autobiography[45] and from his letters to Thomas James. Both Bodley and James came from families which had taken refuge abroad during the Catholic reaction under Queen Mary in centres of protestant and humanist printing, and although the library was from the outset ecumenical in its holdings, if not in its direction, the emphasis was on the creation of a great printed library. But the very visibility and evident permanence of the Bodleian, in a building that had once housed a major collection of manuscripts, ensured that it would be seen also as a safe repository for manuscripts rescued from the dispersals of the early sixteenth century. The presence of Thomas Allen of Gloucester Hall, a great collector of monastic and college manuscripts, on the university's committee to oversee the refoundation of its library, perhaps symbolises the direction the library was to take.[46] Bodley himself did not think it necessary that manuscripts and printed books should be shelved separately.

The vigour of Bodley's approach is nowhere better seen than in his robust use of the import trade. Of our collectors, Dee and Perne had been involved in more ways than one with the Latin traders. Bodley's requirements, however, involved the native Englishmen John Norton and John Bill, who were becoming increasingly expert in the field; he was not merely a recipient and reader of Frankfurt Fair catalogues, as contemporary collectors like Robert Burton and Archbishop Matthew were, but, in true diplomatic style, dispatched booksellers on errands – John Bill's risky journey to Seville is an example. The resources he provided for his library – before they were eroded by the Civil War – enabled the Bodleian curators and librarians not only to use regular trade sources but to call on the expertise of wide-ranging Latin traders such as Henry Fetherstone, Robert Martin, George Thomason and Humphrey Robinson.[47] It is notorious that Bodley was blind to the importance of books from England. The idea of the deposit agreement of 1610 with the Stationers' Company of London came, not from Bodley himself, but from the librarian, Thomas

45 *The life of Sr Thomas Bodley . . . Written by himselfe* (Oxford, 1647).

46 A. G. Watson, 'Thomas Allen of Oxford and his manuscripts', in Parkes and Watson, *Medieval scribes*, 279–314.

47 J. Roberts, 'Importing books for Oxford, 1500–1640', in Carley and Tite, *Books and collectors*, 317–33.

James. Despite Bodley's expressed contempt for English books, the years after his death in 1613 were to see not only the more open policies of the second librarian, John Rouse, but a dramatic rise in the proportion of English books in the college libraries of Oxford and Cambridge.[48]

Only rarely did Bodley's persistence fail him. The royal library, so long a quarry for enterprising collectors, had at last acquired an active custodian; Bodley informed James that his attempts to secure manuscripts from that source had been frustrated by Sir Peter Young.[49]

The series of printed catalogues initiated under Bodley's direction in 1605, and continued as author catalogues from 1620, was an abiding influence in English librarianship. The size to which his foundation grew, and the breadth of its collections, meant that its catalogues, annotated or interleaved, could be used in other and later institutions. The first catalogue to pay the Bodleian the compliment of imitation, even in small matters of layout and typography, was John Spencer's *Catalogus universalis librorum omnium in bibliotheca Collegii Sionii apud Londinenses* in 1650.

Other frontiers were being crossed. Travellers abroad, notably both clerical and secular diplomats, had used their journeys to buy manuscripts and books on a generous scale, no doubt aware of the deficiencies of the English book trade. John Dee's presence in the Low Countries in 1562–4 enabled him to build one of the largest collections of Hebrew books and manuscripts hitherto seen in England.[50] In the early years of the seventeenth century the appetite of English collectors for large-scale acquisitions abroad grew remarkably, and was sustained by the ability of the university libraries to receive and house them. Libraries also became a valued commodity, even as the booty of war. The earl of Essex seized the library of the bishop of Faro in 1596; it was soon transferred to Bodley's new library. That library was also to be enriched through William Laud's acquisition of booty derived from the pillaging of the Thirty Years War (and it was not the only library to do so). Similar grand acquisitions were made in the equally ambitious but more peaceful way of commerce. Henry Fetherstone, that master of the Latin trade, bought the manuscript collection of Giacomo Barocci at Venice, and William Laud persuaded the earl of Pembroke, Oxford University's chancellor, to give it to the Bodleian; similar gifts made to Cambridge University and to Sion College are described below.

48 *Computers and early books: report of the LOC Project*, table 4, 29.

49 Wheeler, *Letters of Bodley to James*, letter 155.

50 G. Lloyd Jones, *The discovery of Hebrew in Tudor England: a third language* (Manchester, 1983), 168–74, 275–7.

The investigations in the Christian East by Laud and his contemporaries should perhaps be viewed in the context of the efforts, discussed below, of Laud's predecessors in office to create a library for the see of Canterbury.

The library left by John, Lord Lumley, at the time of his death in 1609, is one of the best-documented of sixteenth-century libraries, both by the catalogue, so admirably edited in its 1609 version by Sears Jayne and Francis R. Johnson,[51] and by its survivors. It may well have been the largest. Yet although so much is known of the library and of its constituent parts, Lumley's own reticence has ensured that little is known of its purpose and use. Lumley wrote little, and published nothing, and it is unlikely that he, and impossible that any of the library's other creators (Thomas Cranmer, Henry Fitzalan, earl of Arundel, and Humphrey Llwyd), were in any way associated with the Elizabethan Society of Antiquaries, as Jayne and Johnson suggested.[52] It is only in the last decade of his life that Lumley seems to have manifested any purpose or destination for his library.

The earliest 'layer' in the Lumley library is that which originated with Thomas Cranmer, archbishop of Canterbury.[53] David Selwyn suggests that at the time of its confiscation in 1553, the library contained perhaps 700 printed books, a figure well in excess of the 585 books and seventy manuscripts which can be identified today. He attributes the discrepancy to the discarding of overtly protestant books by the strongly Catholic Arundel, when he acquired the library after its confiscation under Queen Mary. Cranmer had owned a significant number of manuscripts from religious houses such as Bath and Christ Church, Canterbury.

The printed books were largely theological – with a significant number of medical works – and were, typically, works of contemporarily published theology from continental sources. If Cranmer had owned protestant books in English, Arundel probably destroyed them. To the library which he thus acquired, Arundel added about 400 volumes described by Jayne and Johnson as 'representing three different interests. First and most important was his own acquisitive interest.' But he was also concerned for the education of his three children – including two daughters – in humanistic style; and they detect also an interest in military matters. Arundel evidently induced his son-in-law, John Lumley, to move from Lumley Castle, near Durham, into his newly completed Nonesuch Palace, where the latter lived until his death in 1609. The next component of the library now developed with Lumley's antiquarian and

51 S. Jayne and F. R. Johnson (eds.), *The Lumley library: the catalogue of 1609* (London, 1956).

52 Jayne and Johnson, *Lumley library*, 7.

53 D. G. Selwyn, *The library of Thomas Cranmer* (Oxford, 1996).

scientific interests being fostered alongside those of the young Welsh scholar Humphrey Llwyd, whom Arundel had brought to Nonesuch as his physician. Llwyd's own interests were, as his publications demonstrated, those of an antiquary, historian – he was a partisan of the 'British History' of Geoffrey of Monmouth – and topographer. Llwyd married Lumley's sister Barbara, and is said to have served as adviser in the accumulation of the Lumley library.[54] Given the congruence between the preoccupations of Lumley and his brother-in-law, this is likely, but the presence in the library of about seventy books bearing Llwyd's *ex libris* is more probably due to the provisions of Llwyd's will, made at his early death in his native Denbigh in 1568;[55] his books were to be kept for his children. Lumley is known to have helped his nephews financially, and they may well have passed on some of their father's books in return. The final 'layer' of books, and the largest, was that of Lumley's own. Jayne and Johnson quote the ownership – overwhelmingly Lumley's – of the 600 books in the 'Historici' section of the catalogue as evidence for his tastes and instincts. Large as was his medical collection, it was in fact dwarfed by John Dee's immense collection of 'Libri Paracelsici'.

Lumley's library was catalogued, probably by Anthony Alcock, in 1596, and the revelation of duplicates by this process led to the gifts to the libraries of the universities: eighty-nine folios to his own university of Cambridge in 1598, and thirty-four to Bodley's refounded library in 1599. This is the earliest hint of a destination for Lumley's books. Both Jayne and Johnson[56] and, later, Selwyn[57] agree on the probability of the gift of Lumley's library to Henry, Prince of Wales, and that this gift may have been stimulated by the attempts of Richard Bancroft, archbishop of Canterbury, towards the provision of a library for the prince. There is a slight incongruity in such a gift from an elderly Catholic nobleman to a prince who was widely seen as a future protestant champion (as there was also in the earlier gift by Lumley of patristic and medieval theology to the strongly protestant foundation of Emmanuel College, Cambridge),[58] but the religious difference may well have been outweighed by the appeal of the prince to the 'old Elizabethans', to whom his father was less congenial.[59]

54 Jayne and Johnson, *Lumley catalogue*, 6.

55 R. Geraint Gruffydd, 'Humphrey Llwyd: some documents and a catalogue', *Transactions of the Denbighshire Historical Society* 17 (1968), 54–107.

56 Jayne and Johnson, *Lumley catalogue*, 13–17.

57 Selwyn, *Library of Thomas Cranmer*, xxxi–xxxiii.

58 S. Bush Jr and C. J. Rasmussen, *The library of Emmanuel College, Cambridge, 1584–1637* (Cambridge, 1986), 14. There were twenty-five such books, all but one of which had belonged to Cranmer.

59 Lumley also gave books to Archbishop Bancroft; see Carley, '"A great gatherer together of books"', 57.

Prince Henry had the Alcock catalogue of 1596 copied, and, even during the remaining three years of the prince's life, specially built accommodation was created for it in St James's Palace,[60] where it continued to attract gifts to the Prince. After Henry's death in 1612, the library became part of, and suffered the vicissitudes of, the royal library, until it was presented to the new British Museum by George II in 1757.

While Archbishop Bancroft was campaigning for funds to establish a library for Prince Henry,[61] he was also building a library of his own at Lambeth, and drawing up a will (dated 28 October 1610), which left his books to his successor 'and to the Archbishops of Canterbury successively forever'.[62] His immediate successor, George Abbot, called him 'for many years a greate gatherer together of bookes', an epithet which suggests that the idea of a library for the see, though a new one, had been long in forming. Of Bancroft's immediate predecessors, such of Cranmer's books as survived were, as we have seen, in the Lumley library, recently in transit from Nonesuch to St James's Palace; some of Cardinal Pole's had been given by him or by his executor, Alvise Priuli, to New College, Oxford;[63] the passing of so many of Parker's and Grindal's books into the libraries of Cambridge and Oxford has already been noted. It seems, however, that, allowing for John Whitgift's substantial bequests of manuscripts to libraries in Cambridge, there still remained at Lambeth a large number of manuscripts and printed books. His library catalogue shows him to have had a printed library, and some part of it remained at Lambeth, somehow to be merged with that of his successor, Richard Bancroft.[64] During Whitgift's tenure, but whether by his own agency, or that of Bancroft (his chaplain, (1592) and successor (1604)) is unclear, there passed into the library at Lambeth portions of several eminent collections; those of John Foxe the martyrologist (d. 1587), Robert Dudley, earl of Leicester (d. 1588), and Sir Christopher Hatton (d. 1591).[65] Armorial bindings (in the case of Foxe) and the dates of death of the others suggest that Whitgift was the next owner of their books; but some, at least, were abstracted by Bancroft's chaplain, Samuel Harsnett (later

60 R. Strong, *Henry, Prince of Wales, and England's lost Renaissance* (London, 1986), 210.

61 Jayne and Johnson, *Lumley catalogue*, 16.

62 A. Cox-Johnson, 'Lambeth Palace Library 1610–1664', *TCBS* 2 (1954–8), 105–26.

63 R. W. Hunt, 'The medieval library', in J. Buxton and P. Williams (eds.), *New College, Oxford, 1379–1979* (Oxford, 1979), 336–7; J. Woolfson, 'Reginald Pole and his Greek manuscripts in Oxford, a reconsideration', *BLR* 17 (2000), 79–95.

64 W. O'Sullivan, 'Archbishop Whitgift's library catalogue', *Times Literary Supplement*, 3 August 1956, 468. The manuscript is TCD, MS E.4.13.

65 For Hatton's books, see W. O. Hassall, 'The books of Sir Christopher Hatton at Holkham', *Library*, 5th ser., 5 (1950–1), 1–13; and R. J. Roberts, 'Sir Christopher Hatton's book-stamps', *Library*, 5th ser., 12 (1957), 119–21; Carley, '"A great gatherer together of books"', 58.

archbishop of York), for the library he established at Colchester.[66] When the next archbishop, George Abbot, had followed Bancroft's precept in the framing of his own will of 25 July 1632, there were 6,065 of Bancroft's books and 2,667 of Abbot's books in the library.

Although Bancroft's will proclaimed his 'chiefest desire' that his books might remain to his successors, alternative provisions were laid down, that, if the bequest to them failed, the books should go to the king's intended college at Chelsea, or to Cambridge University. Cox-Johnson is probably correct in suggesting that the interest of Sir Francis Bacon and of the King himself (mentioned by Abbot) signified King James's own intention to use such a conveniently situated library. The catalogue compiled on Abbot's instructions, and dated 24 April 1612, is a shelf-list showing the books classified along the walls of the upper cloister. Theology, both Catholic and protestant, predictably formed the greatest part of the library, though there were large sections on 'Humanior Literatura' and in the 'Bibliotheca Historica'. Bancroft's manuscripts were apparently shelved separately. The recording of multiple copies among the 'Libri Liturgiarum Ponteficiarum' may mean that Bancroft preserved seized Catholic liturgical books, such as hours and breviaries; he certainly had a little section of 'Libri Puritanici' devoted to his other enemies. Here he kept the little books of the Family of Love, Marprelate tracts and 'Penry varia'. Abbot's books, when added to Bancroft's sequences, were fewer in number, but show that their owner had a greater interest in contemporary literature, and in books on France. He had only thirty-nine manuscripts beside Bancroft's 352.

William Laud, who succeeded Abbot as archbishop in 1633, seems hardly to have augmented the libraries of his predecessors; if he did, few books remain there. He may well have used the library that they left him, but all his own efforts were directed towards the support of the Bodleian Library in the university where he had been a head of house (St John's in 1611) and chancellor in 1629. His support was of an order that no English library had ever received before, both in value and in breadth, qualities which are admirably brought out in Ian Philip's *The Bodleian Library in the seventeenth and eighteenth centuries* (1983). Both Abbot and Archbishop John Williams of York had been involved in gifts of books to and from the Greek Orthodox (notably to the patriarch of Constantinople, Cyril Lucaris),[67] but Laud broadened the scope of these eastern contacts, using his political power to lay a duty on the merchants of

66 Carley, *ibid.*

67 R. J. Roberts, 'The Greek press at Constantinople in 1627 and its antecedents', *Library*, 5th ser., 22 (1967), 13–43.

the Levant Company to bring back Arabic books in their cargoes.[68] The results of his efforts form an important part of the history of the Bodleian Library and in the development of oriental studies in Oxford; as they were strengthened in Cambridge by the accession of Thomas Erpenius's manuscripts, bought at Leiden by the duke of Buckingham in 1625, and presented by his widow in 1632, and by the parliamentary gift of Hebrew books in 1648, from George Thomason's catalogue of 1647.[69] At least in its early years, Lambeth Library seems not to have had the popular support enjoyed, particularly in the City, by Sion College, whose Benefactors' Register, now somewhat ironically deposited at Lambeth, records numerous gifts and bequests, including some from the Stationers' Company.

Sion College was founded under the 1623 will of Thomas White, who died in the following year, and a library was soon added to the foundation.[70] The library depended on donations of money and books, and it is noticeable that, when sums of money were given, such as the £110 collected in 1629 by George Walker, they were used to buy Hebrew books. Some of those in large format (now at Lambeth) can be matched with those in Henry Fetherstone's 1628 *Catalogus librorum in diversis locis Italiae emptorum*. While those in small format were destroyed in the Great Fire of 1666, it is clear that Sion College was the largest purchaser from the Hebrew section of Fetherstone's catalogue, and that the college may be ranked with the two universities as a power in Hebrew studies. When Laud was imprisoned in the Tower in 1641, both the library established by Bancroft and Abbot, and Laud's own books and papers, were at risk. In 1644 the president and fellows of Sion College petitioned for the removal of the 'publick library' to the college. The petition was ineffective, and the library, and Laud's own books and papers – with other papers at Lambeth – underwent different fates. Under the third provision of Bancroft's will, his books were to go to Cambridge; the foundation of Chelsea College of Divinity had not materialised, and episcopacy had been abolished, so that in 1646 the Lords, and in 1647 the Commons, granted Lambeth Library to Cambridge, whither, in 1648–9, it was removed. Parliament seems to have made a distinction between the books of Bancroft and Abbot (and Whitgift), and other books and papers, including Laud's. Cambridge University thanked

68 For this, and for Laud's other activities in securing oriental manuscripts from the Levant, see G. J. Toomer, *Eastern Wisedome and Learning: the study of Arabic in seventeenth-century England* (Oxford, 1996), esp. 108.

69 Oates, *CUL*, 231; and I. Abrahams and C. E. Sayle, 'The purchase of Hebrew books by the English Parliament in 1647', *Transactions of the Jewish Historical Society of England*, 8 (1918), 63–77. This article makes very clear the role of John Selden in this transaction.

70 E. H. Pearce, *Sion College and Library* (Cambridge, 1913).

John Selden for his part in ensuring the translation of Lambeth Library to Cambridge; although Laud's books were subject to pillage during and after his imprisonment, much Lambeth material survived, and the part that Selden played in this, also, has only recently become clearer.[71]

The libraries of the final scholar collectors to appear in this chapter were also touched by the Civil War, though in different ways. Both were ultimately to enrich the libraries of their universities, in such a way that these were to take on the mantle of national libraries for at least another century.

Richard Holdsworth (1590–1649) and John Selden (1584–1654) had, as supporters and creators of libraries, much in common, but their careers, in a time of civil war, diverged widely. Selden, as lawyer, parliamentarian, antiquary and orientalist, published extensively, whereas Holdsworth, clergyman and Cambridge head of house, left little of his own in print, though *The valley of vision, or a clear sight of sundry sacred truths in twenty one sermons*, was published after his death in 1651. Holdsworth's life, as befits the greatest benefactor of Cambridge University Library before Bishop John Moore, is described fully in J. C. T. Oates's history of the library (to which the following account is heavily indebted), where the ambiguity of his intentions towards Emmanuel College and to the University Library – and its ultimate resolution – is set out at length. Holdsworth was elected in 1613 to a fellowship at St John's College, which he had entered in 1607, and he remained at the college until 1623, when he became rector of St Peter le Poer in the City of London, and was professor of divinity at Gresham College in 1629. As a prominent member of the London clergy, he held offices at Sion College during its formative years, and became president in 1639. As such, he would have been involved in the troubles of the library there, notably in the dismissal of the library keeper, Thomas Leech, and in the reinstatement of John Spencer. His name does not, however, appear in the Benefactors' Register of the college. In the years before his return to Cambridge as master of Emmanuel in 1637, he was evidently a frequenter of the London booksellers, since he named two of them, Robert Beaumont and Robert Littlebury, in his will as cataloguers of his books, as 'they know most of my Bookes already'.[72] Many of his books, indeed, as Oates remarks, had also been recycled through Cambridge booksellers and collections. Holdsworth

71 In 1939, James Fairhurst acquired a large collection of papers from the descendants of Selden's executor, Sir Matthew Hale. As a result of subsequent sales at auction, and later gifts, much of this material has found its way back to Lambeth, and successive instalments are described in the *Lambeth Palace Library Annual Review* for 1988, for 1996 and for 2000.

72 Oates, *CUL*, 309.

also served as vice-chancellor of the university from 1640–1 to 1642–3, but his royalist stance led to his confinement to London by Parliament, and he did not return to Cambridge before his death in 1649.

The provenance of some of the most significant groups of his books reflects his patronage of the second-hand stalls of London. His possession of more than a dozen of John Dee's books suggests that they were acquired when the latter's became available in 1625/6; but there were also thirty books in his library which had been looted from Würzburg after its capture by the Swedish army in 1631. There were also books from this source in Archbishop Laud's gift to the Bodleian, and the probability must be that these, too, were acquired in London. Holdsworth's purpose in amassing his library can only be inferred from the somewhat ambiguous terms of his will and correspondence, though he had been a donor of books to his old college of St John's in about 1633; these are alone in bearing his bookplate. Otherwise, he did not personalise his books, either by inscription or binding, and their identification has been rendered more difficult by the fact that the recipients did not keep them together. While Holdsworth was confined to London by Parliament, his books remained in the master's lodgings at Emmanuel College, where they were specifically protected by order of the earl of Manchester. His will of 1649 and the accompanying directions left his books to the University of Cambridge, provided that the Lambeth Library was returned to the see. Although these conditions were not perfectly met at the Restoration, after long discussion Lambeth Library was restored in 1664, and Holdsworth's books – apart from the duplicates, which passed to Emmanuel College – became the largest constituent of Cambridge University Library.

Notwithstanding the provisions of his will and directions, no catalogue of Holdsworth's books seems to have been made until the questions of their disposal came before the adjudicators in 1664. The resulting list ends with an *Index numeralis classium*, according to which there were 10,095 books, including 186 manuscripts.[73] The various branches of divinity, not surprisingly, formed the largest part of the library, though the largest single class was 'Historici'. A notable development – to be seen also in John Selden's library – was the number, more than 200, of incunabula, and these included Cambridge Library's first Caxtons. There were ninety-five 'Libri Hebraei'; like Selden, Holdsworth benefited from the dispersal of John Dee's Hebrew and other oriental books. Of the three Arabic manuscripts, two can no longer be found. Of the 186 manuscripts, 'over thirty' have an English monastic provenance, a relatively

73 *Ibid.*, 327.

small proportion, which may reflect the decreasing number on the market. Oates compares Holdsworth's collection of early English literary texts (unfavourably) with Cotton's; but again, a more revealing parallel would be with Selden's. The study of the early language was becoming academically more popular. Oates sums up thus: 'His motive in amassing a collection so large, multifarious, and impersonal must always have been that it should pass after his death into institutional keeping.'[74] He would, perhaps, not entirely have relished being in the tradition of Andrew Perne, but both men vastly enriched Cambridge University in their generation.

In contrast to the collections already described in this chapter, that of John Selden (1584–1654) was, throughout its owner's life, a resource upon which a long series of scholarly books was based. It is, at first sight, and despite the final ambiguity of Selden's intentions, the most accessible, since it remains as a 'named' collection in the Bodleian Library. No record survives of Selden's purposes in building his vast library, though the phases of his career are a witness to his purposes. He was, until his election to the parliaments of 1624 and of 1626–9, a consulting lawyer, notably to the House of Lords and to the Virginia Company.[75] His concern with the history of law, and particularly of English law and the English constitution, which had been fundamental to his earliest published works, such as the *History of tithes* (1618), was also employed in Parliament, where he was prominent in the opposition to prerogative taxation and to prerogative arrest. The learning he displayed in his early parliamentary career was drawn however, not only from his own books, but from his membership, from his first arrival in London, of Sir Robert Cotton's circle, and from his access to Cotton's library. That the library and its users were seen by the court as a focus of opposition to royal policies was demonstrated by its closure in 1629.

There are several sources for the contents of Selden's library. Unlike Cambridge University Library, which dispersed Holdsworth's books, the Bodleian kept Selden's together, and they may be recognised by the final element, 'Seld.', in their shelf-marks, though the library has occasionally intruded books from other sources into these sequences, and, more culpably, has removed books from them.[76] The duplicates, defined as being 'of the

74 *Ibid.*, 332.

75 D. S. Berkowitz, *John Selden's formative years* (Washington, 1988); P. Christianson, *Discourse on history, law and governance in the public career of John Selden, 1610–1635* (Toronto, 1996).

76 Mr Gerald Toomer – to whom I am indebted for a great deal of information about Selden's library – informs me that more than 100 of Selden's Hebrew books were reclassified into the Oppenheimer collection as 'Opp. adds.' by the library in the nineteenth century.

same kind and edition', were transferred to Gloucester Cathedral Library by Selden's executor, Sir Matthew Hale, in 1663. They numbered about 200, and included a number of Hebrew books. Their provenance is noted in the library catalogue.[77]

A study of the contents of Selden's library must begin with the inventory made after his death on 30 November 1654.[78] It represents the library as it existed on the shelves of Selden's house in White Friars, and lists separately the books of Elizabeth Grey, countess of Kent (1581–1651), who has been variously described as Selden's employer, mistress and, perhaps finally, wife. The inventory gives a total of 6,256 books and, when the manuscripts were added, of 7,466. It is probably a fair copy; its standard of cataloguing is perfunctory, and, in the case of oriental manuscripts, ignorant. It is clear from it that not all of Selden's books and manuscripts reached either the Bodleian or Gloucester Cathedral.[79] The books in the Bodleian were (and still are) classified into the fourfold system then used: 'Jur.' for law, 'Med.' for medicine, 'Th.' for theology, and 'Art.' for the more general arts.[80] The printed books were entered in Hyde's Bodleian catalogue of 1678, and the manuscripts in the *Catalogus librorum manuscriptorum Angliae et Hiberniae* (Oxford, 1697).[81] When the printed books were made over to the Bodleian in 1659, inventories were prepared for the surviving executors.[82]

From his earliest arrival in London, Selden was made familiar with the most important library in the capital, that of Sir Robert Cotton. The library of John Dee, in so far as it remained in the hands of his heir, John Pontois (whom Selden may well have known through the Virginia Company), was probably accessible to him.[83] The Cotton books in Selden's library were probably appropriations,[84] but the Dee books in it were mostly bought after 1625/6.

77 S. M. Eward, *Catalogue of Gloucester Cathedral Library* (Gloucester, 1972).

78 This inventory was acquired by the Bodleian Library in 1947, and is numbered MS Seld. supra 111.

79 D. M. Barratt, 'The library of John Selden and its later history', *BLR* 3 (1950–1), 128–42, 208–13, 256–74. The article is concerned mainly with those manuscripts, 484 in number, which, though listed in the 1654 inventory, did not reach the Bodleian.

80 Tampering with this arrangement has already been noted (above, 315); the category 'S.Seld.' denotes select books.

81 The latter are now most conveniently listed in the Bodleian's *Summary Catalogue* (*SC*).

82 The copy made for Sir Matthew Hale is now in the Houghton Library of Harvard University, MS Eng 1328; that made for Sir John Vaughan has returned to the Bodleian as MS Broxbourne 84.10. Bodleian, MS Add. C 40 is, apparently, not an inventory, but a copy made from the library's original, from which the executors' formal inventories were made.

83 Roberts and Watson, *Dee's catalogue*, 60, 71, n. 52.

84 John Sparrow, 'The earlier owners of books in John Selden's library', *BQR* 6 (1929–31), 263–71. Sparrow counted forty-one, the latest being dated 1622.

The chronological spread of Selden's library is rivalled only by that of Holdsworth. The incunabula are fewer,[85] though a significant proportion is of English origin or in the English language. Books in English have a greater presence in the library than in those of earlier collectors (even without the countess of Kent's books, which were mostly in English, French or Italian). Selden was acquiring books in the last year of his life, 1654.

The linguistic range is no less impressive, and Ben Jonson's compliment that Selden was 'the bravest man in all languages' was perhaps not confined to Selden's fluency in what Jonson would have considered the learned languages, Greek, Latin and Hebrew. The 1654 inventory lists books in all the major romance, though only occasionally the Germanic, languages of Europe, and there are dictionaries of them (usually with Latin equivalents) and guides to their use; but his possession of manuscripts and books in Amerindian languages – his three Mexican manuscripts include the famous Codex Mendoza, and his books embraced some in Nahuatl and Aymara – suggests a very wide linguistic interest. Selden owned books in Japanese printed in western characters. These possessions, set beside the incunabula, suggest that Selden was curious about the spread of the written and printed word.

Unlike the great bulk of his printed library, the manuscripts – oriental, Greek, and one Latin – were specifically bequeathed to the Bodleian in Selden's will, together with such talmudical and rabbinical books as the library did not already have. Books in Arabic were fewer, but he owned most of the products of the Medicean press. In all, 357 manuscripts finally reached the Bodleian, and the largest categories were in Arabic and Hebrew.

Selden's resources in the subjects which engaged his early career went far beyond books in English on tithes, duelling, titles and dignities and the law of the sea, and his authorities were drawn from all over Europe. While he owned most of the significant books hitherto published in England on history and law, he owned French, Italian and Spanish books in these areas, evidently seeking out collections of local legislation and codes. His interest in local Italian history and law was particularly marked. That of the Germanic lands is largely absent, though Danish and Swedish antiquities interested him. Though he seems to have been concerned at the end of his life to proclaim a certain religious orthodoxy, his library demonstrates the catholicity of his *Table talk*: 'Popish Bookes teach and informe us what wee know; we know much out of them; the Fathers, Church story, Schoolmen; all may passe for popish Bookes,

85 The number revealed by the current research for the Bodleian incunable catalogue is about 130. I owe this figure to the kindness of Dr Alan Coates.

and If you take away them: what learning will you leave?' There follows a jibe at the inefficacy of censorship by the Customs: 'Besides Who must be Judge; the Customer or the Wayter? if he disallows a booke it must not be brought into the Kingdome; then Lord have mercy upon all schollers.'[86] This sentiment is amply borne out by his practice; the library is full of such books of doctrine and controversy, and a fair number are indeed of English recusant origin. These are not balanced by large quantities of protestant biblical commentaries, though Selden found space for the Protestant Hebraist Hugh Broughton. Very noticeable among Selden's books are numerous pre-Reformation liturgical works of the uses of Sarum or York. These may have related to Selden's antiquarian studies, alongside the monastic and other manuscripts which are said to have been destroyed by fire after his death. Classical literature in all levels of edition is found all over the library. Selden grouped his oldest English books together, but his taste in literature appears both limited and orthodox, residing in such writers as Chaucer, Gower, Spenser and Jonson; perhaps he relied upon the countess's library for vernacular reading. His name is not normally associated with mathematics and astronomy; yet, particularly on the 'Little Shelves behinde the North doore by the firste wyndow', the compilers of the inventory found an extraordinary range of books in these subjects.[87] It is this, perhaps, that strengthens the belief that Selden was bent on creating an encyclopaedic learned library.

Selden is not known to have left England, and even seems to have avoided doing so. Thus, the wide range of subjects, and dates in his library, prove his expert and continuous use of the second-hand market in London and his patronage of the import trade. He owned a number of Frankfurt Fair catalogues. His eminence as a lawyer and as a scholar ensured that he received numerous authors' presentation copies from both England and abroad (a number of these are recorded by Sparrow); this is in marked contrast with Holdsworth, in whose library Oates could find only four presentation copies. Selden's ownership of Arabic and, in particular, of Hebrew books – of which there was only a limited stock already available in England – argues extensive use not only of learned correspondents but of booksellers. One of these was certainly Menasseh ben Israel of Amsterdam.[88] Selden was well acquainted with 'Latin traders', particularly those connected to the 'firm' of Henry Fetherstone, such as Robert Martin and George Thomason, and a significant number

86 John Selden, *Table talk*, ed. F. Pollock (London, 1927), 23.
87 MS Seld. supra 111, fols. 73–7.
88 I owe this and much more information to Mr Gerald Toomer.

of his Hebrew books can be shown to derive from Fetherstone's 1628 catalogue, and from the series of catalogues published by Robert Martin from 1633 to 1650.

His library also shows evidence of extensive 'borrowing', some of which may charitably be put down to the uncertainties of a time of civil war, and to the undoubted supervision that Selden exercised over libraries at risk. One of these was Cotton's, of which, according to Aubrey, Selden had, during the Commonwealth, 'the key and command'.[89] A 'loan' in 1622 of printed books from Sir Robert Cotton was rather smaller than the forty-one recorded by Sparrow.[90] Selden also borrowed from the royal library.[91] His role as custodian of manuscripts from Lambeth other than those strictly from the Whitgift–Bancroft–Abbott library has already been noted. But his most precious borrowing was the Book of Llandaff, which returned to safe custody in its land of origin only through the collections of Sir John Vaughan and Robert Davies of Gwysaney.

In its owner's lifetime, Selden's was a private library in a private house (if not in his Inner Temple chambers), and recorded use of it is small. An exception revealed in his correspondence is by the Christ Church Hebraist and Arabist John Gregory.[92] In the absence of any surviving catalogue other than a posthumous inventory, it is hard to see how even Selden could have found his way among so many books. The inventory, a shelf-list, does suggest an occasional crude grouping of books by subject or language, though the works of Hugo Grotius, for example, seem to be scattered throughout the library, while the books in oriental languages are crudely grouped.

Selden died on 30 November 1654. His will, dated 11 June 1653,[93] left his oriental and Greek manuscripts and one designated Latin manuscript, and such rabbinical and talmudical printed books as the university did not have, to the University of Oxford. Selden left the remainder of his books to his

89 John Aubrey, *Brief lives*, ed. O. L. Dick, 3rd edn (London, 1958), 272.

90 C. G. C. Tite, 'A "loan" of printed books from Sir Robert Cotton to John Selden', *BLR* 13 (1991), 486–90.

91 Lambeth, MS 4267, fols. 67–8.

92 M. Feingold, 'Oriental studies' in *HUO*, IV. 483. The correspondence is in Bodleian, MS Seld. supra 108.

93 Selden's will is printed in his *Opera omnia*, ed. D. Wilkins (1726), I. lii–liv (will) and lv–lvi (codicil of the same date). The codicil sets out the disposal of his books and marbles, and monetary bequests to his family, offspring and servants. A negative photostat of the filed copy of the will is in Bodleian, MS Seld. supra 110, fols. 43–55. Neither version specifically records that the intended beneficiary, the 'chancellor, masters and scholars', were those of the University of Oxford.

executors, to be parted among them, only willing them not to put them to a common sale. The rather tentative suggestion is made that 'it may do well in some convenient library publick, or some college in one of the universities'. Much ingenuity has been employed in explaining why Selden did not leave the entire library to Oxford. But he did not, and his executors, all lawyers, were sure that he had not, and they offered it to the Inner Temple, on condition that a building would be erected to house it – which the Inn was not prepared to do. In October 1656, Oxford University suggested that it should be given the library as a memorial to Selden; a request which was granted, with the arrival of the books in September 1659. Selden's specific bequest can probably be linked to the gifts which Archbishop Laud had made to the Bodleian Library from 1635, and to his establishment of a chair of Arabic. It is clear that Selden, particularly after his release from custody, was much closer to Laud in matters of learned interest than might be expected from their respective political positions.[94] This was perhaps reinforced, when Selden served as burgess for Oxford University in the Long Parliament, when – at first – Laud was chancellor.

Selden does not seem to have collected coins, and his antiquities were limited to a small number of inscriptions and statues; these were bequeathed to Oxford University in the codicil to his will. Some may have come to him through (and perhaps as a reward for) his work on the *Marmora Arundelliana*, of 1628. Selden wished 'that they may be placed about the publick library walls'. Nine items were handed over in 1659 and, despite this treatment, they are still in the Ashmolean Museum.[95]

How incomplete was the acquisition of Selden's library in 1659 by the Bodleian has become apparent since the library bought the 1654 inventory in 1947, and the extent of the late James Fairhurst's purchase of the Hale family papers has become known. Barratt lists a number of items from the 1654 inventory which did not reach the Bodleian.[96] Most, though not all, are manuscripts, and are those listed on the first six or so folios of the inventory. It is likely that two of the executors, Sir Matthew Hale and Sir John Vaughan, followed, in part, Selden's injunction to distribute his books among themselves. Some of Vaughan's portion may have been destroyed by a fire in the Inner Temple; others passed, perhaps, into Welsh collections. Books from Selden's library were evidently among those acquired – temporarily – by St Paul's Cathedral

94 D. S. Berkowitz, *John Selden's formative years* (1988), 288–91.

95 D. Kurtz, *The reception of classical art in Britain* (Oxford, 2000), 46. I am grateful to both Donna Kurtz and David Sturdy for their help.

96 See above, n. 79.

Library in 1949 (ultimately from the Hale family).[97] Nor do all the countess of Kent's books seem to have reached the Bodleian (though a few did).[98]

The accession of such a scholar's library, however attenuated, and however ambiguous its owner's intentions, was an immense enrichment of Oxford's 'public library'. That, taken with Holdsworth's bequest to Cambridge, ensured that these, more decisively than the libraries of London, were to constitute, for the next hundred years, both magnets for learned donations, and the nation's principal resources for scholarly research.

97 N. Sykes, 'New light on the Tudor epoch: rich collection of manuscripts acquired by St Paul's', *The Times*, 15 June 1949, 5. These were later withdrawn, and sold at Sotheby's in 1963. About twenty were acquired by Lambeth Palace Library.

98 Sparrow ('The earlier owners'), perhaps unable to envisage a female book-owner, thought that the initials 'E G', which are stamped on some books, were those of Edward Gwynne. All those identifiable are in Italian, bound in vellum and stamped in black with a dog (a 'talbot').

12

Matthew Parker's manuscripts: an Elizabethan library and its use

TIMOTHY GRAHAM

Matthew Parker (1504–75) was the foremost collector of medieval manuscripts in the Elizabethan period. The library that he assembled acquired national importance in his own time, and – thanks to Parker's provision for its preservation after his death – it has retained that importance to this day. When Parker became archbishop of Canterbury in 1559, the threat of neglect, loss and destruction still hung over large numbers of books that had belonged to the religious houses dissolved by Henry VIII. The intervening years had witnessed valiant efforts by individual collectors, who, however, had tended to work only on a local or regional scale. What was lacking was a nationally co-ordinated initiative to salvage the written record of England's medieval past. It was just such an initiative that Parker succeeded in instigating and overseeing, even as he laboured to secure the Elizabethan settlement of the Church of England.

During the years of Parker's archiepiscopate, more than 500 manuscripts passed into his hands. These manuscripts included such outstanding treasures as the twelfth-century Bury and Dover Bibles, landmarks of English Romanesque illumination (CCCC, MSS 2 and 3–4); the earliest surviving copy of the Anglo-Saxon Chronicle (CCCC, MS 173); a two-volume copy of Matthew Paris's *Chronica maiora* illustrated by Matthew himself (CCCC, MSS 26 and 16); and a fine copy of Chaucer's *Troilus and Criseyde* with a frontispiece showing the author publicly declaiming his work (CCCC, MS 61). Even more important than the highlights of the collection, however, were its solid depth and the wide geographic range of the source libraries from which it was garnered. Parker succeeded in assembling a collection that, notwithstanding emphases reflecting his own tastes and purposes, was truly representative of the written culture of medieval England. He and his entourage then applied themselves to the detailed study of the books, leaving such ample traces of their work that the modern scholar can reconstruct with precision both the methods by which they proceeded and the purposes that guided them. For Parker's collection was above all a *working* library; it offers a unique picture of how medieval books were explored and exploited for the contribution they could make to major issues that confronted the archbishop and his contemporaries.

The formation of the collection

Parker had already begun to acquire a significant collection of printed books during the earlier part of his career, when he was successively bible clerk, scholar and fellow (from 1527) of Corpus Christi College, Cambridge, dean of Anne Boleyn's college of secular priests at Stoke-by-Clare in Suffolk (1535–44), and master of Corpus Christi College (1544–53). From his undergraduate years Parker had engaged actively in the burning religious debates of his time, and the books that he purchased included major editions of the Church Fathers as well as the writings of contemporary protestant theologians. That he studied these works closely is shown by the wealth of annotations that his copies contain in the small, neat script characteristic of his earlier years. At his death Parker entrusted the majority of his printed books, along with most of his manuscripts, to Corpus Christi College, and they are included in the register of his books given to the college.[1] The register reveals that Parker continued to buy printed books to the end of his life, for it includes over twenty items published in the years 1573–4. Altogether it records more than 850 printed volumes divided into twenty subject categories.

There is little evidence that Parker had any significant interest in collecting manuscripts during his pre-archiepiscopal years. A few acquisitions can be dated to this period, including several manuscripts (CCCC, MSS 113, 125, 172, 185, 418) containing papers of or works by Martin Bucer, who had spent the last three years of his life (1548–51) as regius professor of divinity in Cambridge and whose executor Parker was. Many of the papers that Parker accumulated and generated as dean of Stoke-by-Clare, master of Corpus Christi College and vice-chancellor of Cambridge University (in 1545 and 1548) were later to be bound up as manuscripts and included in his bequest (CCCC, MSS 106, 108, 118 and 170). One medieval manuscript that may have entered his hands relatively early in his career is CCCC, MS 321, a fourteenth-century copy of the commentary on St Matthew's Gospel by the heterodox Franciscan theologian Petrus Johannis Olivi. The script of Parker's annotations in this manuscript is of a kind typical of his younger years.

1 On the Parker Register, see R. I. Page, 'The Parker Register and Matthew Parker's Anglo-Saxon manuscripts', *TCBS* 8 (1981), 1–17; and R. I. Page, *Matthew Parker and his books* (Kalamazoo, 1993), 2–16.

It has been assumed that Parker began to acquire manuscripts on a large scale soon after he became archbishop, and that a major piece of evidence for this is a letter written to him by John Bale on 30 July 1560.[2] Bale, evidently responding to a request from Parker, provides detailed information about medieval texts known to him, whether in printed or in manuscript form, and supplies the names of owners of manuscripts. In requesting this information, however, Parker was not acting on his own behalf, as has been thought; rather, he was seeking to assist his queen, who had been approached by the protestant historian Matthias Flacius Illyricus, who wished to borrow any English materials that he might use for his multi-volume ecclesiastical history then in progress.[3] Bale's letter, if not a symptom that Parker was already attempting to locate manuscripts on his own account at this early stage of his archiepiscopate, nevertheless seems to have had an important impact on Parker's activity as a manuscript collector. It surely helped to alert him to the need to seek actively for manuscripts before they were lost for ever. And it seems to have served in some measure as a finding-list: several of the manuscripts described by Bale eventually came into Parker's hands.[4]

Few of Parker's acquisitions can be precisely dated. Inscriptions in some manuscripts, however, record when and through whom they reached Parker. The earliest of these inscriptions, dated 1564, is in a copy of homilies by John Chrysostom (CUL, MS Ii.3.25) given to Parker by Walter Philips, dean of Rochester Cathedral. A note at the front of CUL, MS Ii.2.11, a copy of the Old English translation of the Gospels, states that the book was presented to Parker by Gregory Dodds, dean of Exeter, and that Parker 'illum in hanc nouam formam redigi et ornari curauit' in 1566; the 'new form' into which Parker cast the manuscript included the provision of a binding of gold-tooled calfskin.[5] CCCC, MS 24, a copy of Thomas Bradwardine's *De causa Dei contra Pelagium*, appears to have been a Christmas gift, for it was presented to Parker on 20 December 1567 by his old acquaintance Andrew Perne, master of Peterhouse.[6] An entry in Parker's own hand in CUL, MS Ii.4.6, a collection of Old English homilies, records that the book was presented to him in Star Chamber on

2 CUL, MS Add. 7489. The letter has most recently been edited in T. Graham and A. G. Watson, *The recovery of the past in early Elizabethan England: documents by John Bale and John Joscelyn from the circle of Matthew Parker* (Cambridge, 1998), 17–30.

3 Graham and Watson, *Recovery of the past*, 2–4; N. L. Jones, 'Matthew Parker, John Bale, and the Magdeburg Centuriators', *Sixteenth Century Journal* 12/3 (1981), 35–49.

4 Graham and Watson, *Recovery of the past*, 4–5, 21 (with 37, n. 55) and 24 (with 43, n. 112).

5 T. Graham, 'A Parkerian transcript of the list of Bishop Leofric's procurements for Exeter Cathedral', *TCBS* 10 (1994), 444; H. M. Nixon, 'Elizabethan gold-tooled bindings', in D. E. Rhodes (ed.), *Essays in honour of Victor Scholderer* (Mainz, 1970), 254–62.

6 Page, *Matthew Parker and his books*, 16.

29 December 1567 by Francis Russell, earl of Bedford. Durham Cathedral Library, MS A.IV.36, an early thirteenth-century copy of Simeon of Durham's *Historia Dunelmensis ecclesiae*, was given to Parker on 11 August 1568 by Robert Horne, bishop of Winchester, as a *quid pro quo* for the gift of a copy of Parker's recently published edition of the *Flores historiarum*.[7] Letters to Parker from the bishop of Salisbury, John Jewel, reveal that in January 1569 Jewel sent Parker the Sherborne copy of King Alfred's translation of the *Pastoral care* of Pope Gregory the Great, now Cambridge, Trinity Coll., MS R.5.22, Part III.[8] Jewel commented that he had 'ransacked' his cathedral library in his search for ancient manuscripts and that this was the only one 'woorthye the findinge'.

These dated acquisitions cluster in the middle and late 1560s. Other evidence confirms that during those years Parker was conducting a major campaign to locate manuscripts. Jewel was not the only one of Parker's bishops writing to him on book-related matters at this time. Other letters survive from John Scory, bishop of Hereford (3 March 1566), Richard Davies, bishop of St Davids (19 March 1566 and 16 February 1568) and Nicholas Robinson, bishop of Bangor (7 October 1567), as well as from John Aylmer, archdeacon of Lincoln (3 November 1567), documenting these churchmen's searches in their cathedral libraries and in the parish churches of their dioceses.[9] The terms in which these letters are couched make it clear that Parker's correspondents were responding to a specific request from the archbishop to provide information about any 'monumentes of antiquitie' (Robinson's phrase) that they could locate. For the most part, their searches had been unsuccessful. Davies, in his first letter, reports that secretary of state William Cecil had already appropriated 'all suche olde monumentes as we had'; Robinson declares that the only items left in his part of the country are 'certaine fabulose histories and that lately written'. Scory, however, was able to locate three 'Saxon bokes' at Hereford. A note in the Hereford Chapter Act Book records that these were a *Vita sancti Marcelini* and collections of *Sermones dominicales* and *Vite quorundam sanctorum saxonice script*';[10] the book of sermons is perhaps CCCC, MS 188, but the others have not been identified.[11]

7 *MMBL* II. 486–7. 8 Jewel's letters are pasted in at the end of CUL, MS Ii.2.4.

9 These letters are in CCCC, MS 114A, p. 447 (Scory), pp. 493–4 and unnumbered pages between pp. 392 and 393 (Davies); and in CCCC, MS 114B, p. 503 (Robinson) and p. 897 (Aylmer). The significant portions of the letters are quoted by C. E. Wright, 'The dispersal of the monastic libraries and the beginnings of Anglo-Saxon studies', *TCBS* I (1951), 221–3; and M. McKisack, *Medieval history in the Tudor age* (Oxford, 1971), 29–32.

10 Hereford Cathedral Library, Chapter Act Book 1512–1566, fol. 210^{v}.

11 M. Budny, *Insular, Anglo-Saxon, and early Anglo-Norman manuscript art at Corpus Christi College, Cambridge*, 2 vols. (Kalamazoo, 1997), I. 572–3.

Confirmation that the middle years of the 1560s were a time of intense research by Parker and his circle into which medieval historical texts survived, and who owned copies of them, comes from a list drawn up by his Latin secretary, John Joscelyn (1529–1603), some time before 1567.[12] Beginning with Gildas, the list names, in approximate chronological order, more than 100 medieval English authors and enumerates their historical writings. When he was able to do so, Joscelyn included a note of who owned manuscripts of the works; many of these notes he added later, as new information came his way. The list seems to have served Parker as an acquisitions guide. Several manuscripts that Joscelyn attributes to other owners were later to become Parker's (for example, the copy of Walter of Coventry's *Memoriale* that was owned by the widow of Sir John Cheke and is now CCCC, MS 175),[13] while Parker also took steps to track down copies of works for which Joscelyn was unable to name an owner. Among these was the *De rebus gestis Ricardi primi* of Richard of Devizes, of which Parker eventually succeeded in obtaining the author's holograph copy, now CCCC, MS 339.[14]

Parker took his searches for manuscripts to a new level, and bolstered his efforts with royal support, when in July 1568 Queen Elizabeth's Privy Council issued letters authorising his agents to search throughout the realm for 'auncient recordes or monumentes written'.[15] Addressed to 'all and singuler her subiectes within her Realme of Englande', the letters underlined the queen's zeal for the preservation of historical records and noted how writings formerly kept in the monasteries 'are nowe come to the possession of sundry priuate persons, and so partly remayne obscure and vnknowne'. The queen assigns to her archbishop of Canterbury 'a speciall care and ouersight in these matters'. Whenever Parker or his agents so request, those who are owners of ancient records must 'gently impart the same' so that the documents may be subjected to perusal. The letters specify that, following such inspection, the records will be returned to their owners for safe keeping on the understanding that, 'when any neede shall require, resort may be made for the testimonie that may be founde in them, and also by conference of them, the antiquitie of the state of these countryes may be restored to the knowledge of the world'.

12 BL, MS Cotton Nero C. iii, fols. 209–12; edited in Graham and Watson, *Recovery of the past*, 61–109.

13 Graham and Watson, *Recovery of the past*, 85–6 (no. J.2.69).

14 Graham and Watson, *Recovery of the past*, 79 (no. J.2.53).

15 A printed copy of the letters, along with the manuscript draft, is preserved in CCCC, MS 114A, pp. 49 and 51. See also J. Bruce and T. T. Perowne (eds.), *Correspondence of Matthew Parker, DD, Archbishop of Canterbury* (Cambridge, 1853), 327–8; Wright, 'Matthew Parker and his circle', 212–13 (where the full text of the letters is quoted); and Page, *Matthew Parker and his books*, 43–4 and pl. 24.

The exact impact of the Privy Council letters is hard to gauge in the absence of precise evidence about when and from whom Parker received the majority of his manuscripts. One of Parker's agents, his chaplain Stephen Batman, claimed that within four years he alone collected 6,700 books that had formerly belonged to the religious houses, and that Parker selected what he wanted from these; if his huge total is to be believed, the books presumably consisted for the most part of printed texts.[16] As many hundreds of manuscripts ended up in Parker's collection, scholars have often doubted whether the archbishop took seriously the assurance in the Privy Council letters that books would be returned to their owners once he had scrutinised them. Yet there is firm evidence that in at least some cases this is indeed what happened. Bodleian, MS Junius 121, an eleventh-century ecclesiastical miscellany, has been annotated by Parker, and even seems to have served his circle as a model for the design of an Anglo-Saxon font;[17] yet it remained the property of Worcester Cathedral until well into the seventeenth century, so Parker's use of it can have been only temporary.[18] That Parker did not become the owner of every manuscript that passed through his hands is also demonstrated by several manuscripts now in the British Library that contain Parkerian markings but for which there is no evidence of actual Parkerian ownership.[19]

It is clear that Parker's 'catchment area' for obtaining manuscripts was far greater than that of previous and contemporary collectors. The identifiable medieval homes of Parker's manuscripts encompass well over forty religious houses, along with some secular institutions.[20] Yet there are distinct regional emphases. Much the largest group of volumes came from the south-east, with the two Canterbury houses, Christ Church and St Augustine's, predominating, and with Rochester, Dover, St Albans and London also represented; next came the east (Norwich and Bury St Edmunds feature strongly, along with Coggeshall, Ely, Peterborough, Lincoln, Cambridge, Thetford and perhaps Thorney); then the west and south-west, with strong showings from

16 S. Batman, *The doome warning all men to the judgement* (London, 1581; facsimile repr. New York, 1984), 400.

17 P. J. Lucas, 'A testimonye of verye ancient tyme? Some manuscript models for the Parkerian Anglo-Saxon type-designs', in P. R. Robinson and R. Zim (eds.), *Of the making of books: medieval manuscripts, their scribes and readers* (Aldershot, 1997), 173 and 178.

18 See also Graham, 'Parkerian transcript', 436–40, for Parker's return of a book borrowed from Exeter Cathedral.

19 For example, MSS Cotton Claudius E. viii (Graham and Watson, *Recovery of the past*, 43, n. 112); Faustina A. ix (owned in 1565 by William Bowyer, keeper of records in the Tower of London; Ker, *Cat. AS*, 193); and Nero D. ii (Graham and Watson, *Recovery of the past*, 101, no. J.2.101).

20 M. R. James, *The sources of Archbishop Parker's collection of MSS at Corpus Christi College, Cambridge* (Cambridge, 1899).

Worcester, Winchester and Exeter, alongside Abingdon, Bath, Hereford, Malmesbury, Oxford, Sherborne and Wigmore. It is striking that hardly any of Parker's manuscripts came from the north. Of all the manuscripts he left to Corpus Christi College, the only ones with a firm provenance north of the Humber are one manuscript each from the Cistercian houses of Jervaulx and Rievaulx and two from Sawley. Parker apparently either did not seek, or was unable, to exert his influence throughout the region that made up the northern province of his church.

The overall fruit of Parker's efforts was the formation of a collection of medieval English manuscripts that was unrivalled in his time for its scope and the quality of its contents. Once the books came into his hands, moreover, they became a working collection in the fullest sense. For Parker's collection more than for any other formed during the Elizabethan period, there is ample evidence to show how the books were treated and for what purposes they were studied.

Treatment and use

Parker seems to have kept the great majority of his manuscripts at his archiepiscopal residence at Lambeth on the south bank of the Thames. The library that he maintained there was very much a private one intended for his own use and that of his associates, even though the purposes that inspired his use were public ones. While the archbishop was prepared to exchange items with close friends and colleagues like Sir William Cecil, there is no evidence that he allowed scholars access and borrowing rights in the way that, a generation later, Sir Robert Cotton was to do with his library. Viewing the manuscripts as his private possessions, Parker allowed himself significant liberties in the ways he handled them. Almost every manuscript that passed into his hands has undergone some transformation as a result of his ownership. Parker's treatment of his manuscripts provides a remarkable insight into the extent to which early modern collectors were prepared to restore and reshape their books.

Parker re-bound most of his manuscripts, at first using the services of several London binders and then, from about 1572, establishing his own bindery at Lambeth.[21] He also provided many of his printed books with bindings, but, whereas the majority of those bindings survive to offer a rich body of evidence

21 Nixon, 'Elizabethan gold-tooled bindings', 238, 242–3, 246, 248, 250, 252 and 254–67; H. M. Nixon, *Five centuries of English bookbinding* (London, 1978), 48, 54, 56 and 58; and H. M. Nixon and M. M. Foot, *The history of decorated bookbinding in England* (Oxford, 1992), 36 and 38–40.

to students of sixteenth-century binding history, the manuscript bindings have almost all perished. None remain at Corpus Christi College, to which Parker left the bulk of his collection.[22] Eight may still be found at the Cambridge University Library, while another is on the ninth-century MacDurnan Gospels in Lambeth Palace Library.[23] All nine bindings have stout wooden boards covered with leather; three, on manuscripts that Parker evidently valued especially highly, have been embellished with gold-tooled decoration.[24] The University Library manuscripts all had metal bosses in the corners of their covers, fore-edge clasps, a parchment title label placed under a transparent piece of horn fixed to the back cover, and a chaining staple mounted in the bottom right area of the front cover. Not all of Parker's manuscripts, however, were given bindings of this degree of elaboration. Some were apparently provided with nothing more than limp vellum covers, for several of the manuscripts given to Corpus Christi are listed within a portion of the Parker Register headed 'Bookes in parchment closures'.

At the time of rebinding, adopting a practice followed by other early modern collectors, Parker would often combine two or more manuscripts into a single volume. His guiding principle was similarity of physical dimensions rather than of content, and some unusual juxtapositions resulted. The most strikingly disparate of his *Sammelhandschriften* is CCCC, MS 197, in which a late fourteenth-century set of continuations of Ranulf Higden's *Polychronicon* is joined with fifteenth-century texts relating to the deposition of Richard II and the execution of Archbishop Richard Scrope, sixteenth-century transcripts of documents concerning the trial of Joan of Arc, fragments of an eighth-century Northumbrian gospel book, and a handful of other miscellaneous items including a sketch of an ancient Jewish coin given to the Calvinist theologian Théodore de Bèze. Despite a general similarity of page size among the various parts, the binder was obliged to trim some of the leaves to reduce them to uniform dimensions; within the gospel fragment this has produced the loss of significant portions of the decoration of the opening of St John's Gospel.[25]

22 The sixteenth-century bindings that survive on two manuscripts at Corpus Christi College (MSS 87 and 217) are pre-Parkerian, being characteristic of the library of Henry VIII, from which the two books in question seem to have come: see J. P. Carley (ed.), *The libraries of King Henry VIII*, CBMLC vii. lxxix–lxxx.

23 CUL, MSS Dd.2.5, Dd.7.3, Dd.8.17, Ff.1.23, Ii.2.4, Ii.2.11, Ii.2.23 and Ii.2.24; and Lambeth, MS 1370.

24 CUL, MSS Ff.1.23 (Anglo-Saxon psalter) and Ii.2.11 (Old English gospels); and Lambeth, MS 1370 (MacDurnan Gospels).

25 T. Graham, 'Changing the context of medieval manuscript art: the case of Matthew Parker', in *Medieval art: recent perspectives. A memorial tribute to C. R. Dodwell*, ed. G. R.

The rebinding process involved equipping the manuscripts with pastedowns and endleaves at both front and back, while Parker also did what he could to repair manuscripts that had suffered damage in one form or another. For both these purposes he was prepared to sanction the reuse of existing manuscript material. Many of the pastedowns and endleaves of his manuscripts consist of portions of early sixteenth-century legal documents cut up by his binders. Fragments of such documents have been used for this purpose in, for example, Cambridge, Trinity Coll., MS R.5.34, CUL, MSS Ii.2.11 and Kk.3.18, and many of Parker's manuscripts at Corpus Christi College, among them MSS 41, 162 and 201. In two manuscripts, CCCC, MS 191 and CUL, MS Ii.2.4, he had smaller strips cut from documents in order to restore the edges of leaves that had rotted away. These legal documents had presumably ceased to have currency by the time his binders made use of them. What is at first sight more surprising is that Parker also permitted leaves from medieval manuscripts to be reused in these ways. The Parkerian pastedowns and endleaves in several manuscripts at Corpus Christi College include leaves that have been removed from a variety of late medieval liturgical manuscripts.[26] In a tenth-century copy of King Alfred's translation of the *Pastoral care* and an eleventh-century Canterbury pontifical (CCCC, MSS 12 and 44), Parker effected repairs to damaged margins by pasting in broad strips cut from a fourteenth-century breviary.[27] He even went so far as to embellish three of his older manuscripts by inserting into them, as frontispiece images, scenes from Christ's passion that had originally belonged to the prefatory cycle of illustrations in a thirteenth-century psalter.[28] It may appear contradictory that the archbishop, so keen to preserve manuscripts, should have been prepared to permit such rank despoliation. Yet, while he valued certain types of manuscripts especially highly – in particular, historical manuscripts and those throwing light on the doctrine and practices of the early English church – he seems to have had much less respect for manuscripts that attested to late medieval liturgical practices. Those practices had been superseded in the reformed English church, and Parker evidently held such manuscripts to be expendable.

Parker's treatment of his manuscripts has in several cases had an impact upon their textual content. Some manuscripts reached him in an incomplete state, with leaves or complete quires missing. Where possible, he would restore the manuscripts by inserting leaves containing transcriptions of the missing

Owen-Crocker and T. Graham (Manchester, 1998), 185–9. The gospel fragment was separated from the rest of the manuscript in 1953 and renumbered as MS 197B.

26 For example, CCCC, MSS 5, 6, 65, 88, 92, 102, 104 and 160.

27 Graham, 'Changing the context', 195–200.

28 *Ibid.*, 189–94.

text; he generally had these transcriptions copied by a practised scribe in calligraphic writing that imitated the original script. For example, he owned an eleventh-century copy of Ælfric's *Grammar* (CCCC, MS 449) that was missing several quires at the beginning. He made good the loss by inserting a new set of quires into which one of his scribes, imitating both Caroline and Anglo-Saxon hands, transcribed the missing text by working from another copy of the *Grammar* (BL, MS Royal 15 B. xxii). Other examples of Parkerian supply leaves containing transcriptions of lost portions of text occur in CCCC, MSS 16 (Matthew Paris's *Chronica maiora*: seven leaves at the front), 188 (an Anglo-Saxon homiliary: one leaf at the front and three in the middle) and 195 (Thomas Walsingham's *Chronica maiora*: a total of seventy-five leaves inserted in batches at six points in the manuscript). Sometimes Parker went yet further and had the manuscript supplied with text that it probably had not at first included. In CCCC, MS 383, a twelfth-century compilation of Anglo-Saxon legal texts, he not only made good the loss of a portion of the laws of King Cnut, but also, for good measure, provided transcriptions of two law codes of King Edgar, even though there is no evidence that the manuscript originally contained these texts. In CCCC, MS 44, his Canterbury pontifical, he inserted twelve leaves that contained, not only the missing ending of a formula for exorcism, but also a further set of texts describing how a provincial synod should be conducted.[29]

But Parker was not always able to find an exemplar from which he could make good a textual loss, and in such cases the ways in which he dealt with the issue produced further loss. His Canterbury pontifical, for example, lacked leaves at the beginning as well as the end. Its first surviving leaf has the concluding lines of an Old English text found in no other manuscript. Unable to supply the missing text, and objecting to the untidiness of having his manuscript begin with an acephalous fragment, Parker had the entire first page erased, turning it into an endleaf on which he then entered his signature of ownership.[30] He erased other fragmentary endings or beginnings of texts in CCCC, MSS 198 and 201, while in CCCC, MS 303, a twelfth-century collection of Old English homilies, he disguised the abrupt opening of the manuscript by erasing the surviving four lines of the end of a homily on page 1, then pasting over this area a parchment strip on which he had the title of the volume entered.[31]

29 M. B. Parkes suggested that the supply leaves had been added to CCCC, MS 44 in the early sixteenth century, when the manuscript was still at Ely, its late medieval home ('Archaizing hands in English manuscripts', in Carley and Tite, *Books and collectors*, 102 and n. 8). I have no doubt, however, that the restoration of the manuscript is Parkerian. See also the account in Budny, *Manuscript art*, I. 681.

30 Page, *Matthew Parker and his books*, pl. 28.

31 Ibid., 47 and pls. 29–30.

Although Parker engaged in practices that may be dubious from the perspective of modern conservation, his many interventions in his manuscripts are evidence of the importance he attached to them. So too are the copious signs of intensive use of the books by him and by members of his circle, notably Joscelyn. Parker did not open his library to outsiders in the way Cotton was to do. He and his associates were, effectively, the sole users of the library, searching through the books for information that bore upon some of the most pressing issues of their own day and using the books as the basis for a major campaign of publication – the first of its kind in England – that saw Parker bring before the public an important series of editions of British historians as well as the first printings of works written in the Old English language. Whereas Cotton would largely be the facilitator of other people's researches, Parker himself played the leading role in and imposed his firm control over the use of his collection.

Often the first need confronting Parker on opening a manuscript was to identify its author and contents. He had contents lists drawn up and entered at the front of many volumes, either making use of existing blank endleaves or having fresh endleaves inserted for the purpose. Identifying an author, when the name was not given in the original title, frequently required a close reading of the text, and in several instances Parker took this work upon himself. CUL, MS Dd.2.5 is a case in point. The manuscript contains an interpolated version of the chronicle of Walter of Guisborough. Parker perceived the relationship with Guisborough's text and noted on the front pastedown, 'hoc chronicum habet historiam Wal. Gisborne, sed multo plura et ordine et materia'. Discovering that many of the interpolations concerned the history of Abingdon, Parker then made the correct deduction that the manuscript had been compiled there: 'ex cenobio Abindoniæ confectum est hoc chronicon', he wrote alongside the opening of the text on folio 1r, while to the pastedown one of his scribes added the observation, 'Author huius operis monachus Abindoniæ', accompanying this comment with references to six pages on which Abingdon interpolations could be found.

Once Parker had identified an author, he often had information about that author – when and where he had lived, what works he had written – entered on an endleaf, where it could provide a reader with some orientation to the manuscript. The main sources he tapped for such information were John Bale's two-volume *Scriptorum illustrium maioris Brytanniae catalogus* (Basel, 1557–9) for British authors and Johannes Tritheim's *Catalogus scriptorum ecclesiasticorum* (Cologne, 1531) for continental ones. At the front of CCCC, MS 150, Part II, a copy of Peter the Chanter's *Verbum abbreviatum*, Parker himself provided a reference to Tritheim's account of Peter: 'Author huius operis Petrus cantor Parisiensis. Claruit anno 1200. Tritheim fol. 81.' In CCCC, MS 292, a copy of Gervase of Tilbury's *Otia imperialia*, a Parkerian scribe has transcribed a lengthy section of Bale's entry on Gervase. The transcription provides biographical information and brief comments on some of Gervase's writings; it continues to the point where Bale mentions the *Otia* but excludes the rest of the entry. Transcriptions of similar passages from Bale's work can be found in, among other manuscripts, CCCC, MSS 175 (Walter of Coventry), 195 (Thomas Walsingham) and 277 (Adam of Barking).

Parker's notes at the front of his books sometimes included comments on their date and former ownership, especially when he believed he could link the books with prominent owners, in particular his archiepiscopal predecessors. It is perhaps not surprising that his observations were of wildly varying degrees of accuracy. When he wrote at the front of CCCC, MS 389, 'Hic liber scriptus ante Conquestum', he was right on target, for this copy of lives of St Paul the Hermit and St Guthlac had been made at St Augustine's Abbey, Canterbury, in the late tenth century. By contrast, his belief that his Northumbrian gospel fragment, CCCC, MS 197B, had belonged to St Augustine, the first archbishop of Canterbury, was wide of the mark, for the manuscript was made about a century after Augustine's death. But the most striking example of Parkerian wishful thinking was his ascription of nine of his manuscripts to Theodore of Tarsus, late seventh-century archbishop of Canterbury.[32] Seven of these manuscripts are in Greek; one is in Arabic; and one is a humanist copy of the *Rhetorica* of Cicero. None of them is earlier than the twelfth century; the Arabic one, indeed, is sixteenth-century; and five are written on paper, which of course was unknown in Europe in Theodore's time and for long afterwards. Yet each has a Parkerian inscription at the front proclaiming it as 'Liber quondam Theodori archiepiscopi' or the like. Parker evidently accorded his 'Theodoran' manuscripts special status within his collection. A note at the front of one of them, a fifteenth-century copy of Homer (CCCC, MS 81), comments that the archbishop regarded it as an immense treasure ('vt ingentem Thesaurum apud se asseruat'); and the antiquary William Lambarde records the special pride that Parker took in these books.[33]

32 CCCC, MSS 81, 158, 401, 403 and 480; CUL, MSS Ff.1.24, Ff.1.26 and Ii.3.25; and Cambridge, Trinity Coll., MS B.10.11.

33 W. Lambarde, *A perambulation of Kent: conteining the description, hystorie, and customes of that shyre* (London, 1576), 233. I am grateful to Carl T. Berkhout for bringing this passage to my attention. See also Parker's own reference to his 'Theodoran' books in his *De antiquitate Britannicæ ecclesiæ*, p. 14 of the second pagination sequence.

Parker and his associates commonly used the front endleaves of the manuscripts to jot down notes drawing attention to passages of particular interest and providing references to the pages on which those passages occurred. These notes, coupled with the frequent Parkerian marginalia to be found throughout the books, help to identify the issues that dominated the Parker circle's use of the collection. One point that emerges is that certain types of manuscript attracted little or no attention. These included technical treatises such as Boethius' *De arithmetica* (CCCC, MS 352); and poetic texts, whether in Latin like Prudentius' *Psychomachia* (CCCC, MSS 23 and 223), or in the vernacular, like Chaucer's *Troilus and Criseyde* (CCCC, MS 61). The manuscripts that were studied most closely included historical chronicles and books attesting to the doctrine and practices of the early English church. The passages that called forth Parkerian annotations tended to relate to a hard core of specific issues: abuses committed by the papacy; the credulousness of the medieval church; the church's doctrine and practice with regard to clerical marriage; church teaching concerning the eucharistic bread and wine; and the history of Canterbury. Most of these issues were central to the reformed English church's stance against Rome. Parker's major purpose in using his collection was to search for material that would bolster the position of the fledgling Church of England, of which he was primate.

The most prolific annotators by far were Parker and Joscelyn. Parker's search for material critical of the papacy emerges frequently, for example in his copy of Peter the Chanter's *Verbum abbreviatum*, where he has sketched a large pointing hand alongside a passage containing a remarkable anecdote attesting to papal capriciousness (CCCC, MS 150, fol. 140^{v}). Of even greater interest to him were passages indicating that there had been a time when clerical celibacy was not enforced, and yielding examples of priests who had been married. Finding no reference to the requirement for a priest to be celibate among the texts prescribing the ritual for the ordination of a priest in his Canterbury pontifical, he noted in the margin, 'In orationibus, in admonitionibus, in benedictionibus nulla mentio cælibatus' (CCCC, MS 44, p. 235); stumbling upon an account of a married clergyman in thirteenth-century England in an interpolated copy of the *Flores historiarum*, he scribbled alongside, 'vxoratus clericus in diebus Iohannis Peccham archiepiscopi Cantuariensis' (CCCC, MS 342, fol. 110^{r}). Both Parker and Joscelyn underlined a passage of one of Abbot Ælfric's *Pastoral letters* that demonstrated that at least some Anglo-Saxon priests had been married (CCCC, MS 265, p. 169). Parker and Joscelyn also found that the Anglo-Saxon manuscripts offered evidence that cast doubt on the historicity of the doctrine of transubstantiation. In a copy of Eadmer's *Vita sancti Odonis*, Parker underlined a passage describing clerics who held that the bread and wine of the Eucharist persisted in their former state after consecration, presenting a mere *figura* of the body and blood of Christ (CCCC, MS 371, p. 95); Joscelyn's attention was caught by a statement by Ælfric, most orthodox of Anglo-Saxon churchmen, to the effect that the bread and wine became Christ's body and blood in a spiritual, not a physical, sense (CCCC, MS 190, p. 156). Joscelyn was able to cross-refer to this passage when coming upon another copy of the same text in which the equivalent lines had been erased (CCCC, MS 265, p. 177); in an accompanying note, he indignantly attributed the erasure to 'quidam papista'. Cross-referencing among the manuscripts, and indeed between the manuscripts and Parker's printed books, was a frequent feature of the two men's annotations, and reveals the extraordinary depth of their familiarity with the books in the collection.

The programme of publication that Parker launched was the means by which he sought to bring manuscript materials before a wider audience and put them in the service of his church.[34] The centrepiece of the programme was a sequence of editions of major English historians based partly on his own manuscripts, partly on others borrowed from fellow collectors. The sequence included the *Flores historiarum*, first published in 1567 and issued in a much expanded second edition in 1570; Joscelyn's edition of Gildas's *De excidio et conquestu Britanniæ* (1567); Matthew Paris's *Chronica maiora* (1571); Asser's *De rebus gestis Ælfredi regis* (1574); and Thomas Walsingham's *Ypodigma Neustriæ* and *Historia Anglicana* (1574). While Parker's intention was in part to make better known as broad a span of English history as possible, from sub-Roman times to the fifteenth century, he also sought to underline what he perceived to be the unwarranted growth of papal power in England as the middle ages progressed; he chose to publish the *Flores historiarum* and *Chronica maiora* specifically because of the frankness with which these works described papal abuses.[35]

Parker claimed that in his editions he added or subtracted nothing from the original authors' words.[36] In practice, however, when he could enlarge on a point by adding material drawn from another source, he quite frequently did so, without signalling the interpolation; he has drawn heavy criticism for

34 For a recent, insightful assessment of Parker's aims and practices in his programme of publication, see B. S. Robinson, '"Darke speech": Matthew Parker and the reforming of history', *Sixteenth Century Journal* 29 (1998), 1061–83.

35 *Flores historiarum per Matthæum Westmonasteriensem collecti*, 2nd edn (London, 1570), Preface, p. [6]; and *Matthæi Paris, monachi Albanensis, Angli, historia maior, a Guilielmo conquestore, ad vltimum annum Henrici tertii* (London, 1571), sig. †.ii^{r}.

36 *Ælfredi regis res gestæ* (London, 1574), sig. ¶.ii^{r}.

this.[37] Two other works that he published offered him a more justifiable opportunity to combine material drawn from a melange of sources. The enlarged edition of *A defence of priestes mariages*, which appeared anonymously in about 1567 but displays unmistakable signs of Parker's controlling hand, includes at the end a section of some seventy pages marshalling and discussing the very passages relating to clerical marriage that have been annotated in his books.[38] In his *De antiquitate Britannicæ ecclesiæ* (1572), Parker sketched the origin and early progress of Christianity in England, the setbacks that the English church experienced at the hands of the papacy, and the sixteenth-century renewal. Especially in its early sections, the work presents a catena of material stitched together from numerous manuscript sources; the three-page chapter on Stigand, for example, draws on no fewer than sixteen sources.

Parker's two major Old English publications also put materials in his collection to the service of specific aims. The principal item in *A testimonie of antiquitie* (1566) was an Easter homily by Ælfric which in Parker's view demonstrated that the primitive English church had not believed in transubstantiation. *The gospels of the fower euangelistes* (1571) showed the public that a vernacular version of the Scriptures had been in circulation before the Norman Conquest and thereby provided a historical justification for contemporary translations; it was no coincidence that the sixteenth-century translation that Parker included in the book, alongside the Old English, was that of the Bishops' Bible of 1568, the very translation that he himself had sanctioned.

Parker's publications present the earliest case of an English collector harnessing the resources of his library to a co-ordinated plan of dissemination. That his manuscripts have continued to serve as the basis for editions and studies is due in no small measure to the care that the archbishop took to ensure the preservation of his books after his death.

Bestowal

Inspired by the desire to preserve the written record of England's medieval past from loss or destruction, Parker took great pains over the formation and maintenance of his collection of manuscripts. It was natural that, as he

37 See especially the sharp comments of Sir Frederic Madden in his *Matthæi Parisiensis, monachi sancti Albani, historia Anglorum, sive, ut vulgo dicitur, historia minor*, RS 44, 3 vols. (London, 1866–9), I. xxxi–xxxvii. See also W. H. Stevenson (ed.), *Asser's life of King Alfred, together with the Annals of Saint Neots erroneously ascribed to Asser*, 2nd edn (Oxford, 1959), xvii–xxi.

38 Page, *Matthew Parker and his books*, 89–92.

approached the end of his life, he should think carefully about how best to secure its continued safe keeping. Cambridge had always been close to his heart, and it was to two Cambridge institutions, the University Library and Corpus Christi College, that he entrusted the bulk of his library under conditions that are the most precise and protective for any bequest of books made in this period.

Not all of Parker's manuscripts, however, ended up in these two institutions. At some point Parker allotted several volumes to his two sons, John (1548–1619) and Matthew (1551–74), whose names he entered at the front of the books. These volumes include scriptural commentaries, Old and Middle English translations of the Scriptures, copies of the Old English *Pastoral care*, and major historical works such as Bede's *Historia ecclesiastica* and William of Malmesbury's *Gesta regum* and *Gesta pontificum*. John Parker inherited several more of his father's manuscripts, for there is a provision in the archbishop's will that any books not specifically bequeathed to anyone else were to pass to him.[39] It could have been in this way that John acquired many of the 109 manuscripts listed in his library catalogue in Lambeth MS 737.[40] Aside from the manuscripts given to his sons, a few other volumes seem to have escaped from Parker's grasp in one way or another. Among these is BL, MS Royal 15 B. xxii, the copy of Ælfric's *Grammar* that served as the exemplar for the Parkerian restoration of the missing text in CCCC, MS 449. At the front of the manuscript, 'Cor. Coll.' has been written in pencil at the top of fol. 5r; yet the manuscript entered the collection of John, Lord Lumley (c. 1534–1609), and passed thence into the royal library.[41]

It was in 1574 that Parker made a major gift of 100 volumes – twenty-five manuscripts and seventy-five printed books – to the University Library in Cambridge. His donation was a key element in the restoration of the library planned by Andrew Perne, master of Peterhouse.[42] Three other donors participated in the effort: Robert Horne, bishop of Winchester, James Pilkington, bishop of Durham, and Sir Nicholas Bacon, the lord keeper. Parker's gift was the most generous and, apart from the Anglo-Saxon psalter that fell within Bacon's donation (MS Ff.1.23), was the only one to include manuscripts. Among the

39 CCCC, Archives XL.A.48, p. 10. The will also includes a bequest of twenty books (to be selected by the archbishop's executors), as well as 'libros, quos illi peculiariter assignaui', to Parker's nephew, the student Samuel Harlestone. These were no doubt printed books.

40 S. Strongman, 'John Parker's manuscripts: an edition of the lists in Lambeth Palace MS 737', *TCBS* 7 (1977), 1–27.

41 S. Jayne and F. R. Johnson (eds.), *The Lumley library: the catalogue of* 1609 (London, 1956), no. 1555. Parker's copy of Asser's *Life of King Alfred* (BL, MS Cotton Otho A. xii) also passed into the Lumley library: Stevenson (ed.), *Asser's life of King Alfred*, xxxvii–xxxix.

42 Oates, *CUL*, 89–118.

manuscripts selected by Parker were six in Old English, as well as major copies of the medieval English chroniclers, including William of Malmesbury, Henry of Huntingdon, Gervase of Canterbury, Richard of Cirencester and Ranulf Higden. The printed books sub-divided into three categories, each comprising twenty-five volumes: protestant commentaries on the Old Testament, protestant commentaries on the New Testament, and a miscellaneous group including scriptural and historical works. Parker's books were given pride of place in Perne's newly restored library, with the commentaries occupying a large desk at the far end of the room, and the manuscripts chained and locked in a cupboard to the left of the entrance.[43] By a tripartite indenture between himself, the university and Corpus Christi College, Parker provided for the upkeep of the books by charging that it was to be the responsibility of the master and fellows of the college to repair and maintain the books and their chains; if the college failed to undertake repairs within forty days of being asked to do so, it was to pay a fine of 3s 4d a week until the repairs were duly completed.[44]

It was Corpus Christi College that acquired the great majority of Parker's books: some 433 manuscripts and well over 800 printed books. The terms under which the college would receive the collection were established in a quadripartite indenture between Parker and the masters and fellows of Corpus Christi, Gonville and Caius and Trinity Hall. This indenture, originally drawn up on Parker's sixty-fifth birthday, 6 August 1569, received its final form on 1 January 1575.[45] Corpus was to receive all the books listed in Parker's register, a copy of which was to be held by each of the colleges.[46] Parker envisaged that the books would be kept in the new library built during the mastership of John Porye (1557–69) specifically with the aim of receiving his books. The premises consisted of two rooms – the *maior bibliotheca* and the *minor bibliotheca* – located above the college's kitchen and buttery, on the south side of Old Court. The *maior bibliotheca*, suitably equipped with stalls, was to receive the folio-sized printed volumes. The remainder of the printed books and all the manuscripts would be stored in chests and cases in the *minor bibliotheca*, which was to have three locks on its door; the keys were to be held by the master and the two keepers of the college chest. In the event, Porye's library was short-lived, for

43 Oates, *CUL*, 113–18, with a diagram of the library on 116.

44 J. Heywood and T. Wright, *Cambridge University transactions during the Puritan controversies of the 16th and 17th centuries*, 2 vols. (London, 1854), I. 164–5.

45 There is a copy of the indenture at the front of CCCC, MS 575.

46 The three copies owned by the colleges are CCCC, MS 575, Gonville and Caius Coll., MS 710/743 and Trinity Hall, MS 29. See further Page, 'Parker Register', 1–17; and Page, *Matthew Parker and his books*, 2–16.

the college was soon provided with a new library in the roof of the chapel begun in 1578 with money given by Sir Nicholas Bacon. It is here that Parker's books were housed for nearly 250 years, until they were moved into the present library in New Court, completed in 1827.

Parker's indenture stipulated that Corpus was to be strictly accountable for the safe keeping of his books. Each year, on or within four days of 6 August, the masters of Gonville and Caius and Trinity Hall, accompanied by those colleges' two Parker scholars, were to conduct an inspection to verify that all the books listed in the Parker Register were present and in good condition. A missing leaf would incur a fine of 4d, a missing quire one of 2s. If a book had been lost, the college must replace it within three months; if it failed to do so, it would be allowed a further three months, after which, if the book was still unreplaced, it would pay an appropriate fine. If the college lost six manuscripts in folio, eight in quarto, or twelve of lesser size and failed to replace them within six months, the entire collection would be delivered into the custody of Gonville and Caius College, which would be held to the same conditions. If it too failed to meet them, the books would pass to Trinity Hall, and, if need be, back to Corpus again.

The indenture also established strict conditions of access, which was permitted only to the master and fellows of Corpus Christi, senior representatives of Gonville and Caius and Trinity Hall, and John Parker.[47] For the fellows of Corpus, the library would be open for six hours a day in winter and for nine during the rest of the year. Books had to be studied within the library, although the master might take up to three books to his lodging (but must not remove them from the college). No one was permitted to write in a book, and all fellows were obliged to swear to treat the books well and not remove them from the library; anyone refusing to take this oath would be denied access. The masters and two senior fellows of the other two colleges might use the library, but only if a fellow of Corpus were present; if either of the masters wished to transcribe from a manuscript, they were to be received in the master's lodging at Corpus, or in a fellow's room, and they would be fined if any leaf went missing. Special provision was made for John Parker to remove from the college any historical manuscript upon surrender of a pledge amounting to twice the value of the book. He must, however, return the book within three months, or he would forfeit the pledge, which the master and fellows could then use to purchase an appropriate new book.

47 The indenture actually names both of Parker's sons. Matthew, however, was no longer alive at the time this final version was drawn up; the text must have been copied without adaptation from an earlier version.

The college's account books for the late sixteenth and early seventeenth centuries show that Parker's directions were generally respected.[48] Every year, the college provided a meal for the officers of Gonville and Caius and Trinity Hall who conducted the annual inspection, and on several occasions it purchased printed books to replace lost items. Before long, however, Parker's conditions of access were modified to enable scholars with specialist interests to study the manuscripts. During the 1620s, William L'Isle, a former fellow of King's College who lived at Wilbraham, close to Cambridge, made transcriptions from Parker's homiliaries in connection with his plan to publish those portions of the Bible that had been translated into Old English; he also transcribed passages from Parker's copy of the Anglo-Saxon Chronicle.[49] There is no record of the arrangements under which L'Isle was granted access. The chance survival of a register of books that were removed from the library for study during the years 1643–8 reveals that Abraham Wheelock, university librarian and lecturer in Anglo-Saxon, was permitted to examine several of the Anglo-Saxon manuscripts.[50] While he was preparing his dual-language edition of Bede's *Historia ecclesiastica*, he even seems to have succeeded in taking the college's copy of the Old English version (CCCC, MS 41) to the University Library to collate it against his base manuscript, CUL, MS Kk.3.18.[51] Notwithstanding Parker's strictures against readers writing in his books, both L'Isle and Wheelock annotated the manuscripts that they studied.

By the late 1640s, the college was even prepared to unlock its library for scholars not resident in Cambridge or its environs. Parker's manuscripts were among the most important sources laid under contribution by the Kentish antiquary Sir Roger Twysden for his monumental collection of medieval English historians, *Historiæ Anglicanæ scriptores decem*, published in 1652. Twysden describes in his preface how his collaborator, Ralph Jennings, was received with all hospitality at Corpus and was permitted to transcribe complete texts.[52] Some forty years later, similar privileges were extended to Archbishop William Sancroft's

48 R. I. Page, 'Audits and replacements in the Parker Library: 1590–1650', *TCBS* 10 (1991), 17–39.

49 S. Lee, 'Oxford, Bodleian Library, MS Laud Misc. 381: William L'Isle, Ælfric, and the *Ancrene wisse*', in T. Graham (ed.), *The recovery of Old English: Anglo-Saxon studies in the sixteenth and seventeenth centuries* (Kalamazoo, 2000), 207–42; and P. Pulsiano, 'William L'Isle and the editing of Old English', in Graham, *The recovery of Old English*, 192–8.

50 The register is CCCC, Archives XXXIX.146.

51 T. Graham, 'Abraham Wheelock's use of CCCC MS 41 (Old English Bede) and the borrowing of manuscripts from the library of Corpus Christi College', *Cambridge Bibliographical Society Newsletter* (Summer 1997), 10–16.

52 R. Twysden (ed.), *Historiæ Anglicanæ scriptores X* (London, 1652), sig. A.3^{r}. For the identity of Twysden's collaborator, see F. W. Jessup, *Sir Roger Twysden, 1597–1672* (London, 1965), 198.

chaplain Henry Wharton, who made extensive use of materials at Corpus for his *Anglia sacra* (1691), a two-volume compilation of sources bearing upon the pre-Reformation history of the English dioceses and their bishops.[53]

These scholars' use of Parker's manuscripts was against the letter of his intentions for his collection, yet in many ways within the spirit, for it had been the archbishop's wish that through the study of the manuscripts 'the antiquitie of the state of these countryes may be restored to the knowledge of the world'.[54] It was in any case inevitable that, with the passage of time and the evolution of scholarship, Parker's restrictive conditions would have to be modified. He had, after all, created a private library of national importance, and the stature of his collection has only increased with the passage of time.

53 For Wharton's use of materials at Corpus, see especially the several references in the preface to vol. II of *Anglia sacra* (pp. x, xii–xiii, xix–xx, xxi and xxvii).

54 The phrase comes from the Privy Council letters of 1568.

PART THREE

★

TOOLS OF THE TRADE

13

Universities and colleges

KRISTIAN JENSEN

The history of college and university libraries in England and Scotland during the early modern period has been described with such knowledge of detail, and with such an awareness of a wider historical framework, that a reader might be excused for feeling that there is no requirement for another article on the topic.[1] Indeed, this chapter mainly aims to provide a survey of existing research, drawing together material published elsewhere. However, important new source material has been published which merits attention and will here be integrated into the discussion of early modern collections.[2] The chosen emphasis of the summary will inevitably articulate my own interests and views.

While there are differences between institutions in England and those in Scotland, and while trade routes vary, it is probably fair to say that trends in library provisions can best be seen as reflecting differences in the size of institutions and in geographical distance from the main European book producing centres, rather than what one might call national differences. I will not, therefore, treat Scotland and England separately, but try to draw out shared trends, problems and solutions.

Books in universities were owned by individual scholars, by colleges and by university libraries. The development of the collections of these three types of owners followed different paths, but they were closely interdependent, all being affected by changing economic, political and intellectual circumstances during the sixteenth and seventeenth centuries.

1 For Oxford, most importantly N. R. Ker, 'The provision of books', in *HUO* III. 441–86; and his *Oxford college libraries in 1556: guide to an exhibition held in 1956* [at the Bodleian Library] (Oxford, 1956); and 'Oxford college libraries in the sixteenth century', *BLR* 6 (1959), 459–515 (repr. in his *Books, collectors and libraries*, 379–436); I. G. Philip and P. Morgan, 'Libraries, books, and printing', in *HUO* IV. 650–85; I. Philip, *The Bodleian Library in the seventeenth and eighteenth centuries* (Oxford, 1983). For Cambridge, in particular J. P. W. Gaskell, *Trinity College Library: the first 150 years* (Cambridge, 1980) and Oates, *CUL*.

2 Notably the lists of books contained in the probate records of the two English universities, published in *BCI* and *PLRE*, and the library catalogues from Cambridge in CBMLC X.

When, in 1540, the monasteries in England and Wales were dissolved, their book collections suffered severely. The same fate befell the collections of those colleges which had been maintained by monastic houses. They had been particularly prominent in Oxford, where the closure of Gloucester College, Durham College and Canterbury College must have meant a significant loss of manuscript books. The collection of Canterbury College was by far the largest and it is well documented,[3] so the scale of its loss can be easily understood. But, even in Oxford, by far the greater number of colleges were non-monastic institutions. They were not dissolved, and their fate was consequently radically different.

In 1535, under Henry VIII, a number of scholastic texts – Duns Scotus, Walter Burley, Antonius Trombetta, Thomas Bricot and Stephanus Brulefer – were excluded from the Cambridge curriculum by direct royal intervention.[4] This coincided with a royal drive for religious reform. Many protestant reformers were vociferous in rejecting parts of the philosophical tradition of the late middle ages, and their arguments were certainly not devoid of theological import. The reformers continued a critique which had been begun in the fifteenth century, and a straightforward causal link between the Reformation and the change to the curriculum cannot be sustained. The authors excluded from the Cambridge curriculum would in the 1520s and 1530s also have seemed old-fashioned and irrelevant at European universities which did not undergo a protestant reform.[5] However, in the increasingly polarised world of the sixteenth century, conservative opposition to religious reform could find expression as opposition to a change in the curriculum and, in an English context, there is a clear correlation between a wish to reform the curriculum and an interest in religious reform.[6] An impression of the complexity of the situation can be seen from the texts which were listed as new standard texts by the Henrician injunctions. In the teaching of philosophy the commentaries and *quaestiones* on Aristotle were eliminated from the curriculum in favour of lectures on Aristotle's own texts, perhaps somewhat unrealistically, and, more realistically, the study of Rudolphus Agricola, Philipp Melanchthon and Georgius Trapezuntius. Of these only Melanchthon was a Protestant.

3 See the inventories published by W. A. Pantin, *Canterbury College, Oxford*, OHS, n.s. 6–8, 3 vols. (1947–50), I. 1–76.

4 *Statuta Academiae Cantabrigiensis* (Cambridge, 1785), 137.

5 See, for instance, A. Seifert, 'Der Humanismus an den Artistenfakultten des katholischen Deutschlands', in W. Reinhard (ed.), *Humanismus im Bildungswesen des 15. und 16. Jahrhunderts*, Mitteilungen XII der Kommision für Humanismusforschung (Weinheim, 1984), 135–54.

6 J. M. Fletcher, 'The Faculty of Arts', in *HUO* III. 159.

It must be emphasised that the production, sale or ownership of the rejected texts was not prohibited. Undoubtedly, royal support for reform of the curriculum will have given succour to reformers within the universities and will have contributed to the diminished importance of certain texts. Their increased irrelevance would have made them more vulnerable to disposal, even at Oxford, where there was no concerted radical reform of the curriculum in the Tudor period, but there is no evidence to support suggestions that medieval book collections in Oxford and Cambridge non-monastic colleges were destroyed for religious reasons under Henry VIII or indeed Edward VI.[7]

Nor is there contemporary evidence connecting the losses suffered by the university libraries of Cambridge and Oxford with the Edwardian visitations in 1550. No money was spent on books in the university library of Cambridge from 1530 to 1573. The accounts survive, but only indicate expenditure on cleaning and maintenance of the building.[8] The library was in practice abandoned in 1546–47.[9] The last documented use of the university library of Oxford is from 1528. John Leland visited the library in the 1530s and listed thirty-one titles, partly based on then existing lists. In the late 1540s John Bale listed eight items of interest for his purpose, but it is not certain whether he actually saw these books or knew about them from other lists. Opened as recently as 1488 but since then bereft of funds and patronage, the medieval university library lacked a voice in a corporate institution consisting of increasingly powerful colleges, and its dispersal was probably down mainly to neglect. Whatever its causes, the process of destruction was complete by January 1556, under Mary Tudor, when the university set up a committee to dispose of the wood used for the library furniture.

If we look at the lists of books which were in the collection of the University of Oxford in the fifteenth century, it is hard to find books which would have caused Edward VI's protestant commissioners much worry. The large sections on civil law were inoffensive, and not even books on canon law were banned. Late medieval biblical commentaries and scholastic theology may have been considered old-fashioned but were certainly not illicit. Manuscripts of classical authors were prominent among those donated by Duke Humfrey, Cicero, Juvenal, Plutarch or Ptolemy, for instance, as were medical manuscripts. It is

7 Despite statements to the contrary, for instance in CBMLC x. Here the changes to the curriculum are repeatedly described as a proscription of books, and it is several times stated that, in contrast to Cambridge, there is evidence for the destruction of books in Oxford as a result of the Edwardian visitations. On the Edwardian visitations at both Oxford and Cambridge see C. Cross, 'Oxford and the Tudor state from the accession of Henry VIII to the death of Mary,' in *HUO* III. 133–9.

8 Oates, *CUL*, 73.

9 *Ibid.*, 81

difficult to imagine that either category would have been offensive to protestant commissioners. Nor would the collection of patristic texts have been suspect. For instance, a manuscript of Athanasius translated into Latin, part of Duke Humfrey's donation from 1444, was in the hands of a private owner by 1550. With a few other surviving items it has been adduced as evidence for the likelihood that books were dispersed in connection with the Edwardian visitation.[10] But Athanasius was a Church Father particularly dear to Luther,[11] who used his work for supporting his opposition to the worship of images. Some works of Athanasius were printed in Wittenberg in 1532 with a preface by Luther and Johannes Bugenhagen,[12] so this book can hardly have given offence to protestants. We must look for other reasons why volumes like this left the university's library at Oxford, and this will help us to understand better the development of book collection within the universities.

Like central university libraries, college libraries undoubtedly suffered losses due to neglect or indifference to earlier books.[13] Many books must have been lost simply because their texts increasingly seemed unimportant, but also manuscripts with texts which were not outdated ran the risk of seeming irrelevant. In this way the disappearance of many medieval manuscripts must in part be due to a similarity between printed books and manuscripts – many standard texts which would have been present in manuscript form became available in printed editions during the first hundred years after the invention of printing and there is evidence that these printed editions were bought by colleges. The years from the mid-1530s to the end of the reign of Edward VI saw colleges in Oxford engaged in a rare level of expenditure on buying books. The period of intense purchasing coincides with the demise of the central university collections, and reflects how power shifted from the university towards colleges. In the years between 1536 and 1550, Magdalen College spend £73 on books, perhaps amounting to 150 volumes, and by 1550 it possessed some modern books in most disciplines of the arts faculty, including history, classics and natural science, but also in medicine, civil law and theology. All Souls spent at least £46 between 1544/5 and 1547/8. Merton spent around £60 in about 1549.

10 BL, MS Royal 5 F. ii, in the hands of George Berche of Brasenose College. On the medieval library, its dispersal and its surviving manuscripts, see in particular A. C. de la Mare in de la Mare and S. Gillam (eds.) *Duke Humfrey's library and the Divinity School, 1488–1988: an exhibition at the Bodleian Library, June–August 1988* (Oxford 1988), 118, no. 32.

11 B. Lohse, 'Luther and Athanasius', *Luther Digest* 4 (1996).

12 *Athanasij libri contra idolatriam gentium, et de fide Sancte Trinitatis. Cum praefatione D. Martini Lutheri et D. Joannis Pommerani* (Wittemberg, 1532).

13 Thus King's College, Cambridge: see W. D. J. Cargill Thompson, 'Notes on King's College Library 1500–1570, in particular for the period of the Reformation', *TCBS* 2 (1954), 39.

In 1543–4 Oriel sold plate to the value of £30 in order to buy books, especially on theology. From 1544 to 1553 New College spent some £40 on buying books. More recent foundations, such as Corpus Christi at Oxford, probably had no need to buy new books as it had the recent bequest of John Claymond of 1537.[14] The purchasing activities of the second quarter of the century must have meant that many older books became vulnerable to disposal. Most college libraries would have been full, and new books required space, and it would have seemed sensible to replace a worn-out old book in an increasingly alien script with an up-to-date edition of the same text.

One might have thought that the books purchased in those years would have reflected a growing interest in Protestantism, and perhaps contemporaries were also under that impression. In the reign of Mary Tudor, during the first months of 1557, Cardinal Pole organised visitations of the two English universities. To assist their work, the Marian visitors required lists to be drawn up of books both in public and in private ownership, for, in contrast to the situation under the Edwardian visitation, the production, sale and mere possession of religiously unacceptable books were by now crimes. The visitation is best documented in Cambridge. A list of books in the university's collection drawn up for the Marian visitors contains a substantial number of medieval manuscripts[15] and, from the college libraries of Clare, King's, Pembroke, St John's and Trinity Hall,[16] as well as perhaps for Corpus Christi College,[17] there is evidence that the medieval college libraries had survived more or less intact. In Oxford, surviving lists of the collections of Merton College and All Souls and probably Brasenose, drawn up for the Marian visitors in 1557, show that numerous medieval books survived in the late 1550s, in the case of Merton some 300, most of which are still in the college's collection today.[18] These books include many of the texts which under Henry VIII had been excluded from the curriculum. Evidence that medieval college collections survived the radical Protestantism of Edward VI is thus abundant from the documentation deriving from the Catholic visitation.

Modern books, on the other hand, are remarkably few among those listed for the Marian visitors. Unsurprisingly, not a single book by a protestant author is found in any of them. The absence of illegal books may mean that college officials simply omitted titles when faced with Pole's oppressive

14 Ker, 'Oxford college libraries', 480 (*Books, collectors and libraries*, 400).

15 Oates, *CUL*, 79.

16 CBMLC x. UC7, UC16, UC 30, UC45, UC56, U 60 and UC25.

17 J. Fletcher and J. McConica, 'A sixteenth-century inventory of the library of Corpus Christi College Cambridge', *TCBS* 3 (1959–63), 187–99.

18 Ker, *Oxford college libraries*, 5.

measure. If they excluded them from their lists they probably also organised their destruction, for no Oxford college now contains any protestant book which can be shown to have been bought before the accession of Elizabeth I, whereas numerous patristic editions can still be identified with books acquired in that period.[19] Although protestant library books must have been lost to the zeal of the commissioners, this aspect should not be exaggerated as far as shared book collections are concerned. Books in university and college libraries were chained to lecterns, on which they were stored lying on their covers. They were meant to be read, or to be used for reference, *in situ* by senior members of the institutions. Small books would not have been considered appropriate for library use and it would have been impractical and a waste of space to have kept them chained on lecterns. The works of patristic authors were perceived to be canonical, above the changing fashions of time, and their authoritative status was given visual expression in the monumental editions of their works. Protestantism was not yet an establishment religion and most protestant authors had not yet achieved the status of authorities. That difference is reflected in the books which protestant authors produced. In the 1550s most protestant books were still fairly small volumes, often of a polemical kind, addressing issues of the day. This was not the sort of book which would have had a natural place in an institutional library designed to hold large folio volumes. They would have been much more likely to have been found in private collections.

Although some protestant authors were to be had in library-type volumes (for instance Martin Bucer, Martin Luther, Philipp Melanchthon and Conrad Pellicanus), their absence from the Marian lists of shared libraries cannot in itself be taken as a sign that the libraries were purged of accessions from the 1530s, 1540s and 1550s. We should perhaps rather read the absence of protestant texts as a useful hint for us to understand the relative importance of shared and private collections. With the growing importance of colleges within the universities, college libraries were subject to less dramatic change than the university collections, but they also seem to have been losing their importance in the middle of the century. They did not have up-to-date books and they were structurally ill-arranged to provide access to the small books which were of often keenest contemporary interest.

As David McKitterick has argued in connection with his study of the library of St John's College, Cambridge,[20] some college collections were so deficient that private collections must have been the mainstay of the work of many

19 *Ibid.*, and Ker, 'The provision of books', 448–9.

20 D. McKitterick, 'Two sixteenth-century catalogues of St John's College Library', *TCBS* 7 (1978), 135–55.

scholars. In other words, during the sixteenth century the affordability of printed books increased to the extent that scholars seem to have had the means required for owning the books which they needed for their work. This meant that college and university libraries were for a time less needed than before. The acquisitions from the reign of Henry VIII and Edward VI did not set a lasting pattern and colleges reverted to the traditional policy of relying on donations for augmenting their collections. Ker pointed out that Trinity College, Oxford, probably spent more on feasting the bishop of Winchester on 2 August 1576 than on the library over forty-five years.[21]

This revolution in the fortunes of private and shared collections would obviously not have been possible without the invention of printing. The impact on academic communication did not follow immediately from Gutenberg's invention, but the change was fairly rapid and, more importantly, the impact continued to gather momentum. While comparisons are difficult, it is clear that prices of books did not fall dramatically immediately following the invention of printing, but that they did fall significantly over a longer period of time.[22] This had a significant impact on collecting patterns. One may, by way of illustration, look at the sizes of collections of books. The Scholar of Oxenford was one of the few virtuous characters in Chaucer's *Canterbury Tales*, written some time before 1400. Chaucer's character bought books for all the money which was donated to him and had at 'his beddes heed | Twenty bookes, clad in blak or reed | Of Aristotle and his philosophie'.[23] Other evidence indicates that this would indeed have been a large book collection for a scholar to have in his private library at that time. Already at the beginning of the sixteenth century a junior scholar might easily have a dozen books or so. Evidence from probate lists drawn up by the authorities in Cambridge[24] and Oxford[25] during the sixteenth century show how things changed. Towards the middle of the sixteenth century a scholar could easily have 100 books in his private

21 Ker, 'Oxford college libraries', 469 (*Books, collectors and libraries*, 389).

22 For a useful survey of information about fifteenth-century book prices see U. Neddermeyer, *Von der Handschrift zum gedruckten Buch: Schriftlichkeit und Leseinteresse im Mittelalter und in der frühen Neuzeit: Quantitative und qualitative Aspekte*, Buchwissenschaftliche Beiträge aus dem Deutschen Bucharchiv München, 61 (Wiesbaden, 1998), II. 831–62; L. Hoffmann, 'Gutenberg und die Folgen: Zur Entwicklung des Bücherpreises im 15. und 16. Jahrhundert', *Bibliothek und Wissenschaft*, 29 (1996), 9. On the point at which printed books began to fall in price, see also L. Hoffmann, 'Buchmarkt und Bücherpreise im Frühdruckzeitalter', *Gutenberg-Jahrbuch* 75 (2000), 73–81; and the section 'Buying printed books' in B. Richardson, *Printing, writers and readers in Renaissance Italy* (Cambridge, 1999), 112–18.

23 Geoffrey Chaucer, *The Canterbury Tales*, the general prologue, lines 293–95 (L. D. Benson (ed.), *The Riverside Chaucer*, 3rd edn (Oxford, 1988), 28).

24 *BCI*. 25 *PLRE*.

collection. Private libraries approaching 200–300 volumes are rare, but they do occur. For instance, when Edward Wygan, the first regius professor of divinity at Cambridge, died in 1545, 186 titles were listed in the probate inventory of his possessions.[26] When Oliver Ainsworth died in 1546, 292 items were listed in the probate inventory of his collection, an evidently Lutheran one which, for instance, contained as no. 70 'Opera Athanasii' valued at 'viij d'.[27] Even more remarkable is the collection of a Richard Cliff, a relatively young scholar who died at about thirty in 1566, leaving no trace of an academic career. Indeed, hardly anything is known about him except that he left a collection of 261 books.[28] If we remember that the total of books given to the University of Oxford by Duke Humfrey between 1435 and 1443/4 was in the order of 280, we can see how things have changed[29] and why scholars had less need for the central collections. By the 1570s and 1580s, junior scholars could easily have more books in their private libraries than even senior scholars in the first half of the century, and more senior scholars could have 300 books or more in their libraries, more books than a very good late fifteenth-century college collection, even if undoubtedly of a different type.

Medieval colleges had had unchained collections of books, said to be *in electione*, which fellows, but not undergraduates, could borrow on an annual rotation basis for use in their studies. These books seem to have been of the same nature as the books chained in the libraries, but were probably second-best or worn-out copies. There can be little doubt that these books were disposed of with little ceremony once they had lost their value, when even students could afford to buy their own books to read in private. In the words of Neil Ker, 'it is well to have these circulating collections in mind when we read of the destruction of books in the middle of the century'.[30]

In 1586 the authorities in Oxford by and large stopped listing people's books for probate purposes, so we no longer have numbers telling us the sizes of private scholars' libraries, but that in itself is an indication: books had become so numerous and so cheap that they were assessed only in the most general way for probate. This tendency is already clear in the busy year of 1577, when

26 *BCI*, i, 138–42. 27 *Ibid.*, 81–6.

28 D. Pearson, 'Richard Cliff. Cleric (chaplain). Scholar (M.A.), probate inventory and will. 1566', *PLRE* 73 (III. 80–118).

29 De la Mare and Gillam, *Duke Humfrey's library*, 18.

30 Ker, 'Oxford college libraries', 464 (*Books, collectors and libraries*, 384). Ker mentions the survival of eighteen circulating books at Lincoln College, Oxford, in the 1590s, half of them being one set of the works of Augustine, and he mentions lists of college books in the rooms of fellows at All Souls in the seventeenth century. These are undoubtedly later printed books.

so many in Oxford died of the plague. The men who drew up the lists of possessions often cut corners. One feels a great deal of sympathy for them when they give up at entry number 228 in the list of books left by James Reynolds, and write 'a hundreth parchment old bokes', only to be followed by another entry, 'xxii Englyshe bokes'.[31] The 228 books which were lumped together by exasperated probate officers under one heading in 1577 would have constituted a collection beyond the dreams of any but the most senior academic at the beginning of the century.

The number of books is not all that counts. Having the right books is at least as important, and that is where a private collection has an advantage over a shared one: it can be put together to reflect the owner's own special interests. This is of evident importance in theology, where the sixteenth century offered so much more controversial diversity of opinion than the late middle ages. We saw that Ainsworth had a collection with a Lutheran bias, while other academic book-owners can be seen to have a Calvinist or a Roman Catholic bias. A shared collection of the late medieval type could not have enough books to cater for such a degree of divergent specialisation, even within a topic as well covered by the traditional college libraries as theology. Also, in fields which were not the subject of religious controversy, private collections could by the mid-sixteenth century exceed in quality and breadth any of the shared collections. Thomas Simons, of Oxford, died in 1553, leaving a preponderantly medical collection of 131 volumes. No contemporary public collection could have matched his collection of the long-established Greek and Arabic authorities and especially not his modern medical literature,[32] which college libraries were particularly slow in acquiring.

However, at least in one respect we are not comparing like with like. Late medieval institutions had large chained folios in their libraries, books deemed to be of lasting importance; the late sixteenth-century scholar might have had a fair number of folios, but his collection would inevitably have contained many small-format items. From *ISTC* we can see that, in the first decade after the invention of printing, from 1456 to 1465, some 45 per cent of surviving editions are in folio; by the last decade of the fifteenth century, the proportion had fallen dramatically to about 30 per cent. This reduction in the proportion of folio volumes continued. As a very rough indication one can see that only 15 per cent of the editions now in the Bodleian Library produced between 1551

31 R. J. Fehrenbach and M. Feingold, 'James Reynolds. Scholar (MA), probate inventory. 1577', *PLRE* 127 (IV. 4–37).

32 M. L. Schwarz, 'Thomas Simons, Scholar (M.A., B.M.); probate inventory. 1553', *PLRE* 65 (II. 222–43).

and 1560 are in folio, and the corresponding figure for 1641 to 1650 is about 7 per cent.[33]

Small-scale books had long been written by students or scholars, whether in the form of lecture notes or as copies of short standard texts, but they were made for private purposes. A medium-term impact of the invention of printing was to turn small, individually inexpensive books into commercially viable merchandise which could be produced for sale throughout Latinate western Europe. The commercially viable small books were the up-to-date tools of the trade for the sixteenth-century scholar.

Acrimonious debate is characteristic of sixteenth-century scholarship in many fields.[34] Controversial books become both commercially possible and commercially desirable. Instead of commentary on Aristotle's Natural History enshrined in a dignified tome, a scholar might own the exchanges of controversial views on natural philosophy between Hieronymus Cardanus and his opponent Julius Caesar Scaliger, printed in quarto and even in octavo. Instead of a commentary on the works of Aristotle, which constituted the elementary logic course, a scholar or even a student might own a small text book summarising the teachings of the philosopher, often from a tendentious point of view, which would require the scholar to own several manuals on the same topic, each taking a different point of view. This cannot be better exemplified than by John Tatham, who died at Oxford in 1576, and left a library of well over 300 items, entry number 222 being 'a great many of lytell bookes in parchment to the nomber of on [one] hundrethe'. Even discounting the 100 small parchment-bound volumes, the collection was in particular strong in small books, abridgements, epitomes, compendia, digests, handbooks and collections of excerpts – whether in theology, philosophy or other subjects, as Charles Huttar, the editor of Tatham's probate list, notes in his introduction. Huttar also notes that Tatham had an interest in the contemporary debates concerning method, a topic which is directly related to the phenomenon of the emergence of the manual as the all-conquering university teaching and learning tool. It is also a strikingly up-to-date collection. Fifteen of Tatham's books were certainly printed in the 1570s and another seventy or so might have been.[35]

33 This evidence can be derived from the CD-ROM version of the Bodleian Library's pre-1920 catalogue.

34 As witnessed, for example, in the field of divinity: P. Milward, *Religious controversies of the Elizabethan age: a survey of printed sources* (London, 1978).

35 C. A. Huttar, 'John Tatham. Scholar (M.A.) Probate Inventory. 1576', *PLRE* 112 (IV. 256–94). While it is true, as stated by Ker, *Oxford college libraries*, 9, that institutions and scholars depended partly on what was to be had at the bookseller's, one should not

Small books typically contained texts and genres which would not have found their way into folio format, but not exclusively. Many of the texts which were frequently found as library texts in the late middle ages, in large chained volumes, could now be found in small format suitable mainly for private collection. There is no better illustration of this than the appearance in 1551–3 of the complete works of Aristotle in octavo format, first in Greek[36] and then in 1560 in Latin, and in duodecimo with the commentaries of Averroes,[37] and in the 1570s even in decimosexto.[38] The Latin Aristotle, a typical medieval library text, was transformed into a set of books for private ownership by individual scholars, as was even the Greek original, which would have been out of reach for most medieval institutions. Many other texts and text types shared this transition. It will have been hard in 1558 to have found a college library which was better in the field of classical Latin and Greek texts than that of William Brown, who, after a successful career at Merton College, died in 1558, leaving a collection of 231 books, covering nearly all the classical poets including the dramatists, and many of the historians, often in both Latin and Greek.[39] The survival of the university's collection of manuscripts of the classics would have been of no importance to him, when he himself had all the main classical authors, and it would not have mattered to him that his copies of the texts were in small formats.

For the individual scholar, the international availability of small scholarly books meant that it became possible to build up a large collection which catered to his private needs. At the level of a specific university, the commercial viability of the Europe-wide export of small cheap books meant that a greater diversity of texts was in circulation, as books were available from many different sources. In particular, for universities and colleges, like the English and Scottish ones, which were not associated with a successful book-producing centre, it also had the effect of obliterating or at least diminishing the importance of local textual traditions, replacing books for local use by the ones which could be imported from abroad. This meant that it became increasingly difficult to impose a specific local academic tradition; the fixed curriculum became ever more fictive.

underestimate the efficiency of the trade. This can be seen from surviving probate lists, where owners often had books which were published only shortly before their death. See also J. Roberts, 'Importing books for Oxford, 1500–1640', in Carley and Tite, *Books and collectors*, 327–8.

36 Apud Aldii filios, Venetiis, 1551–53.

37 Apud iunctas, Venetiis, 1562.

38 Ex officina Salicatiana: Venetiis, 1576.

39 S. Gillespie, 'William Brown. Scholar (M. A.): Probate inventory. 1558', *PLRE* 67 (III. 1–35).

These changes in the fortunes of private and shared collections can thus be seen as the result of a complex interaction between printers and publishers on the one hand and scholars and their institutions on the other. The commercial mass production of books for universities and colleges depended on the publishers catering for a need felt by scholars for books, and on their commercial availability. But, simultaneously, publishers both stimulated and created the scholarly need for which they catered. Most obviously they did this by making excessive claims about the novelty of a production, presenting as a radical revision a barely changed text, or even a set of reissued sheets provided with a new title page. Less directly manipulative but probably much more important, the production itself stimulated demand among a user group which wanted to keep up with developments in their field, and who would in turn produce for the press their own responses and contributions. Religious, scholarly and scientific debate itself became a marketable commodity from which profit could be made.

This trend continued strongly, so that towards the end of the sixteenth century the rapidly expanding book production, alongside a changing and expanding curriculum, had become so large that it was becoming impossible for individual scholars to keep up with the books which they needed. This led to a renewed interest in shared facilities.

According to Neil Ker, there are no extant accounts of disbursements at Balliol before 1572 or at Oriel between 1527 and 1582, and there is only one Christ Church account before 1577.[40] At Merton there is no evidence that money was spent on buying books until 1584, but under Henry Savile, the warden, whose intellectual ambitions were matched by his practical abilities, substantial sums were spent on buying books in Italy and in Frankfurt.[41] Magdalen College, Oxford, as active a purchaser of books under Elizabeth as it had been under Henry and Edward, bought the collection of John Jewel in 1572.

The university libraries began their revival at much the same time as those of the colleges. Cambridge University Library began to regain its importance in 1574 and was well endowed with donations for the rest of the century, making up for the half century of inactivity, before entering another period of repose around 1600.[42] Edinburgh University Library was founded in 1580,[43] and in

40 Ker, 'Oxford college libraries', 460 (*Books, collectors and libraries*, 380).

41 *Ibid.*, 508 (428).

42 Oates, *CUL*, 89–110.

43 J. R. Guild and A. Law (eds.), *Edinburgh University Library, 1580–1980: a collection of historical essays* (Edinburgh, 1982); J. D. T. Hall (ed.), *Edinburgh University Library, 1580–1980: a commemorative exhibition* (Edinburgh, 1980).

Oxford, with the foundation of the Bodleian Library in 1602,[44] the revival of central library provisions was as spectacular as had been the demise of the fifteenth-century institution.

Traditionally, libraries had relied on donations for their new acquisitions. The system of donations had probably worked comparatively well in the fifteenth century, when there was still a relatively contained number of standard texts and standard commentaries which would typically be found in a college library, and large-scale donations continued to be of great importance. Indeed, the revival of the shared collections was strongly reinforced by some large donations, mainly of protestant books collected after the accession of Elizabeth, almost entirely lacking those issued in the 1520s, 1530s and 1540s. Archbishop Matthew Parker's bequest to Corpus Christi, in 1574, and Andrew Perne's bequest to Peterhouse are the two most important examples, both from Cambridge.[45] A gift to All Souls in 1576 brought some protestant books into the library for the first time. Corpus in Oxford received a substantial bequest in 1571, from its president Thomas Greneway; and Queen's College, Oxford, acquired the library of Archbishop Grindal in 1583.[46] Colleges in the 1570s and 1580s finally began to catch up with the most important intellectual change of the sixteenth century. In Scotland, donors who had studied abroad made a significant difference to the collection of continental books in their areas. For instance, Clement Litill's large, chiefly theological collection, valued at 1,000 marks, which was bequeathed in 1580 to Edinburgh, and which became the foundation collection of the university library, may in part reflect his time as a student in Louvain.[47] There were also many books in his collection which can be traced to the dissolution of the monastic collections in 1559. The preponderantly medical bequest to Marischal College, Aberdeen, made by Duncan Liddell (1561–1613), reflects his time as professor of mathematics and medicine at the university at Helmsted,[48] in the same way as the bequest of books on classical languages and philosophy drawn up by Thomas Reid in 1624 reveals his time as teacher of philosophy at Rostock.[49]

44 There is an extensive literature on the Bodleian Library, but see I. Philip, *The Bodleian Library in the seventeenth and eighteenth centuries* (Oxford, 1983).

45 G. H. S. Bushnell and R. I. Page, *Matthew Parker's legacy: books and plate* (Cambridge, 1975).

46 Ker, 'Oxford college libraries', 499 (*Books, collectors and libraries*, 420).

47 Hall, *Edinburgh University Library, 1580–1980*, cf. item 2; C. P. Finlayson, *Clement Litill and his library: the origins of Edinburgh University Library* (Edinburgh, 1980), 21.

48 G. Molland, 'Duncan Liddell (1561–1613): an early benefactor of Marischal College Library', *Aberdeen University Review* 51(1985/6), 485–99.

49 B. Fabian (ed.), *Handbuch deutscher historischer Buchbestände in Europa*, Band 10: *a guide to collections of books printed in German-speaking countries before 1901 (or in German elsewhere)*

The time-honoured system of acquisition by donation had always had its problems. Its inbuilt conservatism might have mattered a little less when libraries were repositories of a shared body of standard texts. By relying on donations, at best reflecting the academic interests of the most recently deceased generation, libraries could not provide scholars with knowledge about the most recent developments or controversies. They would not be able to compete with the currency of the private libraries which we have analysed above. Donations can only ever provide patchy coverage, as is revealed by the continued prominence of retrospective purchasing of books from the early part of the sixteenth century by Edinburgh University Library from bequests of money in the 1620s and 1630.[50] Reliance on donation also increased the risk of duplication. Colleges could risk ending up in the situation of the Augustinian canons at the Abbey of St Mary in Leicester, whose fifteenth-century catalogue records seventeen complete bibles, fifteen of which have names of donors associated with them, mainly canons at Leicester itself, and therefore probably difficult to alienate.[51] Because of the narrower shared universe of reading, one must assume that late medieval college libraries suffered even more from the donation of duplicates than later institutions would, but the problems which Thomas James faced in the newly founded Bodleian Library concerning the donation of duplicates are very telling of how wasteful the reliance on donation could be.[52]

The absence of a collection policy has more of an impact in fields of study which are furthest removed from the core curriculum, for instance law. Books relating to topics which were not frequently taught would not be donated by teachers and students. This explains why Thomas Simons, who died in 1553 in Oxford, whom we mentioned above, would have been better served by his own collection of 131 preponderantly medical volumes than by any institution in

held by libraries in Great Britain and Ireland, x, ed. G. Jefcoate and others (Hildesheim, 2000), 150; I. Bevan, 'Marischal College, Aberdeen, and its earliest library catalogue: a reassessment', *The Bibliotheck: A Journal of Scottish Bibliography* 22 (1997), 4–19.

50 When William Rig in 1619 left a sum of money to Edinburgh University Library, the regents bought twenty-six books, mainly choosing scientific and medical books. These included several sixteenth-century books, for instance Vesalius and Gesner; and in 1635 the library acquired Budaeus, *De asse et partibus eius*, from 1527. C. P. Finlayson and S. M. Simpson, 'The history of the library 1580–1710', in Guild and Law, *Edinburgh University Library, 1580–1980*, 45, state that the sum was 200 Scottish pounds (= 300 marks); see also *ibid.*, 211; and Hill, *Edinburgh University Library, 1580–1980*, item 7.

51 CBMLC VI. A20.1–17.

52 On the problem of duplication in the early years of the Bodleian Library see K. Jensen, 'Problems of provenance: incunabula in the Bodleian Library's Benefactors' Register 1600–1602', in M. Davies (ed.), *Incunabula: studies in fifteenth-century printed books presented to Lotte Hellinga* (London, 1999), 567–9.

Oxford or Cambridge. Large donations of specialist collections could make up for these shortcomings, for a while. The bequest to Exeter College in Oxford of the books of its rector John Dotyn in 1561 was the largest bequest of medical books in the sixteenth century.[53] Upon the death of Sir Thomas Smith in 1576, Queens' College in Cambridge received his outstanding collection, containing an important legal library. But such donations were soon out of date in the rapidly evolving intellectual world. In the case of law, no Cambridge or Oxford library collected legal texts systematically during the sixteenth century.[54]

In Edinburgh, large-scale donations continued to play a role in the development of the university library,[55] but means were sought to make it a more manageable method. The regular acquisition by compulsory donation of books to the university library by students on graduation was by 1635 replaced by a fee, which gave the library more control over a limited budget for acquisitions,[56] and the same happened in Glasgow in 1637.[57] This system was known at Merton College from 1587/8 and later, when the admission money was said to be *ad usum bibliothecae*,[58] and something analogous took place at Christ Church, where individual books were given by groups of MAs jointly, presumably in fact giving money for buying the book.[59] This system was widespread in the seventeenth century.[60] At St Leonard's College in St Andrews, an analogous attempt was made to create a coherent humanities library by co-ordinating small donations from over fifty donors.[61]

Despite these imaginative approaches to donations, few institutions could follow the example set at Merton by Savile, having agents buying the most up-to-date academic books abroad. It is well known that Thomas Bodley and his librarian Thomas James had agents working for the well-endowed Bodleian Library in Germany, Italy and Spain. Glasgow University Library, a little later, in the 1630s, had an agent in Amsterdam to buy books there, after a

53 On the patchy but abundant collection of medical books acquired through donation to Oxford colleges by 1620 see G. Lewis, 'The faculty of medicine', in *HUO* III. 254.

54 For instance, none of the Cambridge academic institutions seems to have followed a deliberate policy of acquiring law books, A. Wijffels, 'Law books in Cambridge libraries, 1500–1640', *TCBS* 10 (1993), 361.

55 Finlayson and Simpson, 'History of the library', 46.

56 Hall, *Edinburgh University Library, 1580–1980*, item 7.

57 J. Durkan, 'The early history of Glasgow University Library: 1475–1710', *The Bibliotheck: A Journal of Scottish Bibliography* 8 (1977), 115, although this money may also have gone to pay the librarian.

58 Ker, 'Oxford college libraries', 469 (*Books, collectors and libraries*, 389).

59 Ker, 'The provision of books', 461.

60 Philip and Morgan, 'Libraries, books, and printing', 673.

61 See V. Pringle, 'An early humanity class library: the gift of Sir John Scot and his friends to St Leonard's College (1620)', *The Bibliotheck* 7 (1974–5), 33–54.

system of occasional funding for purchases had been put on a firmer basis.[62] Throughout the seventeenth century, all institutions, big or small, continued to rely on donations – as is testified, for instance, by the many registers of benefactors – the difference being that some of the larger, more prosperous institutions could make up for imbalances by active selection and purchase, while some smaller institutions, like Marischal College and King's College in Aberdeen, had limited resources for the purchase of books, and relied nearly exclusively on donations from graduates and teachers.[63]

From 1601 to 1640 at Trinity College in Cambridge, donations in money for the library were so substantial that the number of books bought from them amounted to at least 646, whereas donated books numbered at most 810.[64] Trinity was exceptional and exceptionally well connected: most of the donors of books were not fellows of the college, but external benefactors. Even large collections with concerted buying programmes, like the Bodleian Library, continued to depend on donations, for it had problems with securing a steady income for purchases, especially in the years leading up to the Civil War, when the library's income was drastically reduced.[65] The shortcoming of the purchases can be seen from the continued purchasing of second-hand books, books which were not bought, in other words, when they were new. At the Bodleian Library this can be explained to a large extent as an attempt to make up for the 150 years' worth of printed books which preceded its foundation,[66] but when Glasgow University bought books from deceased professors it may be read as a sign that the purchasing policy had not enabled the library to buy the new books which it would have deemed necessary.[67]

The dramatic expansion of the collections of college libraries in Oxford and Cambridge brought practical problems. Throughout the sixteenth century,

62 Durkan, 'Early history of Glasgow University Library', 113.

63 Fabian, *Handbuch*, 151: 'Like Marischal College, seventeenth-century King's made limited provisions for the purchase of books, yet still relied heavily on the beneficence of graduates and teachers.'

64 Gaskell, *Trinity College Library*, 87–8.

65 Philip, *The Bodleian Library*, 25–9, 37–43.

66 A bill dated 27 July 1627 from Henry Featherstone, the library's chief agent, now in Oxford, Corpus Christi College (MS 492, fol. 13), contains eighty-five items, all printed abroad. They were nearly all very recent publications, and the items of the bill give the impression of being a selection of books from a recent Frankfurt fair. This is the first Bodleian bill without a major component of retrospective acquisition. This may indicate that the first great phase of retrospective buying was over. Seven quite recent items were rejected by the Bodleian, as they were already in the library. See K. Jensen, 'The Bodleian Library', in Fabian, *Handbuch*, 270–1.

67 Durkan, 'Early history of Glasgow University Library', 114; the library bought thirty-nine books from Robert Meldrum about 1639, twenty-two books from the widow of James Forsyth in 1646 and thirty-two books from Dr Robert Mayne, professor of medicine in 1649.

college and university libraries had retained the library furniture which had been developed during the late middle ages, rows of sloping lecterns on which chained volumes rested, perhaps with shelves underneath for further chained volumes. Merton College in Oxford, under the dynamic leadership of Henry Savile, was the first to change the medieval lecterns into the stalls system, beginning in 1589, with horizontal bookshelves standing on top of flat desks, designed to have books standing on the shelves, not lying on sloping desks. Merton was followed by a number of other Oxford colleges in the 1590s, and, when Sir Thomas Bodley refurbished the abandoned university library of Oxford for the opening of his library in 1602, he naturally followed the pattern set at Merton by his friend Savile.

This did not, however, sort out the problem of access to library books in smaller formats. It would have been disproportionately costly to chain quartos, and all but impossible for the octavos, although the library of Emmanuel, a newly founded college in Cambridge, shows us how things were changing. It was open to undergraduates,[68] and its first booklist, drawn up between 1586 and 5 March 1598, contains books in octavo.[69] Effective access to small-format books required a completely different type of library management. A system of closed stacks for small-format books was created in the Bodleian Library, in the galleries in the building known as Arts End, completed in 1612. This provided shelving for the octavos, which were of such importance both for teaching and for academic debate, but it required permanent staff to fetch the small books and to supervise readers, preventing them from taking the unchained books away with them. Without dedicated library staff, it was impossible to provide access to these essential small volumes. The provision of library books in small format coincides with growing professionalisation. Marischal College got a librarian's post, probably in association with the transfer of the Common Library of New Aberdeen (the library of St Nicholas Kirk) to Marischal College in 1632,[70] following a pattern known from England. From 1599, Christ Church elected a BA as library keeper to hold office until he took his master's degree. From 1603 a *custos bibliothecae* at St John's, Oxford, was paid to attend for an hour daily. At Brasenose the post of librarian was combined with that of

68 On this development in general see J. McConica, 'The rise of the undergraduate college', in *HUO* III. 1–68, who mentions, for instance, (43) that when Trinity College, Oxford, was founded in 1555 and St John's, Oxford, in 1557, provision was made for the first time in their statutes for undergraduate commoners as well as scholars to form an integral part of the collegiate society.

69 S. Bush and C. J. Rasmussen, 'Emmanuel College Library's first inventory', *TCBS* 8 (1985), 514–56.

70 Bevan, 'Marischal College', 16, n. 4.

keeper of the treasures from 1614, while the earliest record of a library keeper at Lincoln is from 1641.[71] The professionalisation also meant the creation of catalogues. When in 1626–7 William Drummond gave some 550 books to Edinburgh University Library, it occasioned the first surviving catalogue of any part of the library, by then a very substantial collection indeed.[72] Again it is the Bodleian Library which most clearly indicates how far the change had gone in the direction of a professionally run public library, with the remarkable Thomas James and the first printed and published catalogue of a British collection in 1605, followed by his second catalogue in 1620.[73]

In the mid-sixteenth century an individual scholar could own more books than most college libraries and could have collections which in practice obviated the need for a shared collection. For the intellectually ambitious, this was no longer possible by the early seventeenth century. Although individual scholars could also now expect to own even larger libraries, the balance had again shifted towards the shared collections. But, with the re-establishment of university collections and the renewed importance of the shared collections of the colleges, we have not come full circle. Libraries might be set in old buildings, but everything else was new, from their furniture to the types of book which they acquired and the way in which the institutions were run, increasingly dependent on professional staff. Not all to the same extent but each according to their financial means, they had changed to reflect the intellectual and commercial reality of an international market in intellectual products. Libraries had begun their vexed relationship with commercial publishers, whose products they had to acquire in order to remain useful, but whose ever growing output led to an ever more acute problem of money and space.

71 Philip and Morgan, 'Libraries, books, and printing', 678.

72 Finlayson and Simpson, 'History of the Library', 46. See also R. H. MacDonald, *The library of Drummond of Hawthornden* (Edinburgh, 1970).

73 Thomas James, *Catalogus librorum Bibliothecæ publicæ quam vir ornatissimus Thomas Bodleius eques auratus in Academia Oxoniensi nuper instituit* (Oxford, 1605), repr. as *The first printed catalogue of the Bodleian Library: a facsimile* (Oxford, 1986); Thomas James, *Catalogus universalis librorum in Bibliotheca Bodleiana . . .* (Oxford, 1620). See G. W. Wheeler, *The earliest catalogues of the Bodleian Library* (Oxford, 1928).

14

Major ecclesiastical libraries: from Reformation to Civil War

C. B. L. BARR AND DAVID SELWYN

The factor which most dramatically affected ecclesiastical libraries at the time of the Reformation was the dissolution of the monasteries in which most such libraries were situated. It would be easy to assume that, in the majority of monasteries which simply ceased to exist, their libraries disappeared with them; that, in those monasteries which continued to exist as cathedrals or were newly transformed into cathedrals, the libraries were liable to some degree of continued existence; and that, in the non-monastic or secular cathedrals whose status was not significantly altered or interrupted, the libraries continued unchanged. The reality was less simple, and, owing to the limited and haphazard nature of the evidence available to us, is not easy to summarise. Each institution's and each library's history at this period is individual and far from being typical, and the pieces do not add up to a neatly coherent general picture.

When one first looks at Neil Ker's *Medieval libraries of Great Britain (MLGB)*, one is struck by the apparently large number of surviving volumes. This is a misleading impression. If Ker's entries are compared with Knowles and Hadcock's *Medieval religious houses: England and Wales*,[1] it quickly becomes apparent that not a few sizeable houses which may be presumed to have possessed significant libraries are represented by minimal entries or none at all in Ker, and that the numbers of surviving books from the few continuing institutions vary considerably.

Much has been made of the activities of Bale, Leland and Parker. This is more because their activities happen to be well enough documented to be susceptible of our study than because they were typical; each was selective in what he chose to preserve and record. Their activities, however, did not significantly affect or tell us much about what happened to the bulk of ecclesiastical

1 D. Knowles and R. N. Hadcock, *Medieval religious houses: England and Wales*, 2nd edn (London, 1971).

libraries at and after the Reformation. In addition, although the dissolution of the monasteries is certainly the single most dramatic aspect of the Reformation to have affected the libraries, it was not the only one. Even without it, the contents of libraries would have changed considerably from the earlier part of the sixteenth century to the later.

The Reformation itself implied a shift to the new protestant writings – on biblical interpretation and exegesis and religious doctrine in particular, although the picture is far from clear and consistent. In addition, from the later fifteenth century onwards, a more gradual change in scholarship and learning began to take place, albeit less quickly at the cathedrals than at the universities. The spread of printing accompanied and assisted these changes and their impact upon the contents of the libraries. In the past, cathedral libraries had been built up, either in fits and starts or slowly over long periods, almost exclusively by gift and bequest. There was no purchase fund. But in the new situation of reformation and changing scholarly interests, many new books were needed, and were needed fast if the libraries were to continue to be useful. Private benefactors tended to give to the libraries of their institutions such books as they no longer had use for, by which time the books may already have been outdated. So the modernisation of the libraries could not be carried out as quickly as was desirable. Some new books, therefore, had to be bought.

Major benefactions to and redevelopments of cathedral libraries in the century following the Reformation, usually at the instigation and expense of the bishop, are fairly well known and documented – from, for example, Edmund Geste at Salisbury in about 1577 to Tobie Matthew at York in about 1628. But for the equally important picture of how and how much the libraries were organised, maintained, looked after and in particular used, we have less information: a casual remark here and there, mere snippets of information in cathedral act books and accounts, where more remains to be discovered. The most prolific records, studied in detail, are at Canterbury, which, as the senior archiepiscopal see, was not typical. Such records as survive at other cathedrals are incomplete or fragmentary and need to be considered together to give something of an overall picture. Repairs to doors and locks, to windows and roofs and the installation of new shelving (notably at Hereford) all indicate a degree of care and at least occasional use.

Dissolution and Reformation

At the time of the Reformation the libraries of the nine secular (non-monastic) cathedrals – Chichester, Exeter, Hereford, Lichfield, Lincoln, London, Salisbury, Wells, York – had no reason to suffer destruction as did their monastic counterparts, and they could be expected to have continued much as they were. In fact, only three – Hereford, Lincoln, Salisbury – have retained a major part of their pre-Reformation libraries. Similarly with the eight monastic cathedrals – Canterbury, Carlisle, Durham, Ely, Norwich, Rochester, Winchester, Worcester – where their apparent continuity of cathedral status might be assumed to have compensated for monastic dissolution, only two, Durham and Worcester, still possess a sizeable portion of their medieval libraries. At Durham, indeed, the uniquely large proportion of a third of the manuscripts that were in the priory's several book collections in the early fifteenth century has remained at the cathedral to the present day, suggesting that there can have been no systematic policy of disposal.[2]

In fact, these monastic cathedrals did not continue without interruption: while the bishoprics were not affected, their cathedrals were. In most cases, even though the outgoing prior was appointed as the first dean, there was an interval varying from several months to four years between the dissolution of the monastery and the foundation of the new dean and chapter. Only at Norwich were the new dean and chapter appointed immediately at the dissolution of the priory on 2 May 1538.[3] This was the first cathedral priory to be dissolved, and it may be deduced that for some reason it was not thought desirable to repeat this uninterrupted continuity. It is less surprising that, of the six new cathedrals which Henry VIII created out of former non-episcopal monasteries in 1540–42 – Bristol, Chester, Gloucester, Oxford (at Osney 1542–6), Peterborough, Westminster (the last only keeping cathedral status for the ten years 1540–50) – none retains more than a handful of its pre-dissolution books. Again, there was in each case an interval of approximately two years between dissolution and appointment of a dean and chapter, except that in two instances a collegiate church was established immediately after the dissolution until superseded by a dean and chapter (Gloucester and Westminster; the latter reverted to collegiate status in 1550). It was not only the new deans who provided a degree of continuity; at Durham, for example, of the sixty-six members of the priory in 1539, no fewer that thirty-four were appointed to the new chapter in 1541 as major or minor

2 A. I. Doyle, 'The printed books of the last monks of Durham', *Library*, 6th ser., 10 (1988), 218.

3 J. F. Williams and B. Cozens-Hardy (eds.), *Extracts from the two earliest minute books of the dean and chapter of Norwich Cathedral, 1566–1649*, Norfolk Record Soc. 24 (1953), 5–8; D. M. Owen, 'From monastic house to cathedral chapter: the experiences at Ely, Norwich, and Peterborough', in D. Marcombe and C. S. Knighton (eds.), *Close encounters: English cathedrals and society since 1540* (Nottingham, 1991), 10.

canons.[4] To judge by these figures, which are statistically negligible, continuity of cathedral status may count for something, but by itself was not enough to ensure continuity of libraries. Other factors, some general, others local, need to be taken into consideration.

The Henrician statutes issued to individual cathedrals in 1540–2 had little discernible effect on their libraries. The Durham statutes of 1541 instructed that the sacrist was 'to guard diligently in the cupboard or library the scholars' books, which he should exhibit yearly before the Dean'.[5] In 1547, however, a decade after the time when most of the greater monasteries were dissolved, a set of twenty-two royal injunctions was issued to all cathedrals as part of a general ecclesiastical visitation made in the first year of the reign of Edward VI. The eighth ran thus: 'Item they [every dean and chapter] shall maike a librarie in some convenient place within theire churche within the space of one yeare . . . and shall leye in the same Saynte Augustyne's, Basill, Gregorie Nazanzene, Hierome, Ambrose, Chrisostome, Cipriane, Theophilact, Erasmus, and other good writers' workes.'[6] It is significant that nothing is said about maintaining or modernising *existing* libraries, which were presumably considered outdated, for both religious and scholarly reasons. What was required was a *new* library. Erasmus and 'other good writers' were the texts which were now wanted, and the Church Fathers, hitherto represented in manuscript copies, were to be replaced by accurate and convenient printed editions, which it was expected would be within the capabilities of cathedrals to purchase, without waiting for bequests and gifts in the traditional way. It was possibly in compliance with this injunction that in 1549 the Westminster chapter decided 'that . . . the monye [to be raised by selling certain candlesticks and lecterns] . . . be receyvyd . . . for makyng of the lybrary and bying of bookes for the same; and . . . that the lybrary shalbe fynisshed in the northe parte of the cloyster, as sone as the money can be made'.[7] At York a copy of Theophylact's *Enarrationes* on the Gospels and Epistles (Basle, 1540–1), inscribed 'Liber ecclesiae Eborum

4 Doyle, 'The printed books', 214; S. L. Greenslade, 'The last monks of Durham Cathedral Priory', *Durham University Journal* 41 (1948–9), 107–13; D. Loades, 'Monastery into chapter: Durham 1539–1559', *Studies in Church History, Subsidia* 12 (1999), 315–35.

5 J. M. Faulkner (ed.), *The statutes of the cathedral church of Durham*, Surtees Soc. 143 (1929), 138–9; D. Pearson, 'Elias Smith, Durham cathedral librarian 1633–1676', *Library History* 8/3 (1989), 65. At Rochester in 1545, three years after the establishment of the new chapter, the treasurer spent £21 'to buy books for our new library' (W. H. Mackean, *Rochester Cathedral Library* (1953), 14).

6 W. H. Frere (ed.), *Visitation articles and injunctions*, 3 vols. (London, 1910), II. 136.

7 J. A. Robinson and M. R. James, *The manuscripts of Westminster Abbey* (1909), 13; text in C. S. Knighton (ed.), *Acts of the dean and chapter of Westminster, 1543–1609*, pt I, 1543–56, Westminster Abbey record ser. I (1997).

pertinens Cancellario eiusdem', may be a rare surviving purchase in obedience to this injunction, but the mention of the chancellor makes this uncertain; his statutory duties were mainly educational, so that the purchase of the book may have been in connection with his teaching responsibilities rather than for the library; the chancellorship did not come to include responsibility for the cathedral library until Canon James Raine's appointment as chancellor in 1891.[8] At Exeter, John Jewel's commission visiting the western counties in 1559 complained that no copies of the early Fathers were to be found in the cathedral library.[9] Documented purchases of Erasmus's *Paraphrases* on the New Testament were not for cathedral libraries but for the churches themselves, in compliance with other injunctions of 1547.[10]

The disposal of books from cathedral libraries at this period is nowhere systematically documented. The commissioners for dissolution regularly accounted for plate, jewels and 'ornaments', in some cases stated to be taken for the king, and other goods, unspecified, were declared to have been sold; books are in no case specified.[11] As there is no evidence of any significant trade in the sort of books that may have been disposed of from the libraries, it seems likely that any commissioners who were interested simply took any books that attracted them, with or without payment, and that the other books, no doubt the majority, were left to their fates. At Bath, where the Benedictine abbey, though never a cathedral, was nonetheless a seat of the bishops of Bath and Wells, Richard Layton, one of the chief agents in the Dissolution from 1535 and dean of York 1539–44, visited the abbey library in summer 1535 in search of information for Thomas Cromwell's projected Black Book of the Monasteries and sent to him 'a bowke of our lades miracles well able to mache the canterberie tailles, such a bowke of dremes as ye never sawe wich I fownde in the librarie'; and in September of the same year, 1535, Prior William Holleway sent to Cromwell, apparently as some sort of bribe, 'an old boke Opera Anselmi whiche one William Tildysleye after scrutinye made here in my librarye willed

8 York Minster Library, MS XXI.E.12; *The statutes of the Cathedral Church of York* (1900), 6–7; C. B. L. Barr, 'The Minster Library', in G. E. Aylmer and R. Cant (eds.), *A history of York Minster* (1977), 498, 518.

9 W. J. Edmonds, 'The formation and fortunes of Exeter Cathedral Library', *Transactions of the Devonshire Association* 31 (1899), 44–5; W. Schenk, 'An English cathedral library in the 17th century', *Church Quarterly Review* 148 (1949), 73.

10 Frere, *Visitations and injunctions*, II. 117–18 with note; for a purchase e.g. at York in 1551–2, see J. Raine (ed.), *The fabric rolls of York Minster*, Surtees Soc. 35 (1859), 136 (date revised); J. S. Craig, 'Forming a protestant consciousness? Erasmus' *Paraphrases* in English parishes, 1547–1666' in H. Pabel and M. Vessey (eds.), *Holy Scripture speaks: studies in the production and reception of Erasmus' Paraphrases on the New Testament* (Toronto, 2002), 313–58.

11 For example, *LP* XIV (1539), pt ii, no. 475, pp. 170–1, Bury St Edmund's; *ibid.*, XV, 1540, no. 139, pp. 47–9, an added document of 1552 for Winchester.

me to send unto youe by the kynge ys grace and commawndment'; the abbey was dissolved in January 1539.[12]

There are several instances of the retention of monastic books from cathedrals after the Dissolution by the ex-religious. At Ely, the last prior and first dean, Robert Steward, appears to have treated both library books and archives as if they were his personal property as early as 1531, long before he could be given the credit for forethought by concealing them in anticipation of the Dissolution; his inscriptions and heraldic drawings occur among the surviving muniments, and in manuscripts in the Cotton and Harleian collections and at Lambeth.[13] At Winchester, Thomas Dackomb, one of the twelve petty canons appointed on the new foundation in 1541–2, and, despite at heart remaining loyal to the old religion, keeping this position until his death in 1572, collected at least nineteen manuscripts and four printed books, several of which came from St Swithin's Priory. At Durham, the names and dates written in some surviving books from the priory library suggest that not a few of the ex-religious who became prebendaries or parochial clergy took a few books with them, so that these volumes were available for 'rescue' by collectors such as Tobie Matthew (dean 1583–95, bishop 1595–1606, archbishop of York 1606–28) when their temporary owners died.[14] Two of the last monks, probably brothers, Stephen and Nicholas Marley, became canons of the new cathedral chapter. Their sister Anne married Nicholas Tempest of Lanchester and Stanley, both in county Durham, and a number of Durham books thus 'owned' by the Marleys, some of them post-Dissolution acquisitions but mostly identifiable as from the priory collections, passed to the Tempest family, and, after various dispersals, mainly in the eighteenth century, are now in several recusant collections at Ushaw College and in the Harleian Collection at the British Library.[15]

Distinct from the libraries proper, there is some documentation more than a decade after the Dissolution regarding pre-Reformation liturgical books:

> all . . . books or writings whatsoever heretofore used for service of the Church, written or printed in the English or Latin tongue . . . shall be . . . utterly abolished, extinguished, and forbidden for ever to be used or kept . . . And . . . if any person or persons . . . or . . . body politic or corporate, that now have . . .

12 *LP* IX (1535), 11–12, 138; D. G. Selwyn, 'Thomas Cranmer and the dispersal of medieval libraries', in Carley and Tite, *Books and collectors*, 286.

13 D. M. Owen, *The library and muniments of Ely Cathedral* (Ely, 1973), 3–4, 12–13.

14 J. Raine, *A catalogue of the printed books in the library of the dean and chapter of York* (York, 1896), vi–vii; Barr, 'The Minster Library', 501; Doyle, 'The printed books', 214, 218.

15 A. I. Doyle, 'The library of Sir Thomas Tempest: its origins and dispersal', in G. A. M. Janssens and F. G. A. M. Aarts (eds.), *Studies in seventeenth-century English literature, history and bibliography: Festschrift for Professor T. A. Birrell* (Amsterdam, 1984), 83–93.

> any the books or writings of the sorts aforesaid . . . and do not before that last day of June next [1551] . . . deliver . . . all and every the same books to the mayor, bailiff, constable, or churchwardens of the town where such books shall then be, to be by them delivered over openly within three months next following . . . to the archbishop, bishop, chancellor [diocesan legal chancellor, not cathedral chancellor], or commissary and every of them cause them immediately either to be openly burnt or otherwise defaced and destroyed, shall for every such book or books willingly retained . . . forfeit . . . for the first offence twenty shillings, and for the second offence . . . four pounds, and for the third offence shall suffer imprisonment.[16]

An Order in Council dated 25 February 1550/1 to a similar effect, relating to a library at Westminster, which has sometimes been connected with the abbey library, is more likely to refer to a different collection: 'The Kinges Majesties lettre . . . for the purging of his Highnes Librarie at Westminster of all superstitiouse bookes, as masse bookes, legendes and suche like, and to deliver the garnyture of the same bookes, being either of golde or silver . . .'[17] At Lichfield on 4 July 1550, the former choir books, having been defaced in accordance with the act, were sold for a paltry two marks.[18] Otherwise there is little record of any formal destruction by ecclesiastical or civil authorities, and surviving examples show that some copies were surreptitiously kept for private or possible future use by those who secretly clung to the old faith and were prepared to risk discovery and punishment. Ancient gospel books, of the Anglo-Saxon or Norman periods, of which many cathedrals had at least one, were neither library books nor liturgical, but treasures kept in the cathedral treasury and produced on special occasions, and not a few survived, as objects of tradition and heritage and in some cases to continue in use as oath books.[19] In such cases the bookblock, which as a biblical text was unobjectionable, was retained, but the (usually) gilded and jewelled cover would be stripped off, whether in obedience to the other provisions of the statute of superstitious uses or from simple looting of precious metals, stones and similar decorations such as carved ivory plaques.

16 *Act against superstitious books and images*, 1550, sections I and II: J. R. Tanner, *Tudor constitutional documents*, 2nd edn (1930), 113–14.

17 J. P. Neale and E. W. Brayley, *The history and antiquities of the abbey church of St Peter, Westminster*, 2 vols. (1818–23), I. 297, from J. Collier, *An ecclesiastical history of Great Britain*, 2 vols. (1708–14), II. 307; Robinson and James, *Manuscripts of Westminster Abbey*, 12, and n. 3; J. P. Carley (ed.), *The libraries of King Henry VIII*, CBMLC VII. lxxvii.

18 H. E. Savage, 'A secular cathedral under Henry VIII and Edward VI', *Theology* 16 (1928), 70.

19 Barr, 'Oaths', in N. Barker (ed.), *The York Gospels* (London, 1986), 127–31.

The survival of the pre-Reformation books in each cathedral depended greatly on the individuals concerned, both the cathedral clergy who differed in their keenness to follow the 1547 and other instructions to the letter, and the commissioners, both clerical and lay, responsible for dissolving the monastic houses, who appear to have taken action of some sort at non-monastic as well as monastic cathedrals. At Norwich, for example, it was reported in 1538 that 'there was no place convenient for the library and so all the members at that time pillaged it in a most shameful manner';[20] Bale, while listing some fifty-eight books at the cathedral, declared that 'all the library monuments [muniments] are turned to the use of their grossers, candelmakers, sope sellers, and other worldly occupyers . . . O negligence most unfryndly . . . so unenlightened a crime.'[21] Robert Talbot,[22] however, treasurer and a prebendary of Norwich 1547–58, well known as one of the earliest sixteenth-century antiquaries and a collector of manuscripts, especially Anglo-Saxon texts, a generation before Parker, either found or reassembled the cathedral library and took care of it, making notes in at least twenty-one volumes and apparently removing at least three to his own 'museum', where Bale saw them. After his death the Norwich manuscripts were not scattered like Talbot's other books.[23] Nevertheless, at Norwich after Talbot's death 'there was downright neglect',[24] and the survival of the cathedral's medieval books seems to have depended on Andrew Perne, a Norfolk man who was master of Peterhouse from 1554 to 1589, vice-chancellor of Cambridge five times between 1551 and 1580, and dean of Ely from 1557 to 1589, and was responsible for restoring the university library and, posthumously, for a new library at Peterhouse. Somehow Perne gained possession of a number of Norwich manuscripts, and passed them to the university library, possibly in a cartload of books transported from Peterhouse in 1584–5, or in 1589 under the terms of his will, by which he left his printed books

20 Quoted by A. J. Beck, *Norwich Cathedral Library* (Norwich, 1986), 4, from F. Blomefield, *Essay towards a topographical history of the county of Norfolk*, 5 vols. (Fersfield, 1739–75).

21 H. C. Beeching and M. R. James, 'The library of the cathedral church of Norwich', *Norfolk Archaeology* 19 (1915), 85; Bale, *Index*, xx; B. Dodwell, 'The muniments and the library', in I. Atherton *et al.* (eds.), *Norwich Cathedral: church, city and diocese, 1096–1996* (1996), 333, 338.

22 T. Graham, 'Robert Talbot's "Old Saxonice Bede"', in Carley and Tite, *Books and collectors*, 295–316.

23 Talbot's executors are mentioned as holding 'many noble antiquytees' in Bale's letter to Parker, 30 July 1560: T. Graham and A. G. Watson, *The recovery of the past in Elizabethan England*, Cambridge Bibliographical Society Monograph 13 (1998), 25; *BRUO 1501–1540*, 555, 739; Beeching and James, 'The library', 67–116, at 84–90; N. R. Ker, 'Medieval manuscripts from Norwich Cathedral Priory', *TCBS* 1 (1949–53), 4; repr. in *Books, collectors and libraries*, 246; Oates, *CUL*, 137–8.

24 Dodwell, 'Muniments and library', 338.

in folio and quarto to Peterhouse and his manuscripts, 'all the old doctors and Histories that I have in written hande in parchment or in paper at Cambridge or at Ely', to the university library, where he regarded himself as being 'the chief procurer of all the . . . books'.[25] The pre-Reformation Norwich books thus transferred by Talbot and Perne to other libraries were given a greater chance of survival than those left at the cathedral.

Cathedrals were not immune from the activities of other collectors, both in the aftermath of the Dissolution and subsequently, as we have already seen in the case of Perne at Norwich. Among these collectors were major ecclesiastics, such as Cranmer and Parker, who acquired significant numbers of manuscripts for their own personal libraries.

Cranmer's library was primarily a scholar's working library, assembled first at Cambridge in 1503–29, and added to later while he was archbishop, with his and his staff's copious annotations demonstrating their use.[26] But the substantial part of his library that survives also includes fifty-six medieval manuscripts, twenty-seven of them from identifiable monastic houses. Six, possibly nine, are from his own cathedral of Canterbury, where it is clear that books from the medieval library were being dispersed until well into the 1580s, as shown by the copious acquisitions of his successors Parker and Whitgift.[27] No fewer than nine are from Bath, but how they came to Cranmer is not clear, and the same is true of his other ex-monastic books, no more of which are from cathedrals. A fair proportion correspond with his known interests, and some of these have annotations showing his use, but others appear to be random acquisitions. There are reasons for supposing that some may have been acquired in his Cambridge period, before the Dissolution, but this is not certain.

Although only a small number of Cranmer's protestant books survive, his library illustrates a tendency which is common to a number of other similarly large episcopal collections during the period, such as those of Parker, Geste and Bancroft. Despite his protestant acquisitions and the undoubted impact on his collection of the 'New Learning' of the humanists, Cranmer did not discard the older 'scholastic' works from the period when 'he was nosseled

25 E. Leedham-Green and D. McKitterick, 'A catalogue of Cambridge University Library in 1583', in Carley and Tite, *Books and collectors*, 153–235.

26 D. G. Selwyn, *The library of Thomas Cranmer*, OBS Publications, 3rd ser., 1 (1996), esp. 203–8 (appendix A) and 209–28 (appendix B); and 'Thomas Cranmer and the dispersal of medieval libraries', in Carley and Tite, *Books and collectors*, 281–98.

27 N. Ramsay, 'The cathedral archives and library' in P. Collinson, N. Ramsay and M. Spakes (eds.), *A history of Canterbury Cathedral* (Oxford, 1995), 373–5, 378; C. de Hamel, 'The dispersal of the library of Christ Church, Canterbury . . .', in Carley and Tite, *Books and collectors*, 263–79.

in the grossest kind of sophistry' (as his early biographer put it).[28] In fact, he continued to purchase newer editions, particularly of biblical commentaries, by medieval authors such as Peter Lombard, Thomas Aquinas and Denys the Carthusian. His library was also well stocked with the writings of continental theologians hostile to the Reformation, suggesting that he viewed his collection as a resource that would enable him to engage in an informed way in the many ideological issues of the Reformation period and meet his opponents on their own ground.[29]

As one of the first canons of the new foundation at Ely from 1541 to 1554, Matthew Parker[30] may already have acquired the four Ely manuscripts which remain in his collection, though he may equally well have done so later.[31] As dean of Lincoln for the brief period 1552–4, he appropriated to himself some of the archives, but not, as far as is known, anything from the library.[32] Early in his archiepiscopate, Gregory Dodde or Dodds, formerly a Carmelite friar and then dean elect of Exeter, is said to have given Parker Leofric's Anglo-Saxon gospel book, as an encouragement to issue the necessary mandate for his installation.[33] In 1566 Parker thanked Bishop John Scory of Hereford 'that you dydd not forgett to cause Hereford librarie to be serched for Saxon bookes'; and in the preface to his *Testimonie of antiquitie* (1567) he mentions Anglo-Saxon manuscripts 'yet reserved in the libraryes of . . . Worceter, Hereford, and Exeter . . . from which places diverse of these bookes have bene delivered into the handes of . . . Matthewe, Archbyshop of Canterburye'.[34] In 1568, Parker, at his own request, received a royal commission 'for the conseruation of such auncient recordes and monumentes . . . which heretofore were preserued and recorded . . . in diuers Abbeyes . . . and for that most of the same wrytynges

28 BL, MS Harley 417.

29 Selwyn, *Library of Thomas Cranmer*, Introduction, xxx, lxxxv–lxxxviii.

30 M. R. James, *The sources of Archbishop Parker's collection of manuscripts at Corpus Christi College, Cambridge*, Cambridge Antiquarian Soc., octavo publications 32 (1899); W. W. Greg, 'Books and bookmen in the correspondence of Archbishop Parker', *Library*, 2nd ser., 16 (1935–6), 243–79; R. I. Page, *Matthew Parker and his books* (Kalamazoo, MI, 1993).

31 Owen, *Library and muniments*, 4.

32 R. M. Woolley, *Catalogue of the manuscripts of Lincoln Cathedral Chapter Library* (London, 1927), xviii; D. M. Williamson (afterwards Owen), *The muniments of the dean and chapter of Lincoln* (Lincoln, 1956), 7.

33 L. J. Lloyd, 'Leofric as bibliophile', in F. Barlow *et al.*, *Leofric of Exeter: essays in commemoration of the foundation of Exeter Cathedral Library in* AD *1072* (Exeter, 1972), 40, but the date of 1556 there given cannot be right: Parker did not become archbishop until 1559, and his licence to elect Dodds is dated 20 January 1559/60: J. Le Neve, *Fasti ecclesiae Anglicanae*, 3 vols. (Oxford, 1884), I. 387.

34 I. Atkins and N. R. Ker (eds.), *Catalogus librorum manuscriptorum bibliothecae Wigorniensis made in 1622–1623 by Patrick Young* (1941), 9–10.

and recordes so kept in the Monasteries, are now come to the possession of sundry private persons . . . the Queenes . . . pleasure . . . is, that . . . the Archbishop of Canterbury, shoulde haue a speciall care and ouersight in these matters', and that anyone having in his custody 'any such auncient recordes or monumentes' should 'gently impart the same . . . to be safely kept hereafter'.[35] Already in 1564 Walter Philips, last prior and first dean of Rochester, gave Parker a manuscript of Chrysostom from his cathedral library.[36] Later, Dean Nicholas Wotton of Canterbury gave him an important manuscript of the Anglo-Saxon Chronicle from Christ Church, Canterbury.[37] In November 1567, John Aylmer, archdeacon of Lincoln (bishop of London 1577–94), reported to Parker that he could find no 'old wrytten ecclesiasticall historyes' and has only a few 'old fellowes' such as 'scholemen', but was sending what can be identified as a manuscript of Archbishop Stephen Langton's commentary on the Old Testament; there is nothing to show whether the manuscript was from Lincoln Cathedral.[38] In January 1568/9 Bishop John Jewel wrote to Parker: 'I haue ransacked o(u)r poore Librarie of Sarisburie, and haue founde . . . onely one booke written in the Saxon tonge, whiche I minde to send to yo(u)r Grace.'[39]

Cathedrals were, however, sometimes themselves given former monastic manuscripts. The best-known example is Hereford Cathedral, which was one of the beneficiaries of the collecting activities of the Welshman, Sir John Prise, a relation by marriage of Cromwell and a visitor of the monasteries in 1535 and 1539–40. He acquired a considerable number of ex-monastic manuscripts, historical and theological, many of which had come from West Country monasteries visited and dissolved by him, such as the Augustinian abbeys of Cirencester and Bristol, St Guthlac's Priory at Hereford and the Hereford Franciscans, Brecon or Brecknock Priory and the abbeys of Gloucester, Evesham, Pershore, Winchcombe and Tewkesbury. Some of the books that he collected were, like Leland's better-known acquisitions, probably destined for the royal library; but he bequeathed to Hereford Cathedral, 'to be set in their librarye . . . all my written Bookes of Devinite' (thirty volumes identified). He also gave a number of printed books (thirty-one identified). One of the

35 C. E. Wright, 'The dispersal of monastic libraries and the beginning of Anglo-Saxon studies: Matthew Parker and his circle', *TCBS* I (1949–53), 212–13; Page, *Matthew Parker*, 43–4.

36 Wright, 'Dispersal of monastic libraries', 223. 37 *Ibid.*, 217. 38 *Ibid.*, 222.

39 *Ibid.*, 223; J. Ayre (ed.), *The works of John Jewel*, 4 vols. (Cambridge, 1845–50), IV. 1273–4; M. R. James, *Western MSS in the library at Trinity College*, 4 vols. (1900–5), II. 189–192.

two known surviving books from Neath Abbey (which he visited in February 1539), now at Hereford, may additionally be conjectured to have come via Prise.[40] His remaining theological manuscripts (forty-seven items) remained in his family until given in his name to Jesus College at Oxford, probably in 1621–2; his historical texts are now scattered.[41]

One major factor in the history of a library is its physical environment – building and furnishings – and these are subject to the vagaries of destruction, wear and tear, (re)construction and improvement. In the middle part of the sixteenth century and the first half of the reign of Queen Elizabeth, a dearth of information about cathedral libraries suggests that on the whole they were in a state of decay after the upheavals of the Reformation, the Counter-Reformation, and the restoration of Protestantism. In 1549, Lord Protector Somerset demolished much of the great north cloister at St Paul's to provide materials for his new Somerset House in the Strand, so threatening the library, which for a hundred years had been housed in a room over the eastern range, but his work left that side untouched; a fire which destroyed the spire and damaged part of what was left of the cloister in 1561 likewise threatened the library, but it is not known to have been affected.[42] At Christ Church, Oxford, in 1562–3, the former refectory of St Frideswide's was set up as a college (rather than a cathedral) library, furnished with old stalls and desks bought from the divinity school or old university library.[43]

Only at the two metropolitan cathedrals is there evidence of continuous maintenance of a library, which suggests some degree of regular use. At York the royal injunctions of 1547 were supplemented by Archbishops Robert Holgate in 1552 and Edmund Grindal in 1572. Both emphasised security: the former ordered that three vicars choral were to have keys to the library, and to accompany any reader other than a canon or dignitary and allow no harm to come to the books; the latter directed that no book or document 'be tayken out of the tresorye, revestrye, or librarie, except he that tayketh the same write his name in a booke to be provided for the same purpose, testifyeing the contentes of the same wrytinge, and byndinge himself to restore the same

40 Though not listed as such by Ker in 'Sir John Prise', in *Library*, 5th ser., 10 (1955), 1–24, repr. in *Books, collectors and libraries*, 471–95; *MLGB*, 133, *Supplement*, 50 (for the other Neath book now in the National Archives); *LP* XIV, i, (15.39), p. 150.

41 *Books, collectors and libraries*, 471–96; *BRUO 1501–1540*, 463–4; *LP passim* (variously indexed under Ap Rice or Rice); F. C. Morgan (ed.), 'The will of Sir John Prise of Hereford', *The National Library of Wales Journal* 9 (1955), 255–61.

42 W. Dugdale, *History of S. Paul's Cathedral in London* (London, 1658), 132, 276; J. W. Clark, 'On ancient libraries: . . . S. Paul's Cathedral', *Proceedings of the Cambridge Antiquarian Society* 9 (1896–8), 56–8.

43 N. R. Ker, 'The provision of books', in *HUO* III. 466.

againe'. Doubtless they were attempting to put an end to the laxity which had allowed the disappearance of the greater part of the medieval manuscript library. As regards contents, the 'ancient Doctors of the churche' specified by King Edward were probably present in the library, but Holgate ordered the addition of more protestant commentaries on the New Testament, 'Musculus' Commentaries upon Mathue, and John Brentius upon Luke, Calvyne and Bullinger upon the Epistles, Erasmus' Annotacions on the Newe Testament', all to be provided before the following Whitsuntide.[44] Similarly, at Canterbury, Archbishop Thomas Cranmer asked chapter in 1550 if it had a library as ordered in 1547; in the same year the treasurer spent £12 'for the boks off the library', and the following year one prebendary formally handed over to another a group of some twenty books which include seven of the nine named in the Edwardian injunctions and are therefore likely to constitute the new post-Reformation library, distinct from the remains of the medieval collection.[45]

From the Elizabethan settlement to the Civil War

For some cathedrals, the re-establishment of Protestantism at the beginning of Elizabeth's reign prompted some consideration of library resources, but the revival of the libraries was neither immediate nor universal. Salisbury, Westminster and Winchester were swift to respond. At Salisbury, injunctions issued by Queen Elizabeth in 1559 extended the 1547 list of compulsory books by the addition of 'Clemens Alexandrinus, Justinus Martir', and the *Paraphrases* of Erasmus on the New Testament, and it is possible that copies of Erasmus on the Gospels and Acts published in 1551 (English) and on the New Testament in 1555 (Latin) now in the library may have been bought in obedience to these injunctions.[46]

At Westminster, Dean William Bill (1560) drafted new statutes, largely based on those which, as master, he had promulgated for Trinity College, Cambridge, in 1552; these included provision for a library, with books borrowable on a written promise for payment if the book is not returned, the room to be kept clean, £20 a year to be spent on buying books, and donors' names to be recorded both in their gifts and on a board in the library. Bill died a few months later in 1561 before being able to bring this into effect, and the establishment of a new

44 *York Statutes*, 75–6 and 86; Barr, 'The Minster Library', 498–9.
45 Ramsay, 'Cathedral archives and library', 374; J. P. Carley, 'Sir Thomas Bodley's library and its acquisitions', in Carley and Tite, *Books and collectors*, 383, n. 62.
46 C. Wordsworth and D. Macleane (eds.), *Statuta et consuetudines ecclesiae cathedralis . . . Saresberiensis* (London, 1915), 371–2.

library devolved upon his successor, Gabriel Goodman (dean 1561–1601). It was fitted up in 1575 in a new location over the east cloister, where it remained until 1591–2; Goodman himself set the example for donations with the handsome gift of the Complutensian Bible and a Hebrew vocabulary. Within a dozen years the library had flourished to a position where new regulations were required. There were to be new shelves and desks, a catalogue in triplicate, duplicates and triplicates to be sold and the proceeds used for buying new books, the dean and prebendaries to have keys, and the usher or undermaster of the school to be keeper of the library at a fee of 20s a year, the first keeper being none other than William Camden; several books given by him remain in the collection. In 1591, chapter decreed that the library, which had outgrown its quarters, was to be removed into the old monks' dorter, where it has remained ever since.[47]

Bishop Robert Horne's injunctions for Winchester, issued in 1562 and again in 1571, each including instructions about a library, suggest that if any action had ever been taken in consequence of those of 1547 it had not survived the double change of religion:

> the said Dean and Chapter shall within two months next following appoint and prepare within the precinct of the said cathedral church a place both decent and convenient to make and erect a library both with desks and seats . . . and also to furnish the same with such books as shall from time to time be named and appointed by the Ordinary: towards which there shall on this side the Nativity . . . be employed twenty pounds and then forth . . . yearly five marks.

And later:

> that the library be still kept and maintained and increased yearly with books to the yearly value of five marks . . . and that . . . the two last volumes of the Acts and martyrs set forth by Master Fox be provided.[48]

Norwich, however, was especially slow to respond, and was evidently slower than most cathedral libraries in its recovery from the effects of the Dissolution.[49] In 1560, Sir Robert Dudley, high steward of the cathedral (the later earl of Leicester), asked the dean and chapter to grant to a friend of his a

47 Robinson and James, *Manuscripts of Westminster Abbey*, 13–17; L. E. Tanner, *The library and muniment room*, Westminster Papers 1 (1933), 4–5.

48 G. W. Kitchin and F. T. Madge (eds.), *Documents relating to the foundation of the chapter of Winchester, AD 1541–1547*, Winchester Cathedral documents, 1 (1889), 183–5; F. Bussby, *Winchester Cathedral Library*, 2nd edn (Winchester, 1975), 1–2; Frere, *Visitation articles and injunctions*, III. 137, 321.

49 Beck, *Norwich Cathedral Library*, 5.

'little suit' of rooms, which included the library; chapter declined, explaining that the library was 'so erected and joined to other lodgings that the pulling down thereof would be the utter destruction of the lodgings thereto adjoining . . . [and] by God's grace, it shall be furnished again with convenient books, according to the Queen's Majesty's injunctions, having at this present divers books bequeathed by divers good men for the furniture of the same'.[50] The bequests are not specified, but doubtless included the books of Bishop John Hopton, whose will of 1558 bequeathed part of his books to the Black Friars of Norwich if they should be restored to their convent, and the other part thereof to the library of his cathedral, and other books stated in 1568 to have been received from Thomas Tedman, prebendary from 1540 to 1558, though nothing is known of any books of his.[51] In 1568 a royal commission, set up at the instigation of George Gardiner, a 'troublesome' prebendary (nevertheless later made dean, 1573–84), to enquire into the state of the cathedral, encountered difficulty in getting satisfactory answers about the library.[52] Where were the books bequeathed by 'divers good men'? Bishop Hopton's books were detained by his executors, as he died heavily in debt, and held by a Mr Walgrave, who also held books given by Dr Henry King, prebendary from 1548 to 1554.[53] Other books given by Thomas Parker, 'nowe maior', of the gift of Dr John Barrett, prebendary from 1558 to 1563,[54] were conflictingly described as remaining in the library or the vestry. Tedman's and Talbot's books could not be located, but books left in Talbot's house, which was subsequently occupied by Barrett and Thomas Fowle,[55] were said to be in the hands of the current tenant, 'Dr Bounde', apparently Richard Bound, physician to the duke of Norfolk, who 'sent a frivilous Letter of exkuce . . . and departed the Cittie and made no answere'. The commission concluded: 'We finde that there is no convenient place for a Librarie neither the Bookes in the same which have been given by divers persons.' Gardiner later bestowed good books elsewhere: eight books, including the first seven volumes of the *Ecclesiastica historia Magdeburgensis* (Basle, 1562–4), and probably the priory's manuscript of Pseudo-Dionysius, which has Gardiner's name on the flyleaf,[56] and a Nuremberg Chronicle and the Latin New Testament commentary of 'Arelius' (rather, Aretius) to King's

50 *Ibid.*
51 C. H. and T. Cooper, *Athenae Cantabrigienses*, 2 vols. (Cambridge, 1858–61), I. 186, 197.
52 Frere, *Visitation articles and injunctions*, III. 217; Beck, *Norwich Cathedral Library*, appendix D.
53 Le Neve, *Fasti*, II. 499.
54 Cooper, *Athenae*, I. 224–5.
55 'Fowell', prebendary 1563–81: Cooper, *Athenae*, I. 452.
56 CUL, MS Ee.1.4; Beck, *Norwich Cathedral Library*, 6.

College (though his connections were with Christ's and Queens' Colleges).[57] In 1570, Bishop John Parkhurst ordered the dean and chapter 'that they provide ther Bibles and parafrasses wch they nowe wante and repaire and furnish their library w^{t}in sixe moneths',[58] but in 1574, a year after Gardiner became dean, chapter resolved to demolish the old library.[59] Parkhurst's degree of confidence in their compliance with his instructions is demonstrated by his will, which in 1575 left 'to the Lybrarie . . . [of his old school at Guildford] joyning to the Schole the most parte of my Latten bookes'.[60]

Evidence from other cathedrals is more scanty, and permits only glimpses of their state and use during the later sixteenth century. At Ely, for example, Bishop Richard Cox's visitation of 1564 revealed a library in confusion, as replies to a question regarding how many books it contained were remarkably divergent.[61] At Chester in 1582, an order was given for £4 to be spent 'towards the furnishing of their library with books of divinity'.[62] The actual use of York Minster Library envisaged by both Holgate and Grindal is confirmed by roof repairs in about 1574, some binding in 1576, and the chaining of six volumes in about 1579; a few years later regular cleaning began at an annual fee of 10s.[63] At Christ Church, Oxford, chains were purchased frequently; for example, twelve chains in 1583 for the most recent of the many donations of the period, and others in 1592.[64]

Although printed books were affordable, cathedral libraries still relied to a large extent on gifts and bequests. At Wells, William Turner, who, besides being dean from 1551 to 1554 and again from 1560 to 1568, was a noted physician and botanist, gave a five-volume set of the works of Aristotle, besides Galen, Philo, Theophrastus and Alexander Aphrodisaeus (Venice, 1495–8) with signatures

57 Cooper, *Athenae*, II. 55; C. Sayle, *Annals of Cambridge University Library, 1278–1900* (Cambridge, 1916), 54; if these ever reached King's they are apparently not extant.

58 Beck, *Norwich Cathedral Library*, 5.

59 J. F. Williams and B. Cozens-Hardy (ed.), *Extracts from the two earliest minute books of the dean and chapter of Norwich Cathedral, 1566–1649*, Norfolk Record Society 24 (1953), 31.

60 R. A. Christophers, 'Historical introduction', in G. Woodward and R. A. Christophers (eds.), *The chained library of the Royal Grammar School, Guildford: catalogue* (Guildford, 1972), 2–4, 11–13, and appendix D; C. H. Garrett, *The Marian exiles* (Cambridge, 1938), 244–5.

61 Owen, *The library and muniments*, 4.

62 R. V. H. Burne, *Chester Cathedral from its founding to . . . Queen Victoria* (London, 1958), 83–4.

63 Barr, 'The Minster Library', 499.

64 W. G. Hiscock, *A Christ Church miscellany* (Oxford, 1946), 3; Ker, 'Oxford college libraries in the sixteenth century', *BLR* 6 (1957–61), 499; repr. in *Books, collectors and libraries*, 419.

of Erasmus and annotations by him.[65] At Winchester, Dean John Warner (dean 1559–65, previously prebendary 1549–59), who had been the first regius professor of medicine at Oxford (1546–54) and warden of All Souls (1536–55 and 1559–65), gave several scientific books: C. Gesner, *Historiae animalium lib. I–IV* (Zurich, 1551–8, lacking the last volume, published in 1587), L. Fuchs, *De historia stirpium* (Basle, 1542), Dioscorides, *De medica materia* (Cologne, 1529–30), and J. Ruellius, *De natura stirpium* (Basle, 1537); he also gave four printed books to his college of All Souls.[66] Also at Winchester, John Bridges, prebendary from 1565 to 1604 (also dean of Salisbury 1577–1604 and bishop of Oxford 1604–18), presented three manuscripts: Dares, with Geoffrey of Monmouth's *Historia Britonum* and other pieces (from Southwell Minster), *Vita sancti Nicholai*, and *Unum ex quatuor*, a harmony of the Gospels (by Clement of Llanthony, or Zacharias Chrysopolitanus), and John Ebden, prebendary from 1562 to 1614 (also archdeacon of Winchester 1571–75), gave a manuscript containing an anonymous compendium of theology and a printed commentary on Exodus, probably that of J. Brenz (Frankfurt, 1558).[67]

Salisbury fared particularly well in the 1570s, when its bishop, Edmund Geste (1518–77), established by his bequest a new library of printed books without discarding the considerable remains of the medieval manuscript library. Although his predecessor, John Jewel (bishop 1559/60–71), has often been credited with the major role in the new foundation,[68] there is as yet no evidence that any of his books came to the cathedral library. Those that have survived from the bishop's palace were purchased soon after his death by his own college,

65 *CLC* II, A1040; C. M. Church, 'Notes on the . . . library of the dean and chapter of . . . Wells', *Archaeologia* 57 (1901), 216; T. W. Williams, 'Wells Cathedral Library', *Library Association Record* 8 (1906), 376–7; [L. S. Colchester,] *Wells Cathedral Library*, 4th edn (Wells, 1985), 8–9, with facsimiles of inscriptions by Erasmus and Turner; Sir R. Birley, 'The cathedral library', in L. S. Colchester (ed.), *Wells Cathedral: a history* (Shepton Mallet, 1982), 204; illustration in L. S. Colchester, *Wells Cathedral* (London, 1987), 105.

66 *CLC* II, D646, F828, G453, R1070; W. F. Oakeshott, 'Winchester College library before 1750', *Library*, 5th ser., 9 (1954), 13; F. Bussby, *Winchester Cathedral, 1079–1979* (Southampton, 1979), 114–15; *BRUO 1501–1540*, 607–8; N. R. Ker, *Records of All Souls College Library, 1437–1600*, OBS Publications, n.s. 16 (1971), 109, 126, 164.

67 *CLC* II, B2334; J. Vaughan, *Winchester Cathedral Close: its historical and literary associations* (London, 1914), 224–6; Winchester Cathedral, MSS 3, 6, 8 and 9; *MLGB*, 181; *MMBL* IV. 581, 582–3, 586–7.

68 This claim (made by Fuller and Le Bas) probably derives from the inscription formerly placed in the Library, which reads: 'Haec Bibliotheca extructa est sumptibus R. P. ac D. D. Joannis Jewelli quondam Sarum Episcopi, instructa vero libris a R. in Christo P. D. Edmundo Gheast [= Geste] olim ejusdem Ecclesiae Episcopo'. F. Godwin, *De praesulibus Angliae commentarius*, ed. W. Richardson (Cambridge, 1743), 355; H. G. Dugdale, *The life and character of Edmund Geste* (London, 1840), 61; C. W. Le Bas, *The life of Bishop Jewel* (London, 1835), 210.

Magdalen College, Oxford. Eighty-four of them have been traced by Neil Ker, though the 220 chains bought over the same period may more closely indicate the total number bought from Salisbury.[69] Whatever contribution Jewel may have made to the cathedral library, its condition, according to the wording of Geste's will (proved 10 April 1577), was 'now decayed', and Geste may therefore be regarded as the real founder of the present collection of printed books at Salisbury.

To remedy the deficiency, Geste gave and bequeathed to the library

> all my Books there to be kept for perpetual remembrance and token of my favor and good will, to advance and further the Estate and Dignity of the same my Church and See, desiring and trusting that the Dean and Chapter . . . will so ordain and dispose all those my said Books to places and Stalls as may be fit for the preservation and good keeping of the same and this on behalf of God, I require them to do.

His memorial brass describes the bequest in the highest terms as 'ingentem optimorum librorum vim, quantam vix una capere bibliotheca potest, perpetuo studiosorum usui in hac ecclesia conservandam destinavit' – a verdict which is confirmed by the evidence of what remains today.[70] His collection has clearly suffered some losses since then, probably affecting mainly his patristic books. For there are inexplicable gaps in an otherwise comprehensive collection, and some of his copies (as happened not uncommonly in cathedral libraries) may have been supplanted by later, superior editions. There must also have been depredations during the Civil War period, because two of his books were later 'brought in' after the Restoration. But although no contemporary inventory or catalogue survives by which to check these losses, a substantial collection of about 1,300 separate items in over 700 volumes remains – with a preponderance of Reformation writings from the Continent.[71]

A favourite of Elizabeth I – he was her chief almoner from 1560 to 1572 – Geste had been a fellow of King's College, Cambridge, becoming vice-provost in 1548 in the same year that he published his only book (in support of the changes to the mass then being implemented), dedicated to its new provost,

69 N. R. Ker, 'The library of John Jewel', *BLR* 9 (1977), 256–65; C. B. Dobson, 'The "Bel-Ami" volumes in John Jewel's library in Magdalen College, Oxford', *BLR* 16 (1998), 225–32.

70 Dugdale, *Edmund Geste*, 55–8; E. Kite, *The monumental brasses of Wiltshire* (London, 1860), 59–62.

71 S. Eward, *Salisbury Cathedral Library*, 2nd edn (Salisbury, 2004), 6. A separate catalogue in the cathedral library identifying Geste's books is now in preparation. The figures given are provisional and have been supplied by D. G. Selwyn, who is currently preparing a study of Geste's library for publication.

the young Edward VI's tutor, John Cheke.[72] Early in Mary's reign, Geste was expelled by his college on religious grounds, and, like Parker and Cecil, he remained incognito in England (rather than joining the other exiles, like Jewel, on the Continent), though retaining much, if not all, of the collection of printed books he had built up during his years in Cambridge. Under Elizabeth, he played a small yet significant part in liturgical reform, doctrinal definition (Article XXVIII of the Articles of Religion) and as a contributor to the Bishops' Bible – activities well represented by the books that he used in his library.

In bequeathing to his cathedral this new 'foundation collection' of printed books, Geste was providing Salisbury with many of the tools of learning and scholarship considered appropriate for a cathedral in the second half of the sixteenth century – a balance of the best of the old and the new, as envisaged in the various sets of injunctions from the 1540s to those of Elizabeth I. In addition to what was probably the largest collection of Reformation writings to survive from this period,[73] he bequeathed some sixty-five volumes of the early Church Fathers and Councils in the new editions of humanist scholars like Erasmus, though lacking complete editions of Augustine, Ambrose, John Chrysostom and Justin Martyr – this last author specifically listed in the 1559 Injunctions for the cathedral. Among the resources for biblical scholarship were new editions of the biblical text by Erasmus, Pagninus and Sebastian Münster (Hebrew), aids to study such as grammars (especially Hebrew),[74] lexicons and concordances, and a wide range of the 'new' commentaries from Erasmus's brief Annotations and humanists such as Faber Stapulensis to leading Lutheran, 'Reformed' protestant and Catholic exegetes. Geste's collection also comprised resources for liturgical reform (including a number of the new 'church orders'), dogmatics (with a number of doctrinal formularies as well as catechisms from continental Protestantism as well as the Council of Trent), homiletics (with many published sermons and *postilla* from the medieval period as well as both

72 *A treatise against the prevee masse* (London, 1548) (*STC* 11802).

73 Geste possessed unusually large numbers of the major figures of the continental Reformation – Lutheran and Reformed: nearly forty of Luther; over thirty-five of Melanchthon; twenty-eight of Johann Brenz, as well as many items of lesser-known Lutherans. All were in Latin, as were his copies of those in the Reformed tradition: Zwingli (three), Oecolampadius (seventeen), Bucer (eighteen), Calvin (twenty-four), Bullinger (twenty-two) and Theodore Beza (twelve), and those of numerous minor figures. Many of these he annotated and had bound up together by topic or controversy in 'pamphlet' volumes, often indicating the order in which the items were to be assembled. Over 120 such volumes exist, containing between three and eleven items apiece.

74 E.g. Hebrew grammars and other linguistic studies by Sebastian Münster (1536 and 1542), Aurogallus (1539), Capito (1525), Clenardus (1540), Reuchlin (1506), Goeuschelius (1546), Elijah ben Asher (1537) and Robert Stephanus (1558).

sides of the Reformation divide), moral and pastoral theology, ministry and church organisation, clerical training and reform. Like Cranmer, Parker and Bancroft (at the end of the century), Geste did not exclude medieval authors (even scholastics) or his Catholic contemporaries. Over thirty medieval authors are represented, including commentators on Peter Lombard's *Sentences* and scholastics like William of Ockham and Gabriel Biel, and almost 100 contemporary Catholic authors, predominantly continental, but some English. Many of these books (like his copies of protestant authors) are annotated, often in great detail, suggesting that he was anxious to have at hand as broad a conspectus as possible of the diversity of continental opinion – of theological foe as well as friend.[75]

Salisbury is apparently the first cathedral library to have been effectively refounded after the Reformation by a major benefaction. Others followed this pattern during the succeeding century, but it was still more usual for collectors in his position to make lifetime donations and bequests to academic, rather than ecclesiastical institutions, particularly to their own colleges. Geste did not leave any books to his old college (King's) – how much the memory of his expulsion while vice-provost in 1554 had been a factor in that decision can only be conjectured – and it was evidently his concern at the decayed state of the library at Salisbury that was uppermost in his thinking. By contrast, Parker, who could not have been unaware of how far cathedral libraries were falling short of the requirements of the 1559 Injunctions (not least that of his own cathedral at Canterbury, which was to remain woefully inadequate in its holdings of contemporary theology, as the 1634 inventory demonstrates), made a gift of twenty-five manuscripts and seventy-five printed books to Cambridge University in 1574 and chose to bequeath to his old college, Corpus Christi, not only his unique manuscript collection (understandably enough, since he had obtained so many of the medieval items from those very cathedral libraries) but most of his printed books as well. The latter – amounting to over 800 volumes – covered a far wider range of subject-matter than Geste's and would have provided an exceptional resource for any cathedral library that could have been trusted to look after it.[76]

The same trend can be seen in most of the other major collections from this period. Parker's successor, Edmund Grindal, may not have had a large library,

75 For the same tendency among some seventeenth-century bishops, see D. Pearson, 'The libraries of English bishops, 1600–40', *Library*, 6th ser., 14 (1992), 229.

76 B. Dickins, 'The making of the Parker Library', *TCBS* 6 (1975), 18–34; R. I. Page, 'Audits and replacements in the Parker Library: 1590–1650', *TCBS* 10 (1991), 17–39. Records of what remains of his library are now becoming accessible on the Cambridge University college libraries database, which also details provenance evidence.

but the only books that are known to survive as a group are the eighty or so given to his old Oxford college, The Queen's. John Whitgift's – the largest private library of the time at about 6,000 volumes – was dispersed following his death in 1604 and, after other bequests (notably of 150 manuscripts to Trinity College, Cambridge, of which he had been master), the 2,000 or so that came to Lambeth Palace Library were acquired by its founder, Richard Bancroft, perhaps by some arrangement with the relatives who shared the residue of his estate. No books of his, so far as is known, were given to any cathedral library, and the rest of his library may have been sold off.[77] William Laud, the last of the great archiepiscopal collectors before the Civil War, was another who gave the most valuable part of his library to an academic institution (1315 manuscripts to the Bodleian between 1635 and 1640). The fate of his printed books is uncertain, but there is nothing to suggest that any cathedral was a significant beneficiary (although, like Parker, he must have known something of their condition from the visitations he conducted between 1634 and 1637), and only about a dozen have so far been identified at Lambeth Palace.[78]

Similarly, none of the three dioceses with which Lancelot Andrewes had been associated received books when he died in 1626 (at least, none has been identified), and the only significant group that is known today is that of the 400 or so that he bequeathed to his old Cambridge college, Pembroke.[79] Arthur Lake, bishop of Bath and Wells (1616–26), did, it is true, give about forty volumes (mainly patristic) to Wells, volumes I–III of the Eton Chrysostom to Worcester (where he had been dean), and two to the newly endowed public library at Bath Abbey, but four-fifths of his library (estimated at about 500 volumes) went to New College, Oxford, where he had been warden.[80] The case of Samuel Harsnett, archbishop of York (1629–31), was slightly different, for he left his library, not to an ecclesiastical nor an academic institution, but to one which he hoped would nonetheless further clerical education. Perhaps because of the recent munificent bequest of Tobie Matthew (1628), Harsnett did not choose York Minster. But, despite his known concern for the state of cathedral libraries, none of his books went to his two earlier sees of Chichester

77 Pearson, 'Libraries of English bishops', 256; P. Gaskell, *Trinity College Library: the first 150 years* (Cambridge, 1980), 80.

78 A. Cox-Johnson, 'Lambeth Palace Library 1610–1664', *TCBS* 2 (1955), 110; K. Fincham (ed.), *Visitation articles and injunctions of the early Stuart Church*, 2 vols. (Woodbridge, 1994–8), II. 110–15, 257–80.

79 Pearson, 'Libraries of English bishops', 233–4; D. D. C. Chambers, 'A catalogue of the library of Bishop Lancelot Andrews', *TCBS* 5 (1970), 99–121.

80 Pearson, 'Libraries of English bishops', 245, who points out, however, that none of those mentioned in his will for Worcester carries Lake's ownership inscription, which makes any identification uncertain.

or Norwich. In the end, his library of some 900 or more volumes went not to Pembroke Hall, Cambridge (where after some years of friction he had resigned as master), but to his home town of Colchester (still extant, and now housed at the University of Essex), where it was to be freely available 'for the reading and studieinge of them' by the clergy of the town and 'other divines'.[81]

In Scotland, Ireland and Wales, disruption to cathedrals at the Reformation was far more serious than in England, and as a result no identifiable cathedral library collection or major donation to such a library (as distinct from individual items acquired from them by collectors) survives from this period.[82] In Scotland, existing cathedral libraries were either abandoned altogether or transformed (all or part of them) into parish kirks, often under a single minister, with the result that a chapter of canons, with a chancellor or minor canon having responsibility for a cathedral library, played no part in the new church order. Nonetheless, there is evidence for some significant collections built up by individual clerics before and after the upheavals of the Reformation. In most instances, however, the original size of these can only be conjectured from the books that are now widely scattered mainly among academic libraries.

For example, 112 or more printed books have been identified as having come from the library of Henry Sinclair, bishop of Ross (1561–5), and although it is not clear whether these were intended for any ecclesiastical institution after his death, thirty-nine of them came into the possession of his close friend and fellow collector Clement Litill, whose own theological books were bequeathed in 1580 'to the kirk of Edinburgh' and now form part of the foundation collection of the university.[83] Again, about fifty printed books each have survived from the libraries of William Gordon, bishop of Aberdeen (d. 1577) and James Beaton, archbishop of Glasgow (d. 1603),[84] a further fifty-five or so survive

81 *Ibid.*, 242; G. Goodwin, *A catalogue of the Harsnett Library at Colchester* (London, 1888), xxiii–xxv; Harsnett's articles for Chichester Cathedral (1616) ask: 'who should take accoumpt of the safe keeping of the books anciently belonging to your library; and who is the principall cause of your maim and defects that doe appear in these things': Fincham, *Visitation articles*, I. 140.

82 Durkan and Ross, 5–22. In the case of Ireland, no cathedral library collection earlier than that of 1693 appears to be extant (St Canice's, Kilkenny), and the four Welsh cathedral libraries appear to be early eighteenth-century refoundations, though little work has been done on the provenance of the pre-1640 material to establish whether there is evidence of any continuity. These (with the exception of Bangor and St Davids) have been relocated to the National Library of Wales. B. C. Bloomfield, *Directory of rare book and special collections*, 2nd edn (London, 1997), 615, 672, 678, 679, 687.

83 C. P. Finlayson, *Clement Litill and his library* (Edinburgh, 1980), 9–11, 21–8.

84 Durkan and Ross, 24–8 (Beaton), 34–40 (Gordon), 49–60 (Sinclair), 169 (additions). Both Beaton and Gordon owned some Erasmus and patristic authors, but, among

from that of Robert Reid, bishop of Orkney (1541–58), and 400 volumes are listed in the 1594 inventory of Adam Bothwell (c. 1526–93), Reid's successor.[85] As bishop, Reid had included the preservation of the cathedral library and its catalogue among the responsibilities of the chancellor in his measures for the reconstitution of the chapter at St Magnus, Kirkwall, in 1544. Although his own library was dispersed, at least one book found its way into the Bibliotheck bequeathed 'to the ministers of Kirkwall successivelie for a Publick Liberarie to be kept within the town' by William Baikie in 1683, and he left a large legacy for the foundation of a college in Edinburgh, eventually applied to the endowment of the university.[86] In contrast, Bothwell's library provides ample evidence of his acceptance of Renaissance humanism and Protestantism as well as being far wider in subject-matter. Bothwell's much larger library was also dispersed, but there is no evidence that it was ever intended to be passed on as a scholarly resource for the Reformed kirk.[87]

If there was reluctance on the part of most collectors, north and south of the border, to donate their books to ecclesiastical libraries, the difficulty of sustaining these libraries, much less expanding them, was not made any easier when cathedral dignitaries thought fit to give books from their libraries away. In 1566, John Pedder, dean of Worcester, gave to John Dee a manuscript of the *Cosmographia* of 'Aethicus Ister', which had survived Leland's visit a quarter of a century earlier and is now in the Cotton collection with the inscription recording the gift.[88] Later in the sixteenth century, William Thornhill, prebendary of Worcester from 1584 to 1626, more prudently allowed books to leave the cathedral library on loan, and seven manuscripts are known with his inscriptions recording these transactions, two of them dated 1586 and 1590. Four of them had been thus loaned and returned, but, after Patrick Young's visit in 1622, three found their way to the royal library, where they remain.[89]

contemporaries, Catholic rather than protestant writings. Sinclair remained of the old faith and possessed a number of late scholastic authors, although Erasmus and Calvin were represented.

85 Durkan and Ross, 44–7, 170 (Reid), to be supplemented by O. D. Cuthbert, *A flame in the shadows: Robert Reid, bishop of Orkney, 1541–1558* (Kirkwall, 1998), appendix 2, 184–5; A. I. Cameron (ed.), *Warrender papers*, 2 vols., Scottish Historical Soc., 3rd ser., 18–19 (1931–2), 396–413; Durkan and Ross, 29 (Bothwell's pre-1560 survivals).

86 Cuthbert, *Flame in the shadows*, 80, 127. The book (now in Aberdeen University Library) was Reid's Duns Scotus (Paris, 1520), no. 3 in the list given in Durkan and Ross, 44.

87 For an analysis of its contents, see D. Shaw, 'Adam Bothwell: a conserver of the Renaissance in Scotland', in I. B. Cowan and D. Shaw (eds.), *The Renaissance and Reformation in Scotland* (Edinburgh, 1983), 141–69; G. Donaldson, *Reformed by bishops* (Edinburgh, 1987), 22.

88 Atkins and Ker, *Catalogus librorum manuscriptorum*, 11–12; R. J. Roberts and A. G. Watson (eds.), *John Dee's library catalogue* (London, 1990), 14 and no. M80.

89 Atkins and Ker, *Catalogus librorum manuscriptorum*, 12–13.

Young's visit to Worcester was not an isolated incident. He was librarian successively to Prince Henry, James I and Charles I,[90] and it was as 'Keeper of the King's libraries' that in July 1622 he received a royal warrant for payment of £100 'and more if needful . . . to make search in all cathedrals for old manuscripts and ancient records, and to bring an inventory of them to His Majesty'.[91] Within a year he visited and drew up catalogues of the manuscripts at the cathedrals of Lichfield, St Paul's, Salisbury, Worcester and Winchester (in the order of a seventeenth-century list of the catalogues, which were 'in loose sheets').[92] He is not known to have visited any other cathedral libraries. At no cathedral is there any record of his visit, though in several cases his visit must have taken some time, and little is known of the project except for the catalogues themselves, which came to light only in about 1939; they had been removed from the archiepiscopal archives at Lambeth Palace on the fall of Archbishop Laud in 1640–5 by John Selden and passed to his friend and executor Sir Matthew Hale, remaining unknown in the Hale family's Gloucestershire home until found and acquired by James Fairhurst, who returned them to their respective cathedrals.[93] At Winchester, Young's brother John was dean from 1616 to 1645. The Lichfield catalogue lists seventy-nine manuscripts on three folio pages; St Paul's, the only one not yet to have been published, is quite brief; Salisbury, an incomplete listing, records 181 manuscripts on six pages; Worcester, 334 manuscripts on sixteen pages; Winchester, twenty manuscripts, of which the last was 'In Bibliotheca collegij Winton'.[94]

Only at Worcester is there a documented sequel. On 25 November 1623, the dean and chapter deliberated on a letter from James I asking 'for all such dubble maniscripts as we have dubble in our liberary', to be sent to Lord Keeper John Williams towards the furnishing of the library which he was then building at Westminster Abbey, and the chapter duly agreed an order making 'a graunt to my Lord Keeper of such Manuscripts as we have double in our librarie

90 About 1605–49, according to S. Jayne and F. R. Johnson (eds.), *The Lumley library* (London, 1956), 292–3.

91 *Calendar of State Papers Domestic, 1619–1623*, 430; Atkins and Ker, *Catalogus librorum manuscriptorum*, 2.

92 Atkins and Ker, *Catalogus librorum manuscriptorum*, 1–2.

93 *Ibid.*; D. M. Barratt, 'The library of John Selden and its later history', *BLR* 3 (1950–1), 128, 211; Lambeth Palace Library, *Annual review for 2000*, 7.

94 N. R. Ker, 'Patrick Young's catalogue of the manuscripts of Lichfield Cathedral', *Medieval and Renaissance Studies* 22 (1950), 151–68, repr. in his *Books, collectors and libraries*, 273–91; and his 'Salisbury Cathedral manuscripts'; T. Webber, 'Patrick Young, Salisbury Cathedral manuscripts and the Royal Collection', *English Manuscript Studies, 1100–1700* 2 (1990), 283–90; F. Bussby, *Winchester Cathedral, 1079–1979*, 132–3.

towards the furnishing of his library at Westminster'. The canon librarian, John Archbold, died the following month, and it was 3 February 1624/5 before chapter again discussed the matter, recording that, in accordance with a letter from Dean Joseph Hall (1616–27) dated 22 January, they have sent twenty manuscripts, which are listed, to the dean in London 'for the better conveying thereof, and to the said purpose appointed'. There seems no doubt that the books left Worcester, but there is no trace of their ever reaching Westminster, nor are they heard of again. Of the remaining 314 manuscripts, twenty-five are in the Royal Collection and twelve among the Hatton manuscripts in the Bodleian Library.[95] At Lichfield, only one manuscript, and that not certainly, may now survive as part of the Royal Collection, and that not directly from the cathedral.[96] At Salisbury, four, perhaps eight, manuscripts were removed to London, doubtless at Young's request, and in the royal library at St James's they were kept separately from the main collection, perhaps in Young's study; one he annotated carefully, another is a text which he himself edited in 1638.[97] Similarly, one of the Winchester manuscripts came to the royal library.[98] There is no trace of any of the manuscripts catalogued by Young ever coming to the Westminster Abbey Library, nor of Williams complaining that Young and the royal library had deprived Westminster of what should have come there.

A few years before Young's book-hunting expedition, which was in the tradition of Leland and Parker, several cathedral libraries lost books in aid of another good cause. It was in February 1597/8 that Sir Thomas Bodley offered to refound a university library at Oxford, partly 'by procuring benefactions of books', and by June 1600 he had begun to gather books for the new library.[99] Among the first benefactors were Bishop Herbert Westphaling of Hereford, whose gift of £20 was spent to excellent purpose, and George Abbot, who, as bishop of London, contributed £50 in 1610.[100]

Less commendably, several deans and chapters saw fit to respond positively to Bodley's pressing requests for gifts in kind. First, in 1602, was Exeter, where Sir Thomas's brother Laurence was a prebendary from 1580 to 1615; they gave eighty-one Latin manuscripts, eight of them from Leofric's foundation collection, with the result that, of 139 surviving Exeter manuscripts, ninety-eight are now in the Bodleian Library and only twenty-four still at Exeter.[101]

95 Atkins and Ker, *Catalogus librorum manuscriptorum*, 2–7. 96 Ker, 'Lichfield', no. 18.
97 Ker, 'Salisbury', 158–9, repr. as 180–1. 98 *Ibid.*, repr. as 181 n. 1. 99 Macray, 15–19.
100 *Ibid.*, 23, 42; Pearson, 'Libraries of English bishops', 232.
101 G. W. Wheeler (ed.), *Letters of Sir Thomas Bodley to Thomas James* (Oxford, 1926), nos. 13, 19; Macray, 23–4; *MLGB*, 81–5; W. J. Edmonds, 'The formation and fortunes of Exeter Cathedral Library', *Reports and Transactions of the Devonshire Association* 31 (1899), 44;

About 1610–12, Thomas James, the first keeper of Bodley's library, borrowed from Salisbury six volumes of the works of St Ambrose, which he collated in order to expose the corruptions in the Rome and Paris editions of the works of Cyprian, Gregory and Ambrose; the manuscripts have inscriptions 'Liber Bibliothecae Saresburiensis', evidently written at the time of borrowing, and were never returned nor was there any request for them to be given back.[102] Similarly, from Worcester, where Bodley's hope for manuscripts from the cathedral in 1602 was initially unsuccessful, nine manuscripts came to the Bodleian in unrecorded circumstances between 1605 and 1611.[103] In 1611 Bodley enlisted the help of Sir Henry Savile, provost of Eton, in requesting books from the dean, Giles Tomson, and chapter of Windsor (both Savile and Tomson were members of the Oxford committee for the translation of the major part of the New Testament for the Authorized Version of the same year); at first Windsor refused, but, after Dean Tomson's death in June 1612, without any apparent written record, some seventy manuscripts, which must have been the greater part of the collection, were surrendered to Bodley's library.[104]

The immediate loss to these ecclesiastical libraries was Bodley's gain, but, as it is far from certain how many of these manuscripts would have survived the Civil War and other depredations in their original homes, the long-term effect has perhaps been beneficial to scholarship. Windsor, at least, lost little time in using the gained shelf space to good purpose. In 1614, the dean and chapter resolved that any new canon residentiary was to pay £10 'towardes the building and furnishinge of the library', and in 1615 they sought advice from Oxford in order to copy the Bodleian's new shelving.[105]

The appropriation of canons' installation fees to create a library fund, as at Windsor in 1614 (the £10 at that date was doubled to £20 in the nineteenth century, and continued until 1945), was not something new. At Hereford, new statutes of 1583, following on a royal commission of the previous year, which had found the library in a state of neglect, allotted the £2 installation fee, payable by

L. J. Lloyd, The *library of Exeter Cathedral* (Exeter, 1967), 13; F. Barlow *et al.*, *Leofric of Exeter: essays in commemoration of the founding of Exeter Cathedral Library in AD 1072* (Exeter, 1972), 39, 49; M. Swanton (ed.), *Exeter Cathedral: a celebration* (Crediton, 1991), 193–4.

102 Ker, 'Salisbury Cathedral manuscripts', 156–7, repr. as 178–9.

103 *Letters of Sir Thomas Bodley*, nos. 21, 37, 55, 57; Atkins and Ker, *Catalogus librorum manuscriptorum*, 13.

104 *Letters of Sir Thomas Bodley*, no. 215; M. R. James, 'The manuscripts of St George's Chapel, Windsor', *Library*, 4th ser., 13 (1932–3), 67–8; J. Callard, *A catalogue of printed books . . . in the library of St George's Chapel, Windsor Castle* (Windsor, 1976), xii–xiii; *MLGB*, 202–4.

105 S. Bond (ed.), *The chapter acts of the dean and canons of Windsor, 1430, 1523–1672* (Windsor, 1966), 85, 91; Callard, *Catalogue of printed books*, xiii–xiv.

every new canon, to the library.[106] Nevertheless, after the Restoration period, when many cathedral libraries needed to be virtually refounded, this type of library income became the most common form of library fund. It appears to have been of wide appeal because it did not create a new charge on the general finances, and was probably everywhere, as specifically at York by 1707, in lieu of a collation of wine and buns accompanying an installation, the disadvantage being that the income was irregular and unpredictable. As late as 1878, 'fees on installation' were still the only library fund at Winchester and Worcester.[107]

It would be misleading to suggest that there was any general revival in the fortunes of cathedral libraries in the early Stuart period – the surviving archival documentation is often too scanty – but there is evidence for some recovery in a few cathedral and minster libraries, notably at York, Durham, Hereford, Westminster Abbey, Ripon and, to a lesser extent, Canterbury, and a number of new ecclesiastical foundations in London came into being, two of which included notable collections. Even before the accession of James VI and I, the two English universities had experienced something of a revival, first at Cambridge in the form of a major expansion to its collections, resulting from initiatives associated with Andrew Perne, and later at Oxford, which amounted, in effect, to a re-founding of the university library by Sir Thomas Bodley and a succession of donations which this inspired. The impact of the latter on other libraries was not only in the example it set, but in such details as the installation of new shelving and reading desks, the introduction of a benefactors' register, and the publication of Thomas James's catalogue of the Bodleian library (1605, 2nd edition, 1620), which provided not only a practical guide to what might properly be chosen for a scholarly library but a catalogue to record a library's own holdings, which could then be marked up at the appropriate entries.

In the early years of the seventeenth century three new 'public' (that is, institutional) libraries were established, all in London. One never fulfilled its promising beginnings, one remains the leading library of its kind in the country, and the third survived until 1996 and is now partly incorporated in the second.

106 Streeter, 349; B. G. Charles and H. D. Emanuel, 'Notes on old libraries and books', *National Library of Wales Journal* 6 (1950), 361; J. Williams, 'The library', in G. E. Aylmer and J. Tiller (eds.), *Hereford Cathedral: a history* (London, 2000), 515.

107 Barr, 'The Minster Library', 506; H. E. Reynolds, *Our cathedral libraries: their history, contents and uses* (London, 1879), also in the Library Association, *Transactions and proceedings of the second annual meeting . . . 1878* (1879), appendix: tabulated returns.

Chronologically, the first was a bold proposal for a college 'of Divines and other Learned men' at Chelsea, which (as Fuller later described it) was 'intended for a spiritual garrison, with a magazine of all books for that purpose; where learned divines should study and write, in maintenance of all controversies against the papists'.[108] The brain-child of Matthew Sutcliffe, dean of Exeter 1588–1629, who became its first provost and a major benefactor, it was strongly supported by Richard Bancroft, archbishop of Canterbury 1604–10, and King James, who laid the foundation stone on 8 May 1610 (shortly before Bancroft's death) and issued its charter of incorporation on the same day (providing for a provost and nineteen fellows nominated by himself), richly endowing it with lands and privileges. Despite its auspicious beginnings (William Camden was one of its first lay fellows), it never fulfilled the aspirations of its founders; only a part of its buildings was ever completed, and even as early as 1636, Daniel Featley, its second provost, could name only two fellows in residence.[109] Although it survived the Civil War, attempts in 1652 and 1662 to re-establish it, with appeals to Charles II and Archbishop Juxon, met with no success. The extent of its library is uncertain, but it included the books of Matthew Sutcliffe, and Godfrey Goodman, bishop of Gloucester, intended his books to go to the college on his death in 1656 'if ever . . . [it] shall be restored'.[110] In fact, things might have been very different for Chelsea College if Bancroft's proposals for an archiepiscopal library at Lambeth had fallen through, since under his will the college ('if erected within these six years') was the preferred alternative to receive his library.

In the event, that did not happen, and Lambeth Palace Library, the second of these new institutions, came into being. The concept of an archiepiscopal library attached to the see of Canterbury was new. Earlier archbishops had owned personal libraries which were accessible to other scholars (Cranmer's was a case in point), but at death these were disposed of by bequest (e.g. to academic institutions) or sale (Cranmer's was confiscated). In his will (proved on 12 November 1610), Bancroft gave his books 'to his successor, and unto the Archbishops of Canterbury successively forever', on condition that 'he my next successor shall yield to such assurances as shall be devised by such learned Councel as my Supervisor and Executor shall make choice of for the continuance of all the said Books unto the said Archbishops of Canterbury

108 Thomas Fuller, *The Church-history of Great Britain* (London, 1655), book x. 51.

109 7 James I, c.ix (*Statutes of the Realm*, IV. ii, 1165–6); *Survey of London*, XI (Chelsea, part IV) (London, 1927), 3.

110 J. E. B. Mayor, 'Original letters of Godfrey Goodman, together with materials for his life', *Cambridge Antiquarian Communications* 2 (1860), 113–38, at 122.

successively'.[111] The problem facing Abbot was how these 'assurances' were to be given, so that the library did not suffer dispersal at the hands of his successors. His preferred solution (following Bancroft's will) was that each successive archbishop should give a bond to preserve the library intact, but Sir Francis Bacon, the Solicitor-General, suggested as a more reasonable alternative that a catalogue of the collection be made, so that its contents would (so to say) enter the public domain ('that it might be knowne in the ages to come what were those Bookes, which the aforesaid Archbishop Bancrofte did leave to his successors').[112] In some sense Bancroft's was to become a 'public', i.e. institutional, library, therefore, of great use not only to successive archbishops but to the church and to the king (a firm supporter of the proposal) and his successors. In fact, James, a great lover of learning and a considerable bookman himself, became a frequent borrower of books from the library (not all of which were returned).[113]

The catalogue, when it appeared in 1612, listed over 5,580 printed books and about 470 manuscripts in Bancroft's collection, and a copy of it was to be kept by the dean and chapter of Canterbury (but now back at Lambeth), confirming the 'public' nature of Lambeth Palace Library.[114] Like his predecessors, Cranmer and Parker, Bancroft had acquired manuscripts from dissolved religious houses, notably a large group from the Augustinians of Lanthony near Gloucester numbering about 100, perhaps as many as 140.[115] But its largest single component was the cache of two to three thousand or so books from that of his predecessor, John Whitgift; and there is some evidence for thinking that he was interested in drawing into his collection books from other former archbishops, since he had also obtained at different times nearly thirty printed books and manuscripts of Cranmer's, almost all with Lumley's ownership inscription, some probably as direct gifts, others from the old Royal Library, which was another major source of Bancroft's acquisition.[116]

111 Lambeth MS 577, p. 58, in A. Cox-Johnson, 'Lambeth Palace Library', *TCBS* 2 (1955), 105–26, at 105; G. Bill, 'Lambeth Palace Library', *Library*, 5th ser., 21 (1966), 192–206, at 192–3.
112 Cox-Johnson, 'Lambeth Palace Library', 106.
113 Bill, 'Lambeth Palace Library', 194–5.
114 Lambeth Library Records, F.1–2; Cox-Johnson, 'Lambeth Palace Library', 106–7.
115 N. R. Ker identifies about ninety-six MSS (*MLGB*, 109–11, 368–71, and *Supplement*, ed. A. G. Watson, 41–3). M. R. James estimates 130–40 'with certainty or high possibility': 'The history of Lambeth Palace Library', *TCBS* 3 (1959), 13.
116 D. G. Selwyn, *The Library of Thomas Cranmer* (Oxford, 1996), 273–76; for some other examples of these sources, see J. P. Carley, '"A great gatherer together of books": Archbishop Bancroft's Library at Lambeth (1610) and its sources', *Lambeth Palace Library Annual Review* (2001), 50–64.

In its range of subject-matter, the collection was far wider than that of 'a magazine' to serve the needs of polemical theology, even if that may have been among Bancroft's original intentions for Lambeth.[117] The 1612 catalogue listed its contents according to subject classification as well as showing how the classes were disposed around the galleries. While well over half his books were in the biblical and theological disciplines, with both sides of the protestant and Catholic debate almost equally represented, there were more than 1,060 items in the field of history (secular as well as ecclesiastical), over 650 in law (canon, civil and common) and a wide range of general literature (about 530 volumes) devoted chiefly to the Graeco-Roman classics but including other authors such as Chaucer, Bacon, John Dee and James VI and I.[118]

In 1633, a further 2,667 volumes (among them about fifty-seven manuscripts) were added from the library of his successor, George Abbot, who had promised to make such a bequest in 1612 when he first accepted responsibility for Bancroft's donation and outlined his intentions for its future, and these were then added to the relevant subject areas of Bancroft's library rather than kept as a separate collection.[119] In Abbot's case, the subject range was not so very different from that of Bancroft, though with slightly less than half the collection in the biblical and theological fields; there was a similar balance of protestant and Catholic polemic, but with a notably higher proportion of topography and history, and general literature. Cox-Johnson has noted Abbot's preference for contemporary writers such as Burton, Sidney, Drayton and Spenser, and continental literature in translation (though he had all Petrarch's works in Italian), and in some features his collection mirrors that of a gentleman or nobleman with books on political theory, the art of warfare, mathematics, science and architecture, coins and even witchcraft, and a notable collection on the history and contemporary events of France.[120] With over 8,700 volumes, and remarkable for its balance and scope, it was clearly a collection in which Abbot took some pride – 'not much inferiour unto that . . . of any private man in Europe'.[121] It had evidently not expanded much further than that

117 Bill, 'Lambeth Palace Library', 194.

118 Cox-Johnson, 'Lambeth Palace Library', 107–9.

119 *Ibid.*, 106f., 109–10; James, 'The history', 3, estimates this figure from the entries in the Abbot catalogue (two copies, Lambeth Library Records F.3–4), compiled by William Baker, though the manuscripts were not distinguished from the printed books. Cox-Johnson identified only thirty-nine.

120 Cox-Johnson, 'Lambeth Palace Library', 108f. See chapter 21 in this volume, and the case studies of Sir Robert Gordon and the Cecils.

121 Abbot to William Trumball, royal agent at the court of the Archduke Albert of Austria at Brussels, quoted in Cox-Johnson, 'Lambeth Palace Library', 110.

during Laud's primacy on the eve of the Civil War, and there is some evidence that his books were kept apart from the Bancroft–Abbot library in his study, confiscated after his arrest and subsequently dispersed.[122]

The third of these new London foundations was Sion College, founded as a result of the will of Thomas White, rector of a London church (St Dunstan-in-the-West), soon after his death in 1624. Intended as a meeting place for London clergy, with an associated almshouse (Sion Hospital), its library was added in 1630 to house a growing number of donations to the college, in a building above the almshouse, and was endowed initially by White's relative and executor, John Simpson (*c.* 1560–1633), rector of St Olave's, with a librarian, John Spencer, appointed in 1631. During his tenure (1631–80), Spencer maintained a Book of Benefactors (or 'Vellum Book') which had been started in 1629, compiled an author catalogue in manuscript (from 1632) which reached printed form in 1650 as *Catalogus universalis librorum omnium in Bibliotheca Collegii Sionii*, as well as other lists recording items saved and lost in the Great Fire of 1666, and was himself a donor of several hundred books between 1631 and 1658. Although the chief period of the library's expansion occurred in the period 1698–1712, by which time its stock had reached an estimated 10,000 volumes, there were numerous smaller donations in the period before the Civil War, including those of the mathematician Nathaniel Torporley (eighteen manuscripts and 215 printed books) between 1629 and 1633, and the Puritan divine, Walter Travers (*c.* 1548–1635), who bequeathed at least 150 books (including a medieval manuscript).[123] Following Laud's arrest in 1641, there was a proposal to remove the library from Lambeth Palace and settle it at Sion College (successfully resisted by the University of Cambridge, which laid claim to it on the basis of Bancroft's will of 1610), but in 1647 the library of old St Paul's (164 manuscripts and sixty-seven printed books) was moved to Sion College and, together with those donated to the college, was destroyed in a locked rare-books collection of about a

122 See above, 383: 'Scarcely a dozen books in Lambeth . . . bear his arms'; Cox-Johnson, 'Lambeth Palace Library', 110. It seems that Laud's library in his study (regarded as distinct from the Bancroft–Abbot library) was sequestered after his arrest, some ninety-seven of his books being removed for the use of the Assembly of Divines at Westminster on 20 January 1643/4, and that the rest (valued at £140) were given to Hugh Peters, chaplain to the army. Whatever the fate of Laud's printed books, few of them became part of the Lambeth collection; see Cox-Johnson, 'Lambeth Palace Library', 111–13; Jayne, 171.

123 Bloomfield, *Directory*, 366–9; Jayne, 89, 91f., 155, 161f., 168f., 181; *MMBL* 1 (1969), 263. The manuscripts and pre-1850 printed books have now (since 1996) been transferred to Lambeth Palace Library, and the post-1850 material to King's College, London.

thousand books in the 1666 Great Fire.[124] By this time, the Sion College collection, while not rivalling Lambeth in size, may have numbered about 3,000 manuscripts and printed books, of which about 870 folios and quartos escaped destruction as a result of their temporary removal to the Charterhouse before the Fire.[125]

In the cathedrals – despite further losses from their pre-Reformation collections – there were important initiatives which went some way to reverse years of decline and the failure, in many cases, to implement the 1559 Royal Injunctions as these related to their libraries.

Hereford was an early and notable example. Its recovery is particularly associated with the new statutes of 1583 – following on a royal commission of the previous year, which had found the library in a state of neglect (as John Dee had done on an earlier visit in 1574) – and the contribution of Thomas Thornton (*c.* 1541–1629), canon and precentor there from the same year, student and later canon of Christ Church, Oxford, and twice vice-chancellor there, who had two periods as master (*custos*) of the library between 1595 and 1597 and 1610 and 1617. The 1583 statutes introduced a number of reforming measures: a £2 installation fee payable by every new canon to the library, a practice which was followed by other cathedrals and a first start towards funding for cathedral libraries; a list of books to be attached to the end of each desk and the names entered in two books (though not, it seems, fully implemented until a Mr Adams was paid for carrying out this task in 1611/12); and the annual appointment of a residentiary canon as master of the library. By 1596/7 the chapter was keeping separate accounts for the library, and entries exist for the purchase of 'irons and chaines' for the security of the books as well as for new acquisitions.[126]

During the second period of Thornton's custodianship, the impact of the new ideas from Bodley's library at Oxford becomes evident: the introduction from 1611 of a donors' book, the institution of an oath to be taken by readers, and the designing of new chained bookcases – his most abiding legacy –

124 Bloomfield, *Directory*, 366; *MLGB* 120; *MMBL* I. 263, listing nine medieval manuscripts which survived.

125 Bloomfield, *Directory*, 366; Jayne, 91, on the basis of Spencer's alphabetical author catalogue begun in 1632 and used as the basis of the 1650 printed catalogue.

126 E.g. Windsor (1614), where the installation fee was £10, and Durham (1628) on which see below; Streeter, 349; B. G. Charles and H. D. Emanuel, 'Notes on old libraries and books', *National Library of Wales Journal* 6 (1950), 361; for what follows, see J. Williams, 'The library', in G. E. Aylmer and J. Tiller (eds.), *Hereford Cathedral: a history* (London, 2000), 511–35, at 515.

largely modelled on those installed in Duke Humfrey's library, on which he had evidently sought advice from those more experienced in such matters at Oxford. Thornton himself paid for the first two single cases and two of the double cases, and the fact that two more were installed in 1625–7 (with the books placed upright for the first time, fore-edges outwards, for economy of space) suggests a considerable expansion of the library stock during his time by gift and from library funds. A bequest of £20 in the will of Miles Smith, former bishop of Gloucester, purchased about sixty theological books in London, Oxford and Gloucester in 1624, and there were works in Arabic and Hebrew from the same donor; a set of Musculus commentaries (a recommended author) from an earlier bishop of Hereford, Herbert Westfaling, in 1602; twenty-two books from a canon, William St Barbe, in about 1619; and the gift of a manuscript and twenty-eight printed books from Thornton himself when he died in 1629. There were no large acquisitions on the scale of Geste (Salisbury) or Tobie Matthew (York Minster), but cumulatively it is estimated that they had doubled the size of the cathedral library during Thornton's time from some 300 in 1611 (including the inherited manuscripts) to over 600 (by no means exclusively theological) books by 1630. Some money was available, too, for the refurbishment of the older books and manuscripts. During the Civil War, there appear to have been no major losses to the collection despite claims that the library was 'ransacked' after the capture of the city in 1645.[127]

At some cathedrals and minsters, the recovery (not always sustained over a longer period) was associated with the arrival of a particular major donation. In 1623, for example, the dean of Westminster, John Williams (1582–1650), later to become Archbishop of York (1642) and a major benefactor to his old Cambridge college, St John's (1632), presented the library with new book-presses and about 2,000 manuscripts and printed books on a wide range of subjects (including books and pamphlets from the antiquary, William Camden, and a 'gentleman's' collection formed by a Mr Baker [Sir Richard Baker] of Highgate), reorganising the old chapter library as a 'public' library with public access and of more general interest in 1625.[128] At Ripon, where a collegiate church had been

127 Williams, 'The library', 515–21; Jayne, 149, 155; Pearson, 'The libraries of English bishops 1600–1640', 255.

128 The royal printer, John Bill, also gave about 160 books in 1624; Jayne, 80f., 90, 151f.; Bloomfield, *Directory*, 421f. Williams was also instrumental in transferring the library of St Martin's, Leicester (now Leicester Cathedral), to the neighbouring Guildhall, where it remains (Perkin, *Directory*, 265).

re-established in 1608 by James VI and I, following earlier attempts in the 1590s and 1604 to create a clergy training college with 'some reasonable library of books', Dean Anthony Higgin (1608–24) bequeathed his collection of some 1,250 books. Although only the catalogue of the 758 theological items survives, the collection, like that of John Williams' donation to Westminster Abbey, covered a wide subject range, though there were substantial losses either in the Civil War or in 1660, when the central spire collapsed in a winter storm.[129]

Similarly, at York Minster, it was again during the 1620s that signs of a recovery can be detected. Already in 1618, the sub-dean, Edmund Bunny, had made a bequest significant enough to be recorded on his monument, and in 1624 some refurbishment of the collections took place when eight dozen chains were purchased, perhaps for his and other new acquisitions. But it was in 1628–9 that York received its most munificent gift, when to the existing collection of some 200 books was added the private library of its late archbishop, Tobie Matthew, presented to the 'publick use of this church' by his widow Frances, and amounting to over 3,000 items. This was a collection to rival that of almost any contemporary collector or nobleman, rich in theology but also in almost all the other subject-areas and languages that are represented in such libraries (except English literature), and it reflected a lifetime of collecting, from his days at Oxford, where he had been dean of Christ Church until 1583, to his time at Durham (1583–1606), and the wide circle of friends he cultivated during his life. Such a major acquisition necessitated a complete reorganisation of the library building, and this was completed in about 1638 at about the same time that a catalogue was compiled. Fortunately, Matthew's benefaction proved to be an inspiration to others, not least to Ferdinando, Lord Fairfax, who gave several hundred folios himself, and, with his son, Thomas Fairfax, saved the library from destruction after the capture of York in 1644, and even instructed the corporation to pay the salary of a library keeper. As the 'publique librarie in Yorke Minster' it was still receiving donations in 1658.[130]

129 J. E. Mortimer, 'The library catalogue of Anthony Higgin, dean of Ripon (1608–1624)', *Proceedings of the Leeds Philosophical and Literary Society*, Literary and Historical Section, 10, pt 1 (1962), 1–75; Bloomfield, *Directory*, 579; Jayne, 151. William Crashaw, second prebend of Ripon since 1604, bequeathed some of his books to Ripon, while others went to York Minster, and the main part of his library went to St John's College, Cambridge: P. J. Wallis, 'The library of William Crashaw', *TCBS* 2 (1956), 213–28, at 227.

130 C. B. L. Barr, 'The Minster Library', in G. E. Aylmer and R. Cant (eds.), *A history of York Minster* (Oxford, 1977), 487–539, at 499–505; Pearson, 'The libraries of English bishops 1600–1640', 247f. He also gave books to Christ Church while dean there, to Bristol Public

In the same year as Tobie Matthew's gift to York, the chapter at Canterbury, which had witnessed the dispersal of so much of its medieval library in the recent past, resolved 'that every man should endeavour to refurnishe the ancient library of the . . . Church', called for a vellum benefactors' book to register future gifts and, in anticipation of these, ordered that the 'two uppermost desks should be instantly fitted for the receipt of such books'.[131] The dean, Isaac Bargrave, was one who gave books in response to this resolution (these included a copy of the 1620 Bodleian catalogue), and George Abbot gave a further twenty-five when he died in 1633; but on the evidence of the surviving catalogue of 1634 the cathedral's collection was pitiably small and far from up to date. It was during Bargrave's time that the cathedral archives suffered serious losses at the hands of Sir Edward Dering, his cousin, and the issue of security was much in the mind of Archbishop Laud at the time of his visitations the same year and three years later. Both the library and the archives suffered massive disruption during the Civil War and Commonwealth, though most of the books listed in the 1634 catalogue apparently survived and, after the Restoration, were relocated in a new building completed in 1664.[132]

At Durham, recovery came at about the same time. It can probably be traced to a bequest of Francis Bunny in 1617 of £30 'towards the making of a librarie in the vestrie, if Mr Dean and Chapter approve that course, or else to furnish with books (to that value) that which is now in the librarie'. By 1628 refurbishment of the old monastic library room was complete, and some of the existing stock was re-bound when the Dean and Chapter Act for the reform and restoration of the library was passed.[133] This provided, for the first time, a regular income for the library (from burial as well as canons' installation fees), and between 1629 and 1635 £271 2s was raised for library funds, resulting in the acquisition of nearly 300 new books. One of those most involved in this initiative was John Cosin (whose own collection was to form the Cosin Library, founded

Library and to St John's College, Oxford, as well as being an early donor to Bodley's library.

131 N. Ramsey, 'The cathedral archives and library', 378–83; the 1634 inventory is printed in J. W. Legg and W. H. St. J. Hope, *Inventories of Christ Church Canterbury* (Westminster, 1902), 263–5. It contains thirty-one entries for the printed books (c. 80–84 volumes) and twenty-seven manuscripts, but there is no Erasmus, and none of the Reformation commentaries recommended in the Elizabethan Injunctions.

132 Ramsey, 'Cathedral archives', 379–81.

133 Bunny's will was made in 1616. Personal communications from D. Pearson and Dr A. I. Doyle, to whom I am grateful for most of what follows. About 320 manuscripts and sixty printed books had been inherited from the medieval library – a mere torso, though, of what had existed in 1530; D. Pearson, 'Elias Smith, Durham Cathedral librarian 1633–1676', *Library History* 8 (1989), 65–73, at 65.

forty years later in the last years of his episcopate), who had been given the tenth stall in the chapter in 1624, and from 1628 was conspicuously active in library matters, recording in his own hand all the entries in the new register of donations, purchasing books for the library, and in effect carrying out the duties of its librarian until Elias Smith, a minor canon, the first 'librarian curator' since the re-foundation, was appointed in 1633.[134] By the time Smith had made his catalogue of the library (about 1634/5),[135] the collection had grown to 640 items (in 755 volumes), made up of 325 manuscripts and 315 printed books (mostly acquired by gift or purchase during the 1620s and 1630s), and there were further additions up to the Civil War. (Cosin himself, though by this time master of Peterhouse, Cambridge, was still donating books and entering them in the register as late as 1642, during visits to Durham.)[136]

In contrast to the experience of many other cathedral libraries during the Civil War and Commonwealth, Durham was relatively fortunate. About seventy volumes were lost and several of the manuscripts appear to have been scorched, possibly when the cathedral was occupied by 4,500 prisoners taken by Cromwell at the Battle of Dunbar between 1650 and 1652. Both Smith (a strong royalist) and his former assistant at the cathedral school, Isaac Gilpin (a parliamentarian, appointed keeper of the library by the parliamentary commissioners in 1645), have been credited with preserving the collection from destruction, and, when Cromwell's short-lived college at Durham was granted its charter in 1657, the library became its property, with provision in the constitutions for its maintenance and expansion. The restoration of the library to the dean and chapter soon after 1660 saw a revival in its fortunes, with new acquisitions and many small donations increasing its stock of books to about 1,000 by the time Smith, once more its librarian, had died in 1676.[137]

Of the other cathedral libraries, there is less evidence of recovery in the 1620s and 1630s (though individual donations may have continued), but this may be because the necessary archival material no longer exists (because of the widespread disruption to libraries, archives and cathedral chapters during the

134 A. I. Doyle, 'John Cosin (1595–1672) as a library maker', *BC* 40 (1991), 335–57, at 338–40; Pearson, 'The libraries of English bishops 1600–1640', 66. Cosin's draft of the register written in his own hand (though signed by Dean Hunt) is Durham Cathedral Library, MS Hunter 11, no. 20, the fair copy MS A.IV.32.

135 The later date (c. 1670) for this catalogue (Durham Cathedral Library, MS B.IV.47) given by E. A. Read, *A checklist relating to the cathedral libraries of England* (Oxford, 1970), 14, is rejected by Pearson, 'The libraries of English bishops 1600–1640' (72), though additions continued to be made to it up to 1680, even after Smith's death.

136 Doyle, 'John Cosin', 340f.; Pearson, personal communication.

137 Pearson, 'The libraries of English bishops 1600–1640', 67–71.

period 1640–60) or because the relevant provenance research on these collections has still to be undertaken. Even in those cathedrals where some revival had undoubtedly taken place in the early Stuart period, it remained to be seen how their libraries would fare after the Restoration and whether conditions and clerical attitudes would be any more favourable for their preservation and development in the second half of the seventeenth century.

Note: For the most part, the earlier part of this chapter is the work of C. B. L. Barr. David Selwyn is largely responsible for the later part (pp. 379–84, 389–99), but has also supplied sections throughout.

15

Clerical and parish libraries

ARNOLD HUNT

To begin with, a tale of two clergy: John Favour, seventeenth-century vicar of Halifax, and John Wilkinson, one of his fifteenth-century predecessors. Writing in 1619, Favour poured scorn on the pre-Reformation clergy for relying so heavily on 'their golden Legends, Saints lives, Festivals, Martyrologies, *Sermones discipuli*, and such like wholesome books', when 'the Scriptures lay perhaps motheaten in a few libraries, and were scarse to be found in one Priests studie of an hundred'. To illustrate his point, he cited

> the will of a predecessor of mine, in the Vicaridge of Hallifax, dated anno Dom. 1477; who giveth no booke in his will, but one . . . *Item lego Ioanni Wilkinson filio Roberti Wilkinson, unum librum nominatum Legenda Sanctorum, si sit Presbyter: I bequeath to John Wilkinson my brother Robert his sonne, one booke called the Legend of Saints, if he be a Priest*. By which we may see, what store of bookes such a man in those dayes had; perhaps in all likelihood, he had not a better.[1]

At first glance, this appears to present us with the starkest possible contrast between pre- and post-Reformation libraries. Favour was a man of wide learning whose personal library was evidently a large one. In his will, he bequeathed 'my best English Bible' to his son William, his duplicates ('one of every sort of my bookes which I have dubble') to his son-in-law Henry Power, and the remainder of his library to his son John.[2] When he reflected on the solitary volume owned by his medieval predecessor, then glanced round at his own well-stocked bookshelves, it must have seemed to him as though darkness had been succeeded by light. The benighted ignorance of the popish clergy had given way to a new age of learning in which, thanks to the protestant Reformation, the Bible and other religious books were more widely available than ever before.

1 John Favour, *Antiquitie triumphing over noveltie* (London, 1619), 329–30.
2 W. J. Walker, *Chapters on the early registers of Halifax parish church* (Halifax, 1885), 114–16.

Yet I wish to argue in this chapter that there were important threads of continuity running right across this period. The possession of books – as symbols of literacy and learning, aids to the performance of the liturgy, and reference works for the preparation of sermons and homilies – was as important for the medieval clergy as for their sixteenth- and seventeenth-century successors. It was no less important for parish churches. One recent article treats pre- and post-Reformation parish libraries as two completely separate entities, divided by a lengthy interval during which no parish libraries existed at all. 'For some fifty years after the Reformation', we are told, 'nothing that could be described as a library is known to have existed in a parish church.'[3] This chapter will offer an alternative interpretation, in which the existence of a continuous tradition of book-ownership can be seen as bridging the gap between medieval and early modern religious culture.

Clerical libraries

The books owned by the medieval parish clergy were, for the most part, working tools, intended for practical use and reference. The majority were liturgical works, principally missals and breviaries; the remainder were mostly biblical commentaries and model Latin sermons, along with some pastoral treatises and handbooks for confessors. The modest library owned by Thomas Barton (d. 1523), vicar of St Lawrence, York, was probably fairly typical: it contained three service-books (a York breviary, a Sarum breviary, and a 'pye' for calculating the dates of movable feasts), a collection of sermons (the *Sermones discipuli* of Joannes Herolt), a biblical commentary (the *Praeceptorium* of Nicholas de Lyra) and a legal textbook (the *Institutes* of Justinian). The library of another pre-Reformation cleric, Richard Fechett of Bristol (d. 1546), consisted of a couple of mass books, a 'dirige book of vellum with a clasp of silver and gilt', a copy of Herolt's *Sermones discipuli* and the works of 'Vyncentt' (possibly Vincent of Beauvais, more probably St Vincent Ferrer).[4] In Fechett's as in many clergy wills, book bequests are jumbled up with vestments, clothes, monetary gifts, even a bow and arrow – from which it is tempting to infer that the books were not accorded any special status: that the service-books were bundled up with

3 S. Gray and C. Baggs, 'The English parish library: a celebration of diversity', *Libraries and Culture* 35 (2000), 417. See also M. Perkin (ed.), *A directory of the parochial libraries of the Church of England and the Church in Wales* (London, 2004), 30.

4 For Barton, see C. Cross (ed.), *York clergy wills, 1520–1600: city clergy* (York, 1989), 5–7. For Fechett, see Sheila Lang and Margaret McGregor (eds.), *Tudor wills proved in Bristol, 1546–1603* (Bristol, 1993), 1–2.

vestments and other liturgical paraphernalia; and that Fechett's library may have been scattered among his other material possessions rather than set apart as a discrete entity.

H. R. Plomer, one of the first scholars to make a serious study of late medieval book-ownership, believed that even the humblest parish priest would have owned 'at least a breviary of some sort and a missal'. However, more recent research suggests otherwise. Of the northern clergy whose wills are published in the four volumes of *Testamenta Eboracensia*, covering the period from 1346 to 1509, two-thirds had at least one book to bequeath. In a sample of fourteenth- and fifteenth-century wills from the city of Norwich, the figure is one in three; in sixteenth-century wills from the City of London, it is one in three; and in sixteenth-century wills from the diocese of Norwich, it is one in four. Taken together, this evidence suggests that book-ownership, though widespread, was far from universal among the parish clergy. John Shinners has argued that only a minority of the clergy personally owned books, and that, *pace* Plomer, 'the humblest parish priest was quite often bookless'.[5]

However, the reliability of wills as a source of statistical evidence is open to question. Any sample of wills is likely to be skewed towards the wealthier clergy, since their poorer brethren would not have owned enough property to justify the making of a will; and the natural conclusion is that wills probably overrepresent the number of book-owning clergy. But a recent article by Edward Meek points, unexpectedly, to the opposite conclusion. Meek shows that the percentage of clergy wills mentioning books shows a marked fall in the early sixteenth century – just when the advent of print was making books more affordable and more widespread. The most plausible explanation of this apparent paradox is that, as books became cheaper, they were less likely to be singled out for special mention, and more likely to be lumped with other possessions. If so, then it is possible that fifteenth- and sixteenth-century wills may significantly underrepresent the number of book-owning clergy. As Meek concludes: 'it seems likely that there were more printed books in circulation than their occurrence in clerical wills would seem to suggest'.[6]

5 J. T. Rosenthal, 'Clerical book bequests: a *vade mecum*, but whence and whither?', in C. M. Barron and J. Stratford (eds.), *The church and learning in later medieval society: essays in honour of R. B. Dobson* (Donington, 2002), 328; S. Brigden, *London and the Reformation* (Oxford, 1989), 61; J. Shinners, 'Parish libraries in medieval England', in J. Brown and W. P. Stoneman (eds.), *A distinct voice: medieval studies in honor of Leonard E. Boyle, OP* (Notre Dame, IN, 1997), 224.

6 E. L. Meek, 'Printing and the English parish clergy in the late middle ages', *TCBS* 11 (1997), 112–26.

Nor should we make the mistake of assuming that personal possession of books was the same thing as access to books. Many of the poorer clergy may have had access to 'common profit' libraries handed down from one priest to another. William Wilmyncote, a chantry priest in York (d. 1404), left a small but comprehensive collection of liturgical books – a breviary, a missal, an ordinal of York use, a psalter with meditations and prayers, a manual, a *Summa Raymundi* and a bible – with instructions that they were to pass to John Morele, and from him to Wilmyncote's servant Richard de Swayneby. After the latter's death, the collection was to be passed on to other poor priests who did not have books available to them, on condition that if these priests were promoted to a chantry or benefice which had its own books, they were to hand on Wilmyncote's collection to others, and so on until the books were worn out. Similar instructions occur a century later in the will of another York chantry priest, John Fell (d. 1506), who left a 'portas' (breviary) to William White to be handed on 'to a well disposid preist belongyng to the mynster of Yorke; so that it may always retorne to a preist of the said mynstre of Yorke'.[7] Testamentary provisions of this sort, though uncommon, occur with sufficient frequency to suggest that there was a considerable stock of second-hand service books in circulation – books which would not necessarily appear in the owner's will, if handed on by him during his lifetime.

The inclusion of a bible is an interesting feature of Wilmyncote's bequest. While it is true that bibles were far less common than service-books, they were certainly not unknown and may not even have been particularly unusual. The library of William Revetour of York (d. 1446) contained several bibles or biblical commentaries, itemised in his will as 'parvum librum Bibliae integrae cum interpretacione', 'quemdam librum tractatum de Biblia in Anglice', and 'quemdam magnum Rotulum tractatum de Biblia in Latine'. This is perhaps an exceptional case, since Revetour was evidently a man of wide-ranging literary interests, whose sizeable library also contained a copy of a York mystery play and several other English books, including 'librum de Oracione Dominica et Stimulus Conscientiae in Anglica' and 'librum de Evangeliis et Legendam Sanctorum in Anglia [*sic*] tractatam'.[8] But bibles also occur among the possessions of some humbler clergy with fewer books to bequeath. Hugh Smyth, rector of Saundeby in Nottinghamshire (d. 1467), left 'unum librum vocatum

7 J. A. H. Moran, 'A "common profit" library in fifteenth-century England and other books for chaplains', *Manuscripta* 28 (1984), 17–25; J. Raine (ed.), *Testamenta Eboracensia: a selection of wills from the registry at York*, 6 vols., Surtees Soc. 4, 30, 45, 53, 79, 106 (Durham, 1836–69), IV. 244.

8 Raine, *Testamenta Eboracensia*, II. 116–18.

le Byblem' to his brother William, instructing him to pass it on to the church of Saundeby, where it was to be chained for the use and profit of future readers. The library of William Bemond, vicar of Banbury (d. 1509), consisted of 'a book of the Life of Christ', 'a book of the Lives of the Fathers' and 'six books of the Bible'.[9]

On the basis of this evidence, it seems clear that John Favour's polemical characterisation of pre-Reformation clerical learning – with the Bible 'scarse to be found in one Priests studie of an hundred' – was grossly inaccurate. Nor should we go along with Favour in construing the popularity of works like the *Golden legend* as evidence of popish superstition and credulity. On the contrary: the reason the *Golden legend* was popular with the pre-Reformation clergy was that it provided the raw material for sermons; and its appearance in clergy wills, along with biblical paraphrases like the *Vita Christi*, can thus be taken as evidence that the clergy took their preaching duties seriously. The same can be said of moral treatises like the *Destructorium vitiorum* – 'a work in which criticism of the clergy savours of Lollardy', wrote Margaret Bowker, but more likely to have been valued as a source of sermon *exempla*, and common enough in clergy wills to suggest that it was not regarded as suspiciously heterodox.[10] By the early sixteenth century, some clergy had accumulated large collections of sermons. The library of William Lambert, rector of All Hallows, Honey Lane, London (d. 1521/2), included 'Hugonem upon the hole bible; sermones opuscula; Epistolas beati Augustini; Valentinum super psalterium . . . sermones Augustini; sermones Vincentii; sermones Magdalene . . . Iustinis historicus . . . with all my quayres of preching', all of which he bequeathed to Pembroke Hall, Cambridge.[11]

This raises an obvious question. Should clerical ownership of bibles, and concern for preaching, be taken as harbingers of a new 'humanist' spirit presaging the protestant Reformation? An earlier generation of scholars would have had little hesitation in answering this question with a confident 'yes', but the new wave of revisionist scholarship has made this far more problematic. In general, the reading habits of the early sixteenth-century clergy do not seem markedly different from those of their fifteenth-century predecessors; their wills contain few books that would have been unfamiliar a hundred years

9 Raine, *Testamenta Eboracensia*, II. 283; J. R. H. Weaver and A. Beardwood (eds.), *Some Oxfordshire wills proved in the Prerogative Court of Canterbury, 1393–1510* (Oxford, 1958), 100.

10 M. Bowker, *The secular clergy of the diocese of Lincoln, 1495–1520* (Cambridge, 1968), 54; Weaver and Beardwood, *Oxfordshire wills*, 65; M. McGregor (ed.), *Bedfordshire wills proved in the Prerogative Court of Canterbury, 1383–1548*, Bedfordshire Historical Record Soc. 58 (1979), 100.

11 CBMLC X. UC140; S. Brigden, *London and the Reformation* (Oxford, 1989), 61.

earlier. The one noticeable difference is the appearance of a small number of classical texts. Among the books owned by Richard Oliver, vicar of All Saints, North Street, York (d. 1535), were Calepine's Latin dictionary, Erasmus's *Adages*, and Cicero's *De officiis* – on which basis he has been claimed by Claire Cross as a representative of the 'new learning', in contrast to the 'limited . . . intellectual horizons' of an older generation of York city clergy. But such a sharp distinction between old and new is perhaps overdrawn. As Cross admits, Oliver's ownership of these basic classical texts is probably a sign that he was doing some grammar-school teaching, and may therefore tell us little about his own religious opinions or intellectual interests.[12]

Nor was the Reformation necessarily a clean break with the past. In terms of clerical libraries, it may actually have had the reverse effect, in causing a lot of Catholic theological texts to flood out of the dissolved monastic libraries and into the possession of parish clergy, many of whom were themselves ex-monks. One striking example can be found in the will of Robert Barker, vicar of Driffield in Yorkshire, who died in 1581 leaving a library of around 150 volumes. The majority of the books were late medieval sermon collections and biblical commentaries, though the collection was sufficiently up to date to include Erasmus's edition of Jerome, one of the monuments of humanist scholarship. This is an extraordinary collection to find in the possession of a humble parish priest whose living was worth only a few pounds a year and who had few other goods of any value to bequeath. Where had Barker acquired his books? They appear to have come from the library of the Cistercian monastery at Byland Abbey, probably inherited by Barker from a relative who had been the last prior of Byland before its dissolution in 1538. Even as late as 1581, he seems to have regarded them as a working theological library, and left instructions in his will that they were to be kept together and held in trust 'untill such tyme as some one or moe of my naturall blood be able to understande them', though in the event they passed, via Barker's executor John Nettleton, into the collection of the antiquary Henry Savile of Banke.[13]

There are many other examples of medieval books being owned or handed down by Elizabethan clergy. In 1565, Edmund Skelton gave to his parish church of Egton, in North Yorkshire, a Latin bible and two other books which he had probably inherited from the library of Grosmont Abbey, where he had formerly been a monk. In 1572, Robert Pursglove, another Yorkshire cleric, gave

12 Cross, *York clergy wills*, viii, 12–16.

13 C. Cross, 'A medieval Yorkshire library', *Northern History* 25 (1989), 281–90; M. A. Hicks, 'John Nettleton, Henry Savile of Banke, and the post-medieval vicissitudes of Byland Abbey library', *Northern History* 26 (1990), 212–17.

a collection of eight books 'to the use of the schole maister of the grammar schole of Jesus at Gisburne', including works by Augustine, Chrysostom and Aquinas, a five-volume set of the 'Glosa ordinaria cum expositione lire', and a tract volume containing 'Hugo de Sancto Victore super visione Ezechielis, Richardus de Sancto Victore de statu interioris hominis post lapsum, et plures alii sermones'. In 1573, Thomas Marss, vicar of East Markham in Nottinghamshire, bequeathed 'five books of the Bible called Lyre' to the vicar of the neighbouring parish of Tuxford.[14] What we are dealing with here, it seems, is clergy of conservative sympathies who had held on to former monastic books in the hope that the monasteries would eventually be restored. As it became clear that this was not going to happen, they passed their books on to parish churches, grammar schools or like-minded fellow clergy for safe keeping – still, apparently, regarding them as current works of theology, not merely relics of a bygone age.

One clerical library that deserves special attention is that of Robert Parkyn, curate of Adwick-le-Street, near Doncaster. Parkyn – 'the last medieval Englishman', as he has been called – was a reluctant conformist who submitted to the Elizabethan settlement while remaining privately committed to the old religion, and his library is a fascinating time capsule of late medieval Catholicism carried over into the Reformation church. When he died in 1570, he left the majority of his books to his nephew, including 'the holle Byble booke in Latyn and Dionisius Carthusianus his worke uppon the Byble in seven large volumes', a Latin concordance, 'an other fayre booke called Opera Divi Hillarii . . . and also an other fayre prynted booke called Epitome Omnium Operum Divi Aurillii Augustini'. Other books went to neighbouring clergy: to John Hudson, dean of Doncaster, 'a great thicke wrytten booke in parchement' containing a Latin treatise on the seven deadly sins; to Robert Skolaye, vicar of Brodsworth, the sermons of Jodocus Clichtoveus; and to William Watson, curate of Melton, 'a wrytten booke profitable and easye to fynd sentences of the Byble by letters'. Yet, much more surprisingly, Parkyn also owned 'Mr Calvins booke in print', which he bequeathed to one of his parishioners. Strange as it may seem, even this deeply conservative cleric had apparently made some effort to acquaint himself with protestant theology.[15]

14 For Skelton and Marss, see Cross, 'A medieval Yorkshire library', 283. For Pursglove, see North Yorkshire Record Office, Northallerton, ZJL (Lee of Pinchinthorpe papers) / O544.

15 A. G. Dickens, 'Robert Parkyn's Narrative of the Reformation', in Dickens, *Reformation studies* (1982), 290–1.

There is a more general point to be made here about the conservatism of clerical libraries, reinforced by the way that books were handed on within the clerical profession. In the pre-Reformation period, it made obvious sense for books to be handed down from one priest to another, not only because clerical libraries tended to consist of service-books and other tools of the trade, but because the clergy had no wives or children to inherit their goods. One might have expected to find this custom dying out after the Reformation, but the evidence of clerical wills suggests that it still persisted. For example, when Miles Simonson, rector of Stifford in Essex, died in 1567, he left the majority of his goods to his widow, but his library – or, as he modestly described it in his will, 'certain old books remaining here in my house' – to Christopher Eaton, vicar of the neighbouring parish of East Tilbury.[16] Sermon manuscripts, too, though rarely mentioned in wills, may often have been passed down from one preacher to another. This is a significant point of continuity between pre- and post-Reformation habits and patterns of book-ownership; but more importantly, it may have acted as a brake on doctrinal change, since clergy may often have been reading (or even preaching from) books and manuscripts that had come down to them from an earlier generation.

But revisionism should not be carried too far. Margaret Steig's survey of books listed in the wills of Somerset clergy suggests that, by the early seventeenth century, the new theology had almost entirely supplanted the old. A few clergy owned works of medieval theology, like Hugh of Saint-Victor's commentary on the Psalms, or Durandus's commentary on the *Sentences* of Peter Lombard, that may have come down from pre-Reformation libraries; but most of the books in clerical hands were of a more recent vintage. Alongside the Bible (often in a Greek, Hebrew or polyglot edition) and the works of the Fathers (principally Augustine and Chrysostom), there were the writings of the leading continental reformers, their English counterparts, and some of their Catholic opponents: Hieronymus Zanchius, Adrianus Junius, Wolfgang Musculus, William Perkins, John Foxe, Robert Bellarmine.[17] What were these books doing in the libraries of the parish clergy? They were there not simply for the general purposes of preaching and teaching, but also to meet the more

16 F. G. Emmison (ed.), *Essex wills, 1565–1571* (Boston, 1983), 67. For another example, see Lang and McGregor, *Tudor wills*, 31.

17 M. Stieg, *Laud's laboratory: the diocese of Bath & Wells in the early seventeenth century* (1982), 61–2, 353–5. See also R. C. Richardson, *Puritanism in north-west England* (Manchester, 1972), 56–8; C. Cross, 'The incomes of provincial urban clergy, 1520–1645', in R. O'Day and F. Heal (eds.), *Princes and paupers in the English church, 1500–1800* (Leicester, 1981), 79.

specific needs of anti-Catholic (and, to a lesser extent, anti-puritan) controversy, by enabling the clergy to build up a repertoire of arguments drawn from recent polemical works and backed up with scriptural and patristic references. The presence of so many modern works suggests that the clergy felt the need to keep their libraries up to date and were prepared to devote a considerable proportion of their income to buying books.

Outside the ranks of the episcopate, the largest clerical library of its time was that of the veteran anti-Catholic controversialist William Crashaw (1572–1626), who wrote in 1609 that he had 'spent my patrimonye in bookes, and my time in perusinge them'.[18] As a preacher in Yorkshire, and then as lecturer at the Temple Church in London, Crashaw built up a collection of some 4,000 printed books and 200 manuscripts, classified under eight subject-headings: Scriptures, Councils, Fathers, Protestants, Papists, Law, Cosmography and History. He claimed to have spent over £2,000 on the collection, describing it with pardonable pride as 'one of the most complete libraryes in Europe (that of Oxforde excepted)', containing 'as good books as are in any library in Christendom, and some such as are scarce in any other librarye of this land'. However, disaster struck in 1610 when the barristers of the Middle Temple refused to continue paying his salary. Crashaw retired to his benefice of Burton Agnes, in Yorkshire, and sold the bulk of his library to St John's College, Cambridge, where many of the books still survive, easily recognisable by his signature, usually with the date and price, and the motto 'Servire Deo regnare est'. The collection is exceptionally strong in contemporary theology, and the presence of two Frankfurt trade catalogues, the *Bibliotheca exotica* (1610) and *Bibliotheca classica* (1611), suggests that Crashaw was active in seeking out new books from the continent, though the paucity of incunabula would seem to indicate that he had little interest in buying second-hand.

This was a wholly exceptional collection, which went far beyond the needs of an ordinary parish clergyman, as even Crashaw admitted when he described his Yorkshire parish as 'a rude countrye [where] I have no use of such a librarye'. But substantial collections of books were not unknown among the parish clergy. Almost as remarkable as Crashaw's library, in its own way, is the collection of Isaac Lowder of Darlington, who died in 1612. As the editor of his inventory points out, Lowder was by no means a rich man. 'He possessed just enough to furnish one room meagrely. He did not own the bed he slept on. His clothes possibly allowed him one change of attire.' His possessions (other than his

18 On Crashaw's library, see P. J. Wallis, 'The library of William Crashawe', *TCBS* 2 (1956), 213–28, and R. M. Fisher, 'William Crashawe's library at the Temple 1605–1615', *Library*, 5th ser., 30 (1975), 116–24.

books) were valued at £4 12s 3d, he died owing £19 15s 6d, and his assets, including his library, would only just have been enough to clear his debts.[19] Yet he had managed to build up a collection of over seventy volumes, including most of the major protestant reformed authors: Calvin, Peter Martyr, Edward Dering, William Perkins and many other English sermon-writers. He had a good collection of the Latin classics, and textbooks on logic, grammar and rhetoric which would have been useful to him in his role as a schoolmaster. A 'statute booke', a medical textbook and a copy of Angel Day's *English secretarie* suggest that he was called upon for legal and medical advice and for the drafting of wills; and there was even a little light reading, including a copy of *The shepherds calendar.*[20]

Writing in 1626, the Oxfordshire minister Robert Harris complained of the poverty of the clergy: 'I know Preachers of excellent parts . . . who cannot lay out fiftie shillings in five years upon books.'[21] Harris was quite right to point to the enormous disparity in income between the very richest and the very poorest clergy – though in a sense, his remark is a back-handed tribute to the growth of clerical libraries, as it implies that the average parish clergyman would expect to spend at least 10s a year on books. Nevertheless, poor clergy might have had access to books even if they could not afford to buy them. The Derbyshire minister William Hull kept a record of book loans on the flyleaves of his sermon notebooks – 'Mr Peacock, Abbot contr. Bishop', 'Mrs Meverel, Halls peace of the church', 'Mr Taylor, Mr Philips Sermons', 'Mr Cooke, Brightmans Apocalipsis', 'Mr Blackwell, Raynolds contr. Hart' – revealing the existence of a network of local clergy and gentry who were able to borrow new works of theology and religious controversy almost as soon as they were published.[22] The will of Thomas Walker, rector of Grendon, Warwickshire, sheds light on another form of shared access to books. When he died in 1607, Walker left to Richard Latimer, vicar of the neighbouring parish of Polesworth, 'one booke and my part of a booke which are both in his hands', suggesting that the two men had clubbed together to buy a book which they could not have afforded individually.[23]

19 J. A. Atkinson *et al.* (eds.), *Darlington wills and inventories, 1600–1625*, Surtees Soc. 201 (Durham, 1993), 31–3, 122–5, 215–22.

20 It is not clear whether this refers to *The kalender of shepardes* (*STC* 22407 *et seq.*) or to Edmund Spenser's *The shepheardes calendar* (*STC* 23089 *et seq.*).

21 Robert Harris, *Hezekiah's recovery* (London, 1626), D4r.

22 Dublin, Trinity Coll., MS 709, vols. I–III. For another example of clerical book-borrowing, see C. Wilkins-Jones, 'Joseph Lawson, the *Pennarum Nitor*, and the Holt Deanery Book Club', *Notes and Queries* 249/1 (2004), 21.

23 R. O'Day, *The English clergy, 1558–1642* (Leicester, 1979), 163.

The history of clerical libraries thus reflects, in microcosm, the history of the English Reformation as presented in recent scholarship, with a period of slow and reluctant change in the early Elizabethan period followed by rapid consolidation towards the end of the sixteenth century. Paradoxically, it was the survival of medieval patterns of book-ownership and circulation that helped to bring this about. The tendency of the clergy to share books among themselves, and to hand them down to younger successors, meant that Catholic theology took a very long time to drop out of circulation. But it also meant that, once the reformed religion managed to establish a presence in clerical libraries, its subsequent diffusion through the ranks of the clergy was very rapid indeed.

Parish libraries

A decree attributed to Archbishop Winchelsea, first issued in the late thirteenth century, listed eight essential service-books – a lectionary, an antiphonal, a gradual, a psalter, a sequence book, an ordinal, a missal and a manual – which parishioners were required to provide for their churches. The fact that every parish was expected to have its own set of liturgical books does not, of course, mean that every parish did so; yet an inventory of church goods in the archdeaconry of Norwich, compiled in the late fourteenth century, points to an extremely high level of compliance with Winchelsea's decree. Of the 358 churches in the archdeaconry, only six lacked a missal, only twelve lacked a gradual, and the vast majority (94 per cent) had the full set of eight books, while many of the larger city parishes owned very sizeable collections of liturgical texts, sometimes including as many as five or six copies of the same book. What is also interesting is that a small but significant minority of churches owned non-liturgical books. Six parishes had a copy of the Bible, and several others had biblical commentaries or glossed gospel books. Ten had copies of the *Golden legend*, and eleven had William of Pagula's *Oculus sacerdotis*, a handbook for parish priests.[24]

Many of these books had probably been owned by individual clergy before being given or bequeathed to a parish. It was not uncommon for priests to leave a missal or other liturgical book to be used at the altar where they had served, often with a request that their name should be written into the book so that their successors would remember to pray for them. One of the books owned by the parish of Upton, and recorded in the Norwich archdeaconry

24 A. Watkin (ed.), *Archdeaconry of Norwich: inventory of church goods temp. Edward III*, Norfolk Record Soc. 19 (1947–8). See also Shinners, 'Parish libraries', 210.

survey, was a copy of the psalter ('unum bonum psalterium') which had been given to the church by a former vicar on condition that prayers were said for his soul as long as the book remained in use. The will of Christopher Burgh (d. 1469), rector of the Yorkshire parish of Scrayingham, after stipulating that his body was to be buried underneath the high altar, bequeathed 'unum Missale' to the parish with the request that his name be included in the prayers said in church every Sunday. In some cases, priests bequeathed more substantial collections of books. John Spitele (d. 1417) left the parish church of Luton, Bedfordshire, a missal, a manual, a processional, an antiphonal, a copy of the *Pupilla oculi* and Bartholomeus Anglicus, *De proprietatibus rerum*, all except the last written in his own hand.[25]

Increasingly, however, it was the laity who took the initiative in giving and bequeathing books to their parish churches. A recent edition of fifteenth-century wills from the town of St Albans, in Hertfordshire, reveals a pattern that was probably fairly typical of urban parishes across England, with a series of bequests to the parish of St Peter's for the purchase of new liturgical books. In 1482, Margaret Nash left 6d to the high altar and 12d for the purchase of a missal; in 1484, John Man left 12d to the high altar, 4d to St Mary's light and 20d for the purchase of a lectionary; while in the same year, Stephen Newman left 6s 8d to the high altar, 6s 8d to the rood light and 20d for the purchase of a missal for St Mary's altar next to the pulpit. As Eamon Duffy has remarked, bequests of this sort provide 'a detailed picture of the ways in which lay people appropriated the teaching and the priorities of the late medieval Church', and what they suggest is that parishioners attached great importance to the provision of liturgical books and took pride in helping to build up the collection of books belonging to their parish.[26] This sense of local pride is encapsulated in a set of verses written inside a service-book given to the parish of Rushall, Staffordshire, in 1444, which declares that the book has been placed in the church as a permanent heirloom, 'tacched with a cheyn | purposed of entent for to endure | and here perpetuelli stylle to remeyne | fro eyre to eyre'. Parishes set great store by their books and, as legal records show, took steps to recover them if they were lost or stolen.[27]

25 Watkin, *Inventory of church goods*, 37; Raine, *Testamenta Eboracensia*, III. 172; McGregor, *Bedfordshire wills*, 7.

26 S. Flood (ed.), *St Albans wills, 1471–1500* ([Hitchin], 1993), 65, 69, 74; E. Duffy, *The stripping of the altars* (1992), 355.

27 J. W. Clark, 'On some English verses written in a fifteenth-century service-book', *Cambridge Antiquarian Society Proceedings and Communications* 11 (1904); [K. A. Manley], 'An unrecorded medieval parish library?' *Library History* 8/2 (1988), 43–4.

By the late fifteenth century, some parishes had built up very large collections of books. The wealthy parish of All Saints, Bristol, owned a particularly fine collection of liturgical volumes, including eight processionals, seven graduals, six missals, three antiphonals, three lectionaries, two ordinals, two manuals, two breviaries, two psalters, a martyrology, a hymnal and an organ book, all catalogued in painstaking detail in the 1469 inventory of parish property so that they could be easily identified and distinguished from each other: 'Inprimis 1 great mass book, beginning the third leaf *menta sua* . . . Item 1 mass book, beginning the third leaf *unum baptisma* . . . Item 1 little old mass book . . . Item 1 old mass book without boards . . . '[28] Some parishes had also acquired substantial collections of non-liturgical books. Among the books owned by the parish of St Margaret's, Fish Street, London, in 1472 were copies of William Lyndewode's *Constitutiones provinciales*, Hugh Ripelin's *Compendium theologicae veritatis*, Johannes Balbus's *Catholicon*, the works of St Bernard, the popular religious poem *The prick of conscience*, a Latin treatise entitled *De remediis controversorum* and an English collection of miracle tales, *The miracles of Our Ladie* (later printed by Wynkyn de Worde).[29] With collections of this size, one is justified in speaking of a 'library' in the usual sense of the word, not just an accumulation of books.

How were these books used, and who had access to them? Many of the books at St Margaret's, Fish Street, are described as 'cheyned', implying that they were on public display rather than locked in a cupboard or chest. At All Hallows, Barking, there was a copy of the *Pupilla oculi* 'cheyned in the choir', while at St Nicholas Shambles there was a copy of a 'legende in english . . of dyu*ers* seintis lifes', also 'cheyned in the qwere'.[30] It is not absolutely certain that the laity would have had access to the choir or chancel of their parish church, but the likelihood is that they did, and that they could therefore have consulted these books or heard them read aloud. In this connection, there is an intriguing piece of evidence in the post-mortem heresy trial of Richard Hunne, who died in mysterious circumstances while imprisoned in the Lollards' Tower in 1514. Several witnesses testified that Hunne had owned a copy of the Bible in English, but one witness went further, and claimed that 'the sayd book was wont to lye in St Marg*a*ret Cherche in Brigstreet' – Hunne's home

28 C. Burgess (ed.), *The pre-Reformation records of All Saints' [sic], Bristol*, 3 vols. (Bristol, 1995–2004), I. 38–40.
29 F. Kisby, 'Books in London parish churches before 1603: some preliminary observations', in Barron and Stratford, *The church and learning*, 311.
30 Kisby, 'Books in London parish churches', 311.

parish – 'sometyme a month togidders'.[31] If this is true, it suggests that parish libraries may have served as centres for religious discussion, where lay people could meet to read books together or even bring books of their own to share with others.

The Reformation forced parishes to dispose of their existing book collections and acquire new ones. Indeed, it is possible to track the progress of the Reformation simply by looking at the book purchases recorded in churchwardens' accounts, as in the parish of St Mary Woolnoth in London.[32] In 1539 the parish spent 6s 8d on 'the half of the Bybill in the Church': that is, the Bible in English, with the cost split equally between the minister and the parishioners. By the end of Edward's reign the parish had acquired the full complement of books required by law: the Bible, the Book of Homilies and the *Paraphrases* of Erasmus, together with 'two communion books in English' and 'six new psalter books printed in English'. With the reintroduction of Catholicism in the reign of Mary, the parish had to buy a new set of Latin service-books, and in 1553 it spent a grand total of £10 16s 8d on two antiphonals, two graduals, two missals, a lectionary, a manual, a *venite* book (i.e. a Venitare, or music book for the psalms at the beginning of Matins), three processionals and a *dirige* book (i.e. a dirge book, containing the office for the dead).[33] Then in 1559, with the accession of Elizabeth, the parish bought 'four bookes of the English service', and the following year it sold off its Catholic liturgical books at a considerable loss. 'Item', say the accounts, 'receyved of a stacyioner for the lattyn service bookes which weare sold by the consent of the perishoners, 26s 8d', probably no more than the price of the waste paper.

This amounted to a massive upheaval in book-ownership – forcing parishes, in effect, to clear their shelves and start again, not just once but three times. Yet there were significant continuities between the old and the new. The official adoption of the English Bible, for example, could be seen as continuing the existing tradition of placing books in church for the use of the laity. The first royal injunctions, issued in 1536, ordered the clergy to 'provide a book of the whole Bible, both in Latin and also in English, and lay the same in the choir, for every man that will to look and read thereon', while the second royal

31 J. Fines, 'The post-mortem condemnation for heresy of Richard Hunne', *EHR* 78 (1963), 531.

32 J. M. S. Brooks and A. W. C. Hallen, eds., *The transcript of the registers of the united parishes of S. Mary Woolnoth and S. Mary Woolchurch Haw* (1886), xvi–xxx.

33 The *venite* book was in fact obsolete, as its contents were usually incorporated in the antiphonal, so these were probably second-hand books which had survived the Edwardian Reformation.

injunctions, issued two years later, ordered them to place a copy of the English Bible 'in some convenient place within the said church that you have cure of, whereas your parishioners may most commodiously resort to the same and read it'.[34] As we have seen, the choir was the usual place where books were chained before the Reformation. This suggests that, in many churches, the English Bible would have been chained alongside an existing collection of Catholic theological and liturgical books, which would probably not have been removed until the beginning of Edward VI's reign in 1549.

Nor did the Reformation cause the laity to lose interest in providing books for their parish churches. On the contrary, the sense of attachment to a local church, which had previously been expressed in bequests for the purchase of Catholic service-books, was now redirected into the purchase of new protestant texts. The popularity of Foxe's *Acts and monuments* (Foxe's Book of Martyrs) demonstrates this particularly clearly. There was no official requirement for parishes to buy the book, but soon after its publication in 1563, and its republication in a revised and expanded edition in 1570, godly lay people began to leave money in their wills to enable their parish churches to buy a copy. In 1572, James Harris of Great Burstead, Essex, left his bible to his son Isaac and his Book of Martyrs (the only other book mentioned in his will) to his parish church. In 1574, John King of Stebbing, Essex, bequeathed the sum of 10s 'to help to buy the Book of Martyrs so that it may safely remain in Stebbing church to the use of the parishioners'.[35] In the church of St Peter and Paul, Wisbech, the three-volume set of Foxe has long since disappeared, but the reading desk where it was chained can still be seen, with an inscription recording the benefaction of Robert Gooderidge, blacksmith, who 'gave by his last will and testament, £8 to buy theise three books of Marters and to have them set in the church of Wisbeach'.

But perhaps the most important point of continuity lay simply in the high level of compliance with official instructions. Churchwardens may not have been overjoyed at having to sell off their parish's books as waste paper, nor at having to buy an expensive set of new books to replace them; but on the whole they complied, just as their fourteenth-century predecessors had complied with the order to buy the service-books listed in Archbishop Winchelsea's decree. In a recent study of the reception of Erasmus's *Paraphrases*, John Craig lists 155 parishes known to have acquired a copy of the book by 1553.

34 W. H. Frere and W. M. Kennedy, *Visitation articles and injunctions of the period of the Reformation*, 3 vols. (London, 1910), II. 9, 35–6.

35 F. G. Emmison (ed.), *Essex wills, 1571–1577* (Boston, 1986), 64, 421.

The wide range of parishes included in this list, from large urban parishes down to small rural ones such as Wigtoft in Lincolnshire or Leverington in Cambridgeshire, and the fact that many of them went to the extra expense of installing a reading desk and a chain to keep the book secure, all seem to indicate, in Craig's words, 'a level of compliance with the Edwardian injunctions that was extremely high'.[36] This is only one aspect of a general phenomenon familiar to historians of the English Reformation, which Christopher Marsh has labelled the 'compliance conundrum'. We know that many people were deeply attached to the old religion, yet, as Marsh points out, 'recent research has left us in little doubt that, broadly speaking, the people of sixteenth-century England responded to official religious commands by doing what they were told', irrespective of their private opinions.[37]

This is strikingly demonstrated in the records of episcopal and archidiaconal visitations. In 1573, for example, the archdeacon of Nottingham, John Lowth, apparently acting under pressure from the newly appointed archbishop of York, Edmund Grindal, launched a thorough investigation of the church buildings and furnishings within the archdeaconry. He was able to find only one parish lacking a Bible, two lacking the *Paraphrases*, and one lacking both the *Paraphrases* and the Homilies. Even allowing for the fact that some churchwardens probably failed to own up to the lack of books, these are remarkably low figures, which suggest that the great majority of parishes had complied with official requirements.[38] A similar survey in the diocese of Bath and Wells in 1587 uncovered only six parishes lacking the *Paraphrases*. In five of these cases, the churchwardens were ordered to 'provide and gett in sted of the foresaide booke, a booke called Bullingers decades in Englishe, for the use of theire parishe Churche'; in the sixth, the churchwardens were dismissed without further action after reporting that they already possessed a copy of Foxe's Book of Martyrs, this being regarded as an acceptable alternative to the *Paraphrases*. This is of interest as showing that the authorities did not always insist on the books specified in the royal injunctions. It also suggests that, by the 1580s, Erasmus's *Paraphrases* had begun to look rather dated in comparison with the writings of more advanced reformers such as Bullinger and Foxe.[39]

36 J. Craig, 'Forming a protestant consciousness? Erasmus' *Paraphrases* in English parishes 1547–1650', in H. M. Pabel (ed.), *Holy Scripture speaks: the production and reception of Erasmus' Paraphrases on the New Testament* (Toronto, 2002), 313–60.

37 C. Marsh, *Popular religion in sixteenth-century England* (London, 1998), 201.

38 Office act book, 1572–4: Nottingham University Library, AN/A3/1/2.

39 Office act book, 1587–92: Somerset Record Office, Taunton, D/D/Ca 81. Bishop Middleton's visitation articles for the diocese of St Davids, 1583, ordered 'that the Paraphrases

The books required by authority could have served as the nucleus of a parish library. An inventory of 1620 from the parish of St Andrew Undershaft, London, reveals the existence of a small chained library, consisting of 'a booke in folio of Mr Juells workes, three bookes of Mr Perkins workes, two bookes of Martirs the first and second Tome, a booke of Erasmus Expositions on the Gospell, a faire large bible in folio and the workes of Mr Hieron'. The Bible and the *Paraphrases* had been standard for many years, while Jewel's *Works* had been prescribed by Archbishop Bancroft in 1610 as a compulsory purchase for all parishes, but the remainder of these books had presumably been acquired by voluntary purchase or donation. Similar books could have been found in other London parish churches. St Andrew by the Wardrobe had a copy of Peter Martyr's *Commonplaces*, St Botolph without Bishopsgate had Calvin's *Sermons upon the Book of Job*, and St Peter Westcheap had Alexander Nowell's *Catechisme*.[40] The significance of these modest collections is that they gave parishioners access to the writings of some of the leading English and continental Reformed divines – Calvin, Peter Martyr, William Perkins, Samuel Hieron – which, in theological terms, went considerably beyond the official doctrine of the Church of England. It is now widely accepted by historians that the early seventeenth-century Church of England was Calvinist in practice if not in name. Parish libraries helped to disseminate the fruits of this 'Calvinist consensus' to a wider readership.

Some parishes had much larger collections of books formed in a more purposeful manner. A number of towns, including Leicester, Grantham, Norwich and Ipswich, boasted sizeable libraries of theological books for the use of local clergy. One of the earliest of these was at Bury St Edmunds, founded in 1595 and reflecting the commitment of the urban elite to the cause of a godly preaching ministry. Sir Robert Jermyn, the leading local magistrate, led the way by presenting a fifteen-volume set of the works of Calvin, and other local gentry and townsmen followed his lead, in what was effectively a 'sponsor-a-book' scheme whereby individuals could donate a sum of money to have their name attached to a particular volume. Thus Augustine Gooch and John Bye, maltsters, gave the works of St Athanasius; John Man, grocer, gave the works of Cyril of Alexandria; and John Lansdale, clothier, gave Martin Bucer's commentary on the gospels. As these examples suggest, the library was particularly strong in the works of the Fathers and the leading

may be provided in every parish church, or rather Bullinger's *Decades* in English, for it is much more profitable': W. P. M. Kennedy, *Elizabethan episcopal administration*, 3 vols. (1924), III. 150.

40 Guildhall Library, London, MS 4115; Kisby, 'Books in London parish churches', 322.

protestant reformed divines, along with a few medieval scholastic texts that may have come out of pre-Reformation clerical or monastic collections. It was housed in the parish church of St James and was clearly intended primarily for the clergy, but it also contained a few English books – Calvin's *Sermons*, Bullinger's *Decades*, even a few secular works such as Dodoens's *Herball* – and there is evidence that some of these were read and borrowed by the laity as well.[41]

A few country parishes also had substantial libraries endowed by members of the local gentry or nobility. The parish library of Oakham, in Rutland, was founded in 1616 by Lady Anne Harington, widow of John, 1st baron Harington of Exton. In her study of the Oakham library, Anne Herbert suggests that many of the books may have come from the library of Anne's son John Harington, who died in 1614. However, several of the books were published after that date, and it seems more likely that Lady Anne gave a sum of money which was then used to buy a general theological library for use by local clergy.[42] The library is predictably strong in the works of the Fathers and the leading Reformation divines, though there is a distinct leaning towards Lutheran theology (Luther, Melanchthon, Chemnitz) and some surprising gaps among the Calvinist authors (no Calvin, no Beza, no Perkins). The collection as a whole has a slightly impersonal feel to it, and it is hard to avoid the suspicion that the choice of books may have been left to a bookseller who simply assembled a library out of his unsold stock, drawn from recent continental imports with a seasoning of older volumes from the second-hand trade. Much of the library consists of the sort of books that an enterprising London bookseller might have brought back from the Frankfurt book fair, with a preponderance of Paris, Frankfurt and Geneva imprints, while many of the earlier books are in contemporary English bindings and must have come to England soon after their publication, eventually finding their way on to the second-hand market.

But perhaps the most impressive parish library of this period is that of Langley Marish, Buckinghamshire, established between 1613 and 1623 by a local gentleman, Sir John Kederminster, in a purpose-built room adjoining his family pew. It contains about 270 books, mostly Latin works of theology, intended 'for the perpetual benefit of the vicar and curate of the parish of Langley, as for all other ministers and preachers of God's Word that would

41 J. Craig, *Reformation, politics and polemics: the growth of Protestantism in East Anglian market towns, 1500–1610* (Aldershot, 2001), 116–21. The library is now on deposit in Cambridge University Library.

42 A. L. Herbert, 'Oakham parish library', *Library History* 6/1 (1982), 1–11. The library is now on deposit in Nottingham University Library.

resort thither to make use of the books therein'. What makes it extraordinary is its setting, aptly described by the architectural historian John Harris as 'one of the most precious rooms of the whole Jacobean age'. The walls are covered with over 250 painted panels, with landscape scenes, biblical figures and saints in elaborate architectural cartouches; and the room is dominated by a painted chimneypiece in which the Kederminster arms are flanked by the figures of Mars, Mercury and the four Cardinal Virtues, possibly intended to be read as a Neoplatonic allusion to the harmony of the earthly, planetary and heavenly realms.[43] This is plainly a room designed for private reading and meditation, and, although it is attached to a parish church, making it at least a semi-public space, it has more in common with the private closets or studies furnished by individuals for their own use.

In complete contrast to the grandeur of the Kederminster library, the parish library of Measham, in Leicestershire, consisted of only six books. No trace of the library remains in the parish, and we only know of its existence thanks to the fortuitous survival of one of the six books, Francis Rous's *The mysticall marriage . . . between a Soule and her Saviour* (1631), with the rules of the library written on the flyleaf. It was established in 1635 by the parish clergyman, John Jackson, to serve 'as a meanes 1. against deceitfullness of the heart, 2. to know the oracles of God, 3. to increase Christianity, 4. to further practicall Piety, 5. to walk with God in holy peace, 6. lastly to be marryed to Christ in a conjugall yoke, never to be dissolved.' Jackson's plan was that 'the first sixe families (wherein there is any that can read a Chapter) from the North end of the town may have each family one Book a piece quarterly. And every quarter day to be removed by the minister & church-wardens to the next six families and so forward till thei have gone through the whole Parish. After which to begin again as at the first, lending a different Booke to each family from what they last had.' The churchwardens were required to keep a register of borrowers, and to 'putt not any Booke into any mans hand unlesse he will promise to restore it safe againe the next quarter day at the ministers house [or] else at the church'.[44]

Judging from the list of borrowers' names in the sole surviving book, the Measham lending library may not have lasted more than a year. Even so, it is not without significance. It shows that parish libraries could be founded on a small scale, with fairly modest resources. It also suggests that there may have

43 J. Harris, 'A rare and precious room: the Kederminster Library at Langley', *Country Life* (1977), 1576–9; A. Wells-Cole, *Art and decoration in Elizabethan and Jacobean England: the influence of continental prints, 1558–1625* (New Haven and London, 1997), 216–17.

44 Maggs Bros Ltd, *Catalogue 1350: books from the library of James Stevens Cox* (2003), 32–3.

been more of them than we realise – which in turn suggests that many lay people may have had access, through parish libraries, to books that they could not have afforded to buy for themselves. Few parishes had a formally organised library, with a catalogue, shelfmarks, and rules for reading or borrowing, but many had accumulated smaller and less systematic collections of books, and these small collections are arguably just as significant in gauging the impact of protestant ideas. As we have seen, there was great diversity in the size, contents and intended purpose of parish libraries; but what they all demonstrate is that, by the start of the seventeenth century, Protestantism was firmly established at all levels of English society, in the parishes as well as in the universities, and in the countryside as well as in the towns.

16

Schools and schoolmasters (to *c.* 1550)

NICHOLAS ORME

Medieval schools relied on books. Mouths and ears were important too – teachers expounded what had to be learnt, pupils repeated it, and both sides engaged in oral questions and answers – but none of this could happen without the support of writings. Teachers needed copies of the texts they taught. Ideally, so did their pupils. A literate child could work alone with a book, while a bookless child depended on its teacher. At advanced levels of study, both teachers and pupils required access to authoritative grammars and dictionaries. Education was therefore a process which attracted books to itself; it also generated them. Masters might engage in copying texts for themselves, and pupils certainly did. The copies and notes of grammar-school boys, in particular, written on quires of parchment or paper, could grow into volumes and be bound, kept, and passed on to other people as primary sources in their own right.[1]

The variety of such books was wide, and increased during the middle ages. At the most elementary level there were tablets containing the alphabet and, perhaps, basic prayers like the Paternoster – tablets of a single page, yet still referred to as 'books'.[2] Then there were 'primers': prayer-books of several leaves containing basic prayers in Latin or English, sometimes beginning with an alphabet as if they were meant to help with learning to read. More advanced prayer-books and liturgical works were used for instruction or reading practice: psalters, antiphonals, and (from the thirteenth century) books of hours. The study of Latin, centred in grammar schools, was facilitated by a range of texts, often written in manuscript anthologies. Grammar itself was studied from a short simple accidence like that of Donatus, leading on to more comprehensive and systematic grammars like the *Doctrinale* of Alexander de Villa Dei, the

1 On such notebooks, see D. Thomson, *A descriptive catalogue of Middle English grammatical texts* (New York and London, 1979), and N. Orme, *Education and society in medieval and Renaissance England* (London, 1989), 73–85.

2 F. J. Furnivall (ed.), *Political, religious and love poems*, 2nd edn, EETS, OS, 15 (1903), 271.

Grecismus of Evrard of Béthune, and the great classic work of Priscian. Vocabulary was learnt from short word-lists, from longer works like the poems *Synonyma* and *Equivoca* (ascribed to John of Garland) on synonyms and homonyms, and (if available) from Latin dictionaries like those of Papias, Hugutio and John of Genoa (Giovanni Balbi, or *Januensis*), author of the *Catholicon*. Literature was read in the form of classical and medieval Latin poems, notably the *Distichs of Cato*. But not all who learnt to read went on to study Latin. Others deviated into reading French or English, and for them any book in these languages might be employed for reading practice and thereby co-opted for educational use.

The places for learning literate skills were also diverse. Homes were one such context. Teaching by chaplains, clerks or schoolmasters is recorded in the households of kings, bishops, other higher clergy and the lay aristocracy (nobility and gentry) right through the middle ages and into the sixteenth century.[3] Even in small households, fathers or mothers who could read might teach the skill to their children, although such instruction was so informal that it has left little trace. The portrayal of St Anne teaching the Virgin Mary from a book was a popular image in English art from the early fourteenth century onwards.[4] Teaching in homes and households did not always involve Latin grammars. A Latin prayer-book could be used for practising word recognition and pronunciation, and for imparting knowledge of basic prayers. Books in French or English could then be employed for reading. In the later middle ages, commonplace books – anthologies of religious, practical and recreational tracts and poems – sometimes bear signs of usage with children, and one comes across references to adolescent children reading 'adult' authors such as Chaucer, Gower and Lydgate.[5] A family's books might therefore also serve as the library of a domestic school.

Religious houses were other centres of education. The Rule of St Benedict allowed the reception of noble children as monks, and boys and girls are mentioned in English monasteries and nunneries from the seventh century onwards. Child oblation of this kind died out in monasteries in the twelfth century, although it lingered in nunneries and later revived among the friars, who tended to admit recruits in their early teens. In monasteries it was replaced by the practice of maintaining 'almonry boys' to do liturgical duties in the church in return for board, lodging and education. Such boys lived outside the

3 On this subject see N. Orme, *From childhood to chivalry: the education of the English kings and aristocracy, 1066–1530* (London and New York, 1984), esp. 1–60.
4 N. Orme, *Medieval children* (London and New Haven, 2001), 244–5.
5 Orme, *Medieval children*, 276–8, 281–2.

cloister area, and had freedom either to become monks when they reached their late teens or to leave for careers in the world. The *Rites of Durham*, the well-known description of Durham Cathedral Priory as it had been on the eve of the Reformation, records the presence of three groups of young people who typically received education in a late medieval monastery. A dozen or so boys boarded in the almonry and received teaching from a non-monastic schoolmaster in the 'Farmery School' outside the priory gates. Six of their number were also choristers, and received specialised tuition in a song school at the south-east corner of the cathedral. Finally, six novice monks, young adults, attended school for seven years under a senior monk in the west walk of the cloisters.[6]

All such pupils were dependent for their resources on the religious house in which they lived, and the houses had therefore to provide and house the books they needed for their education. Durham and other large monastic communities must therefore have had schoolbook collections. The evidence about books in religious houses includes some references to grammars and other texts relevant to schools. A list of books inserted in the mid-tenth century into a manuscript belonging to St Augustine's, Canterbury, states, 'These are the books that were Æthelstan's', and contains thirteen titles.[7] The works look like a schoolmaster's collection, including Donatus' *Ars Minor* and *Ars Maior* (the *Ars grammatica*), an unnamed 'gloss on Donatus', 'Alcuin' (probably that author's work on grammar or on orthography), 'dialogues' or colloquies, and two books on the art of metre. A list from Christ Church, Canterbury, of about 1170, contains multiple copies of Priscian, classical authors such as Horace, Juvenal, Lucan, Persius, Sallust, Statius and Virgil, and individual copies of the popular school authors Cato, Avianus and Theodulus.[8] At Glastonbury, where a library catalogue was compiled in 1247–8, there were six copies of Priscian, five of Donatus, grammars by Remigius and others, and school authors including Avianus, Cato, Claudian, Persius and Virgil.[9]

The majority of surviving booklists from monasteries come from the period after 1200, when the teaching of boys was done away from the cloister. Perhaps in consequence, many of them contain relatively little in terms of schoolbooks, although there are exceptions. Dover Priory in 1389 had several copies each of Priscian, the *Doctrinale*, Hugutio and a *Catholicon*, and single ones of eleven other popular grammars and reading texts.[10] Eleven years later Titchfield

6 R. C. Fowler (ed.), *Rites of Durham*, Surtees Soc. 107 (1902), 62–3, 84–5, 91–2.
7 BL, MS Cotton Domitian i, fol. 56v; Lapidge, 'Booklists', 50–2.
8 James, *ALCD*, 7–11.   9 CBMLC IV. 203–9.   10 CBMLC II. 151–72.

Abbey, Hampshire, a Premonstratensian house, owned twenty-four volumes of grammar, of which twelve were small *quaterni* or quires. They included four copies of the *Doctrinale*, three of Guillaume Brito's dictionary of words in the Bible, two of Hugutio, and four miscellanies of short grammars and poems.[11] In the late fifteenth century St Augustine's Abbey, Canterbury, possessed a large collection of grammars, including as many as forty-two copies of Priscian, nine of the *Doctrinale*, five of Hugutio, three each of Papias and the *Grecismus*, two of the *Catholicon*, and three grammatical miscellanies.[12] Leicester Abbey had a comparable range of works in the same period, encompassing multiple copies and five miscellanies.[13] Friars' libraries are less well recorded than those of monasteries, but that of the Augustinian Friars of York, catalogued in 1372, was strong on grammar. As well as the usual Priscian, Hugutio, *Doctrinale* and *Catholicon*, it contained several miscellaneous volumes or quires of grammar and poetry.[14]

Lists like these raise problems, too, because they tell us little of how their contents were administered and used. Were the books in the library reserved for the novices and adult monks, or were they available for the teaching of the children of the almonry and other boys in the precincts, such as the noble wards and boarders sometimes brought up in the households of abbots and priors? If not, did the boys have separate book resources? Some grammatical titles, like Priscian, Hugutio and the *Catholicon*, were appropriate works for adults to consult, and do not necessarily indicate use by lay children or their teachers. More suggestive are the miscellanies. The texts they contained were primarily works for grammar-school boys rather than novices or adult monks. Their presence at Leicester, St Augustine's, Titchfield, and the friary at York gives a strong hint that boys were maintained there and used them. Some similar evidence comes from Evesham Abbey, Worcestershire, where Thomas of Hanney's school grammar *Memoriale Juniorum*, a work called *Petagogicum Gramatice*, a *nominale* (list of nouns), and several grammatical *quaterni* (booklets or volumes in limp wrappers) appear among donations made in the late fourteenth century.[15] We should not assume, either, when a religious house owned books, that even its novice or adult members all had access to them. At the very end of monastic history, and admittedly at a disrupted time in 1538, two junior monks of Glastonbury Abbey complained that there was no library

11 CBMLC III. 220–7. 12 James, *ALCD*, 355–68.
13 CBMLC VI. 290–300. 14 CBMLC I. 116–31.
15 CBMLC IV. 139–40. On education at Evesham Abbey, see Orme, *Education and society*, 35–6, 39–42.

or books to which they could resort, although we know that the house was well provided with such resources.[16]

The third great source of education was a school in the sense in which we understand the term today: a free-standing institution, taught by a professional teacher and open to any who could meet the criteria for attendance (usually, in the middle ages, an ability to pay fees). There were private schools in teachers' homes, catering for small groups of pupils, and schools open to the public and taking in larger numbers. Schools of either kind may have existed in Anglo-Saxon England but they are not documented until shortly after the Norman Conquest. Our knowledge of them is based on casual references in documents, so that we can never estimate the total that were open at any one time. It is clear, however, that public schools offering elementary teaching in how to read and more advanced teaching in Latin grammar were to be found in most cathedral cities and county towns by the late twelfth century, and in many smaller market towns by the thirteenth.[17] Most were meant primarily for boys: from perhaps as young as four or five, but usually from a few years older, until the age of eighteen or so. The schooling of girls was more likely to be done privately and informally.[18] This might happen in their own homes, in other people's households, in nunneries, and even with an anchoress or her servant.[19] Occasionally, a girl may have gone to a more public kind of school, as the young heroine of the romance of *Floris and Blauncheflur* is imagined doing in the thirteenth century.[20] There were certainly some such schools for girls later on; we hear of schoolmistresses in Boston, Lincolnshire, London and Oxford during the fourteenth or fifteenth century, as well as an eight-year-old girl in a class of children taught by a London priest.

Numerous references occur to teachers and pupils in schools using books of their own. In 1371, for example, John Burdon, schoolmaster of Carlisle, left 'all my books' to a friend, and John Seward, master of a grammar school in Cornhill, London, did the same in 1435.[21] Pupils might have personal copies of

16 A. Watkin (ed.), *Dean Cosyn and Wells Cathedral miscellanea*, Somerset Record Soc. 56 (1941), 162–3.

17 N. Orme, *Medieval schools* (New Haven and London, 2006), 189–95.

18 Girls' education is discussed by D. Gardiner, *English girlhood at school* (London, 1929), *passim*, and Orme, *Medieval schools*, especially 34–6, 60–1, 77–9, 166–7, 275–8, 285–6, 328–9.

19 J. R. R. Tolkein (ed.), *Ancrene Wisse*, EETS, OS, 249 (1962), 216–17.

20 F. C. de Vries (ed.), *Floris and Blauncheflur* (Groningen, 1986), 73.

21 R. S. Ferguson (ed.), *Testamenta Karleolensia*, Cumberland and Westmorland Antiquarian and Archaeological Soc., extra ser., 9 (1893), 101; V. H. Galbraith, 'John Seward and his circle', *Medieval and Renaissance Studies* 1 (1941–3), 85–99, at 98.

schoolbooks even in the days before printing. Edmund Stonor, a gentleman's son studying grammar at Oxford in the 1390s, possessed his own Donatus, and a chaplain of York named John Fernell bequeathed his nephew Robert a book of grammar and money for school fees in 1466.[22] A will made twenty years earlier by a York scholar, Robert Hunter, disposed of 'all my books' to another young man.[23] Such books were most likely to be grammars, school literary works, or dictionaries: the kind of works cited in writings by schoolmasters and copied into the miscellanies made by them and by their pupils.[24] But masters, at least, might have other interests, and the books in a school (if the boundaries are widened to include the master's chamber) might extend into other areas. John Lelamour, schoolmaster of Hereford, translated a Latin herbal treatise into English in 1373.[25] John Bracebridge, schoolmaster of Lincoln from 1406 and later a chaplain of Syon Abbey, Middlesex, collected some 110 volumes of grammar, philosophy, medicine, canon law and theology, which eventually passed to the library of the abbey.[26] Even the master of a small country school might borrow books, like Arthur Wadington of Alford, Lincolnshire, who was loaned five works of pastoral religion and canon law by nearby Hagnaby Abbey in 1511.[27]

Books which belonged to schools as institutions, as opposed to their members individually, are harder to identify because school records focus on constitutional and economic matters rather than on curricular ones. Still, there are a few stray references which suggest that schools might own texts, or have access to them, as communities. One of the earliest occurs in the records of St Albans Abbey, which governed the school of the local town. It states that in 1328 the school possessed a chest containing its documents and a 'great Priscian', a work which had apparently been given to the school before 1310 by one John Haule. This probably contained books 1–16 of Priscian's work, commonly known as Priscian *Magnus* or *Maior*, while the remaining books 17–18, on constructions, were known as Priscian *Minor*. In 1328 the Priscian was taken out of the chest and given to the headmaster of the school 'so that the boys of the school might inspect it at their will'. The master swore to keep

22 C. L. Kingsford, *The Stonor letters and papers, 1290–1483*, Camden, 3rd ser., 29–30 (London, 1919), Reissued as *Kingsford's Stonor letters and papers, 1290–1483*, ed. and introd. by C. Carpenter (London, 1996), 21 (109); J. Raine (ed.), *Testamenta Eboracensia*, 6 vols., Surtees Soc. 4, 30, 45, 53, 79, 106 (Durham, 1836–69), II. 275.

23 Raine, *Testamenta Eboracensia*, II. 118.

24 Thomson, *A descriptive catalogue*, *passim*.

25 N. Orme, 'The Cathedral School before the Reformation', in G. Aylmer and J. Tiller (eds.) *Hereford Cathedral: a history* (London, 2000), 574.

26 *BRUO* I. 239–40; CBMLC IX. 5–7, 10–11, 13–14, 569–70.

27 A. E. B. Owen, *The medieval Lindsey marsh*, Lincoln Record Soc. 85 (Lincoln, 1996), 69, 73.

custody of the book, and the transaction was recorded.[28] This was evidently a volume belonging to the school and allowed to be used by its pupils, provided that the master took responsibility for it. It clearly had a special status, but this need not mean that such possessions by schools were unusual and always so carefully administered.

Certainly, as time goes on, we hear of books in connection with quite humble schools. In 1371 Nicholas Pontesbury, sub-dean of Wells Cathedral, bequeathed a copy of Hugutio to the parish church of Wellington, Somerset, to be kept by the vicar and churchwardens and delivered, on good security, to the schoolmaster, 'that he and his boys may specially pray for me'.[29] At Hedon, Yorkshire, in 1465 a local chaplain, John Elwyn, left 'all my grammar books, both those in the keeping of William Paynetour, chaplain, and those in my chest' to the local chapel of St Augustine, 'for the teaching and reformation (*reformatio*) of the children learning in the grammar school there'.[30] This chapel was, in effect, the parish church of the town, so that the bequest was analogous to the one at Wellington. A third example comes from Bridport, Dorset. Here we do not have a record of the bequest itself, but an inventory of books, belonging to the parish church in 1476, contains three or four items which look as though they were kept on behalf of the town school: a Hugutio, Thomas of Hanney's *Memoriale Juniorum*, 'an alphabet of Latin words' (presumably a vocabulary) and a book of logic.[31] In each of these cases the local school, while perceived as deserving books, was not felt to have enough status or continuity to look after them safely. Their custody would be better ensured by the clergy and wardens of the local church, who could keep them in the church chest and lend them to the school under supervision.

The size of such collections is unknown; we have only minimum numbers. Bridport's four may not include others on loan to a schoolmaster. Hedon was meant to receive at least four, since the plural term is used of the ones held both by Paynetour and by the donor. That a school library could be far larger than this, even in the fourteenth century, is shown by some exceptional evidence from St Paul's Cathedral in London. The cathedral's clerical staff included a group of eight choristers who lived in a building called the almonry along with the almoner, a priest of the cathedral foundation. The almoner had the duty

28 H. T. Riley (ed.), *Registrum Abbatiae Johannis Whethamstede*, 2 vols., RS (London, 1872–3), II. 314.

29 J. Coleman, 'Four Wells wills of the fourteenth century', *Somerset and Dorset Notes and Queries* 8 (1903), 151–3.

30 Raine, *Testamenta Eboracensia*, II. 270.

31 J. Hutchins, *The history and antiquities of the county of Dorset*, ed. W. Shipp and J. W. Hodson, 4 vols. (Westminster, 1861–73), II. 24.

of ensuring that the boys were fed, clothed, and instructed in the performance of church services, in grammar, and in good manners. He could teach them grammar himself, or he could send them to the cathedral's public grammar school for the purpose, paying 5s a year if he did so. During the mid-fourteenth century the first of these options appears to have been followed; at any rate, book resources for the boys' learning were made available to them in the almonry.

The earliest piece of evidence for this comes from the will of one of the almoners, William of Tolleshunt, in 1329. Tolleshunt bequeathed all his grammar books, except those which were held by Ralph, his clerk, to remain in the almonry in perpetuity 'for the use of the boys living there, on condition that in no way are [the books], lent or alienated'. He also left them 'all the quires of sermons for the Feast of the Holy Innocents, which the boy bishops were wont to pronounce in my time' – a reference to the custom by which the boy bishop, chosen to preside in church on St Nicholas Day (6 December) and Holy Innocents' Day (28 December), preached a sermon. Two of the grammar books are described by name: the better Hugutio with Priscian *Maior* and *Minor*, all bound together, and Isidore of Seville's encyclopaedic dictionary, *Liber Etymologiarum*. These books were for the use of the boys while at school. But Tolleshunt also gave all his books of logic (including the old and new logic) and his books and booklets of natural philosophy 'to be lent to boys apt for schooling when they leave the almonry, on condition that they are restored, subject to a suitable penalty, lest they be alienated'. His medical books and books of civil law, including the *Codex*, *Digestum uetus* and *Autentica*, were disposed of in a similar way. Almonry boys who might go on to higher studies could borrow these books on providing surety that they would return them.[32]

Tolleshunt must have developed a strong loyalty to the almonry and its boys through living there with them. A similar loyalty was expressed with even greater generosity by another almoner, William of Ravenstone, in his will of 1358. He bequeathed three London tenements and a rent charge to the cathedral to maintain one or two extra boys in the almonry, and transferred to his almoner successors all the goods listed in an accompanying inventory. As these goods are mentioned in the will as a bequest, it appears that Ravenstone was handing over, not only goods which he had received as almoner, but ones which he had personally provided while he held office. The inventory seems to confirm this deduction, as it talks of 'books and other things found in the

32 A. F. Leach, 'St Paul's School before Colet', *Archaeologia* 62/1 (1910), 220–2.

aforesaid almonry of old and newly added'. The first section of the document is entirely devoted to books, comprising eighty-two texts in forty-one volumes. How many of the volumes were Ravenstone's own acquisitions, and how many were older, is not clear, because no mention is made of their origins. Some may stem from the bequests of earlier benefactors, including a copy of Hugutio, three of Priscian, a book of natural philosophy and two of logic, which could all be books given by Tolleshunt, although no Isidore is mentioned.[33]

The collection (setting aside the logic and philosophy) was largely concerned with grammar-school subjects. Its largest and most advanced authors were Priscian, Hugutio and Peter Helias, together with a concordance of the Bible. Most of the books were typical school grammars, including seven copies of the *Doctrinale*, two of the *Grecismus* and one each of the *Synonyma* and *Equivoca*. Six were miscellanies of grammatical texts, and there were specimens of the literature read in schools. These comprised two psalters, a book containing hymns and sequences, the *Sex auctores* commonly studied in classrooms up to the fourteenth century (Cato, Theodulus, Avianus, Maximian, Statius and Claudian), the *Metamorphoses* of Ovid, and unspecified works by Juvenal and Persius. Music was represented by a book of polyphonic music (*cantus organicus*), a plainsong gradual, and a quire containing 'rules of the art of music'. The question arises of who used these books: the master or the boys? There was 'a chest in the boys' chamber for the keeping of their books in the same', but this does not mean that the boys had access to it. Only one volume, a *nominale* and *uerbale* (lists of nouns and verbs), is specifically described as 'for the reading and use of the boys so that they may learn from them'. We are left in the dark as to whether these books represented a jealously guarded repository of treasures, or were used primarily by the master, or were issued for classroom use.

The thirteenth and fourteenth centuries saw the gradual evolution of endowed grammar schools, where masters received a stipend in return for teaching wholly or partly without charge. Endowments gave schools more stability. Patrons or governing bodies were established to appoint masters, and the presence of the latter ceased to depend on the uncertainties of fees. The endowment of a school was usually accompanied by the issue of statutes, or of an indenture by which a religious house or group of feoffees assumed the duty of acting as a governing body. Some endowed schools formed part of larger colleges of secular priests of the kind which were popular foundations among rich benefactors in the later middle ages. Winchester College, founded in 1382, is the best-known of these. Others were small independent foundations,

33 Edith Rickert, 'Chaucer at school', *Modern Philology* 29 (1931–2), 257–74.

consisting of a single schoolmaster who often doubled as a chantry priest, saying prayers for the soul of the founder. Here the earliest example is the grammar school of Wotton-under-Edge, Gloucestershire, founded in 1384 by Lady Katherine Berkeley, a widow in an important local baronial family.[34]

School statutes and indentures have a good deal to say about governors, appointments of masters, salaries, terms of employment and sometimes buildings and lands. They are less helpful about books. Wykeham's statutes for Winchester College, issued in 1400, contains a chapter about the books of the college, which talks of the chapel books and other books provided by the founder, given by other people, or purchased by the college, and orders them to be regularly inspected. Books are not to be sold, given away, exchanged, pledged, or taken out of the college except for binding or repair.[35] But the chapter does not make clear if Wykeham supplied books for the school as opposed to the college of clergy to which the school was attached. Much the same is true of Eton College, modelled on Winchester. Its statutes, dating from between 1440 and 1443, are primarily concerned with the college books as a whole, and do not specify those of the school.[36] Those of a third important foundation, St Paul's School, London, issued in 1518, make no allusions to books at all, although they are detailed in other respects. An associated document, setting out the conditions for admitting scholars, states only that the parents or friends of each child shall provide 'convenient books to his learning'.[37] The statutes of smaller schools are usually comparable in omitting the topic.

It would be unsafe, nevertheless, to assume from this that founders did not provide their schools with reading matter. After all, statutes and indentures are silent about other essential matters, such as the furniture of the schoolroom and of the master's lodging. Scraps of other evidence from the thirteenth to the early sixteenth centuries suggest that founders were indeed aware of the importance of books and desirous of making them available. Walter de Merton's statutes for Merton College, Oxford, in 1270, not only arrange for a grammar master to teach the boys and other members of the college, but lay down that 'a supply of books and other necessary things shall be provided for him, decently and competently, from the goods of the aforesaid house'.[38] In

34 Orme, *Medieval schools*, 228–9; *ODNB*, s.n.
35 T. F. Kirby, *Annals of Winchester College* (London and Winchester, 1892), 517.
36 J. Heywood and T. Wright (eds.), *The ancient laws of the fifteenth century for King's College Cambridge and for the public school of Eton College* (London, 1850), 589–91.
37 J. H. Lupton, *A life of John Colet* (London, 1887), 286.
38 J. R. L. Highfield (ed.), *The early rolls of Merton College* (Oxford, 1964), 382.

1410, Henry IV and Roger Ive founded a small chantry college at Battlefield, Shropshire, on the site of the battle of Shrewsbury. The college is not stated to have provided education for the public, but there is a casual reference to a boy at school there in about 1526, and it is likely that some teaching was intended from the start, if only for a few boys employed to serve or to sing.[39] This view is supported by the survival of an anthology of school grammars and reading texts which was compiled, apparently specially for the college, in the early fifteenth century (now Cambridge, Trinity Coll., MS O.5.4). The Venerable Dr David Thomson, who has studied the volume in detail, observes that 'its large size and single clear hand and decoration are not often used for books of elementary treatises and suggest a presentation or dedication volume'.[40]

The Trinity manuscript, it appears, is a rare example of a surviving schoolbook produced for a school at or soon after its foundation. There are at least two other similar pieces of evidence relating to small country grammar schools. One concerns Newland, Gloucestershire, a school founded in 1446 by the widow of a local esquire, Joan Greyndour, a precise lady who not only issued statutes for her foundation but revised them twice as it evolved and developed. The first version says nothing about books, but the second, dating from 1454, includes a clause requiring the schoolmaster to look after 'all the books for the teaching of the scholars' which were evidently part of the school's resources by this time.[41] The other instance relates to the hospital and grammar school at Whitkirk, Yorkshire, founded by Thomas Lord Darcy in 1521. Its statutes do not survive, but we possess a letter written by Darcy to the schoolmaster at about that time, accompanying a delivery of books whose numbers and titles (unfortunately) have not been preserved. The letter orders them 'safely to be kept by the said master to the use of the said hospital and school'.[42]

A little more emerges about schoolbooks at Winchester College from an inventory, made in the mid- or late 1420s, of the books of the college chapel and library.[43] It is divided into subject-categories, the last of which lists nineteen

39 *VCH Shropshire*, II, ed. A. T. Gaydon (London, 1973), 128–31.

40 Thomson, *A descriptive catalogue*, 158–68.

41 J. H. Parry and A. T. Bannister (eds.), *Registrum Johannis Stanbury, Episcopi Herefordensis, 1453–1474*, Canterbury and York Soc. 25 (1919), 28; N. Orme, *Education in the west of England, 1066–1548* (Exeter, 1976), 161.

42 *Letters and papers, foreign and domestic, Henry VIII*, III/1, 394; J. A. H. Moran, *The growth of English schooling, 1380–1548: learning, literacy and laicization in pre-Reformation York diocese* (Princeton, 1985), 36.

43 W. H. Gunner, 'Catalogue of books belonging to the college of St Mary, Winchester, in the reign of Henry VI', *Archaeological Journal* 10 (1858), 59–74.

grammatical volumes with their monetary values. Four had been given by the founder himself: Priscian *Maior*, Hugutio and two copies of the *Catholicon*. As has already been said, books like these need not have been given for school use; they could have been meant for the clergy of the college for whom the library was chiefly intended. The rest of the grammar books had been provided by other donors, apart from the purchase of a copy of Papias. Two of the benefactors, John Shyrfeld and Peter Hert, had given further copies of Priscian and a book of *Dubitabiles in biblia*, and these, like the Papias, could also relate to adult library readers. Some other gifts, however, have a stronger suggestion of the school about them. Thomas Paxton, a priest, had given a Priscian *Maior*, the *Doctrinale* of Alexander of Villa Dei bound with the *Equivoca* ascribed to John of Garland, and a grammatical miscellany. These, the inventory notes, were in the hands of the schoolmaster. A treatise on dictamen had come from John Elmer, an official of the diocese, and two schoolmasters of the college had donated books. Thomas Romsey (in office 1394–1407 and 1414–18) had presented a grammatical work called *Ferrum*, and Richard Darcy (1418–24) a volume containing the *Grecismus* and the *Doctrinale*. Here, as at St Paul's, we see working teachers giving books to the institutions in which they worked. This 'official' list of the college's books therefore includes a few that potentially relate to the school, two of which were being used by the master of the day. And there may have been another, less formal and less valuable collection of schoolbooks in the school itself.

Eton College possesses no inventory as helpful as this. It certainly had a library, as we have seen, and its statutes provide for the lending of books from this both to fellows and to scholars, the latter meaning schoolboys, although such loans had to be authorised by the provost or vice-provost and recorded on small indentures.[44] Here, too, there were probably separate resources for the everyday work of the school, since a college audit roll of 1485–6 mentions payment for binding and repairing 'books of the church, the library, and the school', as if these were separate collections.[45] The Eton schoolmasters certainly had a personal culture of books. William Barrett, usher in the school in 1500–2, owned a volume containing three printed works (Jerome's *Vitae sanctorum patrum*, Aquinas' *De diuinis moribus*, and Bernard's *De consideratione*) which he gave to Robert Dale, fellow of the college from 1497 to 1510, who duly passed it on to William Horman, schoolmaster of Eton from 1486 to 1495 and fellow from 1501 to 1535.[46] Horman was a figure of major importance

44 Heywood and Wright, *Ancient laws . . . for King's College Cambridge and . . . Eton College*, 589–91; R. Birley, 'The history of Eton College library', *Library*, 5th ser., 11 (1956), 231.
45 Birley, 'Eton College library', 231.
46 *Ibid.*, 236–7.

as a grammatical writer and book collector. He was the author of an *Introductorium lingue Latine*, published in 1494 and reissued in 1499, and of a large collection of *Vulgaria* (English sentences with model Latin translations), which appeared in 1519. During his life he acquired a large collection of manuscripts and printed texts including Latin literature, theology and medicine, some fourteen of which he seems to have given to the college library before his death in 1535. He also bequeathed two unspecified volumes from his collection to the schoolmaster and to each college fellow, and three of these subsequently passed to the college as well.[47]

Other endowed schools doubtless acquired volumes by accretion. In 1498, John Austell, canon of Wells Cathedral, willed two printed books to the schoolmaster of Wells Cathedral School, 'for the use of the school there'. Technically, Wells was not one of the new endowed schools, but it was one where the schoolmaster received a small salary for teaching members of the cathedral foundation in his otherwise fee-paying school. The books were John of Genoa's *Catholicon* and a certain *Liber Gutrumni*, which appears likely to be the *Opus grammaticale* 'excerpted from Priscian, Alexander, etc.' by the Spanish friar Andreas Guterius Ceresianus, printed at least three times between 1485 and 1491.[48] In 1542, Wilfrid Borrowe, a cleric of Kirkby Lonsdale, Westmorland, left to its grammar school 'the rest of my books not before given to the school at Kirkby', while Richard Ranson, rector of Wainfleet All Saints, Lincolnshire, gave six books to a similar school in Wainfleet in 1549 – a school of which he had probably been master.[49] In this case some of the titles are listed: Virgil's *Bucolics* with a commentary, an old copy of *Calepine* (probably Ambrogio Calepino's Latin dictionary), a work by Valla and two unnamed books of philosophy.[50] The first three were evidently printed books. These cases resemble those at Winchester College in making the bequests to the school or schoolmaster directly and not, as we saw in some earlier cases, to a local church. Even small endowed schools were now acquiring a reputation for stability sufficient for them to be entrusted with the care of schoolbooks.

Austell's bequest is an early record of the diffusion of printed books into schools. The first known schoolbooks to be printed in England were issued at

47 *Ibid.*

48 F. W. Weaver (ed.), *Somerset medieval wills*, 1, Somerset Record Soc. 14 (1901), 371; Orme, *Education in the west of England*, 85.

49 Moran, *The growth of English schooling*, 36, 259; N. Orme, *Education in early Tudor England: Magdalen College Oxford and its school, 1480–1540* (Oxford, 1998), 72.

50 TNA (Family History Centre), PROB 11/32, lf. 333v–4v (43 Populwell).

Oxford by Theodoric Rood between 1482 and 1485, and others were exported to England by continental printers. The works available gradually included grammars, vocabularies, works on prose composition, poems for reading, such as Cato and Theodulus, and bilingual dictionaries, Latin to English and English to Latin.[51] The impact of the new technology was not immediate, however. It was not until the 1490s that the London printers Wynkyn de Worde and Richard Pynson began printing schoolbooks on a large scale, and not until the first decade of the sixteenth century that particular titles – notably John Stanbridge's simple Latin grammars in English – became bestsellers and were widely used all over the country. By the 1520s, the Oxford bookseller John Dorne was selling numerous copies of printed school grammars to single customers, while his opposite number at Cambridge, Garrett Godfrey, sold sets of such volumes to masters and tutors, presumably for resale to pupils.[52] Printing improved the supply of schoolbooks, but it also led to some confusion as different printers issued standard texts in variant forms, a problem that remained unsolved until 1540, when Henry VIII imposed an authorised grammar. We know almost nothing about the diffusion of printed books into school libraries, except that this must have happened, especially from the 1490s onwards. The references to Wells and Wainfleet show the process in train in grammar schools, and some evidence about Monk Bretton Priory, Yorkshire, reveals it in a monastery. There a list of the priory's books, compiled in 1558 after its dissolution, includes a work by the early Tudor grammarian Robert Whittington, John of Garland's *Synonyma* and *Equivoca*, and Cato with a commentary. The first of these was undoubtedly printed, and probably so were the other two.[53]

The history of book collections in schools before the middle of the sixteenth century is therefore an unrecorded rather than a non-existent subject. It would be quite unsafe to argue, from the paucity of records alone, that schools did not possess or have access to books, apart from those owned privately by their teachers and pupils. We can link books with a range of schools, from well-resourced foundations like Eton, St Paul's, Wells and Winchester, through a major town school (St Albans) and small endowed foundations (Newland and Whitkirk), to humble and unendowed institutions in market towns (Bridport, Hedon and Wellington). They were given by school founders,

51 N. Orme, 'Schools and schoolbooks, 1400–1550', *CHBB* III. 449–69, esp. 456–69.

52 F. Madan, 'The daily ledger of John Dorne', in C. R. L. Fletcher (ed.), *Collectanea (first series)*, OHS 5 (1885); E. Leedham-Green, D. E. Rhodes and F. H. Stubbings (eds.), *Garrett Godfrey's accounts c. 1527–1533* (Cambridge, 1982), e.g. 158.

53 CBMLC v. 287.

schoolmasters, and some external clerical well-wishers. Their titles included, and probably centred on, school texts – grammars, dictionaries, and the kinds of Latin literature read in schools – but might include books on letter-writing (dictamen) or logic. It is possible to envisage such collections, albeit of modest size, as a common resource of those English schools that catered for the public, by the middle of the sixteenth century.

17

School libraries (*c.* 1540 to 1640)

WILLIAM BARKER

Juan Luis Vives, the great Spanish humanist who spent several years in England, wrote a set of schoolboy dialogues under the title *Linguae latinae exercitatio* (1538). In one of them, Spudaeus, the industrious student, gives a tour of his school to Tyro, the new boy. Spudaeus talks about the teachers, the hours of teaching, and then pauses for a quick look through the school library:

> *Spudaeus*. Let us enter. I will show you the public library [*publicam bibliothecam*] of this school. It looks, according to the precept of great men, to the east.
>
> *Tyro*. Wonderful! How many books, how many good authors, Greek and Latin orators, poets, historians, philosophers, theologians, and the busts of authors!
>
> *Spudaeus*. And indeed, as far as could be done, delineated to the life and so much the more valuable! All the book-cases [*foruli*] and book-shelves [*plutei*] are of oak or cypress and with their own little chains [*catenulis*]. The books themselves for the most part are bound in parchment [*membranacei*] and adorned with various colours.
>
> *Tyro*. What is that first one with rustic face and nose turned-up?
>
> *Spudaeus*. Read the inscription.
>
> *Tyro*. It is Socrates and he says: 'Why do I appear in this library when I have written nothing?'
>
> *Spudaeus*. Those who follow him, Plato and Xenophon, answer: 'Because thou hast said what others wrote.' It would take long to go through the things here, one by one.
>
> *Tyro*. Pray what are those books thrown on a great heap there?
>
> *Spudaeus*. The Catholicon, Alexander, Hugutio, Papias, disputations in dialectics, and two books of sophistries in physics. These are the books which I called 'worthy of condemnation'.
>
> *Tyro*. Nay rather, they are condemned to violent death!

Spudaeus. They are all thrown out. Let him take them who will; he will free us of a troublesome burden.[1]

After a few more insulting words about the standard texts of the medieval curriculum, now consigned to oblivion, the two move on, to observe a disputation.

The scene that Vives portrays is in part a fiction, organised around a number of themes: the need to instruct readers in good Latin vocabulary, the promotion of the humanist curriculum and banishment of the old scholastic texts, and the imaging forth of an ideal school. In this school, at its centre, is the library, virtually a shrine to classical authors, who are depicted in busts about the room, their books abundantly provided, the whole a separate and permanent part of the institution, all accessible to students and to other scholars from outside the institution.

Despite the appealing description, few school libraries resembling this ideal were to exist in England for a century and a half. Large and well-organised libraries did exist on the Continent, in some of the larger colleges at Strasbourg and Louvain, but they were a rarity in England until the seventeenth century, and became a normal part of the schools only in the eighteenth century. There were splendid libraries at Eton and Winchester, but these were strictly for the fellows, and were not open to the likes of Spudaeus and Tyro. For most schools, the library, if it can be called that, was a small collection of books, usually dictionaries and other works, that were kept on a shelf, often chained, or in a case, to be used by the master or ushers or the senior boys.

The curriculum of the schools was planned around the mastery of a small number of texts, and only in the last few years of the schoolboy's progress were memory work and oral recitation replaced by complex written composition in prose and verse which required access to supplementary works of an encyclopaedic nature. Until the later stages, they used textbooks in abundance. These might be purchased by individuals or handed down, but they did not form part of a school library. Yet, to read certain authors and to prepare themes or to write their verses, the senior boys needed various dictionaries and guidebooks to the language and lore of the past, including lexicons and collections of phrases and commonplaces and epithets in Latin and Greek. Here is where an institutional collection had an importance. What we would call reference books formed an important part of the humanist curriculum and the habit of

1 Juan Luis Vives, *Linguae latinae exercitatio* (Basel, 1541), 90–1; *Tudor school-boy life: the dialogues of Juan Luis Vives*, trans. F. Watson (London, 1908), 105–6.

using them died hard – it has been shown that many of the classical citations of English Renaissance authors came through the intermediary of dictionaries and not directly from the sources.[2] Schoolmasters also needed a small library of reference books and commentaries to aid in presentation and explication. Most school libraries were built up around the needs of the boys and the master – usually a small number of substantial volumes of humanist collections and scholarship. Few boys owned such books on their own, though the Cambridge scholar Gabriel Harvey makes reference to a dictionary owned by a schoolboy, 'which kost my father at the least xx. good shillinges and twoe'.[3] Instead, the standard books were brought together by donation or by purchase to form a small working library in the school.

After the end of the period under review, all this was to change. In the second half of the seventeenth century, writers such as Charles Hoole (1660) and Christopher Wase (1678) were strongly recommending that a school have a fully developed library of books to supplement the curriculum.[4] John Aubrey, in a set of notes written in the 1680s, provides a long and detailed list of the books that a good school might require.[5] These writers set out in theory a practice that had begun informally in some schools long before. Yet the developed school library, a large body of books (a few hundred or more), in their own room, with a pupil or teacher assigned to care for it, an occasional catalogue or other record of contents, and a set of rules regarding use and borrowing – all this came into fashion only from the second half of the seventeenth century. A library was established at Westminster in 1656, and at other schools about the same time or soon after, such as King Edward's School in Birmingham in 1656, Merchant Taylors' School in London in 1662, the Free School of Wigan in 1664, St Paul's in 1670, Manchester Grammar School in 1680, the Free School of Nottingham in 1693, and King's School in Canterbury in 1702. Most of these were formed by a concerted effort by school governors or by a schoolmaster, or by bequest of a schoolmaster or local cleric. There were a few anomalies – Eton had a very old and very rich library, greatly expanded under Sir Henry Savile from 1596 onwards, yet, as already mentioned, this was for the fellows, not

2 D. T. Starnes and E. W. Talbert, *Classical myth and legend in Renaissance dictionaries: a study of Renaissance dictionaries in their relation to the classical learning of contemporary English writers* (Chapel Hill, NC, 1955).

3 *Letter-book*, BL, MS Sloane 93, fol. 51.

4 C. Hoole, *A new discovery of the old art of teaching schoole, in four small treatises* (London, 1660); P. J. Wallis, 'The Wase school collection: a neglected source in educational history?', *BLR* 4 (1952), 78–104.

5 J. E. Stephens (ed.), *Aubrey on education: a hitherto unpublished manuscript by the author of Brief Lives* (London, 1972).

the boys, as was the library at Winchester, also of late medieval foundation.[6] Shrewsbury had a well-developed library from the sixteenth century onwards. Yet the interesting feature of the library at Shrewsbury and at the other schools that began to have them in the seventeenth century is that their shape and contents may have evolved more from the interests of the masters or from the surrounding community than from the needs of the pupils, and may represent the ideal of a completed education rather than tools for an education in process.

The most important humanist school was St Paul's, founded (or, more technically, refounded from the cathedral school) by John Colet in 1509, the funds for which were given by Colet into the control of the Mercers' Company. Colet's injunctions for the school are well known for their rejection of the old medieval curriculum and the 'blotterature' of bad Latinity.[7] His suggestion that the students read Lactantius and other late Latin authors was not characteristic of the humanist movement, but his emphasis on a total and structured programme of classical reading was very much in the spirit of his friend Erasmus, who was such a massive influence on humanist education throughout Europe. One would expect to find something about a library (perhaps along the lines of what Vives was to recommend so soon afterwards) in Colet's plan for the new St Paul's, but there is nothing. There are, however, continuing records of books having been purchased. Thus, in the account book for 1572–3, we find William Malim, the master, 'allowed . . . for a new Lexicon or Dictionary in Latin, Greek, Hebrew, French, Spanish, and High Dutch, always to remain as an implement to the Schole, well turned and bossed, xix*s*'.[8] This was probably one of the dictionaries that went under the name of Calepine.[9] For 1582–3 there is a list of books purchased by Mr Harrison, the master:[10] a five-volume Greek thesaurus of Henri Estienne and the two-volume Latin thesaurus of Robert Estienne, Thomas Cooper's Latin–English *Thesaurus*, a *Thesaurus Ciceronianus* by Charles Estienne, and various dictionaries and other helps by Johannes Bentz (perhaps his *Thesaurus*, a guide to correct Greek and Latin), Johannes Scapula (his famous Greek lexicon, a revision of Estienne), Marius Nizolius (*Thesaurus Ciceronianus*, a guide to Ciceronian Latin), Theodor

6 R. Birley, 'The history of Eton College library', *Library*, 5th ser., 11 (1956), 231–62; W. Oakeshott, 'Winchester School library before 1750', *Library*, 5th ser., 9 (1954), 1–16.

7 J. H. Lupton, *A life of John Colet, DD, dean of St Paul's and founder of St Paul's School*, 2nd edn (London, 1909), 169.

8 R. B. Gardiner, *The admission registers of St Paul's School, from 1748 to 1876* (London, 1881), 452.

9 Ambrogio Calepino, who lived about 1435–1509/10, revised the *Cornucopia* of Perotti, and this resulting lexicon, in its many different revisions including a series of polyglots, was immensely popular during the period.

10 Gardiner, *Admission registers*, 452.

Zwinger (his *Methodus similitudinum* was published with the *Loci communes* of Conrad Lycosthenes), and Guillaume Budé (any one of a number of his learned works) and a '*Dictionarium historicum et poeticum*' (perhaps the famous encyclopedia of Charles Estienne or something in the same tradition). There are also commentaries on and/or editions of Isocrates, Euripides, Horace, Seneca, Persius, Terence, Sallust, Cicero, Virgil and Caesar. Finally, the Greek grammar of Nicolaus Clenardus, with commentaries, and Petrus Ramus' *Scholae in liberales artes*. In addition Mr Harrison himself gave a New Testament with Theodore Beza's commentary, Silvius Italicus, a Terence, the letters of the younger Pliny, François Hotman's edition of Q. Asconius Pedianus' commentaries on Cicero's orations, Aulus Gellius, Cicero's orations, and another Nizolius. These books form a respectable small collection for reading and reference.[11] In 1590–1, the school purchased the Latin dictionary of Calepine, the Greek dictionary of Scapula, Cicero's works in two folio volumes, and another Cooper, for the lower school.[12] The Cooper obviously got hard use, for another copy of the work (now almost thirty years since last reprinted) was purchased in 1614–15. In 1639–40 the school purchased eight copies of John Rider's *Bibliotheca scholastica* (an English to Latin lexicon, with a Latin index, essential for composition). Despite the recognition that such supplemental texts were needed for the successful instruction of the humanist curriculum, there is no record of a library as such at St Paul's. It is only in 1665–6 that something resembling a library *was* recognised – in that year someone was paid to make 'a schedule of the Books in the School Study'.[13] Many of these books may have been lost in the Great Fire soon after. Only when the school was rebuilt in 1670 was a room set aside for a library.

There was a similar slow movement towards a school library at Merchant Taylors' School. Under its first master, Richard Mulcaster, the school began to accept pupils in 1561 and prospered right from the beginning as one of the principal schools of the time, with some 250 boys and four assistant masters. Yet a school library was built only in 1662.[14] In the same year, a catalogue giving 125 different titles was drawn up. There are, however, donations of books early on. For 7 May 1563 an entry in the records of the Company of Merchant Taylors reads: 'First at this daye Thomas Massheton haberdassher hath geven to the use of the Schole . . . One boke entitelyd Nizolius siue thesaurus Ciceronianus.'[15]

11 *Ibid.* 12 *Ibid.*, 453. 13 *Ibid.*

14 R. T. D. Sayle, 'Annals of Merchant Taylors' School library', *Library*, 4th ser., 15 (1935), 457–80.

15 *Ibid.*, 459.

In 1599 a catalogue of books in the school was made, and it included the following, 'gyven by M Henley for the schoole' (Hugh Hendley having been master of the school in 1590):

Thesaurus linguae grecae Henr: Stephani bownd in three volumes in folio
Cowpers Dictionary folio all rent
Crispin and Grantes Lexicon. 4to
Dictionari*um* poeticum. 4to
Nizolij thesaurus Ciceronianus folio
Epitheta grae: Dinneri. 8°
Epitheta Tectoris [*sic* for Textoris]. 4to all rent
Natalis Comitis muthologia. 8°
Lycosthenis apothegmata. 8° all rent

Along with these were certain others 'gyven by Mr William Gerrard Esquier one of Mr Hyndley executors':

Theatrum humanae vitae in fowre volumes in folio
Erasmi adagia the last in folio
Textoris officina in 4to all rent.[16]

It is interesting to see the *Mythologia* of Natalis Comes (Natale Conti), for this was a standard source of ancient iconology for many authors (Spenser, who attended Merchant Taylors' used it extensively in his *Faerie Queene*, though it was published in 1567, too late for him to have seen it as a pupil). The *Adages* of Erasmus, the collection of Greek epithets by Conrad Dinner and the two works by Ravisius Textor were detailed compilations of ancient language and lore and would have been useful for senior boys looking for words or expressions. The younger boys might have had some use of the Cooper or the Greek lexicon of Jean Crespin (the English edition was prepared by Edward Grant in 1581). The condition of these texts (many 'all rent') must have been a concern, because by 1610 the court minutes read that 'a new supply shalbe presently made of certen Dictionaries, and other bookes, for the necessary vse of the Schollers in the companies $gram^{r}$ schoole'. By 1626, these books must have also been in ruins, because 'Mr Nicholas Gray the cheife Schoolemaster there hath certified this Courte of the great decay and want of bookes'. There is a similar concern in the minutes in 1637 and 1639, showing that the cycle of a reference book used in a large and busy school may have been about ten to fifteen years. In 1650 the court of the Merchant Taylors was again presented with the need to purchase

16 *Ibid.*

books, and the extraordinary thing is how little the list had changed in over a century. They are asked to buy:

> Biblia anglicana in quarto att xiii^{s}. Constantini Lexicon graec. att xx^{s}. Scapulae Lexicon graec. att xxx^{s}. Calepini dictionar*ium* Latinum xxv^{s}. Cooperi dictionar*ium* Lat. att xiij^{s}. Thomae Thomasij dictionar*ium* att x^{s}. Rideri dictionar*ium* att xiij^{s}. Erasmi Adagia att xiij^{s}. Poeticum dictionarium att v^{s}. Epigram*mata* graec. Brodei att x^{s}.[17]

Indeed, in the library catalogue of 1662, which conveniently gives the dates for the books, forty-three of the 125 listed texts were printed before 1600. That there was a busy market in second-hand humanist texts and that these texts were often called for by the schools is further borne out by other existing catalogues for the late seventeenth and eighteenth centuries. The sixteenth century was a great period for the production of lexicons and similar works and these books tended not to be reprinted in the seventeenth century. Yet the schools needed these books to teach the old curriculum.

For an interesting parallel to the development of the collection at Merchant Taylors' School in London, one can look at the company's other school in Crosby. After this school was visited in 1630, the committee of visitors recommended that books be purchased, and the list (full of abbreviations) is found in the company's minutes for 4 May 1630:[18]

> Calepine's Diction, Cooper's Diction, Scapulae Lexicon, Nizolij Diction, Rider's Diction, Seneca Opera, Titus Levius [*sic*], Denneri Epitheta, Licosthenis Apothegmata, Textoris Epitheta, Licosthenis Simil, Textoris Officina, Glocenij Observa, Elegantia Poet, Valerius Maximus, Flores Poetarum, Thesaurus Poeticus, Pliny Histor, Diction Histor Poet., and an English Bible.

It is worth dwelling on this list, because it describes an excellent short collection of reference books for a smaller school. Most of these were sizeable texts, and represented a major outlay for the school authorities. About half of them may have been printed in England, about half on the Continent. The Calepino, Cooper, Scapula and Nizolius are all massive books. The *Bibliotheca scholastica* of John Rider was a substantial quarto. The Seneca and Livy were probably full editions to supplement shorter selections used in the classroom. Then follow a series of collections of epithets, apophthegms and similitudes by Conradus Dinner, Conradus Lycosthenes,[19] Ravisius Textor, Rodolphus Glocenius and

17 *Ibid.*
18 H. M. Luft, *A history of Merchant Taylors' School, Crosby, 1620–1970* (Liverpool, 1970), 41–3.
19 An edition of this text was published in London in 1596 (*STC* 17003.7).

Lorenzo Valla, and the ancient history of Valerius Maximus. The *Flores Poetarum* is probably the *Illustrium poetarum flores* of Octavianus Mirandula and edited by Theodor Pullman.[20] The Pliny *Historia naturalis* was still used in this period as a standard encyclopedia. The 'Diction Histor Poet.' is no doubt the work by Estienne. Other schools purchased books in the same way. Thus the records for Felsted School in 1601 indicate a payment of £6 16s 8d for seven books, 'viz Timelius [*sic*] his bible in Latine, Coopers dictionarye, Eustatius upon Homer in two volumes, T. Livye his history in latine, Xenophon in greek and latine, Erasmus his Chiliads, for the use of the schollers perpetually'.[21] Along with the books, 'Item payd for ix Chaines to fasten the bookes wth a frame of yrone an houerglasse and a padlock ix^{s} ix^{d}' and 'Item payd for a stockelocke and two keyes xvj^{d}'.

At St Albans Grammar School, founded by Sir Nicholas Bacon, the lord keeper, the purchases were also piecemeal, but the collection was more substantial. There were

> twoo verie faire bookes in folio well bound and claspt contayning the whole worckes of Plato: set out by Serranus lately, of the best edition, geven by Mr. Francis Bacon . . . a fayre new Greke Dictionarie in quarto called Crispinus Lexicon newly corrected by Mr. Grant, bound in velume, geven by Mr. Roger Williams our minister . . . an ancient booke of Plinius, *De Historia Naturali*, in majore fo, bound in bord, with a fair margent throughout, lined and ruled, geven by Mr. Thomas, our scholemaster . . an ancient Greke Dictionarie in folio called Cornucopia . . . bound in bord, geven by Mr. Thomas, scholemaster . . . Item a faire nue Bible well bound in red leather, bost and claspt, in iv$^{\circ}$ by Tremellius and the New Testament by Tremelius, and Junius, adding thereunto the Syriack Translation, geven by Mr. Hugh Mantell . . . twoo exellent bookes of many ancient learned men's sentences called for their excellencie Opus Aureum, the Golden Worke, bound in lether, both of a bigness, geven by Mr. William More, minister of St. Peters . . . a faire new Dictionarie, English and Latin, called Cowper's Dictionarie of the last and best edition, geven by Nathanaell Martin, scholler of the schole . . . Moreover there are brought into the librarie twoo verie faire bookes, the one a Homer with enarrations of the best scoliasts, the other Demosthenes of the best and fayrest edition with scutcheons of the armes of my Lord Keeper, reserved since the first Disputations, geven by the sayd Lord Keeper . . . Mr. Addams, Doctor of Physick, gave in his life tyme one Cowper's Dictionarie and a Greke Lexicon . . . The librarie is now worth xv*l*.[22]

20 There was a London edition of 1611 (*STC* 17955).

21 M. Craze, *A history of Felsted School, 1564–1947* (Ipswich, 1955), 42.

22 F. Willcox, 'The accounts of St Albans Grammar School', *Middlesex and Hertfordshire Notes and Queries* 1 (1895), 11–15, 39–42, 138–42; 2 (1896), 40–3.

In 1597–9, there are further additions, this time paid for 'by the Schollers' – 'Erasmus, Adagies . . . Licosthenes Apothegmes . . . Textors Epithetons . . . Tullies Works in two volumes'. An inventory in 1624–6 shows that the library had not grown in the previous twenty-five years, and that the Cooper's Dictionary was now 'vetus et laceratus'. The purchases and donations show that the books are directly related to the business of learning Greek and Latin, and the way they fall off may suggest either a decline in the rigour of the teaching or the readier availability of textbooks.

Few schools attempted to build up a library of books or, if they managed to receive a small library, to maintain one. Of the scores of institutions founded in the sixteenth and early seventeenth centuries, generally the school statutes are silent on the subject of a library, though there might be some mention of the need for books to supplement the curriculum. The Free Grammar School in Sandwich, Kent, was founded in 1563 by Roger Manwood, who, in 1580, drew up a series of statutes: '18. Item, I ordeine, that everie Scholler at his firste admission into this schole shall paie *Six pence*, if his parentes be inhabiting and the Scholler lodged in Sandwich; and *Twelve pence*, if his parentes be not inhabitinge or the Scholler not lodginge there, to the common Boxe; with whiche money the master at his discreacion shall provide necessarie Bookes, as Dictionaries or other, for the common use of the Schollers.'[23] In 1564 Sir Andrew Judd drew up a set of founding statutes for Tonbridge School, also in Kent, and one of the items reads: 'I will that every scholar at his first admission into the School shall pay sixpence to the common boxe, with which money the Master at his discretion shall provide necessary books, to remain in the School for the common use of the scholars.'[24] Often school statutes are copied from those of other schools, and here the repeated requirement of a payment for common books recognises the need for supplemental texts, to be held by the school. Such books were gathered sporadically. The grammar school in Croydon, named after its founder Archbishop Whitgift, has a list of the books held in 1602: 'Imprimis there belonge to the Schole as yet 4 books, viz. A Coper's Dictionarie and Barret's Dictionarie, and two Lexicons bothe of Scapula.'[25] This tiny collection is probably typical – again, Cooper's popular thesaurus, John Baret's *Alvearie or Quadruple Dictionarie, Containing Foure Sundrie Tongues:*

23 N. Carlisle, *A concise description of the endowed grammar schools in England and Wales*, 2 vols. (London, 1818), I. 602.

24 S. Rivington, *The history of Tonbridge School, from its foundation in 1553 to the present date* (London, 1869), 53.

25 F. G. Percy, *History of Whitgift School, Croydon* (London, 1976), 46.

Namelie, English, Latine, Greeke, and French (1580),[26] both published in London, and the Greek–Latin lexicon of Johannes Scapula. The presence of the Scapula shows that either the master of this school or Archbishop Whitgift, who founded the school two years earlier and died two years later, was serious enough about the instruction of Greek to obtain this expensive text. Such a collection for 'the common use of scholars' can hardly be called a library. Yet it is around the lexicons and commentaries that the school libraries began to grow.

The books were valuable property. They were generally kept in a case or chained in the classroom, but not in a library as such. Thus, Coventry Grammar School has as one of its founding statutes of 1628 a rule 'That there be Dictionaries *chained* in the Schoole, for the generall use of the Schollers there, and shall be kept safely by the Head Schoole-maister, and Usher'.[27] The will of Abraham Colfe, who founded the free school at Lewisham, Kent, by his will of 1647, gave his own books 'to be strongly bound in leather' and 'fastened with iron chains' along with 20s per annum for new books, 5s to the usher (or assistant master) as librarian, and 7s to buy new chains.[28] Yet by the end of the century the chains were dropped from many libraries; in 1719 the chains came off the books at Eton. As the transition is made from a small collection to the library housed in a special room, the chains become less necessary for the guarding of the books.

Though Eton and Winchester had their fellows' libraries, very few schools seem to have had early provision for a specially built library. Guildford Royal Grammar School was founded in 1509 by Robert Beckingham of the Grocers' Company, London, and was granted a royal charter in 1552.[29] The library began as a connecting gallery, built in 1586 between two parts of the school. As it was accessible from outside, it seems to have been open to the public (the town of Guildford also had one of the earliest public libraries, founded thirteen years earlier). The core of the library was a bequest made by John Parkhurst, bishop of Norwich, of some sixty-four items consisting entirely of theology (Augustine, Chrysostom, Ambrose, Origen, Cyprian, Gregory of Nazianzus, works of Zwingli, Calvin, Bullinger and others). Almost all these books are still in the school's collection. But the library was to grow through later donations, many items coming one at a time as we have now seen at other schools. For instance, Daniel Bond, in 1588, gave a Cicero, and Thomas

26 Or possibly the earlier *Triple dictionarie*, without the Greek, of 1574.

27 Carlisle, *Endowed grammar schools*, II. 649.

28 *Ibid.*, I. 584.

29 G. Woodward and R. A. Christophers, *The chained library of the Royal Grammar School, Guildford: catalogue* (Guildford, 1972).

Ede in 1578 gave a Foxe's Book of Martyrs. John Birchall, some time before 1606, gave 'Scapula his lexicon for the use of such schoolers in the schole as learne the Greek tongue'.[30] There were gifts by individuals of a Hebrew and Greek Bible of 1584 in 1604, an English New Testament of 1601 in 1618, a Calvin commentary on the Pentateuch (Geneva, 1563) in 1597, an edition of Camden's *Britannia* translated by Philemon Holland (London, 1610) in 1614. In 1635 John Evans gave a copy of Isaacson's *Saturni epherimedes* (London, 1633), and so on, a mixture of theological and academic books. Thus, the collection continued to grow. The library was repaired with new shelves in 1648.[31]

Of all the schools for which records survive, Shrewsbury had the greatest institutional commitment to a library. The school was founded in 1562 and, with 400 boys, was the largest in England. Its first master was Thomas Ashton, a remarkably talented teacher. In its early ordinances of 1578 'a library and gallery' are called for,[32] and books were purchased early and in quantity.[33] There were five lists made in the seventeenth century.[34] The existence of so many lists shows the care with which the collection was treated.

The 1634 list records the purchases and holdings from 1596 up to that time. There were 704 printed books and thirty-seven manuscripts. The list is arranged by author, but also records shelving and pressmarks, so that the organisation of the books is explained in some detail. Many of the books were chained, those not chained being kept 'in the private custodie of the library keeper, and are supposed to bee kept by him either in the Library closett, where small bookes and others not fit to bee chayned are to be looked for; or els in the gallery over the library, where specially mathematicall bookes and instruments are intended to be disposed'.[35] Oldham suggests that the library was organised much along the lines of the nearby cathedral library of Hereford. The books were set out by subject-area, press by press: 'A, Bibles; B, patristic writings; C and D, Biblical commentaries; E, theology; F, Church history; G and H, Law; K, medicine; L, history, &c.; M, mathematics; N, geography and history; O, philosophy; P and Q, Greek historians and dictionaries; R, Latin poets; S, Latin

30 *Ibid.*, 4. 31 Carlisle, *Endowed grammar schools*, II. 568.

32 J. B. Oldham, 'Shrewsbury School library: its early history and organisation', *Library*, 4th ser., 16 (1935–6), 49.

33 J. B. Oldham, 'Shrewsbury School library', *Library*, 6th ser., 14 (1959), 81–99.

34 Oldham, 'Shrewsbury School library: its early history', 50–7; Oldham, 'Shrewsbury School library', 81–99: 1634, a full list in a folio volume; 1654, list of donors, with some books listed; 1659, copy of the preceding, and carried from then to 1736; 'A Catalogue of the Bookes chain'd in the Library of the Free-gram. Schoole of Salop, finished March the last 1664' – a shelf-catalogue; and a roll in parchment from 1606 to 1634 with new purchases listed.

35 Oldham, 'Shrewsbury School library: its early history', 52.

writers; T, dictionaries', with I and J omitted from the sequence.[36] In 1607 there were purchased 'eleven dozen of iron chains for the library'.[37] The books were secured by iron rivets, not by the usual brass plates (as were used at Hereford), and the shelf-marks were first recorded on the rings on the rods of the chains, not on the books themselves. The chaining stopped about 1690, and the chains were sold off fifty years later.

Of the books purchased or given between 1606 and 1634, 36 per cent contained theology and church history, 21 per cent classical works (including translations), 11 per cent philological works, 10 per cent history, 5 per cent law, 4 per cent medicine and 3 per cent mathematics, and a further 10 per cent contained various miscellaneous texts. Comparing these contents with the character of the books at St Albans, Guildford and Kendal, Oldham concludes that 'it is difficult to believe that school libraries of those days were meant for the exclusive use of boys and masters'.[38] He continues:

> By checking the dates at which books were bought at Shrewsbury during the library's first thirty years of life with the date of the books' publication, it will be found that those 'procured with the schole moneye' immediately upon publication bear little relation to the subjects that Ashton ordered to be read. It may have been reasonable for practical purposes to buy, as was done, as soon as they came out, Janson's and Speed's atlases, Camden's *Elizabeth*, Raleigh's *History of the World*, Holyoake's *Dictionary*, Drayton's *Polyolbion*, Ben Jonson's First Folio, and new editions of Tacitus, Livy, Aristotle, Lucian, Pindar, Horace, and Virgil, and, if the authorities felt strongly about it, even *Anti-Christ arraigned*. But of what use to the boys, or even to the presumably overworked four masters teaching some 400 boys, could have been such books, bought as they were immediately on publication, as new editions of Ambrose, Clement, Jerome, Tertullian, Anselm, Calvin, Spelman's *Concilia*, Grotius, *Corpus Iuris Civilis, Lexicon Juridicum*, or Vesalius's *Anatomy*? Still more does one wonder what was the motive of a newly founded and far from affluent school in spending its meagre resources on incunabula such as the *Nuremberg Chronicle*, the *editio princeps* of Aristophanes, Guido Colonna, the works of Pius II, *Gesta Romanorum, Silvae Morales*, Voragine, Clavasio, and, even more curious (in 1606), eleven medieval manuscripts.

Oldham's question about the contents of the library leads him to an interesting conclusion:

> The library may have been intended as a sort of local centre of learning, not merely for the school, but for general use, and perhaps especially for the local clergy, for whose benefit the vast theological and patristic tomes were thought

36 *Ibid.*, 54–5. 37 *Ibid.*, 56, quoting from the school accounts. 38 *Ibid.*, 58.

> to be needed. Or, the selection of books was made on the principle that certain books 'ought to be on the shelves of every gentleman's library', combined with some infection from the new fashion, exemplified at the same time by, for instance, Sir Thomas Bodley, of acquiring valuable books as a 'collector's' hobby. It is not impossible that both motives operated together.[39]

Although Oldham's conclusions seem appropriate for Shrewbury and perhaps for a very few other schools, it should be stressed that the library at Shrewsbury was unusual for its time, and represents a direction that became more widely established only towards the end of the seventeenth century, when the provision of a library came to be seen as a necessity in the organisation of schools.

In the period under review, we see a slow movement towards the establishment of libraries in schools, with a sudden and widespread adoption of the library in both principle and practice only from the 1660s and onwards. The growth of the school libraries by the middle of the seventeenth century can be explained in a number of ways. The most obvious was through a simple process of accumulation. The schools, founded or refounded in such profusion during a period of expansion in the mid-sixteenth century, stabilised as institutions, and therefore tended to retain the large and well-bound books that had been accumulated over the years (if they were not worn to pieces by student use). Many of these books came to the schools by purchase and remained there. The stocks of books also grew through bequest. Schoolmasters and local scholars often left their books to the schools, in part through their recognition of the school's need for books, but also, and perhaps more important, motivated by their desire to maintain the integrity of their personal library, which was more likely to be guaranteed if transferred to institutional ownership.

Finally, by the end of this period, there had emerged the recognition (by writers and by school authorities) that a school library could serve an important function, both to supplement the school curriculum and, in its own way, to provide a separate education for pupils in the school. But the perception of this last possibility was slow in coming. For most schools in the sixteenth and early seventeenth centuries, the books that formed the library were directly connected to the unrelenting work of learning the ancient languages.

39 *Ibid.*, 82.

18

Common lawyers and the Inns of Court

J. H. BAKER

Law is a profession which still requires its leading specialists to own large collections of books, and this was equally true before our period, when Chaucer's serjeant had 'cas and doomes alle | That from the tyme of kyng William were falle'.[1] Indeed, at the start of our period these private libraries were the only libraries of the common law in being, and they could hardly have constituted more than a shelf- or case-full, even for a judge. By 1600 the typical library would have been much larger, and Sears Jayne has been deservedly criticised for not recognising lawyers as a book-owning class in the Renaissance period.[2]

Personal libraries

We do not have any reliably complete inventories of lawyers' libraries before the Stuart period, and there are not many even then. There are plenty of mentions of law books in wills, but these seem to be selective. It was only necessary to make specific bequests of the more valuable or splendid contents of a library, and the workaday volumes were either left generically to a relative who seemed inclined to the law or passed over in silence. Several probate inventories of lawyers have survived and have been published, and they are remarkable for the low proportion of law books: for example, of over forty volumes listed as belonging to Sir Roger Townshend (d. 1493), justice of the Common Pleas, only sixteen were legal;[3] of the thirty-six volumes listed in the

1 Prologue to *The Canterbury Tales* (*c.* 1390), from L. D. Benson (ed.), *The Riverside Chaucer* (Boston, MA, 1987), 28, lines 323–4: 'In termes hadde he cas and doomes alle | That from the tyme of kyng William were falle'. Of course, Chaucer did not mean this literally. For 'termes' see below, 450.

2 R. J. Schoeck, 'The libraries of common lawyers in the Renaissance', *Manuscripta* 6 (1962), 155–67, referring to Jayne, 46.

3 C. E. Moreton, 'The "library" of a late-15th-century lawyer', *Library*, 6th ser., 13 (1991), 338–46.

library of Mr Serjeant Kebell (d. 1500), only four were legal;[4] an inventory of John Holgrave (d. 1487), baron of the Exchequer, lists only a book of chronicles, a *Gesta Romanorum*, two printed books of statutes, a printed Littleton, and 'an olde boke of lawe in paper';[5] while that of Chief Baron Urswyk (d. 1479) included a Chaucer but no professional books at all.[6] The explanation for the paucity of law books in these lists is almost certainly that the inventories were of the libraries kept in the country homes of the deceased subjects, whereas their working law books were kept in the serjeants' inns[7] or Inns of Court and probably disposed of informally through colleagues, clerks,[8] relations in the law or law-booksellers. The law books could have had no value except to other lawyers.

Working law libraries seem at first to have been somewhat unstable in content, not in the sense that law books were common property but because they were freely and widely borrowed within the legal community for reading and copying, or exchanged, or given to friends and colleagues.[9] A note scribbled by John Eltonhede of Lincoln's Inn in the 1450s shows that it was worthwhile to note down who had what manuscripts, for future reference.[10] The free circulation of law books was especially important before the age of printing, which created – for good or ill – some kind of canon of vulgate authorities. Changes of ownership, and even loans, were often recorded on flyleaves. Richard Heigham (d. 1500), serjeant at law, directed his executors that 'all suche bookes as I have in keeping wherof the names of the very owners of theym be writtyn in the first leefe of the same bookes be delivered to the owners of the same bookys', suggesting that he had quite a few volumes on loan.[11] Such inscriptions as survive are usually in the common form 'Iste liber pertinet . . .', occasionally witnessed

4 E. W. Ives, *The common lawyers of pre-Reformation England* (Cambridge, 1983), 445–7.

5 TNA, PROB 2/16.

6 TNA, E154/2/2; F. W. Steer, 'A medieval household: the Urswick inventory', *Essex Review* 63 (1954), 12.

7 Sometimes there are express references in wills to books there. For example, Serjeant Rudhale (d. 1530) bequeathed the contents of his Serjeants' Inn chamber to his younger son, Charles, provided that his elder son, John (a member of the Inner Temple and an attorney), should 'have such bokes there as he will chose for the furtheraunce of his lernyng, levyng to the said Charles bokes convenient for his age and lernyng': PCC 26 Jankyn.

8 Edward Hall (d. 1547), the chronicler, bencher of Gray's Inn, left all his law books to his clerk: PCC 36 Alen.

9 For what follows, see J. H. Baker, *A catalogue of English legal manuscripts in Cambridge University Library* (1996), introduction, xlv–lv; 'The books of the Common Law', in *CHBB* III. 413–17.

10 BL, MS Lansdowne 1176, fol. 188; reproduced (with notes) in Baker, 'Books of the Common Law', 415.

11 PCC 23 Moone.

by fellows of the owner's inn. Sometimes explicits fulfilled a similar role. Legal manuscripts of the fifteenth and early sixteenth centuries frequently end with an 'Explicit . . . quod John Style' (or whatever the name might be). There has been some controversy over whether these names after the *quod* were the names of scribes, as Ker supposed, or of owners.[12] No doubt frequently they were both at once, since law students learnt by copying. In fact, the names are nearly always identifiable as belonging to lawyers or law students. The explicits were evidently treated as ownership inscriptions, substitutions being made by subsequent owners. And there is an example of a legal citation around 1460 which apparently uses *quod* to indicate the owner of the book cited.[13] We even find an early printed year-book with a blank space provided in such an explicit for the owner's name to be inserted.[14] As late as 1549, William Fletewoode used an ownership inscription in the form '. . . quod Willelmus Fletewoode'.[15] Ker's hypothesis is therefore mistaken, at any rate with respect to the generality of law books.

A good indication of the content of a working law library of the fifteenth century is provided in the will of Sir Peter Arderne (d. 1467), justice of the Common Pleas.[16] The books included a *Legenda sanctorum*, a volume of old statutes with a register (*Registrum brevium*) and 'newe tales' (*Novae narrationes*), the new statutes and a 'boke of termes of parchemyn', 'a good book compiled of lawe with a yalowe leddir coveryng', 'a grete boke of lawe of termes of Second Edward in parchemyn', 'my best registre of lawe', 'my booke of assisez of lawe' – that is, a *Liber assisarum*[17] – 'my owne grete compiled booke of lawe covered with reed leddir and a horn upon itt', 'a boke of lawe of parchemyn compiled and bokeled', 'a boke of termes of lawe of paper anno xxxii[do] anno xxxxix and other yeris therin' (i.e. of Edward III). The 'compiled' books were probably abridgements of cases, a recent invention. The 'books of terms' were what later generations called year-books: that is, anonymous law reports cited by regnal year and term.[18] They are what Chaucer meant by the 'terms'

12 See A. W. B. Simpson, 'The circulation of year-books in the fifteenth century', *Law Quarterly Review* 73 (1957), 501; with the further note (referring to Ker) in his 'The source and function of the later year books', *Law Quarterly Review* 87 (1971), 108.

13 BL, MS Add. 65194, fol. 66 ('anno xxii libro assisarum etc. quod Evesham W.'). Citations of specific books are very rare.

14 Pynson's edition of 5 Hen. VII, sig. k6.

15 Yale University, Law MS, G/N21/1.

16 PCC 19 Godyn.

17 Cases on circuit, *c.* 20–50 Edw. III. The printed version (1513/14) extended it back to 1 Edw. III by adding similar cases from the regular year-books.

18 For this terminology, see J. H. Baker, 'Records, reports and the origins of case-law in England', in J. H. Baker (ed.), *Judicial records, law reports and the growth of case law* (Berlin, 1989), 20, nn. 29–30.

containing 'cases and dooms' which had characterised the library of his man of law. Books of terms were sufficiently valued to be mentioned in wills from as far back as the fourteenth century. For instance, Robert Peke (d. 1393) of Gray's Inn bequeathed 'illos libros meos de lege regni Anglie vocatos terminos' and 'omnes terminos meos antiquos';[19] and Richard Bankes (d. 1416), baron of the Exchequer, left to his sons the 'liber terminorum' which had belonged to Chief Baron Plesyngton (d. 1393) and 'alii libri et quaterni pertinentes ad legem terre'.[20]

A leading member of the Bar would have had a comparable collection. Indeed, the most complete pre-1550 catalogue of a working English law library – which seems not to have been noticed before – is the inventory of books left by William Cutler or Cutlerd (d. 1506), serjeant at law.[21] He owned twenty-seven law books (seven of them printed), a manuscript *De dictis philosophorum*, and several service-books kept in his private chapel. The law books included three volumes of statutes, an abridgement of statutes, nine volumes of year-books from Edward III to Edward IV and a *Liber assisarum*, two abridgments of cases (one being the printed Statham), a book of entries,[22] and two books of 'raportes' – which evidently meant readings in the Inns of Court rather than reports of cases.[23] These books were at the time of his death mostly kept in his study at Boston, Lincolnshire, though six printed law books (not described) were found in the chapel.

There was a similar range of law books in the personal library of Sir Thomas Frowyk (d. 1505), chief justice of the Common Pleas. No catalogue exists, but some of his manuscripts can still be identified. His three volumes of year-books of Edward I, Edward II and Edward III are all in the British Library,[24] as is his illuminated volume of *Statuta nova*, which had previously belonged to another judge, William Calow (d. 1487).[25] Calow mentioned in his will a 'book of newe statuts', perhaps this one, together with a book of assizes, a Bracton, and 'ii bookes of abriggements, oon of myne owen labour and thother of Lincolnesin labour'.[26] We know that Frowyk also owned a large book of

19 Lincs. Arch. Office, Reg. Beaufort, fol. 23v (information from Dr N. L. Ramsay).

20 E. F. Jacob (ed.), *The register of Henry Chichele, archbishop of Canterbury, 1414–1443*, 4 vols. (Oxford, 1937–47), II. 66–8. Plesyngton had been chief baron of the Exchequer 1380–6.

21 TNA, PROB 2/472. Though not described as a serjeant, the identity of the deceased is confirmed by his having left a scarlet gown with a hood and a ray gown with a hood, and paid some debts to 'the sargeantes of the comen lawe' (presumably one of the serjeants' inns).

22 That is, precedents of pleading, in Latin, taken from entries on the plea rolls.

23 The second reference is to 'raporttes of statutes'.

24 BL, MSS Add. 37657 (Edw. I), Add. 37659 (Edw. III); Hargrave 210 (Edw. II).

25 BL, MS Cotton Nero C. i (with Calow arms).

26 PCC 7 Milles (dated 1483).

entries, because Lady Frowyk's second husband, Thomas Jakes (d. 1514), left to the Inner Temple an illuminated book of new statutes – quite probably the Calow manuscript – and a 'greate boke of entres', both of which had belonged to the chief justice.[27] Frowyk would certainly have owned other, less valuable books.

The impact of printing is evident from a comparison of these libraries with that of William Rastell, sometime justice of the Queen's Bench, who left over forty books in his chambers in Serjeants' Inn when he fled to exile in Louvain in 1562, about a third of them non-legal.[28] Apart from 'divers bookes of the statutes in parchment', valued at a mere twopence, and perhaps the abridgement 'in paper', the other twenty and more legal titles seem all to have been printed books. Some of them were acquired by Randle Cholmeley, serjeant at law, who left them with others to Lincoln's Inn.[29] The other books in the inventory were mainly classical. Rastell must have taken other books abroad. In the preface to his *Colleccion of entrees*, compiled in Louvain, he mentions a number of important manuscript collections of pleadings which he had perhaps taken with him.[30] The inventory does not mention bookshelves or presses, perhaps because they were fixtures, but it seems probable that the little square table covered with green cloth and the 'stone wrapt in a canvas' served the judge for his reading.

Other law libraries were more modest, though even very modest law libraries usually contained some non-legal books. William Catesby (d. 1485), bencher of the Inner Temple and chancellor of the Exchequer, had eight (unspecified) law books, a psalter, a book of chronicles, and a book *De natura legis naturae* (doubtless Fortescue).[31] Richard Wye (d. 1520), another bencher of the Inner Temple, left not only law books but also 'bookes that concerne devynite, humanite and felocifie'.[32] Richard Isham (d. 1492), a senior but

27 PCC 2 Holder (dated 19 September 1513, proved 13 July 1514): 'I will that my seid good lady and wyff delyver to the company of the Inner Temple my fayer boke of the newe statutes wryten and lymed [i.e. illuminated] and my greate boke of entres which were my singuler good lord Frowykes, there to remayne in the librarie to thentent they shuld the better remember my seid good lord her late husband, her self and me.' The wording suggests that Jakes had only one illuminated statute-book, and it therefore seems likely to have been the Cotton MS.

28 The inventory is printed in 'Legal retrospections', *Law Magazine* 31 (1844), 54–64, at 57–8.

29 J. H. Baker, *Readers and readings in the Inns of Court and Chancery*, Selden Soc. (2000), 528. For the Cholmeley bequest, see below, 456.

30 J. H. Baker (ed.), *The reports of John Spelman*, 2 vols., Selden Soc. 93–4 (London, 1977–8), II. *55–6*.

31 Inventory in TNA, E154/2/4.

32 PCC 26 Ayloffe. One of his law books survives as CUL, MS Ee. 3. 46.

undistinguished member of Lincoln's Inn, seems only to have left a folio bible, priced at 53s 4d, with 'ij lytyll bokys of statutes, a paper boke with ix pamflettes, queyers and papers of divers maters of lawe, price togeder viij s. iiij d.'[33]

By the seventeenth century, a prominent lawyer's library would contain not only manuscript statutes, law reports and digests – both medieval and modern – but also a good number of printed reports and statutes, tracts, pamphlets and other works. Some lawyers, such as Sir Edward Coke (d. 1634) and John Selden (d. 1654), were bibliophiles who amassed remarkably large libraries containing books on a wide range of subjects. These are well known from contemporary catalogues, which have been published,[34] and need no description here. Other notable law libraries from this period, strong in legal history, were those of Mr Serjeant Fletewoode (d. 1594),[35] Francis Tate (d. 1606),[36] Sir Matthew Hale (d. 1676)[37] and Sir John Maynard (d. 1690).[38] A number of more ordinary libraries survived until modern times, though unfortunately the effect of their dispersal has usually been to separate the manuscripts from the printed portions.[39]

Little is known of the construction and appearance of private legal libraries, which were more usually called studies.[40] Of course, many houses still remain which were built by lawyers in our period – Blickling and Montacute spring to mind – and they have libraries, but they no longer contain the original books and may have been altered over the centuries. There are experts who know

33 TNA, PROB 2/58. He had been a member of the inn since the 1450s, but did not achieve distinction in the legal profession.

34 W. O. Hassall (ed.), *A catalogue of the library of Sir Edward Coke* (New Haven, CT, 1950); D. M. Barratt, 'The library of John Selden and its later history', *BLR* 3 (1951), 257–73; J. H. Baker, *English legal manuscripts*, II: *Catalogue of the manuscript year books, readings, and law reports in Lincoln's Inn, the Bodleian Library and Gray's Inn* (Zug, 1978), 18–20.

35 See Baker, *Catalogue of English legal manuscripts*, xlvii–xlviii.

36 *Ibid.*, xlix–l.

37 Baker, *English legal manuscripts*, II. 8–18; D. E. C. Yale, *Sir Matthew Hale's The Prerogatives of the King*, Selden Soc. 92 (London, 1976), appendix, lix–lxxvi. Hale was called to the Bar in 1636.

38 Baker, *English legal manuscripts*, II. 24–5, 57–76; J. Hunter, *A catalogue of the manuscripts in the library of Lincoln's Inn* (1838), 94–123. Maynard was called to the Bar in 1626.

39 Even when they still have a single owner, as with the library of Robert Nicholas (d. 1667) in Cambridge University Library: Baker, *Catalogue of English legal manuscripts*, li–lii. The law manuscripts of Arthur Turnour (d. 1651) and Thomas Powys (d. 1671), serjeants at law, are now in the Harvard Law School: J. H. Baker, *English legal manuscripts in the USA* (1990), II. 101, 186.

40 E.g., TNA, PROB 2/472 (inventory of Serjeant Cutlerd, 1506, listing books in his 'study' at Boston); PROB 11/30, fo. 154^{v} (will of Thomas Lane, bencher of Lincoln's Inn, which mentions 'my study in London', 1544); PROB 2/404B (inventory of Serjeant Lovelace's 'studie at Serjauntes Inne . . . divers law bookes there £3. 6. 8.', 1577).

about such things; but they seem no different in kind from other country-house libraries and ought not to be regarded as law libraries. Of the arrangement and construction of working libraries in chambers very little detailed information is available. There is no portrait of a lawyer, within our period, which has a realistic representation of a library in the background. There is, however, a monument to a judge – Sir Henry Yelverton (d. 1630) – in Easton Maudit church, Northamptonshire, which has shelves of books behind the effigy. The volumes are, naturally, shelved fore-edge to the front, and bear no indication of their titles; an enthusiastic restorer has also painted them in a variety of colours, apparently not recognising them as books.

Institutional libraries

There were no institutional libraries of the common law comparable with the libraries of the universities or large monasteries. The universities and their colleges had law libraries, of course, but little or nothing of the common law was to be found in them until much later. The courts of law at Westminster did not have libraries for use by the judges until Georgian times,[41] though in 1524 the Common Bench ordered the purchase of a book of new statutes, to be kept there 'with the intention that the justices here may inspect the statutes contained in the same book at convenient times'.[42] The officers had collections of precedent books, primarily containing forms of pleading and other entries to be made on the plea rolls. These were mainly their own personal property. However, in 1533 a filazer donated to the King's Bench office a copy of the old book of entries printed in 1510, suggesting that there may have been an office library as well.[43] Yet the book was in private possession by the 1550s, and no other evidence of an office collection has come to light in our period. The books from the King's Bench office, now in the Supreme Court Library, date

41 An engraving of 11 August 1804, by J. G. Walker after E. Pugh, entitled 'The Court of King's Bench, Westminster' (published in R. Phillips, *Modern London: being the history and present state of the British metropolis; illustrated with numerous copper plates* (London, 1805), 233), is the first illustration to show a case of books standing in the court.

42 TNA, CP 40/1044, m. 302 (fines totalling 6s 8d paid 'pro quodam libro novorum statutorum in loco Thesaurarii hujus curie remanando ad intentionem quod justiciarii hic statuta in eodem libro contenta respicere possunt quolibet tempore oportuno').

43 CUL, Syn. 3. 51. 3 (inscribed 'Anno Domini 1533 . . . Memorandum quod Johannes Percyvall gent. donavit hunc librum officine domini Roperi armigeri prothonotarii domini regis in curia domini regis coram ipso rege ex mera et spontanea voluntate sua qu[. . .] ob zelum quem officine antedicte gessit'). It later belonged to Sir William Staundford (d. 1558), justice of the Common Pleas.

back to the seventeenth century but were – at least in some cases – acquired later.

The four Inns of Court each had libraries, which probably appeared during the second half of the fifteenth century, though there is no evidence that the lesser inns – the 'Inns of Chancery' – followed suit. Of the four libraries, enough information has survived to justify considering them one by one.

Lincoln's Inn

The first recorded library in the Inns of Court was at Lincoln's Inn, where in 1475 Roger Townshend – himself a year-book reporter – was paid 30s 'pro bibliotheca',[44] the precise meaning of which is a matter for conjecture. It is hardly surprising, however, that the earliest reference to a library should come from Lincoln's Inn, since it is the only inn which still has records prior to 1500. There is no mention of any new building in 1475, and the smallness of the sum suggests that some existing apartment may have been fitted out under Townshend's direction to receive books. But in 1504 John Nethersole, an attorney of the Common Pleas, left the inn 40 marks 'that the society might build or newly erect a library within the inn, to the increase of learning and the study of the law of England within the inn'.[45] These are the words of the inn's records. There is no mention of such a bequest in the registered copy of Nethersole's will,[46] but, since the chief residuary legatee was Sir John Fyneux, chief justice of the King's Bench and patron of John Roper, chief clerk of Fyneux's court and treasurer of Lincoln's Inn that year, it seems likely that some private arrangement had been made. In any case, the money was received, and the work was mostly completed by 1509, with wainscotting added shortly afterwards.[47] The old library was somewhere in Old Buildings, probably next to the old hall, where it remained until a new library was provided in Stone Buildings in the 1780s. The original building was substantially renovated in 1602–3, when new presses were built for the books, with chains, and the old long table was replaced with desks and stools. The work was promoted by Sir James Ley, one of the benchers and also a noted antiquary, who was later created earl of Marlborough. Ley searched out the arms of the readers of the inn back to 1465, with the intention of placing their shields in the upper

44 W. P. Baildon (ed.), *The records of the Honorable Society of Lincoln's Inn: the Black Books*, 4 vols. (1897), I. 59, 61.

45 Baildon, *Black Books*, I. 136.

46 PCC 25 Holgrave.

47 For what follows, see Baker, *English legal manuscripts*, II. 1–4.

borders of the wainscotting; but in the end the inn settled for a painted 'table' on vellum. At this time the use of the library seems to have been restricted to the benchers, though after physical extension it was formally opened to other members of the inn in 1631.[48]

The earliest recorded acquisition was in 1517, when John Strange (a bencher) left his books to the inn, and two years later Sir John Boteler (d. 1519), justice of the Common Pleas, left his entire law library – 'omnes libros meos de lege quos habeo in domo mea in Silverstrete et Serjaunts Inne in venella Cancellarie'.[49] No lists survive of these bequests, though by 1550 the library had several volumes of medieval reports and a Bracton.[50] But security was weak, and these early gifts were lost. Catalogues were made in 1566, and again in 1606, but the catalogues have fared no better than the books. No doubt mindful of such security problems, Randle Cholmeley, serjeant at law and former bencher of the inn, willed in 1563[51] that most of his lawbooks

> shalbe and remaine in the said librarie to thuse and commoditie of the companie of the said howse, if the governers of the same howse doe take such goode and directe order that the same librarie and bookes may be saved and preserved in good order to the profytt of the saide companye, or elce I will that this my gifte and devise touchinge the same bookes be voide.

The inn accepted the small library on these terms. The books were repaired, and labelled with vellum inscriptions mounted under horn. They were always treated with care, and most or all of them are still there.

The renovation of the library in 1603 was accompanied by an appeal for gifts, resulting in several generous donations, and the establishment of a library fund – which was used, among other things, to procure transcripts of important historical treatises such as *Fleta* (in 1611) and the *Mirror of justices* (in 1615). The office of master of the library was inaugurated in 1609, and in 1629 a librarian (or 'keeper') was appointed.[52] By the 1640s the inn possessed, in addition to several dozen manuscripts (many of which have since disappeared), nearly 300

48 Baildon, *Black Books*, II. 299, 303. For this privilege, members paid a subscription towards the stipend of the library keeper.

49 PCC 22 Ayloffe.

50 Baker, *English legal manuscripts*, II. 2; Baker, *Reports of John Spelman*, II. 131.

51 PCC 23 Chayre; and see Baildon, *Black Books*, I. 340, 352. He excepted from the bequest his books of statutes in English, which he left to Sir Thomas Leigh. Among his other bequests were 'all the bookes of Erasimus whiche he gave me'.

52 Baildon, *Black Books*, II. 117, 290–2, 299. The first library keeper was Abraham Sherman, the chaplain, who held office until 1633. The duties seem thereafter to have devolved on one of the butlers.

printed books, only seventy-eight of which were legal.[53] It was still the rule in 1652 that all 'considerable books' be chained.[54]

Gray's Inn

The extant records of Gray's Inn do not commence until 1569, and the origins of the library were once a matter of doubt.[55] There was even a legend that it was founded by Francis Bacon. It is now known to date from the fifteenth century, since Edmund Pykeryng (d. 1488) left six chained books in his will to the 'libraria de Graysinne',[56] and the inn formerly possessed a fifteenth-century register of writs inscribed 'Iste liber pertinet societati de Greysynn'.[57] From 1514 we often hear of 'library moots' in the inn, showing that the books were housed somewhere sufficiently spacious to permit legal exercises to be held there.[58]

Little is known of the contents of the early library,[59] which were by no means all legal. Indeed, only one of Pykeryng's books was a law book – the statutes of Edward III. The inn still owns a number of non-legal medieval manuscripts of monastic provenance, but these were seemingly acquired long after the Dissolution.[60] In 1555, Robert Chaloner left his law books to the inn, and a small legacy to his kinsman Robert Nowell, 'that he may by [buy] cheines therwith and fasten so manye of them in the librarye at Grauisin as he shall thinke convenyente'.[61] The only book of Chaloner's now in the inn, an important collection of manuscript readings, was not received until 1883, following the Towneley sale.

In 1634 there was evidently an appeal to members and former members[62] of the inn to augment the library in all fields of knowledge, and sixty-nine

53 'A Catalogue of the Names of such law bookes as are at Lincolne Inn taken the 26: of September 1646', BL, MS Harley 7363, fols. 81–5. The list is confined to printed books, but not to law. The subjects are: law (78), divinity (95), philosophy (50), history (68) and physic (1).

54 Baildon, *Black Books*, II. 397.

55 For what follows, see Baker, *English legal manuscripts*, II. 192.

56 PCC 32 Milles (information from Dr A. I. Doyle).

57 Now BL, MS Add. 34901 (inscription no longer present).

58 J. H. Baker, introduction to *Readings and moots at the Inns of Court in the fifteenth Century*, II, Selden Soc. 105 (London, 1990), xxiv.

59 Even the location is uncertain. It was an upper room in Gray's Inn Square, with chambers beneath: R. J. Fletcher (ed.), *The pension book of Gray's Inn*, 2 vols. (London, 1901–10), I. 55 (for 1582), 82–3 (for 1589).

60 *MMBL*, 50.

61 W. R. Douthwaite, *History of Gray's Inn and its associations* (1889), 175–6; Fletcher, *Pension book*, I. xxi–xxii, n.

62 When a bencher took the degree of serjeant at law, he was required to leave his inn of court. He then moved to one of the two serjeants' inns.

volumes still remain which were presented in 1634–5 or shortly thereafter. They are uniformly bound with brass bosses and corners, sometimes with loops for chaining, and with a memorial of the donation either in gilt letters or in inscriptions mounted beneath horn. This interesting library has only recently been the subject of scholarly study, by Professor W. R. Prest, who concludes that it affords clear evidence of the wide cultural interests of members of the legal profession at that date. Only a minority of the books relate to the law,[63] though among them is a manuscript Bracton.[64] As in the other inns, security was a constant problem, and it was only in 1646, after some books were found to be missing, that a librarian was belatedly appointed.[65]

The Inner Temple

The two societies in the Temple probably had libraries in the fifteenth century, like the other two, though no mention has yet been found until slightly later. The Inner Temple certainly had a library by 1506,[66] when it is mentioned in the records – though these records begin only the previous year – and we have seen that in 1514 Thomas Jakes bequeathed to it two of Chief Justice Frowyk's books.[67] A few other donations are known. Sir John Baker (d. 1558), attorney-general to Henry VIII, gave it a famous year-book with annotations by a civilian called Winchedon, a unique feature which attracted the attention of Selden.[68] A year later Sir David Broke (d. 1559/60), chief baron of the Exchequer and a former bencher, left his law books to be divided between a nephew and a cousin:[69]

> excepte my regester written, the booke of entries written whiche was Prowces[70] and a booke of the statutes in Frenche from Edward the thirde dayes, and a booke of Edwarde the thirdes yeares, and a booke of Edward the iiijth yeres, whiche I will shalbe delyvered to the worshipfull companye of the Inner Temple to be fixed and made faste in the librarie there for studentes to looke uppon.

63 W. R. Prest, 'Law, learning and religion: gifts to Gray's Inn library in the 1630s', *Parergon* 14/1 (1996), 205–22 (with an annotated list).

64 Now Gray's Inn MS 21; presented by John Godbold.

65 Fletcher, *Pension book*, I. 356, 359. William Swynfeild was to receive £3 6s 8d per annum in this office.

66 F. A. Inderwick (ed.), *Calendar of Inner Temple records*, 5 vols. (1896–1937), II. 6.

67 See above, 452. There is no record that the books were ever received by the library.

68 J. Selden, *Ad Fletam dissertatio*, appended to *Fleta* (1647), 528–9; ed. D. Ogg (Cambridge, 1925), 149. There is no later reference to it.

69 PCC 10 Mellershe.

70 'Prowce' was Bartholomew Prouz of the Inner Temple (fl. 1505–35), a West Country attorney of the Common Pleas.

The old library was an upper room with chambers beneath it,[71] situated next to the hall, and in 1608 it was extended on to the ground floor.[72] The new library of 1608 cost £129 7s 1d, and evidently became the principal reading room, fitted with iron rods to which books were padlocked.[73] The old or upper library was large enough to be used for learning exercises, as in Gray's Inn. It was also used for receiving noblemen at the readers' feasts,[74] and (after 1608) for 'parliaments', or formal meetings of the benchers.[75] In 1666 it was swept away by the Great Fire, most of the old books disappearing in the flames. (The library was fated to be destroyed twice more. The new library, completed in 1667 – at a cost of over £600[76] – was burned down in 1678, and the Victorian library of 1868 was incinerated during the air-raids of 1941, when about 40,000 volumes were destroyed by enemy action.)

The Middle Temple

There is rather less to be said of the Middle Temple. A report written in 1540 found:[77]

> They now have no library so that they cannot attaine to the knowledge of divers learnings, but to their great chardges by the buying of such bookes as they lust to study. They had a simple library in which were not many bookes besides the law and that library by meanes that it stood allways open, and that the learners had not each a key to it, was [at] last robbed of all the bookes in it.

Little seems to have been done to remedy the position until a new library was founded under the will of Robert Ashley, dated 27 September 1640.[78] As with the Gray's Inn venture of 1634, the object was to establish not a law library but a scholarly library in all subjects. Ashley was a keen collector of books and left them

71 The mention in 1506 is of an admission to chambers beneath it.
72 Inderwick, *Inner Temple records*, II. 35, 43. 73 *Ibid.*, II. 45.
74 *Ibid.*, II. 21; J. B. Williamson, *The history of the Temple*, 2nd edn (London, 1925), 649.
75 Inderwick, *Inner Temple records*, II. 3, 53. Two large curtains were made for the 'upper library' in 1611: *ibid.*, II. 70.
76 *Ibid.*, II. 48 (£430 to John Jordan, bricklayer), 53 (£32 15s to Isaac Row for painting the library and moot chamber, and £136 to William Roundthwayte for wainscotting the library). The library was soon afterwards adorned with painted shields displaying the arms of the readers, later moved to the hall.
77 Baker, *Reports of John Spelman*, II. 132, n. 3.
78 Original will on vellum, Middle Temple archives, MT 9/RAW1.

> to this Noble Society of the Middle Temple in which I have spent so many Yeares of my Life how unworthily soever yett a Member thereof. My desire is That the Bookes may be preserved in such Order as they were left in both Chambers for the Especiall use of the Society Not Excluding any Student whether of our owne or of any forraigne Nation that may bee Curious to see Somewhat which hee cannot so readiely fynd elsewhere.

It was ordered in 1641 that Ashley's books should be kept in presses in the lower parliament chamber 'untill a librarie or place convenient to settle and dispose them in be provided', thereby demonstrating that there was still no library at that time.[79] The library was built in 1650 and escaped the fire of 1666.

Conclusion

These libraries, serving the 'Third University of England', were modest – Professor Prest has described them as 'paltry' by academic standards.[80] Sir Edward Coke's personal library alone was probably larger than those of all the Inns of Court together. In the Inns of Chancery, the younger students and attorneys had no libraries at all at their disposal. The Inns of Court made some effort, as we have seen, but their libraries were more or less unfunded and – until the very end of our period – had no librarians to protect them. The contents were derived largely from haphazard donations, and in the absence of librarians the security was so poor that even these proved to be impermanent assets. We happen to know more about them than about most private collections because of the archival accident that the inns preserved continuous financial records. But the fact remains that the principal means of access to law books before 1640, despite their high cost, was through private ownership.

79 Williamson, *History of the Temple*, 381–4.

80 Prest, *Inns of Court*, 166.

19

Medical libraries

PETER MURRAY JONES

Early British medical libraries owned by practitioners of medicine are not easily distinguished from those owned by persons with a purely theoretical interest in medicine. This is not just a function of our ignorance about the owners of these books – although it is true that we may not know enough to characterise them – but reflects the difficulty of drawing hard and fast lines between theory and practice of medicine. Almost all of the men who can be identified as possessing medical degrees from Oxford, Cambridge and the Scottish or other European universities are known to have practised as well as taught medicine.[1] Conversely, those book-owners we can identify as surgeons or unlicensed medical practitioners did not keep in their libraries books which were of a kind noticeably different from those owned by the university trained men. Both licensed and unlicensed practitioners might own recipe-books, or herbals, or texts on surgery and the medical *practica*. So too with institutions, monastic houses, colleges or gilds of practitioners – they often seem to have owned medical books that reflected both the curriculum of the university medical school and the exigencies of medical treatment of patients.

The most important distinctions that can be drawn in respect of medical libraries are linguistic.[2] Some owners had only books that were in English, in Gaelic or in Welsh. The overwhelming majority of medical libraries in the early period, however, were made up wholly of books in Latin. If other languages were represented in these Latin-dominated libraries, they were French, Italian or German books, rather than English. This has partly to do with the conventions of recording books in the probate inventories that are our best source for

1 For biographical registers of medical practitioners and learned men, including data about book-ownership, see C. H. Talbot and E. A. Hammond, *The medical practitioners in medieval England: a biographical register* (London, 1965), supplemented by F. Getz, 'Medical practitioners in medieval England', *Social History of Medicine* 3.2 (1990), 245–83.

2 These distinctions are discussed in P. M. Jones, 'Medical libraries and medical Latin 1400–1700,' in W. Bracke and H. Deumens (eds.), *Medical Latin from the late middle ages to the eighteenth century* (Brussels, 2000), 115–35.

early medical libraries. Books in Latin or in other European languages were recorded as having more value than books in English. Thus it is possible that English medical books may have remained unrecorded within the library of a learned university practitioner or even lay person. These libraries may in fact have been less latinate than now appears. But, by comparison with the Latin medical libraries, those made up of books only in English, in Gaelic or in Welsh are hard to find. For England, we have a number of wills recording the bequest of medical books in English: for instance, a number of bequests of London surgeons in the fifteenth century leaving their surgical textbook or books to relatives, colleagues or apprentices. These 'libraries' are of course only libraries in the sense of a number of books in the ownership of a named individual, not in the sense of a quantity of books ordered or classified on some principle.[3]

Before 1450 it is hard to identify individuals with significant collections of medical manuscripts. William Rede, later bishop of Chichester, who willed his medical and scientific manuscripts to Merton and to other colleges in Oxford in 1382, is certainly one such; and it is worth reflecting on the fact that we know of his collecting only through the exceptional records remaining in Merton College – that is to say, we know him as a collector because he gave his books to an institution. Perhaps other equally important individuals who owned medical books existed, but are lost to view because the legal and administrative records that might have captured information of this sort were not created, or do not by and large survive from this period.[4] Aside from Rede and Merton College, we know that medical books were owned in some number by monastic houses, for instance St Augustine's and Christ Church, Canterbury.[5]

The principal dynamic at work here is the migration of monks from these houses to Oxford to pursue academic studies before returning to their mother-house. It seems to have been the custom for such students to give the manuscripts they acquired in the course of their studies to their monastery on their return. Some monks pursued medical studies, which accounts for the frequent appearance of the *Articella*,[6] then the corpus of texts at the heart of

3 R. T. Beck, *The cutting edge: early history of the surgeons of London* (London, 1974), lists a number of bequests of these books.

4 F. M. Powicke, *The medieval books of Merton College* (Oxford, 1931), esp. 28–32, and 87–91 (for his will).

5 James, *ALCD*; S. Page, 'Magic at St Augustine's Canterbury in the late middle ages', unpublished PhD thesis, University of London (2000).

6 The *Articella* was the collection of teaching texts that became standard at medical schools in European universities. It included works of Hippocrates and Galen as well as short texts by Byzantine and Arabic authors.

the study of medicine at Oxford and Cambridge, among the books listed in catalogues of these monastic houses. Ownership of multiple copies of these standard texts is a feature of the medical libraries. Perhaps the most striking collection of all is that formed by the Augustinian canons of Leicester Abbey. By the late fifteenth century, there were more than eighty medical volumes (in a total library of over 940), ten of which belonged to a John Bokkedene, 'medicus', from whom they were bought for the use of the community by its abbot William Sadyngton (1420–42).[7] Among some more unusual items that came from Bokkedene or similar sources, we also find multiple copies of the *Articella*, the *Antidotarium Nicolai* and the works of academic surgeons like Lanfranc and Guy de Chauliac. These last are probably to be explained by the academic travel and studies of the canons. Of course, these monastic collections were dispersed at the dissolution of the monasteries in the 1530s.

Around the mid-fifteenth century, however, new academic dynamics had begun to operate. At Oxford and Cambridge, individuals took it upon themselves to attempt to build up medical collections as local institutional resources for medical education and study. In Oxford, the secretary and physician to Humfrey Duke of Gloucester, an Oxford doctor of medicine named Gilbert Kymer, persuaded his master to give his rich library to Oxford in 1439. Kymer also gave his own collection of medical books to the university. Both collections were intended as foundation stones of what was to become the Bodleian Library. Many of Humfrey's books seem to have been diverted or abstracted from their intended home at the University's library. Similarly, most of Kymer's books did not find their way to the university library as he intended they should, one arriving in Merton, and others falling into the hands of private owners before making their way back to the Bodleian later. Yet all of them contain inscriptions in his own hand, recording his gift to the university. Many of Kymer's medical books were written by his servant, the German scribe Herman Zurke. Kymer seems to have had Zurke copy standard commentaries on Galen and practical works of an old-fashioned kind (the *Practica* of Bartholomaeus, the *Rosa Anglica* of John Gaddesden). Some awareness of continental medical scholarship might be inferred from the copying of fourteenth-century commentaries by Bernardus Alberti on the *Canon* of Avicenna, and Pietro da Tossignano on the *Almansor*. Whatever the immediate fate of these books, it is clear that Kymer meant the university to have a nucleus of medical

7 CBMLC vi. A20.1168–250.

books which would serve as a resource for the doctors, MAs and bachelors of Oxford.[8]

In Cambridge a similar development took place, this time under the aegis of the Cambridge doctor Roger Marchall (fl. 1436–77). His role in furnishing Peterhouse and King's colleges with medical books has been studied by Linda Voigts. Forty-four manuscripts survive with evidence of his ownership or use, plus another six manuscripts that were possibly his, and records of twelve more that are now missing. As Linda Voigts has remarked, 'his manuscripts were clearly a personal working library, frequently consulted. However, Marchall must also have seen his books as his contribution to his alma mater and perhaps as his way of furthering the professional training of physicians.'[9] Apart from writing one manuscript himself, Marchall commissioned or assembled others, annotated or illustrated many of them in his own hand, and in nearly all cases supplied readers' aids in the form of lists of the contents of books on flyleaves. These contents lists furnished access to nearly 150 medical texts, and as many on astrology and astronomy. He deliberately excluded from his lists any texts written in the vernacular, clearly showing that his own commitment was to Latin medical learning, not to the dissemination of medical knowledge beyond the academic community in Cambridge. This is the earliest example I know of deliberate segregation of one kind of medical learning from another; as we saw earlier, language was the most consistent basis of this kind of exclusion.[10] Marchall gave or bequeathed medical manuscripts to Peterhouse and King's, the Cambridge colleges which made specific provision for fellows to study medicine in their statutes, and consequently the colleges to which almost all of those who studied medicine in fifteenth-century Cambridge belonged.

The traffic in medical books at these colleges was not restricted to donations to the college library. In his study of early collegiate loan chests at Peterhouse and Corpus Christi colleges, Roger Lovatt has found that twenty-four medical books were pledged at Peterhouse between 1456 and 1500, by ten different fellows (half of the total fellowship). He concludes that ownership of medical books was widespread at the college. But those who pledged medical books

8 On Kymer and his book-collecting and disposals see A. C. de la Mare and S. Gillam (eds.), *Duke Humfrey's Library and the Divinity School, 1488–1988: an exhibition at the Bodleian Library, June–August 1988* (Oxford, 1988); L. E. Voigts, 'Scientific and medical books', in *BPPB*, 345–402, esp. 385–6, and R. C. Ralley, 'The clerical physician in late medieval England', unpublished PhD thesis, University of Cambridge (2005), esp. ch. 2.

9 L. E. Voigts, 'A doctor and his books: the manuscripts of Roger Marchall (d. 1477)', in R. Beadle and A. J. Piper (eds.), *New science out of old books: studies in manuscripts and early printed books in honour of A. I. Doyle* (Aldershot, 1995), 249–315, esp. 265.

10 Jones, *Medical Latin*, 119–21.

were not the medical fellows but other fellows who would quite happily lodge these books in the chest as security against loans of cash, since they did not have frequent need of them. Yet the biggest owner of medical books in the college, Thomas Deynman, later a royal physician, resorted to the chest many times between 1474 and 1487, and not a single book that he pledged was medical. He needed *his* medical books for ready consultation. The *electio* system, by which a portion of the college library was borrowable by the fellows for a year, might seem a promising source of insights into how medical books were actually used within the college, were it not for the fact that *electio* was often abused by the fellows to provide themselves with pledges against loans. So medical books could form a sort of mortgageable capital as well as provide material for study.[11]

The early initiatives in the way of collegiate collection-building did not always, as we have seen at both Oxford and Cambridge, actually achieve the desired results. Despite the intentions of the donors, manuscripts too readily went astray, whether legally or illegally. However, they do constitute evidence that in the manuscript era such institutional collections as those at Merton or the university library in Oxford, and at Peterhouse and King's at Cambridge, were thought of as repositories of medical learning on which students and fellows in medicine might draw – evidence of both co-operation and continuity (to draw on Michael Hunter's observations about archives of a later era) in the husbanding of intellectual resources.[12]

Fate determined that neither co-operation nor continuity would count for much. As Philip Gaskell pointed out, the fate of medical collections in college libraries was largely determined by factors which affected those libraries as a whole, in both Oxford and Cambridge. As well as, first, the replacement of outdated manuscript texts by new printed ones, we must take into account 'secondly, wholesale disposal of the books belonging to the loan [*electio*] collections, which were not replaced; thirdly, the purging of library books on doctrinal grounds by the successive visitations of the Reformation and counter-Reformation; and, fourthly, the loss of library books as a result of maladministration and neglect'.[13] These worked together to produce disastrous consequences, notably for the library at King's, one of the two principal medical collections in Cambridge. From perhaps 500 books in 1528, with a

11 R. Lovatt, 'Two collegiate loan chests in late medieval Cambridge', in P. Zutshi (ed.), *Medieval Cambridge: essays on the pre-Reformation university* (Woodbridge, 1993), 129–65.

12 M. Hunter (ed.), *Archives of the scientific revolution: the formation and exchange of ideas in seventeenth-century Europe* (Woodbridge, 1998).

13 P. Gaskell, *Trinity College Library: the first 150 years* (Cambridge, 1980), 7.

good collection of medical reference works, the total library was only 113 in 1557, and there was only a handful of books left in a room with broken windows and furniture by the late 1560s. The only medical book to survive this holocaust was a manuscript given by Roger Marchall, now MS 21 at King's. At least the fruits of his generosity survive in this single example. Meanwhile, the university library at Oxford, to which some of Gilbert Kymer's medical books had finally found their way, disappeared in total by the mid-century, and the library furniture itself was sold in 1556.

Private libraries were not subject to the full force of these malign influences, of course, and we know that prominent English medical humanists like Thomas Linacre, John Clement and John Caius were able to build useful private collections. Linacre made his the foundation collection of the library of his new College of Physicians, gifting his books with his house to the college in 1518. Unfortunately, neither these books nor any lists that might have been made of them have survived, though we do have lists of the books of Clement and Caius. Ironically, we know of Clement's library only because he had to sue to get it back from confiscation in 1549, when he returned (for a period) from his exile at the hands of the Edwardian reformation. Actually, the collections of Clement and Caius are more remarkable for their conservatism than for any extensive garnering of the fruits of the new humanism. They are more like savings from the wreckage of medical culture than testimonies to a bright new Renaissance dawn, packed as they are with incunabular or early sixteenth-century editions of the Arab and medieval expositors and commentators.[14]

Yet if the mid-sixteenth century was the nadir for institutionalised medical libraries in Oxford and Cambridge, private initiatives on the part of medically qualified academics, allied to changes in the organisation of the book import trade, rapidly changed that. By comparison with the medical humanists who hunted manuscripts in libraries in Europe and the Middle East, the doctors of the Elizabethan era were stay-at-homes, venturing sometimes to Basel or other protestant universities. But they were great buyers of books and, unlike, say, Provost John Argentine of King's in an earlier generation (who had built up his medical library in Padua, even inscribing his books, in Venetian dialect, 'questo libro e mio zouan argentein'), these Elizabethan doctors relied on the book trade and efficient channels of import. They were greatly aided by the development of the biannual Frankfurt book fair and its conveniently arranged subject-catalogues from 1564 onwards. The second half of the

14 A. W. Reed, 'John Clement and his books', *Library*, 4th ser., 6 (1926), 329–39; P. Grierson, 'John Caius' library', *Biographical history of Gonville and Caius College*, VII (1978), 509–25.

sixteenth century saw the creation of several large private medical libraries in Cambridge. Successive regius professors of medicine, John Hatcher, Henry Walker and Thomas Lorkyn, collected medical books avidly, and kept up with the latest continental medical publications.[15]

While the curriculum and academic rituals of Cambridge remained distinctly medieval in character, there is plenty of evidence, not only for the presence of large numbers of medical books among the faculty, but for their being put to use in medical study. Gabriel Harvey was medical fellow at Pembroke Hall, and his predecessor, Lancelot Browne, directed him in a course of reading that depended on this supply of books. What Harvey records in the margins of his copy of Brunschweig's *Homish Apothecary* is the Cambridge equivalent to the printed guide to medical study of Gironimo Mercuriale, edited in 1990 by Richard Durling. He was to start with Pliny and Celsus, along with the modern authors Colombo and Cardano. Brunschweig's useful compilation on distilling medicines should be accompanied by Mattioli, the commentator on Dioscorides' herbal, and Petrus Hispanus, with other antidotaries. A list of further ancient and modern authors on medicine follows.[16]

All these books were to be found among the private libraries of the medical faculty, though not in the university library. These libraries were built up by purchase, but also by bequest or donation from medical colleagues, whose previous ownership is recorded in many of the surviving books of the Cambridge regius professor Thomas Lorkyn (more than 275 separate books from his library remain now in Cambridge University Library). Conversely, Lorkyn was also a lender of books to others, and a list of loans to twenty-one individuals among his colleagues over the five-year period from 1563/4 to 1569 survives. There was clearly a great deal of trafficking in books between these men, and the private reading this enabled was really the driving force of medical study in Cambridge.[17]

The next stage was to institutionalise these 'faculty' libraries. In 1591, Lorkyn left to the university:

> all my phisicke bookes with thos that appertaine allsoe to phisicke to be kept in the inward Librarie in a gret Cubbord locked with two locks the librarie keeper to have on key and the phisicke Reader an other for him and his

15 P. M. Jones, 'Reading medicine in Tudor Cambridge', in V. Nutton and R. Porter (eds.), *The history of medical education in Britain*, Clio Medica (Amsterdam and Atlanta, GA, 1995), 153–83.

16 V. F. Stern, *Gabriel Harvey: his life, marginalia and library* (Oxford, 1979). For Mercuriale see R. J. Durling, 'Girolamo Mercuriale's *De modo studendi*', *Osiris*, 2nd ser., 6 (1990), 181–95.

17 Jones, 'Reading medicine'.

> auditors. Students of phisicke to looke one soe that the said university be at chardge to make convenient cubbords or presses or Cubbord or presse to keepe them in Locked within on yeare after my death.

The university eventually complied with the terms of the bequest, and Lorkyn's intention to create a section of the library specifically dedicated to the use of students of medicine was fulfilled. Previously, the university library had not had any medical books to speak of. Lorkyn's was not an isolated initiative. His successor as regius professor of physic, John Collins, focused on St John's College, Cambridge, as the place in which to found a medical library. He bequeathed his books to the college in 1634, knowing that the fellows of the college had just built an imposing new library, shelved, with presses and book-desks just waiting to be filled. St John's was the college of the lectureship in medicine founded by Thomas Linacre in Cambridge, and thus was a natural focus of medical teaching and learning.[18] So impressed were the medical fellows of other colleges with the library of St John's that at least one of them, Edmund Vintner of King's, added many of his own medical books to those of Collins, and the fellows of St John's followed suit. This culture of benefaction in late sixteenth- and seventeenth-century Oxford and Cambridge colleges was not restricted to medicine, of course, but in some respects the medics seem to have taken the lead. The first English doctor's bookplate is that of John Collins, and this fashion of giving elegant visual expression to the commemoration of the generosity of individuals quickly took hold.[19] Medical books also occupy a considerable place in the new donor-books begun by colleges at about this time for the same purpose, of commemorating and stimulating generosity.

The most spectacular example of commemorating a donor is that of St John's College, Oxford, which was the recipient of the most generous gift of medical books in England before the Civil War. Sir William Paddy, a member of St John's and a wealthy royal physician, gave his medical library of some 1,200 works in over 700 volumes to the college in 1602,and he followed this up by paying for a librarian and giving further large gifts of medical books before and at his death in 1634. As in the case of St John's, Cambridge, the

18 E. Quarmby-Lawrence has made extensive use of the records of donation and purchase at St John's College, Cambridge, and is currently writing a PhD thesis entitled 'The Cambridge college library in its social and intellectual context *ca.* 1550–1700'. P. M. Jones is working on a study of the lists of medical books at St John's College in the seventeenth century.

19 C. C. Peachey, 'The bookplates of medical men', *Proceedings of the Royal Society of Medicine* 23 (1930), 493–5.

college had already built a new library which was waiting to receive such gifts, but, once Paddy's gift was secured, St John's was encouraged at the expense of William Laud to build a yet more splendid library to give the books appropriate housing (where they may still be seen). St John's was not passive in the matter of building up its collections, but actively solicited such donations as that of Paddy.[20]

Similar proactive policies can be found in colleges with much smaller collections. As mentioned earlier, the library of King's College, Cambridge, was desolate by 1570, but the new provost, Roger Goade, set about changing all that. He encouraged donations from wealthy benefactors and insisted that those who were not members of the foundation, but who paid to share the commons of the fellows or scholars, should each make a parting gift of books to their alma mater. Many of these gifts were of medical books, and those fellow commoners and fellow scholars who made them had no academic or professional interest in medicine. Clearly, they were being instructed to add certain chosen medical titles to the library as their parting gift to the college. In return, they had their names inscribed in the books themselves and recorded in the splendid new donors' book of the library. The successor to John Collins as regius professor of physic in Cambridge, Ralph Winterton, a fellow of King's, was prevailed on to donate some of his books before his early death in 1636. Goade and his successors as provost were also able to tap one or two eminent medical practitioners of the day, unconnected to King's, particularly the surgeon John Banister and the royal physician Leonard Poe, both of whom gave books, and in Banister's case an anatomical model, to King's College Library.[21]

Sir Thomas Bodley was just as purposeful, of course, in rebuilding the library named after him in Oxford. The Bodleian Library started with nothing (the former library room was used as the 'phisicke scholes' by the 1570s) and had to purchase all its medical books, as in the other subjects. Many great benefactions were received in the seventeenth century as the result of the arm-twisting of Bodley or later curators of the library, but these brought in medical manuscripts (in the Digby and Ashmole collections, for example) rather than up-to-date medical books. For this purchasing of new medical books, Bodley employed the two London booksellers John Norton and John Bill. Norton imported

20 J. F. Fuggles, 'A history of the library of St John's College, Oxford, from the foundation of the college to 1660', unpublished BLitt thesis, Oxford (1975). Paddy's medical books are now catalogued and records for them are available via the Oxford Libraries Information System (http://www.lib.ox.ac.uk/olis/).

21 These remarks are based on study of the early library catalogues of King's. See also W. D. J. Cargill Thompson, 'Notes on King's College Library, 1500–1750, in particular for the period of the Reformation', *TCBS* 2 (1954), 38–54.

stock direct from Frankfurt, purchasing at the twice-yearly fairs, while Bill visited Paris, Rome, Venice and other Italian towns, picking up books for Bodley and dispatching them to London as he went. By the time the library opened to readers in 1602, the imported books had been moved from London to Oxford, and the shelving in Duke Humfrey's was organised spatially, faculty by faculty. However, by 1605, when Thomas James's pioneering catalogue was published, that principle of subject-location was already breaking down under the pressure to fill vacant shelf-space with books of a suitable size.[22] In 1605 there was already a respectable medical collection of 204 folio volumes, 113 quarto, and 221 octavo or below, giving 538 (another 120 were added between 1605 and 1612). Counting each volume as containing, on average, two different works within the same book, this would come out as something like 1,100 works out of a library total in 1612 of 15,000.[23] Thereafter this kind of count becomes even more difficult, as catalogues subsequent to that of 1620 onwards were published in author-order rather than subject-order, and the physical division of the library into faculties became lost in the overcrowding of shelves. The 1610 agreement with the Stationers Company, that the Bodleian should receive a copy of every book registered with its members, was for most of the seventeenth century unenforced, and probably unenforceable. Yet we can be reasonably certain that the steady growth of the Bodleian as a whole – which slowed down in mid-century with political disturbances and loss of patronage, but never stopped – was matched by the growth of the medical library there.[24]

While medical libraries at the Scottish universities followed the same lines of development as those in England, the culture of Gaelic Scotland and Ireland was distinctive. The study of medicine was carried out in 'schools' maintained by the more important hereditary families of doctors, under the patronage of ruling families. The schools provided the setting within which the copying of Gaelic medical manuscripts took place, apparently as the work of students. These manuscripts became the property of the writers, who might pass them on to their own pupils or at least have their pupils copy from them. Literacy among the Gaels, or at least the 'professional' classes, stemmed from the increasing part that Scots played as a language of government in the Highlands of the sixteenth century. The Beatons were the best-known and probably most important of the hereditary medical families, and they owned many medical

22 See below, 608–9.

23 The total of medical books bears comparison with the largest private medical libraries of the period (e.g. of Sir William Paddy, see above).

24 See I. Philip, *The Bodleian Library in the seventeenth and eighteenth centuries* (Oxford, 1983), and references cited there.

manuscripts. Unfortunately, most of our evidence for their collections comes from the end of the seventeenth century. When Martin Martin met Fergus Beaton, physician in South Uist, in about 1695, he reported that the latter possessed 'the following ancient Irish manuscripts in the Irish character; to wit, Avicenna, Averroes, Joannes de Vigo, Bernardus Gordonus, and several volumes of Hippocrates'. This is a representative list of the authorities on which European medicine of the late medieval period was based, and there can be no doubt that these manuscripts had been long treasured within the family. Surviving medical manuscripts in the Pennycross of Mull collection, now Society of Advocates manuscripts in the National Library of Scotland, were listed by Edward Lhuyd as in the possession of John Beaton in 1700. Again, this is predominantly a medieval collection, though John Beaton was a practising physician who kept up to date, citing, for instance, his older contemporary William Harvey.[25]

By comparison with what we know of Gaelic Scotland, our knowledge of vernacular medical libraries in Wales of the period is slim indeed. One surviving Welsh manuscript from the Myddfai area, dating from around 1400, is Bodleian, MS Rawlinson B 467. It may represent a survivor of similar traditions of family medical learning as in Gaelic Scotland, since the semi-legendary 'Physicians of Myddfai' were a Welsh medieval family of practitioners through whom such manuscripts may have descended. Other medieval Welsh manuscripts have been connected with less good reason to the 'Physicians of Myddfai', and in truth we have no certain knowledge of medical collections or libraries owned by Welsh practitioners.[26]

25 J. Bannerman, *The Beatons: a medical kindred in the classical Gaelic tradition* (Edinburgh, 1986), 89 (for Martin), 114–19 (for the Pennycross collection), and 89–119 (in general).

26 M. E. Owen, 'The medical books of medieval Wales and the physicians of Myddfai', *The Carmarthenshire Antiquary* 31 (1995), 34–44.

20

Heralds' libraries

PAMELA SELWYN

The College of Arms and its library

As early as the fifteenth century, rules began to be laid down concerning heralds and their use of books.[1] Although there is some doubt about the authenticity of the 'Ordinances and Statutes . . . for the good Government of the Office of Arms', said to have been promulgated by Thomas of Lancaster, duke of Clarence, when lieutenant-general of the army in France and Normandy between 1417 and 1421, it is probable that those parts which do not concern the office of Garter were based on genuine originals of the fifteenth century. One of these ordinances laid down that at convenient times the officers of arms were to apply themselves to the study of books of good manners and eloquence, chronicles and accounts of honourable and notable deeds of arms, and the properties of colours, plants and precious stones, so that they might be able most properly and appropriately to assign arms to each person.[2]

Under the terms of their charter of incorporation of 1484, the heralds were to establish a library in Coldharbour (their original headquarters) which was to be common to all the heralds, under the control of chapter. There, each king of arms 'had his place several for his own library'. When the house was taken away from the heralds by Henry VII, there is some conflict of evidence regarding what happened to their corporate library, but it seems that all the books were taken to the house of John Wrythe, then Garter King of Arms.

Having been granted a new home in 1555 by Philip and Queen Mary, the heralds were directed by the earl marshal, in 1568, to once again establish a library, but little seems to have been done immediately to give effect to this, and the kings of arms continued to maintain their separate libraries.[3] In 1597

1 For a concise description of the history, composition, duties and library of the College of Arms, see the website of the college: www.college-of-arms.gov.uk/About.htm.

2 A. R. Wagner, *Heralds of England: a history of the office and College of Arms* (London, 1967), 66–8; also his *Heralds and heraldry*, 2nd edn (London, 1956), 59–61 and appendix C.

3 R. Dennys, *The heraldic imagination* (London, 1978), 55 *passim*.

the ancient records and books of the kings of arms and heralds were acquired by chapter, and the nucleus of the college's unique library was established.[4] The earliest full catalogue of the college library is that made in 1618 by Samson Lennard, Bluemantle Pursuivant.[5] By that time it had become very much a professional library, reflecting the heralds' day-to-day work.[6]

Heralds and their libraries in the later sixteenth century

During the sixteenth century, the College of Arms became increasingly concerned with the custody and preservation of the pedigrees and other documents compiled during the course of their visitations and day-to-day work of granting arms to newly created noblemen and gentry – the main source of their fees then, as it still is today. It had been customary in the early years of the century for rolls of arms and other documents to be handed down from one herald to his successor in office. As has already been mentioned, there was a central library, but it lacked most of the important documents, as even those which were part of the college library were borrowed by heralds and not returned.

The distinction should perhaps be made between the day-to-day work of the heralds and their wider role in the development of Elizabethan antiquarianism. C. E. Wright wrote that 'the strongest continuous force in the fostering of antiquarian studies in the sixteenth century . . . was the College of Arms and its officers'.[7] The considerable contribution of the heralds to the furtherance of antiquarian studies arose naturally out of their duties, especially out of the researches needed to compile the genealogies associated with the visitations that were carried out regularly from the time of Henry VIII. In the course of these visitations the heralds also examined private muniments as well as public records, and it is in the books of visitations made by Robert Glover, Somerset, that copies of charters and drawings of seals first appear. In their journeying up and down the country, the heralds had the opportunity to inspect and record monuments and inscriptions in the churches of towns and villages they passed through. From these developed the invaluable class of manuscripts usually

4 Wagner, *Records and collections of the College of Arms* (London, 1952).
5 London, Coll. of Arms, MS I.II, pt ii, 1–29: 'Arms in Trick and Calendar of Bookes'.
6 Dennys, *The heraldic imagination*, 56.
7 C. E. Wright, 'The Elizabethan Society of Antiquaries and the formation of the Cotton library', in Wormald and Wright, *English Library*, 179.

designated as 'Church Notes'. The earliest of these were collected by Robert Cooke, Clarenceux, in 1569.[8] Therefore, their work made them antiquaries *manqués*. It is, nevertheless, true that several leading lights in the Elizabethan Society of Antiquaries combined the roles of antiquary and 'working' herald. William Camden, for instance, best known as the author of *Britannia*, was also Clarenceux Herald from 1597 until 1623.

Some clauses of the new code of practice drawn up in 1568 by the earl marshal, Thomas Howard, duke of Norfolk and briefly mentioned above, were the cause of considerable contention among the heralds and none more so than the one which dealt with books and libraries! In this clause all the 'Records, Rolls, Books and pedigrees' already in the library and those subsequently delivered to it by the heralds were to remain there permanently and were to be borrowed only with the consent of Garter and at least one other king of arms.[9] The only exception to this rule was that Clarenceux and Norroy or their deputies were allowed to remove books to take with them on their visitations. Although this seems a sensible arrangement, it led to numerous, and sometimes bitter, disputes. The problem lay in the question of the ownership of books already in the library and those in the possession of individual heralds which Norfolk ruled should be deposited in the library. Not surprisingly, heralds were reluctant to hand over 'their' books. Robert Glover, Somerset, questioned the wisdom of this regulation on the grounds that, as a result, every herald and pursuivant had the right of free access and 'there hath been much cuttinge out of leaves out of sondrey recordes, such entrance of Armes and pedigrees not justifiable, such stealinge away of the bookes and recordes them selfes' that 'the lyke hath not ben heard of'.[10]

These disputes about the ownership of the heralds' 'tools of the trade' rumbled on and featured prominently in complaints against William Dethick, Garter, by Glover and others, and indeed in Dethick's complaints about other heralds. Dethick was accused of removing all the best books and records into his own private study, and when he was forced to allow search to be made, eighteen folio volumes were found which proved to be 'office books'. Dethick promised to return the books, but it was not until the year after his deprivation

8 Wright, 'The Elizabethan Society of Antiquaries', 179.

9 Wagner, *Heralds of England*, 190. The 'Orders' were printed in G. D. Squibb (ed.), *Munimenta Heraldica: MCCCCLXXXIV* to *MCMLXXXIV*, Publications of the Harleian Society, n.s., 4 (London, 1985). A full text appears on the Web at http://renaissance.dm.net/heraldry/earl_marshal.html.

10 London, Coll. of Arms, Heralds MS VIII, fol. 194^{v}, quoted by Wagner, *Heralds*, 192. A librarian in the twenty-first century might be tempted to say, 'Plus ça change, plus c'est la même chose.'

of office in 1605 that eleven books were handed in.[11] In 1588, Dethick accused Robert Cooke, Clarenceux King of Arms, and Knight, Chester Herald, of stealing forty or fifty books from the library at one time. He added, with what appears to have been typical malice, that Flower Norroy and Glover Somerset had 'their parts like'.[12]

In 1595, Thomas Lant, Portcullis Pursuivant, was complaining about the sorry state of the College of Arms and raking up the old complaints about the breaking open of the office by Cooke, Glover and Knight, when it was 'rifled of many ancient books, Visitations, pedigrees, and other records'.[13] Such items are obviously considered to be of prime importance in a herald's ability to pursue his 'trade', and it seems equally obvious that by the close of the sixteenth century they were still more likely to form the 'private' library of the individual herald than to form a comprehensive collection in the 'institutional' library of the College of Arms.

Nevertheless, moves were still ongoing to gather the records together. After the death of George Talbot in 1590, following an ineffective period of office as earl marshal, a commission was set up to look into the parlous state of the College of Arms and to reform it. The commission was headed by Sir William Cecil, 1st Baron Burghley, a man who was not only Elizabeth's first minister but a man well known to have a great interest in genealogy and heraldry. Pedigrees were a decorative feature throughout Theobalds, his sumptuously decorated country house, and several coats of arms were set into the house's windows. The 'Green Gallery' at Theobalds was painted 'round the walls' with trees, 'one for every county in England, and from their boughs hang the coats of arms of those earls, barons and nobles who lived in that particular county'.[14] Under his direction, there seems to have been a move towards making inventories of the libraries of individual heralds on their deaths. This had happened earlier, as Wagner states – in connection with the unlawful removal of books from the library of the College of Arms – that 'a great number of books of arms and pedigrees were said to have been brought out of Glover's chambers after his death in 1588 and left in the public office and an inventory made'.[15] Later, these

11 BL, MS Add. 35213, fol. 33, contains 'A catalogue of such books as Sir Robert Cotton had of one Jacob Chaloner', apparently a note in answer to some official enquiry respecting Sir William Dethick's books. Jacob Chaloner (1566–1613), arms painter and genealogist, acquired the books from Dethick.

12 Wagner, *Heralds*, 220. 13 *Ibid.*

14 Quotation from S. Watkins, *In public and in private: Elizabeth I and her world* (London, 1998), 107–8. Burghley's acquisition of many of Robert Glover's manuscripts will be discussed below.

15 Wagner, *Heralds*, 220.

disappeared, but Cooke Clarenceux and Norroy saw the inventory in Dethick's hands, which suggested he had the books also. However, this appears to be largely hearsay evidence, as the surviving inventory of Glover's books, dated 1 June 1588 (discussed in greater detail below) is almost certainly of the books in his house rather than any he may have had in his office at the College of Arms.[16] It is certain that after the death of Robert Cooke, Clarenceux, in penury and debt, in 1593 an inventory was made in October of that year and Burghley pressed the heralds to purchase them for the college library.[17] Cooke's books, rolls, and records, along with those of Clarenceux Lee were finally purchased in 1597.[18] However zealous Burghley might have been to ensure that heralds' books and rolls were purchased for a 'central' library at the College of Arms, when it came to the library of Robert Glover, Somerset, Burghley himself finally contrived to secure a large part of it.[19] However, the fate of Glover's library after his death in 1588 goes some way to illustrate how the College of Arms was attempting to gather together a 'working library' for the college as a whole in the latter years of the sixteenth century, while individual heralds felt that their personal library was their greatest asset for their work while alive and as a means of raising money for their family after their death.

The library of Robert Glover, Somerset (1544–1588): a case study

Robert Glover was born in 1544, appointed Portcullis Pursuivant in 1568 and Somerset Herald in 1570, a position he held until his death in April 1588.[20] Glover, regarded by the late A. R. Wagner as the founder of modern critical genealogy, was one of the first heralds to found pedigrees on record evidence.[21] As has been mentioned above, he was also among the earliest scholars to make antiquarian extracts from monastic cartularies for use in the compilation of

16 The inventory is BL, MS Lansdowne 58, fols. 103–6.

17 The inventory is BL, MS Lansdowne 75, item 31, fols. 68–74. Wagner, *Heralds*, 221 and n. 4, draws attention to Dethick's letter to Burghley on the matter dated 5 January 1593/4. This inventory provides further insights into the make-up of a herald's library at this time.

18 Wagner, *Heralds*, 221.

19 See P. M. Selwyn, 'Such speciall bookes of Mr. Somersettes as were sould to Mr. Secretary': the fate of Robert Glover's collections', in Carley and Tite, *Books and collectors* (London, 1997), 389–401. Material from this paper is used extensively throughout this present chapter.

20 For information on Glover's career see T. C[ooper], 'Glover, Robert', *DNB*, XXII. 7–8.

21 A. R. Wagner, *English genealogy*, 2nd edn (Oxford, 1972), 364.

genealogies.[22] He was also the first to appreciate the value of early rolls of arms, of which he copied no fewer than thirty, with a 'care and reverence for the originals' which is attested by the headings which prefix some of his copies.[23] In 1584 he compiled *Glover's Ordinary*, comprising some 15,000 coats of arms, each neatly 'tricked' by him.

In the years immediately preceding his death, Glover was closely involved in the problems arising from the general unrest at the College of Arms. He wrote a paper identifying the underlying causes of the unrest and drew up a plan for their reform.[24] One result of this was to antagonise William Dethick, Garter, a violent and choleric man, who had already put Glover in fear of his life 'because of an opinion on the succession to the Crown which he had expressed in private conversation'. In fact, Glover had merely said that 'he was of the opinion of Polydore Vergil that the issue of Henry VIII were to be preferred before others'.[25] Dethick continued to persecute Glover, who finally wrote to Burghley seeking help and protection 'wher I never yet missed in tyme of need'.[26] In the course of this letter Glover provided a thumbnail character sketch of himself as a man who was 'of nature studyous and quyette abhorring contention'. He also said that he had been accustomed to draw his 'confortes' from the 'springes of yor [Burghley's] favor and goodnes' which have hitherto 'proved themselves bottomless'. Glover also noted that it was Burghley himself who had created him Portcullis Pursuivant twenty years before. In the final sentence of the letter, Glover made what was to prove a prophetic statement. He was, he wrote, 'lykely for the time to come to have few more good dayes, yf this man (being the only man lyvinge that wisheth me any ill) may have his will as he pourposeth'. Glover's fears proved well founded. Within a year, in April 1588, he was dead.

In the course of his duties Glover built up a library of medieval manuscripts as well as a considerable collection of transcripts from medieval chronicles, cartularies, state papers and rolls of arms. At his death, the disposal of his collections became a matter of concern, not only to his immediate family but also to the College of Arms; Sir Francis Walsingham, one of his executors;

22 G. R. C. Davies, *Medieval cartularies of Great Britain* (London, 1958), xv; J. H. Round, *Family origins*, ed. W. Page (London, 1930), 6.
23 A. R. Wagner, *A catalogue of English mediaeval rolls of arms* (London, 1950), xx, and 143 for a list of rolls owned and copied by Glover.
24 Preserved in London, Coll. of Arms, Heralds MS VIII. The problems are discussed at length in Wagner, *Heralds*, 169–221.
25 Quoted by Wagner, *Heralds*, 216, from 'Causes why Sir William Dethick was put from his office, 1603'.
26 The letter occurs in BL, MS Lansdowne 54, item 84, fol. 193.

George Talbot, earl of Shrewsbury; and Sir William Cecil, 1st Baron Burghley. One result of these concerns has been to provide us with much information about Glover's library.

Glover's will, drawn up on 4 April 1588, shows a great concern for the fate of his library.[27] The relevant section of the will reads: 'it may be that my bookes and other thinges which I have painefully and derely gotten may be saughte by others to the great preiudice of my saide wife and children beinge the principall parte of my substance that I shall leave unto them'. He saw his library not just as essential for his profession but as the main means of supporting his family after his death.[28] To safeguard his family he petitioned Walsingham to be their protector and friend. Further, he requested his friends Thomas Randolph and Robert Beale to 'be ayding and assistinge unto them that they maye not be defrauded of that which apperteynethe unto them'.[29] The will is remarkable for the fact that the books are the only valuables mentioned.

Glover was obviously concerned that the main part of his library would be claimed by the College of Arms as belonging to them under the terms of the 'Orders' of 1568. On 15 July 1588, Glover's executor, Thomas Milles, his nephew, wrote a long letter to the earl marshal, George Talbot, 6th earl of Shrewsbury, suggesting that Talbot himself might like to purchase the books.[30] However, Milles reveals that the College of Arms had, as feared, already intervened. He explained that the 'Officers of Arms freely confess that upon the disposing of his books depends the welfare and ruin, or discredit, of their office', and in order to facilitate this disposal they had considered petitioning the queen to provide for his family by taking his books and collections into her own hands. However, this plan appears to have failed, although Robert Cooke, Clarenceux, a friend of Glover's, had suggested to his widow that the queen should give at least 1,000 marks in return for the books, which Milles saw as providing an ongoing pension for the widow. Four months after the will was drawn up, as the widow's poverty increased, Milles heard that Talbot had 'put on a mind' to

27 The will is PCC 7 Leicester; TNA, PROB 11/73 RH 53.

28 There is evidence for the widows of other heralds sellling their husbands' libraries. For instance, Sir Edward Dering purchased books from the library of Nicholas Paddy, Lancaster Herald, from his widow for £20. N. H. Krivatsky and L. Yeandle, 'Books of Sir Edward Dering of Kent (1598–1644)', *PLRE* 4, item 475 (I. 246).

29 Thomas Randolph, Master of the Queen's Posts, had acted as Burghley's agent in Scotland and had brought the antiquary Laurence Nowell to Burghley's attention. Robert Beale, clerk to the Privy Council, *c.* 1580–90, and Walsingham's brother-in-law, had borrowed several manuscript cartularies from Glover, and extracts from them, made for Beale, occur in BL, MS Add. 32100.

30 The letter was printed, from a copy said to be in the Duke of Norfolk's collections, in the *Gentleman's Magazine* 90 (1820), 595–6. Talbot became earl marshal in January, 1572/3 and held the office until his death in 1590.

take them into his own hands. A 'Mr. Hercy' had already inspected the books and written to Talbot about them.[31] So in July 1588, the expectation was that the books and transcripts would come to Talbot, the earl marshal. It is unclear whether George Talbot subsequently purchased any of the books, and he was, himself, dead by the end of 1590.

It is tempting to speculate that events may have followed a course similar to those which attended the death of Robert Cooke, Clarenceux, in 1593. On this occasion the inventory, already mentioned above, was made on 12 October 1593 and Burghley himself pressed the heralds to purchase the books for the college library. Cooke's books, rolls and records, however, reached the college library only in 1597. Whatever may have been the true circumstances, Glover's books and collections *were* sold and a considerable number came into the possession of Burghley. Many eventually found their way by somewhat circuitous routes to the College of Arms Library and several appear to have been handed on – or indeed to have found their way back – to his successors as Somerset Herald.[32]

We are fortunate to have two main sources for details of books known to have been in Glover's library at the time of his death. In addition to the inventory made on 1 June 1588, a further list survives among the collections of Elias Ashmole at the Bodleian Library.[33] The Lansdowne document is headed 'An account of old books, rolls, and heraldic papers belonging to him [Glover Somerset] & found in his house at the time of his death in 1588'.[34] The Ashmole document is 'A Noate of such speciall Bookes of Mr. Somersettes as were sould to Mr. Secretary', copied by Ashmole on to the last folio of a collection of Glover's transcripts.[35] The inventory in Lansdowne 58 and that copied by Ashmole are by no means mutually exclusive, although the Ashmole list is almost entirely made up of genealogy and heraldry, whereas Lansdowne 58 lists

31 'Mr. Hercy' is almost certainly the John Hercy decribed as servant to the earl of Shrewsbury in the indexes to both volumes of *A calendar of the Shrewsbury and Talbot papers in Lambeth Palace Library and the College of Arms* (London, 1971), although most of his letters there calendared relate to the seventh earl. It seems likely that he acted as man of business to both earls.

32 The 'Testa de Neville', a manuscript which came into Burghley's hands, was subsequently sold with other Burghley manuscripts at auction in 1687, being purchased by the Greys of Wrest Park. It remained at Wrest Park and in the Grey family until very recently, when it was auctioned in London and purchased by the then Somerset Herald, Thomas Woodcock – so after 400 years its ownership had reverted to Somerset Herald. For a full discussion of the fate of Glover's collections see Selwyn, 'Such speciall bookes'.

33 Bodleian, MS Ashmole 836, fol. 767. For a discussion of this list and its relation to Lansdowne 58, see Selwyn, 'Such speciall bookes'. I hope to publish a fuller account of Glover's collections, identifying, where possible, the books and manuscripts in these lists and those which have survived elsewhere.

34 BL, MS Lansdowne 58, fols. 103–6.

35 I have discussed the significance of this note in Selwyn, 'Such speciall bookes', 393–4.

a considerable number of medieval chronicles as well as heraldry. In general, the lists exhibit a different approach to cataloguing. The Lansdowne inventory lists Glover's medieval manuscripts in a classified sequence numbered A to Z, A1 to Z1, and A2 to I2, suggesting that this may echo their original arrangement on his shelves. The Ashmole list, on the other hand, mentions very few of the chronicles and medieval treatises but gives far more precise details of the genealogical and heraldic items. Lansdowne contains phrases such as 'a greate heape of large paper-books piled together', whereas Ashmole has much more precise descriptions such as 'a faire greate thick booke of pag[e] Royall bound in black lether full of Armes in trick, & commonly tearmed the greate booke of Tricke'.

The Lansdowne list of 'Olde books, etc.' has been examined by Dennys from the point of view of a typical herald's library.[36] He notes that, 'as might be expected from the Ordinances and Statutes . . . for the good Government of the Office of Arms' (1417–21), Glover owned no fewer than thirty-six 'cronicques, actes et gestes d'honneur [et] faictz d'armes', which ranged from Eutropius' *History of Rome*, Bede's *Historia ecclesiastica*, William of Malmesbury's *Historia regum Anglorum*, Geoffrey of Monmouth, Gildas and Giraldus Cambrensis' *Expugnatio Hibernica*, to three copies of the *Flores historiarum*, and a copy of the Brut.[37] The fifteenth-century 'Ordinances' also enjoined heralds to read 'livres de bonnes moeurs [et] elequence', but these are poorly represented in Glover's library, although he did have a copy of John Gower's *Confessio amantis*, a Bible and a 'Booke of cardinoll vertues', which might fall into this category. Of the remaining books, at least six concerned matters of law or state and four concerned ceremonies such as coronations and funerals, which loomed large among the heralds' duties and which, in the case of the latter, were a rich source of fees.[38] Among his books were three identifiable treatises on heraldry. There was a copy of Bado Aureo's *Tractatus de armis*, and a copy, made by Glover himself in 1572, of Baddesworth's version of Nicholas Upton's *De studio militari*.[39] There was also a book of the statutes of the Order of the Golden Fleece. Dennys comes to the conclusion that, although Glover acquired his library in the mid-sixteenth century, 'all the chronicles and heraldic treatises

36 Dennys, *The heraldic imagination*, 56.

37 *Ibid*. The Brut MS can be identified as College of Arms, MS Vincent 421.

38 Glover, in his letter to Burghley, was particularly bitter that Dethick had failed to summon him to attend the funeral of Mary, Queen of Scots.

39 Dennys identifies this with the beautifully illustrated College of Arms, MS Vincent 444. There are versions of these works by Bado Aureo and Upton in at least two other manuscripts known to have passed through Glover's hands, BL, MSS Add. 37, 526, and Stowe 668, which contains a French translation.

were either originals or copies of works compiled at a much earlier period', suggesting the 'kind of library that a fifteenth-century herald would also have collected and used'.[40] However, the chronicle texts listed above were largely to be found in monastic libraries prior to the Dissolution and were beginning to circulate more widely among scholars only after 1550.

The Lansdowne inventory is valuable, not only for the list of manuscripts which it provides, but also for the description of the 'furniture' and arrangement of Glover's library. It is the account of 'old books, rolls, and heraldic papers' in the first section of the inventory that best illustrates the nature of a herald's 'working library' – both its content and the way it was stored.[41] His collections, including the unbound documents and rolls, were housed in two 'studies', described as the 'Upper Study towards the gardin', and the 'great Study next the Streat', which also contained a 'Gallery'.[42] The inventory also gives a graphic description of the library 'furniture' in which the books, rolls, and pedigrees were stored.

The 'Upper Study' contained a press which was divided into '2 boxes' which were 'full of divers rolls, pedigrees, etc.', and another 'large Roome' which was divided by 'partitions' into further boxes which were also full 'of Rolles & Bundles of matters of pedegrees & heraldry'. The room also contained a 'cubbord' with six boxes, 'eche Box full of wrytinges of sevrall natures', which touched upon 'thorder of ye Garter, Coronations, Burialls, Parliament Rolls, etc.' Another three 'cases of boxes', each marked with 'alphabet Letres on ech Box', were full of 'armours, Evidences & Sealles'. Yet another 'large case of boxes' housed 'more thinges of sundrie natures touchinge heraldry', and a further 'Frame of shelves' – presumably the equivalent of an upright bookcase – contained 'Bagges of parchemyn of sundry natures'. A familiar sight in most modern scholars' libraries, there was also a 'great heape of large paper-books piled together'. These had been 'bought sometimes of Richmond Herald' and were 'all heraldry'.[43] This illustrates the way in which books were not only passed on from office-holder to office-holder but were also 'sold on'. This 'Upper Study' also housed 'sondrie faier paper Books endorsed *Confuseanor[u]m*, beinge collections & readinges: all of his owne hande and sett together by themselves'. These transcripts are also noted in the Ashmole list as 'Ten other Bookes of his Collec[ti]ons bound in Velim & endorsed Confuseanea'.[44]

40 Dennys, *The heraldic imagination*, 56. 41 *Ibid.* 42 BL, MS Lansdowne 58, fol. 103.

43 'Richmond Herald' may be identified as either Hugh Cotgrave (in office from 1566 to 1584) or Richard Lee (in office from 1584 to 1594), but more probably Cotgrave.

44 There is further evidence of these *confuseana* in a manuscript of transcripts by William Smith, Rouge Dragon, made in about 1600, which is now BL, MS Harley 245. Part 2 of this

The inventory of the Upper Study then lists 'divers other paper books of visitations of xxiiij Shires' which are all 'of his owne hand'. These are the books compiled by Glover during his visitations and form the core of a herald's library. The Ashmole list notes 'Thirteene Bookes of visitac[i]ons' which have been compiled 'out of the pedigrees' of gentlemen in 'Yorkshire, Staffordshire, Suff: Huntingdon, Dorsett, Devon, Kent, Wiltsh: Oxfordsh: Bedford, Northumberland, Durham, North[amp]ton, Lancaster & Norff.' In other words, they had been copied from personal records and muniments presented to the heralds by local gentry during their visitations of these counties.

Several of these visitation records certainly passed into Burghley's hands, as they occur in a third document that provides information on the make-up of Glover's library, namely the 1687 *Sale catalogue* of the library of the earl of Ailesbury, which included a large number of manuscripts which belonged to Burghley, several of which are annotated in some copies as being in Glover's hand.[45] The 1574 visitation of Kent was copied in 1677 by Gregory King, Rouge Dragon, into College of Arms, MS H2, and was collated with 'an Original of Robert Glover, Somerset Herald now in the Library of the right Honourable Robert, earl of Aylesbury' which had been 'borrowed for that purpose by Sir William Dugdale'.[46]

Three more shelves in this study contain yet more 'books of his owne hand & travaill' which contain collections of pedigrees, 'armes' and 'matters of hearaldry'. Other parts of the study contain yet more books of heraldry and 'papers of historie' and 'a smale grope of bookes bought of Turpyn sometimes Herald'.[47] This is another example of heralds selling books to fellow professionals. Finally, there were 'Certain books bound in velym full of Armes tricked by his self'. It was the function of a herald, not to produce printed books dealing with genealogy, but to use the information he had copied from documents and muniments seen on his visitation journeys, from chronicles and cartularies both in private ownership and kept in 'public' collections such

manuscript contains on fol. 74^{r} (O. F.76) the words 'Incipit Liber / CONFUSANEARUM, B / Robti. Gloveri Somersettj Heraldi'. The manuscript was subsequently owned by Sir Simonds D'Ewes; see A. G. Watson, *The library of Sir Simonds D'Ewes* (London,1966), 145, List A, [346].

45 The catalogue, published by T. Bentley and Benjamin Walford, offered for sale the 'Bibliotheca illustris . . . viri cujusdam praenobilis ac honoratissimi olim defuncti'. Among the 'Manuscripts of Heraldry, &c in Folio' (Lots 1–38), lots 25–31 list books of visitations. In some copies of the *Catalogue*, lots 27–30 are marked in ink as being 'per Glover'. Several other items in this section and elsewhere in the *Catalogue* are also marked as being written by Glover.

46 Wagner, *Records and collections of the College of Arms*, 70.

47 Richard Turpin was Windsor Herald between 1562 and 1581.

as those in the Tower of London, to draw up pedigrees for noble families[48] – often beautifully painted and 'tricked' – and to devise coats of arms for those newly ennobled.

The contents of the 'great Study next the Streat' are not listed in such detail, but echo the pattern of storage in the Upper Study. There is a press in which are placed 'sondrie Bookes', bound in vellum, 'endorsed *Miscellaneor[u]m*' and again 'all of his owne hande'. These 'miscellanea' are also mentioned in the Ashmole list as '12: Bookes faire bound in Velim & endorsed on the back Miscellanea'. Ashmole MS 848 is one of these miscellaneous collections.[49] In the 'same presse' are to be found yet more 'faire books of his owne hande-writinge of sundrie matters'.

Glover's large collections of transcripts have survived in many collections and show him collecting information from cartularies, charters in the possession of individuals, chronicles, 'state papers' and inscriptions found in churches, as well, of course, as the heraldic rolls and books borrowed from other heralds. For example, the extracts in Harley 245 consist of pedigrees taken *inter alia* from the monastic register of Blyth Priory, from charters held by families such as the Lisles of Gosford and the Shirleys of Staunton – these presumbly collected during visitations he conducted – and extracts from 'records in the Tower', such as the Close and Patent Rolls, and Exchequer documents. Similarly, in BL, MS Cotton Otho D. iv – a manuscript from the collection of Sir Robert Cotton – are extracts in Glover's hand from the monastic registers of the 'Monasterij de Furnesia' (Furness in Cumbria) and from the Abbey of 'Oseney in Com. Oxon.', and pedigrees from 'Scotichronico cap. 19, 1265'(Fordun's *Scotichronicon*). Exchange of papers and information between heralds is illustrated in the same manuscript by an entry containing a pedigree of the Chaloner family.[50] This pedigree, Glover writes, was: 'copyd and sent to Sr Arthur Champernoun knight, and that copy was lent unto me Somerset by R. Lea Portcullys. In January 1582 by the which this was here copyd.'

Finally, the same press in the Great Study contains four 'drawers or boxes' of 'armours, Rolles of Armes, etc.' These 'armours' and rolls of arms form

48 For instance, the magnificent roll compiled and painted for the Cecils by Cooke Clarenceux and Glover, which is now at Hatfield House.

49 In a transcript of Bodleian, MS Ashmole 848 in MS Ashmole 860, Ashmole refers to the former as 'Robert Glovers book "D" of manuscript collections'. William Smith's transcripts in pt 1 of BL, MS Harley 245 are headed 'Liber Miscellaneorum Roberti Gloveri Somerseti Heraldi'.

50 BL, MS Cotton Otho D. iv, fol. 157. This manuscript was said by Thomas Smith in his *Catalogue of the manuscripts of the Cottonian Library, 1696*, ed. C. G. C. Tite (Woodbridge, 1984), 75, to have once belonged to Lord Burghley – another of Glover's books that came into his possession after 1588.

the most basic 'tools of the trade' used and compiled by heralds. Glover was the owner of at least two important medieval rolls of arms (*Thomas Jenyns II*, a vellum book given by Jenyns to Glover in 1578, and the early fourteenth-century *Holland's Roll*).[51] Glover owned the *Rous Roll* – also called the Beauchamp Pageant – one of the most spectacular of the medieval rolls of arms. This is listed among his books as item X.1 in the Lansdowne list, where it is described as 'The life of Richard Beauchamp Erle of Warwick'.[52] In addition, Glover made copies of at least thirty-two medieval rolls, several of which survive only in the copies made by him, the originals having been lost.[53] Twenty-three of these transcripts are in Oxford, Queen's Coll., MS 158, a manuscript bequeathd to the college by Sir Joseph Williamson (1633–1701).[54]

Glover also copied from such documents and created his own pedigrees and rolls of arms. BL, MS Cotton Otho D. iv, for instance, contains on folios 187–92, 'Armes des chevaliers qui furent al tournement fait á Donstaple, 1333'. These are extracts by Glover from the Second Dunstaple Roll, which is usually dated to 1334. The original roll of 136 names and blazoned arms is apparently lost and it is only through transcripts such as this that it survives.[55] In 1584 he compiled his *Ordinary*.[56] A further manuscript compiled by Glover is his 'Baronagium Angliae'. This also came into Burghley's possession and, with many other Glover manuscripts, was sold in the 'Ailesbury' sale in 1687, and finally reached the British Library as MS Egerton 3792.

The last entry relating to the Upper Study states that there were yet more books of heraldry stored in the same press but these were 'sett by themselves', presumably meaning that they were shelved separately, away from the other items. This study also boasted a gallery, presumably shelves arranged at a higher level and reached by steps leading to a narrow walkway. This contained 'two cases of boxes full of old Evidences & Seales'. This seems to imply that there were yet more transcripts, pedigrees and seals which were placed – no doubt – in neatly labelled boxes. Possibly these were used less frequently, as they were housed in a less accessible part of the library.

Given the number of surviving transcripts in Glover's hand, it is not surprising that so much space was given over to them in the cases and boxes

51 For a list see Wagner, *Catalogue of English medieval rolls of arms*, 143.

52 It is now BL, MS Cotton Julius E. iv. A facsimile edition of the manuscript is Viscount Dillon and W. H. St John Hope (eds.), *The Pageant of the birth, life and death of Richard Beauchamp, earl of Warwick, KG, 1389–1439* (London, 1914).

53 These are listed and discussed in Wagner, *Catalogue of English medieval rolls of arms*, 143 and *passim*.

54 For a list of the transcripts in this manuscript, see *ibid.*, 132–3.

55 *Ibid.*, 40–1 and 76.

56 Wagner, *Heralds*, 343–4.

forming his library. This inventory provides a fascinating picture of a herald's library towards the close of the sixteenth century, with its shelves, boxes and cubbyholes holding piles of loose papers, copies of pedigrees, rolls of arms, some stored in boxes or perhaps kept in the kind of velvet bag that is used today. Glover's library may have been exceptional in its size and in the number of medieval manuscripts and original rolls of arms that he owned, but it must have been very typical of the working library of a herald towards the end of the sixteenth century.

PART FOUR

*

LIBRARIES FOR LEISURE

21

'The profession of a gentleman': books for the gentry and the nobility (*c.* 1560 to 1640)

PAMELA SELWYN AND DAVID SELWYN

The great era of country-house libraries – often perceived as 'libraries for leisure' – was undoubtedly the eighteenth century, but evidence survives for more than a hundred 'gentry' libraries during the period 1560–1640 and many more have, no doubt, disappeared without trace. By any standards, some of these were significant collections, rivalling in size those of many institutions and many belonging to professional men such as churchmen and lawyers. We aim to look at the libraries of both the nobility and the gentry for this period and attempt to place them in the context of the great social and political changes that were taking place in the period encompassing the end of the Tudor dynasty and that of the first of the Stuarts, culminating in the anarchy of the Civil War, which destroyed and dispersed many libraries.

Gentlemen's libraries come in all shapes and sizes during the eighty years covered by our survey and a similar diversity can be seen in the attitude of their owners to books and learning in general. Ownership of a library did not of itself imply a scholarly outlook or deep learning.[1] The stereotype of the pleasure-loving, hunting and hawking country gentleman is certainly well attested in our period: 'never a lover of bookes, butt of all corporall exercises and pleasures, as dancing, hunting, hauking, and such country sports, which made him of a robust complexion' was a grandson's tribute to Sir William Guise of Elmore.[2] But this was only part of the picture, as surviving gentlemen's libraries, catalogues, inventories and their own scholarly activities bear witness. Henry Knappe, for example, let it be known that a work he had just completed (now BL, MS Stowe 41) had been 'translated by myselfe at Pyrton in the intervalls of my Hunting & Hawking times, Anno 1632'. This suggests a good

1 F. Heal and C. Holmes, *The gentry in England and Wales, 1500–1700* (Basingstoke, 1994), 80.

2 Quoted in J. T. Cliffe, *The world of the country house in seventeenth-century England* (New Haven, CT, 1999), 156.

balance of the cerebral and the outdoor life, but the implied antithesis between reading and physical pursuits occurs again and again, and the scales could also be tipped the other way, as in this tribute to the gentleman scholar, Sir Richard Worsley of Appledurcombe House in the Isle of Wight, from his neighbour Sir John Oglander: 'wonderful studious, insomuch as he affected no counterye spoortes, eythor hawking or huntinge, but whollie spent his tyme when he wase alone att his booke'.[3]

However, it would be unwise to generalise. There were some, like Sir Thomas Lucy III (d. 1640), Sir Henry Yelverton, and Lady Anne Clifford (d. 1676), who were proud to be remembered by posterity for their love of books; in Sir Thomas's case, by having the titles of his favourite classical authors carved on his funerary monument at Charlecote Church, Warwickshire, in a scene which also shows him in the very gentlemanly pursuit of riding the 'great horse' (ironically, a fall from just such a horse was the cause of his death).[4] Sir Henry Yelverton and his wife are shown semi-reclining on their elbows in front of a portion of their library in a memorial at Easton Maudit, Northamptonshire;[5] and in Lady Anne's case, the celebrated 'Great Picture' of 1646, a triptych now displayed at Appleby Castle, depicts her with shelves of books in the background, emblematic of her bookishness and learning.[6]

What made a man a gentleman between 1560 and 1640? In the case of the sons of noblemen, it was undoubtedly their birth. However, the redistribution of land in the wake of the monastic dissolutions (from the 1540s) resulted in the creation of many new 'gentlemen', who sought to mirror the lifestyle of the older aristocracy, using their newly acquired lands and wealth to build houses in the new style, with long galleries to display their newly acquired pictures and a library room to display their newly purchased books as well as their 'cabinets of curiosities'. Shakespeare at the end of the century would bemoan the fact that now 'every Jack has become a gentleman'.

During the course of the sixteenth century the whole concept of a gentleman's role in society had been undergoing a sea change. It was no longer conceived narrowly in terms of military service to one's liege lord – in the case of noblemen, the king. Noblemen increasingly found a new role as administrators. They served as ambassadors and diplomats in the king's service, on duty

3 Cliffe, *World of the country house*, 168.
4 Heal and Holmes, *Gentry in England and Wales*, 267, pl. 22.
5 N. Pevsner, *The buildings of England: Northamptonshire* (Harmondsworth, 1961), 192 and pl. 34b.
6 D. J. H. Clifford (ed.), *The diaries of Lady Anne Clifford* (Stroud, 1990), 98–99; for a fuller study of Lady Anne and her 'Great Picture' see also G. Parry, *The seventeenth century: the intellectual and cultural context of English literature, 1603–1700* (New York, 1989), 80.

in foreign embassies, or as holders of one of the great offices of government such as lord treasurer or secretary of state.

The change is signalled in the series of manuals for those who wished to be a 'perfect gentleman', published over the century from 1530 to 1630, setting out 'rules' for the conduct of a gentleman's life. Among the earliest – and undoubtedly the most influential in a European context – was Castiglione's *Il cortegiano* (*The courtier*), published in Italy in 1527 and translated into English by Sir Thomas Hoby during his years of 'retirement' in Mary's reign – finally appearing in print during the year 1561.[7] A Latin version by Bartholomew Clerke appeared in 1571 (*STC* 4782), frequently reprinted on the Continent as well as in England (*STC* 4783–7) and an Italian, French and English version, in parallel columns, was published in London in 1588 (*STC* 4781). Castiglione's work epitomised the changing attitudes, giving wider currency to a new social ideal: that of the educated and 'refined' Renaissance man for whom the Court (as Lawrence Stone has put it) was 'the natural centre of the universe'.[8] Hoby's dedicatee was Henry, Lord Hastings, son and heir of the earl of Huntingdon, one 'trayned up all his life time in Court, and of worthy qualities', and it was Hoby's intention that the new translation, under such noble patronage, would enable Castiglione's precepts to reach a wider audience.The purpose of *The courtier* is summed up as follows:

> To princes and Greate men, it is a rule to rule themselves that rule others . . . To men growen in yeres, a pathway to the behoulding and musing of the mind, and to whatsoeuer elles is meete for that age: To yonge Gentlemen, an encouraging to garnish their mindes with morall vertues, and their bodye with comely exercises, and both the one and the other with honest qualities to attaine unto their noble ends: To Ladyes and Gentlewomen, a mirrour to decke and trimme themselves with vertuous condicions, comely behauiours and honest entertainment toward al men: And to them all in general a storehouse of most necessary implements for the conuersacione, use, and training up of mans life with Courtly demeaners.[9]

Such a rule would fit both men and women, young and old, to enter the 'profession' of a gentleman or gentlewoman at court.

Castiglione's work occurs widely in surviving gentry libraries of the period – in the original Italian, Hoby's English translation, Clerke's Latin version, and in

7 B. Castiglione, *The courtyer; done into Englyshe by Sir Thomas Hoby* (London, 1561) (*STC* 4778).

8 L. Stone, *The crisis of the aristocracy, 1558–1641* (Oxford, 1965), 400. 'The Court [Stone continues] was as essential to the good life . . . as the City State to Aristotle.'

9 Quoted from Lord Lumley's copy of *STC* 4778, now at the British Library, 1030.c.13, A3^{v}.

other European languages. It is listed, for example, in the 1615 Salisbury House shelf-list of the Cecils,[10] in the catalogue of Sir Thomas Knyvett's library at Ashwellthorpe (1618),[11] the inventory of about 1625 of Sir Roger Townshend (two copies of Clerke's Latin version),[12] and in the library of Sir Edward Coke (1634 – a copy of the French edition).[13] It also occurs among the books of William Drummond of Hawthornden (both Hoby's and the Italian original) in the 1620s.[14] John, Lord Lumley's copy of Hoby's translation, once at Nonsuch and transferred with the rest of his library to that being assembled for Prince Henry in 1609, is now in the British Library (Lumley 1643; BL, 1030.c.13). The library of the Hamilton family, earls of Haddington, formerly at Tyninghame House and now housed in the National Library of Scotland, actually contained two editions of the Spanish translation by Juan Boscan as well as a copy of the Italian original, but seemingly no copy of Hoby's English translation.[15] Castiglione is also among the authors whose books are depicted in Lady Anne Clifford's 'Great Picture' of 1646.[16]

Castiglione's work, however, did not hold complete sway in England. Running parallel to it were anglicised versions which emphasised service to the prince in the country as well as at court. This theme runs from Sir Thomas Elyot's *The boke named The Governour* (published in 1531, *STC* 7635) down to Richard Brathwait's *English gentleman* and his *English gentlewoman* which appeared in 1630 and 1631 respectively.[17] The full title of Brathwait's books give a clearer idea of their purpose:

> The English gentleman: containing sundry excellent rules, or exquisite observations, tending to the direction of every gentleman of selecter ranke and qualitie: how to demeane or accomodate himselfe in the manage of publike

10 In the case 'Bookes of Diverse sortes'. Now at Hatfield House. We are much indebted to the librarian and archivist, Robin Harcourt-Williams, for allowing us to use his transcript of the shelf-list and to the marquess of Salisbury for permission to quote from it. On the reception and influence of *The courtier* see Peter Burke, *The fortunes of The Courtier: the European reception of Castiglione's* Il Cortegiano, Pennsylvania studies in the history of the book (Pennsylvania State University Press, 1996).

11 D. McKitterick, *The library of Sir Thomas Knyvett of Ashwellthorpe, c. 1539–1618* (Cambridge, 1978), entries 748 and 1123.

12 R. J. Fehrenbach, 'An inventory of books in the possession of Sir Roger Townshend, ca. 1625', *PLRE* 3 (1. 79–135), items 41 and 53.

13 W. O. Hassall (ed.), *A catalogue of the library of Sir Edward Coke* (New Haven, CT, 1950), item 1095, the French edition, Paris, 1569.

14 R. H. McDonald (ed.), *The library of Drummond of Hawthornden* (Edinburgh, 1971), entries 719 and 1212.

15 The copies are now in the National Library of Scotland with the shelf-marks *Tyn. 90* (Anuers, 1574), *96* (Anuers, 1561) and *4* (Venice, 1587).

16 G. Parry, *Seventeenth century*, 80; Clifford, *Diaries of Lady Anne Clifford*, 98–9.

17 *STC* 3563 and 3565 respectively.

> or private affaires [and] The English gentlewoman, drawne out to the full body expressing what habilliments doe best attire her, what ornaments doe best adorne her, what complements doe best accomplish her.

Another work in the same tradition was Henry Peacham's highly successful book entitled *The compleat gentleman*, which appeared in 1622.[18] This contained a eulogy of the Renaissance ideal for the aristocracy, which shows how well Castiglione's courtly model had endured,[19] even if somewhat tempered by first-hand experience of the 'new' court of King James I and his Scottish courtiers, as Lady Anne Clifford found on her first introduction to the court in 1603, when it was meeting at Robert Cecil's great house, Theobalds. She and her mother were received 'very graciously' but 'we all saw a great change between the Fashion of the Court as it is now and that in the Queen's time'.[20]

It was, above all, the education of the gentleman which was receiving increasing emphasis as the sixteenth century progressed. Sir Thomas Smith (1513–77) and Sir John Cheke (1514–57) would have heartily endorsed the slogan 'Education. Education. Education' for the young gentleman of the time. In the 1530s Thomas Starkey had lamented that 'with us . . . gentlemen study more to bring up good hounds than wise heirs' and 'First and most principall of all ill customs used in our country commonly . . . [is] that which toucheth the education of the nobility, whom we see customarily brought up in hunting and hawking, dicing and carding, eating and drinking, and, in conclusion, in all vain pleasure, pastime and vanity.'[21] However, by the middle of the century, gentlemen were increasingly being urged to obtain 'professional training'. As a result, there was an explosion in the number of gentlemen attending the universities and the Inns of Court. Young women, too, were included in this push towards education, resulting in what has been called the 'first great age of the bluestocking', notable among the learned ladies being the famous Cooke sisters, Lady Jane Grey and Elizabeth I herself. Mildred Cooke – William Cecil's second wife – read and wrote Greek and Latin fluently, having greater fluency in Greek than her husband. She made many donations of books to Oxford and Cambridge colleges and to schools such as Westminster and King's, Canterbury, as well as owning a collection of her own, well stocked with editions of the Greek Fathers and contemporary writers, and making considerable use of her husband's library. Her books, annotated in the language of the text, are

18 *STC* 19502. 19 Stone, *Crisis of the aristocracy*, 401.

20 Clifford, *Diaries of Lady Anne Clifford*, 22.

21 Stone, *Crisis of the aristocracy*, 674–5. See also Roger Ascham, *The scholemaster*, London, 1570 [*STC* 832], dedicated to Sir William Cecil, especially *A preface*, where the same point is made.

now widely dispersed, but some nineteen survive at Hatfield House, alongside those of her husband. The Howard family also ensured that their children – boys and girls alike – were given a good education. Lady Katherine Howard, daughter of the ill-fated earl of Surrey and wife of Henry, Lord Berkeley, kept up with her Latin grammar, was skilful in French, 'perfect', we are told, in Italian, a student of natural philosophy and astronomy, familiar with globes and quadrants, as well as the more usual female accomplishments such as playing the lute.[22] Care also had to be taken to ensure that appropriate books were made available to the fledgling gentleman and gentlewoman. Thomas, 3rd Lord Paget, was making purchases in 1580 with the education of his son, William, and the needs of his tutor, Adam Robyns (a fellow of King's College, Cambridge), in mind.[23]

There was no shortage of good advice available for – and from – fathers, for the education of their children. Elyot himself, for example, had advocated a study of Latin and Greek from the ages of seven to thirteen to be followed by a rigorous university education – although even he advocated physical education to strengthen the body.[24] Again, Lord Burghley – half a century later – was among the most fervent advocates of a sound classical grounding for young gentlemen, and the Cecils' library at Salisbury House in the Strand was well stocked with just such reading. As chancellor of Cambridge University, he advised Sir John Harington, of Kelston, who was at Cambridge in 1578, to read Cicero for the Latin language, Livy and Caesar for Roman history 'exceeding fitt for a gentleman to understande', and Aristotle and Plato for logic and philosophy. His object was to produce 'a fytte servaunte for the Queene and your countrey for which you weare born and to which, next God, you are most bounde'.[25] As master of the Court of Wards, Burghley presided over the education of many fatherless young gentlemen entrusted to his care, and has provided us with details of a typical day in the education of the twelve-year-old Edward, earl of Oxford – a ward in his household in 1562. At 7 in the morning, the day began with a dancing lesson, followed at 7.30 by half an hour for breakfast; from 8 until 9 it was French, followed by an hour's Latin from 9 to 10. From 10 to 10.30, writing and drawing provided some relief, and the morning was rounded off by prayers and dinner at 10.30. The afternoon began with cosmography from 1 to 2, more Latin from 2 to 3, and French again from 3 to 4. Lessons ended with writing from 4 to 4.30, and the boy was finally released

22 Stone, *Crisis of the aristocracy*, 676–7.

23 A. H. Anderson, 'The books of Thomas, Lord Paget (c. 1544–1590)', *TCBS* 6 (1975), 226–42, esp. 228–9.

24 Stone, *Crisis of the aristocracy*, 677.

25 *Ibid.*, 679.

at 4.30 with prayer and supper. Even during the holidays, he was enjoined to read the epistle in Latin and English before dinner, and afterwards, the gospel in English or Latin. What remained of the holiday, however, could be spent in riding, shooting, dancing and other exercises.

A gentleman's library reflected not only the collecting tastes of its owner but the needs of the household for which he was responsible. Several surviving libraries and inventories of the period provide evidence of being well stocked with books for the education and recreation of the young gentleman in mind, as well as exercises once penned by children to impress their parents. After her marriage (c. 1552/3), Jane, Lady Lumley, dedicated and sent her translations of 'Isocrates orations ad Nicolem. &c. out of Greeke into Latin' and 'Euripides tragedie called Iphygenia, translated likewise by hir out of greeke into English and written with hir owne hande' to 'my lorde of Arundell' her father. These childhood exercises became part of the Arundel-Lumley collection and are now in the British Library with other items from the Old Royal Library.[26] Similarly, 'Lady Anne Cecil's French grammar in English and French' was listed in the catalogue of the Ailesbury Sale of 1687, which contained considerable numbers of books and manuscripts once owned by Burghley.[27] Lady Anne's autographed copy of a French grammar published by Robert Stephanus (Estienne) in 1549 survives at Hatfield House.[28]

While the sons of protestant gentlemen were increasingly being sent away to school, the pre-university education of most young noblemen and gentlemen and the entire education of the gentlewoman was generally carried out at home by means of a private tutor – usually a graduate straight from university – who became part of the household, drawing on what resources were available to him in its library. Such tutors were often a major influence in forming the tastes of their charges. Thus Samuel Daniel, having once been her tutor, was a great influence on the reading tastes of Lady Anne Clifford. For instance, in a diary entry for 28 January 1618, she notes that 'Rivers used to read [to] me in Montaigne's *Plays* and Moll Neville in *The Faerie Queene*'. Both these authors were a strong influence on the poetry of Daniel and, obviously sharing in his enthusiasm, in 1620 she 'mad a monument for Mr. Spenser the pouett and set it up at Westminster'.[29] Spenser's works are also prominent on the shelves

26 BL, MS Royal 15.A.ix; no. 1920 in S. Jayne and F. R. Johnson (eds.), *The Lumley library: the catalogue of 1609* (London, 1956).

27 *Bibliotheca illustris: sive catalogus variorum librorum . . . viri cujusdam praenobolis ac honoratissimi olim defuncti* (London, 1687). 'Manuscripts in English, folio', 89, lot 36.

28 *Traictes de la grammaire françoise*. At Hatfield House (no. 15742).

29 Clifford, *Diaries of Lady Anne Clifford*, 47–8 and p. 48n*.

behind the young Lady Anne on the left-hand panel of her 'Great Picture' of 1646.

It is also clear that young gentlemen furthered their education in mainland Europe, a course of action strongly recommended by Peacham himself,[30] though they were no doubt well aware of the objections of such as Joseph Hall, voiced in his *Quo vadis?* (1617). Brian Hillyard has suggested that a group of forty-five books formerly in the library of Thomas Hamilton, 1st earl of Haddington (1563–1637) – now part of the Tyninghame collection at the National Library of Scotland – may have been acquired while he was a student in France, which was a common destination for young Scots pursuing their education in the sixteenth century and later.[31] All these books are signed 'MTHamiltoun' in an italic hand, and they include a number with French imprints which bear annotations suggestive of notes made during lectures.

The sons of English noblemen also travelled abroad to polish their French and attend the great French riding school at Paris, where they learned how to school and manage the 'great horse' and also the finer points of fencing, dancing and music. Knowledge of how government worked in Europe was also useful and necessary for a young man who intended a career as a diplomatist. For those who still sought a career in the military arena, knowledge of fortification and techniques of siege-warfare could best be learned in the camps of Europe.[32]

Several letters have survived written by anxious parents to their sons on the eve of their departure for mainland Europe or written to the luckless tutor whose task it was to control the high spirits of the young man but who had to report certain worrying trends in his conduct. It is clear that in the eyes of most parents their son's continental visit was not to be in any sense a holiday. In 1541 Lord Cobham had laid down strict ground rules for the conduct of his son, William.[33] The young man was to 'pray each morning, go to mass, study civil law, rhetoric, and Greek, obey his tutor in all things, keep his body chaste, write home regularly, practise on the lute and other musical instruments, observe foreign forms and customs – and not talk too fast'. At the bottom of this formidable list, the boy had solemnly written, 'I wyll performe aull thes thynges bi the grace of God by me your sonne/ Wylliam Brooke.'

Thomas Cecil's visit to Europe in 1561 certainly multiplied the grey hairs on his father's – William Cecil's – head. His tutor, Thomas Windebank, constantly

30 H. Peacham, *The compleat gentleman* (1622), ch. 16.

31 B. Hillyard, '"Durkan and Ross" and beyond', in A. A. MacDonald, M. Lynch and I. B.Cowan (eds.), *The Renaissance in Scotland: studies in literature, religion, history and culture offered to John Durkan* (Leiden, 1994), 367–83.

32 Stone, *Crisis of the aristocracy*, 692.

33 *Ibid.*, 693.

complained that his charge was completely out of control, throwing away money on horses, gambling, and generally ignoring any pretence of learning. Windebank, completely at the end of his tether, begged to be recalled to England, as he could cope no longer. Thomas had been enjoined to write to his stepmother, Mildred, in French on a regular basis, although one can imagine that the formidable Mildred would not have been easy to please. In fairness, Cecil was well aware of his eldest son's intellectual limitations and only required him to be able to cope with conversational French and Italian.[34] However, when it came to the proposed visit to Italy, Cecil put his foot down and forbade Windebank to take his charge across the Alps, where untold temptations and dangers awaited the young. He advised fellow parents: 'suffer not thy sonnes to passe the Alpes'. Thomas somewhat redeemed himself in later years, distinguishing himself as a soldier, building a fine house with magnificent gardens in the latest style at Wimbledon, and donating several fine volumes of classical texts to the Bodleian Library, Oxford.[35] However, Thomas never really regained his father's affection, his brother Robert in effect became Lord Burghley's heir, and (rather poignantly) there are books from his library which have 'W. Burghley for my son Thomas', with the 'Thomas' crossed through and Robert's name substituted.[36]

The turn of the century saw the first stirrings of 'cultural tourism' to Europe. Englishmen began to visit France and Italy to see the paintings and architecture inspired by the Renaissance and to view the antiquities. 'Guide-books' for the gentleman abroad were also appearing in significant numbers for the first time. Sir Robert Dallington, a member of the circle around Henry, Prince of Wales, wrote his *View of France* in 1598 (it was published in 1604),[37] a copy of which is listed in the inventory (*c.* 1625) of Sir Roger Townshend,[38] and one also survives from the library of Sir Thomas Egerton.[39] Published in 1605, Dallington's *A method of travell*[40] – a reissue of his previous work, with new preliminaries – gave detailed and practical advice to the intending gentleman

34 *Ibid.* For a fuller discussion of Thomas Cecil's 1561 tour of Europe with his tutor, Windebank, see P. M. Black, 'Some new light on the career of Laurence Nowell the antiquary', *Antiquaries Journal* 62 (1982), 116–23.

35 List of nineteen Greek MSS given in 1618, listed in the *Bodleian benefactors' register*, 220–1; also in *Bodleian library records: 1613–1620 day book*, II, fols. 86^r–87^r. This was one of many such donations that enriched university and college libraries at this time.

36 One such example occurs at the foot of the title page of John Baret, *An alvearie or triple dictionarie* (London, 1573, *STC* 1410); dedicated to Burghley (Hatfield, 7945).

37 London: printed by Symon Stafford, 1604, *STC* 6202.

38 Fehrenbach, 'Sir Roger Townshend', *PLRE* 3, item 253.1.

39 At Harvard University Library (*STC* 6202).

40 London: printed by Thomas Creede (1605?); *STC* 6203.

traveller, warning him of the dangers of changing his religion, advising him of the best centres and recommending 'readers' to develop his language skills and practise conversation. This would be a far better use of his time than attending their universities, which, in the liberal sciences, were 'farre inferiour to ours' ($B2^v$). Dallington also suggested what money to bring and the likely expenses to be incurred for fencing, riding and paying his servants. Particularly pertinent was Dallington's advice about bringing books: 'let them be few or none', lest books be found which were prohibited by the inquisition or subject to some local tax ('gabell'). Better to buy what is needed on the spot, especially books 'not to be got here in England' and, on leaving, 'send them home by his merchants meanes' (Ci^v). His advice may go some way to explaining the large number of standard texts in French and Italian that occur in gentlemen's libraries. How far such gentlemen were encouraged to seek inspiration and reading matter in continental libraries – institutional and private – in the course of their travels is not clear. It was to be some years before Lomeier published his guide to European libraries,[41] but Dallington included a brief description of the Medici library at San Lorenzo in Florence in his *Survey of the great Dukes State of Tuscany in . . . 1596*, published in 1605 (*STC* 6200), with its 'three thousand nine hundred books very finely bound in leather, after one sort, all bound to their seates . . . in number sixty eight' ($C2^v$) – a book which was owned by Sir Roger Townshend.[42] Such guide-books included places to visit, architecture and other sights to view, and much information about the country, the people and its government.

Armed with such books – though not always heeding their advice – young men set out with new enthusiasm. In 1603, the twenty-three-year-old Dudley, Lord North, was in Antwerp, where he was clearly enjoying himself, gambling, going to plays, playing tennis and generally seeing the sights. However, in the midst of this he did find time to buy a copy of Camden's *Britannia* and obtain a 'new binding' for a book of fortifications, and may possibly have read Plato's *Republic* and a history of the Low Countries.[43] The Scottish gentleman poet, William Drummond of Hawthornden, as a young man purchased over 300 books while in France studying law between 1606 and 1608.[44]

41 Johannes Lomeier, *De bibliothecis liber singularis*, 2nd edn (Utrecht, 1680), ch. x. The first edition had appeared in 1669.

42 Fehrenbach, 'Sir Roger Townshend', *PLRE* 3, item 253.2 (1.130). Sir Roger also owned Joseph Hall's dissuasive *Quo vadis?* (item 3.185).

43 Stone, *Crisis of the aristocracy*, 696–7.

44 McDonald, *Library of Drummond of Hawthornden*, 37–40.

The product of this new emphasis on education, acquired both at home and in the course of travel abroad, was an aristocracy that now often comprised men of letters, scholars, collectors and connoisseurs, willing to act as 'Maecenas' to the poets, dramatists and writers of the age. Some were also men of letters themselves. For instance, Henry Percy, the 9th earl of Northumberland – better known as the 'wizard earl' – prepared a vast treatise on the art of warfare,[45] while his interest in horse-racing (in which he himself took part in the 1580s), military strategy and philosophy, led to works on the care and training of horses, the building of forts and the immortality of the soul being dedicated to him.[46]

The libraries

What is known about the number, size and content of the libraries of gentlemen and the nobility during the Elizabethan and early Stuart periods? Not nearly as much as we would like, and this is even more the case with those of gentlewomen.[47] Despite the pioneering work of Sears Jayne in identifying contemporary catalogues, inventories, donations, household and booksellers' accounts,[48] and the current *Private libraries in Renaissance England* (*PLRE*) project, no full-scale study of gentlemen's libraries has yet been attempted, and the database for such a study is still small and largely unresearched. The position is not helped by the omission of most private collections – no doubt for very good reasons – from the two editions of the *Directory of rare book and special collections* (1985 and 1997).[49] Heal and Holmes are substantially correct in claiming that 'gentry libraries have been researched only patchily for our period'.[50]

The book collections of gentlemen and the nobility were subject to the same vagaries and accidents of survival as institutional libraries and those of the professions during the period: loss through fire and other physical damage and war, and disposal, dispersal and division, arising from collections passing

45 G. R. Batho, 'The library of the "Wizard" Earl: Henry Percy Ninth Earl of Northumberland (1564–1632)', *Library*, 5th ser., 15 (1960), 249–50.

46 Batho, 'Library of the "Wizard" Earl', 249.

47 See D. McKitterick, 'Women and their books in seventeenth-century England: the case of Elizabeth Puckering', *Library*, 7th ser., 1 (2000), esp. 363.

48 Jayne.

49 *Directory of rare book and special collections in the United Kingdom and the Republic of Ireland* (London, 1985); 2nd edn, ed. B. C. Bloomfield (London, 1997).

50 Heal and Holmes, *The gentry in England and Wales*, 278.

from owner to heir, and from the rise and fall of family fortunes – political, economic and marital. A number of potentially important collections were lost or dispersed during the Civil War, such as those at Raglan Castle (the Royalist marquis of Worcester) and Wardour Castle (the Royalist Arundells). Of the 139 collections for which at least some statistical information exists (twelve from Scotland, four from Wales, and the remainder from England), thirty-six fall within the period up to and including 1600. For the period as a whole, only a little over fifty have been, or are in the course of being, edited, and a further thirty have been described in varying detail. There are round-figure, or in some instances more precise, numbers for many of these libraries, but the figures given in some inventories are very approximate estimates, like the '3 cart loads' of the 1st Lord Hatton at the end of our period. In some cases the existence of a collection is known only from a few identified armorial bindings.

A further difficulty occurs with collections which are known only by donations to university and college libraries, for this was a period when such institutions were actively soliciting gifts to restore libraries which had suffered much in the turmoil of the Reformation period. Many of these books came from gentry and the nobility, often from donors who had no obvious links with the institutions concerned and far more in number than the figures suggested in the pioneer survey by Sears Jayne: some thirteen up to 1600, and twenty-eight from 1601 to 1640. In such instances, it may not be known, for example, whether the donation represents the whole library of the donor or only a part of it; or even whether the donor had a library at all, since the books may have been purchased (perhaps after advice) with money given by the donor – the purchases sometimes being made long after the donor's death. Moreover, it may not be known how far the subject-matter of the books donated is truly representative of what was in the donor's own collection (if he even had one) and how far they were a selection of what was judged to be appropriate to the needs or preferences of the receiving institution. Consequently, inferences drawn from records of donations have to be treated with some caution.

There are problems, too, about estimating the size of some of the larger libraries even when catalogues or inventories have been edited or identified. Some lists are clearly incomplete. Only music volumes, for example, are recorded in the case of Sir Thomas Kitson of Hengrave,[51] and by contrast

51 *Ibid.*

the shelf-list for the Cecils' library at Salisbury House in the Strand (1614/15) gathers all the musical material under the single entry, 'Diverse Bookes of musicke and songes'.[52] The music may well have been much more than a minor component in that collection, since Robert Cecil (1563–1612), 1st earl of Salisbury, was a notable patron of music.[53]

Again, the gentry and, even more, the nobility often owned London properties as well as houses in the country, with libraries or at least smaller collections in each, and some of these may not figure in surviving booklists. The eighty books listed in the 1577 inventory at Longleat are not the totality of Sir John Thynne's collection, for he had books in his other residences,[54] and there were books of Edward Paston's in three of his Norfolk homes.[55] Estimating the size of a particular collection is also complicated by the fact that some owners disposed of books to friends or institutions during their lifetime. In the case of Lord Lumley, for example, while we have details of his gifts to Oxford and Cambridge, books donated to friends come to light from time to time only as a result of chance discoveries. Some collections were divided among several children on their owner's decease. That of William Cecil, 1st Baron Burghley (1520–98), for example, was divided between his sons, Thomas and Robert. Again, a collection like that of Henry Fitzalan, 12th earl of Arundel, is difficult to reconstruct with any accuracy because 'duplicates' were disposed of when it was merged with that of his son-in-law, Lord Lumley, after the latter joined him at Nonsuch in 1557.

The library of William Cecil, 1st Baron Burghley, poses a special problem. Cecil is known to have had books 'at court', as well as in residences in the Strand, London, Theobalds, north of London (neither of which, sadly, survives) and in Burghley House in Northamptonshire. The shelf-list of the printed books at Salisbury House in the Strand (now at Hatfield House) was made some years after his death and includes books of his son Robert, who had died in 1612, just as Hatfield House was nearing completion. We have no lists relating to Theobalds, Burghley House in the Strand or Burghley, his great 'prodigy house' in Northamptonshire. The problem in Cecil's case is further

52 The entry occurs at the end of the section, 'Philologie'.

53 On Robert Cecil, see L. Hulse, 'The musical patronage of Robert Cecil, First Earl of Salisbury (1563–1612)', *Journal of the Royal Musical Association* 116 (1991), 24–40.

54 For this information we are grateful to Dr Kate Harris, who is preparing the list for publication.

55 P. Brett, 'Edward Paston (1550–1630): a Norfolk gentleman and his musical collection', *TCBS* 4 (1964), 67.

complicated by the existence of a sale catalogue of 1687,[56] which purported to offer his library for sale but failed to distinguish genuinely 'Cecil' items (such as many of the manuscripts) from later printed books and some other manuscripts, which could never have belonged to him because of their date. Over 200 of his books are now at Hatfield House, built by his younger son, Robert; a very few (originally through his son Thomas) still remain at Burghley House, and what remains of the rest is scattered throughout the world as a result of the 1687 sale and earlier dispersals. To a large extent (and this must be the case with many libraries of the period) the size and content of such libraries have not only to be inferred from such catalogues, inventories and household accounts as survive but also supplemented from the books that remain.

In the face of such uncertainties, it may be unhelpful to ask what constitutes a large library in this period, particularly since what may have been a comparatively large collection in the 1560s – of (say) 200 or more books – may seem relatively insignificant in the 1630s. In the period up to 1600 there is sufficient information to suggest that two libraries – both of noblemen – exceeded 1,000 books: those of Arundel (d. 1580) and Burghley (d. 1598), while that of Francis Russell, 2nd earl of Bedford, may have exceeded 600 printed books and manuscripts (list of 1584). Among gentlemen, there is evidence for three libraries of about 400 books: those of Sir Thomas Smith (1566), Richard Stonley (1597) and William Gent (1600). In the period up to the 1640s, the surviving collections increase in number and size, as we should expect. The largest for which evidence exists is that of the 2nd earl of Arundel, Thomas Howard (1646), at some 4,500 books, and that of the Sidney family at Penshurst may have been of a similar size. Earlier, Lumley's library at Nonsuch had consisted of about 3,000 items in 1609 (excluding earlier donations and disposals), and Sir Thomas Tresham's (*c.* 1605), which has been estimated by Sears Jayne at about 2,600.[57] Two other notable collections exceeding 2,000 books were those of Sir Robert Gordon of Gordonstoun (about 2,350 by 1640, but continuing to expand up to the time of his death in 1656) and Henry Wriothesly, 3rd earl of Southampton (1624). Another eight, although smaller than these, exceeded in size any collection of the gentry or nobility in the period up to 1600:

56 *Bibliotheca illustris*.

57 Jayne, 138, xii (where the list is assigned to Tresham). Closer examination of BL, MS Add. 39, 830, fols. 155^v–214^r, reveals that there are here two overlapping lists with much duplication. The total number of items may actually have been much smaller than suggested.

Owner	Date	Approximate size
Richard Branthwaite	1620	1,750
Henry Percy, 9th earl of Northumberland	1632	1,500–2,000
William Paget, 4th Baron Paget	1628	1,550–1,600
Sir Thomas Knyvett, of Ashwellthorpe	1630	1,484
William Drummond, of Hawthornden	1627	1,407
Cecil library at Salisbury House	1615	1,314
Sir Edward Coke	1634	1,227+
Lord Edward Herbert, baron of Cherbury	1648	940+ books at Montgomery Castle

On a smaller scale, an increasing number of women had collections in their own right in addition to using those of their husbands. Before 1600, however, information is only sketchy. The puritan Catherine, duchess of Suffolk, is reputed to have had a 'chest full' of books in 1580, and a few survive with ownership inscriptions of Jane, Lady Lumley (Arundel's daughter) and Mildred Cecil, wife of Lord Burghley (some of these being donations to colleges). In the period after 1600, there were donations of probably over 100 books to Oakham parish church in 1616 by Ann Harington, wife of John, 1st Baron Harington of Exton, and 180 to Sidney Sussex, Cambridge, by her daughter, Lucy, countess of Bedford, in 1628. Class catalogues of somewhat larger collections are extant for those of Frances Egerton, countess of Bridgewater, in 1633 (241 items) and Frances Wolfreston, who owned about 240 books by 1641. This growth is what we might expect and it reflects the expansion of private libraries in general during the seventeenth century.

Studies, closets and library rooms

Simon Jervis, in his recent discussion of country-house libraries, has suggested that the origins of private libraries lie in rooms such as the 'little study called the newe Librarye', which Henry VIII had at Westminster.[58] He had many other studies, at Westminster, at Windsor and at Greenwich.[59] The 'little study' at Westminster did, it is true, house a few books, but its use resembled that of a muniment room rather than a library, as it contained 'sundry wrytinges from sondrie places beyond the Sea', 'bulle's', 'treatise & commissions for

58 S. Jervis, 'The English country house library', in N. Barker, *Treasures from the libraries of National Trust country houses* (New York, 1999), 13.

59 BL, MS Harley 1419 A and B, fols. 186^{r}–188^{v}.

peace', 'wrytinges concerning the ordre of Saynte Mychaell', and 'plattes and petygrees' in leather and canvas bags, in coffers, in boxes, and in a 'cupboard full of tilles' (i.e. 'drawers'). There were also two oak desks containing writing instruments (silver ink boxes, scissors, penknives and a pencil) and spectacle cases. Shelves supported 'paternes for Castles and engynnes of warre', and the room also contained measuring and surveying instruments and a 'great globe of the descripcion of the Worlde'. The presence of an elephant's 'toothe', a series of handsome cabinets and coffers covered in velvets or painted leather, two coffers of mother-of-pearl with silver mounts, twenty-four enamelled plaques of the Nine Worthies and other subjects (presumably from Limoges) and an unfinished portrait of Henry VIII himself suggests that this room most closely resembled the 'cabinet of curiosities' of art and nature associated with the collectors of the early seventeenth century (such as Sir Robert Cotton) and referred to by Sir Henry Wotton in his *Elements of architecture*, published in 1624, as 'Repositories for workes of rarity in Picture or other Arts, by the Italians called Studioli'. Some of the other items stored in the little study or 'newe librarye' suggest that it more closely resembled an up-market lumber room. Among these were 'one Angling roode of rede' and no fewer than fifteen velvet collars for hounds. Also at Westminster, the 'Kynges secrete studie', called the 'chaier house', was fitted with forty-four compartments in four tiers of eleven. This, however, contained no books, but another miscellaneous collection of treasures.

In an inventory of the goods belonging to Henry, Lord Stafford (1501–63), drawn up in 1565/6, the books seem to have been kept in four classes or cases in the gallery of Stafford Castle, but were actually used in a well-lit study on the ground floor near the garden. This study was furnished with a reading desk, two cupboards and a large trestle table. Such a room might have had some resemblance to the later Kederminster Library (1631).[60] Peacham, in *The compleat gentleman* (1622), had timely advice to give about the location of such studies and the general care of books: 'To auoide the inconuenience of moathes and moldiness, let your studie be placed, and your windows open if it may be, towards the East' rather than to the south or west, and 'suffer them not to lie neglected', but 'haue a care of keeping your bookes handsome and well bound'. His warnings were as pertinent then as they are now: 'our mappes and pictures will quickly become pale, loosing their life and colours, or rotting vpon their cloath, or paper, decay past all helpe and recouerie'.[61]

60 Illustrated in Heal and Holmes, *The gentry in England and Wales*, pl. 23.
61 1622 edn, 54f.

As collections grew in size, books were often distributed in different parts of the house. Sir William Ingleby's books, according to the 1618 inventory of Ripley Hall, Yorkshire, drawn up after his death, had been kept in the new study, the old study and the dining parlour, and where no separate library room existed this practice continued throughout the seventeenth century.[62] Sometimes there is information about how the books were distributed among these different locations. The 1588 inventory of Robert Glover, Somerset Herald, for example, describes in some detail the way in which his books and papers were stored in the various 'studyes'. Here, again, the various rolled up pedigrees, charters and seals were kept in sets of drawers, with the books arranged on shelves in numbered presses.[63] Books, however, were frequently kept in chests. In a 'noet of my lo[rds] books' made in 1584, the collection of Francis Russell (*c.* 1527–85), 2nd earl of Bedford, seems to have been kept 'in the long Trunck', and, 'in the great cheast bound with iron', there were no fewer than 190 books.[64] Business papers were also kept in chests. Lady Anne Clifford wrote in 1619 that she 'brought down with me my lady's [her mother, the countess of Cumberland] great trunk of papers to pass away the time, which trunk was full of writings of Craven and Westmorland and other affairs, with certain letters of her friends and many papers of philosophie'.[65] Books were still being kept in this way in the 1650s by John Holles, 2nd earl of Clare.

Gentlemen's book collections were frequently distributed among their various residences. For instance, Edward Paston (1550–1630), a Norfolk gentleman, kept some of his many music manuscripts in a chest, a closet and four 'trunckes' in the gallery in Appleton Hall (near Sandringham in Norfolk) as well as other items in the 'Study next the Parlor', but there were other books at his properties of Thorpe Hall and Town Barningham.[66]

Evidence exists, too, for a number of compact travelling libraries early in the seventeenth century made up of a selection of miniature books. Four examples have been identified, each with three shelves of small gold-tooled vellum-bound volumes, containing about forty-four books each, on theology and philosophy, history and poetry, placed in a wooden box, the lid of which contains on the inside an ornately decorated catalogue, while the outside of

62 Cliffe, *World of the country house*, 163–6.
63 The inventory is BL, MS Lansdowne 58, fols. 103–6. See also above, 476–84.
64 M. St Clare Byrne and G. S. Thomson,'My Lord's books: the library of Francis, second earl of Bedford in 1584', *Review of English Studies* 7 (1931), 396–405.
65 Clifford, *Diaries of Lady Anne Clifford*, 66, annotation 51.
66 P. Brett, 'Edward Paston', 67.

the box gives the appearance of a leather-bound folio volume. These were evidently all gifts, very probably by the same donor, the barrister William Hakewill, to friends and patrons who included Sir Thomas Egerton (who died in 1617), Sir Julius Caesar, Master of the Rolls, a member of the Madden family, and one of the sons of Sir Nicholas Bacon. Other collections of miniature books with the same purpose in mind were made for Henry, Prince of Wales, and Prince Charles.[67]

Closets – small rooms within the private apartments of a gentry family – were frequently used both to store and to read books. A design for a closet made by the English architect Richard Smythson in about 1600 shows four elevations fitted out, apart from door, chimneypiece and window, with shelves divided into compartments and with four built-in desks. Some of the compartments are identified as 'For a mape', 'For loose papers', 'for writings' and 'For Incke'. This rather austere room seems more akin to a muniment room or an estate office than a room in which to enjoy a leisurely read. Nevertheless, we have a diary entry of Lady Anne Clifford for the use of a closet as a 'reading room'. She writes on 26 April 1617 at Knole: 'I spent the evening in working and going down to my Lord's Closet where I sat and read much in the Turkish History [*The Generall historie of the Turkes*, by Richard Knolles] and Chaucer.'[68] Again, a month later, on 24 May, she provides further evidence of the use of the closet as a library: 'The 24th we set up a great many of the books that came out of the North in my closet.'[69] The reference is to her library which had recently been brought down from the Clifford estates in the north, left to her uncle on her father's death.

The inventory drawn up on the death of Henry Percy, the 'Wizard Earl', in 1632 shows both chests and closets still being used for books. However, 'chests of books of all sorts fifty-two, and to fill twelve small chests besides' were kept in the library itself along with seventy-seven pictures, including 'twelve Turks' and 'twenty-four Emperors' and many 'curiosities'. Also, 'in the closet belonging to the Old Earl's chambers' were 'books in folio forty-four, in vellum of all sorts twenty-eight, pamphlets of all sorts thirty-three'. The inventory provides no evidence of shelving.[70] Again, in 1618, Sir William

67 W. A. Jackson and H. M. Nixon, 'English seventeenth-century travelling libraries', *TCBS* 7 (1979), 294–32.

68 Clifford, *Diaries of Lady Anne Clifford*, 54.

69 *Ibid.*, 56.

70 Batho, 'Library of the "Wizard" Earl', 250. For a recent reassessment suggesting 'an early form of the Pepys-type freestanding bookcase' see S. West, 'Studies and status: spaces for books in seventeenth-century Penshurst Place, Kent', *TCBS* 12 (2002), 266–92, esp. 271.

Ingleby's books shared the old study at Ripley Hall, Yorkshire, with items such as a sparrow net, a lark net, horse collars and bridles.[71]

The idea of a separate library room for the display of books on shelves took hold only gradually even among the wealthier gentry, as Cliffe points out.[72] Early in the period there is evidence from Longleat, the residence of Sir John Thynne, where in 1563 two Frenchmen, a sculptor and a joiner, were hired for work which included the decoration of the porch, the panelling of the gallery and work on bookcases for the library.[73] At the end of the period, an inventory of 1634 drawn up on the death of Sir Edward Zouch describes a room in his newly completed Jacobean mansion as a library containing 250 books. If the class-catalogue of Lord Lumley's library made by Anthony Alcock in 1596 was based simply on an inspection of the books on the shelves, then the collection at Nonsuch was arranged in a large room according to seven subject classes, with some, particularly theology, occupying a number of cases.[74] This seems to have been the case at Salisbury House in the Strand. The 1614/15 catalogue of books 'in your lordships library' – one of the many London houses of the Cecils – suggests a large library room with three cases on the left and four on the right, accommodating in all about 1,300 books. If a survey and plan made by Sir Christopher Wren in 1706 is to be believed, the library built at St James's in 1609–10 to accommodate the book collection of Henry, Prince of Wales, was located on an upper floor of the palace at the extreme south-east corner. The room was 25ft by 35ft, divided lengthways by a fitting which seems to have had a double stack of shelves or boxes. The interior was not exclusively utilitarian, as payments to the master sculptor Maximilian Colt reveal the addition of an elaborate fireplace and 'four greate arches over the passages in the library, with architrave round aboute them and the Princes armes in the spandrils'. The decoration also included both Ionic and Corinthian capitals, pyramids, pendants and satyrs.[75] It was not, however, until the end of the seventeenth century that the libraries of English country houses became the elegant rooms with ornate decoration, lined with books in uniform bindings, that we see today.

A library room furnished with bookcases rather than chests or trunks was a place where finely bound books could be displayed to advantage and shown to visitors, and there are many examples of owners from this period who valued their books in this way. Lumley, despite the size, range and historical

71 Cliffe, *World of the country house*, 163. 72 *Ibid.*

73 D. Burnett, *Longleat: the story of an English country house* (London, 1978), 32, 34.

74 Jayne and Johnson, *Lumley library*, 9–10, 32–3.

75 R. Strong, *Henry, Prince of Wales and England's lost Renaissance* (London, 1986), 210.

importance of his collection, does not seem to have cared much for the elegance of his bindings,[76] and in this respect he differed from his father-in-law, the 12th earl of Arundel, whose fascination with things Italian, his love of music (evident in the music section of what remains of his library) and for books as beautiful objects in themselves may explain the presence of such items as a finely bound Aldine Aristotle (the work of the Medallion binder),[77] the *Psalter and ten canticles*, calligraphically written by the Florentine Petruccio Ubaldini in 1565 (BL Royal MS 2 B.ix) and the copy-book *Specimens of calligraphy and illumination* from the same source (*c.* 1550–3), dedicated to his young son, Lord Maltravers, who died tragically young in 1556 (BL, MS Royal 14.A.i), three examples among many.

Two other such owners may be mentioned: Thomas Wotton (1521–87), the 'English Grolier', whose library was distinguished by books which were elegantly printed and adorned with fine bindings, often in the French style, some of which he may have acquired when he was in France in 1547;[78] and Robert Dudley (1532/3–88), earl of Leicester, who was almost as much a patron of English bookbinders as a friend and patron of scholars and poets, and whose surviving books can be identified by the quality of their bindings.[79]

Lord Burghley's library may have been essentially a working collection – witness the large number of his books and manuscripts covered in functional vellum covers – but his 'private passions' included genealogy and cartography, and these are combined in his interleaved, hand-coloured copy of Ortelius' Atlas at Burghley House with its additional maps, annotations, inserted genealogies and memoranda in his own hand, noting the correct mode of address of such luminaries as the tsar of Russia.[80] Despite much rebinding of his books in the early eighteenth century, several examples of fine bindings – some of them presentation copies – survive from his library, such as his copy of Ariosto's *Orlando furioso* (in the translation of another gentleman scholar, Sir John Harington) – now in the British Library (C.57.h.1) – and another atlas, this time by Mercator (1589), Jan Laski's presentation copy of his *De sacramentis* (1552), and the Dutch edition of Wagenaar's *Mariner's mirror* (1584), all now at Hatfield House.[81]

76 Jayne and Johnson, *Lumley library*, 12, n. 1.

77 H. M. Nixon, *Five centuries of English bookbinding* (London, 1978), pl. 15 (42).

78 M. M. Foot, *The Henry Davis gift: a collection of bookbindings* (London, 1978), 1. 139–55.

79 Foot, *Henry Davis gift*, 1. 27–34; for examples, see Nixon, *Five centuries of English bookbinding*, pls. 16 and 17.

80 We would like to express our thanks to Lady Victoria Leatham for allowing us to examine the 'Burghley Atlas'.

81 Nixon, *Five centuries of English bookbinding*, pl. 24 (60) for the Ariosto.

Libraries and their contents

Although a number of booklists have been published and some dispersed libraries reconstructed, a great quantity of future research, publication and analysis is necessary before anything like a comprehensive view of gentlemen's libraries can be attempted.[82] Until then, the way forward lies in particular case studies. This is just as well. No two libraries – nor the preferences of any two book-collectors – are the same, whatever the degree of similarity.

Two case studies in particular will be considered, though reference will be made to other published catalogues already mentioned. Both were relatively large collections for the time: one of a family of noblemen and state servants, the other of a Scottish gentleman. Neither has yet been published. The first is the library of the Cecils' London house in the Strand (Salisbury House), for which there is a 'Catalogge' of their printed books (more accurately a shelf-list) dating from 26 January 1614/15. This evidently includes books formerly owned by William, 1st Baron Burghley, who had died in 1598, those of his son Robert (d. 1612), 1st earl of Salisbury, and William, who had very recently succeeded to the earldom. Slightly more than 1,300 volumes are listed. Only the author, short title-description and the format (folio, quarto, etc.) are given.

The second is that of Sir Robert Gordon of Gordonstoun (1580–1656), historian of the House of Sutherland, courtier (when he had time from his other activities), active soldier, part-time diplomat, landowner and (it might be added) traveller, because he must have spent much of his time on the move between his Sutherland estates, the court of James I and VI in London, and the Close at Salisbury, home of his wife Lucy, Dean John Gordon's daughter, whom he married in 1613. Gordon's library, now dispersed, can be reconstructed with some certainty from the manuscript catalogue of 1743 now in the National Library of Scotland (MS 3804), and the printed sale catalogue of 1816. By 1640, Gordon's library was considerably larger (at about 2,350 items) than that of the Cecils at Salisbury House, but the difference may be more apparent than real, since Gordon's included a very large number of pamphlets (political, historical

82 The important library of William, Lord Howard of Naworth, currently being researched by Dr Richard Ovenden, is discussed below, 539–43, and the 1577 inventory of Sir John Thynne's at Longleat is being prepared for publication by Dr Kate Harris. The *Libri pertinentes* series has a number of studies in progress, such as that on the 9th earl of Northumberland (the 'Wizard Earl'), and that on William Cecil, 1st Lord Burghley, and it is hoped to include the 1615 inventory of the Cecils' library in the Strand. The inventories associated with the Hattons (now at the Northampton Record Office), and the library of some 3,000 books built up by the Robartes family at Lanhydrock in Cornwall (now in the care of the National Trust) are also being researched.

and ecclesiastical) which are individually listed in the index, while the Salisbury House catalogue is a shelf-list describing only the first item in each bound volume.

On the evidence of these and other contemporary catalogues it is abundantly clear that such libraries were not exclusively for 'leisure'. It might have been expected that a 'recreational' component (such as is detailed in Marcia Vale's survey of gentlemen's recreations)[83]and the known interests of the owner, would figure prominently in, if not dominate, such lists, but this is not the case (Gordon's, though including a generous measure of such writing, being no exception). In fact, the content of these collections often follows the conventional subject-divisions and classification of other contemporary libraries, such as those of institutions and the professions, as if seeking to provide (albeit on a smaller scale) something of a 'repository of human knowledge' for the owner and his household. What impresses is the wide subject-range of these libraries – indicative of a deliberately well-stocked collection, combining the known special interests and 'private passions' of the present owner with the recreational and utilitarian needs of his household: divinity (a major element), the education and general upbringing of the young, appropriate to the 'profession of a gentleman' (as detailed, for example, by Peacham and others),[84] the management and development of the estates (for which he would need books on agriculture, husbandry, accounting, architecture, etc.), his civil, military and legal responsibilities as landowner, soldier and politician, and so on.

This wide subject-range is very evident in the Cecils' collection at Salisbury House (1615). The library room contained seven cases of books, three on the left and four on the right, divided by subject. 'Divinity' occupied two of these at the 'Upper End', accounting for just under 30 per cent of the entire library, and this section had evidently been under pressure from expansion with books moved from one case to the other. The other five 'cases' covered somewhat elastic subject areas: history (over 22 per cent), which also included travel and discovery, some bibliography (including two copies of the 1605 Bodleian catalogue), perspective and architecture; a philology case (22 per cent), which included the literary texts, ancient and modern, which Cecil had recommended (along with the histories) as 'fitt for a gentleman to understand', and unspecified 'Bookes of musicke and songes' no doubt for recreational performance in the

83 M. Vale, *The gentleman's recreations: accomplishments and pastimes of the English gentleman, 1580–1630* (Cambridge, 1977).

84 Peacham, *The compleat gentleman*. Peacham includes chapters on the cultivation of 'style' in speaking and writing, the study of history, cosmography, geometry, poetry, music, drawing, limning and painting, and heraldry, as well as bodily exercise, 'reputation and carriage', and, as appropriate, travel.

house; natural philosophy (9.5 per cent) – which included herbals, gardening and medical books, astronomy and meteorology, agriculture and mineralogy, military strategy and fortifications, and more on architecture; law (just under 8 per cent) and a final, 'catch-all' case – 'Bookes of Diverse sortes' (8.5 per cent), on chivalry, military ceremonial, politics, government and commerce, and more of the 'lighter' literature.

Two further observations need to be made about the Salisbury House collection. The books were predominantly in Latin (about 57 per cent) and of continental printing (about 75 per cent). Neither the English language nor English printing alone could provide anything like what was needed for the household, the owner's recreations or his responsibilities as servant of the state, any more than for those in the professions. English-language books – many of them pamphlets dating from after Burghley's death in 1598 – account for about 22 per cent of the library, and there are substantial collections of French (13 per cent) and Italian (4.5 per cent), with smaller numbers in Greek, Spanish, Dutch, German and Irish. In Lord Lumley's library of slightly earlier date, the low number of vernacular items was even more striking, amounting to about 12 per cent of the entire collection (187 English books, sixty-eight Italian, fifty-eight French, while Spanish, Dutch, German and Welsh were represented by not more than one or two each), Latin, Greek and Hebrew being the main languages.[85] A similar pattern is found in the library of Henry, 1st Baron Stafford, at the beginning of the period (1563). All his law books were Latin and of continental printing, and English-language books, some of them relating to gentlemanly pursuits (such as husbandry, surveying and hawking), accounted for only thirty-two of the total of 300 items, and English printing only forty.[86] Sir Thomas Knyvett's much larger and more comprehensive library (1618) lies somewhere between that of Lumley's and the Cecils': nearly 74 per cent of the stock is in Latin, 11 per cent in English, 7 per cent in French, 6.5 per cent in Italian, and the rest (Greek, Hebrew, German and Spanish) 1.5 per cent. Only just under 15 per cent of the books were printed in England. In Gordon's case, English-language books certainly occupy a much larger proportion of his library, but there is wide variation between the subjects. All his books on husbandry were of English printing, while at the other extreme over 90 per cent of those on chemistry were printed on the Continent. His large collection of history lay somewhere in between, with 43 per cent of continental printing,

85 Jayne and Johnson, *Lumley library*, 11–12.
86 Anderson, 'Books of Thomas, Lord Paget'.

54 per cent in the English language, 20 per cent in French and about 25 per cent in Latin, with a few examples of Italian.

The 1743 manuscript catalogue of Gordon's library comprises an alphabetical shelf-list (in which three of the eighteen cases have been much expanded) and a subject index (probably reflecting eighteenth-century notions of library science) divided into no fewer than sixteen categories. Direct comparison with the Cecils' collection is less easy, therefore, but divinity (12 per cent) is again a major component – probably nearer 20 per cent when the large number of items relating to religion in the sections on politics (36 per cent) and history (20.4 per cent) are taken into account. Other significant areas in Gordon's library were poetry (206 items, which included plays, novels and romances, nearly 9 per cent, with an additional forty-one grammars and dictionaries), law (5 per cent) and medicine (3.8 per cent). There were also small designated sections on philosophy (twenty-nine items), natural philosophy (thirty-three), mathematics (thirty-nine), chemistry (twenty-two), husbandry (twenty), the art of war (twenty) and astrology (six), and, like the Cecils' library, a large miscellaneous section (115 items). Gordon's books on heraldry were to be found under politics, and those on genealogy under history. His library also included a substantial quantity of 'lighter literature' with more than sixty French romances from the 1620s and 1630,[87] for his own entertainment and that of his household.

The relatively high proportion of divinity in both libraries is far from exceptional during this period, reflecting the quantity of publishing in this field and the importance of religion particularly at a time of upheaval and controversy. Lumley's theology section (1609) stood at about 36 per cent, though it included, of course, much of Archbishop Cranmer's library, dispersed in 1553. For comparison, Henry, 1st Baron Stafford (1563), had just under 16 per cent; Sir Thomas Knyvett (1618) just under 23 per cent; William, 4th Lord Paget (1628), 24 per cent, and Scipio Le Squyer (1632) just under 29 per cent.

In the Cecils' case, beside numerous bibles (whole or parts in a number of European languages in addition to those in Latin and Greek), commentaries and other scholarly aids, patristic and recent, there were whole sets of the early Church Fathers (but, notably few medieval scholastics) and much contemporary theology: controversial – on both sides of the Reformation

87 T. A. Birrell, 'Reading as pastime: the place of light literature in some gentlemen's libraries of the 17th century', in R. Myers and M. Harris (eds.), *Property of a gentleman: the formation, organisation and dispersal of the private library, 1620–1920* (Winchester, 1991), 121–3. Sir Edward Dering clearly collected material of this kind, buying over 225 playbooks between 1615 and 1624.

divide – practical divinity, sermons, and works of edification, instruction and spirituality. As Elizabeth's first secretary and later lord treasurer, Burghley had to be fully briefed on religious matters, with his special responsibilities for detecting religious and political subversion ('knowing the enemy'), and the pressing controversies of the day. His copy of Pietro Martire Vermigli's *Tractatio* (1549) – a key work in the eucharistic controversies of Edward VI's reign (now at Hatfield House) – had been thoroughly annotated, as had a section in Musculus' *Commonplaces* on the same matter. As secretary of state, William Cecil had taken part in a 'Conference' of divines on these matters with his brother-in-law, the distinguished Greek scholar, Sir John Cheke, at his own house in November 1551.[88] In his position, he would receive dedication or presentation copies such as the copy of Jan Laski's *De sacramentis* (London, 1552), now at Hatfield, bearing not only Laski's presentation inscription but a number of authorial corrections to the text in his hand. But this section of the library has a wider context than matters of state, his own religious leanings and those of his wife, Mildred; he needed to have a well-stocked collection – for those involved in the religious and moral education of his sons, for the conduct of daily prayers for the household, and for the use of his chaplains and visiting clergy, who might well use the library for scholarly purposes as well as more pressing needs such as sermons.

Sir Robert Gordon, while not having the same political responsibility for these matters as William Cecil, had nonetheless a wide range of biblical and patristic texts in the divinity section of his library as well as some scholastics such as Duns Scotus on Lombard's *Sentences* (Venice, 1612). He also had a large number of contemporary writings on both sides of the Reformation divide (his mother was a practising Catholic and his own position had been under suspicion): twenty-three volumes of pamphlets, recent Catholic authors such as Bellarmine (nine volumes, 1606–26), *The Catholike Moderator* (1624: *STC* 5636.8) and *The life and death of Mr Edward Geninges*, martyred in 1591 (St Omer, 1614), balanced by protestant texts such as *The canons and constitutions of the Scottish [episcopal] church* (Aberdeen, 1636), and works by Melanchthon, Calvin, Cranmer, John Foxe, Jewel and Thomas Morton. Such eclecticism was far from unusual. The Cecils' own library included a number of Roman breviaries, missals, manuals and Marian offices.

Like other gentlemen, Gordon had many books relating to world history, exploration, discovery and travel, particularly to the new world. In 1625, he

88 J. Strype, *Life of Sir John Cheke* (Oxford, 1821), 70–86, printed from CCCC, MS 102, fols. 253–66. For the Cecils, see P. Croft (ed.), *Patronage, culture and power: the early Cecils* (New Haven, CT, 2002).

had been created the first baronet of Nova Scotia, had been granted 16,000 acres on the coast, and was involved in the plantation of a colony there. In addition to books on New England, the West and East Indies and Virginia, he had items of more direct relevance, like Richard Eburne's *A plaine pathway to plantations* (London, 1624, *STC* 7471) and John Bonoeil's *A treatise of the art of making silke . . . together with instructions how to plant and dresse vines* (London, 1622, *STC* (2nd edn) 14378), as well as a copy of his namesake's (Sir Robert Gordon of Lochinvar, d. 1627?), *Encouragements for such as shall have intention to bee undertakers in the plantation of Cape Breton* (Edinburgh, 1625, *STC* 12069).

But it is the sections of his library that relate to the 'profession of a gentleman' which are of particular interest. He had, as might have been expected, *The courtier* of Castiglione, in a French translation (Lyons, 1580), and Peacham's *The compleat gentleman* (London, 1627). There are books on courtly conduct, honours and political life, letter-writing and 'civil conversation' (by Stephano Guazzo, in the Italian, French and English versions), Philippe de Bethune's *Counsellor of estate* (French and English versions), a work on *The court of James the First* (London, 1620, *STC* 1022) and ten works on court entertainments and masques performed on special occasions, such as the visit of the emperor of Morocco's ambassador in 1637 (*STC* 18165). His library was also well stocked with books for the education of young gentlemen: *The court of civill courtesie* (London, 1591), William Martyn's *Youths instruction* (1612, *STC* 17531), George Moore's *Principles for young princes* (1611, *STC* 18068) and James Cleland's *Institution of a young nobleman* (Oxford, 1607, *STC* 5393), along with William Browne's *Arte of riding the Great Horse* (London, ?1628, *STC* 3913.5) and pamphlets on duelling. Like other landowners, he had two of the standard works on architecture, Vitruvius (Venice, 1567) and Sir Henry Wotton's *Elements of architecture* (London, 1624, *STC* 26011).

Clearly, a major interest of Gordon's reflected in his library was husbandry, and gardening in particular, and these books were mostly in English. In addition to Conrad Heresbach, *Four bookes of husbandry* (1606), examples of the prolific [recycler] Gervase Markham, and John Crawshey's *Countryman's instructor on diseases in animals* (1636), he had works on bee-keeping (by Edmund Southerne, 1593, John Levett, 1634, and Charles Butler, 1623), planting, propagation and grafting, by Simon Harward (1623) and Leonard Mascall (1625), Thomas Hill's *Profitable art of gardening* (1593) and *The countryman's recreation* (1640). There were books on orchards and kitchen gardens by William Lawson (1623) and John Parkinson (1629), hop gardens by Reginald Scot (1576), and the less glamorous side of horticulture such as 'Platte of manures' (1594), that is, Sir Hugh Plat's *Diuerse new sorts of soyle not yet brought into any publique vse for manuring both of pasture and arable ground* (*STC* 19989). This interest in gardens and architecture, albeit at the level of formal garden design, was something shared with the Cecils.

Architecture and gardening were in fact two other interests which commonly feature in gentlemens' libraries of the period, particularly from the 1570s and 1580s onwards,[89] and some of the rarer titles (less easy to obtain in this country) feature in their desiderata sent to agents or friends travelling to the Continent. The 1615 shelf-list of the Cecils' library in Salisbury House lists a number of architectural works, including several editions of Vitruvius, and one each of Salomon de Caus, *La perspective* (dedicated to Henry, Prince of Wales) and Albrecht Dürer, *De vrbibus, arcibus, castellisque condendis* . . . (Paris, 1535), a book on fortification and architectural drawing, while William Cecil's copy of Jean Cousin, *Liure de perspectiue* (Paris, 1560), which he had asked Throckmorton to obtain for him, is now in Lambeth Palace Library, bound with a copy of Jacques Androuet du Cerceau's *De architectura* (Paris,1582), which may also have belonged to him.[90] It is also known from a letter of his to Sir Thomas Smith, the queen's ambassador in Paris, that there was one such book that he particularly coveted and was clearly hoping that Smith would procure for him. This was a copy of Philibert de L'Orme, *Nouvelles inventions pour bien bastir*, published in Paris in 1561,[91] and it is thought that the extraordinary obelisk that tops the clock-tower at Burghley House may derive from one of de L'Orme's illustrations of Anet, even though Cecil's own copy of the book has yet to be found.

This was the period of the great formal garden of Tudor and Stuart England so memorably described by Roy Strong,[92] gardens that were to be uprooted by exponents of the 'landscape' style in the eighteenth century. Gardening was a particular personal interest of Lord Burghley's – Strong describes it as a 'weakness which he freely admitted'.[93] It was an interest that received expression both in the gardens of Burghley's London house in the Strand and at Theobalds. Both these gardens were superintended by the great herbalist John Gerard, who dedicated his *Herball* – a work found in many libraries

89 See M. Airs, *The making of the English country house, 1500–1640* (London, 1975), 26–8, who mentions Sir Thomas Smith, who owned over twelve books on architecture, Sir Thomas Tresham (over twenty) and Henry Percy, the 'Wizard Earl' (over twelve).

90 It is known that du Cerceau's book influenced the construction of the gardens at Theobalds. See R. Strong, *The Renaissance garden in England* (London, 1979), 53.

91 A. Wells-Cole, *Art and decoration in Elizabethan and Jacobean England: the influence of continental prints, 1558–1625* (New Haven,CT, 1997), 38 and n. 36.

92 Strong, *Renaissance garden in England*.

93 *Ibid.*, 52. The gardens at Theobalds are discussed on 51–6.

of the period – to Burghley in 1597.[94] Theobalds was acquired by Burghley in 1564, and during the 1570s and 1580s it developed into a kind of auxiliary royal palace for the queen's frequent visits there towards the end of her reign. The gardens were constructed in the latest fashion between 1575 and 1585. His London house also had elaborate gardens, though we know little about them. Burghley's 'weakness' is reflected in the books and manuscripts in his library. Hatfield preserves a number of garden plans in his own hand. In one of his notebooks that survive, there are notes in his hand relating to the planting and care of crops, and there is a letter from him in 1561 (25 March) to Sir Thomas Windebank, who was in Paris with Cecil's son Thomas, requesting him to procure 'a lymon, a pomgranat, and a myrt tree' (to add to his existing orange tree) so that these could be included with other items that Sir Francis Carew was intending to send home. He particularly requests Sir Thomas that 'before hand [he] send me in wryting a perfect declaration howe they ought to be used kept and ordered'.[95] Books relating to gardening and agriculture with Cecil's signature now at Hatfield include his much annotated 'Geoponica' (or *De agriculturae* (Basle, 1540) attributed to 'Constantine VII', with commentary by Cornarius), the *De re hortensi libellus, vulgaria herbarum florum et fructum* by Charles Estienne in 1539, bound with the same author's *Seminarium, et plantarum fructiferarum* (Paris, 1540) – the former annotated by Burghley throughout.

The garden at Theobalds seems to owe something to the gardens presented by Vredeman de Vries in his *Hortorum viridariorumque formae*. De Vries's work was widely used for its garden patterns by builders in England. There is a plan of the Great Garden at Theobalds endorsed by Burghley. The approach to this garden was through a loggia painted with genealogies (another of Burghley's interests), and the garden was surrounded by a moat on which visitors could be rowed in boats. The design echoes Androuet du Cerceau's engravings of French gardens in his *Le plus excellents bastiments de France* (1576) – one of the very few architectural books to give actual views of gardens, and a book which was known and studied in England.[96]

His son Robert inherited his father's passion for gardening. As a young man he had created a remarkable emblematic garden at his house at Pymms (4 miles distant from Theobalds)[97] in honour of Elizabeth I, and as soon as he inherited Theobalds, on Burghley's death in 1598, he started new garden

94 *STC* 11750, with Burghley's arms, as dedicatee, on the verso of the title page.

95 R. Strong, 'Sir Francis Carew's garden at Beddington', in E. Chaney and P. Mack (eds.), *England and the continental Renaissance* (Woodbridge, 1990, 1994), 234.

96 Strong, *Renaissance garden in England*, 53.

97 *Ibid*., 46.

developments. The garden at Hatfield House, built between 1607 and 1612 (which he had exchanged with James I for Theobalds in 1607) was created by Cecil's gardener, Mountain Jennings. When it came to stocking the garden, John Tradescant took over, being to Hatfield what Gerard had been to Theobalds. Tradescant brought shiploads of rare trees, fruits, flowers, plants and seeds back from Europe. Marie de Medici sent Cecil 500 fruit trees and two gardeners to supervise their planting. Robert Cecil died on 24 May 1612 and never lived to enjoy either his great house or its magnificent garden.

The gentleman as 'virtuoso'

The early seventeenth century saw the emergence of the new cultural phenomenon of the 'virtuoso'. A virtuoso was someone whose main concern in life was with the collecting of natural or artifical 'curiosities' – accompanied by some antiquarian 'research', aesthetic appreciation, and the acquisition of classical sculpture and 'old-master' paintings. He often dabbled in a little 'science' and engineering, on the side. The collecting of 'curiosities' was certainly not new in the early seventeenth century. John Stowe tells us that Reyner Wolfe (d. 1573), the printer and also the instigator of Holinshed's *Chronicles*, had just such a collection, including 'curiosities' found among the numerous cartloads of bones he removed from the charnel house in St Paul's Churchyard when setting up his business there. Antiquarians such as John Twyne, of Canterbury, began excavating at ancient sites, and William Camden, Lord Howard of Naworth and Sir Robert Cotton were interested in Roman antiquities being found at Hadrian's Wall. Lord Howard, who lived very close to the wall, formed his own collection of Roman altars and inscribed stones to adorn the gardens at Naworth, sending some examples south to add to Cotton's growing collection of antiquities.[98] Pottery, bones and above all coins found their way into their collections – notably that of Sir Robert Cotton – and were proudly displayed to visitors, along with their shelves of books. William Cecil also had a coin collection to accompany his books at Theobalds, and evidence of his interest in coin and medal collecting survives in his library, which included Sebastiano Erizzo, *Discorso sopra le medaglie antiche* (Venice, 1559), which he acquired in 1565, now at the National Art Library (V&A, Clements Coll. CLE LL2). Henry Herbert, 2nd earl of Pembroke (?1534–1601), was another, collecting not only

98 G. Ornsby (ed.), *Selections from the household books of the Lord William Howard of Naworth Castle*, Surtees Soc. 68 (Durham, 1878), lvii, lix.

manuscripts, but ancient sculpture, coins, medals and gems. Others had begun to purchase sculpture and works of art from abroad, often to decorate their new homes and 'fantasticall' gardens. In the 1560s, for example, William Cecil was buying statues of Roman emperors from Venice and importing marble doorframes, basins and tables from France to be set up eventually in his new residence, Theobalds. The 'Wizard Earl' was interested in scientific experiments, as William Drummond of Hawthornden was in trying to invent weapons of war. The libraries of such men reflect these interests and we have to see their libraries in this wider context.

However, it was Thomas Howard, 2nd earl of Arundel (1585–1646), who was to be dubbed by Horace Walpole in the eighteenth century as 'the father of virtu' in England. A man of great *hauteur* – whom many found insufferable – he was nevertheless to set before his contemporaries a new ideal for the life of a gentleman. It was this side of him that stands out in this description of him by his one-time secretary, Sir Edward Walker:[99]

> He was the greatest favourer of Arts, especially painting, sculpture, Designs [i.e. drawings], carving, Building and the like, that this age has produced; his Collection of Designs being more than any person living, and his Statues equal in number, value and antiquity to those in the Houses of most Princes . . . And he had the Honour to be the first Person of Quality that set a value on them in our Nation.

Arundel's visit to Italy in 1613/14 with his friend Inigo Jones saw the beginning of his collecting activities. While in Rome he obtained a licence to import Roman antiquities, and commissioned four statues from a Roman sculptor. He was also purchasing books in Italy. These antiquities had a considerable impact when they arrived in England. His great-uncle, John, Lord Lumley, had owned the largest collection of pictures in England – over 200 – but these were mainly portraits of ancestors and notable 'worthies' of the day. Lumley also had the second largest library of the time, and another relative, Lord William Howard of Naworth, had formed another large library in the north. What was different about Arundel's collection was not only its size and scope, but its intention – 'art for art's sake' – as opposed to the often utilitarian outlook of his predecessors.

Inigo Jones designed a new italianate picture and sculpture gallery at Somerset House to house the collection. The collection was viewed by Lady Anne Clifford in December 1616: 'Upon the 27th . . . Presently after Dinner

99 R. Strong, *The spirit of Britain: a narrative history of the arts* (London, 1999), 238. Chapter 18 (239–51) deals in detail with Thomas Howard, earl of Arundel, the 'Virtuoso'.

came my Lord thither and we went together to my Lady Arundel's where I saw all the Pictures and Statues in the Lower Rooms.'[100]

As well as sculpture, paintings and antiquities, Arundel owned a huge library. This was augmented, when he was a part of the 1636 embassy to Vienna, by the purchase of the library of Willibald Pirckheimer, the wealthy Renaissance humanist and friend of Dürer, which included priceless books and incunabula – some of them illustrated by the great German artist.

Arundel's circle included Sir Robert Cotton, John Selden, William Camden, Sir Henry Spelman and William Harvey. His librarian was Francis Junius. In his *Compleat gentleman*, Henry Peacham, who was tutor to Arundel's children, sums up the changes in the education of a gentleman largely inspired by Arundel. In a chapter entitled 'Of the dignities and necessitie of Learning in Princes and Nobilitie', he writes: 'Since learning then is an essential part of Nobilitie, as vnto which we are beholden, for whatsoeuer dependeth on the culture of the mind; it followeth, that who is nobly borne, and a Scholar withal, Deserveth Double Honour, being bothe εὔγενης and πολυμαθης.'[101] These were fine words for a lofty ideal. We have come a long way from the perceived stereotype of the hunting and hawking gentleman who had little if any time for his books. Let Peacham have the last word in his timely advice to those who would be 'compleat gentlemen' in 1622:

> Affect not as some doe, that bookish Ambition, to be stored with books and haue well furnished Libraries, yet keepe their heads emptie of knowledge: to desire to haue many bookes, and neuer to vse them, is like *a childe that will haue a candle burning by him, all the while he is sleeping.*[102]

100 Clifford, *Diaries of Lady Anne Clifford*, 43.
101 Peacham, *The compleat gentleman*, ch. 2, 18.
102 Peacham, *The compleat gentleman*, 54.

22

Libraries of the 'common sort'

MARGARET SPUFFORD

Libraries built up by professionals – theologians, lawyers, doctors, heralds – for the purposes of their work could be, and often were, as we have seen, both large and valuable. The libraries for leisure built up by gentlemen and by literary figures and their patrons were likewise costly and extravagant. Where money has been expended, and where collecting has been notable, there are likely to be records, maybe in the shape of account-books or even booklists. The history of the libraries of notable men, and sometimes women, is traceable by the sixteenth and seventeenth centuries. If we turn to the possible collections of cheaper and much less beautiful print turned out for lower groups in society, but also read by their social superiors, we immediately run into difficulties.

There is a general rule which lays down that, paradoxically, the cheaper, commoner and more ephemeral an object is, the rarer are its survivals. In the wills of the 'common sort of people', on whom we are now focusing, books are mentioned if they were prestigious or of value. Copies of the Bible in a good binding, or of Foxe's 'Book of Martyrs', might well be bequeathed in a will. Anything cheap was not likely to be found there. Similarly, the probate inventory, the list of movable goods made after a death, was highly unlikely to bother to include very inexpensive items. There was a catch-all phrase at the end of an inventory. It did not have the pejorative ring it has to us now, but an entry 'Item, other trash' or 'item, other lumber', or simply 'for things forgot' with a small value attached, was very often there. In the seventeenth century, ballads cost 1d or ½d new. The cheapest of the genre of chapbooks, 'small merries, small godlies and pleasant histories' new in the 1620s for an expanding market, cost 2d or 3d new.[1] So did a news-book. If a householder's goods did include this sort of item, only an obsessive appraiser would make a note of individual copies of such books, although there is a chance that a collection of ballads or such books making up a noticeable value might be jotted down.

1 T. Watt, *Cheap print and popular piety, 1550–1640* (Cambridge, 1991), ch. 7, esp. 273.

Among 1,500 inventories from urban and rural Norfolk and Suffolk, discussed at a day conference on book ownership and readership at the University of East Anglia in 1978,[2] only five references were found to 'little books' priced at under 6d, that were within the range of the pocket of a common man on wages of 12d a day. These books were all for sale, not in private hands. A widow who had kept a shop in Lowestoft when she died in 1590 had seventy-nine volumes worth only 22s 2d together. They included twenty-two primers in English and eighteen ABCs. We do not know, but would like to, what the other thirty-nine books were. Such cheap little books, at a price accessible to the agricultural labourer, were not worthy of record in a probate inventory, unless the owner had a collection, a 'library', worth a pound or so. The little books wore out, tore, disappeared, like the ephemera they were, just as the single-sheet ballad and woodcut did.[3]

For this reason, in general we depend for our knowledge of the sixteenth- and seventeenth-century chapbooks and ballads on the gentry who collected them for pleasure alongside the first-folio Shakepeares and copies of Chaucer. The work of the scholar concentrating on cheap print would be gloomy indeed if she did not have Samuel Pepys, Anthony Wood and, strictly in our period, Mrs Frances Wolfreston to fall back on. This anachronistic use of evidence seems permissible, because of the 'timeless' quality of many of the stories and songs related in them. The origins of some of them lay deep in the middle ages, but their printing history reached forward well into the nineteenth century. *Guy of Warwick* originated in a French source around 1200, and was collected by Samuel Pepys in the 1680s in two versions, one a twenty-four-page octavo with the hero 'meanly born', and the other in a much longer quarto more likely to appeal to the gentry, in which the hero has a genealogy stretching back to Cassivellaunus, king of the Belgae, even though he had now fallen on hard times.[4] *Amadis de Gaul*, probably of fourteenth-century Catalonian origin, was translated into English in 1588. It was printed repeatedly, once by Charles Tias to sell at 6d in 1664, and appears, rather oddly, with Southey as the author, in an edition issued in 1803.

However, even though the 'libraries' of working men and women do not survive, and we are reduced to what we hope is intelligent surmise, there are

2 M. Spufford, *Small books and pleasant histories: popular fiction and its readership in seventeenth-century England* (London, 1981), 48, 125–6.

3 M. Martin, 'The case of the missing woodcuts', *Print Quarterly* 4 (1987), 343–61.

4 Spufford, *Small books*, 225–7 and 259–60. See D. Hall, 'The world of print and collective mentality', in his *Cultures of print: essays in the history of the book* (Amherst, MA, 1996), 83–9, for a discussion of this long-lived corpus of what he calls 'traditional culture'. The specifically English additions to this corpus do have poor heroes who 'make good'.

a very few precious scraps of information which do give us proof that at least some tiny 'libraries' for pleasure were made in the sixteenth and seventeenth centuries, and some of these same working men and women did manage to assemble a little hoard of books.

In 1576, a very intriguing man, John Maulden, died. He had worked as both a weaver and a barber, to judge from the weaving shop, spindles and two looms in his house in Suffolk, as well as scissors, razors, comb and '5 cases for a barber'. His dual occupation had not brought him prosperity, for his goods were worth only about £12. But he also had a third occupation. The inventory included 'sarten parelle for morres dancers and other empellementes with the bels', valued at £1. So he was a member, or the leader, of a local group of morris dancers. But why did he also have as many as four chests, containing sixty-seven books worth 13s 4d? If they were averaged out, they would not have been worth more than 2½d each. Yet it was worth putting them in the inventory, since their combined value was a significant sum. Why did he have them, and the chests in which to put them? Did he read them to himself for pleasure, sell them, or did he perhaps read them aloud, to add to the attractions of his troupe of dancers? We do not know, but this example shows that 'little books' were attractive and were read by the poor.[5]

John Maulden was not alone. An even poorer man, William Bane, labourer, worked in the Forest of Arden, and died in 1614, leaving goods worth £8 19s 4d. He lodged in a sparsely furnished room, probably in his master's house, with a 'Course Chaffe bedd' with 'the Course furniture to the same belongeing' and two small coffers. His tools were in his room too: one hook, one bill, and 'other od Implementes'. Astonishingly, the appraisers also found 'Certayne small bookes' valued at 10s. If they were worth 2d each, there were as many as sixty. Here is a labourer reading for pleasure, and, even more surprising, writing, for there was also 'one penne and inke horne'.[6] He upsets all our convenient categorisations. I was driven to suggest, by some very odd evidence from the wood-pasture parish of Eccleshall in Staffordshire, where people were teaching writing who should not have been teaching writing (according to the painstaking doctrine worked out by social historians including myself), and other people were fluent readers who should not have been,[7] that, just possibly,

5 D. Dymond, 'Three entertainers from Tudor Suffolk', *Records of Early English Drama* 16/1 (1991), 3–5. I am very grateful to David Dymond for drawing this example to my attention.

6 V. Skipp, 'Economic and social change in the Forest of Arden, 1530–1649', in J. Thirsk (ed.), *Land, church and people: essays presented to H. P. R. Finberg* (Reading, 1970), 111.

7 M. Spufford, 'The importance of religion in the sixteenth and seventeenth centuries', in M. Spufford (ed.), *The world of rural dissenters, 1520–1775* (Cambridge, 1995), 44–70.

people in wood-pasture regions, where there was more time than in the back-breaking ceaseless round of arable regions, might have had more leisure to cultivate literate skills. We may now add John Maulden and William Bane, both from wood-pasture regions, not to speak of John Aubrey's 'melancholy, contemplative and malicious . . . fanatiques' of north Wiltshire, who 'only milk the cows and make cheese', as opposed to their neighbours of arable south Wiltshire, where, 'being weary after hard labour, they have not leisure to read and contemplate of religion, but goe to bed to their rest'.[8]

Dr Michael Frearson has found a very remarkable list of the books of a shoemaker and glover of Gloucestershire, John Tayer, who put down the titles of his books in his account book in 1627. It is, to my knowledge, a unique listing of the titles of the 'small books' in personal ownership. Shoemakers and men in the leather trades were frequently drawn to dissent, or at least to piety, and John Tayer was no exception. He had two bibles and a testament, as well as three psalters and two catechisms. He also had practical aids to living. A 'Statute Book' and 'the bookes of the assize of Bread' were with 'divers Almanackes bound together'. A book on 'the duties of constables' tything men and such low and lay ministers of the peace' surely indicated John Tayer had held such offices in his own community, and was a man of standing. He was interested in the world beyond Gloucestershire. He had two books on travel to Turkey and Persia. But his 'small books' indicated that the bibles and psalters were not there merely for display. He had copies of *The rich cabinet*, *The garden of spiritual flowers*, *A godly garden of comfortable hearbes*, *Smug the smith*, *A subpena* [*sic*] *from heaven* and *The treasure of gladness*. Men such as John Tayer were deeply important, whether as separatists or men of conviction, for in their shops customers met, waited, talked and exchanged ideas. John Tayer could draw upon his books for both ideas and the stories to illustrate them.[9]

The rare references found thus far suggest that these small, precious collections of books were kept loose, or in book-chests. References to studies are, not surprisingly, even more rare, but one or two are known. It is perhaps no coincidence that one of them would seem to have existed by virtue of the office held by the individual concerned. William Tassell was the parish clerk of Balsham in Cambridgeshire from the 1530s onwards. He died in 1574/5. He had been a scribe of local wills and inventories, and a witness to many more, as well

8 M. Spufford and J. Went, *Poverty portrayed: Gregory King and the parish of Eccleshall* (Keele, 1995), 50–2.

9 I am indebted to Dr Frearson for this information, as yet unpublished in full. See M. C. Frearson, 'The English corantos of the 1620s', unpublished PhD thesis, University of Cambridge (1994), 16; Spufford, 'Importance of religion', 53–4.

as making the most substantial bequest to the poor of Balsham in a hundred years. However, in 1551 he had had an uncomfortable fortnight in London, bound to appear daily before the Privy Council on a charge of astrological fortune-telling. His reputation apparently spread as far as Lincolnshire. He probably became one of the early members of the Family of Love in Balsham; his son was certainly a member, and the mystical ideas of the indwelling of God in man in this life would probably have appealed to an astrologer. However that may be, he escaped the accusations, and continued to live in Balsham. When he died in 1574/5, he left one of his sons 'all my Studdye as it standeth'. This would argue not only the high degree of literacy we would already assume from his history, but a larger collection of books than we have so far found.[10]

It is another hundred years before evidence is known to survive of the notion of setting aside space in houses in the county of Cambridgeshire, as opposed to any of the colleges of Cambridge or by the clergy, for the enjoyment of reading as a pleasurable private occupation. Even then, this practice was restricted only to the most prosperous in village society, those with larger houses, who had perhaps benefited from 'The Great Rebuilding'.[11] Of nearly 350 inventories which survive from between 1660 and 1670, only a single house, apart from those of the clergy or gentry, had a 'study' in it. Thomas Laurence, a yeoman of Trumpington, whose goods were worth £138 when he died in 1669, had at least ten books in his study. Nevertheless, Richard Wootton, a yeoman of Ickleton, had 'his books' and money with a desk in his chamber, which indicates that the idea of creating a private space, if not designating a room a 'study', was present. Best of all, perhaps, and most tempting to the modern scholar, is the sense of leisure created by the appraisers' description of the little closet off the chamber over the parlour in the house of Robert Tebbutt, a very substantial yeoman of Chippenham, who died in 1682. It contained a silver tankard, two tumblers, two wine cups, seven silver spoons and a 'parcel' of books. It sounds as if Robert Tebbutt practised a very enviable type of civilised living. But very few of the Cambridgeshire yeomen can have sipped wine as they read of an evening.[12]

Despite these precious fragments of information, we do not, with the exception of John Tayer, know the titles of the books owned by these people and their like. It is therefore impossible to tell whether these little collections were handed down as treasures to be guarded and kept with care by the next generation or generations. There is just one method we can use, and that is

10 C. Marsh, *The Family of Love in English society* (Cambridge, 1994), 70–4.

11 R. Machin, 'The Great Rebuilding: a reassessment', *Past and Present* 77 (1977), 33–56.

12 M. Spufford, *Contrasting communities: English villagers in the sixteenth and seventeenth centuries*, 2nd edn (Stroud, 2000), 211.

to search in the reverse direction, looking later for the record of a collection that had been handed down and carefully kept. This method turns out not to be fruitless.

James Raine was born in 1791, the son of a village smith and a dressmaker, in the North Riding of Yorkshire, and later wrote his memoirs. He was a quiet and sickly boy, and spent much time with both his grandmothers, who fed his interest in print and in stories. His paternal grandmother spent her Sunday afternoons reading the New Testament and her favourite devotional book, 'the Countess of Morton's *Devotions*'. James wrote:

> she also had two books in which I took great interest . . . one a life of Christ ornamented at the head of each chapter with a rude [crude] woodcut . . . It belonged to the earlier part of the seventeenth century. She also had a copy of Aesop's Fables, tattered and torn and imperfect, equally ornamented with woodcuts, over which I used to pore with infinite delight. This book was of an earlier date. I spent every hour . . . revelling in the glories of an immense bundle of penny histories and ballads, made myself intimately familiar with giants, witches, fairies and their doings and had the Seven Champions of Christendom and the ballade of Robin Hood at my fingers' ends.

But also, he wrote,

> My grandmother's stock of tales was very considerable, turning chiefly on giants and ghosts with not a few touching tales of the dark deeds of faeries [*sic*] and witches . . . Many of my grandmother's tales had a religious object in view, the promotion of the due observance of the sabbath day . . . But giants and ghosts and faeries were the staple in which not only she but every other house in the village delighted most to deal . . . it is extremely easy to account for the way in which our ancestors spent their evenings even centuries ago before the invention of printing.

His paternal grandfather had in the evenings read aloud to a whole circle of neighbours whom he would gather round him, and to whom he read such books as he owned for their amusement or edification. In the summer evenings this was done in the open air; Josephus' *Wars of the Jews* was the book that was most welcomed by the villagers and most captivated their attention. James's maternal grandmother, who had been a servant in her youth, was blind, and had no books, but she did have a good memory. She took particular pleasure in 'teaching me Watts's Hymns', which she knew by heart, as well as telling him many other tales.[13]

13 'James Raine's memoir', in A. Marsden (ed.), *A Raine miscellany*, Surtees Soc. 200 (Newcastle-upon-Tyne, 1989), 10, 13–18.

So not only were this boy's grandmothers storytellers, in a fashion which John Clare immortalised in *The shepheard's calender*, but one of them had inherited a tiny library, of the kind we are talking about. It contained two late sixteenth- or early seventeenth-century books, and a 'great bundle' of small books and ballads. These, like his grandmother's inherited pewter, were obviously precious possessions. Some books and print did descend in the family, although you would never find them in a will or inventory.

23

The libraries of the antiquaries (*c*. 1580–1640) and the idea of a national collection

RICHARD OVENDEN

The libraries formed by the group of individuals known as antiquaries during the period 1580 to 1640 were of crucial importance for the long-term development of the great research collections of the modern period. They are, for this reason alone, worthy of consideration, but the study of these libraries illuminates other aspects of early modern society and culture, since the context in which they were formed, and the impact they made, impinged significantly on the political, religious, cultural and intellectual life of Britain. In order to shed light on these collections, the individuals who formed them, and the emergent concept of a national collection which they helped to develop and articulate, a number of questions arise concerning the contents of the collections, why and how they were acquired and the uses to which they were put. But before these questions are answered, we must first turn our attention to the antiquaries themselves, and what distinguished them from their contemporaries.

To be an antiquary in the period 1580 to 1640 was not be a member of a profession, or to belong to a specific sector of society, for individuals who could in some circumstances be described as antiquaries could also be described and categorised in different circumstances in other ways, such as noblemen, clerics, politicians or heralds. Although antiquity was not specifically a subject studied at university,[1] in general antiquaries were those who engaged in the study of antiquity, defined in Renaissance Britain as not only the classical past, but the classical and medieval periods together. To be an antiquary in early modern Britain meant engaging in a number of different kinds of activities, or betraying certain traits which, when identified, can help in determining those individuals during this time-span who could be so described.

1 L. Brockliss, 'Curricula', in H. De Ridder-Symoens (ed.), *A history of the university in Europe*, III: *Universities in the early modern age, 1500–1800* (Cambridge, 1996), 575–7; K. Thomas, 'The life of learning', *Proceedings of the British Academy* 117 (2001), 201–35.

Some of these activities and traits related to books, and were described by John Earle in his often quoted *Microcosmographie* of 1628. Antiquaries were, in his opinion, 'strangely thrifty of times past', they were 'enamour'd of old age', and loved 'all things . . . the better for being mouldy and worme-eaten', and he identified the antiquary as 'a great admirer . . . of the rust of old Monuments'. More specifically, Earle characterises an antiquary thus: 'a manuscript he pores on everlastingly, especially if the cover be all Moth-eaten'.[2]

There were a handful of individuals, however, who did earn their living by antiquarian activity. John Leland had been given an official title as King's Antiquary (or recorder of antiquities) by Henry VIII, and some of the royal librarians undertook activities which were those of an official antiquary in all but name. John Joscelyn was employed by Matthew Parker 'as one of his Antiquaries', to judge by an inscription in an ex-Parker manuscript (now Lambeth, MS 959).[3] The paradigm case, however, was that of Patrick Young, royal librarian, who was charged by James I 'to make a search in all cathedrals for old manuscripts and ancient records, and to bring an inventory of them to His Majesty'.[4] Young made catalogues of the contents of a number of English cathedral libraries. The visits he made and the catalogues he compiled were used to assist the transfer of books from the cathedral libraries to newer collections, including the royal collection itself, but Young was also responsible for alienating books from the royal collection. He made numerous gifts of royal library books to his fellow antiquaries, including James Montagu, Sir Robert Cotton, and a number of influential Scottish antiquaries, including James Reid, and Sir James Balfour of Denmilne, the Lyon King of Arms.[5] Heralds were another group of individuals whose living to some extent depended

2 C. E. Wright, 'The Elizabethan Society of Antiquaries and the formation of the Cottonian library', in Wormald and Wright, *English library*, 176.

3 J. P. Carley, 'The manuscript remains of John Leland, "The King's Antiquary"', *TEXT: Transactions of the Society for Textual Scholarship*, 2 (1985), 11–120; J. Evans, *A history of the Society of Antiquaries* (Oxford, 1956), 9. For the fate of Leland's own collections, see O. Harris, '"Motheaten, mouldye, and rotten": the early custodial history and dissemination of John Leland's manuscript remains', *BLR* 18 (2005), 460–501.

4 I. Atkins and N. R. Ker, *Catalogus librorum manuscriptorum bibliothecae Wigorniensis, 1622–1623, by Patrick Young* (Cambridge, 1944), 1–2. See also T. Webber, 'Patrick Young, Salisbury Cathedral manuscripts and the Royal Collection', *English Manuscript Studies 1100–1700* 2 (1990), 283–90; J. P. Carley, 'The royal library as a source for Sir Robert Cotton's collection: a preliminary list of acquisitions', in C. J. Wright (ed.), *Sir Robert Cotton as collector: essays on an early Stuart courtier and his legacy* (London, 1997), 208–29; J. Kemke (ed.), *Patricius Junius (Patrick Young), Bibliothekar der Könige Jacob I. und Carl I. von England: Mitteilungen aus seihem Briefwechsel* (Leipzig, 1898).

5 For Balfour see most recently I. C. Cunningham, 'Sir James Balfour's manuscript collection: the 1698 catalogue and other sources', *Edinburgh Bibliographical Society Transactions* 6/6 (1997–9), 191–255.

on antiquarian pursuits. Some of these men will be discussed in this chapter, but for the most part they are dealt with elsewhere (see above, chapter 20).

To be an antiquary implied both learning and constant study and curiosity. William Camden was described by a contemporary as 'our learned and studious Antiquarie'.[6] William Somner, registrar of the ecclesiastical courts in Canterbury, writing the preface to his *Antiquities of Canterbury* at the end of our period, outlined his motivation for writing the book:

> My thoughts and affections ever much inclined to the search and study of Antiquities, (to which also my particular calling did in some manner lead me) I have more particularly as bounde in duty and thankfulnesse, applyed my selfe to the Antiquities of Canterbury, the place of my birth and abode. And to me this was sufficient motive why I should of all other places desire to know the antiquities and former estate thereof.[7]

He goes on to describe the sources for his information: 'This work was chiefly collected from old Manuscripts, Leiger-Bookes and other Records of credit', and it is largely this process of collecting information in manuscript form that will make up the remainder of the discussion in this chapter.

The College of Antiquaries

Before the books and libraries are discussed in detail, it is necessary to provide a brief account of the development of the College or Society of Antiquaries, the most formal expression of antiquarian behaviour developed in this period.[8] The college began to meet in 1585 or 1586, according to John Spelman in his *The original of the four terms of the year* (London, 1614), attended by

> divers Gentlemen in London, studious of Antiquities [who] framed themselves into a College or Society of Antiquaries, appointing to meet every Friday weekly in the Term, at a place agreed of, and for Learnings sake to confer upon some Questions in that Faculty . . . The Society increased daily: many persons of great worth, as well noble as other learned, joining themselves unto it.[9]

6 William Warner, *Albion's England* (London, 1632), 351.
7 William Somner, *The antiquities of Canterbury* (London, 1640), sig. ** r.
8 For the following account see Evans, *Society of Antiquaries*; L. Van Nordern, 'Sir Henry Spelman on the chronology of the Elizabethan College of Antiquaries', *Huntingdon Library Quarterly* 13 (1950), 131–60; Wright 'Elizabethan Society of Antiquaries'; D. R. Woolf, *The social circulation of the past: English historical culture, 1500–1730* (Oxford, 2003), 162–3.
9 Quoted in Evans, *Society of Antiquaries*, 8–9.

After 1607 the College of Antiquaries vanished, despite a brief revival in 1614, the concept of the organisation having fallen foul of royal approbation.

Although there is no definitive list of members, we do know that most were knights, that almost all the rest were gentlemen, of whom there were twenty-one graduates of Oxford, and sixteen of Cambridge, and that there were no clergy. Many of the members had some connection either with the law or with the College of Heralds, and they bound themselves to consult only English sources in their deliberations. The legal profession was particularly prominent among the membership of the society: a number of scholars have drawn attention to the centrality of antiquarian investigation to the establishment of modern civil law, and, in turn, to the articulation of early modern political theory.[10] It is also worth mentioning that there were others connected with the Inns of Court and the legal profession who had active antiquarian interests, but who were not members of the College of Antiquaries – the Cornish Catholic Nicholas Roscarrock being one.[11] A record of the attenders at a meeting of the college in 1591 indicates the spread of interests and backgrounds among the members who participated: William Dethicke (Garter King of Arms), William Camden (Clarenceux King of Arms), William Fleetwood (recorder of London), Francis Thynne (who would become Lancaster Herald), Francis Tate (a lawyer), John Dodderidge (a judge), Thomas Talbot (clerk of the records in the Tower of London), Arthur Agarde (deputy chamberlain of the Exchequer), Henry Spelman (MP and lawyer), Sir Walter Cope (chamberlain of the Exchequer, and master of the Court of Wards); and John Stow and Robert Cotton, both of whom earned their living by a variety of means. The membership of the college changed over the period, but we know enough to be sure that the interests of the generality did not differ much from the examples cited above.

One striking feature which the members had in common was their interest in book-collecting, and in particular the collecting of manuscripts associated with the British medieval past. A crucial turning point in the history of the College of Antiquaries came in 1603, when they petitioned Elizabeth I for the foundation of both a library and an academy dedicated to the study of British antiquity (see below, 548–50), but the antiquaries also formed personal libraries. These took many forms. The defining characteristic common to all,

10 See especially R. J. Schoeck, 'The Elizabethan Society of Antiquaries and men of law', *Notes and Queries* (1954), 417–21; and J. G. A. Pocock, *The Ancient Constitution and the feudal law* (Cambridge, 1987).

11 N. Orme (ed.), *Nicholas Roscarrock's Lives of the saints: Cornwall and Devon*, Devon and Cornwall Record Society, n.s., 35 (Exeter, 1992), 5–7.

however, was the fact that most contained medieval manuscripts. These were largely volumes which had been in religious collections at the dissolution of the monasteries, but other kinds of documents such as charters, as well as printed books, were also collected. In addition to religious texts, historical works were considered especially important and valuable. Some collectors, however, had particular subject-areas where their acquisitions were focused: John Dee's scientific collections and Lord William Howard's illuminated books are two examples. Some collectors considered administrative documents as of equal if not greater importance to literary texts: thus Cotton, D'Ewes and Dering were responsible for saving large collections of medieval charters and cartularies from both religious and secular sources.

Some of these collections were very large, took many years to form, and became considerable resources for a wide variety of users. Sir Robert Cotton's is an extreme example, whose collection will be considered in some detail below (550–7), but there were other major collections of considerable size: those of Lord William Howard of Naworth (1563–1640), Sir Simonds D'Ewes (1602–50), Sir Edward Dering (1598–1644), and the Scottish collector Sir James Balfour of Denmilne (1600–57), for example, are significant for both their size and for the importance of some of the individual volumes. At the other extreme, many antiquaries, who existed in more modest financial and social circumstances, nonetheless formed small but significant collections – men such as the Welsh antiquary Jaspar Gryffyth (1568?–1614) and, from Kent, Sir Peter Manwood (d. 1625). What is distinctive about all these collections, however, is that they were deeply interconnected, the small with the large, the provincial with the metropolitan, the courtly with the professional. The networks of collecting, sharing, and exchanging for the purpose of sharing information, in terms of both reading and of the subsequent stage of copying, were often very complex, and can be hard to unravel, but understanding them is essential to explain the *mentalité* of the antiquaries, and on a more practical level, to explain the ways in which the collections were formed, used and dispersed.

As will be seen in the case of Sir Robert Cotton, the major antiquaries attracted circles of like-minded men. The humbler sort of antiquary could also operate in a similar way, however, and this activity often took place away from London, parliament and the court. One example of this can be found in the case of Sir Peter Manwood (1571–1625).[12] Manwood's library can be reconstructed

12 P. W. Hasler, *The history of Parliament: the House of Commons, 1588–1603*, 3 vols. (London, 1981), III. 14–15; H. R. Woudhuysen, *Sir Philip Sidney and the circulation of manuscripts, 1558–1640* (Oxford, 1996), 130–3; and L. A. Knafla, 'Sir Peter Manwood', *ODNB* XXXVI. 572–3.

only from evidence in surviving volumes. To judge from the remnants, it was a small but interesting group of medieval manuscripts, with perhaps an even more interesting group of fair manuscript copies largely of older manuscript exemplars, executed by a variety of individuals (and especially by his men of business, the brothers John and Henry Crispe). Of the older manuscripts, a small number were inherited from the collection of his father, Sir Roger Manwood, lord chief baron of the Exchequer under Elizabeth, including a collection of pieces on the claim of the English kings over France, which Peter 'founde the 26th of Marche 1605 of my fathers bookes'.[13] Sir Peter noted Camden's hand in the volume, and had it rebound soon after its reappearance. Sir Roger had several connections with Matthew Parker, and at least one volume, a copy of John Day's printed edition of *A testimonie of antiquitie*, seems to have been owned by Parker.[14] Some of his medieval manuscripts may share the same provenance. Peter Manwood also received volumes through gifts. His ownership of the Ashmole Bestiary (Bodleian, MS Ashmole 1511) contains Manwood's ownership inscription recording the gift of the volume from his friend William Man, on 3 August 1609.[15] The manuscript had probably been an East Anglian production, but in any case had been in the possession of William Wryght, vicar of Chepynge Wycombe, in 1550. Little is known about William Man other than that he was called to the Bar at the Middle Temple in 1605, that he served first as an official at the Court of King's Bench, and then as filazer for Kent, thus moving in circles which would have given him the opportunity to flatter Manwood in either a county or a court context. Manwood also received volumes from leading antiquaries, receiving a copy of John Stow's *Annales* from the author himself on 24 February 1601; in an inscription on the title page, Manwood refers to Stow as 'my freinde'.[16]

Manwood, as a local grandee in Kent, translated his antiquarian interests into his local Kentish setting, as well as indulging them as part of his London activities. Thus we have a group of writers such as Richard Knolles, Edward Grimestone and Thomas Menfeilde, all of whom received patronage from Manwood. Knolles wrote an influential *Generall historie of the Turkes* (1603), as well as translating Jean Bodin's *Six bookes of a commonweale* (1606), and at the same time was appointed by Manwood to the post of master of the school founded by his father at Sandwich. Knolles borrowed books from his patron to

13 Bodleian, MS Bodley 885.
14 Now BL, MS Add. 18160. I owe my knowledge of it to Henry Woudhuysen.
15 R. Poole, 'A MS from the Tradescant collection', *BQR* 6 (1931), 221–2.
16 Woudhuysen, *Circulation of manuscripts*, 131, n. 7. Stow also gave a copy of his *Survey of London* in 1598, which is now in the Folger Shakespeare Library.

help him complete both works. Four volumes of state papers were presented by Manwood to the Bodleian in 1620.[17] Menfeilde's annotations on a copy of Camden's *Britannia* given to him by Manwood reveal that the recipient thought of the donor as a Maecenas.[18]

Another antiquary who operated in both metropolitan and provincial contexts, and as the centre of distinct circles of fellow users and consumers of books, was Lord William Howard of Naworth.[19] Howard was not just a great collector of books, but a reader and annotator of them. He was a copyist of the records possessed by others, but also happy to open up his collections for the use of his immediate circle and other, more distant antiquaries. The evidence for these networks can be seen principally from annotations and marginalia found on volumes which survive from his collections. Lord William's own hand can be clearly identified in a number of instances: he often supplies chapter or sectional headings in a spiky, quasi-gothic hand, and more commonly, we find him making brief marginal notes, clearly intended to mark out the subject of a passage, in a careful italic. His interests can be clearly identified from these pithy summaries. Names of families and individuals predominate, although he also makes reference to other writers, or indeed to other manuscripts. Thus, in the unique copy of the life and passion of St William of Norwich (CUL, MS Add. 3037), we find neat little genealogies, and various dates in the margins. The second half of the manuscript is a copy of the first recension of the *Life and miracles of St Godric* by Reginald of Durham, and this has also been annotated by Howard, bringing to attention, for example, the passage referring to Godric's death in 1170.[20] His notes are quite often accurate, especially when citing the deaths of heads of religious houses or identifiable members of noble households. Occasionally his pen intervenes in a more substantial way. In BL, MS Arundel 11, for example, Howard created a form of index by repeating the supplied chapter headings. His hand does appear elsewhere in the manuscript, but this activity is clearly aimed at assisting the consultation of the volume on subsequent readings, either by himself or by others with access to his books.

17 One is in a handsome contemporary gilt-tooled centrepiece binding, now Bodleian, MS Bodley 966; see G. Barber, 'Notes on some English centre and corner piece bindings *c.* 1600', *Library*, 5th ser., 17 (1962), 93–5.

18 Maggs Catalogue 1121, no. 15.

19 G. Ornsby (ed.), *Selections from the household books of the Lord William Howard of Naworth Castle*, Surtees Soc. 68 (Durham, 1878); H. S. Reinmuth, 'Lord William Howard (1563–1640) and his Catholic associations', *Recusant History* 12 (1973–4), 226–34; D. Mathew, 'The library at Naworth', in D. Woodruff (ed.), *For Hilaire Belloc* (London, 1942), 117–30; and R. Ovenden and S. Handley, 'Lord William Howard', *ODNB* XXVIII. 452–4.

20 CUL, MS Add. 3037, fol. 159^r.

Other hands habitually appear in the margins and flyleaves of the volumes owned by Howard, not all of them positively identifiable. One of them is certainly that of Nicholas Roscarrock, who was a close companion of Howard's from the 1580s, and lived at Naworth after 1607.[21] Howard's factor, Thomas Widmerpoole, was also a man of learning, and annotated some of the manuscripts and printed books. Father Augustine Hungate, Howard's chaplain, would also have had access to the library at Naworth and may well be among the annotators. The others await further study.[22]

To whom outside this inner circle (focused on the Howard stronghold at Naworth) were the Howard collections made available? Cotton and Camden made use of Howard's manuscripts following their first contacts in London in the 1580s, when both were members of the College of Antiquaries.[23] They were certainly not alone. The antiquary and herald Francis Thynne examined material in Howard's collections in the 1590s, seeing one of the volumes of the Fountains cartulary, and notes on the funeral ceremonies of earls from an unidentified book in his possession.[24] The parliamentarian and collector Sir Simonds D'Ewes owned the cartulary of Bermondsey Priory which had been Howard's, possibly indicating a personal connection between the two.[25] Sir George Buc, master of the revels, was another literary figure to make use of the library, making reference to charters and other records seen in 'the cabinet of my good Lord, my Lord William Howard'.[26] James Ussher, a collector and antiquary of the 'first eleven', borrowed one of the four manuscripts of Aldhelm's letters, which he used for his edition, and his antiquities of the British church contains a reference to the Magna Tabula of Glastonbury Abbey, then in Howard's possession at Naworth.[27] In January 1639 Roger Dodsworth visited Howard in the north.

From the end of our period Sir Edward Dering can also be seen as a focus for both metropolitan and provincial collecting, exchanging and related

21 Orme, *Roscarrock's Lives of the saints* (1992).

22 The present author is preparing a comprehensive account of Howard and his circle.

23 There is no documentary evidence for Howard's being a member of the Society until 1617, when his name appears first on a list of those 'living persons fit to keep up and celebrate that Round Table', on a list presented to Buckingham in an attempt to revive the society, printed by Richard Gough in *Archaeologia* 1 (1770), xv–xix.

24 D. Carlson, 'The writings and manuscript collections of the Elizabethan alchemist, antiquary, and herald Francis Thynne', *Huntington Library Quarterly* 52 (1989), 214, 254.

25 BL, MS Harley 231: G. R. C. Davis, *Medieval cartularies of Great Britain* (London, 1958), no. 46.

26 Sir George Buc, *The history of King Richard the Third, 1619*, ed. A. N. Kincaid (Gloucester, 1979), 113.

27 J. Krochalis, 'Magna tabula: the Glastonbury tablets (part 1)', *Arthurian Literature* 15 (1997), 117–18. I owe this reference to James Carley.

antiquarian activity. In 1638, Dering, together with Sir Christopher Hatton, Sir Thomas Shirley and Sir William Dugdale, constituted themselves as a 'Society of Antiquaries' in imitation of the, by then, defunct organisation of the same name. Sharing information concerning original sources was at the heart of their agreement: 'that every one doe helpe and further each others studyes and endeavours by imparting and communicating . . . all such bookes, notes, deedes, rolles, etc., as he hath' and that 'every one do severally gather all observable collections w*hi*ch he can, concerning the foundation of any religious house, or castle, or publike worke, and all memorable notes for historicall illustration of this kingdome' and that 'every one do endeavour to borrowe of other strangers, with whom he hath interest, all such bookes, notes, rolles, deedes, etc., as he can obteyne'. Furthermore, the responsibilities of collecting and copying different classes of materials was divided up between the four men in order to make their activities more efficient.[28] Of the four, Dering was active as an antiquary throughout the period 1580 to 1640, and was the prime mover in the establishment of this society, which flattered its forebear, rather than being a serious attempt at revival. Dering's library has been studied to some degree, but still warrants a detailed examination.[29] Like most of the antiquaries, he owned a substantial reference library of printed books as well as extensive manuscript collections, and many of his printed books survive today, easily identifiable by both ownership inscriptions and armorial bookbindings. Dering was a great annotator of his books: his copy of the 1632 edition of John Guillim's *Display of heraldry*, now in Eton College Library, contains his extensive annotations, and his copy of Lodovico Beccadelli's *Vita Reginaldi Poli, Britanni* (Venice, 1563) shows his close reading of the text, and his ability to draw parallels between the historical events of the previous century and the effects of religious zeal in his own times.[30]

Like Cotton, Dering was educated at both Cambridge and the Middle Temple, and likewise, his dynastic ties were to country estates, with Dering's belonging to rural West Kent, but not far from Canterbury. His county associations, both to Canterbury and Dover, where he was lieutenant, greatly assisted his antiquarian efforts: his position as an antiquary was such that Dugdale referred to him as 'a most complete gentleman in all respects, and an excellent

28 L. B. L[arking], 'On the Surrenden charters', *Archaeologia Cantiana* 1 (1858), 55–9.

29 C. E. Wright, 'Sir Edward Dering: a seventeenth-century antiquary and his "Saxon" charters', in C. Fox and B. Dickens (eds.), *The early cultures of north-west Europe* (Cambridge, 1950), 369–93; and also N. H. Krivatsy and L. Yeandle, 'Books of Sir Edward Dering of Kent (1598–1644)', *PLRE* 4 (1. 137–269).

30 Patrick King, *Catalogue 16*, no. 2.

Antiquarye, and will in some things stand us in stead, out of his ritch treasurye of collections in that kynde'.[31] Dering sat in Parliament during the eventful years leading up to the English Civil War, and sided with the king. He probably owned around 2,000 printed books, and the subjects represented betray a number of interests, and include a passion for contemporary theatre, with many purchases of English dramatists, notably Shakespeare and Jonson, being recorded in his Booke of Expenses. His library also included sections on history, heraldry, genealogy, law, agriculture, education, mathematics, natural history, travel and medicine, as well as English, French and Italian literature. Dering's own deep political interest in contemporary religious debates is reflected in the large number of books on contemporary theological controversies, but his accounts record especially purchases of books on heraldry, both new and second-hand, and include a reference, for example, to the £18 he spent on heraldry books from the sale of the library of Ralph Brook, York Herald.[32]

Dering's collection of charters and manuscripts was of sufficient stature to rank him in the 'first eleven' of British antiquaries. Not only did he secure for Cotton a contemporary copy of Magna Carta from Dover Castle (see below, 537), but he also possessed a huge number of early charters, many of which passed into the Cottonian collection, others remaining at Surrenden until they were sold between 1861 and 1865,[33] although many of the pre-Conquest charters were acquired by the antiquary Thomas Astle in the eighteenth century.

Dering's manuscripts have long since been dispersed, but, although no significant contemporary list survives, many can be identified from inscriptions or armorial bindings. They include an important copy of Thorne's Chronicle of St Augustine's abbey (CUL, MS Add. 3578), and a copy of the *Historia Britonum*, probably the result of an exchange with Cotton (now National Library of Wales, MS Llanstephan 175), a cartulary from Christ Church, Canterbury, another from St Augustine's, and a fragment of a register from Dover Priory (BL, MSS Add. 25109, 46352, 26766), a twelfth-century glossed gospel of St John also from St Augustine's, a thirteenth-century French copy of the *Summa* of Raymundus de Pennafort (Bodleian, MSS Lyell 1 and Lyell empt. 3), a fifteenth-century Italian manuscript of Cornelius Nepos (now Harvard University Library, MS Lat. 1), a Wycliffite bible (London, British and Foreign Bible Society, MS Eng. 1, 2), and another Middle English manuscript (now JRUL, MS Eng. 92). The Dering Roll of Arms, now in the British Library, was one of

31 Krivatsy and Yeandle, 'Sir Edward Dering', 139.

32 Wright, 'Sir Edward Dering', 386.

33 The collection, estimated to include over 2,000 charters, as well as numerous printed books, was sold by Puttick and Simpson in four sales in their London rooms.

two manuscripts purchased from the antiquary Ralph Starkey in 1597, and he also owned an important Roll of Arms containing copies by Robert Glover, Somerset Herald (now Oxford, Queen's Coll., MS 158).[34] His pocket-book records copies of Joscelyn's Anglo-Saxon–Latin Dictionary and Laurence Nowell's *Vocabularium Saxonicum* (copied from originals in the Cottonian library), and a copy of Thomas Stubbs's Chronicles of the archbishops of York; a volume containing transcripts of Cinque Ports records, 1540–50, was sold recently.[35]

The antiquaries did not rely solely on interdependent collecting for the formation of their libraries. Other methods played their part. Those with access to the sites of medieval collections clearly had an advantage. The acquisition of manuscripts from these sites has been seen, to some extent, as an activity of the early phases of the dispersals: in the 1540s, and later in the 1560s. Books and other documents, especially charters, however, could be had by those with the ability to gain access to muniment rooms and other storage areas as late as the 1630s. Dr William Wats, for example, was carefully gathering evidence of manuscripts that had been removed from the muniment room at Canterbury Cathedral in the 1630s, and announced to the dean and chapter that he had discovered a trove of materials: 'For plainly gentlemen there are other manuscripts in the same nest which some time were your or the moncks' before you.'[36] Tantalisingly, Wats also referred in his letter to activities he undertook on behalf of Sir Robert Cotton in Cambridge 'some 20 yeares ago' (i.e. 1618). As we have seen, Sir Edward Dering had access to significant quantities of charters, many of which he passed on to Sir Robert Cotton. Most significant among these was a copy of Magna Carta which Dering gave to Cotton in 1630 and which he had discovered among the muniments of Dover Castle, a repository to which he had free access, as lieutenant of the castle, and to which he liberally helped himself.[37]

Dering was not the only collector of charters. Sir Simonds D'Ewes, another antiquary with a penchant for medieval manuscripts, amassed an enormous collection of deeds and charters, some from sources within his own family, but others from landowners with no interest in retaining ancient deeds, and others by acquisition *en bloc* from other sources: many hundreds of charters relating to Lincolnshire monastic houses came into his possession in the early

34 A. Wagner, *A catalogue of English medieval rolls of arms*, Harleian Society publications, 100 (Oxford, 1950), 14–16.

35 H. P. Kraus, *Catalogue 176*, no. 57.

36 C. E. Woodruff and W. Danks, *Memorials of the Cathedral Priory of Christ in Canterbury* (London, 1912), 393; N. Ramsay, 'The cathedral archives and library', in P. Collinson *et al.* (eds.), *A History of Canterbury Cathedral* (Oxford, 1995), 381.

37 Wright, 'Sir Edward Dering', 375–7.

1640s through a gift from Montagu Bertie, 2nd earl of Lindsey, and others came from gifts from the heralds Sir William Le Neve, Sir Richard St George and John Philpot in the 1630s. A further significant tranche came in 1628, when D'Ewes acquired the printed and manuscript collections of the recently deceased antiquary Ralph Starkey, which collection itself included a significant quantity of John Stow's own papers.[38]

Antiquaries gave and received books and manuscripts for a variety of reasons. One reason was to seek friendship or favour on behalf of the giver. Thomas Sparke, for example, gave a manuscript treatise on the Ten Commandments to John Sanford, a prebend of Christ Church, Canterbury, in 1622. Describing Sanford as 'a most worthy favourer of learning and lover of antiquities', Sparke gave the manuscript 'in regard of your care and good ende towards the preferment of my child in his learning'.[39] Sanford had been a prominent Oxford don in his time, teaching French, Italian and Spanish at Balliol and Magdalen, in addition to publishing grammars of Latin, Italian and Spanish.[40]

How were these libraries formed, and in particular what were the sources for the supply of medieval manuscripts to the libraries of the antiquaries? The period 1580 to 1640 witnessed the rise of the phenomenon of the second-hand trade in manuscripts. This particular aspect of the book trade has not been the subject of much concerted study, to some extent because the existing evidence for the activities of commercial booksellers in the trade in manuscripts is somewhat scant. Booksellers, of course, became interested in medieval manuscripts as soon as the Dissolution began to encourage the depopulating of libraries of the old learning. But for the most part, these manuscripts were acquired only to be broken up and used as all manner of waste material. By the middle of the century, however, the markets for these manuscripts changed. It became clear that there were those who placed a value on the intact material, and as a result some booksellers began to play a part in the preservation of manuscripts, as opposed to their destruction. Thus in 1574 John Dee acquired a manuscript 'from a stall in London'.[41] By the early seventeenth century a little more evidence becomes extant; here are just a few examples. Particularly active in this area was Stephen Potts, who gave manuscripts to St John's College,

38 A. G. Watson, 'Sir Simonds D'Ewes' collection of charters and a note of Sir Robert Cotton's charters', *Journal of the Society of Archivists* 2 (1962), 247–54; *The library of Sir Simonds D'Ewes* (London, 1966).

39 BL, MS Cotton Cleopatra A. v, fol. 13.

40 M. Feingold, 'The Humanities', in *HUO* IV. 271.

41 J. Roberts and A. G. Watson (eds.), *John Dee's library catalogue* (London, 1990), 17.

Oxford, and who also sold manuscripts to Sir Roger Twysden.[42] Even more important seem to have been Laurence Sadler and Cornelius Bee, both of whom acted as suppliers of quite important manuscripts for figures such as Archbishop Laud, Sir Roger Twysden and Sir Simonds D'Ewes.[43] Scipio Le Squyer patronised Launcelot Toppyn, another London dealer, who had access to medieval manuscripts which had been at Exeter in the middle ages.[44] In 1628, moreover, we have a list returned to the Privy Council of thirty-nine dealers in 'old libraries, mart bookes or any other'.[45]

The rise in the number of booksellers dealing, or to some extent specialising, in medieval manuscripts naturally went hand in hand with a rise in the commercial values attached to such books. William Wats, a Canterbury cleric, wrote in 1638 that he had seen a 'book of the Obites and particular places of burialls of the Priors' and that 'The Bookseller asked me 20s for it, which I being loth to give, and fearing to buye lest you should have said I found it amongst Dr Sympson's books'.[46]

The activities of Lord William Howard also betray some evidence of the liveliness of the second-hand trade in manuscripts. In 1589, Howard's busiest year for acquiring manuscripts (to judge by his dated ownership inscriptions), he purchased the Arundel or Eadui Psalter from John Proctor, who had a shop on Holborn Bridge. On only one manuscript does he appear to have written the price he paid for the book: £5 for a collection of Irish medical texts, now MS Arundel 333 in the British Library. In 1628 we find Howard paying 7s for 'an olde manuscript and 2 other bookes . . . bought at Worcester',[47] one of the few hints we have that Howard was actively pursuing manuscripts outside of London and his network of like-minded scholars and antiquaries, although which book the comment refers to is not known. By and large Howard seems to have had a lengthy relationship with the London trade for printed books. Throughout the seventeenth century he patronised London booksellers, and in the 1620s and 1630s he gave a good deal of custom to Humphrey Robinson, a bookseller

42 Potts sold a manuscript of Jacobus de Voragine, *Legenda aurea*, to Twysden in 1626 (now BL, MS Stowe 49). R. W. Hunt, 'Donors of manuscripts to St John's College Oxford during the presidency of William Laud 1611–1621', in R. W. Hunt, I. G. Philip and R. J. Roberts (eds.), *Studies in the book trade in honour of Graham Pollard*, Oxford Bibliographical Society publications, n.s., 18 (Oxford, 1975), 68.

43 M. A. F. Borrie, 'The Thorne Chronicle', *British Museum Quarterly* 31 (1966–7), 87–90.

44 R. Ovenden, 'Scipio Le Squyer and the fate of monastic cartularies in the early seventeenth century', *Library*, 6th ser., 13 (1991), 325.

45 W. W. Greg, *A companion to Arber* (Oxford, 1967), 40–1.

46 Woodruff and Danks, *Memorials*, 393.

47 G. Ornsby (ed.), *Selections from the household books of Lord William Howard of Naworth*, Surtees Soc. 68 (Durham, 1878), 244.

at the Three Pigeons, St Paul's Churchyard, and one of the most important figures in the London trade. In 1620 we find no less a figure than William Laud purchasing manuscripts from George Loftus, a London bookseller. Laud also purchased manuscripts from his neighbour at Croydon, Daniel Harvey, a merchant, amounting to the substantial sum of £50 in 1638.[48]

One question remains about the operation of the book trade in making medieval collections available – that of the dispersal of large collections. The death of John Dee in 1609 produced a great dispersal of important manuscripts and printed books, many of which were to be found in the collections of other antiquaries soon after Dee's death. How did they get there? What is clear from the work of Julian Roberts and Andrew Watson is that Patrick Saunders and John Woodall, who had come by the largest remnant of the Dee library, had recourse to a bookseller in London – possibly identifiable with John White in Little Britain, a prominent stationer who was involved with the Latin trade – and it is possibly he who marked many of the Dee books with a cipher. Certainly, from the accounts of Sir Simonds D'Ewes, it is clear that a number of Dee's books were being sold in 1625 and early 1626, at least two groups being marked in his accounts as 'Ex Bibliotheca Joh Dee Doctoris 1626'.[49]

One aspect of the collecting activities of the antiquaries which should be considered as culturally significant is the emerging interest in and appreciation of medieval art, which can be detected through their libraries. Ascribing 'modern' notions of concepts so notoriously difficult as aesthetics, taste and appreciation to Renaissance individuals is a dangerous area to become involved with, but some of the libraries of contemporary antiquarian collectors display such a remarkable array of significant examples of medieval art that it would be misleading to ignore it altogether.

The collections of Lord William Howard are particularly revealing in this regard. Of the books which Howard possessed, we see some of the most significant examples of late medieval English illumination, and several examples of highly important work from earlier periods. Howard possessed the Gospels of Queen Margaret of Scotland, for example, a small but highly significant gospel lectionary of the mid-eleventh century (Bodleian, MS Lat. liturg. f.5), and possibly identifiable with one of the five gospel books regarded as relics in a late fourteenth-century inventory of the books at Durham Cathedral Priory. It is not a *de luxe* book, but it does have a group of illustrations – portraits of the four evangelists – and, given its Scottish royal and Durham monastic

48 H. O. Coxe, *Laudian Manuscripts*, ed. R. W. Hunt (Oxford, 1973), xxvii, xxxiii.
49 Roberts and Watson, *Dee's library*, 64–5.

provenance, is a book of considerable significance. The manuscript was one of five in Howard's library which had been previously owned by John Stow. There have been serious claims made for Stow to have been, like Howard, a Catholic, but a shared passion for the past would have been enough to cement the friendship of the two, and certainly enough for them to have exchanged manuscripts as fellow members of the College of Antiquaries.[50] Howard also acquired the manuscript now known as the Arundel or Eadui Psalter (BL, MS Arundel 155). Originally written in the second quarter of the eleventh century, in both Latin and Anglo-Saxon, with the text altered to Gallican use after the Conquest, it is one of a number of manuscripts written by the scribe Eadui Basan, a monk at Christ Church, Canterbury.[51] It is illustrated with a combination of line-drawings and a single full-page miniature carefully executed in full colour and gold, illustrating Eadui holding the psalter at the feet of St Benedict. From Howard's inscription in the volume we know that he purchased the book in 1592. With such significant Christ Church connections, the book would undoubtedly have had a value among the antiquaries of the late sixteenth century as a historical document from the latter stages of the Anglo-Saxon period, but such a beautiful book – the Caroline minuscule is as much an element of its aesthetic value as the illustrations – seems to have avoided the fate of the extensive annotation which befell Howard's other manuscripts.

From the high middle ages, Howard's collection included three of the most important English examples of the illuminator's art. Two of these passed down through the Fitzalan and Howard families, and, given his own regard for the Howard name, their presence raises no eyebrows. The Luttrell Psalter (BL, MS Add. 42130) is one of the most famous of all English medieval manuscripts, known chiefly for the astonishing marginal illustrations by five different artists, which convey a strange and bizarre picture of medieval life.[52] It descended through the Fitzalan family to Mary Fitzalan, who married Lord William's father, from whom Lord William no doubt inherited the volume. Another important work of medieval art with family connections is that now known as the Howard-Fitton Psalter, which is, like Luttrell, now in the British Library (MS Arundel 83, pt 1). This is an important early

50 R. Gameson, 'The Gospels of Margaret of Scotland and the literacy of an eleventh-century queen', in L. Smith and J. H. M. Taylor (eds.), *Women and the book: assessing the visual evidence* (London, 1996), 149–71. For Stow's Catholicism see I. W. Archer, 'John Stow, citizen and historian', in I. Gadd and A. Gillespie (eds.), *John Stow (1525–1605) and the making of the English past* (London, 2004), 20–1.

51 M. Gibson, T. A. Heslop and R. W. Pfaff (eds.), *The Eadwine Psalter: text, image, and monastic culture* (London, 1992).

52 J. Backhouse, *The Luttrell Psalter* (London, 1989).

fourteenth-century manuscript, written and illuminated in East Anglia. The manuscript contains, in addition to its superb illumination, the arms of the Howard family juxtaposed with those of Fitton, probably referring to Lord William's ancestors Sir William Howard and his wife, Alice Fitton. Given these firm family connections, it seems likely that this volume also remained within the Howard family, passing down to Lord William on the death of his father. The same cannot be said for the manuscript which is today bound inside the same covers as the Howard-Fitton Psalter, namely that masterpiece of early fourteenth-century illumination, the De Lisle Psalter (fols. 117–35^{v}). De Lisle, unlike its close neighbour, bears no apparent connection with the Howard family. Codicologically, and palaeographically, the two manuscripts can be shown to have been originally separate. De Lisle is considerably the smaller of the two, now consisting of only nineteen folios, as opposed to the 116 of the Howard Psalter. Howard was not prone to dismembering his own books, unlike many of his contemporaries, Cotton in particular. Furthermore, Howard-Fitton is the larger of the two manuscripts, a fact that whoever had them bound together respected, as to have trimmed it down to the size of De Lisle would have been an act of serious vandalism.[53] The De Lisle Psalter certainly outshines the Howard-Fitton Psalter in the quality of the remaining illumination. The twenty-four illustrations, all large miniatures, comprise a narrative cycle of the life of Christ and a group of theological diagrams and pictorial moralities. The text is lost, suggesting forcefully that whoever preserved what remains did so on account of the quality and beauty of the illuminations. Was Lord William responsible for the pairing? This is suggested by the separate, dated ownership inscriptions on the two manuscripts: on Howard-Fitton, 1591, and on De Lisle, 1590. De Lisle's original recipients were nuns at the Gilbertine house at Chicksands in Bedfordshire. The house was dissolved in 1538, the lands passing through the Snowe and Osborne families, neither of which appears to have any connection with the Howards; it may have been acquired by Lord William through the trade. Given that De Lisle seems to have been acquired first, probably in a fragmentary state, from an unknown source, it seems highly likely that Howard bound the book up with the Howard-Fitton Psalter, and in so doing displayed an understanding and appreciation of the stylistic affinities of these two *de luxe* books. Such a scenario must of course remain conjecture – and indeed it is equally possible that the two manuscripts were bound together in the early seventeenth century, when they were acquired by Howard's nephew Thomas Howard, 2nd earl of

53 L. F. Sandler, *The Psalter of Robert De Lisle in the British Library*, rev. edn (London, 1999).

Arundel, who not only had a sophisticated appreciation of art, but employed a librarian, Franciscus Junius, who may have had a hand in binding books in the Arundel collection (see below, 544).[54]

The nature of Howard's attitude to these books was probably a mixture of several different motives. The presence of the Howard-Fitton and Luttrell Psalters may easily be explained as the evidence of descent through the family, but their preservation within the collection, and the additional presence of other illuminated manuscripts which were undoubtedly purchased, and the fact that all were kept free from the kind of annotation that is a characteristic of other volumes, suggest that some element of appreciation of the books as works of art was present in his consciousness. We must not, however, forget that the English recusants played a major role in the physical preservation of sacred objects. Not only books, but other artefacts were preserved, most famously the body of St Chad and the Syon cope.[55] Howard, too, played his part in this. The Langdale Rosary, a late medieval English rosary of gold with enamelled panels now in the Victoria and Albert Museum, is one example. The piece is connected to both Lord William and Nicholas Roscarrock, who had beads added to the piece with depictions of both St Endelient, a Cornish saint, and St William of Norwich, to whom Howard appears to have held a special devotion, as he owned one of the most important manuscripts of the life of William, now in Cambridge University Library.[56] Howard also had the ornate ceiling transferred from Kirkoswald Castle and placed in his own library room at Naworth – behaviour which further indicates aesthetic appreciation, as well as a taste for medieval heraldry. Given his ownership of altars and inscribed stones from Hadrian's Wall, we can perhaps build a picture of a collector, and one with multiple motives lying behind the basic impulse to collect. It is tempting to conjecture, given the variety of his collections, that Howard was partaking in that aristocratic habit of withdrawing from the world into a place occupied with uncommon objects: books, jewellery, coins and stones (for example), which reflect his own multi-faceted interest in, and relationship with, the past.[57]

One other example can be identified which strengthens the argument for identifying the period 1580 to 1640 as the birth of appreciation of medieval

54 D. Howarth, *Lord Arundel and his circle* (New Haven, CT, 1985).

55 D. Rogers, 'The English recusants: some mediaeval literary links', *Recusant History* 23 (1997), 485–6.

56 Orme, *Roscarrock*, 11–12; R. W. Lightbown, *Medieval European jewellery* (London, 1992), 526–8.

57 A. Emery, *Greater medieval houses of England and Wales, 1300–1500*, I: *Northern England* (Cambridge, 1996), 233–5.

books as works of art. Some of Sir Robert Cotton's practices with the volumes he has bound up show an aesthetic sensibility at work. For example, Cotton occasionally identified his books in his own catalogues as being beautiful, normally referring to decoration or illumination rather than to script. He also wrote about books that he had seen and to which he took a liking – partly because of their decoration. More tellingly, Cotton was frequently to be found removing decorated leaves from highly illuminated manuscripts (often psalters and other liturgical books) to be found homes in undecorated volumes as frontispieces; such acts were not normally undertaken without thought by Cotton, for he clearly had an eye for the significance of iconography, provenance or decorative schemes both in the inserted leaves and in the places where they were inserted. Clearly, the inserts and the recipients were consciously and carefully chosen to complement one another. Such actions are not normally regarded as the behaviour of the connoisseur, but examples of artistic appreciation from this period are scarce: Cotton's behaviour, if we can see beyond our twenty-first-century sensibilities, can be identified with fledgling aesthetic judgements.[58]

At the very end of our period emerges the first clearly identifiable connoisseur of medieval and Renaissance illumination, in the person of Thomas Howard, 2nd earl of Arundel, the nephew, as has already been noted, of Lord William Howard.[59] Arundel's collection, partly inherited from his uncle, became one of the greatest in England, and must be seen as one facet of a much broader and equally impressive collecting strategy, ranging from architectural drawings to antique sculpture (the famous 'Arundel Marbles', now in the Ashmolean Museum, Oxford). In the 1630s, Arundel became the head of a diplomatic mission to Nuremberg, and there acquired the library of the great Renaissance collector Wilibald Pirckheimer, which included a number of books illustrated by Dürer. The most significant example of illumination in the Arundel collection, however, was the Gritti / Arundel Psalter, which was given to Arundel by Francesco Barberini's secretary Cassiano dal Pozzo, who was closely attuned to Arundel's collecting interests – the book was therefore a supremely well-chosen diplomatic gift. Although he cannot be regarded as specifically an antiquary, Howard as a courtier and officer of the state did encourage antiquarian activity (through employment of Franciscus Junius as his own librarian, promoting the antiquarian work of the artist and printmaker

58 M. Brown, 'Sir Robert Cotton, collector and connoisseur?', in M. P. Brown and S. McKendrick, *Illuminating the book: makers and interpreters: essays in honour of Janet Backhouse* (London, 1998), 281–98.

59 Howarth, *Lord Arundel*.

Wenceslaus Hollar, and financing the research of Selden and others on the Arundel Marbles). The combination of Arundel as antiquary, collector and connoisseur can therefore allow him to be identified as the heir of the generation of Howard and Cotton, and the prototype of the 'modern' collectors that were to follow.[60]

An integral part of building the collections of antiquaries was the exchange of originals for the purpose of obtaining copies. Until the recent work of Henry Woudhuysen and Peter Beal, this particular aspect of collecting has not been widely recognised.[61] There is much evidence to demonstrate this kind of activity as being integral to the development of the libraries of antiquaries during this period. Peter Manwood, for instance, regularly borrowed manuscripts from his fellow antiquaries, and the fair copies survive: a copy of the English translation of Camden's *Britannia* by Richard Knolles; he borrowed Stow's original of the life of Henry V; and in the letter from Manwood to Cotton already referred to, there is mention of Manwood 'writing oute of an oulde booke, but itt goeth forward slowely because of ye ould hande out of use with us'.[62] The Society of Antiquaries established by Dering, Dugdale and others in 1638 had copying as a central facet of its activities, and we know a good deal about Dering's own antiquarian methods, thanks to the copies he made of his substantial collection of charters, long since dispersed, but often relating closely to his relationship with Cotton, to whom he would send the originals of his Saxon charters 'as fast as I can coppy them'.[63] Ussher recommended 'Mr Thomas Downes, stationer' as a copyist 'who dwelleth at White Hart Court in Warwick Lane'.[64]

Exchanges also took place of original manuscripts. Sir Robert Cotton and Sir Simonds D'Ewes, for example, shared a manuscript from Dee's library in 1626, probably as part of an exchange of manuscripts between the two, and passed some of these parts on to Thomas Allen of Oxford.[65] The Welsh antiquary

60 D. Jaffé *et al.*, 'The earl and countess of Arundel: Renaissance collectors', *Apollo* 164/414 (August 1996), 24–6; H. G. Fletcher *et al.*, *The Wormsley Library* (London, 1999), 62–7; R. Ovenden, 'Thomas Howard, second [=14th] earl of Arundel', in W. Baker and K. Womack (eds.), *Pre-nineteenth-century British book collectors and bibliographers* (Detroit, 1999), 155–63.

61 Woudhuysen, *Circulation of manuscripts*, 116–33; P. Beal, *In praise of scribes: manuscripts and their makers in seventeenth-century England* (Oxford, 1998).

62 BL, MS Lansdowne 85, fol. 185^{r}.

63 These volumes are now BL, MSS Add. 5481, Add. 43471, Stowe 853 and Stowe 924: see Wright, 'Sir Edward Dering', and B. S., 'A Dering Manuscript', *British Museum Quarterly* 8 (1933–4), 26–7, citing the letter from Dering to Cotton (BL, MS Cotton Julius C. iii, fol. 143^{r}).

64 C. R. Elrington (ed.), *The whole works of the Most Rev. James Ussher, DD* (1847–64), XVI. 46–7.

65 A. G. Watson, 'A Merton College manuscript reconstructed', *BLR* 9 (1976), 207–17.

Jaspar Gryffyth regularly borrowed books from Cotton, and on one occasion in 1613 sent him a lot of over forty manuscripts from his own collection for borrowing in return. Gryffyth was clearly anxious to demonstrate that he also was a serious collector, who had items worth borrowing, no doubt to maintain access to Cotton's burgeoning library: 'I would gladlie knowe wherin I might anyway gratifie you & requite in some measur your greate kindnesse'.[66]

Not surprisingly, such a situation conspired to encourage not only circles of antiquaries working closely together, bound by ties of religion, family and shared interest, but also rivalry, envy and suspicion. The evidence for these aspects of collection-building is scant, but there are hints to be found. In a letter from Sir Peter Manwood to Sir Robert Cotton, for example, he asks Cotton 'to please remember me for H. the 8. Lyff wch I exsedingly desire to reade. I will keepe itt p*ri*vatt to my self',[67] which suggests that Cotton himself might be anxious not to let others have access to the volume. Likewise the death of antiquaries and collectors also created the opportunity for competitive instincts to come to the surface among the antiquaries of early seventeenth-century London. In his autobiography, D'Ewes described the size and importance of the collection, formed by a man for whom D'Ewes himself had few kind words to say, while he nonetheless 'had an earnest desire to buy the librarie, but mine owne wants, and diuers other men being about the acquiring of it likewise made mee feare I should misse of it'.[68] The Society of Antiquaries formed by Dering, Hatton, Shirley and Dugdale drew up clauses which insisted that their rough copies 'be not imparted to any stranger without the gene*ra*ll consent of this society'.[69]

Many antiquaries, especially those from titled families, were able to acquire materials from within their own family. Simonds D'Ewes, for instance, wrote to Dering in 1633 complaining that he could not get 'the great harvest of old deedes touching my wives seuerall families out of the Ladie Tracies hands'.[70] Lord William Howard was able to benefit from family connections to acquire books, such as the Luttrell and Howard-Fitton Psalters noted above. Of course, his connections were rather better than most of his fellow countrymen, so this was a considerable advantage. Several printed books have a dated *ex libris* of Lord William's father, the 4th duke of Norfolk. The Yale copy of Upton's *De officio*

66 R. Ovenden, 'Jaspar Gryffyth and his books', *BLJ* 20 (1994), 107–39.

67 BL, MS Lansdowne 85, fol. 185r. The manuscript may be BL, MS Cotton Vespasian B. xvii: C. G. C. Tite, *The early records of Sir Robert Cotton's library: formation, cataloguing, use* (London, 2003), 178.

68 Watson, *Library of Sir Simonds D'Ewes*, 24.

69 L[arking], 'Surrenden charters', 56.

70 Watson, 'Sir Simonds D'Ewes' collection', 248.

militari has the inscription of Henry Fitzalan, 12th earl of Arundel, one of the greatest book-collectors of the sixteenth century, and was presumably acquired by Howard through the same route. In the early stages of the production of the 1607 edition of the *Britannia*, Camden was forced to hold up the printing, as his friend Lord William Howard of Naworth, 'for the love that he beareth the studies of antiquity, willingly imparted unto me the Manuscript Annales of Ireland . . . which I thought good to publish'.[71] The volume (Bodleian, MS Laud Misc. 526) had been acquired by his grandfather, Thomas Howard, 2nd earl of Surrey, Henry VIII's viceroy in Ireland, and Lord William no doubt acquired the volume through family descent. He also owned two other Irish manuscripts, both collections of Irish medical texts, but they appear not to have come to him by the same route.

Howard seems to have been particularly close to his uncle Henry Howard, the earl of Northampton. Northampton, too, was deeply interested in literature, learning and antiquarian pursuits. After his death, the majority of Northampton's books were acquired by his nephew Thomas Howard, 2nd earl of Arundel, in 1615 for £529. But not everything passed in this direction. Of particular importance are the five volumes of Northampton's commonplace books, four of which are with the remnants of the Howard library now at Durham; one strayed with part of the Howard estate papers and is now at Castle Howard. As with his medieval illuminated manuscripts, Lord William resisted the temptation to annotate the books, leaving them reverentially alone. Further evidence of this respect is the fact that Lord William purchased one of the most important pieces of English Renaissance silverware from Northampton's estate (of which he was an overseer and a financial beneficiary) for £7 12s. The item in question is known as the Howard Grace Cup, and is now in the Victoria and Albert Museum. It is hallmarked 1525–6, but encompasses an ivory bowl which tradition has ascribed to Thomas Becket.[72]

The acquisition of the Dacre estates in the late sixteenth century also brought new sources of books. One case in point is the Lanercost cartulary, missing since the eighteenth century, but now safely residing in the Cumbria County Record Office. Lanercost, a short stroll from Naworth Castle, had been granted to the Dacres after the Dissolution, and many of the outbuildings had been appropriated by the family for residential purposes. Cartularies, of course, tended to be transferred along with the lands which they document, and so the Dacres would have taken possession of the cartulary of

71 William Camden, *Britannia* (London, 1607), 794.

72 L. Levy Peck, *Northampton: patronage and policy at the court of James I* (London, 1982); P. Glanville, *Silver in Tudor and early Stuart England* (London, 1990), 394–7.

the Augustinian Priory at Lanercost at the same time as they acquired the priory buildings and the lands which had accrued to it since its foundation in 1169.

The idea of a national collection

Despite, or perhaps because of, the multitude of substantial private collections of antiquaries, and the frequent and significant interaction between them during this period, a number of these individuals recognised the need for a 'national' collection. In 1602 or early 1603, three prominent members of the Society or College of Antiquaries – Sir Robert Cotton, Sir James Ley and John Dodderidge – drew up a petition which was presented to Elizabeth I outlining 'A proiect touching a petition to be exhibited vnto her maiesty for the erecting of her library and an Academy'.[73]

The scheme focused on preserving what the antiquaries regarded as the memory of the nation, and embraced both the formation of a collection, governed by specific collection development policies, and the arrangements for the continued management of it, alongside proposals to develop an 'Accademye for the studye of Antiquity and Historye' which they hoped would be populated with persons 'studious of antiquitie for the better preservation of the said Library & encrease of knowledge in that behalfe'. The forming of a central repository for materials crucial to the nation's past was at the heart of the proposal: they highlighted 'divers old bookes concerninge mater of history of this Realme originall Charters & monuments' which they regarded as needful of preservation, for these materials are 'rare & . . . otherwise maye perishe'. Numerous examples are cited: 'their ar divers & sundry monuments worthe observation whearof the orygynall is extant in the hands of some privat gentleman & allso divers others excellent monumentes whearof there is no record now extant which by theise meanes shall have publick & salfe [*sic*] custody for vse when occasion shall serve'. Furthermore, the public good is not being served, for 'there are divers treatises published by auctoryte for the satisfaction of the world in divers matters publicke which after they are by publik auctoryte prynted & dispersed they do so after som tym become

73 The petition is found in two copies in the Cottonian collection (MSS Faustina E. v (fols. 89–90) and Titus B. v (fol. 210)). The text was printed in part by Richard Gough in his preface to *Archaeologia* 1 (1777), i–xxix, and completed by J. Ayloffe in his edition of Thomas Hearne's *Collection of curious discourses* (London, 1771), 324. The most recent and accessible printing is to be found in N. Barker (ed.), *Treasures of the British Library* (London, 1996), 43.

very rare for that there is no publick preservation of historye & Antiquity of which the vniversityes being busyed in the artes tak little care or regard'. The centralisation of these manuscripts should also include material at present in the royal library, which was known to be in the doldrums during Elizabeth's reign.[74] One of the clauses of the petition therefore suggested 'that it may please her Maiesty to bestow out of her gratious library sutche & so many of her bookes concernying history & Antiquity as yt shall please her highnes to graunt for the better furnishing of this library'.

The benefits of such a scheme are not detailed in the petition, but from some of the clauses we can see that the antiquaries clearly felt that such a state-driven development could derive clear benefits for the state. The members of the academy would be 'enabled to do vnto her Maiesty & the Realme sutche service as shall be requisite for their place', and they were quick to point out that such persons would be above reproach in terms of loyalty: 'none shall be admitted . . . except that he take the othe of the Supremacy'. The petitioners were anxious that the deliberations of the academy should be flexible enough to allow for the members to be able to indulge their own curiosities without fear or suspicion from the state, but indeed for the state's long-term benefit: 'To this corporation may be added the Study of forreyn modern Tongues of the nations our neighbors Countryes & regard of their historyes & state whereby this Realm in a short tyme may be furnished with sundry gentlemen enabled to do her Maiesty & the realme service as agentes or otherwise to be Imployed.'

By this final strategically placed suggestion that the knowledge to be derived from antiquarian and related studies could be placed at the state's disposal, especially in relation to foreign affairs, the petitioners were clearly hoping that Elizabeth's own sense of her vulnerable international position would lead to a favourable answer. The end result is clear: no such endeavour was embarked upon, but the reasons for inaction are less obvious. As no formal reply has survived, some have doubted whether the petition was ever formally delivered, suggesting that the copies in the Cottonian collection are merely drafts.[75] If the petition was presented, then it is also clear that it was drafted for Elizabeth, in the last year of her reign, but that it probably remained for James VI and I to consider a response. The inaction can be explained in a variety of ways. The Scottish king had little knowledge of antiquaries, and therefore no reason to favour their proposals. He also had reason to dislike the

74 Birrell, *English monarchs and their books* (London, 1987), 24–6.
75 Barker, *Treasures*, 42–4.

suggestion that the royal library be dismembered; not only was James scholarly, but he brought his own librarian, Peter Young (later to be succeeded by his son Patrick), down from Scotland with him.[76] More importantly, the strategic value of the academy and its library disappeared with James's attempts to cease the war with Spain.[77]

Whatever the reasons, the attempt of the antiquaries to establish a national collection and an academy of scholars to go alongside it failed. But, perversely, a by-product of this failure can be perceived to be the creation of the most important private collection of the seventeenth century, for Sir Robert Cotton went on from the failure of the petition to amass what would in the eighteenth century be one of the founding collections of the Britain's national library itself.

The library of Sir Robert Cotton

The library of Sir Robert Cotton is of pivotal importance in the history of libraries, not just of the period 1580 to 1640 (a period which, in fact, spans Cotton's own career in collecting), or indeed of the seventeenth century as a whole, but in the history of libraries *per se*. Cotton's collection is so vast, and the materials it contains so important for such a wide range of studies, that the collection itself to some extent still defies a single comprehension. Indeed, Cotton himself was a man of such diverse interests and activities that, until Kevin Sharpe's monograph of 1979, he had not been the subject of a comprehensive biographical study. Fortunately, the Cottonian collection received a good deal of scholarly attention in the latter part of the twentieth century, and as a result it is now possible to attempt to place Cotton and his library in the context of the antiquarian movement and the libraries of the antiquaries in the period 1580 to 1640.[78]

Cotton is one of the more difficult antiquaries of this period to categorise. Born in 1571 into gentry stock, he would, had he been of a different

76 Birrell, *English monarchs*, 26–30.

77 S. Adams, 'Spain or the Netherlands?', in H. Tomlinson (ed.), *Before the English Civil War* (London, 1983).

78 See especially Wright, 'Elizabethan Society of Antiquaries'; K. Sharpe, *Sir Robert Cotton, 1586–1631: history and politics in early modern England* (Oxford, 1979); C. C. G. Tite, *The manuscript library of Sir Robert Cotton* (London, 1994); the contributions to C. J. Wright (ed.), *Sir Robert Cotton as collector: essays on an early Stuart courtier and his legacy* (London, 1997); G. Parry, *The trophies of time: English antiquarians of the seventeenth century* (Oxford, 1995); and, most recently, Tite, *Early records of Sir Robert Cotton's library*. The following account of Cotton is particularly indebted to the published and unpublished contributions and friendship of Colin Tite, the doyen of all Cotton scholars.

temperament, perhaps have been satisfied with a life managing his inherited estates. But thanks to a series of influences during Cotton's education, he was spurred with an extraordinary impetus to embark on a life of antiquarian pursuits. The first of these occurred during his time at Westminster School, where William Camden had recently been appointed master and was working toward the first edition of his *Britannia*. Camden and Cotton were to remain close friends for the rest of their lives. From Westminster School Cotton went up to Jesus College, Cambridge, where Richard Bancroft was a tutor, prior to his taking up a post at St Paul's Cathedral and eventually appointment to the see of London. Bancroft, a serious book-collector, although not an antiquary, may have exerted an early influence on Cotton, but some of the Cambridge contacts he made were more tangible.[79] More significantly, Cotton entered the Middle Temple in 1588. As we have seen, the College of Antiquaries, founded just a few years earlier, drew many of its early members from the legal profession, and confined its meetings to the law terms. The milieu around the Inns of Court in the 1580s was clearly conducive both to antiquarian discussions and to fostering nascent collecting instincts. In 1588, Cotton's first recorded acquisitions take place: three manuscript volumes: a mid-tenth-century collection of pieces on confession and penance, a fifteenth-century copy of Higden's *Polychronicon*, and a compendium which included Giles of Rome's *De regimine principum*.[80]

Throughout the next decade more manuscript acquisitions followed, including manuscripts from the collection of John, Lord Lumley, and perhaps his first really significant acquisition – the remarkable Vespasian Psalter (Cotton Vespasian A. i), which bears Cotton's signature dated 1599. As Colin Tite has pointed out, one indication of both the size and the notoriety of Cotton's collection at this time is the fact that Sir Thomas Bodley thought Cotton worth approaching to solicit manuscripts for his library in Oxford.[81] The failed petition to Elizabeth in the early years of the seventeenth century therefore came at a time when not only was Cotton establishing himself in the middle of a network of men with similar antiquarian interests, but his own collecting was beginning to become a major part of his life. The petition's failure also coincided with a time when Cotton's own library was becoming an institution, not only within the circle of cognoscenti, but for a wider audience within both erudite and political circles of London. In 1604, for example, we have the first

79 D. Pearson, 'The libraries of English bishops, 1600–1640', *Library*, 6th ser., 14 (1992), 235.
80 Tite, *Manuscript library*, 5.
81 Tite, *Manuscript library*, 6; H. Ellis, *Original letters of eminent literary men of the sixteenth, seventeenth, and eighteenth centuries* (London, 1843), 103.

evidence that Cotton was lending material from his collection, and on a scale which prompted him to record the items in a list (the first of many); and the fact that the borrowers included Cotton's own patron, the earl of Northampton, suggests that the range of uses to which his collection was being put matched the aims outlined in the petition to Elizabeth. His collection has been described as 'effectively the library of the Society of Antiquaries', but, as later events would show, contemporaries also viewed it as a potent political force.[82]

The library grew at a remarkable rate during the following thirty years, and by a variety of means. A surprisingly high proportion of the acquisitions consisted of gifts: William Lambarde, Richard Carew and of course Camden and Arthur Agarde were donors from among his Society of Antiquaries friends (the latter two leaving him a proportion of their libraries in their wills). Significant books were given by parliamentarians such as Sir Edward Dering and Sir John Selden, and by contacts outside of London such as the Irish collectors James Ussher and Sir James Ware.[83]

But Cotton could not have built up such a large collection through the gifts of his friends and admirers alone. Like many of the antiquaries, Cotton used every method available to acquire his favoured materials. Manuscripts, as has already been shown, were freely exchanged and traded among the antiquaries, and in this respect Cotton must be regarded as the centre of this trading network. Patrick Young, Sir Simonds D'Ewes, Archbishop Richard Bancroft and others all engaged in exchanging and trading manuscript volumes with Cotton. This activity did, however, encourage the kind of breaking up of volumes now regarded as highly unethical, as it destroyed much vital provenantial evidence. From the scale of dismemberment in the context of exchanges, however, contemporaries clearly regarded it as a valid method of building a collection, and there is therefore a danger of being overly critical in hindsight.[84]

Cotton also had access to the principal official repositories of records and documents, a fact that certainly aided his efforts to build up the part of his

82 Parry, *Trophies*, 78; Sharpe, *Cotton*, 80; Tite, *Manuscript library*, 20–5.

83 Parry, *Trophies*, 78–9, and Sharpe, *Cotton*, 57–9.

84 See generally Tite, *Manuscript library*, 13–19; and specifically A. G. Watson, 'Sir Robert Cotton and Sir Simonds D'Ewes: an exchange of manuscripts', *British Museum Quarterly* 25 (1962), 19–24; A. G. Watson, 'A St Augustine's Abbey, Canterbury, manuscript reconstructed: Trinity College Cambridge MS R.14.30 and British Library MSS Egerton 823 and 840A', *TCBS* 6 (1975), 211–71; A. G. Watson, 'A Merton College manuscript reconstructed: Harley 625; Digby 178, fols. 1–14, 88–115; Cotton Tiberius B. IX, fols. 1–4, 225–35', *BLR* 9 (1976), 207–17; J. P. Carley and C. G. C. Tite, 'Sir Robert Cotton as collector of manuscripts and the question of dismemberment: British Library MSS Royal 13. D.I and Cotton Otho D. VIII', *Library*, 6th ser., 14 (1992), 94–9.

ollection that dealt with more recent history – the state-paper collections relat-
ng to the sixteenth and early seventeenth centuries. This aspect of Cotton's
ibrary is the least well investigated, but it was perhaps the most sought-after
art of the collection for those who searched for evidence for political pur-
oses. Cotton, Camden, D'Ewes and other antiquaries were aware that the
tate records were not well cared for, and this may have been their excuse for
ppropriating those materials which they could into their own collections, for
he sake of better safeguarding. As the seventeenth century progressed, how-
ver, some of the custodians of public records, at least, were beginning to fear
hat the utility of the collections in their care – as at the Tower of London, and
he Court of Exchequer Records in Westminster Hall – was being undermined
y Cotton's acquisitiveness.[85] But Cotton was not the only antiquary to exploit
hese public collections. Scipio Le Squyer, an official of the Court of Exchequer in the early seventeenth century, is found in 1635 being paid for 'searching,
ligesting, transcribing, and copeying' various public records in the Exchequer
or an unnamed user, and Sir Simonds D'Ewes in his autobiography recorded
earching the 'rare and useful records' of the Exchequer, including consulting
he Domesday Book under Le Squyer's supervision.[86] Cotton certainly had
lealings with Le Squyer, lending him a cartulary from Exeter. Le Squyer's
rofessional interests spilled into his private antiquarian pursuits – the 1632
atalogue of his own collection records over 200 manuscripts, and includes
hree cartularies, and he later listed as many cartularies then in private hands
s he could. This category of 'public' record was highly sought after in the
eriod 1580 to 1640, both from a historical and an antiquarian viewpoint, and
nore importantly for legal reasons. John Selden, for example, used 'those
uthorities . . . both printed and manuscript Annalls, Histories, Councels,
Chartularies, Laws, Lawiers, & Records as only were to be used in the most
ccurat way of search that might furnish for the subiect' in his *Historie of tithes*,
nd specifically listed the cartularies he consulted in the Cottonian library for
he work.[87] Cartularies in early modern England became a crucial weapon

85 For the public records in general see R. B. Wernham, 'The public records in the sixteenth and seventeenth centuries', in L. Fox (ed.), *English historical scholarship in the sixteenth and seventeenth centuries* (London, 1956), 18–20; E. M. Hallam, 'The Tower of London as a record office', *Archives* 14 (1979), 3–10; E. M. Hallam and M. Roper, 'The capital and the records of the nation: seven centuries of housing the public records in London', *London Journal* 4 (1978), 73–94; and on the contemporary fears concerning Cotton's activities with the public records, Tite, *Manuscript library*, 14; K. Sharpe, 'Introduction: rewriting Sir Robert Cotton', in Wright, *Sir Robert Cotton as collector*, 14–15.

86 Ovenden, 'Le Squyer', 323–37; J. O Halliwell-Phillips (ed.), *The autobiography and correspondence of Sir Simonds D'Ewes* (London, 1845), I. 432.

87 John Selden, *The historie of tithes* (London, 1618), p. xii and sig. ** 3^{v}.

in the claims of aspiring gentry for land-ownership, and became sought after as sources of evidence and precedence.[88] They therefore became increasingly protected, and difficult to access. In 1620, William Yonge attempted to act as go-between for Roger Dodsworth in his efforts to consult the cartulary of the Augustinian house at Healaugh Park in Yorkshire, 'which lyes dormant within the precincts of York'. He reported to Dodsworth that 'before [his kinsman] could obtayne a sight thereof', he was ordered to 'conceale it especially from you'. The owner, Philip Padmore, was clearly concerned that he should not be seen to give Dodsworth sight of the book, 'otherwise it would be very preiudiciall to both your future searches',[89] possibly because the volume was to be acquired very shortly afterward by Sir Robert Cotton, who would perhaps have preferred to be the first antiquary to gain access to the volume.

By the early 1620s, Cotton's various collecting methods had brought his collection to a considerable size, large enough for a catalogue to be a necessary tool in managing it. The earliest catalogue of the collection, compiled in about 1621–3, lists over 400 volumes (as can be seen from the dismembering activities, this really means many more manuscripts, the volume in the Cottonian sense normally referring to a *Sammelband*).[90] The remainder of the 1620s saw collections arrive in the Cottonian library in bulk rather than as piecemeal acquisitions. Thus eighty manuscripts arrived from the collection of Sir Henry Savile of Banke after his death in 1617, but in time to be recorded by Cotton in 1621,[91] and a smaller but no less significant number came from the remnants of John Dee's library after its final dispersal in the 1620s, although some may have arrived earlier, probably through direct purchase from John Pontois rather than through the trade.[92] In 1623 he inherited all the manuscripts and printed books from Camden's library (except those on heraldry), including his working papers, such as the copy-text for his *Annales*.[93]

By the time of Cotton's death in 1631, the collection had grown to over 900 volumes, and additions were still being made to it after his death. It contained a staggering number of manuscripts now regarded as national treasures, including highly significant pre-Norman manuscripts such as the Lindisfarne Gospels (MS Cotton Nero D. iv), the eighth-century Vespasian Psalter (MS Cotton

88 Ovenden, 'Le Squyer', 327–8. 89 Bodleian, MS Dodsworth 113, fol. 97.

90 C. C. G. Tite, 'The earliest catalogues of the Cottonian library', *BLJ* 6 (1980), 144–57.

91 A. G. Watson, *The manuscripts of Henry Savile of Banke* (London, 1969), 11.

92 Roberts and Watson, *Dee's library*, 65.

93 Sharpe, *Cotton*, 58; P. Collinson, 'One of us? William Camden and the making of history', *TRHS*, 6th ser., 8 (1998), 152–4.

Vespasian A. i), the ninth-century Carolingian Coronation Gospels (MS Cotton Tiberius A. ii), five of the seven surviving manuscripts of the Anglo-Saxon Chronicle (MSS Cotton Domitian viii, fols. 30–70; Otho B. xi; Tiberius A. vi; Tiberius B. i, fols. 112–64; Tiberius B. iv), King Alfred's translation of Orosius (MSS Cotton Tiberius B. i, fols. 3–111), two of the oldest manuscripts of Bede's *Historia ecclesiastica* (MSS Cotton Tiberius A. xiv and Tiberius C. ii), and the unique manuscript of *Beowulf* (MS Cotton Vitellius A. xv). A huge number of histories and chronicles were collected by Cotton, including a twelfth-century manuscript of the *Historia Britonum* (MSS Cotton Nero D. viii, Titus A. xxvii, and Titus C. xvii), Knighton's Chronicle (MS Cotton Tiberius C. vii), Simeon of Durham's *Historia ecclesiastica Dunelmensis* (MS Cotton Caligula A. viii), and Thomas of Elmham's biography of Henry V (MS Cotton Claudius E. iv). There were literary texts in abundance, such as the *Ancrene Riwle*, Laȝamon's *Brut*, the *Coventry mystery plays*, and the unique manuscript of *Pearl* and *Sir Gawain and the Green Knight* (MS Cotton Nero A. x).

In addition to the cartularies and single-sheet charters described above, the Cottonian collection also possessed a substantial quantity of materials relating to the English Parliament. These were of various types, but principally consisted of the medieval records of a series of volumes of the Parliament rolls, and dated, more or less complete, from 1376 to 1533, a mixture of original documents and scribal copies. There was also a number of volumes of abridgements and extracts from the rolls, as well as collections of writs of summons and writs for the payment of members. A very important aspect of Cotton's collection of parliamentary materials was of course the collections of manuscript volumes of statutes, one of the most important of which, a fifteenth-century set of statutes, bears his ownership inscription dated 1598, and was lent to John Selden in 1622. This material was acquired from a variety of sources, some of it from antiquarian friends such as Sir Peter Manwood and Francis Tate, other parts no doubt harvested from the various repositories containing such records: the Tower, the Exchequer records in and around Westminster Hall, the records kept in Westminster Abbey chapter house, and in the Rolls Chapel in Chancery Lane. As Colin Tite has observed, as Cotton relocated to a house in the close vicinity of the Palace of Westminster in 1622, his collection became increasingly accessible to members of parliament, who began to treat the collection less as a circulating library and more as a reference collection.[94]

94 C. C. G. Tite, 'The Cotton library in the seventeenth century and its manuscript records of the English Parliament', *Parliamentary History* 14 (1995), 121–38.

From the medieval sources of the Cottonian collection, much can be learnt about the availability of ex-monastic books in the period: no fewer than 141 volumes of British medieval cartularies are recorded by Godfrey Davis as being in the Cottonian collection, ranging from those of the Benedictines at Abingdon to St Leonard's Hospital at York, taking in eight of the Ely cartularies and registers, four of those from Christ, Church, Canterbury, and six from St Augustine's, Canterbury, five from St Albans and two from Reading.[95] Of the medieval literary manuscripts, an even more impressive tally can be recorded: no fewer than 337 manuscripts in whole or in part have been identified in *Medieval libraries of Great Britain* (*MLGB*) as being from identifiable British medieval institutional collections, from sources as diverse as Glasgow and St David's, and Dover and Furness; in fact, these 337 books came from a total of 109 separate medieval institutional collections. Few patterns are discernible from the list, save the obvious point that there are few manuscripts from houses where the books had largely remained *in situ* since the Dissolution. Thus there are only seventeen books from Durham Cathedral Priory in the Cottonian library, whereas almost 300 remain in Durham to this day. Likewise, neither Hereford, Lincoln nor Salisbury Cathedral manuscripts are well represented in the Cottonian collection. The houses which did have large collections, and which did witness a widespread dispersal, are therefore well represented, but two houses stand out from the rest as supplying the greatest number: Christ Church Cathedral Priory and St Augustine's Abbey at Canterbury supplied no fewer than fifty-seven manuscripts, with twenty-eight from Christ Church and twenty-nine from St Augustine's. There is no single reason for such an accumulation of Canterbury books (a further singleton from the Franciscan house at Canterbury must be added); rather, a variety of factors accounts for this phenomenon. First, the two Canterbury houses both had very large libraries indeed – it has been estimated that both houses had in the region of 2,000 volumes at the Dissolution,[96] and both libraries were of course dispersed. Secondly, the proximity of Canterbury to London made it easy for books to transfer to the metropolitan area, either through the activities of intermediaries, such as antiquaries like John Twyne, or through anonymous routes, to the London trade. The age and importance of the Canterbury collections no doubt also played their part in attracting Cotton to the available books. Indeed, the fact that Canterbury had been home to some of the really iconic books of the early middle ages – such as the Vespasian Psalter – had attracted collectors like Cranmer and Parker in the generation before Cotton.

95 Davis, *Medieval cartularies*.
96 James, *ALCD*, liii, lxii–lxiii.

As such, many of these valuable books (in the historic as well as the financial sense) stood a good chance of becoming available to Cotton, either through the intermediaries from the preceding generation, or from sources in Kent who had access to troves of material, such as Edward Dering, or the Canterbury prebendary Nicholas Simpson.[97] In addition to the great collections of manuscripts, charters and other administrative documents described above, Cotton clearly also owned a substantial collection of printed books, about which we know tantalisingly little.[98]

The Bodleian Library

If the Cottonian collection was to be considered ultimately as the founding element of the British National Library Collection (the British Museum Library, to become the British Library), one institutional collection was founded during our period which rapidly became a storehouse for manuscripts sourced by antiquaries and other collectors, and which can therefore lay some claims to having served as the *de facto* national collection for over 150 years, until the establishment of the British Museum Library: the Bodleian Library in Oxford. The history of the establishment of the Bodleian Library is very well known, both from contemporary sources and from more recent studies. One aspect of the Bodleian's early collections that has not been studied comprehensively, however, is its acquisition of antiquarian materials – medieval manuscripts and other primary documents collected from a variety of British sources, but often from antiquaries themselves. From the inception of his idea to refound Oxford's University Library in the 1590s, Sir Thomas Bodley recognised the need to establish a 'great store of honourable friends' to help him further his design.[99] In reality, this meant individuals who would contribute either books or financial resources to set the new institution on a firm footing. To some extent the motivations both in Bodley's mind and in those of the early donors was to create a 'great storehouse or magazine of antiquities' and, tellingly, 'a most admirable ornament *aswell of the state*, as of the Vniversitie', or a national library in all but name.[100] The fact that the library was open not just to the senior members of the University of Oxford but to the 'whole republic of

97 Wright, 'Sir Edward Dering'; Ramsay, 'Cathedral archives and library', 377–8.

98 C. G. C. Tite, 'A catalogue of Sir Robert Cotton's printed books?', *BLJ* 17 (1991), 1–11.

99 *The life of Sir Thomas Bodley. written by himself* AD *1609*, in *Trecentale Bodleianum: a memorial volume for the three-hundredth anniversary of the public funeral of Sir Thomas Bodley, March 29, 1613* (Oxford, 1913), 19.

100 G. W. Wheeler (ed.), *Letters of Sir Thomas Bodley to Thomas James, first keeper of the Bodleian Library* (Oxford, 1926), 88.

the learned' also encouraged the notion that those who gave to the Bodleian gave to support the learned throughout the realm. Associated with both the establishment of a rich manuscript collection and the wide access to it that lay at the heart of the university's policy, the other fact that encourages the view that the Bodleian held the 'national library' banner for Britain during the seventeenth and eighteenth centuries was the establishment of the deposit of books from the Stationers' Company from 1610 onwards, which became the cornerstone both of the Legal Deposit legislation of subsequent centuries and of the Bodleian's own collection of printed books.[101]

The petition to Elizabeth was not the first attempt to form a national collection. John Leland, John Bale and John Dee (1556) had all made similar attempts,[102] but it was perhaps the most eloquent statement in favour of establishing a collection which would match the reality of the functions which Cotton's library had begun to fulfil, and would come to deliver in substantial measure during the 1620s and 1630s – so successfully, in fact, that it would ultimately lead to Cotton's arrest and the closure of his library. But if the legacy of this period was not the formation of a national library, it can be found perhaps in the origins of historical scholarship, for the period 1580 to 1640 witnessed the coming of age of British historical writing and editing.[103] From the first efforts of the later Elizabethan era, from Camden's brilliant *Britannia* in 1586 through to the monumental production by William Dugdale and Roger Dodsworth known as the *Monasticon Anglicanum* (published in 1654 but first planned in the late 1630s), publishing was an important facet of antiquarian activity. The publication of editions of medieval texts in particular was a significant by product of the collecting of manuscripts, and can perhaps be seen as the end result of a connected series of activities that began with the acquisition of manuscripts. The antiquaries eagerly pursued copies of the best chronicles Henry of Huntingdon, Ralph of Diss, Roger Howden, Thomas Walsingham Matthew Paris, Geoffrey of Monmouth and Walter of Guisborough were the most sought after. Of the forty-three surviving medieval copies of the *Historia Anglorum* of Henry of Huntingdon, for example, Lord William Howard owned two, Henry Savile (1549–1622), editor of the *Rerum anglicarum post Bedam*

101 For a general account of the arrangement see I. Philip, *The Bodleian Library in the seventeenth and eighteenth centuries* (Oxford, 1983), 27–30; see also J. Barnard, 'Politics, profits and ?idealism: John Norton, the Stationers' Company and Sir Thomas Bodley', *BLR* 17 (2002), 385–408. Roberts and Watson, *Dee's library*, 194–5.

102 Roberts and Watson, *Dee's library*, 194–5.

103 J. W. Binns, *Intellectual culture in Elizabethan and Jacobean England: the Latin writings of the age* (Leeds, 1990), 178–95.

scriptores praecipui (1596) (which included editions of William of Malmsebury and Roger Howden as well as Henry of Huntingdon) owned three, Sir James Balfour one, and Sir Robert Cotton two. Of the six earliest manuscripts of 'Florence' of Worcester's Chronicle, Parker owned one, John, Lord Lumley another, and Lord William Howard (the first editor of the text) two, one given to him by the Kentish antiquary William Lambarde, who in turn had acquired it from John Stow.[104]

Very often the chief collectors were also responsible for ground-breaking publications, often editions of medieval historical sources. This phenomenon can be traced back as far as 1567 with Jocelyn's edition of Gildas, made possible thanks to Parker's collections, and continued through our period with Parker's edition of Matthew Paris in 1571, with Asser and Thomas Walsingham following in 1574, Gerald of Wales's *Itinerarium Cambriae* (1585) edited by the Welsh antiquary David Powel, and Lord William Howard of Naworth's edition of 'Florence' of Worcester's *Chronicon ex chronicis* in 1592. Other collectors followed this lead, the most significant of whom was Sir Henry Savile, who oversaw the first printings of William of Malmsbury, Henry of Huntingdon and Roger Howden, published as *Rerum anglicarum scriptores post Bedam praecipui* in 1596. Sir James Ware published lists of Irish bishops and archbishops in 1626 and 1628, and the first biographical dictionary of Irish writers in 1639. John Selden's edition of Eadmer's *Historia novorum* (1623) and Camden's *Annales* of 1615 – albeit based on his great friend Cotton's collections, and dealing with the more recent past, but nonetheless based on the fruits of antiquarian collecting, were also important contributions to what Hugh Trevor-Roper has called 'the intellectual re-validation of the English heritage'.[105]

Although the antiquaries of our period did not see the foundation of a national, co-ordinated collection, and a series of 'harvesting' activities for its development, they did begin the process of forming what today can be termed a distributed national collection, as a number of the antiquaries gave books to what were to become great research collections. Sir Henry Savile gave

104 For Stow's collecting of historical sources, see A. Gillespie, 'Stow's "Owlde" manuscripts of London chronicles', in Gadd and Gillespie, *John Stow*; and, for a more general account of the connection between early modern historiography and the collecting of medieval sources, D. Woolf, *The social circulation of the past: English historical culture, 1500–1730* (Oxford, 2003), 168–73.

105 W. O'Sullivan, 'A finding list of Sir James Ware's manuscripts', *Proceedings of the Royal Irish Academy* 97C (1997), 69–99; R. R. Darlington and P. McGurk (eds.), *The Chronicle of John of Worcester* (Oxford, 1995), II. lxxxi–lxxxiii; H. Trevor-Roper, 'John Stow', *Renaissance essays* (London, 1985), 97.

over forty manuscripts to the Bodleian in 1620; Sir Peter Manwood gave a number between 1613 and 1620; Sir James Ley, one of the men behind the Society of Antiquaries' petition of 1601, gave four manuscripts between 1611 and 1620. Thomas Nevile, dean of Canterbury and master of Trinity College, Cambridge, gave the college a large number of its most important manuscripts including the Eadwine Psalter from Christ Church, Canterbury, in 1611–12; and John, Baron Lumley, although not a great antiquary, was nonetheless a significant collector of the period, with pronounced historical interests, and gave eighty-seven manuscripts and printed books to Cambridge University Library in 1598. Moreover, as Neil Ker noted almost half a century ago, by 1640 most of the great collections of manuscripts had reached a point where many of them were to remain substantially intact, and form the cornerstones of the major research collections of modern Britain.[106] At the time of Sir Robert Cotton's death, that great library, which was to become the nucleus of the national collection in the British Museum and subsequently the British Library, had more or less reached stasis; with the exception of a few strays, the vast bulk of the collection was to remain together for almost 400 years. The larger part of the substantial collection formed by Sir Simonds D'Ewes was also to remain in the family until swallowed by that great acquirer of collections, Humfrey Wanley, for Robert Harley. Likewise, the collections of Lord William Howard were in significant number absorbed into the library of Thomas Howard, 2nd earl of Arundel (himself no mean antiquary), and were to become the nucleus of the collections of the Royal Society in 1678, whence they were eventually for the most part to find their way into the library of the British Museum in 1831. In Scotland, Sir James Balfour's manuscripts remained together until acquired by the Faculty of Advocates in Edinburgh in the late seventeenth century, and were then to form the cornerstone of the National Library of Scotland. In Ireland, Sir James Ware's manuscripts may have been largely dispersed (although the largest concentration is now in the Bodleian Library), but that of James Ussher came to form the basis of the great manuscript library of Trinity College, Dublin. The collections of Thomas Allen, Kenelm Digby and William Laud were all to become landmark collections in the Bodleian Library, and remain there to this day. This generation of collectors therefore built significantly on the work of those in the first phase of collectors – men who were responsible for the dispersals immediately following the dissolution of the monasteries.[107]

106 N. R. Ker, 'The migration of manuscripts from the English medieval libraries', *Library*, 4th ser., 23 (1942–3), 1–2; repr. in his *Books, collectors and libraries*, 459–60.
107 See above, chapter 10.

The antiquaries of the generation following Matthew Parker made their mpact, not simply through the piecemeal survival of individual collections, ut through the formation of a new vision of what collecting meant. They were ble to articulate the need, not only for an institutional role in building research ollections, but for the activity of historical research itself to be recognised as function inseparable from that of collecting.

PART FIVE

★

ORGANISATION AND ADMINISTRATION

24

Library administration (*c.* 1475 to 1640)

C. Y. FERDINAND

From the beginning of library history, the same fundamental administrative issues have preoccupied the keepers of libraries. Librarians have in the first place sought to establish, build and maintain collections of information – whether in tablets, scrolls, documents, manuscript books or printed books. They have always been concerned about the ordering of knowledge represented in their collections. On a more practical level, they have had to find physical space for their texts and readers. They have had to look to the conservation and preservation of collections and, when storage space was limited or there were compelling reasons to modernise, librarians have had to turn their attention to the orderly disposal of books. Defining and regulating readership are recurring issues too. Record-keeping – of the books and objects in the collection, of readers, of benefactors – while not always formally practised or preserved, continues to concern anyone who has ever had to manage a large library. All of these issues have been incorporated into library administrative policy, formally in statutes and written rules, and more casually in the policies that can be deduced from what is known of early modern library practice.

While the underlying principles have remained more or less the same, some of the details of library administration evolved, or at least changed, during the period between 1475 and 1640. British library collections at the beginning of the early modern period were generally smaller ones, limited by the expense of handwritten books and the technologies of making printed books. Their keepers and readers might well have been expected to use their common knowledge of the more informal collections, rather than a catalogue or marks on books or shelves, to find their reading material. The art of bibliography was in its infancy: collectors had to work harder to build up their collections, and catalogues, with some notable exceptions, were often fairly primitive inventories or lists of short titles, usually designed more for keepers' purposes than for readers'. Fairly sophisticated union catalogues, for example Henry de Kirkestede's *Catalogus de libris autenticis et apocrifis* (which itself drew upon the earlier *Registrum Angliae*),[1] did pre-date the early modern period, but there was evidently little thought in the fifteenth century of building upon this earlier work, or of following it to the logical conclusion of the establishment of a central or national library.[2] The relatively small size of these early book collections also meant that they could often be accommodated in the furniture – usually cupboards and chests – already available. The attitude towards library space began to change more rapidly by the end of the fifteenth century, though when founders of new institutions routinely included plans for separate library rooms in their proposals and others, with established libraries, began to look for more formal and extensive space for them. The introduction of cheaper mass-produced books from the second half of the fifteenth century obviously played a big role in the expansion of library collections. The continental printers had a natural head start in supplying the British market with printed books, particularly Latin books, but the focus of supply gradually shifted as continental printers moved to Britain and the British trade in bookselling and printing matured, to be formalised with the incorporation of the Stationers' Company in 1558.

The concept of a regular book-acquisitions budget remained relatively undeveloped in the fifteenth and sixteenth centuries and most institutional collections were established and enlarged by donation, following the precedent set in the monastic houses. Administrative ingenuity therefore was at first directed more towards imaginative ways of securing gifts of books than towards the apportioning of any formal budget for books or library. Expenses were usually met on an *ad hoc* basis: if a large number of gift volumes arrived one year, then money would be found from general institutional funds to pay for their carriage or for chains to secure some of the books in the library – facts that might be recorded in the annual account-books. Indeed, account-books often provide the only evidence we have for long-disappeared book benefactions. Administrative policy was sometimes only sketched out in institutional statutes that suggested who might use the collection and which officers should look after it. The keepers themselves could not be said to have had much formal library training, and individual library administration varied with the experiences and inclinations of the different men – and they were always men – in charge. Running a library was almost never a full-time post in the

1 CBMLC XI and II.
2 For early union catalogues and their origins in patristic bio-bibliography, see R. H. and M. A. Rouse, 'Bibliography before print: the medieval *De viris illustribus*', in P. Ganz (ed.), *The role of the book in medieval culture: proceedings of the Oxford International Symposium, 26 September–1 October 1982* (Turnhout, 1986), 133–53.

fifteenth century. In monastic communities the duties were often fulfilled by the precentor, whose other responsibilities included looking after the music and service-books.[3] Likewise the head of house, his deputy or the bursar might have administrative responsibility for a college library, along with his other college jobs. Library keepers may have been appointed in local libraries, but the post invariably came with other duties such as preaching. Very wealthy private collectors were the only ones who might have the luxury of a full-time librarian.

By the beginning of the seventeenth century, a somewhat more professional approach to library administration was becoming evident in Britain. This trend might be attributed to the influence of continentals such as the Swiss-German scientist and bibliographer Konrad Gesner (1516–65), the Jesuit professor of classical studies Claude Clément (*c.* 1594–1642) and Gabriel Naudé (1600–53), librarian to Cardinal Barbarini and Cardinal Mazarin. From further afield the fame of Italian libraries such as those of the dukes of Urbino or the Ambrosiana Library in Milan no doubt contributed. Francis Bacon (1561–1626), Thomas Bodley (1545–1613) and Bodley's first librarian, Thomas James (1573?–1629), were among those who interpreted the trend in Britain. Gesner's *Bibliotheca universalis* (1545) and his *Pandectae* (1548–9) were relatively successful attempts to record everything that had ever been written. His methods for constructing library catalogues and the suggestion that librarians use his *Bibliotheca universalis* as a basic catalogue for their own collections as well as a tool for acquisitions helped promote at least the principle of consistency in library practice. While Naudé's directions for a professionally run library were not published in English until John Evelyn's translation in 1661,[4] his work had been available to anyone who could read French from the 1620s. Linked to these developments was a growing appreciation of the benefits of the large scholarly library accessible to anyone who needed to use it. Clément's contribution, *Musei sive bibliotheca* (1628), discussed libraries more in terms of their iconography and architecture and helped to raise the status of seventeenth-century libraries in other ways.[5]

The British were precocious in the early conception of a national collection, although it took a couple of hundred years for the idea to be developed fully. As

3 See above, chapter 8.

4 Gabriel Naudé, *Instructions concerning erecting of a Library: presented to My Lord the President de Mesme, now interpreted by Jo. Evelyn, Esquire* (London, 1661); *Advis pour dresser une bibliothèque* was published in 1627.

5 M. V. Rovelstad, 'Two seventeenth-century library handbooks, two different library theories', *Libraries & Culture* 35 (2000), 540–56.

early as 1556, John Dee (1527–1608) suggested to Queen Mary that a royal library be established to store a collection of ancient books, retrieved from endangered libraries.[6] Another great private collector, Sir Robert Cotton (1571–1631), along with fellow antiquaries Sir John Doddridge (1555–1628) and Sir James Ley (1550–1629), proposed to Queen Elizabeth at the very beginning of the seventeenth century that something along the lines of a national library be formed.[7] Bacon was similarly concerned and published a related plan, 'The Advancement of Learning', in 1605. This was the same year that James I paid a visit to the new Bodleian Library, suggesting that 'if I were not a King, I would be an University-Man; and if it were so that I must be a Prisoner, if I might have my wish, I would desire to have no other Prison than that Library, and to be chained together with so many good Authors'.[8] The concept of king- or book-as-prisoner may be retrograde, but royal bibliographical support boded well for libraries in the early seventeenth century, as of course did the re-establishment of the Oxford University Library as a public academic library, 'an Ark to save learning from Deluge'.[9]

The natural progression in British library administration from the fairly unstructured and diverse tradition at the end of the fifteenth century to the precursors of professional librarianship in the seventeenth was seriously disrupted in the mid-sixteenth century. The process was begun when Henry VIII decided he needed textual support for his divorce from Catherine of Aragon and sent his colleagues to scour the major collections for relevant volumes. Key books had already begun to disappear from the abbey libraries long before the official start of the dissolution of the monasteries, sometimes evidently with the collaboration of the abbots.[10] Christ's College, Cambridge, was endowed in 1507 with lands, as well as books and jewels, from a dissolved abbey.[11] After Henry found his plans temporarily thwarted by the Catholic

6 R. J. Roberts and A. G. Watson (eds.), *John Dee's library catalogue* (London, 1990); J. Carley, 'Monastic collections and their dispersal', in *CHBB* IV. 339.

7 See above, 304–5.

8 Thomas Bodley, *Reliquiæ Bodleianæ: or some genuine remains of Sir Thomas Bodley. Containing his life, the first draught of the statutes of the publick library at Oxford, (in English) and a collection of letters to Dr. James, &c. published from the originals in the said library* (London, 1703), introduction (sig. A7ᵛ).

9 R. A. Beddard, 'The official inauguration of the Bodleian Library on 8 November 1602', *Library*, 7th ser., 3 (2002), 255–83; *Sir Thomas Bodley and his library: an exhibition to mark the quatercentenary of the Bodleian, February to May 2002* (Oxford, 2002); *Letters and life of Francis Bacon*, ed. J. Spedding, 7 vols. (London, 1861–74), III. 253.

10 For the substantial payments made to the abbots or priors of Ramsey, Sempringham, Gloucester, Evesham, and St Augustine's, Canterbury, see J. P. Carley, in CBMLC VII. xxxvii–xxxviii.

11 Carley, 'Monastic collections', 340.

authorities, he ordered Thomas Cromwell to oversee changes to the university curriculum that established new public lectures, encouraged humanistic learning in the arts and more or less replaced the study of canon law with that of civil law.[12] Cromwell's visitors could report on the success of this campaign, in their famous description of a New College quad 'full of the leaves of Dunce [Duns Scotus], the wind blowing into every corner'. From the 1530s British library keepers found themselves in unusual administrative roles, overseeing the dispersal of some libraries, attempting to protect their collections from opportunistic sales or acquisitive royal agents, finding ways to support or ignore a new university curriculum, or perhaps simply capitulating in their neglect of administrative duties. The extent of real book destruction in Britain during these reforms and the role the library keepers played then are still under debate, but no one doubts there were big changes. Religious reforms affected libraries on the Continent too, but the evidence suggests that the English and Scottish tackled the job of purging their various libraries and chapels of newly offensive material with greater vigour than did their continental colleagues. Books from the old monasteries found new homes in other collections, were broken up for binders' waste, or worse. Recent collaborative projects such as *Medieval libraries of Great Britain* (*MLGB*) and the Corpus of British Medieval Library Catalogues (CBMLC) have helped gauge the magnitude of book loss and dispersal: for example, books from the library of the Benedictine priory in Durham are now to be found in more than forty-five libraries. Evidence for book loss in one college library may be found in the University College benefactors' book, which was compiled from scratch in 1674, evidently by opening the books in the library to check for notes of provenance. The very few pre-Reformation books listed suggest a fairly comprehensive sixteenth-century clear-out.

The pace of book replacement in the academies quickened when the ready availability of attractive printed editions coincided with efforts by the universities to support a changing curriculum and political situation. As a result of these policies the furniture of the Oxford University Library, which had fallen into disuse anyway, was completely emptied and then sold, while the Cambridge University Library, which had enjoyed a stock of about 600 books in 1500, was reduced to only about 175 books by 1556. The colleges, which more directly serviced the academic needs of their fellows and sometimes enjoyed

12 For the background to the Cromwellian reforms, see C. I. Hammer Jr, 'Oxford town and Oxford University', in *HUO* III. 90–4; the effects of the Cromwellian visitations on both Oxford and Cambridge are discussed in C. Cross, 'Oxford and the Tudor state from the accession of Henry VIII to the death of Mary', *ibid.*, 127–9.

great autonomy, were less susceptible, and many retain sizeable medieval collections today despite the depredations of the mid-sixteenth century. College accounts record increased expenditure for printed books after 1535. Other libraries – Henry VIII's and other private collectors' in particular – positively flourished under these conditions. Attempts to rebuild and protect institutional book collections after this contributed to the development and consolidation of library administration in the late sixteenth and early seventeenth centuries. That books and libraries had played some part in settling the Henrician disputes no doubt helped to raise bibliographical profiles.

The keepers

In larger libraries the different roles undertaken by the modern professional librarian – selecting books, organising them on the shelves and in catalogues, supervising circulation, and so on – were often shared among various institutional officers and members at the beginning of the early modern period. Until the collapse of the monastic system made them redundant, the precentor-librarians usually oversaw the day-to-day administration of their libraries according to the rules set out by the institution, although they would still have had other non-library tasks to perform. A more variable hierarchy was adopted within the academic communities, where a variety of senior members, including heads of houses, shared responsibilities, usually for two libraries: a circulating collection and a reference or chained library. At Merton College, Oxford, early statutes made the warden and sub-warden jointly in charge of distributing the books, while the bursar officially had custody of both the circulating and chained books. By the end of the fifteenth century the sub-warden had effectively become acting librarian in that he regulated the distribution of books from the circulating collection. The Peterhouse, Cambridge, statutes of 1344 require that books and other college valuables should be listed on indentures, the two parts of which were to be kept by the master and the deans; keys to the book-chests were kept by the senior dean and the master; and books were distributed to the fellowship under the direction of the deans. When a bibliophile master, John Warkworth, took up his post in 1473, he oversaw the enactment of statutes that outlined a redistribution of library responsibility: the master and all resident fellows had the authority to approve the loan of any chained book outside the college, unless the donor of a specific book had stipulated that it should never leave the library; the master and two deans should value the books; and so on. Similar statutes, giving primary library responsibilities to senior college officers but sometimes also including the general fellowship, were enacted in Oxbridge colleges into the middle of the sixteenth century.[13]

In other institutions, such as the two semi-public clerical libraries set up in Bristol and Worcester in the fifteenth century, clerics were appointed to the post of library keeper. These two libraries were governed by nearly identical rules, promulgated in 1464, that required the keeper to have a Bachelor's degree, know his Scriptures well enough to interpret them for his more ignorant readers, give public lectures, preach, and take responsibility for the welfare of the book collection – a familiar combination of library and religious administration. Each keeper was to be paid a fairly generous salary of £10 per annum, while the Worcester librarian received in addition a length of woollen cloth as well as a gown and hood.[14]

In the higher academic institutions, such as the colleges in Oxford and Cambridge, there seemed to be a general awareness of what might be termed 'best practice' when it came to issues such as library rooms, collections and furniture. So, in Oxford, Magdalen College explicitly modelled its new library on All Souls, which had imitated New College library to some extent. All the colleges had to take into account changes in the curriculum when stocking their libraries. When Bodley's librarian made a visit to Cambridge, he was urged '*to take good notice of their Orders, in placing and disposing their Library-Books: Whether they do it by the Alphabet, or according to the Faculties*'.[15] There was more diversity to be found in administrative strategies. Magdalen College, Oxford, seems to have been the first to appoint a fellow librarian, of the sort that is still to be found today. That is, one of the governing body, but not necessarily the head of house or his deputy, was placed in charge of library administration, and for that extra service he was paid a stipend. The first, in 1549, was the controversial Henry Bull, who had been associated with library duties such as writing inscriptions in new books since at least 1531.[16] According to the college account-books, he was paid 15s 'pro diligentia sua circa bibliothecam'. It is no coincidence that the 1549–50 academic year saw other intense library activity there, including the compilation of a library catalogue for which Bull and another fellow, John

13 Clark, *Care of books*, 127–33.

14 Worcestershire County Record Office, Register of Bishop Silvestro de' Gigli, fol. 134, cited in T. Kelly, *Early public libraries: a history of public libraries in Great Britain before 1850* (London, 1966), 33.

15 Bodley, *Reliquiæ Bodleianæ*, 61.

16 For example, in 1531 he was paid 6s 4d for preparing the leaves of manuscript service-books (Magdalen Coll. Archives, LCE/4, p. 7). For some of Bull's other activities see C. Y. Ferdinand, 'Magdalen College and the book trade: the provision of books in Oxford, 1450–1550', in A. Hunt, G. Mandelbrote and A. Shell (eds.), *The book trade and its customers, 1450–1900* (Winchester, 1997), 183.

Slade, were paid 20s.[17] Although some fellow librarians fell short (John Day, who was fellow librarian from 1558 to 1572, attracted the bursar's comment in the account-books that his stipend was 'pro *negligentia* circa bibliothecam'),[18] Magdalen followed this style of librarianship through the rest of this period, and indeed until 1992. On the other hand, Trinity College, Cambridge, employed until 1608 a library keeper who enjoyed the same status as the college butler or janitor. This changed when the posts of librarian and sub-librarian were endowed by the enlightened Sir Edward Stanhope in the early seventeenth century. Stanhope thought the job demanded a scholar, preferably one who was unmarried.[19] An older tradition was still apparent at University College in 1640, when the librarian was ordered to obtain the master's permission before lending any book or globe from the library.[20]

At the university level, Cambridge established a university librarianship in 1577, after nearly 300 years of chaplain librarians. The post was endowed with neither great status nor salary, and was initially described as 'the keepeing of the Bookes in the common Library, for the convenient accesse of Students thereunto, and the good preservation of the Bookes'. The first library keeper, William James, happened to be a fellow of Peterhouse at the time of his appointment, but his successors were not always scholars. James had no trouble combining the light duties of his library post with that of registrar at King's College, when he migrated there.[21]

Promulgating library rules themselves was likely to have been outside the remit of most early modern librarians, but they left their marks in other ways. For example, the custodianship of Clement Canterbury, who had charge of the library at St Augustine's, Canterbury, in the late fifteenth century, is still evident in the records he kept of the books in his care, in their foliation and in the leather bindings he arranged for them.[22] The marks left by his numerous anonymous colleagues in surviving books are evidence of the ways other keepers tackled

17 Magdalen Coll. Archives, LCE/5, fols. 86^v–87^r. Magdalen College, under the direction of its founder, William Waynflete, was library-oriented from the beginning: Waynflete endowed the just-built college library with 800 books in 1481. While the college had been founded in 1458, its account-books (*libri computi*) did not begin until 1481; the first account-book included a heading for library expenditure.

18 W. D. Macray, *A register of the members of St Mary Magdalen College, Oxford, from the foundation of the college*, II: *Fellows, 1522–1575* (London, 1897), 128.

19 P. Gaskell, *The library of Trinity College, Cambridge: a short history* (Cambridge, 1971), 8–9.

20 University Coll. archives, UC:GB3/A1/1, p. 49. References from the University College Archives have been supplied by Robin Darwall-Smith, archivist of University and Magdalen Colleges, Oxford.

21 Oates, *CUL*, 119–20.

22 B. C. Barker-Benfield, 'Clement Canterbury, librarian of St Augustine's Abbey, Canterbury', in *MSS at Oxford*, 89.

the job of organising their libraries, and indeed reflect late medieval attitudes towards organising knowledge in general: the shelf-marks they attached to them are clues to how the collections were arranged on the lecterns or shelves, and to which books first greeted readers; the position of the marks left by their chains suggests how individual volumes were actually stored; manuscript indexes record serious attention to readers' needs; inscriptions in the books might record provenance, price or other evidence of the book's physical and reading history. The addition of library duties to the job description of one member or the appointment of a library keeper suggests growing institutional concern for the preservation of book collections and the needs of readers. But it was really not until the end of the sixteenth century and the beginning of the seventeenth that the role of library keepers assumed much prominence in Britain.

The learned Thomas Bodley was among the first in England to act on the idea that the proper administration of a large public library required the undivided attention of a full-time, well-paid scholar. Bodley evidently drew on classical precedents – among them the library of Ptolemy Philadelphus and the first Roman public library built by Asinius Pollio[23] – to define his ideal librarian; and he might well have been influenced by practice on the continent, where he had spent a considerable time.[24] The description of the duke of Urbino's early sixteenth-century librarian has a courtly but remarkably modern ring to it in its roll of administrative duties. Among other things, he should be

> learned, of good presence, temper, and manners; correct and ready of speech . . . He must . . . keep [the books] arranged and easily accessible . . . He must preserve the books from damp and vermin, as well as from the hands of trifling, ignorant, dirty, and tasteless persons. To those of authority and learning, he ought himself to exhibit them with all facility, courteously explaining their beauty and remarkable characteristics, the handwriting and miniatures, but observant that such abstract no leaves. When ignorant or merely curious persons wish to see them, a glance is sufficient.[25]

No British library of the time could match the opulence of the Urbino collection, but its administrative details were most of them worth imitation. Bodley's

23 Bodley, *Reliquiæ Bodleianæ*, sig. A3.

24 *The life of Sr Thomas Bodley, the honourable founder of the Publique Library in the University of Oxford. Written by himself* (Oxford, 1647), 1–8. David Vaisey, Bodley's librarian emeritus, has discussed Bodley's continental activities in several unpublished lectures.

25 J. Dennistoun, *Memoirs of the dukes of Urbino, illustrating the arms, arts and literature of Italy, 1440–1630*, new edn, ed. E. Hutton (London, 1909), I. 167–8. I am grateful to Martin Davies for drawing this to my attention.

Oxford librarian was to have similar qualifications, as well as a wholehearted dedication to library duty. He would be

> noted and known for a diligent Student, and in all his Conversation to be Trusty, Active, and Discreet; a Graduat also, and a Linguist, not encumbred with Marriage, nor with a Benefice of Cure. For it cannot stand with Piety, that such a Charge should admit the continual Society of other publick Imployments; and Marriage is too full of Domestical Impeachments, to afford him so much time from his private Affairs, as almost every Day's necessity of his private Presence will require.[26]

The post of Bodley's librarian was an important one: his election was to be held in Convocation, similar to that for university proctors. Bodley found his man in Thomas James, who fulfilled most of his patron's requirements, even after he married and had to contend with Domestical Impeachments. His nephew Richard James (1592–1638) was to assist Cotton with his library.

That libraries – and their keepers – had also become an accepted and important part of life outside the academic and religious communities by the middle of the seventeenth century is evident in letters written by John Williams, bishop of Lincoln in the 1630s. In his discussions about the move of the library from the chancel of the cathedral to a new location in town, he takes it for granted that not only will there be 'a faire & decent Roome for a Library in that place', but that money can be raised for 'some Meanes to Mayntaine a Keeper of the Bookes that shalbee there sett up'. In another letter he urges the mayor of Lincoln to pay the new librarian as much as the town could afford.[27]

Acquisitions

Established institutional libraries continued to increase their collections in the traditional ways during the fifteenth century. Desiderata could be found and copied out by individual scholars, transcribing from whole books, or perhaps from exemplars rented in parts – *peciae* – from approved local stationers.[28]

26 Bodley, *Reliquæ Bodleianæ*, 17–18.

27 John Williams, bishop of Lincoln (1582–1650) to Henry, 5th Earl of Huntingdon, 18 September 1633; and to the mayor of Lincoln, 18 September 1633 (San Marino, Huntington Library, MSS HA13330–1), a reference kindly supplied by Keith Lindley. It is worth mentioning that, at about the same time (1631), the duke of Urbino bequeathed his library to the community of Urbino, ensuring that revenue from his land (the Campo dei Galli) would support the post of librarian to look after the collection (Dennistoun, *Memoirs of the dukes of Urbino*, III. 242).

28 M. B. Parkes, 'The provision of books', in *HUO* II. 462–70.

By design or by accident, some of this personal property ended up in communal libraries. Monasteries, cathedrals, parishes and university colleges still relied heavily on donations for their libraries, and were sensible enough not to leave the process entirely to chance. Institutional policies required, or at least encouraged, members to contribute books to their libraries when they joined, died or moved on, or they set up schedules of fees or compensation to pay for communal books. Books themselves were occasionally left as pledges for loans of money or books, a practice that continued into the early modern period until the mass production of books diluted their relative value. Confiscation of these pledged books, which sometimes had been borrowed from other libraries, was another occasional means of replenishing library stock, or the pledges could be sold, with the revenue, in theory, going to the library.[29] Such practices could easily be abused, particularly when no one officer was dedicated to the interests of the library and its readers. There is no evidence to show that library keepers themselves framed any of these rules, and it is probably anachronistic to describe these traditions in terms of a formal acquisitions policy, but clearly such institutional practices had a direct effect on the size and composition of library collections.

When Archbishop Kilwardby decided to straighten out the affairs of Merton College in 1276, he included an injunction that the books belonging to its individual fellows should ultimately become part of the communal library – 'probably the most important service which Kilwardby rendered the college' – and certainly a library administrative decision that continued to affect the pattern of Merton acquisitions for centuries.[30] The 1292 statutes of Oxford's (arguably) oldest college, University College, include two relating to the library, and neither entertains the possibility of acquisitions by any means other than gift or legacy. The chest of books given by Richard de Lyng to Cambridge in 1355 no doubt set a precedent for other gifts to the university, and the same might be said of the beneficence of Humfrey, duke of Gloucester, who gave about 280 books to Oxford about a century later, although Oxford's very casual approach to major gifts – it took about thirty years to house Humfrey's gift – has to be mentioned. The practice of noticing these gifts in book inscriptions, formal lists of donors, or incidentally in institutional accounts is evidence that book donations were encouraged throughout the early modern period. The

29 H. W. Garrod, 'The library regulations of a medieval college', *Library*, 4th ser., 8 (1928), 314–15.

30 G. H. Martin and J. R. L. Highfield, *A history of Merton College, Oxford* (Oxford, 1997), 49–50; H. W. Garrod (ed.), *Merton College: injunctions of Archbishop Kilwardby, 1276* (Oxford, 1929).

elaborate benefactors' books of the early seventeenth century, some of them with illuminations, rich leather bindings, and chains and clasps of precious metal, suggest the continuing commitment of institutions to the tradition of building libraries by gift.[31]

Early acquisitions policies were relatively passive then, based on the institution's economic priorities and further limited by the extent to which donors could be guided to contribute according to library needs. A persuasive personality could make up for the obvious deficiencies of such a policy. One such was William Waynflete, bishop of Winchester and chancellor of England, who, as soon as he had secured permission to incorporate his new college in Oxford in 1458, set about stocking its library. His tactics might have been questionable, particularly in diverting to Magdalen College gifts intended by John Fastolf to set up another college in Caister, but they worked.[32] By 1481, when Bishop Waynflete made a visit to inspect the new buildings, which included a spacious first-floor library room in the cloisters, he had collected around 800 books from various benefactors for his library. That probably made Magdalen College's the largest in town then, and the survivors attest to its range.[33] Consistent practice could secure similar results. The earliest extant catalogue of Cambridge University Library, compiled between the 1420s and 1440s, 'clearly reflects a sustained attempt to secure books for the Library', according to J. C. T. Oates.[34] It records 122 books covering the various fields of religion, moral philosophy, medicine, logic, grammar and canon law.

This tactic had built-in drawbacks of course – gift acquisitions were naturally sporadic and sometimes surprising, and often came with strings attached, even if they appeared at first to be free. Some of the monastic libraries, built up in this manner, 'even the greatest, had something of the appearance of a heap . . . at the best, it was the sum of many collections, great and small, rather than a planned articulated unit'.[35] Nevertheless, donations-led acquisitions policies evidently met most readers' expectations, if not all their scholarly needs. There are many examples of fifteenth- and sixteenth-century library collections that

31 In this light it is interesting to note that current plans to rebuild the ancient Alexandrian Library do not include provision for a book budget: the organisers expect to rely entirely on book donations, according to newspaper reports (A. Philps and A. Palmer, 'Alexander's library rises from the ashes', *Sunday Telegraph*, 12 March 2000, 27).

32 V. Davis, *William Waynflete, bishop and educationalist* (Woodbridge, 1993), 131–9.

33 Ferdinand, 'Magdalen College and the book trade', 176. Macray speculates that fewer than 100 remain; their different provenances make them difficult to identify (*Register*, I. 8).

34 Oates, *CUL*, 9.

35 D. Knowles, *The religious orders in England*, 3 vols. (Cambridge, 1948–55), II. 332.

were able to support the university curriculum in this way. All Souls College in Oxford had a particular strength in law books, following the lead of the Chichele donation in 1438, but the medical section was developed too, and included gift books such as Hippocrates' *Aphorisms* and Galen's *Tegni*. One old member, William Goldwin, supplemented those with a large collection of other medical books in 1482.[36] By 1502, it is estimated that there were about 250 manuscripts and 100 printed books in the All Souls Library. The small and relatively poor University College seems to have followed a similar plan, but on a lesser scale. An unpublished calendar of the library benefactors' book, compiled by that college's archivist, Robin Darwall-Smith, shows that on the whole gifts given over the period 1513 to about 1650 generally conformed to library needs; the majority were folio volumes of theological works, almost certainly editions the college could not well afford to buy for itself. The donors were nearly always fellows of the college and would have known the library well enough to donate the appropriate books or at least see the academic point of a gift suggestion.[37] Judging from institutional records, the donation tradition was widely accepted and there does not seem to have been any concerted movement to set up even informal acquisitions budgets until well into the sixteenth century.

Most of the recorded expenditures for libraries in the late fifteenth and early sixteenth centuries are for items and services relating to donated books: payment for carriage of gift books is commonly recorded; entries for chaining new acquisitions and binding them often feature. There are occasional records of building work and repairs to the library fabric. This is not to say that there were no early book purchases. Accounts for Bolton Abbey showed that there was deliberate book-buying there as early as the 1300s, and Geoffrey Martin has deduced that there were eleven purchases against 184 donations recorded in a list of theological books compiled for Merton College in the 1370s.[38] Entries under the *Custus librariae* heading in the first volume of the Magdalen College account-books record that five copies of Alexander de Hales's *Expositio super tres libros Aristotelis de anima* (Oxford: Theodoric Rood, 11 October 1481) were

36 E. Craster, *The history of All Souls College Library* (London, 1971).

37 University College Archives, UC: BE1/MS1/3. One interesting exception is Mary Bishop, who gave a copy of Foxe's *Acts and monuments* in thanks for her son John's time at university (fol. 3r).

38 F. Wormald, 'The monastic library', in Wormald and Wright, *English library*, 29, 31, n. 37; I. Kershaw and D. M. Smith (eds.), *The Bolton Priory compotus, 1286–1325: together with a priory account roll for 1377–1378* (Woodbridge, 2000); Martin and Highfield, *History of Merton College*, 83.

purchased almost as soon as the edition left the press.[39] These were almost certainly bought to be lent to the college fellows, so it is surprising to find that two of the five copies have actually survived.[40] Clare Sargent notes the purchase of twenty-nine books for £7 17s 4d from the estate of Henry Bullock for the library of Queens' College, Cambridge, in 1526. In this case it is unclear whether the college dealt directly with Bullock's estate or worked through an intermediary bookseller, but evidently it was the college president who was behind the transaction.[41]

While gifts of books continued to be the mainstay of acquisitions, the balance of purchased books in the university libraries began to change noticeably from the 1530s. The government's attempt to modernise university teaching in the 1530s was one of the forces behind the upsurge in college library purchases then. Neil Ker records increases in bought acquisitions in many of the Oxford college libraries about this time: 'over £73 at Magdalen between 1536 and 1550; £30 at Oriel in 1543/4; at least £46 at All Souls between 1544/5 and 1547/8; more than £60 at Merton in or about 1549; some money almost certainly at Balliol, where there are no accounts before 1568'.[42] Some progressive colleges were more enthusiastic than others, and not only began buying printed editions to support the new curriculum, but also discarded manuscript editions that now seemed out of date. The culmination was probably the aggressive acquisitions policy pursued by Thomas Bodley, who actively employed booksellers such as John Norton and John Bill to supply the new Oxford University Library with imported books through the Latin trade.[43] Bodley pursued donations with the same determination, and once tried unsuccessfully to convince James I's librarian, Peter Young (1544–1628), that he had been given a warrant by the king 'for the choice of any books that I shall like in any of his houses or librarys'.[44] On the other hand, a determined head of house could promote a more conservative policy to ensure the survival of medieval manuscripts. One such was Richard Fitzjames, warden of Merton College from 1483 to 1507, who 'kept the

39 Magdalen Coll. Archives, LCE/1, fol. 11^{v}.

40 Both volumes were rebound, probably during the big rebinding drive Magdalen undertook in the late fifteenth century. This has obscured any evidence of early chaining. There are post-1610 chain-staple scars on the new bindings.

41 Cambridge, Queens' Coll., Misc B, fol. 77b (C. Sargent, 'The archaeology of a Cambridge library: the records of Queens' College, Cambridge, 1448–1672', forthcoming).

42 N. R. Ker, 'The provision of books', in *HUO* III. 448.

43 J. Roberts, 'The Latin trade', in *CHBB* IV. 160.

44 I. Michael, 'King James VI and I and the count of Gondomar: two London bibliophiles, 1613–18 and 1620–22', in E. H. Friedman and H. Sturm (eds.), *'Never-ending adventure': studies in medieval and early modern Spanish literature in honor of Peter N. Dunn* (Newark, DE, 2002), 430, 427.

place medieval', a policy that seemed to have enduring influence.[45] This *ad hoc* approach to acquisitions prevailed into the seventeenth century and beyond for many academic libraries.

Another way of finding acquisitions funds is recorded in the University College account roll for 1575/6–1576/7 in an entry under the 'Extraordinary Rents' heading: 'pro pecunia collata in bibliotec', which suggests that certain rentals may have been set aside for the library.[46] Occasionally donors were persuaded to give money to purchase books rather than donating the books themselves. The important protestant library of Bishop John Jewel was purchased by Magdalen College in the 1570s for £120 – 'the largest sum spent by an Oxford college until the very end of the century' – under the direction of the then president, Laurence Humphrey, who evidently persuaded his colleagues to come up with personal contributions to do so.[47] University College was able to attract a substantial cash gift in 1632, from a former master, George Abbot, archbishop of Canterbury, who gave £100 specifically to buy books. The college seems to have taken some time to consider its library purchases, for, according to their accounts, carriage for the eight-volume works of Chrysostom bought with Abbot's gift was not arranged until 1634/5.[48]

Acquisition by donation experienced something of a revival after the Reformation, as benefactors and institutions collaborated to reconstruct and renew library collections. In Cambridge, Andrew Perne and Matthew Parker worked hard to attract gifts to the university and college libraries. Perne donated many volumes he had liberated from Norwich Cathedral Library and indeed from the University Library, and left a bequest of a sizeable part of his private collection to Peterhouse in 1589.[49]

Private collectors, from better-off students to princes, were in a different category. Most of them purchased the books they needed to develop their collections, drawing on a number of resources from local stationers and booksellers to personal agents who could supply books from continental and British *scriptoria* and presses.[50] Others showed greater ingenuity in their approach to collection-building. Key books were borrowed and never returned; or

45 *Ibid.*, 446.

46 University Coll. Archives, UC: BU1/F/169 (A. D. M. Cox and R. H. Darwall-Smith (eds.), *Account rolls of University College, Oxford*, II: *1471/2–1596/7*, OHS, n.s. 40 (2001), 443).

47 N. R. Ker, 'The library of John Jewel', *BLR* 9 (1977), 256–64.

48 University Coll. Archives, UC: BU2/F1/1. The Chrysostom was probably the 1612 Greek edition, published from Eton.

49 E. Leedham-Green and D. McKittterick, 'A catalogue of Cambridge University Library in 1583', in Carley and Tite, *Books and collectors*, 154–5; *BCI*, I. 419–79.

50 Recent discussions of individual libraries include M. L. Ford, 'Private ownership of printed books', *CHBB* III. 205–28.

collectors seized the many acquisitions opportunities offered during the turbulent mid-sixteenth century. John Leland (1506?–52) travelled the country in the 1530s systematically recording books in libraries and later saved a great many from destruction.[51] John Bale (1495–1563) managed to rescue some 150 manuscript books from destruction, only to be forced to abandon them in Ireland when the political tide turned and he had to flee England in 1553. Both collected for Henry VIII, and many of these volumes ended up in the royal collections. The royal libraries were also enlarged when Henry began borrowing and purchasing treatises that supported his case for divorce. Garbrand Harks, the protestant Oxford bookseller, was said to have rescued many books discarded from the college libraries in the mid-sixteenth century and later almost certainly managed to place some of them in private collections. There are also records of sales of books to Harks – £1 6s 8d – from the All Souls College Library in 1549/50.[52] During most of this period an exchange of students from northern and southern Europe, including Britain, as well as the competitive nature of library-building, fuelled private collecting. While many bibliophiles were generous in making their private collections available to scholars, one need only list some of the big named collections – such as the King's Library and the Cottonian collection at the British Library, or that of Clement Litill (d. 1580), now in Edinburgh – in any of the major research libraries today to understand that private collecting is often, eventually, for the public good.

Losses

The same forces that were behind early acquisitions budgets also, conversely, assisted book losses in various ways. The price of printed books was dropping in the sixteenth century, as larger and more editions of standard texts came off continental and British printing presses, and libraries could more readily afford to buy the books they needed. So could individual readers, who might donate ever larger collections to their college, university or local library. In the minds of some sixteenth-century library keepers, uniform printed editions must have seemed more attractive and up to date than their old medieval manuscript stock. The larger collections were outgrowing the restricted storage space of the lectern-furnished library too, which meant that old editions were sometimes easily discarded in favour of the new; there simply was not room enough

51 J. P. Carley, 'The royal library under Henry VIII', in *CHBB* III. 275.
52 A. G. Watson, 'The post-medieval library', in *Unarmed soldiery: studies in the early history of All Souls College* (Oxford, 1996), 65–91.

to keep everything. Curriculum changes in the universities, with new subjects and classical Renaissance learning replacing the old medieval schools, accelerated the process.

Reports that whole cartloads of manuscript books were removed from libraries in the mid-sixteenth century – John Bale's 'tyme of the lamentable spoyle of the libraryes of Englande' – can be shocking to generations who place a high value on the handwritten book.[53]

> A great nombre of them which purchased those superstycyouse mansyons, reserved of those lybrarye bokes, some to serue theyr iakes, some to scoure theyr candel styckes, & some to rubbe their bootes. Some they solde to the grossers and sope sellers, & some they sent ouer see to the bokebynders, not in small nombre, but at tymes whole shyppes full, to the wonderynge of the foren nacyons.[54]

Anthony Wood alleges that Oxford students at one college turned from desecrating religious services to 'borrow hatchets and went into the Choir and chopped in pieces such books that were not bought for forty pound'.[55] There were similar reports from Scotland. The seventeenth-century Scots historian John Spottiswoode wrote about this, and a witness in 1562 described the 'insane fury' of those who destroyed both images and books.[56] The drive to buy new textbooks, the increasing availability of affordable printed material, the lack of library space, along with government pressure to purge libraries of undesirable material, all promoted a more rapid turnover of book stock. In many mid-sixteenth-century cases, where the fervour of educational and religious reformers went much further, the results might be described as devastating. It is likely that many of the discarded books ended up, as John Bale describes, in the hands of continental bookbinders and collectors.[57]

N. R. Ker's pioneering work on medieval pastedowns – the waste parchment and paper used by binders to reinforce their work – in later Oxford bindings enabled him to chart a pattern of book loss and replacement in one university

53 Bale to Matthew Parker, 30 July 1560: T. Graham and A. G. Watson (eds.), *The recovery of the past in early Elizabethan England: documents by John Bale and John Joscelyn from the circle of Matthew Parker* (Cambridge, 1998), 17.

54 *The laboryouse journey & serche of Johan Leylande, for Englandes antiquitees . . . with declaracyons enlarged: by Johan Bale* (London, 1549; repr. Amsterdam, 1975), fol. Bi^{r}.

55 Anthony Wood, *The history and antiquities of the University of Oxford, in two books*, ed. and tr. John Gutch (Oxford, 1796), II. 105.

56 Durkan and Ross, 6.

57 Andrew Watson notes at least seventeen Oxford books in Antwerp, including 'seven from All Souls, eight from Balliol and two from Abingdon Abbey' ('The post-medieval library', 84).

town.[58] From the evidence of the remnants of these recycled books, it is clear (but not surprising) that Oxford libraries were deliberately getting rid of medieval theology and canon and civil law manuscripts from about 1490 to 1540, for leaves from these volumes can be identified in the structures of later bindings. Durkan and Ross record the sighting decades later of out-of-date canon-law books that had been abandoned from the library at St Andrews during the Reformation.[59] The removal of books – whether they were manuscripts, incunables or later printed books – to make space for what were viewed as superior copies is, however, a recurrent feature of library practice.

Readership and circulation

While England was arguably 'massively illiterate' into the seventeenth century, with an estimated literacy rate of one-third for men and only one-tenth for women, this was also a time of increasing concerns about reading (particularly of the Bible) and a contingent growth in literacy. Literacy rates in Scotland were probably slightly higher than in England.[60] Even a cursory look at the output of the British printing press during this period is suggestive. A search of the online *English short-title catalogue* demonstrates a trend to publish more and more in print: in the first quarter-century of printing, the *ESTC* records 472 items; in 1501–25 there are 1,381; in 1525–50, 2,930; in 1551–75, 3,636; in 1576–1600, 6,879; and in 1601–25, 11,935. In the second full quarter of the seventeenth century, that figure actually rose to 28,971, although those inflated numbers reflected the political turmoil of the 1640s. These figures are fairly crude ones that do not distinguish between books and pamphlets, or between new titles, new editions and reissues, and they do not of course include the continental imprints that made their way across the Channel in large numbers, which would have made up the vast majority of books in libraries; nevertheless they do suggest a growing population of readers, many of whom would have turned to libraries to supply some of their needs.

Most institutions limited their readership to members and perhaps certain categories of associated membership. Evidence suggests that qualified laymen

58 Oxford is a useful example, for, as Ker notes, binders there continued to use old books in their bindings up to the seventeenth century, long after their Cambridge colleagues had abandoned the practice. N. R. Ker, *Fragments of medieval manuscripts used as pastedowns in Oxford bindings, with a survey of Oxford binding,* c. *1515–1620* (Oxford, 1954).

59 Durkan and Ross, 7.

60 D. Cressy, *Literacy and the social order: reading and writing in Tudor and Stuart England* (Cambridge, 1980), 2; R. A. Houston, *Scottish literacy and the Scottish identity: illiteracy and society in Scotland and northern England, 1600–1800* (Cambridge, 1985).

were occasionally allowed to borrow books from monastery libraries.[61] There were a few semi-public libraries in Great Britain in the fifteenth and sixteenth centuries. One John Carpenter at his own expense founded a small library in Worcester, which was intended to be open to all clergy. A Bristol library with similar readership was founded in 1464, associated with the Gild of Kalendaries. Provision was made for the library to be open 'for two hours before None and two hours after None . . . all who wish to enter that library for the purpose of study shall be free to come and go', supervised by a salaried library keeper. Another early public library was the Guildhall Library in London, a chained collection described in 1549 as 'a house appointed by the saied maior [Richard Whittington] and cominalitie for . . . resorte of all students for their education in Divine Scriptures'.[62]

The restored University Library at Oxford was generous about who could consult its collections too: 'only Doctors and Licentiats of the Three Faculties, Batchelors of Divinity, Masters of Arts, Batchelors of Physick, and Law, Batchelors of Arts of two Years standing, and all other Batchelors; if they come thither in their Habits and Hoods, and there demean themselves with Reverence'.[63]

Thomas Bodley was the most conspicuous early British proponent of a more open policy of admissions. He could be said to be part of a new wave of enlightened library policy-makers in the early seventeenth century that included Federigo Borromeo (1564–1631), who founded the Ambrosian Library in Milan in 1609. Bodley's original policy, which later became more relaxed, was that the University Library would be open five hours each day to anyone who could prove he was a graduate. At the same time, Bodley had learnt hard lessons about what happens when books are lent, which convinced him of the merits of a reference-only collection: any qualified scholar who needed to use Bodley's collection could do so, but he was not allowed to take the books out of the library. For most libraries, institutional membership equalled some form of readership. Even then, readers were usually further restricted to certain categories of member.

Libraries commonly maintained a reference collection, separate from the circulating library, that could more or less be guaranteed to be made available when required for consultation. These books were often secured in chests

61 D. M. Norris, *A history of cataloguing and cataloguing methods, 1100–1850: with an introductory survey of ancient times: a thesis accepted for the honours diploma of the Library Association* (London, 1939; repr. Detroit, 1969), 11.

62 Schedule of possessions in Guildhall College, quoted in Thomas Kelly, *Early public libraries: a history of public libraries in Great Britain before 1850* (London, 1966), 30.

63 Bodley, *Reliquiæ Bodleianæ*, 33.

or cupboards until the fourteenth and fifteenth centuries, and then located (sometimes chained) on lecterns or horizontally on shelves until the early seventeenth century, and even later in some libraries; after that, reference books continued to be chained, but in an upright position to bars running along bookshelves. Chaining was a practice that endured well into the eighteenth century. Indeed, the last college in Oxford to unchain its books did not do so until 1799, while Cambridge libraries began unchaining from the 1620s. In the mutually contrary spirit that can occasionally be detected even now, Cambridge continued to use lecterns long after Oxford had abandoned them. There was a prevailing need to make certain that all qualified readers had ready access to a body of material necessary for their studies, but the relative rarity and value of manuscripts and early printed books also contributed to the chained-book policy. Under normal circumstances these reference books had a fighting chance of survival, unless they were superseded and deliberately discarded during routine library modernisation: many of the older books in institutional libraries still bear the marks of the metal staples that once connected book to chain.

Library administrators early understood the value of allowing readers to borrow books too, and some part – often the larger part – of many collections was set aside to endure the uncertainties of circulation. The circulation system in common use at the beginning of the early modern period was the *electio*, a practice akin to the annual distribution of books within Benedictine communities, introduced at Oxford and Cambridge colleges during the fourteenth century; it had become the prevailing book circulation system in the British universities by the end of the fifteenth century.[64]

Borrowing had advantages not just for the readers; library keepers would have appreciated the benefits of freeing up limited book storage space, particularly before more efficient book shelving had become a regular feature of library rooms. Circulation records took the form of simple indentures at some institutions: Eton College Library recorded borrowed books by the first words of second folio (*secundo folio*) on small indentures to be retained by the provost or vice-provost.[65] Others required security of some sort, often the deposit of another book of roughly equal value, or readers would have to write their own names in the borrowed book, almost as if they were new owners.[66]

64 For the medieval period, see above, chapter 6; for the continuation of the practice into the sixteenth century, see E. S. Leedham-Green, 'University libraries and book-sellers', in *CHBB* III. 323–6.

65 R. Birley, 'The history of Eton College Library', *Library*, 5th ser., 11 (1956), 231.

66 C. de Hamel, 'The dispersal of the library of Christ Church, Canterbury, from the fourteenth to the sixteenth century', in Carley and Tite, *Books and collectors*, 265.

Lincoln College, Oxford, was still conducting book elections in 1596,[67] but most others had abandoned the idea long before then. The demise of the *electio* can be read in the archives of Merton College. There was a long record of complaints against the lax administration of the system, beginning in the fourteenth century. The system was definitely in trouble by the end of the fifteenth century, when in 1488 the return of five volumes from the election of one Mollond is recorded: he had borrowed the books twelve years earlier when he had been working on an arts degree, and had failed to return them when he began a degree in theology.[68] Merton fellows borrowed unmanageably large numbers of books, both for themselves and for their colleagues; some of them returned books different from those they had borrowed; others were fined for books they had lost. In a disastrous theological election of 1508, fifty-two books were found to be missing. One fellow, Matson, was unable to account for a single one of the twenty-eight volumes he had borrowed. After 1519 there is no further record of elections there.[69] Extant records for other colleges suggest that many had true elections rather than assignments, and that poorer colleges, able to provide only one or two books per fellow, fared better with their elections. There was probably as much variety in the rules around the return of books as in their borrowing. Merton's elected books were not supposed to be returned piecemeal as their readers no longer needed them, but were expected to be returned in one lot at election time. The absence of a full-time librarian and the space to store the books made this a practical option. Institutions with fewer books were readier to handle more irregular book returns.

Another sort of loan, from institution to institution, is evident in the early part of this period. That is the loan of large parts of collections from monastic libraries to sister institutions, such as from the cathedral library at Christ Church, Canterbury, to Canterbury College in Oxford. There seems to have been some attempt to keep track of these books through stock-taking and inventories, but in fact most did not make it back to the original library.[70]

The policies that determined whether books went into the reference or the circulating collection were governed both by the needs of the library community and by the wishes of benefactors. It is safe to say that the rules

67 Ker, 'Provision of books', in *HUO* III. 456.

68 Garrod, 'Library regulations', 318.

69 *Ibid.*, 323–6.

70 De Hamel, 'Dispersal of the library of Christ Church', 266. Alan Coates discusses a similar relationship between the book collections of Reading Abbey and its dependent cell at Leominster in his *English medieval books: the Reading Abbey collections from foundation to dispersal* (Oxford, 1999), 19–23.

were usually framed by the leaders of those communities, rather than by an one person who could be designated a librarian. The Jesuits, who include British recusants in the sixteenth century, set out rules for their continenta libraries that suggested that deciding who could borrow books was beyon the authority of the library keeper. That was the rector's job.[71] Donors wer influential too, often stipulating in their bequests exactly how their gift book should be stored and used. Others were more accommodating, specificall allowing the library keepers to place books in either the circulating or th reference collection, depending on space, scholarly need and so on. Richar Wylleys, warden of Higham Ferrers (1504–23), gave New College, Oxfor a manuscript copy of Gratian's *Decretum* with the provision that it shoul always be available for loan to any fellow who had to leave town to avoid th plague.[72]

Smaller institutional libraries, such as those designed to serve the need of colleges, kept reference collections but continued to lend books to thei members through this whole period. Thomas Bodley, setting up a much large library with a different clientele in the early seventeenth century, set out detailed administrative policy for the renewed Oxford University Library i his draft of the statutes. It is clear that he had given careful thought to book lending and decided that it was too risky:

> And sith the sundry Examples of former Ages, as well in this University, as in other Places of the Realm, have taught us over-often, that the frequent Loan of Books, hath bin a principal Occasion of the Ruin and Destruction of many famous Libraries; It is therefore ordered and decreed to be observed as a Statute of irrevocable Force, that for no Regard, Pretence, or Cause, there shall at any time, any Volume, either of these that are chained, or of others unchained, be given or lent, to any Person or Persons, of whatsoever State or Calling, upon any kind of Caution, or offer of Security, for his faithful Restitution.[73]

Bodley was determined about not lending library books, and expected hi librarian, Thomas James, to be just as strict. Indeed, Bodley took pride in th fact that he had once personally refused the bishop of Gloucester's request t borrow Oxford books.[74] This reference-only policy is one that has been effec tively adopted in some of the major academic and copyright-deposit librarie

71 B. Connolly, SJ, 'Jesuit library beginnings', *Library Quarterly* 30 (1960), 246.
72 Ker, 'Provision of books', in *HUO* III. 456.
73 Bodley, *Reliquiæ Bodleianæ*, 27–8. 74 *Ibid.*, 207.

as a means of ensuring that obligations to readers, both current and future, are met.

Inside the sixteenth-century college library room, security measures did not seem to extend much beyond book-chains and trust in library readers, who, in academic institutions, were, after all, the trustees of all their college collections. There were plenty of rules for key-holders: they were asked to close the books they had been reading, or required to shut the windows on their way out, but there is little evidence that they needed supervision. That so many illuminations and initials have been removed from the college manuscript books suggests not so much a casual attitude towards supervision of readers as the fellows' proprietorial attitude towards college property.

The ordering of books

Cataloguing and classification were probably the two most important administrative tasks facing early modern librarians, for these exercises ensured that collections were recorded for security, individual books could be found by readers and keepers, and, if the books were borrowed by readers, they could be more readily traced. There seems to be an irresistible human impulse behind this, to plot a hierarchy of knowledge and to arrange books of written human knowledge in the same order. The evidence for the cataloguing and classification schemes of libraries, many of which were dispersed centuries ago, can be found in marks left in the books and sometimes on library furniture, but it is primarily in their catalogues, discussed in depth by David McKitterick (below, chapter 25), that the work librarians put into organising their collections can best be seen.

Books in larger libraries were most often arranged on their lecterns or shelves according to a subject-classification scheme that was mirrored in their catalogues. That is not to say that every early library followed this plan. Books in very small collections, with readers accustomed to finding their own way around, could manage without strict subject-arrangement and corresponding catalogues. Larger libraries were not necessarily bound to arrange their collections in subject-order, so long as the books had shelf-marks and there was a key – usually a catalogue – to the shelf-marks and perhaps someone to fetch the books. The British Library and the Bodleian Library today, each storing millions of books on closed access, many of them in the order in which they were acquired, follow such a system.

Dorothy May Norris's study of the cataloguing methods in hundreds o libraries provides evidence for general cataloguing and classification trend in Britain.[75] Norris discusses several kinds of documents in her study, includ ing inventories, shelf-lists, lists of donations, and catalogues. The fifty or sc library catalogues she considers suggest that the most common way to begin arranging entries in catalogues in the fifteenth and sixteenth centuries was by subject, and the evidence of the marks in books confirms that books were often placed on lecterns and shelves in more or less the same arrangement as in their catalogues.

Preservation and conservation

There are many signs that early library keepers were concerned both to preserve their collections and to keep them in good repair. Much of the evidence is in account-books that record the purchase of chains to confine books to the library, or sporadic payments for the services of binders to repair and bind books, some of which would have arrived in the library in sheets, or roughly bound under vellum wrappers. Fifteenth-century statutes, too, record rules that reference books must not leave the library or that circulating books have to stay within the walls of the lending institution. They often give instructions on how readers should care for library books: users should ensure that books are never left open on the lecterns overnight, or they were instructed to resist the impulse to raise extra cash by selling or pawning books. The rules themselves suggest that such carelessness was a real threat. Various marks in the books show that occasionally they were indeed left as pledges for loans, while wine and water stains, and mutilated leaves, suggest other conservation dangers.

However developed library conservation and preservation practice might have been by the sixteenth century, it suffered setbacks during the Reformation. Numerous book collections were dispersed, changed hands or were even destroyed. For a time, preservation came to mean a great deal more than just preserving the books in good condition in the library; keepers had to devise tactics simply to keep their books at all. The libraries in dissolved monasteries were of course the most vulnerable, although academics must have worried whether their libraries might be next. There is evidence in one booklist of heroic efforts to salvage at least the remnants of a monastic library in Yorkshire. Much of the credit has to go to William Browne (d. June 1557), prior at Monk Bretton, who removed his colleagues Thomas Frobisher

75 Norris, *A history of cataloguing*.

d. March 1557), Thomas Wilkinson (d. before 1564?), and Richard Hinchcliff d. 1574), and what was left of his priory library, to nearby Worsborough. Browne's will suggests that his intention was to preserve the collection in the hope that it could be restored to the monastery when the authorities came to their Catholic senses. Richard Sharpe has identified many of the 142 volumes in the inventory as printed books.[76] We will never know if Prior Browne and his brethren had simply selected printed books from a much larger collection, or if the collection had already been depleted of manuscripts, or whether the priory had a modern policy of replacing old manuscript editions with printed texts.

When Henry turned his attention to modernising the curricula at Oxford and Cambridge, college library keepers seemed to have had more options than their religious counterparts in the monasteries. But here again there were attempts to circumvent the new regime by removing books, until it seemed safe to restock the libraries. Andrew Perne (1519?–89), master of Peterhouse in Cambridge, is said to have removed a large number of books from Norwich Cathedral Library, which he presented to Cambridge University Library in 584.[77] Cargill Thompson suggests that this discovers another part of the roblem: the ease with which books were removed by Perne – and by others who may have had no intention of returning them – indicates a neglectful style of library administration that may have made the reformers' job asier.[78]

Booksellers like Garbrand Harks in Oxford also played an adjunct role in the preservation of libraries. Harks evidently purchased or reclaimed manuscript books that were destined for destruction; some of these probably went to replenish private and institutional libraries when the coast was clear. Private collectors played their part too, even when serving their own ends. Neil Ker draws attention to what he calls the 'one systematic attempt to preserve books t the time of the Dissolution'. Most of the manuscripts in Henry VIII's library were from the monasteries: 'Out of more than four hundred of the king's books now in the Royal Collection of the British Museum [Library], about two hundred and fifty can be assigned to fifty-five medieval libraries.'[79] Other monastic books, still preserved in national and academic libraries, found their ay into the relative safety of the libraries of collectors such as Henry Savile 568–1617), John Dee, Matthew Parker and Sir Robert Cotton.

76 CBMLC IV. 266–87. Carley cites other examples in 'Monastic collections', 341.
77 N. R. Ker, 'Medieval manuscripts from Norwich Cathedral Priory', *TCBS* 1 (1949), 1–28.
78 W. D. J. Cargill Thompson, 'Notes on King's College Library 1500–1570, in particular for the period of the Reformation', *TCBS* 2 (1954), 48.
79 *MLGB*, xi. For further details, see Carley, CBMLC VII.

From the mid-sixteenth century, preservation practice settled back for a while into the usual routine of binding, chaining and keeping the library tidy. There seems to have been a little renaissance in Oxford around the beginning of the seventeenth century though, perhaps partly as a result of the introduction of library shelving. This new furniture (discussed more fully above, chapter 1) made a dramatic difference – probably every bit as dramatic as mobile shelving did in the twentieth century – by effecting a huge increase in book storage space without any change to the fabric of the building. Many institutions took the opportunity offered by the shift from lectern to shelf to enhance the overall appearance of their libraries. Oxford still chained its books, but often placed them on the new furniture fore-edge forward. Blacksmiths had to be recruited to make the longer, pivoted chains to allow shelved books to be read at the desks attached to the bookshelves, and each book had to be handled, so it made sense to check the books' condition and repair, rebind or replace them. Magdalen College, Oxford, embarked on a systematic rebinding campaign in the early seventeenth century, employing the bookseller-binder Robert Way, among others, to cover both manuscript and printed books in reverse calf with ribbon ties.[80] On the other hand, Cambridge was slower to adopt shelving, but began to unchain its books around 1627, long before Oxford did. It could be argued that library books were less secure this way, but removing metal chains and staples obviously brought other benefits, both for readers, who could read anywhere in the library, and for books, whose condition was improved.

The activities in the field of preservation and conservation of that dynamic library duo, Bodley and his librarian, are well documented. On his book-purchasing jaunts, Bodley sometimes sent duplicates back to Oxford, where James was supposed to replace defective, badly bound or marked copies with the better ones. This exercise was to be performed with discretion. As Bodley wrote, '*I would always intreat you, that any Defects among your Books, may be but known to your self, and not descanted abroad.*' And Bodley's statutes determined that one of the librarian's duties was 'to trim every Volume, that is not in good Plight, with fit Reparations, for Use and Continuance'.[81]

Conclusion

The variety of administrative practice in British libraries, fragmentary evidence that is often hidden deep in institutional archives, the sporadic nature of

80 See numerous entries in Magdalen College Archives Libri Computi.
81 Bodley, *Reliquiæ Bodleianæ*, 22, 57–9.

library activity in Britain with all its disruptions, and the breakdown of important libraries in the sixteenth century make it risky to generalise. Some developments might cautiously be suggested, though. Collections did not develop because of any systematic approach to acquisitions; rather, they became great or were neglected depending on the personalities who oversaw them, on the gifts they received, and on occasional purchases, usually in response to a specific demand. Readership and circulation varied from library to library, too, when institutions defined their own readership and set their own rules for borrowing and reference, based on their particular requirements. Although modern professional librarianship in Britain is a phenomenon that really began in the nineteenth century, with the establishment of the Library Association in the 1870s and the development of proper library training, the ground was being prepared in the seventeenth century.

25

Libraries and the organisation of knowledge

DAVID MCKITTERICK

When, in 1574, the year after his death, John Caius's *Historia Cantebrigiensi Academiae* was published in London, it contained a catalogue of most of th books in Cambridge University Library. The list was the first to be printed c any institutional British library. It represented a collection depleted after fou decades of scholarly, educational and religious turmoil.[1] The mid-sixteenth century revolution in the universities had roots in secular learning as well a in religion and politics, in debate and in neglect, as well as in violence an prejudice.[2] Like those at Oxford, and those of the colleges at Cambridge, th catalogue of the library belonging to the University of Cambridge bore witnes to these educational and religious upheavals, in losses as well as in what ha survived.

As presented in Caius's account, the catalogue was of manuscripts an printed books, the two media listed separately but under the same subjec heads. Thus it included not only the manuscript of Boethius' *De consolatior philosophiae* that had belonged to the university since the fifteenth centur but also Greek books presented by Cuthbert Tunstall in 1529: editions fro the presses of Aldus Manutius and others, the *editio princeps* of Homer, an a number of Greek manuscripts.[3] The list in Caius's book was, furthermor a list of what were here called *veteres libri*, and the purpose in offering was at least partly as an invitation to others to provide the necessary moder complement – especially of printed books. By arranging this survey in an ord

1 John Caius, *Historiae Cantebrigiensis Academiae ab urbe condita liber primus* . . . (1574). For identities of most of the manuscripts, see the notes by M. R. James in John Caius, *Works*, ed. S. C. Roberts (Cambridge, 1912), 115–16. See also G. Pollard and A. Ehrman, *The distribution of books by catalogue to AD 1800* (Cambridge, 1965), 250, 257. For Caius's own library, see P. Grierson, 'John Caius's library', in M. J. Prichard and J. B. Skemp (eds.), *Biographical history of Gonville and Caius College*, VII (Cambridge, 1978), 509–25.

2 For some of the issues, see for example R. W. Hunt, 'The medieval library', in J. Buxton and P. Williams (eds.), *New College, Oxford, 1379–1979* (Oxford, 1979), 335–6.

3 Oates, *CUL*, 60–9. For catalogues of the library down to the mid-sixteenth century, see CBMLC x.

opening with Greek literature and language, perhaps Caius and his colleagues made clear their humanist intent. Grammar was followed by *Dialectica* with *Philosophica*; then *Rhetorica* and *Historica*; and a trio of books headed rather grandly *Arithmetica, Geometria, Astronomia,* comprising Boethius' *Ars metrica*, Tunstall's *De arte supputandi* and Aristotle. This in turn was followed by a still more ambitious section, *Cosmographia, Musica*, comprising Dionysius' *De situ orbis*, Ptolemy and Strabo, before the final large sections of bibles, patristics and theology, and civil and canon law.

The arrangement was that of Caius or his assistants, not of the library, where Tunstall's books were shelved together, and where even in the past few months the vice-chancellor, Andrew Perne, had given instructions for the room to be rearranged against the arrival of substantial donations for which he was negotiating.[4] It was an arrangement quite different from that of the traditional faculties, for which the inscriptions in the stained glass in the windows of the libraries at Jesus College, Cambridge (*c.* 1500) and at Eton (1521) stood as guides and, now, historical documents.[5]

Caius's book is, furthermore, a reminder that there are always two fundamental ways (with many further subsidiaries) of arranging books: one on the library shelves, the other on paper and according to the priorities chosen by one individual for a particular selection, and for the particular purposes of the moment. In his history of the university, Caius was concerned to show, not only that Cambridge was older than Oxford, but also that it was alert to modern scholarly trends. As they stood on the shelves in the mid-century, the University Library's books showed little consistency in their ordering or arrangement. Tunstall's books had been shelved together but scant attention had been paid to subject, or faculty, elsewhere, and such traces as there were of older benefactions were at best piecemeal, even accidental. Terence stood next to Aquinas, Strabo next to Ambrose, Thucydides (in Latin) next to Gregory on Job. To any contemporary eye in the 1560s, the contents of the University Library were hardly representative of the Reformation; and it was not simply because of the religious purges to which libraries at Cambridge had been subject. The situation, manifestly unsatisfactory by the 1570s, where a university was expected to defend the reformed faith but lacked the most obvious of resources in its own library, was being addressed by Matthew Parker even as Caius's book

4 J. C. T. Oates and H. L. Pink, 'Three sixteenth-century catalogues of the University Library', *TCBS* 1 (1952), 310–40; Oates, *CUL*, 93–4.

5 M. R. James, 'Description of the stained glass in the windows of Election hall', *Etoniana*, 30 November 1904, 38–9; A. Masson, *The pictorial catalogue: mural decoration in libraries* (Oxford, 1981), 64–5, figs. 6, 18–19.

was passing through the press. In parallel developments, some Oxford colleg libraries likewise saw a renaissance in the last quarter of the century.[6]

Much earlier in our period, the library at Syon Abbey contained over 1,30 books by 1504. The catalogue begun by Thomas Betson shows it organise under letters of the alphabet, A–V, with grammar and classical texts at th beginning, followed by medicine and astrology. Bibles were placed in class I followed by commentaries, but history and dictionaries intervened befor theological topics returned for classes M–S, the whole concluding with cano and civil law. The classification is notable, not only for placing humanist inte ests at the beginning of the alphabetical sequence, but also for separating th Bible from theology. Unfortunately we do not know how the arrangement (the room (or rooms) may have made this seem less disrupted than appea to be the case on the evidence of the order of the catalogue alone.[7] A simil principle had been followed at the Sorbonne in the fourteenth century, but was one that was to look odd to later generations, who became accustomed in the Vatican, Paris and Britain alike – to seeing theology at the beginning (classification schemes, with bibles generally first of all.[8]

The history of library classification is dominated by innumerable tension between ideas, the ordering of knowledge, the activities of authors and publis ers, accessions policies, fortunes and practices, and the sheer physical deman of finding space for books on shelves. Such issues are further complicated b demands to keep books together according to some other order, such as b donor, or by date of acquisition, and by the accidents and vagaries of ho books on wholly different subjects can be bound up together, whether on th instruction of a librarian or at the whim of a bookbinder. In the hands of a owner such as Matthew Parker, even the integrity of volumes as publishe was at risk, as he rearranged their contents to suit his own ways of thin ing. Manuscripts were even more liable to reorganisation: both Parker and S Robert Cotton separated and rebound parts in different volumes so as to me their particular needs.[9] In most libraries, private and institutional, and as o of the arrangements most economical of space, ordering by size is a freque

6 N. R. Ker, 'The provision of books', in *HUO* iii. 453–4.

7 V. Gillespie, in CBMLC ix. xlviii–xlix.

8 For the Sorbonne arrangement, see H.-J. Martin, R. Chartier and J.-P. Vivet (eds.), *Histoire de l'édition française*, i: *Le livre conquérant, du moyen âge au milieu du xviie siècle* (Paris, 1982), 436.

9 R. I. Page, *Matthew Parker and his books* (Kalamazoo, MI, 1993), 46–55; E. Leedham-Green and D. McKitterick, 'A catalogue of Cambridge University Library in 1583', in Carley and Tite, *Books and collectors*, 157, 159. For Cotton, see C. G. C. Tite, *The manuscript library of Sir Robert Cotton* (London, 1994), 43–6, and *The early records of Sir Robert Cotton's library: formation, cataloguing, use* (London, 2003).

henomenon – a distinction sometimes being made between the larger (and herefore deemed more important) books, which were organised by subject, nd the smaller ones, to which less attention was paid.

Libraries, the book trade and scholarship had different needs in the ways hat books were organised. When Conrad Gesner assembled his *Bibliotheca niversalis* (Zurich, 1545),[10] a book that was to remain a standard work of eference, for private and institutional owners alike, long into the seventeenth entury, he organised his entries alphabetically, by author. Three years later, in is *Pandectarum, sive partitionum universalium . . . libri xxi*, he rearranged much of is matter by twenty-odd subject-heads, breaking each head down into further livisions. His work was a guide to reading and, thanks to its incorporating everal catalogues of the publications from the main continental scholarly rinters (Froschouer, Aldus Manutius, Gryphius, Froben, etc.), it was also a uide to the book trade. It offered little or nothing to aid in the organisation f libraries, as distinct from their assembling.

Gesner's work was valued, and used by subsequent generations as well, ecause it was firmly based on what had been written and published, in nanuscript or print. So, too, was the work of François Grudé de La Croix lu Maine, who in 1584 published the first (and, as it proved, only) volume f his *Bibliothèque française*. But La Croix du Maine had further ambitions, in roposing to the king of France a scheme whereby a library might be created ased on a hundred-odd *buffets*, or bookcases, of which the illustration he provided is often accepted as the first depiction of a bookcase in a recognisably nodern form. Each *buffet* would contain 100 volumes. His proposed scheme egan with God, and concluded with the sequence *Livres de récréation*; *Paradis, urgatoire & Enfer*; and *La fin du monde*. But, unlike Gesner (who had, incidenally, placed *Theologia* at the end), La Croix du Maine was in effect proposing kind of vast commonplace book, an arrangement, not of books as they had een published (the basis of a library), but of the contents of books.[11]

By the first half of the seventeenth century, knowledge in libraries was nvested not just in books, but also in coins and medals, maps, globes, rints, pictures and sculpture. In the 1590s, the university printer at Cambridge produced a list of the coins in the possession of the University Library,

10 See, with further references to a substantial literature, A. Serrai, *Conrad Gesner* (Rome, 1990).

11 François Grudé de La Croix du Maine, *Premier volume de la bibliothèque* (Paris, 1584). For a further discussion of 'libraries without walls', see R. Chartier, *The order of books* (Cambridge, 1994, originally published as *L'ordre des livres*, 1992). For other aspects, not concerned directly with libraries, see A. Taylor, *General subject-indexes since 1548* (Philadelphia, 1966).

recently received by bequest from Andrew Perne, master of Peterhouse.[12] A Oxford, it was ordered in 1652 that a catalogue of the coins and other raritie should be made, following the arrival in the Bodleian of the collections of Si Thomas Roe and William Laud.[13] In both public and private collections, coin provided illustrative and iconographic complements to books, and survey such as Occo's *Imperatorum Romanorum numismata*, a work widely distribute among larger libraries of all kinds, provided the crucial links.[14] The follow ing pages are concerned with books and manuscripts alone. To a greater c lesser degree, these were complemented by other forms of knowledge whos organisation, historical, chronological or thematic, was an often essenti accompaniment.

When in the first years of the century Sir Thomas Bodley worked wit Thomas James to establish a new university library in Oxford, some of th assumptions of the two men concerning the arrangement of books wer straightforward. But one fundamental issue was to affect the new library fc centuries. In 1599, James was visiting Cambridge libraries, collecting materia for his catalogue of manuscripts in the two universities. Bodley pursued hi with letters. 'You must by no meanes omitte, to take good notice of the orders, by placing and disposing their librarie bookes: whether they doe it, b the Alphabet, or according to the faculties.'[15] Whatever James reported fro Cambridge, where the libraries were by no means uniformly organised, th decision was soon taken at Oxford that the books should be ordered accordir

12 Oates, *CUL*, 139–41. For Perne, see D. McKitterick (ed.), *Andrew Perne: quatercentenary studies* (Cambridge, 1991). The contents of his library are listed in *BCI*, 419–79. His coins are now in the Fitzwilliam Museum, though the confusions of centuries mean that it is no longer possible to distinguish them from the rest of the old university collection.

13 Macray, 72, 84, 108. In 1650, Sir Simonds d'Ewes borrowed a number of coins: 107, and BL, MS Harley 298, fol. 173.

14 For the collection of Sir Robert Cotton, with further references to others, see G. van der Meer, 'An early seventeenth-century inventory of Cotton's Anglo-Saxon coins', in C. Wright (ed.), *Sir Robert Cotton as collector: essays on an early Stuart courtier and his legacy* (1997), 168–82; for those of Prince Henry and his brother Charles I, see A. MacGregor, 'The king's disport: sports, games and pastimes of the early Stuarts', in A. MacGregor (ed.), *The late king's goods: collections, possessions and patronage of Charles I in the light of the Commonwealth sale inventories* (1989), 403–21, esp. 411–12. After 1649, the coins in the royal collection, like the books, were in the care of John Dury. Many aspects of the interrelationships of book collections with non-book collections during this period remain imperfectly explored, but see J. Cunnally, *Images of the illustrious: the numismatic presence in the Renaissance* (Princeton, 1999). See also above, 517–8.

15 Bodley to James, 24 December 1599, G. W. Wheeler (ed.), *Letters of Sir Thomas Bodley to Thomas James* (Oxford, 1926), 2. For two of the Cambridge libraries at this time, see S. Bush Jr and C. J. Rasmussen, *The library of Emmanuel College, Cambridge, 1584–1637* (Cambridge, 1986), and P. Gaskell, *Trinity College Library: the first 150 years* (Cambridge, 1980), ch. 6.

o faculties: of theology, law, medicine and arts. The first printed catalogue, of 605, showed the system in operation.

Whatever the variations later in the order, a system employing letters of he alphabet for the case, followed by numbers for the shelf and volume, ecame widely accepted practice. In some libraries, including Peterhouse,[16] mmanuel College,[17] the public library at Norwich,[18] and the reserved cupoards *australe* and *boreale* in the Bodleian, words indicating the compass orintation – north, east, south, west – were employed, but it was as easy to se the tripartite system alone. It was common to place bibles first, typically ollowed by commentaries, which themselves might be divided between Old nd New Testaments, or between Catholic and Protestant. The system was eadily adaptable to libraries' own needs and emphases. In the 1630s, Edinurgh University Library began the sequence with theology, and kept most f the books of William Drummond of Hawthornden together in class K, for *elles-lettres*.[19] At Ipswich, where the books were intended primarily to aid the own preacher, the books were organised so as to give the Church Fathers pride of place in the alphabetical order.[20]

Despite growing unease at the inadequacies of the old headings, librarians remained conservative. When, in the Interregnum, the entire library of Lambeth Palace was removed to Cambridge, to be absorbed into the University Library, the two libraries had to be rearranged – the Lambeth arrivals far outnumbering what was already at Cambridge. Now, letters of the alphabet were used to signify the presses, followed by Greek letters for the shelves, and numbers to indicate order on the shelves. But though one of the two library rooms was organised by subject, the other, holding the older collection, remained arranged mostly according to benefactor.[21] The same principles, using Greek letters, were adopted in Trinity College, Cambridge, which likewise retained a mixed arrangement whereby the old library was left intact, and more recent additions were shelved by benefactor: the college library was not reclassified in a single subject sequence until the 1660s.[22]

Organisation was not only by letters of the alphabet or numbers. Little has so far been recovered of ways in which colour was used in British libraries, as

16 Cambridge, Peterhouse, MS 405. 17 Cambridge, Emmanuel Coll., MS III.1.20.

18 D. M. Norris, *A history of cataloguing and cataloguing methods, 1100–1850* (1939), 168.

19 C. P. Finlayson and S. M. Simpson, 'The history of the library, 1580–1710', in J. R. Guild and A. Law (eds.), *Edinburgh University Library, 1580–1980: a collection of historical essays* (Edinburgh, 1982), 43–54, at 49.

20 J. Blatchly, *The town library of Ipswich, provided for the use of the town preachers in 1599* (Woodbridge, 1989), 33.

21 Oates, *CUL*, 264–6. 22 Gaskell, *Trinity College Library*, 113–15.

it was (for example) in the Cistercian library at Altzelle, near Dresden. There the catalogue of 1514 specified red for theology, black for law, and so forth, each book being further identified by a letter and number according to its *pulpitum*.[23] The Benedictine Florian Trefler also suggested the use of colour, in a different way.[24] Colour could easily be applied to fore-edges, and thus (since the books stood with their spines facing inwards) be readily visible on the shelf, but so far little evidence has been found of its being employed for subject-classification in post-Reformation England. In some libraries, other decorative devices were employed. At Ipswich, for example, the books were organised according to a scheme that employed letters, numbers and astronomical or astrological signs, the books being marked on the fore-edges so that when a shelf was complete it showed a continuous line from end to end.

If the emergence of a new literature of librarianship in the late sixteenth and early seventeenth centuries was a response to increasing numbers of books that came from the presses of Europe, it was also a movement that was by no means confined to the British Isles. Questions of arrangement, management, selection and distribution were at least as urgent in continental Europe as they were in London, Oxford or Edinburgh. In England, the dissolution of most of the monastic libraries, and the subsequent redistribution of their surviving manuscripts, with what seems to have been a rather smaller number of their printed books, added further complexities. But the underlying issues were the same: how to deal with books, new and old, in quantities such had never before been encountered. By the first half of the seventeenth century, these posed considerable difficulty. Many recalled Polydore Vergil's words from the end of the fifteenth century, that a man could print as much in a day as it had taken to write in many months.[25] Writers repeatedly recalled the libraries of Alexandria and of Constantinople, the sources for Alexandria suggesting figures as high as 400,000 or even 700,000 items – far larger than any seventeenth-century library, but a warning of what could happen again, and (since Alexandria was the greatest of all) also a goal to be sought.[26] Ever since classical times there had been complaints at the numbers of books and of authors, whether by Juvenal or by Amianus Marcellinus. The impression of overwhelming floods of publications was strengthened by the omnipresence of the printed word, and

23 L. Schmidt, *Altzelle*, Beiträge zur Geschichte der Wissenschaftlichen Studien in Sächsischen Klostern I (Dresden, 1897), 35.

24 Florian Trefler, *Methodus exhibens per varios indices . . . bibliothecae . . ordinationem* (Augsburg, 1560?).

25 Polydore Vergil, *De inventoribus rerum libri VIII*, lib. II, cap. VII.

26 For some figures, see Louis Jacob, *Traicté des plus belles bibliothèques publiques* (Paris, 1644), 146–8.

t remained a difficulty to be met with guides not just to particular literatures law, chemistry, sermons, etc.) but also to study and to the selection of books and reading more generally.

Figures for output are difficult to estimate with any accuracy. In seventeenth-century France, one of the most reliable measures remains the series of calculations made by H.-J. Martin in the 1960s, based on the (then still incomplete) author catalogue of the Bibliothèque Nationale.[27] In this alone, he discovered that the annual numbers of French books just in that library and published in the first years of the seventeenth century had roughly doubled by about 1640 and had more than tripled by the 1660s. Obviously the annual figures are subject to the distortions of political activity, and the whole is biased as the holdings of a single library; but there is no reason to question the scale of the trend.

The figures for the much smaller printing industry in the British Isles are more comprehensive, thanks to the *STC*, Wing, and the detailed survey of late seventeenth-century periodicals by Carolyn Nelson and Matthew Seccombe.[28] The very comprehensiveness of these works has to be treated with some care lest a bookplate count as much as the eight-volume Eton folio Chrysostom. Losses also vary in different periods; but it seems fairly clear that between the early 1590s and the late 1630s numbers of publications each year at least doubled.[29]

For Germany, on the other hand, the Thirty Years War created an environment in which the book trade laboured under serious difficulties. The figures for the Frankfurt fair catalogues show an activity in the second decade of the century not to be matched until the eighteenth century. They may mislead in their detail, in that there is considerable evidence from across Europe to suggest that at times of political turmoil the volume of pamphlet production actually increases – and this is just the kind of literature that was never strongly represented in the fair catalogues. But the upward trend of the figures seems inescapable.

27 H.-J. Martin, *Livre, pouvoirs, et société à Paris au xviie siècle*, 2 vols. (Geneva, 1969). See also Martin, Chartier and Vivet, *Histoire de l'édition française*, I: *Le livre conquérant*, 441–9.

28 C. Nelson and M. Seccombe, *British newspapers and periodicals, 1641–1700: a short-title catalogue of serials printed in England, Scotland, Ireland and British America* (New York, 1987).

29 J. Barnard and M. Bell, 'Statistical tables', in *CHBB* IV. 779–85. For more detail in the period to 1640, see the chronological tables by P. Rider in *STC* III. More generally, for some of the dangers in quantification, see H. Amory, 'Pseudodoxia bibliographica, or When is a book not a book? When it's a record', in L. Hellinga (ed.), *The scholar and the database*, CERL Papers 2 (2001), 1–14.

Britain drew on different kinds of books, and different languages, to different degrees. Though the church and the universities made this especially noticeable in institutional libraries, it was also true of politics, schools and much of everyday life. In many libraries, domestically produced books were outnumbered by those printed overseas. The increasing activity of foreign publishers was as important to the British library economy as was that of the printing trade in London, Oxford, Cambridge and Edinburgh.[30]

International trade was implicit in the acquisition and sharing of knowledge. As a result, national figures of output have to be interpreted in wider contexts. They do not in themselves provide a reliable guide as to the real scale of increase in the retail book trade, nor do they offer a scale by which to judge increases in the stocks of libraries. Nor, of course, can they take account of books surviving from past years. The losses from ecclesiastical and university libraries in England during the turbulent years of the mid-sixteenth century are only one aspect of a larger question. It is now impossible to determine the scale of loss, and partly for reasons having nothing to do with religion. Humanist scholarship displaced older traditions which were, literally, thrown out. New curricula replaced old. For texts of lasting appeal, the longstanding practice of replacing manuscripts with new copies as old ones wore out continued into the world of printed books. Volumes were discarded from libraries, and the space was used for replacements, or for new books entirely.[31]

These were European questions, not just British. The literature of librarianship during the period covered by this volume likewise tended to be international. The Jesuit Claude Clément's *Musei, sive bibliothecae extructio, instructio, cura, usus libri IV* (Lyon, 1635) was one of the most widely available, if not most thoroughly read, of all general manuals in the seventeenth century. Angelo Rocca on the Vatican Library (1591) was read in Germany and England, as well as in Italy.[32] Naudé's *Advis pour dresser une bibliothèque* (Paris, 1627, 1644) was printed in English in 1661, in a translation by John Evelyn.

Clément was criticised for his over-ambition. Nonetheless, his book was widely disseminated, and became well known as a kind of textbook on its subject, even in England. It discussed not just the organisation of books and

30 See for example J. Roberts, 'Importing books for Oxford, 1500–1640', in Carley and Tite, *Books and collectors*, 317–33; J. Roberts, 'The Latin trade', in *CHBB* IV. 141–73.

31 See for example Gillespie, CBMLC IX. l–li.

32 For a summary of the contents of this book, and for much else on the literature of libraries in the sixteenth and seventeenth centuries, see A. Serrai, *Storia della bibliografia*, V: *Trattatistica biblioteconomica*, ed. M. Palumbo (Rome, 1993). See also L. Desgraves, 'Naissance de la "science" des bibliothèques', *Revue française d'histoire du livre* 70–1 (1991), 3–30.

libraries but also what other kinds of collections were appropriate to accompany books (such as coins, medals, globes) and, further, the architecture and decoration of libraries (with inscriptions as well as images). It was dedicated to Philip IV of Spain, as was only appropriate for a book that concluded with a long section on the Escorial: Clément larded his dedication with references to other royal collectors from Philip of Macedon and Ptolemy Philadelphus to Charlemagne. Altogether, his book stands, at nearly 600 pages of small type in quarto, as one of the most comprehensive books on the design and organisation of libraries to have been published in the seventeenth century.

Unlike some authorities who wrote about libraries, Clément was not tolerant of all literature; and he firmly believed that some books, such as plagiaries, obscene books or heretical books, should be excluded. In one sense he was not, therefore, encyclopaedic. But he was right to emphasise the size of the problem as the world faced the inexhaustible activities of printing presses. It was one that was more obviously acknowledged by Alsted in his *Encyclopaedia* (1630). It concerned the organisation of knowledge in libraries: the ordering of ideas in a specific context, in setting books in due order on the shelves, in such a way that they could be recalled for use and so that they presented a coherent portrait of knowledge within a particular environment. After all, the first two purposes of a library stated by Clément were those that few would have disputed: *utilitatis publica* and *eruditionis ostentatio* – public value, and the demonstration of knowledge.

One of the most familiar visual models for libraries in a novel world is Woudanus's well-known engraving of the interior of the recently founded university library at Leiden, dated 1610. On each side of the room stand eleven cases, or *plutei*, shelves with sloping desks on which the chained books could be rested so as to be read. They are divided by an aisle, and they set out in order an intellectual progression under seven heads: mathematics, philosophy, literature, theology (six out of the twenty-two cases available), history, medicine and law – the last taking up five cases, as only appropriate in a university that was already established as a notable legal centre. At the far end are two long cupboards, their solid doors presumably normally locked, while in the foreground is another, larger and more ornate cupboard containing the legacy of Joseph Scaliger, a couple of pairs of globes (one globe is being measured by two scholars). Maps, portraits and a long landscape decorate the walls.[33]

33 This has been much copied and reproduced. See for example Clark, *Care of books*, between 164–5; E. Hulshoff Pol, 'The library', in Th. H. Lunsingh Scheurleer and G. H. M. Posthumus Meyjes (eds.), *Leiden University in the seventeenth century: an exchange of learning* (Leiden, 1975), 394; *Leidse Universiteit 400: stichting en eerste bloei 1575–ca. 1650* (Amsterdam,

By 1610, swollen with ordinary additions and with the Scaliger books having arrived only in the previous year, the Leiden library was already substantially bigger than it had been in 1595, when the first printed catalogue had been published.[34] By then an important principle had already been established, in the separation of the smaller format books from those in folio that stood in the main rank. By 1640, when a new catalogue was issued, the various further places that had been contrived for the books were leading to a still further breakdown of the original scheme, where space had long since run out. Neither the 1595 catalogue nor that of 1640 was indexed. Books were listed simply shelf by shelf, and subject-arrangements grew in parallel. As a result, it became progressively more time-consuming to discover whether or not a particular book or author was in the library.

The Leiden library was well known to British visitors and scholars.[35] Its problem was universal. As successive proposals for the ordering of knowledge in libraries were published across Europe in the seventeenth century, so the subject-heads represented in the engraving of 1610 tended to become more numerous, eventually, Hydra-like, sprouting further sub-heads.

As numbers of printed books increased, so also did questions of how far subjects could be divided up, beyond the traditional arts. Gabriel Naudé, writing in Paris in 1627, proposed a simple division under broad heads: theology, medicine, law, history, philosophy, mathematics and *humanités*. Under each of these headings, subjects were then to be broken down into smaller units.[36] By 1635, Clément was suggesting a sequence of twenty-four *armaria*, beginning with the Bible, passing through theology to canon and civil law, and thence to

1975), 134; P. Thornton, *Seventeenth-century interior decoration in England, France and Holland* (New Haven, CT, 1978), fig. 297. For different versions of the scene, see C. Berckvens-Stevelinck, *Magna commoditas: geschiedenis van de Leidse Universiteitsbibliotheek, 1575–2000* (Leiden, 2001), 39.

34 (Petrus Bertius), *Nomenclator autorum omnium quorum libri . . . exstant in Bibliotheca Academiae Lugduno-Batavae* (Lugduni Batavorum, 1595), repr. in facsmile, with an introduction by R. Breugelmans (Leiden, 1995). See also E. Hulshoff Pol, 'The library', 395–459, and Berckvens-Stevelinck, *Magna commoditas*.

35 Quite apart from tourists and academic visitors, British students at Leiden are listed in *Album studiosorum Academiae Lugduno Bataviae, 1575–1875* (Leiden, 1875). See also for example R. W. Innes Smith, *English-speaking students of medicine at the University of Leyden* (Edinburgh, 1932); and J. A. van Dorsten, *Poets, patrons and professors: an outline of some literary connexions between England and the University of Leyden* (Leiden, 1962).

36 Gabriel Naudé, *Advis pour dresser une bibliothèque* (Paris, 1627): the same framework was proposed in the later edition of 1644; facsimile edn, introd. C. Jolly (Paris, 1990). See also C. Jolly, 'Naissance de la "science" des bibliothèques', in *Hbf* II. 380–5. For Naudé, see in particular M. Cochetti, 'Gabriel Naudé, *mercurius philosophorum*', *Il Bibliotecario* 22 (1989), 61–106, and P. Nelles, 'The library as an instrument of discovery: Gabriel Naudé and the uses of history', in D. R. Kelley (ed.), *History and the disciplines: the reclassification of knowledge in early modern Europe* (Rochester, NY, 1997), 41–57, with further references.

Philosophia contemplativa (headed by Seneca) and *moralis*, followed by mathematics, medicine, history, philology and literature, ending with *Pii* and *Ascetici* before manuscripts and books in oriental languages. He was but one of several who proposed similar arrangements for knowledge.

Something of this development or, rather, answer to the twin demands of knowledge and of the publishing industry, can be seen in what happened to ideas for library classification in the hands, not of librarians, but of booksellers, who (presumably then as now) considered that it was easier to trap customers by ensuring that they searched as widely as possible in their own and cognate subjects, and so chose rather broad classifications – much like modern online booksellers. Though the functions and ambitions of libraries and booksellers were very different, both had need to classify their books. The London bookseller Andrew Maunsell, who departed from much former practice (including Gesner) by arranging his work by surnames rather than Christian names, devoted most of his 1595 catalogue to divinity, before a shorter section on mathematics, physic and surgery. Part of his purpose was to help people to discover what they perhaps only half remembered, and so under Divinity he set his sub-headings in roughly alphabetical order: Adultery, Adversity, Anabaptists, Antichrist, etc.

In booksellers' and library schemes alike, we witness the gradual identity of new subjects of study, the resolution between (for example) mathematics and geography, the identification of modern political reality, the acknowledgement of modern literature. Such schemes sit beside others of the seventeenth and eighteenth centuries, in natural philosophy by Ray, Willughby, Linnaeus or others, or by Wilkins in the study of language. They ignored alphabetical ordering by author (as, for example, in Gesner's bibliographical work of the 1540s) just as the natural world was reduced into classifications based on analysis and, increasingly, on observation.[37] But the new bibliographical schemes have a distinct character all of their own, in that books, as physical objects, are not as susceptible to organisation as is much of the knowledge or opinion that they contain.

Since the books in them had to be shared, and be easily identified by many people, the need for some formal arrangement by subject was greater in institutional libraries than in private ones, and greater in larger than in smaller collections. In private houses, there is some evidence that distinctions might be

37 For related observations on Milton and modern classifications of the natural world, see K. L. Edwards, *Milton and the natural world: science and poetry in Paradise lost* (Cambridge, 1999), especially ch. 6; see also, more generally, K. Thomas, *Man and the natural world: changing attitudes in England, 1500–1800* (1983), esp. 51–70.

made between books kept in different rooms, for different purposes (domestic or professional, recreational or learned, for example), and for different parts of the family.[38] There is substantial evidence that at least in the larger formal private libraries some attempt was made at classification, either on the shelves or in the catalogues, and sometimes in both. The library of Lord Lumley contained about 3,000 works. During the 1590s it was catalogued in two sequences, one by subject and the other an alphabetical one by author. The catalogue copied from these in 1609, made at the instance of Prince Henry, did not represent the order of the books on the shelves, but instead also set them out by subject: *theologi, historici, artes liberales et philosophi, medici, legistae, cosmographi et geographi, common lawe* and *musici*, each subject being divided according to format but with the different languages – Latin, Greek, Hebrew, English and Italian – being mingled indiscriminately.[39] Each section was in turn organised roughly alphabetically by the first name of authors, Thomas More, Sir Thomas Smith and Sir Thomas Elyot thus appearing near each other. This was a consequence of copying out the former catalogue of the mid-1590s, written at the very time that (as we have seen) the bookseller Andrew Maunsell made a virtue of choosing to arrange authors by surnames instead. A few years later, when the collection of a Norfolk country gentleman, Sir Thomas Knyvett, was catalogued, a sustained effort was made to separate subject and language.[40] By the time of his death in 1618, Knyvett owned over 1,400 books, and this catalogue went far beyond the ordinary post-mortem inventory both in its bibliographical detail and in its organisation. He was sufficiently concerned with the order of his library to ensure that each volume had a shelf-mark written in it – a feature common enough in the larger private libraries of the eighteenth and nineteenth centuries, but unusual in such a library at this date. His catalogue was organised in the sequence *theologi, medici, historici, politici et geographici, mathematici, libri philosophici et aliarum artium humaniorum, libri poetici et musici* and *libri utriusque iuris*, each broad discipline being arranged so as to distinguish the folio books from the smaller formats, and with the books in French, English, Spanish and Italian likewise under separate heads.

Such arrangements, being those in private libraries, were perhaps open to fewer public criticisms, but they must, even to their owners, have seemed

38 S. West, 'Studies and status: spaces for books in seventeenth-century Penshurst Place, Kent', *TCBS* 12 (2002), 266–92.
39 S. Jayne and F. R. Johnson (eds.), *The Lumley library: the catalogue of 1609* (London, 1956).
40 D. J. McKitterick, *The library of Sir Thomas Knyvett of Ashwellthorpe, c. 1539–1618* (Cambridge, 1978).

inadequate: in the Lumley catalogue, for example, Copernicus and Ovid both fell under the same head, whereas in the Knyvett catalogue Copernicus was more strategically placed with *libri mathematici*, and so with Alhazen, Vitruvius and Dürer. Though it has since been much quoted in discussions about institutional libraries, and its arguments were cast on a large scale, Gabriel Naudé's *Advis pour dresser une bibliothèque* (translated into English in 1661) was intended as a contribution to the development of a private one. Naudé was librarian to Henri de Mesmes, and his book reflected many of the concerns shared across Europe. In a wide-ranging consideration of the purposes and means of collection-building, at a period when, for the first time, it was commonplace for private libraries to be numbered by thousands of volumes rather than dozens or hundreds, Naudé insisted on the need for library organisation, what he called *ordre* and *disposition*:

> for without this, doubtless, all inquiring is to no purpose, and our labour fruitless; seeing Books are for no other reason laid and reserved in this place, but that they may be serviceable upon such occasions as present themselves; Which thing it is notwithstanding impossible to effect, unless they be ranged, and disposed according to the variety of their subjects, or in such other sort, as that they may easily be found, as soon as named. I affirm, moreover, that without this Order and disposition, be the collection of Books whatever, were it of fifty thousand Volumes, it would no more merit the name of a *Library*, than an assembly of thirty thousand men the name of an *Army*, unlesse they be martiall in their several quarters, under the conduct of their Chiefs and Captains; or a vast heap of stones and materials, that of a palace or a house, till they be placed and put together according to rule, to make a perfect and accomplished structure.[41]

Unlike theories of knowledge, libraries have to deal with the practicalities of storage, of cost, of accessibility. Those such as Naudé or (later) Pierre Le Gallois,[42] who proffered advice in the seventeenth century on forming a substantial private library, emphasised not only the need to select, but also the need for a long purse: they could hardly have been more frank.

Meanwhile, when, in 1650, John Dury addressed his *Reformed librarie-keeper* to the learned world, as an accompaniment to his tract on education, *The reformed school*, he had principally in mind the libraries of universities, where he

41 Gabriel Naudé, *Instructions concerning erecting of a library*, 74–5. Translated quotations from Naudé's *Advis* are taken from John Evelyn's version, published in 1661 as *Instructions concerning erecting of a library*.

42 Pierre le Gallois, *Traitté des plus belles bibliothèques de l'Europe* (Paris, 1680).

found librarians falling far short of his ideals: 'Their places are but Mercenarie and their emploiment of little or no use further, then to look to the Books committed to their custodie, that they may not be lost; or embezled by those that use them, and this is all.'[43] If expectations had fallen since the time of Thomas James at the Bodleian, just a generation earlier, Dury's allegation also questioned how far librarians thought it necessary to arrange books in any particular order. In his own mind, there was a distinction between the ways in which books were set on the shelves, and the more informative ways by which they could be presented to readers by the organisation of the catalogue. The ordering of the shelves was not so much secondary to the subject-catalogue as a wholly separate issue that had nothing to do with the ordering of knowledge. The task of the librarian, 'to keep the public stock of Learning, which is in Books and Manuscripts to increas it, and to propose it to others in the waie which may be most useful unto all', was left vague in its details. When Dury came, therefore, to the question of the catalogue, he had raised no special expectations. His proposal was as limited in its lack of detailed development as his earlier requirements had ben unspecific.

> And to do all this, First a Catalogue, of the Treasurie committed unto his charge is to bee made, that is all the Books and Manuscripts, according to the Titles whereunto they belong, are to bee ranked in an order most easie and obvious to bee found, which I think is that of Sciences and Languages; when first all the Books are divided into their *subjectam materiam* wherof they Treat, and then everie kinde of matter subdivided into their several Languages.[44]

Though he clearly had in mind both a manuscript catalogue, to be maintained in the library, and a printed catalogue for publication, it is noticeable that he did not press for an alphabetical ordering of authors. Nor was there any suggestion that the ranking of the titles in the catalogue need correspond in any way with the arrangements on the shelves. The idea of ordering of languages was well established, and it was to remain in use for many years more, albeit more in the catalogues of booksellers than in those of libraries.

Though the primary purpose for Thomas James's *Ecloga Oxonio-Cantabrigiensis* (1600) was as a union catalogue of manuscripts in the libraries of the two universities, James had also used this book to address European themes

43 John Dury, *The reformed librarie-keeper, with a supplement to the reformed-school . . . Whereunto is added, I. An idea of mathematicks (by J. Pell). II. The description [Lat.] of one of the chiefest libraries . . . in Germany* [viz. that of Wolfenbüttel, edited by S. Hartlib] (London, 1650), 16.

44 *Ibid.*, 19.

with his attack on the effects of censorship on the texts of the Fathers of the Church. For James, libraries were much more than places in which knowledge was accumulated and organised. They were also places in which knowledge was generated, and from which it was to be dispersed. This more active role was sought increasingly in the seventeenth century, albeit sometimes more as an ideal than as the reality. When Francis Bacon had written in 1605 of libraries as 'the shrines where all the relics of the ancient saints, full of true virtue, and that without delusion or imposture, are preserved and reposed',[45] he was expressing a conservative view. The notion of repose, of passive storage, was one that sat slightly oddly next to his arguments and proposals, both in *Of the proficience and advancement of learning* (1605) and in the *Instauratio magna* (1620), for a more active approach. In 1650, Dury, a member of the circle of Samuel Hartlib that was committed to the international exchange (or 'trade', as Dury insistently, and revealingly, called it) of information, added an account of the library at Wolfenbüttel to his tract *The reformed librarie-keeper.*[46] So that it could be more easily understood by the international community of scholars, he printed this part of his book in Latin. The growth of that library, the energy with which studies were pursued, and the international role it assumed in the learned world, offered an example to be emulated.[47]

For such 'trade', better organisation was necessary. To this end, librarians and those who used libraries increasingly worked to ensure that knowledge was organised according to contemporary needs and disciplines. Naudé's insistence on the importance of arranging books was so that they could be serviceable: 'Without this Order and disposition, be the collection of Books whatever, were it of fifty thousand Volumes, it would no more merit the name of a *Library*, than an assembly of thirty thousand men the name of an *Army* unlesse they be martiall in their several quarters, under the conduct of their Chiefs and Captains.'[48] To Naudé, the ideas advanced by La Croix du Maine in 1584

45 Francis Bacon, *Of the advancement of learning* (1605) Bk 2, Dedication to James I. For Bacon and the ordering of knowledge, see S. Kusukawa, 'Bacon's classification of knowledge', in M. Peltonen (ed.), *The Cambridge companion to Bacon* (Cambridge, 1996), 47–74.

46 For Dury, see C. Webster, *The great instauration: science, medicine and reform, 1626–1660* (London, 1975): for Dury, Hartlib and the 'Office of Address', see 67–77. For another view, see R. Garnett, 'Librarianship in the seventeenth century', in his *Essays in librarianship and bibliography* (London, 1899), 174–90.

47 *Sammler Fürst Gelehrter Herzog August zu Braunschweig und Lüneburg, 1579–1666* (Wolfenbüttel, 1979); for the organisation of the library, and the introduction of a system of decimal points to allow extensions to its classification, see M. von Katte, 'Herzog August und die Kataloge seiner Bibliothek', *Wolfenbütteler Beiträge* 1 (1972), 168–99.

48 Naudé, *Instructions*, 75.

for 100-odd presses on different topics, were simply unhelpful. Instead, and using arguments based on Cicero's *De oratore*, Naudé emphasised memory as an aid to access and classification. The best order for books was that which was 'le plus facile, le moins intrigué, le plus naturel, usité'. The familiar, even the traditional, order was best since, in complementary fashion, order aided memory and vice versa.[49] The faculties (developing the medieval ones, he named theology, medicine, jurisprudence, history, philosophy, mathematics and *humanitez*) should serve as main headings which could then be divided further. 'That all Books of like argument and subject be precisely reduced, & disciplin'd in their destin'd places; since in so doing, the memory is so refreshed that it would be easie in a moment onely to find out whatever Book one would choose or desire, in a Library that were as vast as that of Ptolomy.' To support this, there should be two catalogues, one 'so precisely dispos'd according to their several Matters and Faculties, that one may see & know in the twinkling of an eye, all the Authors which do meet there upon the first subject that shall come into ones head; and in the other, they should be faithfully ranged and reduced under an Alphabetical order of their Authours.'[50] If, for Naudé, the purpose of a library was essentially as a historical repository, and in this he differed from those who later regarded it as an extension to the laboratory, he had also formulated a crucial point: that the library was not simply to be comprehensive, but was to be able to be extended at any point, in accordance with extensions in knowledge itself.

The old faculties that had contented Bodley in the first years of the century, and that were reflected in the arrangement of portraits painted in the frieze above the books at Oxford,[51] were abandoned. But the process at Oxford was a slow one, and in the 1650s Gerard Langbaine was but one of several who found the old system, and the old catalogue, inadequate to their needs. In 1652, Seth Ward, professor of astronomy, reported on the conclusion of some months' deliberation:

> We have conceived it requisite to examine all the bookes of our public library (everyone takeing his part) and to make a catalogue or index of the matters and that very particularly in philosophy, physic, mathematics and indeed in all

49 For *Ad Herennium*, *De oratore* and other texts in this context, see F. Yates, *The art of memory* (London, 1966), ch. l. For aspects of the Baconian background, see also P. Rossi, *Clavis universalis: arts de la mémoire, logique combinatoire et langue universelle de Lulle à Leibniz* (Paris, 1993; originally published in Italian, 1983).

50 Naudé, *Instructions*, 78, 90.

51 For this frieze, see the articles by J. N. L. Myres, 'The painted frieze in the picture gallery', *BLR* 3 (1950), 82–91, 'Thomas James and the painted frieze', *BLR* 4 (1952), 30–51, 'Further notes on the painted frieze', *BLR* 5 (1956), 290–307. See also Masson, *The pictorial catalogue*.

> the other facultyes, that so that greate numbers of bookes may be serviceable and a man may at once see where he may find whatever is there concerneing the argument he is upon.[52]

It was only several generations later that the Bodleian began to shelve most of its books according to a new classification scheme, one no longer based on the old faculties. For all libraries using one or other version of the old heads, perhaps the greatest difficulties in lack of specificity lay in the section of *Libri artium*. Even in the printed Bodleian catalogue of 1605, this was used as a kind of sump into which were tossed books that could not be counted as falling in one of the other faculties.[53] The main part of this catalogue consisted of shelf-lists, and so readers were able to scan the shelves, and at the same time were at the mercy of a demonstrably crude classification system. Thus books on history were placed with those on architecture, on grammar, on natural philosophy and mathematics. A manuscript bestiary was shelved next to a printed book on Parma, and a book on agriculture next to a life of Julius Caesar. In order to help his readers, James provided an alphabetical list of authors, but the old university faculties were not so much inadequate to modern needs as mostly irrelevant. When a new edition of the catalogue appeared in 1620, it presented the books in alphabetical order of author, as they had been recorded in the library's own manuscript catalogue since 1612.[54] But the shelving distinctions stayed the same.

Like the Bodleian catalogue of 1620, that of Sion College in 1650 was organised by author. Both catalogues had behind them purposes that were very largely theological. Thomas James was an outspoken critic of Roman Catholicism, and at Sion John Spencer was employed to manage a library intended primarily for Anglican clergy. In both cases, the author catalogue by itself was thought insufficient. For clergy wishing to obtain commentaries on the Bible, Spencer provided an index organised according to the books of the Bible, adding also lists of commentators on the Creed, the Ten Commandments, on the church's major feasts, on Thomas Aquinas, and some others. Unlike in the body of his printed catalogue, he left ample space in this part for further

52 Seth Ward to Sir Justinian Isham, 27 February 1652, quoted in I. G. Philip and P. Morgan, 'Libraries, books, and printing', in *HUO* IV. 663.

53 Thomas James, *Catalogus librorum bibliothecae publicae quam vir ornatissimus Thomas Bodleius . . . nuper instituit* (Oxoniae, 1605), repr. in facsimile as *The first printed catalogue of the Bodleian Library, 1605* (Oxford, 1986).

54 For reproductions of pages from these catalogues, see G. W. Wheeler, *The earliest catalogues of the Bodleian Library* (Oxford, 1928).

references to be added in manuscript, in this respect following the example of the Bodleian catalogue.

Whether on the continental mainland or in Britain, there was no generally accepted order for placing books on shelves. Size was the most obvious way of doing so, whether in broad distinctions or (after the period with which this volume is concerned) in the carefully graded arrangements of Samuel Pepys, who reorganised his books on several occasions so as to proceed by steps from the largest to the smallest, with small wooden blocks on which to stand volumes that would otherwise disrupt the visual effect.

For most libraries, the printed book was no different from a manuscript. Each contained particular works, required by or given to the library concerned and requiring to be placed on a shelf. At Syon Abbey, the largest late medieval collection in Britain of which a full catalogue survives, manuscript and print were shelved together, according to subject but without regard for medium. There is some evidence of efforts to replace manuscript with print, though there had to be a considerable measure of chance in what was possible in this respect. The strength of tradition, and the fact that many people saw no need to separate the two, is to be seen in the influential publications of Gesner, who mingled manuscript and print. In most libraries, the two media were not systematically separated for several generations.

More commonly, many libraries reflected the arrival of donations. In Cambridge University Library, the various gifts of Matthew Parker, Sir Nicholas Bacon, Robert Horne and others were in large part shelved as groups, though there were elements of compromise with other ideas. The gifts seem to have been organised from within Cambridge so as to obtain from each donor books (or the cash wherewith to buy them) within particular subjects. As a result, when each gift was shelved as a group, the subjects – *theologia, astronomia, cosmographia, dialectica, rhetorica, geometria, musica, arithmetica, grammatica, historia* – on the whole fell naturally together.[55] At Oxford, the manuscripts received in the mid-seventeenth century, whether acquired by purchase or by donation, were all shelved according to collection.

Issues of organisation applied to manuscripts as well as to printed books, on the one hand (thanks to their smaller numbers) in much less degree but on the other with complications of their own. The tendency of manuscript volumes to contain works of different writers, and often on quite different subjects, made consistent shelf-classification by subject impossible. The first major post-Reformation attempt at a union catalogue of manuscripts, and that

55 Leedham-Green and McKitterick, 'A catalogue of Cambridge University Library', 153–235.

limited enough in its scope, was by Thomas James, in 1600.[56] He restricted himself to the libraries of Oxford and Cambridge. For recent major donations, such as Matthew Parker's to Cambridge University Library, or those of William Smart, of Ipswich, to Pembroke College, Cambridge, he listed the books according to their provenances. At Gonville and Caius College, he noted those manuscripts in the college library, and the rather larger number *in archivis*.

But there was a much greater difficulty for any user of James's catalogue, in that the miscellaneous ordering of much of it, and its arrangement library by library, meant that there was no immediate way of discovering the whereabouts of any given text. James sought to meet this by various strategies. His interests in compiling the handbook were primarily theological, as a part of what became an obsession with the ways by which the Roman Catholic Church had corrupted and excised the works of the Church Fathers. Not surprisingly, therefore, he gave most energy to ensuring that theological works could be found; and for these he provided a detailed index, besides a chronological list of authorities from Dionysius and Josephus in the first century to Thomas Walsingham in the fifteenth. Then, after an analysis of Aristotelian manuscripts, James turned to the arts faculties, first providing a list of subjects, with those who had written on them, and then an alphabetical and detailed index to the library catalogues. Finally came lists of writers on medicine and on civil and canon law, but none of these was accompanied by a similar index to the main catalogue. The grand design petered out, and in the last pages of his work James returned to his concerns with the texts of Cyprian and Augustine. In his everyday work as librarian to Sir Thomas Bodley, James was in a much more restricted position, and the catalogues that he saw through the press for his patron show both more sustained analysis and the same impatience.

The impetus for the fundamental division between manuscript and print that now characterises the management of large libraries seems to have originated less with scholars – bibliographers, historians or librarians – than with the book trade. When in 1595 Maunsell issued his *Catalogue of English printed books*, he addressed himself to the Stationers' Company, drawing attention to the differences between his own work and that of his predecessors Gesner, Simler and John Bale: 'They make their Alphabet by the Christen name, I by the Sir name: They mingle Diuinitie, Law Phisicke, &c. together, I set

56 T. I[ames], *Ecloga Oxonio-Cantabrigiensis tributa in libros duos* (1600).

Diuinitie by it selfe: They set down Printed and not Printed, I onely Printed . . .'[57] By the 1630s, English booksellers' catalogues were regularly distinguishing print from manuscript. Maunsell's purpose was to determine not just what had been printed, but also, therefore, what was available for sale to his current customers. Unlike Bale or the others, he was not compiling a subject- or author-bibliography, from all sources, but a trade list. Where the trade led, libraries followed. In Oxford as in Paris, print and manuscript were gradually separated. By the time that John Spencer compiled his catalogue of Sion College Library (1650), the manuscripts there were listed with the printed books but were evidently stored apart, since Spencer provided no shelf-mark for them as he did for the printed books.

Only in the late seventeenth century was it all but universally accepted that manuscripts and printed books should be separated. At the beginning of the century, Sir Thomas Bodley insisted on their being kept on the shelves, and listed in the catalogue, mingled one with the other. This was followed by Thomas James, his long-suffering librarian, in the printed catalogue of 1605. But by the time of the printed catalogue of 1674, the two were firmly apart, a point emphasised in the very title of Thomas Hyde's work, *Catalogus impressorum librorum in Bibliothecae Bodleianae*. A few years later, Edward Bernard, also working from Oxford, and with the help of Humfrey Wanley, concentrated in the *Catalogi librorum manuscriptorum Angliae et Hiberniae* (Oxford, 1697–8) on the manuscripts in both private and public libraries, though even here there were occasions on which printed books were admitted, for example in the celebrated group of early specimens in the library of John Moore (d. 1714). For some purposes the two media remained muddled together even long after Mabillon and Montfaucon had in effect founded the discipline of palaeography, and Mallinckrodt and others had begun to define the history of printing by the enumeration of early editions.[58]

Separation was not only a question of manuscript and print. Segregation between different parts of the library, for different purposes, on open and closed shelves, was a long-established concept. But the reasons varied, and application varied still more. At Cambridge, Parker's manuscripts were set aside in a cupboard on their own together with his coloured copy of the Nuremberg Chronicle: this last offers an unusual early example of a high value set on a printed book. At Leiden, the need for a secure office, or *musaeum*,

57 Andrew Maunsell, *The first part of the catalogue of English printed bookes* (1595), dedication 'To the Worshipfull the Master, Wardens, and Assistants of the Companie of Stationers, and to all other Printers and Booke-sellers in generall'.

58 D. McKitterick, *Print, manuscript and the search for order, 1450–1830* (Cambridge, 2003).

was expressed in 1595: during the first decades of the seventeenth century the most valuable manuscripts were set aside, in secure conditions, though many others were left interspersed with printed books.[59] It was the same at Oxford, where Bodley's determination ensured that books of all kinds were organised primarily by subject rather than according to any notion of fragility or rarity.

> I hold opinion, that among the printed, there will be very many, not much lesse to be respected, then som of your rarer manuscriptes. And therfor my opinion is still, that they should be cheined as the rest, reserving onely the most singular and rare for your closets or the grates, and committing all the rest, to the trust which we must repose in mens othes, and consciences.[60]

Only a few were at first placed in cupboards, or *archiva*, and it was not until the arrival of the large Roe (1628), Barocci (1629) and Digby (1634) collections that segregation was established as regular policy. The fact that manuscripts and printed books existed side by side in libraries raises two key questions. First, how were the two differently valued? Secondly, how was this reflected in the organisation of libraries? Clément, writing in 1635, drew on Martial, Jerome and others when justifying the separation of the older manuscripts, with some other categories, from the more ordinary run.[61] Some books had been valued for their annotations for centuries, though it was less usual for the names of the annotators to be remembered.

At Sion College,[62] a library for the clergy of the diocese of London and therefore to some extent a public one, some books were marked in the catalogue as being *Arch.*, a term probably borrowed from Oxford. In 1639, the Sion library was arranged in eighteen stalls, nine down each side of the room. By 1650 this seems to have been extended, in that the letters ran now from A to W. In addition, the *archivium* was arranged also by letter, but with a single number; a similar arrangement pertained for unbound pamphlets. The manuscripts must have been kept separate again, since they are not allocated any sigla. Printed books designated *Arch.* were available on application to the librarian.

59 Bertius, *Nomenclator*, fol. B2^{v}; E. Hulshoff Pol, 'The library', 413, 417, 420–1.

60 Bodley to James [February 1602]: Wheeler, *Letters of Sir Thomas Bodley to Thomas James*, 25–6; see also R. W. Hunt, *Summary catalogue of western manuscripts in the Bodleian Library at Oxford*, I: *Historical introduction* (Oxford, 1953), ix.

61 Claude Clément, *Musei, sive bibliothecae tam privatae quam publicae extructio, instructio, cura, usus* (Lugduni, 1635), 370–2.

62 J[ohn] S[pencer], *Catalogus universalis librorum omnium in bibliotheca Collegii Sionii apud Londinenses* (1650). The standard history is E. H. Pearce, *Sion College and library* (Cambridge, 1913). Much of the library was destroyed in the Great Fire, 1666. Some of the most valuable books were sold at Sotheby's, 13 June 1977, and the residue was subsequently dispersed, the earlier books passing to Lambeth Palace Library.

As in some other libraries, the books reserved in this way were those, generally in smaller formats, perhaps thought likely to be of less immediate use to the London clergy, and less needful to be immediately to hand. However, the distinction was one of size, the larger (and therefore deemed more important) books being placed on the open shelves. Greek and Latin grammars were all, for example, set aside. So, too, were Jesuit works, and many of the publications of William Prynne. Inevitably there were some results that now seem odd. Drayton's *Poems* (an octavo) was set aside, whereas his *Polyolbion* (a folio) was left on the open shelves. The reason was certainly nothing to do with possible antiquarian value. Some early rarities were placed on the ordinary shelves, such as the copy of Caxton's *Recuyell of the historyes of Troye*, presented in 1646 and placed at T.9.8. The Mercator atlas (1585–95), given in 1636, was likewise placed on the open shelves.

Between the 1650s and the 1690s, the world of the learned library was transformed, in the wake of ideas brought back from continental Europe with the Restoration, in a growing perception of links between libraries and national interest, and in the rapid development of attention to private libraries. Emulation, imitation and rivalry, stimuli in private and public libraries alike, were often as much social as scholarly. The Bodleian Library, in effect Britain's national library, was most prominent of all. When in 1697 Humfrey Wanley was asked his opinion for a new catalogue of the library, to replace Hyde's of 1674, he replied to the curators as follows:

> One way of taking such a general Catalogue may be this. Suppose a dozen or more Learned men, who are likewise supposed to *know books* better than others, meet so many times a week, for a month or two, and consult together for the best method in placing the books, as whether it be best to place all books of a bigness together promiscuously or all books of a Faculty, Science, &c. together, and that with respect to their heighth; or not, placing the different editions of every author together, the oldest, first. To consult whether books with gilt backs should stand with their backs out or not; whether Authors should be placed in Alphabetical order as to their names or not; whether a Donation should be placed by it self in the Library or in the Benefaction book. Whether particular notice ought to be taken of any different Readings, or other Learned Notes written in the books, by knowing men.
>
> Whether the Title & date of every book should not be expressed in the Language of the book.
>
> To consult about the Method of drawing up a Catalogue from the books so placed. As whether it be not the best way to express the book, that a Scholar may know what book is meant tho' he does not see the book it self. Whether when a book contains many different Tracts of several Authors,

> under one general Title, Every author & Tract ought not to be expressed in the Catalogue. Whether upon any General Head, or Author, the names of all those Authors or books that any way illustrate the others ought not to be carefully put down.[63]

From this, Wanley proceeded to what should be included in the descriptions, and in what order the catalogue should be arranged. It is noticeable that, though he set out the questions clearly enough, none was new other than how the books should be displayed. Many of the questions that had been unresolved at the beginning of the century remained unresolved at the end, on a larger scale than ever. But one had in effect been abandoned. The Bodleian catalogue of 1674 became known across Europe. Both it and the Barberini catalogue published at Rome in 1681 were in alphabetical order of author. For the next several generations, independently published subject-indexes were the natural complements to author-catalogues. The distinction between subject-bibliography and library-classification underpinned the compromises inherent in the organisation of books. Furthermore, whatever the hopes that were periodically expressed (and they were heard in both Oxford and Cambridge), the largest libraries could not be expected to provide subject catalogues as well. In this at least, some of the anxieties attaching to libraries in the sixteenth and early seventeenth centuries became a lesser issue.

63 Humfrey Wanley, memorandum to the curators of the Bodleian Library, 1697, printed in *Bodleian Quarterly Record* 1 (1915), 106–12 and quoted in Norris, *History of cataloguing*, 152–3. This is Wanley's revised version, omitting outspoken criticism of the Librarian, Thomas Hyde. For the first, and fuller, version, see S. G. Gillam and R. W. Hunt, 'The curators of the library and Humphrey Wanley', *BLR* 5 (1954–6), 85–98.

Select bibliography

PRINTED PRIMARY SOURCES

Adams, S. (ed.), *Household accounts and disbursement books of Robert Dudley, earl of Leicester, 1558–1561, 1584–1586*, Camden 5th ser., 6 (Cambridge, 1995).

Allen, P. S., and H. W. Garrod (eds.), *Merton muniments*, OHS 86 (1926).

Anstey, H. (ed.), *Munimenta academica or Documents illustrative of academical life and studies at Oxford*, 2 vols., RS (London, 1868).

Epistolae academicae Oxon., 2 vols., OHS 35–6 (1898).

Bacon, F., *Letters and life of Francis Bacon*, ed. J. Spedding, 7 vols. (London, 1861–74).

Baildon, W. P. (ed.), *The records of the Honorable Society of Lincoln's Inn: the Black Books* (London, 1897).

Bale, J., *Index Britanniae scriptorum*, ed. R. L. Poole and M. Bateson, new edn with intro. by C. Brett and J. P. Carley (Woodbridge and Rochester, NY, 1990).

Bernard, E. *Catalogi librorum manuscriptorum Angliae et Hiberniae* (Oxford, 1697–8).

[Bertius, P.], *Nomenclator autorum omnium quorum libri . . . exstant in Bibliotheca Academiae Lugduno Batavae* (Lugduni Batavorum, 1595), repr. in facsmile. with an introduction by R. Breugelmans (Leiden, 1995).

Blake, E. O. (ed.), *Liber Eliensis*, Camden 3rd ser., 92 (London, 1962).

Boase, C. W. (ed.), *Register of rectors and fellows . . . of Exeter College* (Oxford, 1879).

Registrum Collegii Exoniensis, OHS 27 (1894).

Bodley, T., *The life of Sr Thomas Bodley, the honourable founder of the Publique Library in the University of Oxford. Written by himself* (Oxford, 1647).

Reliquiæ Bodleianæ: or some genuine remains of Sir Thomas Bodley. Containing his life, the first draught of the statutes of the publick library at Oxford – in English – and a collection of letters to Dr. James, &c., ed. T. Hearne (London, 1703).

Letters of Sir Thomas Bodley to Thomas James, ed. G. W. Wheeler (Oxford, 1926).

Bullarium diplomatum et privilegiorum sanctorum Romanorum pontificum Tauriensis editio, 24 vols. (Turin, 1857–72).

Caius, J., *Historiae Cantebrigiensis Academiae ab urbe condita liber primus . . .* (London, 1574).

Cambridge University, *Statuta Academiae Cantabrigiensis* (Cambridge, 1785).

Castiglione, B., *The book of the courtier* [*Il libro del cortegiano*, Venice, 1528], tr. Sir Thomas Hoby, introduction by J. H. Whitfield (London, 1974).

Catalogi veteres librorum ecclesiae cathedralis Dunelm., Surtees Soc. 7 (London, 1839).

Clark, J. W., *The observances in use at the Augustinian Priory of S. Giles and S. Andrew at Barnwell, Cambridgeshire* (Cambridge, 1897).

Clément, C., *Musei, sive bibliothecae tam privatae quam publicae extructio, instructio, cura, usus* (Lugduni, 1635).

Clifford, D. J. H (ed.), *The diaries of Lady Anne Clifford* (Stroud, 1990).

Cox, A. D. M., and R. H. Darwall-Smith (eds.), *Account rolls of University College, Oxford*, II: *1471/2–1596/7* (Oxford, 2001).

Cross, C. (ed.), *York clergy wills, 1520–1600: city clergy* (York, 1989).

Dinter, P. (ed.), *Liber tramitis aevi Odilonis abbatis*, Corpus Consuetudinum Monasticarum 10 (Siegburg, 1980).

Documents relating to the university and colleges of Cambridge, 3 vols. (London, 1852).

Dury, J., *The reformed librarie-keeper, with a supplement to the reformed-school. Whereunto is added*, I. *An idea of mathematicks* (by J. Pell). II. *The description* [Lat.] *of one of the chiefest libraries in Germany* [viz. that of Wolfenbüttel], ed. S. Hartlib (London, 1650).

Fletcher, R. J. (ed.), *The pension book of Gray's Inn*, I (London, 1901).

Fowler, J. T. (ed.), *Rites of Durham*, Surtees Soc. 107 (1903).

Foxe, J., *The acts and monuments of John Foxe*, 8 vols., ed. S. R. Cattley (London, 1837–41).

Frere, W. H. (ed.), *Visitations and injunctions*, 3 vols. (London, 1910).

Garrod, H. W. (ed.), *Merton College: injunctions of Archbishop Kilwardby, 1276* (Oxford, 1929).

Gesner, C., *Bibliotheca universalis* (Zurich, 1545).

Pandectarum, sive partitionum universalium . . . libri xx (Zurich, 1548).

Gibson, S. (ed.), *Statuta antiqua Universitatis Oxoniensis* (Oxford, 1931).

Gordon, Sir R., *A catalogue of the singular and curious library, originally formed between 1610 and 1650, by Sir Robert Gordon of Gordonstoun . . . with some additions by his successors . . . which will be sold by auction by J. G. Cochrane, bookseller, at No. 1 Catherine Street, Strand, on Thursday, March 14, 1816, and eleven following days (Sundays excepted), at half past eleven o'clock* [in 2,421 lots].

Gransden, A. (ed.), *The customary of the Benedictine abbey of Eynsham in Oxfordshire*, Corpus consuetudinum monasticarum 2 (Siegburg, 1963).

Hanslik, R. (ed.), *Regula S. Benedicti*, 2nd edn, *CSEL* 75 (Vienna, 1977).

Hassall, W. O. (ed.), *A catalogue of the library of Sir Edward Coke* (New Haven, 1950).

Highfield, J. R. L. (ed.), *The early rolls of Merton College, Oxford* (Oxford, 1964).

Hildemar, *Expositio regulae*, ed. R. Mittermüller, *Vita et regula SS. P. Benedicti una cum expositione regulae a Hildemaro tradita* (Regensburg, 1880).

Hingeston-Randolph, F. C. (ed.), *The register of Walter de Stapeldon, bishop of Exeter, 1307–1326* (London and Exeter, 1892).

Humbertus de Romanis, OP, *Opera de vita regulari*, ed. J. J. Berthier, 2 vols. (Rome, 1888–9).

Hyde, T., *Catalogus impressorum librorum in Bibliothecae Bodleiana* (Oxford, 1674).

Inderwick, F. A. (ed.), *A calendar of the Inner Temple records*, 5 vols. (London, 1896–1937).

Jacob, L., *Traicté des plus belles bibliothèques publiques* (Paris, 1644).

James, M. R., *The ancient libraries of Canterbury and Dover* (Cambridge, 1903).

James, T., *Ecloga Oxonio-Cantabrigiensis tributa in libros duos* (London, 1600).

Catalogus librorum bibliothecae publicae quam vir ornatissimus Thomas Bodleius . . . nuper instituit (Oxoniae, 1605), repr. in facsimile as *The first printed catalogue of the Bodleian Library, 1605* (Oxford, 1986).

Catalogus universalis librorum in Bibliotheca Bodleiana . . . (Oxford, 1620).

Jayne, S., and F. R. Johnson (eds.), *The Lumley Library: the catalogue of 1609* (London, 1956).
Jocqué, L., and L. Milis (eds.), *Liber ordinis S. Victoris*, *CCCM* 61 (1984).
Ker, N. R., 'The library of John Jewel', *BLR* 9 (1977), 256–64.
Kershaw, I., and D. M. Smith (eds.), *The Bolton Priory compotus, 1286–1325: together with priory account roll for 1377–1378* (Woodbridge, 2000).
Knowles, D. (ed.), *The monastic constitutions of Lanfranc*, rev. C. N. L. Brooke (Oxford, 2002).
Krivatsky, N. H., and L. Yeandle, *Sir Edward Dering*, *PLRE* 4 (I. 137–269).
La Croix du Maine, François Grudé de, *Premier volume de la bibliothèque* (Paris, 1584).
Lang, S., and M. McGregor (eds.), *Tudor wills proved in Bristol, 1546–1603* (Bristol, 1993).
Leathes, S. M. (ed.), *Grace book A*, Cambridge Antiquarian Society (Cambridge, 1897).
Leedham-Green, E. S., *Books in Cambridge inventories: book-lists from Vice-Chancellor's Court probate inventories in the Tudor and Stuart periods*, 2 vols. (Cambridge, 1986).
Leedham-Green, E. S., and D. McKitterick, 'A catalogue of Cambridge University Library in 1583', in Carley and Tite, *Books and collectors* (1997), 153–235.
Leland, J., *The laboryouse journey & serche of Johan Leylande, for Englandes antiquitees geuen of hym as a New Yeares gyfte to Kynge Henry the VIII. In the XXXVII. Yeare of his reygne, with declaracyons enlarged by Johan Bale* (London, 1549; repr. Manchester 1895, Amsterdam and Norwood, 1975).
De rebus Britannicis collectanea, ed. T. Hearne, 2nd edn, 5 vols. (London, 1774).
Commentarii de scriptoribus Britannicis, ed. J. P. Carley and C. Brett (forthcoming).
MacDonald, R. H. (ed.), *The library of Drummond of Hawthornden* (Edinburgh, 1971).
McKitterick, D. J., *The library of Sir Thomas Knyvett of Ashwellthorpe, c. 1539–1618* (Cambridge, 1978).
'Two sixteenth-century catalogues of St John's College Library', *TCBS* 7 (1978), 135–55.
Maclagan, M. (ed.), *Philobiblon Richardi de Bury: the text and translation of E. C. Thomas* (Oxford, 1960).
Macray, W. D. (ed.), *Register of the members of Magdalen College, Oxford*, 8 vols. (London, 1894–1915).
Maunsell, A., *The first part of the catalogue of English printed bookes* (London, 1595).
Naudé, G., *Advis pour dresser une bibliothèque* (Paris, 1627); tr. J. Evelyn as *Instructions concerning erecting of a Library: presented to My Lord the President de Mesme, now interpreted by Jo. Evelyn, Esquire* (London, 1661).
Nicolas, N. H. (ed.), *The privy purse expenses of King Henry the Eighth* (London, 1827).
Oates, J. C. T., and H. L. Pink, 'Three sixteenth-century catalogues of the University Library', *TCBS* 1 (1952), 310–40.
Palgrave, F. (ed.), *The antient kalendars and inventories of the Treasury of her Majesty's Exchequer* . . . , 3 vols. (London, 1836).
Pantin, W. A., and W. T. Mitchell (eds.), *The register of congregation, 1448–1463*, OHS, n.s. 22 (1972).
Plummer, C. (ed.), *Venerabilis Baedae, Historia ecclesiastica gentis Anglorum, Historia abbatum* . . . , 2 vols. (Oxford, 1896).
Raine, J. (ed.), *Testamenta Eboracensia: a selection of wills from the registry at York*, 6 vols. Surtees Soc. 4, 30, 45, 53, 79, 106 (Durham, 1836–69).
Riley, H. T. (ed.), *Gesta abbatum sancti Albani*, 3 vols., RS (London, 1867–9).
Roberts, R. J., and A. G. Watson (eds.), *John Dee's library catalogue* (London, 1990).
Salter, H. E. (ed.), *Registrum Annalium Collegii Mertonensis, 1483–1521*, OHS 76 (1923 for 1921).

argent, C. D., *The archaeology of a Cambridge library: the records of Queens' College, Cambridge, 1448–1672* (forthcoming).
elden, J., *Opera omnia*, ed. D Wilkins (London, 1726).
hadwell, C. L., and H. E. Salter, *Oriel College records*, OHS 85 (1926).
tatutes of the colleges of Oxford, 3 vols. (Royal Commission, 1853).
teer, F. W., 'A medieval household: the Urswick inventory', *Essex Review* 63 (1954), 4–20.
pencer], [J.], *Catalogus universalis librorum omnium in bibliotheca Collegii Sionii apud Londinenses* (London, 1650).
tevenson, J. (ed.), *Chronicon monasterii de Abingdon*, 2 vols., RS (London, 1858).
homas of Marlborough, *History of the abbey of Evesham*, ed. J. Sayers, and tr. L. Watkiss (Oxford, 2003).
hompson, E. M. (ed.), *Customary of the Benedictine monasteries of Saint Augustine, Canterbury and St Peter, Westminster*, 2 vols., HBS 23, 28 (1902–4).
ite, C. G. C., *The early records of Sir Robert Cotton's library* (London, 2003).
oulmin Smith, L. (ed.), *The itinerary of John Leland in or about the years 1535–1543*, 5 vols. (London, 1906–10).
refler, F., *Methodus exhibens per varios indices . . . bibliothecae . . . ordinationem* (Augsburg, 1560?).
William of Malmesbury, *De gestis pontificum Anglorum*, ed. N. E. S. A. Hamilton, RS (London, 1870); tr. D. Preest as William of Malmesbury, *The deeds of the bishops of England* (Woodbridge, 2002).
Gesta regum Anglorum, ed. R. A. B. Mynors, R. M. Thomson and M. Winterbottom, 3 vols. (Oxford, 1998–9).

SECONDARY LITERATURE

Alexander, J. J. G., 'Painting and manuscript illumination for royal patrons in the later middle ages', in Scattergood and Sherborne, *English court culture*, 141–62.
Amory, H., 'Pseudodoxia bibliographica, or When is a book not a book? When it's a record', in L. Hellinga (ed.), *The scholar and the database*, CERL Papers 2 (London, 2001).
Anderson, A. H., 'The books of Thomas, Lord Paget (*c.* 1544–1590)', *TCBS* 6 (1975), 226–42.
Backhouse, J., 'Founders of the royal library: Edward IV and Henry VII as collectors of illuminated manuscripts', in D. Williams (ed.), *England in the fifteenth century: proceedings of the Harlaxton Symposium for 1986* (Woodbridge, 1987), 23–41.
'Illuminated manuscripts associated with Henry VII and members of his immediate family', in B. Thompson (ed.), *The reign of Henry VII: proceedings of the 1993 Harlaxton Symposium* (Stamford, 1995), 175–87.
'The royal library from Edward IV to Henry VII', *CHBB* III (1999), 267–73.
Baker, J. H., *English legal manuscripts*, 2 vols. (Zug, 1975–8).
'The books of the common law', in *CHBB* III (1999), 411–32.
Ball, R. M., 'The opponents of Bishop Pecok', *JEH* 48 (1997), 230–62.
Barber, G., *Arks for learning: a short history of Oxford library buildings* (Oxford, 1995).
Barker-Benfield, B. C., 'Clement Canterbury, Librarian of St Augustine's Abbey, Canterbury', in *MSS at Oxford* (1980), 89–92.
Baron, F. (ed.), *Les fastes du Gothique: le siècle de Charles V* (Paris, 1981).

Barr, C. B. L., 'The Minster Library', in G. E. Aylmer and R. Cant (eds.), *A history of York Minster* (Oxford, 1977), 487–539.

Barratt, A., 'Small Latin? The post-Conquest learning of English religious women', in S. Echard and G. R. Wieland (eds.), *Anglo-Latin and its heritage: essays in honour of A. G. Rigg on his sixty-fourth birthday* (Turnhout, 2001), 51–65.

Barratt, D. M., 'The library of John Selden and its later history', *BLR* 3 (1950–1), 128–42, 208–13, 256–74.

Bartle, R. H., 'A study of private book collections in England between *c.* 1200 and the early years of the sixteenth century, with special reference to books belonging to ecclesiastical dignitaries', unpublished BLitt thesis, Oxford University (1956).

Bartlett, A. C., *Male authors, female readers: representation and subjectivity in Middle English devotional literature* (Ithaca, NY, 1995).

Batho, G. R., 'The library of the "Wizard" Earl: Henry Percy ninth earl of Northumberland (1564–1632)', *Library*, 5th ser., 15 (1960), 246–261.

Beddard, R. A., 'The official inauguration of the Bodleian Library on 8 November 1602', *Library*, 7th ser., 3 (2002), 255–83.

Bell, D. N., 'A Cistercian at Oxford: Richard Dove of Buckfast and London, B. L., Sloane 513', *Studia monastica* 31 (1989), 69–87.

What nuns read: books and libraries in medieval English nunneries (Kalamazoo, MI, 1995).

'The library of Cîteaux in the fifteenth century: *primus inter pares* or *unus inter multos?*', *Cîteaux: commentarii cistercienses* 50 (1999), 103–33.

'Monastic libraries: 1400–1557', in *CHBB* III (1999), 229–54.

'Printed books in English Cistercian monasteries', *Cîteaux: commentarii cistercienses* 53 (2002), 127–62.

Bell, H. E., 'The price of books in medieval England', *Library*, 4th series, 17 (1937), 312–32.

Bellenger, A., 'A medieval novice's formation: reflection on a fifteenth-century manuscript at Downside Abbey', in Ferzoco and Muessig, *Medieval monastic education* (2000), 35–40.

Bennett, H. S., 'The production and dissemination of vernacular manuscripts in the fifteenth century', *Library*, 5th ser., 1 (1946–7), 167–78.

Benton, J. F., 'The court of Champagne as a literary center', *Speculum* 36 (1961), 551–91.

Berckvens Stevelinck, C., *Magna commoditas: geschiedenis van de Leidse Universiteitsbibliotheek, 1575–2000* (Leiden, 2001).

Besson, A., 'Private medical libraries', in A. Besson (ed.), *Thornton's medical books, libraries and collectors* (London, 1990), 267–300.

Bevan, I., 'Marischal College, Aberdeen, and its earliest library catalogue: a reassessment', *Bibliotheck* 22 (1997) 4–19.

Birley, R., 'The history of Eton College Library', *Library*, 5th ser., 11 (1956), 231–61.

Birrell, T. A., *The library of John Morris: the reconstruction of a seventeenth-century library* (London, 1976).

English monarchs and their books: from Henry VII to Charles II (London, 1987).

'Reading as pastime: the place of light literature in some gentlemen's libraries of the 17th century', in R. Myers, and M. Harris (eds.), *Property of a gentlemen* (Winchester, 1991), 113–31.

Bischoff, B., and M. Lapidge (eds.), *Biblical commentaries from the Canterbury school of Theodore and Hadrian* (Cambridge, 1994).

:shop, T. A. M., *English Caroline minuscule* (Oxford, 1971).

ishop, W. J., 'Some medical bibliophiles and their libraries', *Journal of the History of Medicine* (1948), 229–62.

latchly, J., *The town library of Ipswich, provided for the use of the town preachers in 1599* (Woodbridge, 1989).

liss, P. (ed.), *Athenae Oxonienses*, 4 vols. (London, 1813–20).

loomfield, B. C. (ed.), *Directory of rare book and special collections in the United Kingdom and the Republic of Ireland*, 2nd edn (London, 1997).

odleian Library, *Sir Thomas Bodley and his library: an exhibition to mark the quatercentenary of the Bodleian, February to May 2002* (Oxford, 2002).

offey, J., and J. T. Thompson, 'Anthologies and miscellanies: production and choice of texts', *BPPB*, 279–315.

rett, P., 'Edward Paston (1550–1630): a Norfolk gentleman and his musical collection', *TCBS* 4 (1964) 51–69.

roadhurst, K. M., 'Henry II of England and Eleanor of Aquitaine: patrons of literature in French?', *Viator* 27 (1996), 53–84.

romwich, J., 'The first book printed in Anglo-Saxon types', *TCBS* 3 (1962), 265–91.

rook, V. J. K., *A life of Archbishop Parker* (Oxford, 1962).

rooke, C. [N. L.], *A history of Gonville and Caius College* (Woodbridge, 1985).

rooks, N. P., *The early history of the Church of Canterbury* (Leicester, 1984).

rown, T. J., 'The oldest Irish manuscripts and their late antique background', in P. Ní Chatháin and M. Richter (eds.), *Irland und Europa* (Stuttgart, 1984), 311–27; repr. in *A palaeographer's view: the selected writings of Julian Brown*, ed. J. Bately *et al.* (London, 1993), 221–41.

illough, D. A., *Alcuin: achievement and reputation* (Leiden, 2004).

irtt, J., 'Notes upon ancient libraries', *Notes and Queries* 1 (1849–50), 21–3.

ish, S., Jr, and C. J. Rasmussen, *The library of Emmanuel College, Cambridge, 1584–1637* (Cambridge, 1986).

ishnell, G. H. S., and R. I. Page, *Matthew Parker's legacy: books and plate* (Cambridge, 1975).

ixton, J., and P. Williams (eds.), *New College, Oxford, 1379–1979* (Oxford, 1979).

yrne, F. J., *A thousand years of Irish script* (Oxford, 1979).

irgill Thompson, W. D. J., 'Notes on King's College library 1500–1570, in particular for the period of the Reformation', *TCBS* 2 (1954), 38–54.

irley, J. P., 'John Leland and the contents of English pre-dissolution libraries: the Cambridge friars', *TCBS* 9 (1986), 90–100.

'John Leland and the contents of English pre-dissolution libraries: Lincolnshire', *TCBS* 9 (1989), 330–57.

'Sir Thomas Bodley's library and its acquisitions: an edition of the Nottingham benefaction of 1604', in Carley and Tite, *Books and collectors* (1997), 357–86.

'The royal library under Henry VIII', in *CHBB* III (1999), 274–81.

'"A great gatherer together of books": Archbishop Bancroft's library at Lambeth (1610) and its sources', *Lambeth Palace Library Annual Review* (2001).

'Monastic collections and their dispersal', in *CHBB* IV (2002), 339–47.

'Religious controversy and marginalia: Pierfrancesco di Piero Bardi, Thomas Wakefield and their books', *TCBS* 12 (2002), 206–45.

'Pre-Conquest manuscripts from Malmesbury Abbey and John Leland's letter to Beatus Rhenanus concerning a lost copy of Tertullian's works', *Anglo-Saxon England* 33 (2004), 195–223.

Carley, J. P., and V. Law, 'Grammar and arithmetic in two thirteenth-century English monastic collections', *Journal of Medieval Latin* 1 (1991), 140–67.

Carley, J. P., and C. G. C. Tite (eds.), *Books and collectors, 1200–1700: essays presented to Andrew Watson* (London, 1997).

Catto, J., 'Franciscan learning in England, 1450–1540', in Clark, *Religious orders* (2002), 97–104.

Cavanaugh, S. H., 'A study of books privately owned in England 1300–1450', 2 vols., unpublished PhD thesis, University of Pennsylvania (1980).

'Royal books: King John to Richard II', *Library*, 6th ser., 10 (1988), 304–16.

Cerdeira, C. 'Early modern English medical wills: book ownership, and book culture', *Canadian bulletin of medical history* 12 (1995), 427–39.

Chadwick, N. K., 'Early culture and learning in North Wales', in N. K. Chadwick *et al.* (eds.), *Studies in early British history* (Cambridge, 1954), 34–46.

Chaney, E., 'Quo vadis? Travel as education and the impact of Italy in the sixteenth century', in P. Cunningham and C. Brock (eds.), *International currents in educational ideas and practices* (London, 1988), 1–28.

Charles-Edwards, T. M., 'The context and uses of literacy in early Christian Ireland', in Pryce, *Literacy*, 62–82.

Chartier, R. *The order of books* (Cambridge, 1994; originally published as *L'ordre des livres* (Aix-en-Provence, 1992)).

Cheney, C. R., 'English Cistercian libraries: the first century', in C. R. Cheney, *Medieval texts and studies* (Oxford, 1973), 328–45.

'Richard de Bury, borrower of books', *Speculum* 48 (1973), 325–8.

'A register of MSS borrowed from a college library, 1440–1517', *TCBS* 9 (1987), 103–29.

Christ, K., *The handbook of medieval library history*, rev. A. Kern, ed. and tr. T. M. Otto (Metuchen, NJ, and London, 1984).

Church, C. M., 'Notes on the . . . library of the dean and chapter of . . . Wells', *Archaeologia* 57 (1901), 201–28.

Clanchy, M. T., *From memory to written record: England, 1066–1307*, 2nd edn (Oxford, 1993).

Clark, J. G., 'University monks in late medieval England', in Ferzoco and Muessig, *Medieval monastic education* (2000), 56–71.

'Reformation and reaction at St Albans Abbey, 1530–58', *EHR* 115 (2000), 308–9.

'The religious orders in pre-Reformation England', in Clark, *Religious orders* (2002), 3–33.

'Thomas Walsingham reconsidered: books and learning at late-medieval St Albans', *Speculum* 77 (2002), 832–60.

'Print and pre-Reformation religion: the Benedictines and the press *c.* 1470–*c.* 1550', in J. Crick, and A. Walsham (eds.), *The uses of script and print, 1300–1700* (Cambridge, 2004), 76–7.

Clark, J. G., (ed.), *The religious orders in pre-Reformation England* (Woodbridge, 2002).

Clark, J. W., *Libraries in the medieval and Renaissance periods* (Cambridge, 1894).

The care of books (Cambridge, 1901).

Coates, A., 'Benedictine monks and their books in Oxford', in Wansbrough and Marett-Crosby, *Benedictines in Oxford* (1997), 79–94, 289–93.

English medieval books: the Reading Abbey collections from foundation to dispersal (Oxford, 1999).

Cobban, A. B., 'Robert Wodelarke and St Catharine's', in E. E. Rich (ed.), *St Catharine's College, Cambridge, 1473–1973* (Cambridge, [1973]), 1–32.

Cochetti, M., 'Gabriel Naudé, mercurius philosophorum', *Il Bibliotecario* 22 (1989), 61–106.

Coleman, W. E., 'Chaucer, the *Teseida*, and the Visconti library at Pavia: a hypothesis', *MÆ* 51 (1982), 92–101.

Collinson, P., N. Ramsay and M. Sparks (eds.), *A history of Canterbury Cathedral* (Oxford, 1995).

Constable, G., *The reformation of the twelfth century* (Cambridge, 1996).

Courtenay, W. J., *Schools and scholars in fourteenth-century England* (Princeton, NJ, 1987).

'The fourteenth-century booklist of Oriel College Library', *Viator* 19 (1988), 283–90.

Cox-Johnson, A., 'Lambeth Palace Library 1610–1664', *TCBS* 2 (1955), 105–26.

Crook, E. J. 'Manuscripts surviving from the Austin friars at Cambridge', *Manuscripta* 27 (1983), 82–90.

Cross, C., 'Oxford and the Tudor state from the accession of Henry VIII to the death of Mary', in *HUO* III (1986), 117–49.

'A medieval Yorkshire library', *Northern History* 25 (1989).

'Monastic learning and libraries in sixteenth-century Yorkshire', in J. Kirk (ed.), *Humanism and reform: the church in Europe, England, and Scotland, 1400–1643*, Studies in church history, Subsidia 8 (Oxford, 1991), 255–69.

Cross, C., and N. Vickers (eds.), *Monks, friars and nuns in sixteenth-century Yorkshire* (Leeds, 1995).

Cross, J. E., 'On the library of the Old English martyrologist', in Lapidge and Gneuss, *Learning and literature* (1985), 227–49.

Cunnally, J., *Images of the illustrious: the numismatic presence in the Renaissance* (Princeton, 1999).

Davenport, C., *English heraldic book-stamps* (London, 1909).

Davies, G. R. C., *Medieval cartularies of Great Britain* (London, 1958).

Davis, V., *William Waynflete: bishop and educationalist* (Woodbridge, 1993).

Davison, P. (ed.), *The book encompassed: studies in twentieth-century bibliography* (Cambridge, 1992).

D'Avray, D. L., 'Portable *vademecum* books containing Franciscan and Dominican texts', in *MSS at Oxford* (1980), 61–4.

Dean, R. J., and M. B. M. Boulton, *Anglo-Norman literature: a guide to texts and manuscripts*, ANTS Occasional publications series 3 (London, 1999).

De Hamel, C. F. R., *Glossed books of the bible and the origins of the Paris booktrade* (Woodbridge, 1984).

Syon abbey: the library of the Bridgettine nuns and their peregrinations after the Reformation (London, 1991).

A history of illuminated manuscripts, 2nd edn (London, 1994).

'The dispersal of the library of Christ Church, Canterbury, from the fourteenth to the sixteenth century', in Carley and Tite, *Books and collectors* (1997), 263–79.

de la Mare, A. C., and B. C. Barker-Benfield (eds.), *Manuscripts at Oxford: an exhibition in memory of Richard William Hunt* (Oxford, 1980).

de la Mare, A. C., and S. Gillam (eds.), *Duke Humfrey's library and the divinity school, 1488–198* (Oxford, 1988).

de la Mare, A. C., and R. W. Hunt (eds.), *Duke Humfrey and English humanism in the fifteent century* (Oxford, 1970).

Delisle, L., *Le cabinet des manuscrits de la Bibliothèque (impériale) nationale*, 4 vols. (Paris 1868–81).

Dennys, R., *The heraldic imagination* (London, 1978).

De Ricci, S., *English collectors of books and manuscripts (1530–1930) and their marks of ownershi* (Cambridge, 1930).

A handlist of the manuscripts in the library of the earl of Leicester at Holkham Hall, Transaction of the Bibliographical Society, Supplement 7 (Oxford, 1932).

Desgraves, L. 'Naissance de la "science" des bibliothèques', *Revue française d'histoire du livr* 70–1 (1991), 3–30.

Dickins, B., 'The making of the Parker library', *TCBS* 6 (1972), 19–34.

Dodwell, B., 'The muniments and the library', *Norwich Cathedral: church, city and dioces 1096–1996* (London, 1996), 325–38.

Dorsten, J. A. van, *Poets, patrons and professors: an outline of some literary connexions betwee England and the University of Leyden* (Leiden, 1962).

Doughty, D. W., 'The library of James Stewart, earl of Moray, 1531–1570', *Innes Review* 2 (1970), 17–29.

Douthwaite, W. R., *Gray's Inn, its history and associations* (London, 1886).

Doyle, A. I., 'English books in and out of court from Edward III to Henry VII', in Scattergoo and Sherborne, *English court culture* (1983), 163–81.

'The printed books of the last monks of Durham', *Library*, 6th ser., 10 (1988), 203–19.

'Publication by members of the religious orders', in *BPPB* (1989), 109–23.

'Book production by the monastic orders in England (*c.* 1375–1530)', in L. L. Brown rigg (ed.), *Medieval book production: assessing the evidence* (Los Altos Hills, CA, 1990 1–19.

'Stephen Dodesham of Witham and Sheen', in P. R. Robinson and R. Zim (eds.), *Of th making of books: medieval manuscripts, their scribes and readers: essays presented to M. Parkes* (Aldershot, 1997), 94–115.

Drogin, M., *Anathema! Medieval scribes and the history of book curses* (Totowa and Montcla NJ, 1983).

Duffy, E., *The stripping of the altars* (New Haven and London, 1992).

Dugdale, W., *Monasticon Anglicanum*, ed. J. Caley, H. Ellis and B. Bandinel, 6 vols. (Londo 1846).

Dumville, D. N., 'English libraries before 1066: use and abuse of the manuscript ev dence', in M. W. Herren (ed.), *Insular Latin studies* (Toronto, 1981), 153–78; rep in M. Richards (ed.), *Anglo-Saxon manuscripts: basic readings* (New York, 1994), 16 220.

'Liturgical books for the Anglo-Saxon episcopate: a reconsideration', in D. N. Dumvill *Liturgy and the ecclesiastical history of late Anglo-Saxon England* (Woodbridge, 199 66–95.

urkan, J., 'The early history of Glasgow University Library: 1475–1710', *Bibliotheck* 8 (1977), 102–26.

urkan, J., and A. Ross, *Early Scottish libraries* (Glasgow, 1961).

urling, R. J., 'Girolamo Mercuriale's *De modo studendi*', *Osiris*, 2nd ser., 6 (1990), 181–95.

dwards, K., 'Bishops and learning in the reign of Edward II', *Church Quarterly Review*, 138/275 (1944), 57–86.

nmison, F. G., 'Jacobean household inventories', *Bedfordshire Historical Record Society* 20 (1938), 50–143.

ler, M. C., 'Syon Abbey's care for books: its sacristan's account rolls 1506/7–1535/6', *Scriptorium* 39 (1985), 293–307.

'Devotional literature', in *CHBB* III (1999), 495–525.

Women, reading, and piety in late medieval England (Cambridge, 2002).

chingham, C., *Church organization in Ireland AD 650 to 1000* (Maynooth, 1999).

ans, J., *A history of the Society of Antiquaries* (Oxford, 1956).

hrenbach, R. J., *Sir Roger Townshend's Books, PLRE* 3 (I. 79–135).

rdinand, C. Y., 'Magdalen College and the book trade: the provision of books in Oxford, 1450–1550', in A. Hunt, G. Mandelbrote and A. Shell (eds.), *The book trade and its customers, 1450–1900* (Winchester, 1997), 175–87.

rzoco, G., and C. Muessig (eds.), *Medieval monastic education* (London, 2000).

nlayson, C. P., and S. M. Simpson, 'The history of the library 1580–1710', in Guild and Law (eds.), *Edinburgh University Library 1580–1980* (1982), 43–54.

etcher, J. M., 'The faculty of arts', in *HUO* III (1986), 157–99.

etcher, J . M., and J. McConica, 'A sixteenth-century inventory of the library of Corpus Christi College, Cambridge', *TCBS* 3 (1961), 187–99.

etcher, W. Y., *English book collectors*, ed. A. Pollard (New York, 1902).

ot, M. M., *The Henry Davis gift: a collection of book-bindings*, 2 vols. (London, 1978–83).

The history of bookbinding as a mirror of society (London, 1998).

rd, M. L., 'Importation of printed books into England and Scotland', in *CHBB* III (1999), 179–201.

'Private ownership of printed books', in *CHBB* III (1999), 205–28.

rdyce, C. J., and T. M. Knox, 'The library of Jesus College, Oxford, with an appendix on the books bequeathed thereto by Lord Herbert of Cherbury', OBS 5 (1936), 75–115.

edman, J. B., *Northern English books, owners and makers in the late middle ages* (Syracuse, NY, 1995).

meson, R., 'The origin of the Exeter Book of Old English poetry', *ASE* 25 (1996), 135–85.

The manuscripts of early Norman England (c. 1066–1130) (Oxford 1999).

The scribe speaks? Colophons in early English manuscripts, H. M. Chadwick Memorial Lectures 12 (Cambridge, 2001).

meson, R., and A. Coates, *The old library, Trinity College, Oxford* (Oxford, 1988).

rnett, R., 'Librarianship in the seventeenth century', in R. Garnett, *Essays in librarianship and bibliography* (London, 1899), 174–90.

rrod, H. W., 'The library regulations of a medieval college', *Library* 8 (1927–8), 312–35.

rrod, H. W., and J. R. L. Highfield, 'An indenture between William Rede, bishop of Chichester, and John Bloxham and Henry Stapilton, fellows of Merton College, Oxford, London, 22 October 1374', *BLR* 10 (1978–82), 9–19.

Gaskell, [J.] P., *Trinity College library: the first 150 years* (Cambridge, 1980).
Getz, F., 'Medical practitioners in medieval England', *Social History of Medicine* 3 (199
245–83.
Gibson, M., *Lanfranc of Bec* (Oxford, 1978).
'The twelfth-century glossed bible', *Studia Patristica* 23 (Leuven, 1989), 232–44; repr. M. Gibson, *'Artes' and bible in the medieval West* (Aldershot, 1993), no. XIV.
Gillam, S., *The divinity school and Duke Humfrey's library at Oxford* (Oxford, 1988).
Gillam, S., and R. W. Hunt, 'The curators of the library and Humphrey Wanley', *BLR* (1954–6), 85–98.
Gillespie, V., 'Vernacular books of religion', in *BPPB* (1989), 317–44.
'Syon and the New Learning', in Clark, *Religious orders* (2002), 75–95.
Gneuss, H., 'Liturgical books in Anglo-Saxon England and their Old English terminolog in Lapidge and Gneuss, *Learning and literature* (1985), 91–141.
Handlist of Anglo-Saxon manuscripts: a list of manuscripts and manuscript fragments writt or owned in England up to 1100 (Tempe, AZ, 2001).
Golding, B., *Gilbert of Sempringham and the Gilbertine order, c. 1130–c. 1300* (Oxford, 1995).
Gougaud, L., 'The remains of ancient Irish monastic libraries', in J. Ryan (ed.), *Féil-Sgríbhi Eóin Mhic Néill: essays and studies presented to Professor Eoin MacNeill* (Dublin, 1940), 3 34.
Gray, S., and C. Baggs, 'The English parish library: a celebration of diversity', *Libraries a Culture* 35 (2000), 417.
Graham, T., 'A Parkerian transcript of the list of Bishop Leofric's procurements for Exe Cathedral: Matthew Parker, the Exeter Book, and Cambridge University Library M Ii.2.11', *TCBS* 10 (1994), 421–55.
'Matthew Parker and the conservation of manuscripts: the case of CUL MS Ii.2.4', *TC* 10 (1995), 630–41.
'Changing the context of medieval manuscript art: the case of Matthew Parker', in G. Owen-Crocker and T. Graham (eds.), *Medieval art: recent perspectives. A memorial trib to C. R. Dodwell* (Manchester, 1998), 183–205.
Graham, T., and A. G. Watson, *The recovery of the past in early Elizabethan England: docume by John Bale and John Joscelyn from the circle of Matthew Parker*, Cambridge Bibliograp ical Society Monographs 13 (Cambridge, 1998) (an annotated edition of Cambrid University Library, MS Add. 7489 and other documents).
Greatrex, J., 'English cathedral priories and the pursuit of learning', *JEH* 45 (1994), 396–4
'From cathedral cloister to Gloucester college', in Wansbrough and Marett-Crosby, *Be dictines in Oxford* (1997), 48–60.
'The scope of learning within the cloisters of the English cathedral priories in t later middle ages', in Ferzoco and Muessig, *Medieval monastic education* (200 41–55.
Green, R. F., 'King Richard II's books revisited', *Library*, 5th ser., 31 (1976), 235–9.
Greg, W. W., 'Books and bookmen in the correspondence of Archbishop Parker', *Libra* 4th ser., 16 (1935), 243–79.
Gribbin, J. A., *The Premonstratensian order in late medieval England* (Woodbridge, 2001).
Grierson, P., 'John Caius' library', in *Biographical history of Gonville and Caius College*, (1978), 509–25.

Gruffydd, R. G., 'Humphrey Llwyd: some documents and a catalogue', *Transactions of the Denbighshire Historical Society* 17 (1968), 54–107.

Gruffydd, R. G., and R. J. Roberts, 'John Dee's additions to William Salesbury's dictionary', *Transactions of the Honourable Society of Cymmrodorion*, n.s. 7 (2001), 19–43.

Guild, J. R., and A. Law (eds.), *Edinburgh University Library, 1580–1980: a collection of historical essays* (Edinburgh, 1982).

Gullick, M., *Extracts from the precentors' accounts of Ely Cathedral Priory concerning books and bookmaking* (Hitchin, 1985).

'The bindings', in Mynors and Thomson (1993), xxvi–xxxii.

'The hand of Symeon of Durham: further observations on the Durham martyrology scribe', in D. Rollason (ed.), *Symeon of Durham: historian of Durham and the North* (Stamford 1998), 14–31, 358–62.

'Professional scribes in eleventh- and twelfth-century England', *English Manuscripts Studies 1100–1700* 7 (1998), 1–24.

'The scribal work of Eadmer of Canterbury to 1109', *Archaeologia Cantiana* 117 (1998), 173–89.

'The scribes of the Durham cantor's book (Durham, Dean and Chapter Library MS B.IV.24) and the Durham martyrology scribe', in D. Rollason, M. Harvey and M. Prestwich (eds.), *Anglo-Norman Durham, 1093–1193* (Woodbridge, 1994), 93–109.

Gwynn, A., 'Archbishop FitzRalph and the friars', *Studies: an Irish Quarterly Review* 26 (1937), 50–67.

The Irish church in the eleventh and twelfth centuries, ed. G. O'Brien (Dublin, 1993).

Gwynn, A., and R. N. Hadcock, *Medieval religious houses: Ireland* (London, 1970).

Harris, E., and N. Savage, *British architectural books and writers, 1556–1785* (Cambridge, 1990).

Harris, K., 'Henry V's books', in K. B. McFarlane (ed.), *Lancastrian kings and Lollard knights* (Oxford, 1972), 233–8.

'Patrons, buyers and owners: the evidence for ownership and the role of book owners in book production and the book trade', in *BPPB* (1989), 163–99.

Hart, V., and P. Hicks (eds.), *Paper palaces: the rise of the Renaissance architectural treatise* (New Haven and London, 1998).

Harvey, B., 'A novice's life at Westminster Abbey in the century before the Dissolution', in Clark, *Religious orders* (2002), 51–73.

Hassall, W. O., 'The books of Sir Christopher Hatton at Holkham', *Library*, 5th ser., 5 (1950–1), 1–13.

Heal, F., and C. Holmes, *The gentry in England and Wales, 1500–1700* (Basingstoke, 1994).

Herbert, A. L., 'Oakham parish library', *Library History* 6 (1982), 1–11.

Hervey, M. F. S., *The life, correspondence and collections of Thomas Howard, earl of Arundel* (Cambridge, 1921).

Herzog August Library Wolfenbüttel, *Sammler Fürst Gelehrter Herzog August zu Braunschweig und Lüneburg, 1579–1666* (Wolfenbüttel, 1979).

Higgitt, J., 'Manuscripts and libraries in the diocese of Glasgow before the Reformation', in R. Fawcett (ed.), *Medieval art and architecture in the diocese of Glasgow*, The British Archaeological Association Conference Transactions 23 (Leeds, 1999), 102–10.

Hillyard, B., '"Durkan & Ross" and beyond', in A. A. MacDonald, M. Lynch and I. B. Cowa (eds.), *The Renaissance in Scotland: studies in literature, religion, history and culture offere to John Durkan* (Leiden, 1994), 367–83.

Hinnebusch, W. A., *The early English Friars Preachers* (Rome, 1951).

Houston, R. A., *Scottish literacy and the Scottish identity: illiteracy and society in Scotland an northern England, 1600–1800* (Cambridge, 1985).

Howarth, D., *Lord Arundel and his circle* (New Haven, 1986).

Hughes, K., 'The distribution of Irish scriptoria and centres of learning from 730 to 1111', i N. K. Chadwick, K. Hughes *et al.* (eds.), *Studies in the early British church* (Cambridge 1958), 243–72.

'The Welsh Latin chronicles: *Annales Cambriae* and related texts', in K. Hughes, *Celti Britain in the early middle ages: studies in Scottish and Welsh sources* (Woodbridge, 1980) 67–85.

'Where are the writings of early Scotland?', in K. Hughes, *Celtic Britain in the early midd ages: studies in Scottish and Welsh sources* (Woodbridge, 1980), 38–52.

Hulse, L., 'The musical patronage of Robert Cecil, first earl of Salisbury (1563–1612)', *Journa of the Royal Musical Association* 116 (1991), 24–40.

Humphreys, K. W., *The book provisions of the mediaeval friars, 1215–1400* (Amsterdam 1964).

Hunt, R. W., 'The manuscript collection of University College, Oxford: origins and growth' *BLR* 3 (1950), 13–34.

'The library of Grosseteste', in D. A. Callus (ed.), *Robert Grosseteste, scholar and bisho* (Oxford, 1955), 121–45.

'The library of the abbey of St Albans', in Parkes and Watson, *Medieval scribes* (1978) 251–77.

'The medieval library', in Buxton and Williams, *New College* (1979), 317–45.

Hunter, J., *A catalogue of the manuscripts in the library of Lincoln's Inn* (London, 1838).

Hunter, M. (ed.), *Archives of the scientific revolution: the formation and exchange of ideas i seventeenth-century Europe* (Woodbridge, 1998).

Huws, D., *Five ancient books of Wales*, H. M. Chadwick memorial lecture 6 (Cambridge 1996); repr. in D. Huws, *Medieval Welsh manuscripts* (Cardiff, 2000), 65–83.

'The medieval manuscript in Wales', in Jones and Rees, *A nation and its books* (1998), 25–39 repr. in D. Huws, *Medieval Welsh manuscripts* (Cardiff, 2000), 1–23.

Irwin, R., *The heritage of the English library* (London, 1964).

The English library: sources and history (London, 1966).

Ives, E. W., *The common lawyers of pre-Reformation England* (Cambridge, 1983).

Jackson, W. A., and H. M. Nixon, 'English seventeenth-century travelling libraries', *TCBS* 7 (1979), 294–321.

Jackson-Stops, G., 'Gains and losses: the college buildings, 1404–1750', in Buxton and Williams, *New College* (1979), 193–264.

'The buildings of the medieval college', in Buxton and Williams, *New College* (1979), 147–92.

Jackson-Stops, G., and J. Pipkin, *The English country house: a grand tour* (London, 1984).

James, M. R., *On the abbey of St Edmund at Bury*, Cambridge Antiquarian Society Octavo Publications 28 (1895).

The sources of Archbishop Parker's collection of MSS at Corpus Christi College, Cambridge, with a reprint of the catalogue of Thomas Markaunt's library (Cambridge, 1899).
ardine, L., *Worldly goods: a new history of the Renaissance* (London and Basingstoke, 1996).
ayne, S., *Library catalogues of the English Renaissance* (Berkeley and Los Angeles, 1956; reissued, Godalming, 1983).
efcoate, G., and others, *Handbuch deutscher historischer Buchbestände in Europa* (gen. ed. B. Fabian), x: *A guide to collections of books printed in German-speaking countries before 1910 (or in German elsewhere) held by libraries in Great Britain and Ireland* (Hildesheim, 2000).
ensen, K., 'Problems of provenance: incunabula in the Bodleian Library's Benefactors' Register 1600–1602', in M. Davies (ed.), *Incunabula: studies in fifteenth-century printed books presented to Lotte Hellinga* (London, 1999), 559–602.
'Text-books in the universities: the evidence from the books', in *CHBB* III (1999). 354–79.
ohnstone, H., *Edward of Carnarvon* (Manchester, 1946).
olly, C. 'Naissance de la "science" des bibliothèques', in *Hbf* II (1988), 381–5.
ones, P. H., and E. Rees (eds.), *A nation and its books: a history of the book in Wales* (Aberystwyth, 1998).
ones, P. M., 'Reading medicine in Tudor Cambridge', in V. Nutton, and R. Porter (eds.), *The history of medical education in Britain* (Amsterdam and Atlanta, GA, 1995), 153–83.
'Book ownership and the lay culture of medicine in Tudor Cambridge', in H. Marland and M. Pelling (eds.), *The task of healing: medicine, religion and gender in England and the Netherlands, 1450–1800* (Rotterdam, 1996), 49–68.
'Medicine and science', in *CHBB* III (1999), 433–48.
'Medical libraries and medical Latin 1400–1700', in W. Bracke and H. Deumens (eds.), *Medical Latin from the late middle ages to the eighteenth century* (Brussels, 2000), 115–35.
Katte, M. von, 'Herzog August und die Kataloge seiner Bibliothek', *Wolfenbütteler Beiträge* 1 (1972), 168–99.
Kelly, T., *Early public libraries: a history of public libraries in Great Britain before 1850* (London, 1966).
Kenney, J. F., *The sources for the early history of Ireland: ecclesiastical* (New York, 1929); repr. with revisions by L. Bieler (New York, 1966).
Ker, N. R., 'The migration of manuscripts from the English medieval houses', *Library*, 4th ser., 23 (1942–3), 1–11, repr. in *Books, collectors and libraries* (1985), 459–470.
'Medieval manuscripts from Norwich Cathedral Priory', *TCBS* 1 (1949–53), 1–28; repr. in *Books, collectors and libraries* (1985), 243–72.
'Chaining from a staple on the back cover', *BLR* 3 (1950–1), 104–7, repr. in *Books, collectors and libraries* (1985), 327–30.
'Richard de Bury's books from the library of St Albans', *BLR* 3 (1950–1), 177–9.
Fragments of medieval manuscripts used as pastedowns in Oxford bindings, with a survey of Oxford bindings, c. 1515–1620 (Oxford, 1954).
'The chaining, labelling, and inventory numbers of manuscripts belonging to the old University Library', *BLR* 5 (1954–6), 176–80, repr. in *Books, collectors and libraries* (1985), 321–6.

'Sir John Prise', *Library*, 5th ser., 10 (1955), 1–24, 471–96, repr. in *Books, collectors and librari* (1985), 471–96.

Oxford college libraries in 1556: guide to an exhibition held in 1956 [at the Bodleian Library (Oxford, 1956).

'Oxford college libraries in the sixteenth century', *BLR* 6 (1959), 459–515, repr. in *Book collectors and libraries* (1985), 379–436.

English manuscripts in the century after the Norman Conquest (Oxford, 1960).

'Books at St Paul's Cathedral before 1313', in A. Hollaender and W. Kellaway (eds.), *Studi in London history presented to Philip Edmund Jones* (London, 1969), 41–72; repr. in *Book collectors and libraries* (1985), 209–42.

Records of All Souls College Library, 1437–1600, OBS, n.s., 16 (1971).

'Oxford college libraries before 1500', in J. Ijsewijn and J. Pacquet (eds.), *The universiti in the middle ages* (Louvain, 1978), 293–311; repr. in *Books, collectors and libraries* (1985 301–20.

'Cardinal Cervini's manuscripts from the Cambridge friars', in R. Creytens and P. Künz (eds.), *Xenia medii aevi historiam illustrantia oblata Thomae Kaeppeli OP* (Rome, 1978 repr. in *Books, collectors and libraries* (1985), 437–58.

'The books of philosophy distributed at Merton College in 1372 and 1375', in P. Heywort (ed.), *Medieval studies for J. A. W. Bennett* (Oxford, 1981), 347–94; repr. in *Books, collecto and libraries*, 331–78.

Books, collectors and libraries: studies in the medieval heritage, ed. A. G. Wastson (Londo and Ronceverte, 1985).

'The provision of books', in *HUO* III (1986), 441–519.

Keynes, S., 'King Æthelstan's books', in Lapidge and Gneuss, *Learning and literature* (1985 143–201.

Kisby, F., 'Books in London parish churches before 1603: some preliminary observations', i C. Barron and J. Stratford (eds.), *The church and learning in late medieval society: studi in honour of Professor R. B. Dobson* (Donington, 2002), 305–26.

Knowles, D., *The religious orders in England*, 3 vols. (Cambridge, 1955).

The monastic order in England, 2nd edn (Cambridge, 1969).

Knowles, D., and R. N. Hadcock, *Medieval religious houses: England and Wales*, 2nd ed (London, 1971).

Kottje, R., 'Klosterbibliotheken und monastische Kultur in der zweiten Hälfte des 1 Jahrhunderts', *Zeitschrift für Kirchengeschichte* 4/18 (1969), 145–62.

Kren, T., and S. McKendrick (eds.), *Illuminating the Renaissance* (Los Angeles and Londo 2003).

Krochalis, J. E., 'The books and reading of Henry V and his circle', *Chaucer Review* 23 (1988 50–77.

Kusukawa, S., 'Bacon's classification of knowledge', in M. Peltonen (ed.), *The Cambrid companion to Bacon* (Cambridge, 1996), 47–74.

Laistner, M. L. W., 'Bede as a classical and a patristic scholar', *TRHS*, 4th ser., 16 (1933 69–94.

Lapidge, M., 'The Welsh-Latin Poetry of Sulien's Family', *Studia Celtica* 8–9 (1973–4), 68–10

'Gildas's education and the Latin culture of sub-Roman Britain', in M. Lapidge an D. Dumville (eds.) *Gildas: new approaches* (Cambridge, 1984), 27–50.

'Surviving booklists from Anglo-Saxon England', in Lapidge and Gneuss, *Learning and literature* (1986), 33–89.

Lapidge, M., and H. Gneuss (eds.), *Learning and literature in Anglo-Saxon England: studies presented to Peter Clemoes on the occasion of his sixty-fifth birthday* (Cambridge, 1985).

Lawless, G., *Augustine of Hippo and his monastic rule* (Oxford, 1987).

Lawlor, H. J., 'Notes on the library of the Sinclairs of Rosslyn', *PSAS* 32 (1897–8), 90–120.

Leach, A. F., 'Wykeham's books at New College', *Collectanea*, 3rd ser., OHS 32 (1896), 213–44.

Leader, D. R., *A history of the university of Cambridge*, I: *The university to 1546* (Cambridge, 1988).

Leedham-Green, E. [S.], 'Private libraries in Renaissance England: a progress report', PBSA 91 (1997), 563–71.

'University libraries and book-sellers', in *CHBB* III (1999), 316–53.

Le Gallois, P., *Traitté des plus belles bibliothèques de l'Europe* (Paris, 1680).

Legge, M. D., *Anglo-Norman literature and its background* (Oxford, 1963).

'Anglo-Norman as a spoken language', in R. A. Brown (ed.), *Proceedings of the Battle conference on Anglo-Norman studies*, II: *1979* (Woodbridge, 1980), 108–17.

Lehmann, P., 'Bücherliebe und Bücherpflege bei den Karthäusern', *Miscellanea Francesco Ehrle: scritti di storia e paleografia*, Studi e testi 41 (Rome, 1924), 364–89; repr. in P. Lehmann, *Erforschung des Mittelalters*, III (Stuttgart, 1960), 121–42.

Lekai, L., *The Cistercians: ideals and reality* (Kent, OH, 1977).

Lewis, G., 'The faculty of medicine' in *HUO* III (1986), 213–56.

Little, A. G., and F. Pelster, *Oxford theology and theologians c. AD 1282–1302*, OHS 96 (1934).

Lloyd Jones, G., *The discovery of Hebrew in Tudor England: a third language* (Manchester, 1983).

Lovatt, R., 'Two collegiate loan chests in late medieval Cambridge', in P. Zutshi (ed.), *Medieval Cambridge: essays on the pre-Reformation university* (Woodbridge, 1993), 129–65.

'The triumph of the colleges in late medieval Oxford and Cambridge', *History of Universities* 14 (1998, for 1995–6), 95–142.

Lowe, E. A., *Codices Latini antiquiores: a palaeographical guide to Latin manuscripts prior to the 9th century*, 12 vols. (Oxford, 1934–72).

Lucas, P. J., 'The growth and development of English literary patronage in the later middle ages and early Renaissance', *Library*, 6th ser., 4 (1982), 219–48; repr. in Lucas, *From author to audience* (1997), 249–80.

From author to audience: John Capgrave and medieval publication (Dublin, 1997).

'A testimonye of verye ancient tyme? Some manuscript models for the Parkerian Anglo-Saxon type-designs', in P. R. Robinson and R. Zim (eds.), *Of the making of books: medieval manuscripts, their scribes and readers: essays presented to M. B. Parkes* (Aldershot, 1997), 147–88.

MacGregor, A., 'The king's disport: sports, games and pastimes of the early Stuarts', in A. MacGregor (ed.), *The late king's goods: collections, possessions and patronage of Charles I in the light of the Commonwealth sale inventories* (London and Oxford, 1989), 403–21.

McKendrick, S., '*La grande Histoire Cesar* and the manuscripts of Edward IV', *EMS* 2 (1990), 149–69.

'The Romuléon and the manuscripts of Edward IV', in N. Rogers (ed.), *England i the fifteenth century: proceedings of the 1992 Harlaxton Symposium* (Stamford, 1994), 149–69.

McKitterick, D., 'Women and their books in seventeenth-century England: the case c Elizabeth Puckering', *Library*, 7th ser., 1 (2000), 359–80.

Print, manuscript and the search for order, 1450–1830 (Cambridge, 2003).

McKitterick, D. (ed.) *Andrew Perne: quatercentenary studies*, Cambridge Bibliographical Society Monographs 11 (Cambridge, 1991).

MacNeill, E., 'Beginnings of Latin culture in Ireland', *Studies: an Irish Quarterly Review* 2 (1931), 39–48 and 449–60.

McPherson, D., *Ben Jonson's library and marginalia: an annotated catalogue*, Studies in Philology: Texts and Studies, 71/5 (Chapel Hill, NC, 1974).

Macray, W. D., *Annals of the Bodleian Library, Oxford*, 2nd edn (Oxford, 1890).

Mapstone, S., *Scots and their books in the middle ages and the Renaissance: an exhibition in the Bodleian Library, Oxford* (Oxford, 1996).

Martin, G. H., and J. R. L. Highfield, *A history of Merton College, Oxford* (Oxford, 1997).

Martin, H.-J., *Livre, pouvoirs, et société à Paris au xviie siècle*, 2 vols. (Geneva, 1969).

Martin, H.-J., R. Chartier and J. P. Vivet (eds.), *Histoire de l'édition française*, 1: *Le livre conquérant du moyen âge au milieu du xviie siècle* (Paris, 1982).

Masson, A., *The pictorial catalogue: mural decoration in libraries* (Oxford, 1981).

Meale, C., 'Patrons, buyers and owners: book production and social status', in *BPPB*, 201–38.

Mews, C. J., 'Monastic educational culture revisited: the witness of Zwiefalten and the Hirsau reform', in Ferzoco and Muessig, *Medieval monastic education* (2000), 182–97.

Molland, G., 'Duncan Liddell (1561–1613): an early benefactor of Marischal College Library', *Aberdeen University Review* 51 (1985/6), 485–99.

Moreton, C. E., 'The "library" of a late-15th century lawyer', *Library*, 6th ser., 13 (1991), 338–46.

Morgan, P., 'Francis Wolfreston and "Hor Bouks": a seventeenth-century woman book-collector', *Library*, 6th ser., 11 (1989), 197–219.

Munby, A. N. L., 'Notes on King's College Library in the fifteenth century', *TCBS* 1 (1949–53), 280–6.

Mynors, R. A. B., *Durham Cathedral manuscripts to the end of the twelfth century* (Oxford, 1939).

Catalogue of the manuscripts of Balliol College, Oxford (Oxford, 1963).

Myres, J. N. L., 'The painted frieze in the picture gallery', *BLR* 3 (1950), 82–91.

'Thomas James and the painted frieze', *BLR* 4 (1952), 30–51.

'Further notes on the painted frieze', *BLR* 5 (1956), 290–307.

'Oxford libraries in the seventeenth and eighteenth centuries', in Wormald and Wright, *English Library*, 236–55.

Myers, R., M. Harris and G. Mandlebrote (eds.), *Libraries and the book trade: the formation of collections from the sixteenth to the twentieth century* (New Castle, DE, 2000).

Nebbiai-Dalla Guarda, D., 'Les listes médiévales de lectures monastiques', *RB* 96 (1986), 271–326.

'La bibliothèque commune des institutions religieuses', *Scriptorium* 50 (1996), 254–68.

Nelles, P. 'The library as an instrument of discovery: Gabriel Naudé and the uses of history', in D. R. Kelley (ed.), *History and the disciplines: the reclassification of knowledge in early modern Europe* (Rochester, NY, 1997).

Nelson, C., and M. Seccombe, *British newspapers and periodicals, 1641–1700: a short title catalogue of serials printed in England, Scotland, Ireland and British America* (New York, 1987).

Newman, C. E., 'The first library of the Royal College of Physicians', *Journal of the Royal College of Physicians of London* 3 (1968–9), 299–307.

Nixon, H. M., *Five centuries of English bookbinding* (London, 1978).

Nixon, H. M., and M. M. Foot, *The history of decorated bookbinding in England* (Oxford, 1992).

Norris, D. M., *A history of cataloguing and cataloguing methods, 1100–1850: with an introductory survey of ancient times: a thesis accepted for the honours diploma of the Library Association* (London, 1939).

Oakeshott, W. F., 'Winchester College library before 1750', *Library*, 5th ser., 9 (1954), 1–16.

'Sir Walter Ralegh's library', *Library*, 5th ser., 23 (1968), 285–327.

Oates, J. C. T., 'The libraries of Cambridge, 1570–1700', in Wormald and Wright, *English library* (1958), 213–35.

Cambridge University Library: A history, 1: *From the beginnings to the Copyright Act of Queen Anne* (Cambridge, 1986).

Oliver, G., *Lives of the bishops of Exeter and a history of the cathedral* (Exeter, 1861).

Ó Néill, P. P., 'The impact of the Norman invasion on Irish literature', *Anglo-Norman Studies* 20 (1998 for 1997), 171–85.

Orme, N., *Medieval schools* (New Haven and London, 2006).

O'Sullivan, W., 'Archbishop Whitgift's library catalogue', *Times Literary Supplement* (1956), 468.

'The palaeographical background to the Book of Kells', in F. O'Mahony (ed.), *The Book of Kells* (Aldershot, 1994), 175–82.

'The Irish "remnaunt" of John Bale's manuscripts', in R. Beadle and A. J. Piper (eds.), *New science out of old books: studies in manuscripts and early printed books in honour of A. I. Doyle* (Aldershot, 1995), 374–87.

Owen, M. E., 'The medical books of medieval Wales and the physicians of Myddfai', *The Carmarthenshire Antiquary* 31 (1995), 34–44.

Pächt, O., and J. J. G. Alexander, *Illuminated manuscripts in the Bodleian Library, Oxford*, 3 vols. (Oxford, 1966–73).

Page, R. I., 'The Parker Register and Matthew Parker's Anglo-Saxon manuscripts', *TCBS* 8 (1981), 1–17.

'Audits and replacements in the Parker Library: 1590–1650', *TCBS* 10 (1991), 17–39.

Matthew Parker and his books (Kalamazoo, MI, 1993).

Pantin, W. A., *Canterbury College Oxford*, 4 vols., OHS, n.s. 6–8, 30 (1950–85).

Parkes, M. B., 'The literacy of the laity', in D. Daiches and A. K. Thorlby (eds.), *Literature and western civilization: the medieval world* (London, 1973), 555–76; repr. in Parkes, *Scribes, scripts and readers* (1991), 275–97.

'The contribution of Insular scribes of the seventh and eighth centuries to the "grammar of legibility"', in A. Maierù (ed.), *Grafia e interpunzione del latino nel medioevo* (Rome, 1987), 15–29; repr. in Parkes, *Scribes, scripts and readers* (1991), 1–18.

The scriptorium of Wearmouth-Jarrow (Jarrow, 1982); repr. in Parkes, *Scribes, scripts and readers* (1991), 93–120.

Scribes, scripts and readers: studies in the communication, presentation and dissemination of medieval texts (London, 1991).

'The provision of books', in *HUO* II (1992), 407–83; abridged in Parkes, *Scribes, scripts and readers* (1991), 299–310.

Parkes, M. B., and A. G. Watson, *Medieval scribes, manuscripts and libraries: essays presented to N. R. Ker* (London, 1978).

Parry, G., *The seventeenth century: the intellectual and cultural context of English literature, 1603–1700* (London, 1989).

Peachey, C. C., 'The bookplates of medical men', *Proceedings of the Royal Society of Medicine* 23 (1930), 493–95.

Pearce, E. H., *Sion College and library* (Cambridge, 1913).

Pearson, D., *Provenance research in book history: a handbook* (London, 1994).

'The libraries of English bishops, 1600–1640', *Library*, 6th ser., 14 (1992), 221–57.

Peden, A., 'Science and philosophy in Wales at the time of the Norman Conquest: A Macrobius manuscript from Llanbadarn', *Cambridge Medieval Celtic Studies* 2 (1981), 21–45.

Perkin, M. (ed.), *A directory of the parochial libraries of the Church of England and the Church in Wales*, 2nd edn (London, 2004).

Pfaff, R. W., 'Bishop Baldock's book, St Paul's Cathedral, and the Use of Sarum', in Pfaff, *Liturgical calendars, saints and services in medieval England* (Aldershot, 1998), no. XI.

'The Anglo-Saxon bishop and his book', *BJRL* 81 (1999), 3–24.

Philip, I. G., 'Sir William Pickering and his books', *BC* 5 (1956), 231–8.

The Bodleian Library in the seventeenth and eighteenth centuries (Oxford, 1983).

Philip, I. G., and P. Morgan, 'Libraries, books, and printing', in *HUO* IV (1997), 659–85.

Piper, A. J., 'The libraries of the monks of Durham', in Parkes and Watson, *Medieval scribes* (1978), 213–16.

'Dr Thomas Swalwell: monk of Durham, archivist and bibliophile (d. 1539)', in Carley and Tite, *Books and collectors* (1997), 71–100.

Plummer, C., 'On the colophons and marginalia of Irish scribes', *Proceedings of the British Academy* 12 (1926), 11–44.

Pollard, G., 'Medieval loan chests at Cambridge', *Bulletin of the Institute of Historical Research* 17 (1940), 113–29.

'The construction of English twelfth-century bindings', *Library*, 5th ser., 17 (1962), 1–22.

'The loan chests', in W. A. Pantin and W. T. Mitchell (eds.), *The register of congregation, 1448–63*, OHS, n.s. 22 (1972), Appendix III, 418–20.

Pollard, G., and A. Ehrman, *The distribution of books by catalogue to AD 1800* (Cambridge, 1965).

Pollard, J. G., 'England and the Italian medal', in E. Chaney and P. Mack (eds.), *England and the continental Renaissance: essays in honour of J. B. Trapp* (Woodbridge, 1990), 191–201.

Powicke, F. M., *The medieval books of Merton College* (Oxford, 1931).

Prest, W. R., 'Law, learning and religion: gifts to Gray's Inn library in the 1630s', *Parergon* 14/1 (1996).

Pringle, V., 'An early humanity class library: the gift of Sir John Scot and his friends to St Leonard's College (1620)', *Bibliotheck* 7 (1974–5), 33–54.

Pronger, W. A., 'Thomas Gascoigne', *EHR* 53 (1938), 606–26; 54 (1939), 20–37.

Pryce, H. (ed.), *Literacy in medieval Celtic societies* (Cambridge, 1998).

Purser, J., *Scotland's music: a history of the traditional and classical music of Scotland from earliest times to the present day* (Edinburgh, 1992).

Ramsay, N., 'The cathedral archives and library', in P. Collinson, N. Ramsay and M. Sparks (eds.), *A history of Canterbury Cathedral* (Oxford, 1995), 341–407.

'The library and archives 1109–1541', in P. Meadows and N. Ramsay (eds.), *A history of Ely Cathedral* (Woodbridge, 2003), 157–68.

'The library and archives to 1897', in D. Keene, A. Burns and A. Saint (eds.), *St Paul's: the cathedral church of London, 604–2004* (London, 2004), 413–25.

Reed, A. W., 'John Clement and his books', *Library*, 4th ser., 6 (1926), 329–39.

Rhodes, D. E., *John Argentine, provost of King's: his life and his library* (Amsterdam, 1967).

Richards, M. P., 'Texts and their traditions in the medieval library of Rochester Cathedral Priory', *Transactions of the American Philosophical Society* 78/3 (1988).

Rickert, E., 'Richard II's books', *Library*, 4th ser., 13 (1933), 144–7.

Rijksmuseum, Amsterdam, *Leidse Universiteit 400: stichting en eerste bloei 1575–ca. 1650* (Amsterdam, 1975).

Ringrose, J., 'The medieval statutes of Pembroke College', in P. Zutshi (ed.), *Medieval Cambridge: essays on the pre-Reformation university* (Woodbridge, 1993), 93–127.

Roberts, R. J., 'Sir Christophers Hatton's book-stamps', *Library*, 5th ser., 12 (1957), 119–21.

'The Greek press at Constantinople in 1627 and its antecedents', *Library*, 5th ser., 22 (1967), 13–43.

'John Dee and the matter of Britain', *Transactions of the Honourable Society of Cymmrodorion* (1991), 129–43.

'Importing books for Oxford, 1500–1640', in Carley and Tite, *Books and collectors* (1997), 317–33.

'The Latin trade', in *CHBB* IV (2002), 141–73.

Robinson, B. S., '"Darke speech": Matthew Parker and the reforming of English history', *Sixteenth Century Journal* 29 (1998), 1061–83.

Robinson, J. A., and M. R. James, *The manuscripts of Westminster Abbey* (Cambridge, 1909).

Rogers, D., *The Bodleian Library and its treasures, 1320–1700* (Henley-on-Thames, 1991).

Rogers, N., 'The early history of Sidney Sussex College Library', in D. E. D. Beales and H. B. Nisbet (eds.), *Sidney Sussex College, Cambridge: historical essays* (Woodbridge, 1996), 75–88.

Rosenberg, E., *Leicester, patron of letters* (New York, 1955).

Rosenthal, J. T., 'Aristocratic cultural patronage and book bequests, 1350–1500', *BJRL* 64 (1982), 522–48.

'Clerical book bequests: a *vade mecum*, but whence and whither?', in C. Barron and J. Stratford (eds.), *The church and learning in late medieval society: studies in honour of Professor R. B. Dobson* (Donington, 2002), 327–43.

Roth, F., *The English Austin Friars, 1249–1538*, 2 vols. (New York, 1961–6).

Round, J. H., *Family origins*, ed. W. Page (London, 1930).

Rouse, R. H., 'The early library of the Sorbonne', *Scriptorium* 21 (1967), 42–71; repr. in Rouse and Rouse, *Authentic witnesses* (1991), 341–408.

Rouse, R. H., and M. A. Rouse, 'Bibliography before print: the medieval *De Viris Illustribus*', in P. Ganz (ed.), *The role of the book in medieval culture: proceedings of the Oxford International Symposium 26 September–1 October 1982* (Turnhout, 1986), 133–53.

'La bibliothèque du collège de Sorbonne', *Hbf*, I (1989), 113–23.

Authentic witnesses: approaches to medieval texts and manuscripts (Notre Dame, 1991).

'"*Potens in opere et sermone*": Philip, bishop of Bayeux, and his books', in Rouse and Rouse, *Authentic witnesses* (1991), 33–59.

'The Franciscans and books: Lollard accusations and the Franciscan response', in Rouse and Rouse, *Authentic witnesses* (1991), 409–24.

Manuscripts and their makers: commercial book producers in medieval Paris, 1200–1500, 2 vols. (Turnhout, 2000).

Rovelstad, M. V., 'Two seventeenth-century library handbooks: two different library theories', *Libraries & Culture* 35 (2000), 540–56.

Rundle, D., 'Two unnoticed manuscripts from the collection of Humfrey, duke of Gloucester', *BLR* 16 (1997–9), 211–24, 299–313.

St Clare Byrne, M., and G. S. Thomson, 'My lord's books', *Review of English Studies* 7 (1931), 396–405.

Sammut, A., *Unfredo duca di Gloucester e gli umanisti italiani* (Padua, 1980).

Sanders, V., 'The household of Archbishop Parker and the influencing of public opinion', *JEH* 34 (1983), 534–47.

Sangwine, E., 'The private libraries of Tudor doctors', *Journal of the History of Medicine and Allied Sciences* 33 (1978), 167–84.

Sayer, M., and H. Massingberd, *The disintegration of a heritage: country houses and their collections, 1979–1992* (Norwich, 1993).

Saygin, S., *Humfrey, duke of Gloucester (1390–1447) and the Italian humanists* (Leiden, 2002).

Sayle, C., 'The library of Thomas Lorkyn', *Annals of Medical History* 3 (1921), 310–23.

Scase, W., 'Reginald Pecock, John Carpenter and John Colop's "Common Profit" books', *MÆ* 61 (1992), 261–74.

Scattergood, V. J., 'Literary culture at the court of Richard II', in Scattergood and Sherborne, *English court culture* (1983), 29–43.

Scattergood, V. J., and J. W. Sherborne (eds.), *English court culture in the later middle ages* (London, 1983).

Schoeck, R. J., 'The libraries of common lawyers in the Renaissance', *Manuscripta* 6 (1962), 155–67.

Selwyn, D. G., *The library of Thomas Cranmer* (Oxford, 1996).

'Thomas Cranmer and the dispersal of medieval libraries: the provenance of some of his medieval manuscripts and printed books', in Carley and Tite, *Books and collectors* (1997), 81–94.

Selwyn, P. M., '"Such speciall bookes of Mr. Somersettes as were sould to Mr. Secretary": the fate of Robert Glover's collections', in Carley and Tite, *Books and collectors* (1997), 389–401.

Serrai, A., *Storia della bibliografia*, v: *Trattatistica biblioteconomica*, ed. M. Palumbo (Rome, 1993).

Sessions, W. K., *A printer's dozen: the first British printing centres to 1557 after Westminster and London*, 2nd edn (York, 1983).

Shadwell, C. L., 'The catalogue of the library of Oriel College in the 14th century', *Collectanea*, I, OHS 5 (1885), 59–70.

Sharpe, R., 'Accession, classification, location: shelfmarks in medieval libraries', *Scriptorium* 50 (1996), 279–87.

'Reconstructing the medieval library of Bury St Edmunds: the lost catalogue of Henry of Kirkstead', in A. Gransden (ed.), *Bury St Edmunds: medieval art, architecture, archaeology, and economy*, BAA Conference Transactions 1994 (1998), 204–18.

Titulus: identifying medieval Latin texts (Turnhout, 2003).

'Monastic reading at Thorney Abbey (1323–1347)', *Traditio* 60 (2005), 243–78.

'Medieval library catalogues and indexes', in N. J. Morgan and R. M. Thomson (eds.), *CHBB* II (forthcoming).

Sheppard, J. M., 'Magister Robertus Amiclas: a Buildwas benefactor?', *TCBS* 9 (1988), 281–8.

The Buildwas books: book production, acquisition and use at an English Cistercian monastery, 1165–c. 1400, OBS, 3rd ser., 2 (1997).

Sherman, W. H., *John Dee: the politics of reading and writing in the English Renaissance* (Amherst, MI, 1995).

Shinners, J., 'Parish libraries in medieval England', in J. Brown and W. P. Stoneman (eds.), *A distinct voice: medieval studies in honor of Leonard E. Boyle, OP* (Notre Dame, IN, 1997), 207–30.

Shire, H. M., *Song, dance and poetry in the court of Scotland under King James VI* (Cambridge, 1969).

Short, I., 'Patrons and polyglots: French literature in twelfth-century England', *Anglo-Norman Studies* 14 (1991), 229–49.

Simpson, A. W. B., 'The circulation of year-books in the fifteenth century', *Law Quarterly Review* 73 (1957), 492–505.

'The source and function of the later year-books', *Law Quarterly Review* 87 (1971), 94–118.

Sims-Williams, P., 'The uses of writing in early medieval Wales', in Pryce, *Literacy* (1998), 15–38.

Smith, L., 'Lending books: the growth of a medieval question from Langton to Bonaventure', in *Intellectual life in the middle ages: essays presented to Margaret Gibson*, ed. L. Smith and B. Ward (London, 1992), 265–79.

Southern, R. W., *Saint Anselm and his biographer* (Cambridge, 1963).

Robert Grosseteste: the growth of an English mind in medieval Europe, 2nd edn (Oxford, 1992).

Sparrow, J., 'The earlier owners of books in John Selden's library', *BQR* 6 (1929–31), 263–71.

Spufford, M., *Small books and pleasant histories: popular fiction and its readership in seventeenth-century England* (London, 1981).

Stern, V. F., *Gabriel Harvey: his life, marginalia and library* (Oxford, 1979).

Stirnemann, P., 'Les bibliothèques princières et privées aux xiie et xiiie siècles', in *Hbf* I (1989), 173–91.

'Une bibliothèque princière au xiie siècle', in *Splendeurs de la cour de Champagne au temps de Chrétien de Troyes* (Troyes, 1999), 36–42.

Stokes, H. P., *The chaplains and the chapel of the University of Cambridge*, Cambridge Antiquaria Society, Octavo Series 41 (1906).

Stratford, J., 'The manuscripts of John, Duke of Bedford: library and chapel', in D. William (ed.), *England in the fifteenth century: proceedings of the 1986 Harlaxton Symposium* (Wood bridge, 1987), 329–50.

The Bedford inventories: the wordly goods of John, duke of Bedford, regent of France (1389–1435 (London, 1993).

'The early royal collections and the Royal Library to 1461', *CHBB* III (1999), 255–66.

'"La Somme le Roi" (Reims, Bibliothèque municipale, MS. 570): the manuscript of Thomas of Woodstock, duke of Gloucester, and the scribe, John Upton in M.-C. Hubert, E. Poulle and M. H. Smith (eds.), *Le statut du scripteur au moyen âge: actes du XIIe colloque scientifique de paléographie latine* (Paris, 2000), 267–82.

Stratford, N., 'Bishop Grandisson and the visual arts', in M. Swanton (ed.), *Exeter Cathedral a celebration* (Exeter, 1991), 145–55.

Streeter, B. H., *The chained library: a survey of four centuries in the evolution of the English librar* (New York, 1931).

Strong, R., *The Renaissance garden in England* (London, 1979).

Strongman, S., 'John Parker's manuscripts: an edition of the lists in Lambeth Palace MS 737', *TCBS* 7 (1977), 1–27.

Summerson, H. [R. T.] 'The Lucys of Charlecote and their library', *National Trust Studie* (1979), 148–59.

'An English bible and other books belonging to Henry IV', *BJRL* 79 (1997), 109–15.

Taburet-Delahaye, E. (ed.), *Paris 1400: les arts sous Charles VI* (Paris, 2004).

Talbot, C. H., 'The universities and the medieval library', in Wormald and Wright, *Englis library* (1958), 66–84.

'The English Cistercians and the universities', *Studia monastica* 4 (1962), 197–220.

Talbot, C. H., and E. A. Hammond, *The medical practitioners in medieval England: a biographica register* (London, 1965).

Taylor, A., *General subject-indexes since 1548* (Philadelphia, 1966).

Taylor, F., 'The books and manuscripts of Scipio Le Squyer, deputy chamberlain of the Exchequer, 1620–59', *BJRL* 25 (1941), 137–64.

Taylor, J. H. M., and L. Smith (eds.), *Women and the book: assessing the visual evidence* (London and Toronto, 1997).

Taylor-Vaisey, R. D., 'Regulations for the operation of a medieval library', *Library*, 5th ser 33 (1978), 47–50.

Thomas, A. G., *Great books and book collectors* (London, 1975).

Thomas, G. G. C., 'The Stradling library at St Donat's, Glamorgan', *National Library of Wales Journal* 24 (1985–6), 402–19.

Thompson, B., 'Monasteries, society and reform in late medieval England', in Clark, *Religious orders* (2002), 165–95.

Thomson, R. M., 'The library of Bury St Edmunds Abbey in the eleventh and twelfth centuries', *Speculum* 47 (1972), 617–45; repr. in Thomson, *England and the twelfth-century renaissance* (Aldershot, 1998), no. I.

'The Norman Conquest and English libraries', in P. Ganz (ed.), *The role of the book in medieval culture*, 2 vols. (Turnhout, 1986), II. 27–40; repr. in R. M. Thomson, *England and the twelfth-century renaissance* (Aldershot, 1998), no. XVIII.

Manuscripts from St Albans Abbey, 1066–1235, 2nd edn, 2 vols. (Woodbridge, 1987).

'Robert Amiclas: a twelfth-century Parisian master and his books', *Scriptorium* 49 (1995), 238–43; repr. in R. M. Thomson, *England and the twelfth-century renaissance* (Aldershot, 1998), no. III.

William of Malmesbury, 2nd edn (Woodbridge, 2003).

Books and learning in twelfth-century England: the ending of 'Alter Orbis' (forthcoming).

hornton, P., *Seventeenth-century interior decoration in England, France and Holland* (New Haven, 1978).

'ite, C. G. C., 'A "loan" of printed books from Sir Robert Cotton to John Selden', *BLR* 13 (1991), 486–90.

The manuscript library of Sir Robert Cotton (London, 1994).

'A catalogue of Sir Robert Cotton's printed books?', in C. J. Wright (ed.), *Sir Robert Cotton as collector* (London, 1997), 183–93.

'ale, M., *The gentleman's recreations: accomplishments and pastimes of the English gentleman, 1580–1630* (Cambridge, 1977).

'oigts, L. E., 'Scientific and medical books', in *BPPB* (1989), 345–402.

'A doctor and his books: the manuscripts of Roger Marchall', in R. Beadle and A. J. Piper (eds.), *New science out of old books: studies in manuscripts and early printed books in honour of A. I. Doyle* (Aldershot, 1995), 249–314.

'olk, P., *Der liber ordinarius des Lütticher St Jakobs-Klosters*, Beiträge zur Geschichte des alten Mönchtums und des Bendiktinerordens 10 (Münster, 1923).

/agner, A. R., *A catalogue of English mediaeval rolls of arms* (London, 1950).

Records and collections of the College of Arms (London, 1952).

Heralds and heraldry, 2nd edn (London, 1956).

Heralds of England: a history of the office and College of Arms (London, 1967).

English genealogy, 2nd edn (Oxford, 1972).

/ainwright, J. P., *Musical patronage in seventeenth-century England: Christopher, first Baron Hatton (1605–1670)* (Aldershot, 1997).

/allis, P. J., 'The library of William Crashaw', *TCBS* 2 (1956), 213–28.

/alsh, K., *A fourteenth-century scholar and primate: Richard FitzRalph in Oxford, Avignon and Armagh* (Oxford, 1981).

/ansbrough, H., and A. Marett-Crosby (eds.), *Benedictines in Oxford* (London, 1997).

/arkentin, G., 'The world and the book at Penshurst: the second earl of Leicester (1595–1677) and his library', *Library*, 6th ser., 20 (1998), 325–46.

/aterer, J. W., 'Irish book-satchels or budgets', *Medieval Archaeology* 12 (1968), 70–82.

/atson, A. G., *The library of Sir Simonds d'Ewes* (London, 1966).

'Thomas Allen of Oxford and his manuscripts', in Parkes and Watson, *Medieval scribes* (1978), 279–314.

'John Twyne of Canterbury (d. 1581) as a collector of medieval manuscripts: a preliminary investigation', *Library*, 6th ser., 8 (1986), 135–6; repr. in his *Medieval manuscripts in post-medieval England* (Aldershot, 2004), IV. 135–36.

'The manuscript collection of Sir Walter Cope', *BLR* 12 (1987), 262–97.

'The post-medieval library', in *Unarmed soldiery: studies in the early history of All Souls College* (Oxford, 1996).

A descriptive catalogue of the medieval manuscripts of All Souls College, Oxford (Oxford, 1997).

A descriptive catalogue of the medieval manuscripts of Exeter College, Oxford (Oxford, 2000).

Watt, T., *Cheap print and popular piety, 1550–1640* (Cambridge, 1991).

Webb, C. J., 'Note on books bequeathed by John of Salisbury to the cathedral library of Chartres', *Mediaeval and Renaissance Studies* 1 (1941), 128–9.

Webber, T., *Scribes and scholars at Salisbury Cathedral, c. 1075–c. 1125* (Oxford, 1992).

'The patristic content of English book collections in the eleventh century: towards a continental perspective', in P. R. Robinson and R. Zim (eds.), *Of the making of books: medieval manuscripts, their scribes and readers: essays presented to M. B. Parkes* (Aldershot, 1997), 191–205.

Weiss, R., 'The earliest catalogues of the library of Lincoln College', *BLR* 8 (1937), 343–59.

'Henry VI and the library of All Souls College', *EHR* 57 (1942), 102–5.

'The private collector and the revival of Greek learning', in Wormald and Wright, *English library* (1958), 112–35.

Wells, E. B., 'Scientists' libraries: a handlist of printed sources', *Annals of Science* 40 (1983), 317–89.

Wheeler, G. W., *The earliest catalogues of the Bodleian Library* (Oxford, 1928).

Wijffels, A., 'Law books in Cambridge libraries, 1500–1640', *TCBS* 10 (1993), 359–412.

Williams, T. W., 'Wells Cathedral Library', *Library Association Record* 8 (1906), 372–7.

Williman, D., and K. Corsano, 'Tracing provenances by *dictio probatoria*', *Scriptorium* 53 (1999), 124–45.

Willis, R., *The architectural history of the University of Cambridge*, ed. J. W. Clark, 4 vols. (Cambridge, 1886).

Wood, A., *The history and antiquities of the University of Oxford, in two books*, ed. and tr. J. Gutch (Oxford, 1792–6).

Woolfson, J., *Padua and the Tudors: English students in Italy, 1485–1603* (Toronto, 1998).

'Reginald Pole and his Greek manuscripts in Oxford: a reconsideration', *BLR* 17 (2000), 79–95.

Wormald, F., 'The monastic library', in Wormald and Wright, *English library* (1958), 15–31.

Wormald, F., and C. E. Wright, *The English library before 1700* (London, 1958).

Wright, C. E., 'The dispersal of the monastic libraries and the beginnings of Anglo-Saxon studies. Matthew Parker and his circle: a preliminary study', *TCBS* 1 (1951), 208–37.

'The Elizabethan Society of Antiquaries and the formation of the Cottonian library', in Wormald and Wright, *English library* (1958), 176–212.

'The dispersal of the libraries in the sixteenth century', in Wormald and Wright, *English library* (1958), 148–74.

Wright, N., 'Gildas's reading: a survey', *Sacris erudiri* 32 (1991), 121–62.

General index

Index of manuscripts